Norman Cohn

The Pursuit
of the Millennium

Revolutionary Millenarians and Mystical
Anarchists of the Middle Ages

PALADIN
GRANADA PUBLISHING
London Toronto Sydney New York

Published by Granada Publishing Limited
in Paladin Books 1970
Reprinted 1970, 1972, 1978

ISBN 0 586 08002 3

First published in Great Britain by
Secker & Warburg Ltd 1957
Copyright © Norman Cohn 1957, 1961, 1970

Granada Publishing Limited
Frogmore, St Albans, Herts AL2 2NF
and
3 Upper James Street, London W1R 4BP
1221 Avenue of the Americas, New York, NY 10020, USA
117 York Street, Sydney, NSW 2000, Australia
100 Skyway Avenue, Toronto, Ontario, Canada M9W 3A6
Trio City, Coventry Street, Johannesburg 2001, South Africa
CML Centre, Queen & Wyndham, Auckland 1, New Zealand

Made and printed in Great Britain by
Hazell Watson & Viney Ltd
Aylesbury, Bucks
Set in Monotype Fournier

Contents

Illustrations

Acknowledgements

The illustrations are reproduced by courtesy of the British Museum, the Bibliothèque Royale de Belgique, the Courtauld Institute of Art and Mrs J. P. Sumner. I am indebted to the late Professor G. R. Owst and the Cambridge University Press for permission to quote from the translation of John Bromyard in *Literature and Pulpit in Medieval England*.

Foreword to the Paladin Edition

The publication of a third edition of *The Pursuit of the Millennium* has provided an opportunity for a thorough revision. Almost a quarter of a century has passed since I began work on the book, and thirteen years since I finished it. It would be a poor comment on the progress of scholarship, or on my mental elasticity, or on both, if I could find nothing in it now to modify or clarify. In point of fact I have found plenty. The new version has thirteen chapters instead of twelve, and a different Introduction and Conclusion; two other chapters have been substantially altered; and innumerable minor changes have been made throughout. Some readers may like to know what, in general terms, all this amounts to. The changes, then, can be summarized as follows.

In the first place, the results of recent research have been taken into account. *The Pursuit of the Millennium* is still the only book on its subject, i.e. the tradition of revolutionary millenarianism and mystical anarchism as it developed in western Europe between the eleventh and the sixteenth centuries. But there have been many fresh contributions, ranging from short articles to long books, on individual aspects and episodes of that story. In particular the picture of that mysterious cult, the Free Spirit, has been filled out by the labours of Professor Romana Guarnieri, of Rome. These labours have included the identification and editing of *The Mirror of Simple Souls* of Marguerite Porete – a basic text of the Free Spirit, which admirably complements the much later Ranter texts that form the Appendix to the present work. Professor Guarnieri has also produced the nearest approach that has yet been made to a complete history of the cult, in Italy as well as in northern and central Europe. Our knowledge of the Taborites, *Pikarti* and Adamites of Bohemia has likewise been deepened, not only by the constant flow of Marxist studies emanating from Czechoslovakia but also by an impressive and enlightening series of articles by an American scholar, Professor Howard Kaminsky. These major additions to knowledge, along with many minor ones, have been incorporated into the relevant chapters of this book.

As *The Pursuit of the Millennium* never was intended to be a general history of religious dissent or 'heresy' in the Middle Ages, most of the recent research in that field – which is abundant – leaves its argument untouched. Nevertheless it is a thought-provoking experience to read such wide-ranging and authoritative works as *Dissent and Reform in the Early Middle Ages* by Professor Jeffrey Russell; *Heresy in the Later Middle Ages* by Professor Gordon Leff; and *The Radical Reformation* by Professor George Williams. None of these works overlaps with *The Pursuit of the Millennium* in more than a couple of chapters, but between them they offer a grandiose history of dissent extending from the eighth century to the sixteenth. Viewed in this wider context, the sects and movements described in the present volume emerge all the more clearly as exceptional and extreme: in the history of religious dissent, they form the most absolute, anarchic wing. The new Introduction defines their peculiarities, while the new Chapter 2 shows how they fit into the larger picture.

The social composition of these sects and movements, and the social setting in which they operated, were adequately indicated in the first edition; and it proved unnecessary to make any changes on that score. It may be that economic historians could, by detailed research into individual cases, bring further enlightenment; but certainly none is to be expected from the current exchange of dogmatic generalizations between Marxist and non-Marxist historians of 'heresy'. Nothing, for instance, could be more sterile than the debate between certain historians in West and East Germany as to whether 'heresy' can or cannot be interpreted as a protest of the unprivileged; the former being, apparently, unable to imagine how a religious movement can express social animosities, and the latter how dissent can come from the privileged strata. The best protection against such oversimplification is some acquaintance with the sociology of religion. So fortified, one is unlikely to imagine that all medieval 'heresy' was of one kind, reflecting the same kind of discontent and appealing to the same segments of society.

So far as revolutionary millenarianism is concerned, its socio-logical import emerges from chapter after chapter of this book; but I have also tried to summarize it, as concisely as possible, in the Conclusion. The Conclusion is indeed the part of the book that has attracted most attention of all; in particular, much comment, both favourable and unfavourable, has been provoked by the suggestion that the story told in this book may have some relevance to the revolutionary upheavals of our own century. This argument has been discussed at length not only in reviews and articles but also, and most profitably, in spontaneous debates at the universities, British, Continental, and American, where I have been invited to lecture. All this has helped me to clarify my ideas on the matter; and while I am still convinced that the argument is valid, I think that it needed to be expressed both more briefly and more clearly. I have attempted this in the new Conclusion.

Finally, the Bibliography. The old Bibliography, which was purely historical, has been revised to include historical works which have appeared since the original version of the book was written; they are marked with an asterisk. But *The Pursuit of the Millennium* belongs at least as much to the comparative study of millenarianism as to the study of medieval history; and in that field too very considerable progress has been made in recent years. A selection of recent works and symposia, mostly anthropological and sociological, is given as a supplement to the Bibliography; and many of these themselves contain bibliographies which will enable the interested reader to explore further in this difficult but vitally important field.

N.C.

The University of Sussex
February 1969

Introduction: The Scope of this Book

The original meaning of 'millenarianism' was narrow and precise. Christianity has always had an eschatology, in the sense of a doctrine concerning 'the last times', or 'the last days', or 'the final state of the world'; and Christian millenarianism was simply one variant of Christian eschatology. It referred to the belief held by some Christians, on the authority of the Book of Revelation (XX, 4–6), that after his Second Coming Christ would establish a messianic kingdom on earth and would reign over it for a thousand years before the Last Judgement. According to the Book of Revelation the citizens of that kingdom will be the Christian martyrs, who are to be resurrected for the purpose a thousand years in advance of the general resurrection of the dead. But the early Christians already interpreted that part of the prophecy in a liberal rather than a literal sense, in that they equated the martyrs with the suffering faithful – i.e. themselves – and expected the Second Coming in their lifetime. And in recent years it has become customary amongst anthropologists and sociologists, and to some extent amongst historians too, to use 'millenarianism' in a more liberal sense still. The word has in fact become simply a convenient label for a particular type of salvationism. And that is the way it will be employed in this book.

Millenarian sects or movements always picture salvation as

(a) collective, in the sense that it is to be enjoyed by the faithful as a collectivity;

(b) terrestrial, in the sense that it is to be realized on this earth and not in some other-worldly heaven;

(c) imminent, in the sense that it is to come both soon and suddenly;

(d) total, in the sense that it is utterly to transform life on earth, so that the new dispensation will be no mere improvement on the present but perfection itself;

(e) miraculous, in the sense that it is to be accomplished by, or with the help of, supernatural agencies.

Even within these limits there is of course room for infinite variety: there are countless possible ways of imagining the Millennium and the route to it. Millenarian sects and movements have varied in attitude from the most violent aggressiveness to the mildest pacifism and from the most ethereal spirituality to the most earthbound materialism. And they have also varied greatly in social composition and social function.

There was certainly great variety amongst the millenarian sects and movements of medieval Europe. At the one extreme were the so-called 'Franciscan Spirituals' who flourished in the thirteenth century. These rigorous ascetics came mainly from the mixture of noble and merchant families which formed the dominant class in the Italian towns. Many of them renounced great wealth in order to become poorer than any beggar; and in their imaginings the Millennium was to be an age of the Spirit, when all mankind would be united in prayer, mystical contemplation and voluntary poverty. At the other extreme were the various millenarian sects and movements that developed amongst the rootless poor of town and country. The poverty of these people was anything but voluntary, their lot was extreme and relentless insecurity, and their millenarianism was violent, anarchic, at times truly revolutionary.

This book deals with the millenarianism that flourished amongst the rootless poor of western Europe between the eleventh and the sixteenth centuries; and with the circumstances that favoured it. But if that is the main theme, it is not the only one. For the poor did not create their own millenarian faiths, but received them from would-be prophets or would-be messiahs. And these people, many of them former members of the lower clergy, in turn took their ideas from the most diverse sources. Some millenarian phantasies were inherited from the Jews and early Christians, and others from the twelfth-century abbot Joachim of Fiore. Others again were concocted by the heretical mystics known as the Brethren of the Free Spirit. This book examines both how these various bodies of millenarian belief originated and how they were modified in the course of being transmitted to the poor.

The world of millenarian exaltation and the world of social unrest, then, did not coincide but did overlap. It often happened that certain segments of the poor were captured by some millenarian prophet. Then the usual desire of the poor to improve the material conditions of their lives became transfused with phantasies of a world reborn into innocence through a final, apocalyptic massacre. The evil ones – variously identified with the Jews, the clergy or the rich – were to be exterminated; after which the Saints – i.e. the poor in question – would set up their kingdom, a realm without suffering or sin. Inspired by such phantasies, numbers of poor folk embarked on enterprises which were quite different from the usual revolts of peasants or artisans, with local, limited aims. The conclusion to this book will attempt to define the peculiarities of these millenarian movements of the medieval poor. It will also suggest that in certain respects they were true precursors of some of the great revolutionary movements of the present century.

No other overall study of these medieval movements exists. The more strictly religious sects which appeared and disappeared during the Middle Ages have indeed received ample attention; but much less attention has been given to the story of how, again and again, in situations of mass disorientation and anxiety, traditional beliefs about a future golden age or messianic kingdom came to serve as vehicles for social aspirations and animosities. Though there is no lack of excellent monographs dealing with single episodes or aspects, the story as a whole remained untold. The present work aims, so far as may be, at filling that gap.

To open up this largely unexplored field entailed combing many hundreds of original sources in Latin, Greek, Old French, sixteenth-century French, and medieval and sixteenth-century German, both High and Low. Research and writing took, in all, some ten years; and it was because that seemed long enough that I decided – reluctantly – to limit the investigation to northern and central Europe. Not that the Mediterranean world of the Middle Ages has no similar or equally fascinating spectacles to offer; but it seemed to me less important that the survey should be geographically all-embracing than that it should be, for the area covered, as exhaustive and accurate as I could make it.

The raw material has been supplied by contemporary sources of the most varied kinds – chronicles, reports of inquisitorial investigations, condemnations uttered by popes, bishops and councils, theological tracts, polemical pamphlets, letters, even lyric poems. Most of this material was produced by clerics who were utterly hostile to the beliefs and movements which they were describing; and it has not always been easy to know just how much allowance to make for unconscious distortion or conscious misrepresentation. But fortunately the other side also produced a large body of literature, much of which has survived the sporadic efforts of secular and ecclesiastical authorities to destroy it; and so it has been possible to check clerical sources not only against one another but against the written pronouncements of quite a number of millenarian prophets. The account given here is the end-product of a long process of collecting and collating, appreciating and re-appreciating a vast mass of evidence. If in the main it is an unhesitating account, that is because almost all the major doubts and queries which arose in the course of the work had answered themselves before the end. Where uncertainties still remain they have of course been indicated.

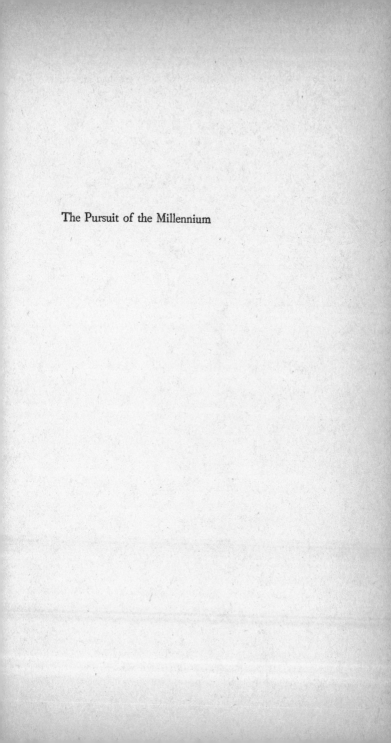

The Pursuit of the Millennium

1 The Tradition of Apocalyptic Prophecy

Jewish and early Christian apocalyptic

The raw materials out of which a revolutionary eschatology was gradually built up during the later Middle Ages consisted of a miscellaneous collection of prophecies inherited from the ancient world. Originally all these prophecies were devices by which religious groups, at first Jewish and later Christian, consoled, fortified and asserted themselves when confronted by the threat or the reality of oppression.

It is natural enough that the earliest of these prophecies should have been produced by Jews. What so sharply distinguished the Jews from the other peoples of the ancient world was their attitude towards history and in particular towards their own role in history. Save to some extent for the Persians, the Jews were alone in combining an uncompromising monotheism with an unshakable conviction that they were themselves the Chosen People of the one God. At least since the exodus from Egypt they had been convinced that the will of Yahweh was concentrated on Israel, that Israel alone was charged with the realization of that will. At least since the days of the Prophets they had been convinced that Yahweh was no mere national god, however powerful, but the one and only God, the omnipotent Lord of History who controlled the destinies of all nations. It is true that the conclusions which Jews drew from these beliefs varied greatly. There were many who, like the 'Second Isaiah', felt that divine election imposed a special moral responsibility on them, an obligation to show justice and mercy in their dealings with all men. In their view Israel's divinely appointed task was to enlighten the Gentiles and so carry God's salvation to the ends of the earth. But alongside this ethical interpretation there existed another which became ever more attractive as the fervour of an ancient nationalism was subjected to the shock and strain of repeated defeats, deportations and dispersals. Precisely because they were so utterly certain of being the Chosen People, Jews tended to react to peril, oppression and hardship by phantasies of the total triumph and boundless prosperity which Yahweh, out of his omnipotence, would bestow upon his Elect in the fulness of time.

Already in the Prophetical Books there are passages – some of them dating from the eighth century – that foretell how, out of an immense cosmic catastrophe, there will arise a Palestine which will be nothing less than a new Eden, Paradise regained. Because of their neglect of Yahweh the Chosen People must indeed be punished by famine and pestilence, war and captivity, they must indeed be subjected to a sifting judgement so severe that it will effect a clean break with the guilty past. There must indeed by a Day of Yahweh, a Day of Wrath, when sun and moon and stars are darkened, when the heavens are rolled together and the earth is shaken. There must indeed be a Judgement when the misbelievers – those in Israel who have not trusted in the Lord and also Israel's enemies, the heathen nations – are judged and cast down, if not utterly destroyed. But this is not the end: a 'saving remnant' of Israel will survive these chastisements and through that remnant the divine purpose will be accomplished. When the nation is thus regenerated and reformed Yahweh will cease from vengeance and become the Deliverer. The righteous remnant – together, it was held latterly, with the righteous dead now resurrected – will be assembled once more in Palestine and Yahweh will dwell amongst them as ruler and judge. He will reign from a rebuilt Jerusalem, a Zion which has become the spiritual capital of the world and to which all nations flow. It will be a just world, where the poor are protected, and a harmonious and peaceful world, where wild and dangerous beasts have become tame and harmless. The moon will shine as the sun and the sun's light will be increased sevenfold. Deserts and waste lands will become fertile and beautiful. There will be abundance of water and provender for flocks and herds, for men there will be abundance of corn and wine and fish and fruit; men and flocks and herds will multiply exceedingly. Freed from disease and sorrow of every kind, doing no more iniquity but living according to the law of Yahweh now written in their hearts, the Chosen People will live in joy and gladness.

In the apocalypses, which were directed to the lower strata of the Jewish population as a form of nationalist propaganda, the tone is cruder and more boastful. This is already striking in the earliest apocalypse, the 'vision' or 'dream' which occupies Chapter VII of the Book of Daniel and which was composed about the year 165 B.C., at a peculiarly critical moment in Jewish history. For more than three centuries, since the end of the Babylonian exile, the Jews in Palestine had enjoyed a fair measure of peace and security, at first under Persian, later under Ptolemaic rule; but the situation changed when in the second century B.C. Palestine passed into the hands of the Syro-Greek dynasty of the Seleucids. The Jews themselves were bitterly divided, for while the worldly upper classes eagerly adopted Greek manners and customs the common people clung all the more resolutely to the faith of their fathers. When the Seleucid monarch Antiochus IV Epiphanes, intervening on behalf of the pro-Greek party, went so far as to forbid all Jewish religious observances, the response was the Maccabean revolt. In the 'dream' in the Book of Daniel, which was composed at the height of the revolt, four beasts symbolize four successive world-powers, the Babylonian, the (unhistorical) Median, the Persian and the Greek – the last of which 'shall be diverse from all kingdoms, and shall devour the whole earth, and shall tread it down, and break it in pieces'. When this empire in turn was overthrown Israel, personified as the 'Son of Man',

came with the clouds of heaven, and came to the Ancient of Days. . . . And there was given him dominion, and glory, and a kingdom, that all peoples, nations and languages should serve him: his dominion is an everlasting dominion, which shall not pass away. . . . The greatness of the kingdom under the whole heaven [was] given to the people of the saints of the most High . . .

This goes much further than any of the Prophets: for the first time the glorious future kingdom is imagined as embracing not simply Palestine but the whole world.

Already here one can recognize the paradigm of what was to become and to remain the central phantasy of revolutionary eschatology. The world is dominated by an evil, tyrannous power of boundless destructiveness – a power moreover which is imagined not as simply human but as demonic. The tyranny of that power will become more and more outrageous, the sufferings of its victims more and more intolerable – until suddenly the hour will strike when the Saints of God are able to rise up and overthrow it. Then the Saints themselves, the chosen, holy people who hitherto have groaned under the oppressor's heel, shall in their turn inherit dominion over the whole earth. This will be the culmination of history; the Kingdom of the Saints will not only surpass in glory all previous kingdoms, it will have no successors. It was thanks to this phantasy that Jewish apocalyptic exercised, through its derivatives, such a fascination upon the discontented and frustrated of later ages – and continued to do so long after the Jews themselves had forgotten its very existence.

From the annexation of Palestine by Pompey in 63 B.C. down to the war of A.D. 66–72 the struggles of the Jews against their new masters, the Romans, were accompanied and stimulated by a stream of militant apocalyptic. And precisely because it was addressed to the common people this propaganda made great play with the phantasy of an eschatological saviour, the Messiah. This phantasy was of course already ancient; if for the Prophets the Saviour who was to reign over the Chosen People at the end of time was usually Yahweh himself, in the popular religion, on the other hand, the future Messiah seems to have played a considerable part ever since the nation entered on its political decline. Originally imagined as a particularly wise, just and powerful monarch of Davidic descent who would restore the national fortunes, the Messiah became more superhuman as the political situation became more hopeless. In 'Daniel's dream' the Son of Man who appears riding on the clouds seems to personify Israel as a whole. But already here he may have been imagined as a superhuman individual; and in the Apocalypses of Baruch and of Ezra, which belong in the main to the first century A.D., the superhuman being is incontestably a man, a warrior-king endowed with unique, miraculous powers.

In *Ezra* the Messiah is shown as the Lion of Judah at whose roar the last and worst beast – now the Roman eagle – bursts into flame and is consumed; and again as the Son of Man who first annihilates the multitudes of the heathen with the fire and storm of his breath and then, gathering together the lost ten tribes out of alien lands, establishes in Palestine a kingdom in which a reunited Israel can flourish in peace and glory. According to *Baruch* there must come a time of terrible hardship and injustice, which is the time of the last and worst empire, the Roman. Then, just when evil has reached its greatest pitch, the Messiah will appear. A mighty warrior, he will rout and destroy the armies of the enemy; he will take captive the leader of the Romans and bring him in chains to Mount Zion, where he will put him to death; he will establish a kingdom which shall last until the end of the world. All the nations which have ever ruled over Israel will be put to the sword; and some members of the remaining nations will be subjected to the Chosen People. An age of bliss will begin in which pain, disease, untimely death, violence and strife, want and hunger will be unknown and in which the earth will yield its fruits ten-thousand-fold. Would this earthly Paradise last for ever or for some centuries only, pending its replacement by an other-worldly Kingdom? On this matter opinions differed but the question was in any case an academic one. Temporary or eternal, such a Kingdom was worth fighting for; and these apocalypses had at least established that in the course of bringing the Saints into their Kingdom the Messiah would show himself invincible in war.

As, under the rule of the procurators, the conflict with Rome became more and more bitter, messianic phantasies became with many Jews an obsessive preoccupation. According to Josephus it was chiefly the belief in the imminent advent of a messianic king that launched the Jews upon the suicidal war which ended with the capture of Jerusalem and the destruction of the Temple in A.D. 70. Even Simon bar-Cochba, who led the last great struggle for national independence in A.D. 131, was still greeted as Messiah. But the bloody suppression of that rising and the annihilation of political nationality put an end both to the apocalyptic faith and to the militancy of the Jews. Although in later centuries a number of self-styled messiahs arose amongst the dispersed communities, what they offered was merely a reconstitution of the national home, not an eschatological world-empire. Moreover they very rarely inspired armed risings, and never amongst European Jews. It was no longer Jews but Christians who cherished and elaborated prophecies in the tradition of 'Daniel's dream' and who continued to be inspired by them.

A messiah who suffered and died, a kingdom which was purely spiritual – such ideas, which were later to be regarded as the very core of Christian doctrine, were far from being accepted by all the early Christians. Ever since the problem was formulated by Johannes Weiss and Albert Schweitzer some sixty years ago experts have been debating how far Christ's own teaching was influenced by Jewish apocalyptic. If that question lies far outside the scope of the present study, some of the sayings which the Gospels attribute to Christ lie well within it. The celebrated prophecy recorded by Matthew is certainly of great significance, and remains significant whether Christ really uttered it or was merely believed to have done so: 'For the Son of Man shall come in the glory of his Father with his angels; and then he shall reward every man according to his works. Verily I say unto you, there be some standing here, which shall not taste of death, till they see the Son of Man coming in his kingdom.' It is not surprising that many of the early Christians interpreted these things in terms of the apocalyptic eschatology with which they were already familiar. Like so many generations of Jews before them they saw history as divided into two eras, one preceding and the other following the triumphant advent of the Messiah. That they often referred to the second era as 'the Last Days' or 'the world to come' does not mean that they anticipated a swift and cataclysmic end of all things. On the contrary, for a long time great numbers of Christians were convinced not only that Christ would soon return in power and majesty but also that when he did return it would be to establish a messianic kingdom on earth. And they confidently expected that kingdom to last, whether for a thousand years or for an indefinite period.

Like the Jews, the Christians suffered oppression and responded to it by affirming ever more vigorously, to the world and to themselves, their faith in the imminence of the messianic age in which their wrongs would be righted and their enemies cast down. Not surprisingly, the way in which they imagined the great transformation also owed much to the Jewish apocalypses, some of which had indeed a wider circulation amongst Christians than amongst Jews. In the apocalypse known as the Book of Revelation, Jewish and Christian elements are blended in an eschatological prophecy of great poetic power. Here, as in the Book of Daniel, a terrible ten-horned beast symbolizes the last world-power – now the persecuting Roman state; while a second beast symbolizes the Roman provincial priesthood which demanded divine honours for the Emperor:

And I stood upon the sand of the sea and saw a beast rise up out of the sea, having . . . ten horns. . . . And it was given to him to make war with the saints, and to overcome them: and power was given to him over all kindreds, and tongues, and nations. And all that dwell upon the earth shall worship him, whose names are not written in the book of life. . . . And I beheld another beast coming up out of the earth. . . . And he doeth great wonders . . . and deceiveth them that dwell on the earth by means of those miracles which he had power to do . . .

And I saw heaven opened, and behold a white horse; and he that sat upon him was called Faithful and True, and in righteousness he doth judge and make war. . . . And the armies which were in heaven followed him upon white horses, clothed in fine linen, white and clean. And out of his mouth goeth a sharp sword, that with it he should smite the nations. . . . And I saw the beast, and the kings of the earth, and their armies gathered to make war against him that sat on the horse, and against his army. And the beast was taken, and with him the false prophet that wrought miracles before him, with which he deceived them that had received the mark of the beast, and them that worshipped his image. These both were cast alive into a lake of fire burning with brimstone. And the remnant were slain with the sword of him that sat upon the horse . . . and all the fowls were filled with their flesh . . .

And I saw the souls of them that were beheaded for the witness of Jesus and for the word of God, and who had not worshipped the beast . . . and they lived and reigned with Christ a thousand years . . .

At the end of which period – the Millennium in the strict sense of the word – there follow the general resurrection of the dead and the Last Judgement, when those who are not found written in the book of life are cast out into the lake of fire and the New Jerusalem is let down from heaven to be a dwelling-place for the Saints for ever:

And I saw a new heaven and a new earth: for the first heaven and the first earth were passed away; and there was no more sea. And I John saw the holy city, new Jerusalem, coming down from God out of heaven, prepared as a bride adorned for her husband. And I heard a great voice out of heaven saying, Behold, the tabernacle of God is with men, and he will dwell with them, and they shall be his people, and God himself shall be with them, and be their God. And God shall wipe away all tears from their eyes; and there shall be no more death, neither sorrow, nor crying, neither shall there be any more pain: for the former things are passed away. And he that sat upon the throne said, Behold, I make all things new. . . . And he carried me away in the spirit to a great and high mountain, and showed me that great city, the holy Jerusalem, descending out of heaven from God, having the glory of God: and her light was like unto a stone most precious, even like a jasper stone, clear as crystal . . .

How literally people could take this prophecy and with what feverish excitement they could expect its fulfilment is shown by the movement known as Montanism. In A.D. 156 it happened in Phrygia that a certain Montanus declared himself to be the incarnation of the Holy Ghost, that 'Spirit of Truth' who according to the Fourth Gospel was to reveal things to come. There soon gathered around him a number of ecstatics, much given to visionary experiences which they confidently believed to be of divine origin and to which they even gave the name of 'the Third Testament'. The theme of their illuminations was the imminent coming of the Kingdom: the New Jerusalem was about to descend from the heavens on to Phrygian soil, where it would become the habitation of the Saints. The Montanists accordingly summoned all Christians to Phrygia, there to await the Second Coming, in fasting and prayer and bitter repentance.

It was a fiercely ascetic movement, which thirsted for suffering and even for martyrdom; for was it not, above all, the martyrs resurrected in the flesh who were to be denizens of the Millennium? Nothing was so propitious to the spread of Montanism as persecution; and when, from the year 177 onwards, Christians were being once again persecuted in many provinces of the Empire, Montanism suddenly ceased to be merely a local movement and spread far and wide, not only through Asia Minor but to Africa, Rome and even Gaul. Although Montanists no longer looked to Phrygia, their confidence in the imminent appearance of the New Jerusalem was unshaken; and this was true even of Tertullian, the most famous theologian in the West at that time, when he joined the movement. In the early years of the third century we find Tertullian writing of a wondrous portent: in Judaea a walled city had been seen in the sky early every morning for forty days, to fade away as the day advanced; and this was a sure sign that the Heavenly Jerusalem was about to descend. It was the same vision which (as we shall see) was to hypnotize the masses of the People's Crusades as they toiled towards Jerusalem, some nine centuries later.

In expecting the Second Coming from day to day and week to week the Montanists were following in the footsteps of many, perhaps most, of the earliest Christians; even the Book of Revelation had still expected it to happen 'shortly'. By the middle of the second century such an attitude was however becoming somewhat unusual. The tone of the Second Epistle of Peter, which was written about A.D. 150, is hesitant: out of compassion, Christ may tarry 'until all should have come to repentance'. At the same time a process began by which Christian apocalypses which had hitherto enjoyed canonical authority were deprived of it, until only the Book of Revelation survived – and that only because it was mistakenly attributed to St John. Yet if a growing number of Christians thought of the Millennium as a remote rather than as an impending event, many were still convinced that it would come in the fulness of time. Justin Martyr, who was certainly no Montanist, establishes the point clearly enough in *Dialogue with the Jew Trypho*. There he makes his Jewish interlocutor ask: 'Do you Christians really maintain that this place, Jerusalem, will be built up again, and do you really believe that your people will assemble here in joy, under Christ, and together with the patriarchs and the prophets?' To which Justin replies that, while not all true Christians are of that persuasion, he and many others are united in the confident belief that the Saints will indeed live a thousand years in a rebuilt, adorned and enlarged Jerusalem.

Remote or imminent, the Kingdom of the Saints could no doubt be imagined in many different ways, from the most material to the most spiritual; but certainly the imaginings of many even of the most highly educated Christians were material enough. An early specimen of these phantasies is provided by the 'Apostolic Father' Papias, who was probably born about A.D. 60 and who may have sat at the feet of St John. This Phrygian was a man of learning who devoted himself to preserving first-hand accounts of Christ's teaching. Although the millennial prophecy which he attributes to Christ is spurious – counterparts are to be found in various Jewish apocalypses such as *Baruch* – it is of great interest as showing what at any rate some educated and earnest Christians of the sub-apostolic age expected – and what moreover they could believe Christ himself to have expected:

The days will come in which vines shall appear, having each ten thousand shoots, and on every shoot ten thousand twigs, and on each true twig ten thousand stems, and on every stem ten thousand bunches, and in every bunch ten thousand grapes, and every grape will give five-and-twenty metretes of wine. And when any one of the Saints shall take hold of a bunch, another bunch shall cry out, 'I am a better bunch, take me; bless the Lord through me.' Likewise [the Lord] said that a grain of wheat would bear ten thousand ears, and every ear would have ten thousand grains, and every grain would give ten pounds of the finest flour, clear and pure; and apples and seeds and grass would produce in similar proportions; and all animals, feeding only on what they received from the earth, would become peaceable and friendly to each other, and completely subject to man. Now these things are credible to believers. And Judas, being a disbelieving traitor, asked, 'How shall such growth be brought about by the Lord?' But the Lord answered, 'They shall see who shall come to those times.'

Irenaeus, who was also a native of Asia Minor, brought these prophecies with him when he came to settle in Gaul towards the end of the second century. As Bishop of Lyons and a distinguished theologian he probably did more than anyone to establish the millenarian outlook in the West. The concluding chapters of his massive treatise *Against Heresies* form a comprehensive anthology of messianic and millenarian prophecies culled from the Old and New Testaments (and including also the passage from Papias). In the opinion of Irenaeus it is an indispensable part of orthodoxy to believe that these things shall indeed come to pass on this earth, for the benefit both of the righteous dead, who are to be resurrected, and of the righteous living. And the reason which he gives for his conviction shows that the part played by compensatory phantasies was no smaller than it had been in the days of 'Daniel's dream':

For it is just that in that very creation in which they toiled and were afflicted and were tried in every way by suffering, they should receive the reward of their suffering; and that in the very creation in which they were killed for the love of God they should be revived again; and that in the very creation in which they endured servitude, they should also reign. For God is rich in all things, and all things are his. It is fitting, therefore, that the creation itself, being restored to its primeval condition, should without qualification be under the dominion of the righteous ...

The pattern was still the same in the fourth century. When the eloquent Lactantius set about winning converts to Christianity he did not hesitate to reinforce the attractions of the Millennium with those of a bloody vengeance on the unrighteous:

But that madman (Antichrist), raging with implacable anger, will lead an army and besiege the mountain where the righteous have taken refuge. And when they see themselves besieged, they will call loudly to God for help, and God shall hear them, and shall send them a liberator. Then the heavens shall be opened in a tempest, and Christ shall descend with great power; and a fiery brightness shall go before him, and a countless host of angels; and all that multitude of the godless shall be annihilated, and torrents of blood shall flow. . . . When peace has been brought about and every evil suppressed, that righteous and victorious King will carry out a great judgement on the earth of the living and the dead, and will hand over all heathen peoples to servitude under the righteous who are alive, and will raise the (righteous) dead to eternal life, and will himself reign with them on earth, and will found the Holy City, and this kingdom of the righteous shall last for a thousand years. Throughout that time the stars shall be brighter, and the brightness of the sun shall be increased, and the moon shall not wane. Then the rain of blessing shall descend from God morning and evening, and the earth shall bear all fruits without man's labour. Honey in abundance shall drip from the rocks, fountains of milk and wine shall burst forth. The beasts of the forests shall put away their wildness and become tame . . . no longer shall any animal live by bloodshed. For God shall supply all with abundant and guiltless food.

It is in the pages of Commodianus, a very inferior Latin poet of (probably) the fifth century, that the usual phantasies of vengeance and triumph suddenly crystallize into an urge to take up arms and fight – a first foreshadowing of the crusading millenarianism which was to burst upon Europe in the later Middle Ages. For according to Commodianus when Christ returns it will be at the head not of an angelic host but of the descendants of the ten lost tribes of Israel, which have survived in hidden places, unknown to the rest of the world. This 'hidden, final, holy people' is shown as a singularly virtuous community which knows nothing of hatred, deceit or lust and which carries its dislike of bloodshed to the point of vegetarianism. It is also a divinely favoured community, for it is wholly immune from fatigue, sickness and premature death. Now this host hastens to liberate Jerusalem, 'the captive mother'. 'They come with the King of Heaven. . . . All creation rejoices to see the heavenly people.' Mountains flatten themselves before them, fountains burst forth along their route, clouds bow down to protect them from the sun. But these Saints are fierce warriors, irresistible in war. Raging like lions, they devastate the lands they cross, overthrow the nations and destroy the cities. 'By God's permission' they loot gold and silver, singing hymns for the favours thus lavished upon them. Antichrist in terror flees to the northern parts and returns at the head of an army of followers who are obviously those fabulous and fearsome peoples known collectively as Gog and Magog, whom Alexander the Great was said to have imprisoned in the far North. But Antichrist is defeated by the angels of God and cast into hell; his captains are reduced to be the slaves of the Holy People and so, later, are the few survivors of the Last Judgement. As for the Holy People themselves, they live for ever in a Holy Jerusalem – immortal and unaging, marrying and begetting, unafflicted by rain or cold, while all around them a perpetually rejuvenated earth pours forth its fruits.

The apocalyptic tradition in medieval Europe

The third century saw the first attempt to discredit millenarianism, when Origen, perhaps the most influential of all the theologians of the ancient Church, began to present the Kingdom as an event which would take place not in space or time but only in the souls of believers. For a collective, millenarian eschatology Origen substituted an eschatology of the individual soul. What stirred his profoundly Hellenic imagination was the prospect of spiritual progress begun in this world and continued in the next; and to this theme theologians were henceforth to give increasing attention. Such a shift in interest was indeed admirably suited to what was now an organized Church, enjoying almost uninterrupted peace and an acknowledged position in the world. When in the fourth century Christianity attained a position of supremacy in the Mediterranean world and became the official religion of the Empire, ecclesiastical disapproval of millenarianism became emphatic. The Catholic Church was now a powerful and prosperous institution, functioning according to a well-established routine; and the men responsible for governing it had no wish to see Christians clinging to out-dated and inappropriate dreams of a new earthly Paradise. Early in the fifth century St Augustine propounded the doctrine which the new conditions demanded. According to *The City of God* the Book of Revelation was to be understood as a spiritual allegory; as for the Millennium, that had begun with the birth of Christianity and was fully realized in the Church. This at once became orthodox doctrine. Now the very fact that the eminently respectable Irenaeus could have regarded such a belief as an indispensable part of orthodoxy was felt to be intolerable. Determined efforts were made to suppress the millenarian chapters of his treatise *Against Heresies*, and to such good effect that it was only in 1575 that they were rediscovered in a manuscript which the expurgators happened to have overlooked.

Nevertheless the importance of the apocalyptic tradition should not be underestimated; even though official doctrine no longer had any place for it, it persisted in the obscure underworld of popular religion. It was largely thanks to that tradition that the idea of the Saints of the Most High became as potent in some Christian circles as it had ever been amongst Jews – although, since Christianity claimed to be a universal religion, it was no longer interpreted in a national sense. In Christian apocalyptic the old phantasy of divine election was preserved and revitalized; it was the body of literature inaugurated by the Book of Revelation which encouraged Christians to see themselves as the Chosen People of the Lord – chosen both to prepare the way for and to inherit the Millennium. And this idea had such enormous attractions that no official condemnation could prevent it from recurring again and again to the minds of the unprivileged, the oppressed, the disoriented and the unbalanced. The institutionalized Church did indeed show the utmost skill in controlling and canalizing the emotional energies of the faithful, and particularly in directing hopes and fears away from this life and towards the next. But although its efforts were normally successful, they were not invariably so. Particularly at times of general uncertainty or excitement people were always apt to turn to the Book of Revelation and the innumerable commentaries upon it – alongside which there gradually emerged another and equally influential body of apocalyptic writings, now known as the medieval Sibylline Oracles.

The apocalyptic of Hellenistic Judaism included some books which, like the famous Sibylline Books preserved at Rome, claimed to record the utterances of inspired prophetesses. In reality these 'oracles', written in Greek hexameters, were literary productions which were intended to convert pagans to Judaism and which did in fact enjoy a great vogue amongst them. When proselytizing Christians in turn began to produce Sibylline prophecies they drew heavily on these Jewish Sibyllines. This new prophetic literature still knew only one eschatological Saviour: the warrior-Christ as he had appeared in the Book of Revelation. But ever since Alexander the Great the Graeco-Roman world had been accustomed to deify its monarchs. There had been Hellenistic kings who carried the title of 'Saviour' and Roman Emperors who were accorded divine honours in their lifetime. It was therefore not surprising that, as soon as Christianity joined forces with the Empire, Christian Sibyllines should greet the Emperor Constantine as the messianic king. After Constantine's death the Sibyllines continued to attach an eschatological significance to the figure of the Roman Emperor. Thanks to them, in the imagination of Christians for more than a thousand years the figure of the warrior-Christ was doubled by another, that of the Emperor of the Last Days.

The oldest of the Sibyllines known to medieval Europe was the *Tiburtina*, which in its Christian form dates from the middle of the fourth century. From 340 to 350 the Empire was divided between the two surviving sons of Constantine: Constans I, who ruled in the West, and Constantius II, who ruled in the East. The Arian controversy was at its height; and whereas Constans was a staunch upholder of the Nicene faith and a protector of Athanasius, Constantius inclined – more on political than theological grounds – to favour the Arian party. In 350 Constans, who had proved a vicious ruler, was murdered by his troops and Constantius became the sole ruler of the Empire. The Tiburtine Sibylline reflects the reactions of Catholics to this setback. It tells of a 'time of sorrows', when Rome will be captured and tyrants will oppress the poor and innocent and protect the guilty. But then there comes a Greek Emperor called Constans who unites the western and eastern halves of the Empire under his rule.

Of commanding presence, tall, well-proportioned, with handsome and radiant face, Constans reigns 112 (or 120) years. It is an age of plenty: oil, wine and corn are abundant and cheap. It is also the age which sees the final triumph of Christianity. The Emperor lays waste the cities of the heathen and destroys the temples of the false gods. He summons the heathen themselves to Christian baptism; those heathen who refuse to be converted must die by the sword. At the end of the long reign the Jews too are converted and when this happens the Holy Sepulchre shines forth in glory. The twenty-two peoples of Gog and Magog break loose, multitudinous as the sands of the sea; but the Emperor calls his army together and annihilates them. His task accomplished, · the Emperor journeys to Jerusalem, there to lay down the imperial crown and robes on Golgotha and so hand over Christendom to the care of God. The Golden Age and with it the Roman Empire have come to an end, but before the end of all things there remains a short time of tribulation. For now Antichrist appears and reigns in the Temple at Jerusalem, deceiving many by his miracles and persecuting those whom he cannot deceive. For the sake of the Elect the Lord shortens those days and sends the Archangel Michael to destroy Antichrist. Then at last the way lies open for the Second Coming to take place.

The figure of the Emperor of the Last Days, introduced for the first time by the *Tiburtina*, looms still larger in the Sibylline known as the *Pseudo-Methodius*. This prophecy, which was disguised as a work of the fourth-century bishop and martyr Methodius of Patara, was in reality composed towards the end of the seventh century. Its original purpose was to bring consolation to Syrian Christians in their galling and still unfamiliar position as a minority under Moslem rule. It opens with a survey of world-history from the Garden of Eden to Alexander and then passes at one bound to the author's own time. Under the guise of a prophecy of things still to come it describes how the Ishmaelites, once defeated by Gideon and driven back into their deserts, return and ravage the land from Egypt to Ethiopia and from the Euphrates to India. The Christians are punished for their sins by being subjected for a time by these hordes, who of course stand for the conquering armies of Islam. The Ishmaelites kill Christian priests and desecrate the Holy Places, by force or guile they seduce many Christians from the true faith, they take from the Christians one piece of land after another, they boast that the Christians have fallen into their hands for ever.

But – and here the prophecy for the first time really ventures into the future – just when the situation is worse than it has ever been, a mighty Emperor, whom men had long thought to be dead, shakes off his slumber and rises up in his wrath. He defeats the Ishmaelites and lays waste their lands with fire and sword, he sets upon them a yoke a hundred times more oppressive than that which they had set upon the Christians, he rages also against those Christians who have denied their Lord. There follows a period of peace and joy during which the Empire, united under this great ruler, flourishes as never before. But then the hosts of Gog and Magog break out, bringing universal devastation and terror, until God sends a captain of the heavenly host who destroys them in a flash. The Emperor journeys to Jerusalem, there to await the appearance of Antichrist. When that dread event occurs the Emperor places his crown upon the Cross at Golgotha and the Cross soars up to heaven. The Emperor dies and Antichrist begins his reign. But before long the Cross reappears in the heavens as the sign of the Son of Man and Christ himself comes on the clouds in power and glory, to kill Antichrist with the breath of his mouth and to carry out the Last Judgement.

The particular political situations which had evoked these prophecies passed away and the very memory of them was lost, yet the prophecies themselves kept all their fascination. Throughout the Middle Ages the Sibylline eschatology persisted alongside the eschatologies derived from the Book of Revelation, modifying them and being modified by them but generally surpassing them in popularity. For, uncanonical and unorthodox though they were, the Sibyllines had enormous influence – indeed save for the Bible and the works of the Fathers they were probably the most influential writings known to medieval Europe. They often dictated the pronouncements of dominant figures in the Church, monks and nuns such as St Bernard and St Hildegard whose counsel even popes and emperors regarded as divinely inspired. Moreover they proved infinitely adaptable: constantly edited and reinterpreted to fit the conditions and appeal to the preoccupations of the moment, they catered at all times for the craving of anxious mortals for an unquestionable forecast of the future. Already when the only versions known to the West were in Latin and therefore accessible only to clerics, some knowledge of their purport penetrated even to the lowest strata of the laity. From the four-teenth century onwards translations began to appear in the various European languages, and when printing was invented these trans-lations were amongst the first books to be printed. At the very close of the Middle Ages, when the fears and hopes which first shaped the Sibylline prophecies lay a thousand years and more in the past, these books were being read and studied every-where.

The Johannine tradition* tells of one warrior-saviour who is to appear in the Last Days, the Sibylline tradition tells of two, but both traditions agree that in those times there will arise an arch-enemy of God, the prodigious figure of Antichrist. This was a figure to which the most diverse traditions had contributed and which had become a symbol as potent as it was complex. Here again the influence of 'Daniel's dream' was decisive. When that prophecy spoke of a king who 'shall exalt himself, and magnify himself above every god', and 'speak great words against the most High', it was referring cryptically to the persecuting monarch Antiochus Epiphanes, who was in fact a megalomaniac. But the origin of the prophecy was soon forgotten, even while the Book of Daniel continued to be regarded as a sacred scripture which foretold future things. Disengaged from its historical context the figure of the god-hating Tyrant of the Last Days passed into the common stock of Jewish and later of Christian apocalyptic lore. In St Paul's warning to the Thessalonians and in the Book of Revelation this figure reappears as the pseudo-messiah 'who op-poseth and exalteth himself above all that is called God, or that is worshipped; so that he as God sitteth in the temple of God, showing himself that he is God . . .'. By the 'signs and lying

* i.e. stemming from the Book of Revelation, which is attributed to S John.

wonders' which the false prophet will work through the power of Satan he will deceive the world. On the surface he will seem all virtue and benevolence. His wickedness, though absolute, will be most cunningly masked and this will enable him to establish a tyrannical rule of great strength: 'And it was given unto him to make war with the saints, and to overcome them: and power was given him over all kindreds, and tongues, and nations.'

This figure, to which the name of Antichrist was now given, could therefore be regarded as a human being, a despot at once seductive and cruel, and as such a servant and instrument of Satan. But Antichrist never was thought of as being merely a man, however wicked. The Persian (Mazdean) expectation of the overthrow of the arch-devil Ahriman at the end of days, interwoven with the Babylonian myth of a battle between the supreme God and the Dragon of Chaos, penetrated into Jewish eschatology and profoundly influenced the phantasy of the Tyrant of the Last Days. Already in the prophecy of 'Daniel', Antiochus appears not only as the king of fierce countenance but also as the horned creature which 'waxed great, even to the host of heaven; and it cast down some of the host of heaven and of the stars to the ground, and stamped upon them.' In the Book of Revelation the traditional role of Antichrist is divided between the First Beast – the great red dragon which appears in the heavens or rises out of the sea, with seven heads and ten horns – and the Second Beast – the horned monster which 'speaks as a dragon' and which comes up out of the bottomless pit inside the earth.

Here the figure of Antichrist has merged into the figure of that other horned monster who dwelt in the depths of the earth, 'the dragon, that old serpent', Satan himself; and during all the centuries when he continued to preoccupy and fascinate the imagination of men, Antichrist retained this demoniacal quality. Throughout the Middle Ages he was portrayed not only as an enthroned tyrant but also as a demon or dragon flying in the air surrounded by lesser demons, or trying to fly aloft in order to prove himself God and being hurled to his death by God [Plate 1]. In the middle of the twelfth century St Hildegard of Bingen saw him in a vision as a beast with monstrous, coal-black head, flaming eyes, ass's ears and gaping, iron-fanged maw. In fact Antichrist was, like Satan, a gigantic embodiment of anarchic, destructive power. To appreciate how boundless that power was felt to be, how superhuman and how terrifying, one has only to look at Melchior Lorch's portrayal of Satan-Antichrist (here identified with the Pope) [Plate 2]. This picture dates from the middle of the sixteenth century but the emotion which it expresses, compounded of horror, hatred and disgust, had been troubling Europeans for many centuries before.

The Sibylline and Johannine prophecies deeply affected political attitudes. For medieval people the stupendous drama of the Last Days was not a phantasy about some remote and indefinite future but a prophecy which was infallible and which at almost any given moment was felt to be on the point of fulfilment. Medieval chronicles show clearly enough how particular political judgements were coloured by these expectations. In even the most unlikely reigns chroniclers tried to perceive that harmony amongst Christians, that triumph over misbelievers, that unparalleled plenty and prosperity which were to be the marks of the new Golden Age. In almost every new monarch his subjects tried to see that Last Emperor who was to preside over the Golden Age, while chroniclers bestowed on him the conventional messianic epithets, *rex justus* or maybe David. When each time experience brought the inevitable disillusionment people merely imagined the glorious consummation postponed to the next reign and, if they possibly could, regarded the reigning monarch as a 'precursor' with the mission of making the way straight for the Last Emperor. And there was never any lack of monarchs to appeal, with varying degrees of sincerity or cynicism, to these persistent hopes. In the West both French and German dynasties exploited the Sibylline prophecies to support their claims to primacy, as the Byzantine Emperors had done before them in the East.

The coming of Antichrist was even more tensely awaited. Generation after generation lived in constant expectation of the all-destroying demon whose reign was indeed to be lawless chaos, an age given over to robbery and rapine, torture and massacre, but was also to be the prelude to the longed-for consummation, the Second Coming and the Kingdom of the Saints. People were always on the watch for the 'signs' which, according to the prophetic tradition, were to herald and accompany the final 'time of troubles'; and since the 'signs' included bad rulers, civil discord, war, drought, famine, plague, comets, sudden deaths of prominent persons and an increase in general sinfulness, there was never any difficulty about finding them. Invasion or the threat of invasion by Huns, Magyars, Mongols, Saracens or Turks always stirred memories of those hordes of Antichrist, the peoples of Gog and Magog. Above all, any ruler who could be regarded as a tyrant was apt to take on the features of Antichrist; in which case hostile chroniclers would give him the conventional title of *rex iniquus*. When such a monarch died, leaving the prophecies unfulfilled, he would be degraded, just like the *rex justus*, to the rank of 'precursor'; and the waiting would be resumed. And here too was an idea which lent itself admirably to political exploitation. It frequently happened that a pope would solemnly declare his opponent – some turbulent emperor or maybe an anti-pope – to be Antichrist himself; whereupon the same epithet would be flung back at him.

But if traditional phantasies about the Last Days constantly influenced the way in which political happenings and personalities were viewed and the language in which political struggles were conducted, it was only in certain social situations that they functioned as a dynamic social myth. In due course we shall consider what these situations were. But first it is necessary to glance at the tradition of religious dissent which always existed in medieval Europe and which could at times produce claimants to messianic or quasi-messianic roles.

2 The Tradition of Religious Dissent

The ideal of the apostolic life

The tradition of apocalyptic prophecy was only one of several preconditions of the movements with which this book is concerned. Another was the tradition of religious dissent which persisted throughout the Middle Ages. Not that these movements were typical expressions of religious dissent; on the contrary, in many respects – in their atmosphere, their aims, their behaviour and (as we shall see) their social composition – they were altogether untypical. Nevertheless, these particular upheavals can be fully understood only in the context of widespread religious dissatisfaction.

Of course the Church played a huge part in creating and sustaining medieval civilization, its influence permeated the thoughts and feelings of all sorts and conditions of men and women – and yet it always had difficulty in satisfying completely the religious aspirations it fostered. It had its religious elite, the monks and nuns, whose lives – at least in theory, and often in practice too – were wholly devoted to the service of God. Monks and nuns served society as a whole by their prayers, and often they also cared for the sick and needy; but it was not, generally, their task to minister to the spiritual needs of the laity. That was the responsibility of the secular clergy, and it was a responsibility which they were often ill equipped to discharge. If the monks and nuns tended to be too remote from the world, the secular clergy, from bishops to parish priests, tended to be over-involved in it. Wealth and political ambitions amongst the higher clergy, concubinage or sexual laxity amongst the lower clergy – these were the things that layfolk complained of. And there was also a great hunger for evangelism; people longed to hear the Gospel preached simply and directly, so that they could relate what they heard to their own experience.

The standards by which the Church was judged were those which the Church itself had set before the peoples of Europe as an ideal; for they were the standards of primitive Christianity, as portrayed in the Gospels and in the Acts of the Apostles. To some extent those standards were enshrined in the monastic way of life, which was modelled on the way of life of the Apostles. 'For then,' says the Rule of St Benedict, 'are they truly monks when they live by the labour of their hands, like our fathers and the apostles.' And when, in the tenth and eleventh centuries, the monasteries of Cluny and Hirsau launched their great movement of reform, the object was to bring monastic life more closely into line with the life of the first Christian community as described in *Acts*: 'And all that believed were together, and had all things in common ... neither said any of them that aught of the things which he possessed was his own ...' But all this, enclosed within monastery walls, was only of limited interest to the laity. There were always some layfolk who noted, with bitterness, the gulf that separated the poverty and simplicity of the first Christians from the wealthy, hierarchically organized Church of their own time. These people wanted to see, in their midst, men in whose holiness they could trust, living and preaching like the original Apostles.

Men did exist who were prepared to fill that role, even if it meant going against the Church. In the eyes of the Church, only its duly ordained ministers were entitled to preach; laymen who presumed to do so fell under the Church's ban. Yet there hardly seems to have been a time in medieval Europe when there were no lay preachers wandering through the land, in imitation of the Apostles. Such people were known already in sixth-century Gaul; and they continued to appear from time to time until, from about 1100 onwards, they suddenly became both more numerous and more important.

The change can be regarded as a by-product of one of those great efforts to reform the Church from within that punctuate the history of medieval Christianity; and in this case the dynamism behind the reform came from the papacy itself. In the Middle Ages the Church, including the monasteries, had fallen into dependence on secular monarchs and nobles, who controlled ecclesiastical appointments at all levels. But during the eleventh century a succession of vigorous popes set out to establish the autonomy of the Church; and this involved a new emphasis on the special status and dignity of the clergy, as a spiritual elite standing clearly apart from and above the laity. The formidable Gregory VII in particular made strenuous efforts to suppress simony, or the purchase of ecclesiastical offices, and to enforce clerical celibacy (at a time when many priests were married or living in concubinage).

In their efforts to carry out this papal policy, the propagandists of reform did not hesitate to whip up the feelings of the laity against refractory clerics. Some even went so far as to call simoniac bishops servants of Satan, and to suggest that ordinations made by such bishops were invalid. Diocesan councils repeatedly forbade married or concubinary priests to say mass; and so did Gregory VII himself. Orthodox reformers did not, of course, argue that sacraments administered by unworthy priests were invalid; but it is not surprising that such ideas should have begun to circulate amongst the laity. The great reform movement had itself intensified the religious zeal of laymen and laywomen; the yearning for holy men of apostolic life was stronger than ever. By the end of the eleventh century newly awakened religious energies were beginning to escape from ecclesiastical control and to turn against the Church. It was now widely felt that the test for a true priest lay not in the fact of ordination but in his fidelity to the apostolic way of life. Henceforth unauthorized wandering preachers could expect a following such as they had never known before.

It is worth while to glance at a typical freelance preacher who flourished in France at the beginning of the twelfth century. He was a former monk called Henry, who had left his monastery and taken to the roads. On Ash Wednesday in 1116 he arrived at Le Mans, and he did so in some state: he was preceded by two disciples, as Christ had been on his last approach to Jerusalem; and these disciples bore a cross, as though their master were a bishop. The real bishop, Hildebert of Lavardin, took all this in good part; he even gave Henry permission to preach Lenten sermons in the town, and then imprudently took himself off on the long journey to Rome. As soon as the bishop's back was turned Henry – a bearded young man, dressed only in a hair shirt, and endowed with a mighty voice – began to preach against the local clergy. He found willing listeners. The people of Le Mans were very ready to turn against their clergy, for these were a venal and loose-living lot. Moreover, the bishops of Le Mans had long been active in local politics, and in an unpopular cause – they had lent their support to the counts, from whose overlordship the burghers were struggling to free themselves. All in all, it is not surprising that after a short course of Henry's preaching the populace was beating priests in the streets and rolling them in the mud.

One need not believe the accusations of sexual licence and perversion which the clerical chroniclers brought against Henry, for these were clichés which were regularly brought against religious dissidents. On the contrary, Henry seems to have been a preacher of sexual austerity, who persuaded women to throw their rich clothes and ornaments on to bonfires specially lit for the purpose, and who reformed prostitutes by marrying them off to his own followers. But about his anticlerical ardour there is no doubt. In later years, when he was active in Italy and Provence, he rejected the authority of the Church altogether, denying that ordained priests had the power to consecrate the host, to give absolution, or to preside at marriages. Baptism, he taught, should be given only as an external sign of belief. Church buildings and all the trappings of official religion were useless; a man could pray anywhere as well as he could in a church. The true Church consisted of those who followed the apostolic life, in poverty and simplicity; love of one's neighbour was the essence of true religion. And Henry regarded himself as directly commissioned by God to preach this message.

Henry was to have many successors. Throughout the Middle Ages the demand for religious reform persisted; and the ideal behind that demand, if it varied in detail from time to time and from place to place, remained the same in essentials. Over a period of some four centuries, from the Waldensians through the Franciscan Spirituals to the Anabaptists, one finds men wandering through the land, living a life of poverty and simplicity in imitation of the apostles, and preaching the Gospel to a laity avid for spiritual guidance.

Admittedly, that ideal was not confined to dissenters or (as they were called) heretics. Already in Henry's time there were other monks, such as Robert of Arbrissel and St Norbert of Xanten, who went out into the world as wandering preachers with the full permission of the pope; and when, in the thirteenth century, the Franciscan and Dominican orders were created, they were quite consciously modelled on the apostolic life. Indeed, without the various attempts to realize the ideal of primitive Christianity within the framework of the institutionalized Church, the movement of dissent would certainly have been far larger than it was. Yet these attempts were never wholly successful. Again and again the preaching monks or friars withdrew behind their monastery walls, or else abandoned the pursuit of holiness for that of political influence. Again and again reforming orders, originally devoted to apostolic poverty, ended by acquiring great wealth. And whenever that happened, some part of the laity felt a spiritual vacuum, and some dissenting or heretical preachers came forward to fill that vacuum.

Normally these preachers offered themselves simply as spiritual guides. But sometimes they claimed to be much more – divinely inspired prophets, messiahs, even incarnate gods. This phenomenon lies at the very heart of the present study, and it is time to consider in more detail some early instances of it.

Some early messiahs

The sixth-century historian of the Franks, St Gregory, Bishop of Tours, is noted for the care with which he collected information about contemporary happenings; and in the town of Tours, which was situated on the high road between the north and south of France, he had an excellent listening post. The last six books of the *Historia Francorum*, which are written in the form of a diary and record each event as it occurred, are of particularly great historical value. Under the year 591 Gregory tells of a freelance preacher who set himself up as a messiah.

A man of Bourges, having gone into a forest, found himself suddenly surrounded by a swarm of flies; as a result of which he went out of his mind for two years. Later he made his way to the province of Arles, where he became a hermit, clad in animal skins and wholly dedicated to prayer. When he emerged from this ascetic training he claimed to possess supernatural gifts of healing and prophecy. Further wanderings took him to the district of Gévaudon, in the Cevennes, where he set himself up as Christ, with a woman whom he called Mary as his companion. People flocked to him with their sick, who were cured by his touch. He also foretold future events, prophesying sickness or other misfortunes for most of those who visited him, but salvation for a few.

The man displayed such powers that Gregory attributed them to the Devil's help. Certainly they were remarkable enough to secure him a large and devoted following – even if, as always with medieval statistics, one must regard the figure of 3,000 as a wild exaggeration. Nor did these followers consist solely of unlettered folk – they also included some priests. They brought him gold, silver and clothing; but the 'Christ' distributed all these things to the poor. When the gifts were offered he and his female companion would prostrate themselves and offer up prayers; but then, rising to his feet, he would order the assembly to worship him. Later he organized his followers in an armed band, which he led through the countryside, waylaying and robbing the travellers they met on the way. But here too his ambition was not to become rich but to be worshipped. He distributed all the booty to those who had nothing – including, one may assume, his own followers. On the other hand, when the band came to a town, the inhabitants, including the bishop, would be threatened with death unless they worshipped him.

It was at Le Puy that the messiah met his doom. When he arrived at this important episcopal city he quartered his 'army' – as Gregory calls it – in the neighbouring basilicas, as though he were about to wage war against the bishop, Aurelius. Then he sent messengers ahead to proclaim his coming; they presented themselves to the bishop stark naked, leaping and somersaulting. The bishop in his turn sent a party of his men to meet the messiah on the way. The leader of the party, pretending to bow, grabbed the man round the knees; after which he was quickly secured and cut to pieces. 'And so,' comments Gregory, 'fell and died that Christ, who should rather be called Antichrist.' His companion Mary was also seized, and was tortured until she revealed all the diabolic devices that had given him his power. As for the followers, they dispersed, but still remained under their leader's ban. Those who had believed in him continued to do so; to their dying day they maintained that he was indeed Christ and that the woman Mary, too, was a divine being.

In Gregory's experience the case was by no means unique. Several similar personalities appeared in other parts of the country, and they too attracted a devoted following, particularly amongst women; people regarded them as living saints. Gregory himself had met several such and had tried, by exhortation, to retrieve them from the paths of error. Yet he himself saw these happenings as so many 'signs' of the approaching End. Plague and famine were abroad, so surely false prophets must also be expected? For, he reflected, Christ himself said: '... there shall be famines, and pestilences, and earthquakes, in divers places.... Then if any man shall say unto you, Lo, here is Christ, or there; believe it not. For there shall arise false Christs, and false prophets, and shall show great signs and wonders; insomuch that, if it were possible, they shall deceive the very elect.' And these things were to mark the coming of the Last Days.

A century and a half later St Boniface, when functioning as papal legate and labouring to reform the Frankish church, came across a very similar figure called Aldebert. This man had come as a stranger to the district around Soissons, where the local bishop forbade him to preach in churches, even though he claimed to have been ordained. Aldebert was of humble origin and his audiences too consisted of simple country folk. Like the anonymous sixth-century messiah, he practised apostolic poverty; and he too claimed to perform miraculous cures. To begin with he merely set up crosses in the countryside and preached beside them, in the open air; but soon his followers built proper accommodation for him to preach in – first little chapels, then churches.

Aldebert was not content to be merely a reformer, he claimed to be a living saint. People, he said, ought to pray to him in the communion of saints, for he possessed extraordinary merits which could be put at the service of his devotees. And because he regarded himself as the equal of the saints and apostles he declined to dedicate his churches to any of them; instead, he dedicated them to himself. But indeed Aldebert went much further than that – he laid claim to at least some of Christ's distinctive attributes. Thus he declared that he was filled with God's grace while still in his mother's womb and, by God's special favour, was already a holy being when he was born. Before his birth his mother dreamed that a calf came out of her right side; inevitably one thinks of the Annunciation to Mary, and of Jesus as the Lamb of God – especially as Jesus was popularly believed to have been born through the right side of the Virgin.

A prayer composed by Aldebert, which Boniface sent to Rome for the Pope's consideration, shows how sure he was of a special relationship with God: God, it appears, had promised to give him whatever he desired. The prayer ends with a plea for support from eight angels; and from another source we know that Aldebert enjoyed the services of an angel who would bring him, from the ends of the earth, miracle-working relics, thanks to which he could obtain whatever he wanted for himself and his followers. He also possessed a letter from Christ, which he used as a basis for his own teachings – a phenomenon which we shall meet again and again in later chapters.

Aldebert's impact was certainly great. People abandoned their priests and bishops and flocked in multitudes to hear him. Over his immediate followers, who included many women, his hold was absolute. They were convinced that he knew all their sins, without their confessing them; and they treasured as miracle-working talismans the nail parings and hair clippings he distributed among them. His influence spread so far afield that Boniface regarded him as a serious menace to the Church, and even asked the Pope for help in 'leading the Franks and Gauls back to the right path' which Aldebert had caused them to abandon.

In fact a whole series of synods were concerned with his activities. In 744 Boniface held a synod at Soissons, with the approval of Pope Zachary and the active support of the Frankish kings Pepin and Carloman; it was decided to defrock Aldebert and to take him into custody, and to burn the crosses he had set up. But Aldebert escaped and continued to preach; so the following year another synod met, presided over by Boniface and King Carloman; this time Aldebert was declared not only deposed from the priesthood but also excommunicated. Still he managed to continue preaching, and to such effect that some months later yet another synod was convened, this time in Rome, consisting of twenty-four bishops and presided over by Pope Zachary himself. The Roman synod had before it not only a full account from Boniface but also a biography of Aldebert which that messiah had officially approved, and a prayer which he himself had composed. These documents convinced the synod that the man was a lunatic. As a result, he was treated leniently; for he was given a chance to recant and so avoid excommunication. Boniface had wanted him excommunicated and imprisoned at once; and he was certainly right in thinking that so long as Aldebert remained at liberty he would continue to preach his peculiar doctrine and to win adherents. In 746 an embassy from King Pepin to Pope Zachary reported that the eccentric preacher was still active. However, he seems to have died soon afterwards.

Four centuries later, at a time when wandering preachers of apostolic life were becoming a serious threat to the institutionalized Church, a 'Christ' was active in Brittany. The fullest account we possess of this man is given by William of Newburgh, who wrote half a century later. Normally, one would tend to discount such a belated source; but William is one of the more reliable of medieval chroniclers, and as in this instance most of his information faithfully repeats sources contemporaneous with the events, it seems likely that the remaining details come from some other early source, now lost.

William of Newburgh calls the Breton 'Christ' Eudo de Stella, and most modern historians have taken over this name or its French equivalent, Eudes de l'Etoile. The extant contemporary chronicles however refer to the man as (*inter alia*) Eys, Eon, Eun, and Eons, and know nothing of the 'de Stella'. There is similar uncertainty about his status. William of Newburgh is alone in saying that he was of noble origin; but there is general agreement that he came from Loudéac in Brittany and that he was not a monk or an ordained priest but a layman who had picked up a smattering of Latin.

He assumed the priestly prerogatives nevertheless. Around 1145 he began preaching in the open air; one may assume that, like other wandering preachers, he exalted the apostolic way of life. He also celebrated some kind of mass for the benefit of his followers. He was certainly a man of magnetic personality; those who had dealings with him were caught, we are told, 'like flies in a spider's web'. In the end he organized his followers in a new church, with archbishops and bishops whom he called by such names as Wisdom, Knowledge, Judgement and by the names of the original apostles. As for himself, he was convinced that it was his name that was indicated in the phrase at the end of prayers: 'per eundem Dominum nostrum Jesum Christum' really meant not 'through the same Jesus Christ our Lord' but 'through Eun Jesus Christ our Lord'. So he had no hesitation in calling himself the Son of God.

Eon was followed by great multitudes of the rough populace; and some of these people must certainly have been driven by sheer desperation. One of the original chroniclers of Eon's adventures comments that at that time such a famine was raging that the charitable were unable to support the starving masses of the poor, while even those who normally enjoyed a superfluity of goods were reduced to begging for food. It is known that the winter of 1144 was a terrible one and was followed by two years of appalling dearth. Multitudes of poor folk left lands which could no longer support them and migrated, even overseas. Brittany had been so utterly devastated by the Northmen some two centuries before that in the twelfth century it still resembled a colonial territory, sparsely populated by free peasants, and much of it covered by dense forests. It was in these forests that Eon had his base.

When a man decided to become a wandering preacher, whether orthodox or dissenting, he often started by going into a forest and living for some time as a hermit. During this period of ascetic training he would acquire the spiritual power for his mission; he might also acquire a reputation as a holy man and attract his first followers. That is how the pseudo-Baldwin was to begin his career in 1224; and Eon may well have followed the same course. What is certain is that, once his following was organized, it terrorized the forest-dwellers of Brittany. It was a restless and violent horde which delighted in raiding and destroying churches, monasteries and hermits' cells; wherever it passed, many perished by the sword and many more died of starvation. That much emerges from the contemporary chronicles. William of Newburgh adds that Eon's followers themselves lived in luxury, magnificently dressed, never doing any manual labour, always in a state of 'perfect joy'; it was even believed that demons provided them with splendid banquets, and that anyone who partook of these forfeited his understanding and became one of the community for ever. From all this one may conclude that, like similar hordes in later centuries, Eon's following lived largely by plunder.

Eon's influence extended far beyond his immediate followers.

In fact he became such a menace that in the end the Archbishop of Rouen sent an armed band against him. In 1148 he was taken prisoner – it was noted that the capture was signalled by that familiar portent of great happenings, the sudden appearance of a comet. Brought before a synod which was held in Rheims cathedral by Pope Eugenius he had a new observation to make about his name: the formula 'Per *eum* qui venturus est judicare vivos et mortuos et seculum per ignem' also referred to him, who was indeed the one who must come to judge the quick and the dead, and the world by fire. According to William of Newburgh Eon also explained that a forked staff which he carried regulated the government of the universe: when the fork pointed upwards two-thirds of the world belonged to God and one to himself; when it pointed downwards the proportions were reversed.

The synod handed Eon over to the custody of the Archbishop of Rouen. Imprisoned in a tower at Rouen, and fed on water and little else, the unfortunate man soon died. William of Newburgh tells also of the fate of his principal disciples. Captured along with their master, they steadfastly refused to deny him and bore proudly the titles he had given them. They were accordingly condemned to be burnt as impenitent heretics. They remained unshaken to the last. One of them threatened destruction to their executioners and as he was led to the stake cried out continuously: 'Earth, divide thyself!' 'For such,' comments William, 'is the power of error when once it has taken hold of the heart.'

No modern historian, it would seem, has ever denied that the anonymous 'Christ' in the sixth century, or Aldebert in the eighth century, or Eon in the eleventh century, really behaved as their contemporaries said they behaved. The picture in each case is much the same. These men all started as freelance preachers devoted to the apostolic way of life, but ended by going much further. All three developed messianic pretensions, claiming that they themselves were living saints, equals of the original Apostles or even of Christ. All three found big followings, which they organized into 'churches' devoted to the worship of themselves. In two of the three cases some of the followers were also organized as armed bands, for the purpose not only of protecting the new messiah but of spreading his cult by force. All this has been accepted by historians as substantially accurate. But in the case of another, very similar figure, Tanchelm of Antwerp, there is less general agreement.

There are some grounds for thinking that Tanchelm was once a monk. In any case he had certainly acquired literacy such as was normally the monopoly of clerics, and he was also noted for his eloquence. Some time around 1110 he found it necessary to flee from the diocese of Utrecht to the county of Flanders. There he won the favour of the Count, Robert II, who sent him on an important diplomatic mission to the Holy See. The Count was interested in weakening the power of the German Emperor in the Low Countries; and the task with which he charged Tanchelm was to persuade the Pope to partition the diocese of Utrecht, which was allied with the Emperor, and attach part of it to a diocese under the Count's control. Accompanied by a priest called Everwacher, Tanchelm journeyed to Rome; but the Archbishop of Cologne persuaded Pope Paschal II to reject the scheme.

So Tanchelm's essay in diplomacy was a failure; moreover, in 1111 his patron Count Robert died. It was a turning-point, and Tanchelm set out briskly in a new direction. From 1112 onwards he was active as a wandering preacher, no longer in Flanders but in the islands of Zeeland, in Brabant, in the prince-bishopric of Utrecht and above all at Antwerp, which became his headquarters.

What happened then is a matter of controversy, owing to the nature of the principal sources. These consist of a letter from the Chapter of Utrecht to the Archbishop of Cologne, probably written between 1112 and 1114, asking the Archbishop, who had already seized Tanchelm and Everwacher, to keep them in prison; and a life of Tanchelm's orthodox opponent, St Norbert of Xanten. But if the authors of these documents all had an interest in defaming Tanchelm, it does not follow that everything they tell is necessarily untrue; and in fact much of it is very familiar and correspondingly convincing. In particular the Chapter of Utrecht deserves to be taken seriously; for it was describing events which were supposed to be occurring at that very moment, and for the benefit of a neighbouring prelate who would surely have been able to check the information.

According to the Chapter, Tanchelm began his preaching in the open fields, dressed as a monk; we are told that his eloquence was extraordinary and that multitudes listened to him as to an angel of the Lord. He appeared to be a holy man – the Chapter of Utrecht complained that like his master the Devil he had all the appearance of an angel of light. Like so many other wandering preachers, he started by condemning unworthy clerics – such as the priest at Antwerp, the only one in the town at that time, who was living in open concubinage – and then broadened his attack to cover the Church as a whole. He taught not merely that sacraments were invalid if administered by unworthy hands but also that, things being as they were, holy orders had lost all meaning, sacraments were no better than pollutions, and churches no better than brothels. This propaganda proved so effective that people soon stopped partaking of the Eucharist and going to church. And in general, as the Chapter ruefully remarked, things came to such a pass that the more one despised the Church the holier one was held to be. At the same time Tanchelm exploited a very material grievance; as the Chapter complained, 'he easily persuaded the populace to withhold tithes from the ministers of the Church, for that is what they wanted to do.' Tithes were indeed detested by medieval peasants, who bitterly resented having to surrender a tenth of all their produce, from corn to the herbs in their gardens and the down on their geese. And the resentment was all the greater when the priest who received the tithes was not respected.

So far Tanchelm's teaching reminds one of the monk Henry, who was active at just the same time. Moreover, both men operated in the same social context, which was that of the rise of the communes. When Henry arrived at Le Mans, the burghers were still furious with their bishop for supporting the Count, from whose overlordship they were struggling to free themselves. The area where Tanchelm carried on his apostolate had also for many years been swept by communal insurrections. Starting in 1074, one town after another in the Rhine valley, Utrecht, Brabant, Flanders and northern France had set about extricating itself so far as possible from the dominion of its feudal suzerain, ecclesiastical or secular. These movements, the earliest of the social risings which were to punctuate the history of medieval towns, were mostly organized by merchants in furtherance of their own interests. Merchants wanted to be rid of laws which, originally formulated for a population of dependent peasants, could only impede commercial activity. They wanted to escape from dues and levies which had once been the price of protection but which seemed mere arbitrary exactions now that burghers were able to defend themselves. They wanted to govern their towns themselves and according to laws which recognized the requirements of the new economy. In many cases these aims were achieved peacefully; but where the suzerain or lord proved intransigent, the merchants would organize all the men of the town into an insurrectionary society to which each member was bound by solemn oath.

Insurrections occurred chiefly in episcopal cities. Unlike a lay prince, a bishop was a resident ruler in his city and was naturally concerned to keep his authority over the subjects in whose midst he lived. Moreover the attitude of the Church towards economic matters was profoundly conservative; in trade it could for a long time see nothing but usury and in merchants nothing but dangerous innovators whose designs ought to be firmly thwarted. The burghers, for their part, if once they decided to break a bishop's power, were quite capable of killing him, setting fire to his cathedral and fighting off any of his vassals who might try to avenge him. And although in all this their aims usually remained severely limited and entirely material, it was only to be expected that some of these risings should be accompanied by an outcry against unworthy priests. When the lower strata of urban society were involved such protests tended in fact to rise shrilly enough.

Such was the social context both of Henry's agitation and of Tanchelm's. But unless we are to discount altogether all the contemporary sources, Tanchelm must have gone much further than Henry. According to the Chapter of Utrecht, Tanchelm formed his followers into a blindly devoted community which regarded itself as the only true church; and he reigned over them like a messianic king. On his way to deliver a sermon he would walk surrounded by an escort and preceded, not by a crucifix, but by his own sword and banner, borne like royal insignia. Indeed, he openly proclaimed that he possessed the Holy Spirit in the same sense and in the same degree as Christ and that like Christ he was God. On one occasion he had a statue of the Virgin Mary brought to him and in the presence of a vast crowd solemnly betrothed himself to her. Coffers were placed on either side of the statue to receive wedding gifts from male and female followers respectively. 'Now,' said Tanchelm, 'I shall see which sex bears the greater love towards me and my bride.' The clergy who witnessed it record with horror how people rushed to make their offerings and how women threw in their ear-rings and necklaces.

The clergy were convinced that Tanchelm's motive on this occasion was greed, but in reality he may well – like the sixth-century 'Christ' or his own contemporary Henry the monk – have been more concerned to lead the rich away from the paths of worldly vanity. One may also discount the tales of erotic debauches, for these were always told of heretics of any kind. On the other hand there seems no reason to doubt that Tanchelm really did set himself up as a divine being. The Chapter of Utrecht describes how one of Tanchelm's followers, a smith called Manasses, organized a fraternity of twelve men, in imitation of the Apostles, and a woman representing the Virgin Mary. This is not the kind of story that people invent – especially not for the benefit of a neighbouring archbishop. Again, the Chapter of Utrecht and the biographer of St Norbert both state that Tanchelm distributed his bath-water among his followers, some of whom drank it as a substitute for the Eucharist, while others treasured it as a holy relic. One is reminded of Aldebert, who distributed his nail-parings and hair-clippings amongst his followers. And to anyone familiar with anthropological findings concerning *mana*, or indwelling power, and the ways in which it can be transmitted through material vehicles, such performances too will be immediately comprehensible.

The biography of St Norbert adds other details. It tells how Tanchelm organized an armed bodyguard, with whom he used to hold splendid banquets. It also says that it was unsafe for anyone, even the great princes of the neighbouring territories, to approach Tanchelm save as a follower and that those who did so were commonly killed by the bodyguard. The Praemonstratensian Continuator of Sigebert of Gembloux even says that Tanchelm and his followers carried out 'many massacres'. However, this is all doubtful evidence. The biographer of St Norbert probably wrote about 1155; and though he may have been drawing on an earlier biography, now lost, he may also have been influenced by the story of the sixth-century 'Christ' in Gregory of Tours. As for the Praemonstratensian Continuator of Sigebert, he wrote after 1155, and the source of his information is obscure.

But even if these late additions to the story are discounted, it is clear that Tanchelm did exercise, by whatever means, a very real dominion over a large area. The canons in the Chapter of Utrecht freely admitted their helplessness. Tanchelm, they insisted, had long been a danger to the church of Utrecht; if he were to be released and allowed to resume his work they would not be able to resist him and the diocese would be lost to the Church without hope of recovery. And even after his death (he is believed to have been killed by a priest, around 1115) Tanchelm long continued to dominate the town of Antwerp. A congregation of canons specially established for the purpose was unable to counteract his influence but on the contrary succumbed to it. It was at this point that Norbert of Xanten was called in. A great noble who had renounced a brilliant career at the imperial court to wander through the world in apostolic poverty, Norbert was famed as a worker of miracles, a healer of the sick and insane, a tamer of wild beasts. Because of this he was able, though with difficulty, to win the common people away from their allegiance to Tanchelm and recapture Antwerp for the Church.

Wandering preachers of holy and 'apostolic' life found listeners in all strata of society. Not only when they were orthodox, like Robert of Arbrissel or Norbert of Xanten, but even when they were clearly heretical, like the Cathars in Languedoc, they often enjoyed the support of great nobles and prosperous burghers. But it does appear that the kind of preacher who claimed to be a divine or semi-divine being – a living saint, or a messiah, or an incarnation of the Holy Spirit – appealed particularly to the lower strata of society.

It is true that, even here, what one finds is only a tendency, not an invariable rule. Some of the followers of the sixth-century 'Christ' were able to bring him gold and silver, and some of Tanchelm's female devotees had necklaces and ear-rings to offer. On the other hand, it is hardly conceivable that the armed band whom the 'Christ' set to waylay and rob travellers, so that he could distribute the booty to the poor, were not themselves poor. Tanchelm found his first followers among the inhabitants of Walcheren and the other islands lying in the mouths of the Meuse and the Scheldt. These can only have been poor fisherfolk and peasants; and even later, at Antwerp, his closest associates were such as would let themselves be organized by a blacksmith. As for Eon, he too was followed by 'multitudes of the rude populace' in the wild and remote forests of Brittany.

All in all, it seems clear enough that these messiahs drew the bulk of their support from the lowest social strata. More than half a century ago the great sociologist of religion, Max Weber, drew attention to the tendency underlying such phenomena:

A salvationist kind of religion can very well originate in socially privileged strata. The charisma of the prophet ... is normally associated with a certain minimum of intellectual culture. ... But it regularly changes its character ... when it penetrates to under-privileged strata. ... And one can point to at least one feature that normally accompanies this shift; one result of the unavoidable adaptation to the needs of the masses. This is, the appearance of a *personal* saviour, whether wholly divine or a mixture of human and divine; and of the religious relationship to that saviour as the precondition for salvation. The further one descends the ladder of social stratification, the more radical the ways in which this need for a saviour is wont to express itself ...

The tendency indicated by Weber has been observed in many colonial or ex-colonial territories during the present century. As one example out of hundreds one may consider the Zulu messiahs studied by Dr Bengt Sundkler. Just like the medieval personalities, these men called themselves Christians and drew their basic inspiration and imagery from the Scriptures. But they also made the greatest possible claims for themselves, and these were enthusiastically accepted by their followers. 'Most Zulu prophets,' writes Dr Sundkler, 'are regarded by their followers as semi-divine beings. The Prophet becomes the Black Christ, and it is because of this that he acquires his tremendous influence over his followers.'

The career of the most celebrated of Zulu messiahs, Isaiah Shembe (1870–1935) is illuminating. Shembe was a lay preacher of great eloquence and magnetic personality, who built up a church of his own in opposition to the White-sponsored Mission churches. At first he claimed only to be a prophet, and to the White authorities he would never admit to more. But to his followers he eventually divulged that he was 'the Promised One', a true successor and replacer of Jesus. What Jesus, in his day, had done for Whites and their salvation, he was now doing for Zulus and their salvation. He claimed that the Lord had called him when still in his mother's womb. And he foretold that in due course he would stand at the gate of the Heavenly Jerusalem, when he would turn away the Whites and those Blacks who had followed the Mission churches, and admit only his own followers.

All this quite strikingly recalls the messiahs of medieval Europe; and it is worth reflecting on the circumstances in which Shembe and similar Zulu messiahs have flourished. Sundkler points out that such a messiah both resembles and differs from a ruler of the Zulus in the days when they were still an independent nation. Messiah and ruler were both seen as divine beings, but whereas the ruler incorporated the power of the Zulus, the messiah 'will always claim to be the spokesman of the despised.'

Typically, messiahs of this kind tend to flourish not amongst the poor and oppressed as such, but amongst the poor and oppressed whose traditional way of life has broken down and who have lost faith in their traditional values. Now, during the Middle Ages certain areas of western Europe experienced just such crises of mass disorientation. This was particularly the case from the end of the eleventh century onwards. From that time on one can discern quite clearly, within the great stream of religious dissent, one current which can properly be called the religious dissent of the poor. From that time on one can speak without qualification of messiahs of the poor and messianic movements of the poor.

It is with such figures and such movements that most of this book will be concerned. But first it is necessary to consider briefly who these poor were – what distinguished them from the poor of earlier centuries, to what new pressures they were reacting and what new needs they were trying to express.

3   The Messianism of the Disoriented Poor

The impact of rapid social change

Revolutionary movements of the poor, headed by messiahs or living saints and drawing their inspiration from the Sibylline or Johannine prophesies concerning the Last Days, occurred with increasing frequency from the end of the eleventh century onwards. They did not however occur in all periods or in all regions. So far as northern Europe is concerned, it is only in the valley of the Rhine that one can detect an apparently unbroken tradition of revolutionary millenarianism continuing down to the sixteenth century. In some areas of what are now Belgium and northern France such a tradition can be traced from the end of the eleventh to the middle of the fourteenth century, in some areas of southern and central Germany from the middle of the thirteenth century down to the Reformation; after which the beginnings of a tradition can be observed in Holland and Westphalia. On the fringe of far bigger upheavals, a millenarian commotion occurred around London and another in Bohemia.

With one or two minor exceptions, all the movements with which the present study is concerned arose within these fairly precise limits; and one is prompted to ask why this should be so. However hazardous it may be to pursue the causation of social phenomena in a society which cannot itself be directly observed, the incidence of revolutionary millenarianism is here far too clearly defined, both in space and in time, to be without significance. A bird's-eye view suggests that the social situations in which outbreaks of revolutionary millenarianism occurred were in fact remarkably uniform; and this impression is confirmed when one comes to examine particular outbreaks in detail. The areas in which the age-old prophecies about the Last Days took on a new, revolutionary meaning and a new, explosive force were the areas which were becoming seriously over-populated and were involved in a process of rapid economic and social change. Such conditions were to be found now in one area, now in another, for in these respects the development of medieval Europe was anything but uniform. Wherever they occurred life came to differ vastly from the settled agricultural life which was the norm throughout the thousand-year span of the Middle Ages; and it is worth considering in what precisely the difference consisted.

It was certainly not that the traditional life on the land was easy. Agricultural techniques, though they improved, were never such as to keep the peasantry in a state of plenty even under favourable circumstances; and for most peasants life must always have been a hard struggle. In every village there were numbers of peasants living near or at subsistence level; and agricultural surplus was so small and communications so precarious that a bad harvest often meant mass famine. For generations on end large areas of northern and central Europe were devastated by invading North-men and Magyars and for centuries on end much larger areas were repeatedly thrown into turmoil by the private wars of feudal barons. Moreover the bulk of the peasantry normally lived in a state of permanent and irksome dependence on their lords, ecclesi-astical or lay. Many peasants were serfs, who carried their unfreedom in their blood and transmitted it from generation to generation. A serf belonged by birth to the patrimony of a lord; and this was felt to be a uniquely degrading condition. But there also existed other conditions which, if less humiliating, were nevertheless almost as hard to bear as serfdom itself. During the long centuries of constantly recurring warfare, when no effective central government existed, most small landowners had found it necessary to surrender their lands to the local lord who, with his band of mounted retainers, was alone in a position to offer protection. The descend-ants of these men were also dependent on a lord; and although their dependence was regulated by a permanent and hereditary contract, it was not necessarily less onerous than that of a serf. In an age when the most effective guarantees of personal independence lay in the possession of land and in the ability to bear arms, the peasants were at a great disadvantage; for only nobles could afford armour, and almost all the land in the agricultural regions was held either by nobles or by the Church. Land on which to live had to be rented, protection had to be earned; and this meant that most peasants had to supply their lords with a formidable amount of labour services, of regular dues in kind and of special fines and levies.

Admittedly the conditions of peasant life were extremely varied. The proportion of bond and free in the peasant population differed greatly from century to century and from region to region, and again within these two main categories there were to be found infinite variations both in juridical status and in prosperity; even amongst the population of a single village there were usually great inequalities. But when every allowance has been made for these complexities it is still true that if poverty, hardships and an often oppressive dependence could by themselves generate it, revolutionary millenarianism would have run strong amongst the peasantry of medieval Europe. Yet this was not normally the case. A marked eagerness on the part of serfs to run away; recurrent efforts on the part of the peasant communities to extract concessions; brief, spasmodic revolts – such things were familiar enough in the life of many a manor. But it was not often that settled peasants could be induced to embark on the pursuit of the Millennium. And when they did so it was either because they were caught up in some vast movement which had originated in quite different social strata, or because their own traditional way of life was becoming impossible, or – which was the commonest case – for both these reasons together.

It is possible to see why, despite all the poverty and the hardships and the dependence, the agricultural society of the early Middle Ages – and of the later Middle Ages too in many regions – should have been relatively unreceptive to the militant eschatology of the unprivileged. To an extent which can hardly be exaggerated, peasant life was shaped and sustained by custom and communal routine. In the wide northern plains peasants were commonly grouped together in villages; and there the inhabitants of a village followed an agricultural routine which had been developed by the village as a collectivity. Their strips of land lay closely interwoven in the open fields, and in ploughing, sowing and reaping they must often have worked as a team. Each peasant had the right to use the 'common' to a prescribed extent and all the livestock grazed there together. Social relationships within the village were regulated by norms which, though they varied from village to village, had always the sanction of tradition and were always regarded as inviolable. And this was true not only of relationships between the villagers themselves but of the relationship between each villager and his lord. In the course of long struggles between conflicting interests each manor had developed its own laws which, once established by usage, prescribed the rights and obligations of each individual. To this 'custom of the manor' the lord himself was subject; and the peasants were commonly most vigilant in ensuring that he did in fact abide by it. Peasants could be very resolute in defending their traditional rights and even on occasion in extending them. They could afford to be resolute, for population was sparse and labour much in demand; this gave them an advantage which to some extent offset the concentration of landed property and of armed force in the hands of their lords. As a result the manorial regime was by no means a system of uncontrolled exploitation of labour. If custom bound the peasants to render dues and services, it also fixed the amounts. And to most peasants it gave at least that basic security which springs from the hereditary and guaranteed tenancy of a piece of land.

The position of the peasant in the old agricultural society was much strengthened, too, by the fact that – just like the noble – he passed his life firmly embedded in a group of kindred. The large family to which a peasant belonged consisted of blood-relatives by male and female descent and their spouses, all of them bound together by their ties with the head of the group – the father (or, failing him, the mother) of the senior branch of the family. Often this kinship-group was officially recognized as the tenant of the peasant holding, which remained vested in it so long as the group survived. Such a family, sharing the same 'pot, fire and loaf', working the same unpartitioned fields, rooted in the same piece of earth for generations, was a social unit of great cohesiveness – even though it might itself be riven at times by bitter internal quarrels. And there is no doubt that the individual peasant gained much from belonging to such a group. Whatever his need, and even if he no longer lived with the family, he could always claim succour from his kinsfolk and be certain of receiving it. If the ties of blood bound they also supported every individual.

The network of social relationships into which a peasant was born was so strong and was taken so much for granted that it precluded any very radical disorientation. So long as that network remained intact peasants enjoyed not only a certain material security but also – which is even more relevant – a certain sense of security, a basic assurance which neither constant poverty nor occasional peril could destroy. Moreover such hardships were themselves taken for granted, as part of a state of affairs which seemed to have prevailed from all eternity. Horizons were narrow, and this was as true of social and economic as of geographical horizons. It was not simply that contact with the wide world beyond the manor boundaries was slight – the very thought of any fundamental transformation of society was scarcely conceivable. In an economy which was uniformly primitive, where nobody was very rich, there was nothing to arouse new wants; certainly nothing which could stimulate men to grandiose phantasies of wealth and power.

This state of affairs began to change when, from the eleventh century onwards, first one area of Europe and then another became sufficiently peaceful for population to increase and commerce to develop. The first areas in which this occurred lay partly in French, partly in German territory. In the eleventh, twelfth and thirteenth centuries, in an area extending almost from the Somme to the Rhine and centring on the great principality which the counts of Flanders were governing with singular firmness and efficiency, population expanded rapidly. Already by the eleventh century north-east France, the Low Countries and the Rhine valley were carrying a population beyond what the traditional agricultural system could support. Many peasants set about reclaiming land from sea, marsh and forest, or migrated eastwards to take part in the great German colonization of lands hitherto inhabited by Slavs; and with these pioneers things generally went well enough. But many remained for whom there were no holdings, or whose holdings were too small to support them; and these had to shift for themselves as best they could. Some of this surplus population went to form a rural proletariat; while some flowed into the new commercial and industrial centres and produced an urban proletariat.

The Vikings, having brought ruin upon many parts of Europe, gave the first impetus to the development of industry in and around the County of Flanders, which at that time extended from Arras to Ghent. Weaving had been carried on there since Roman times and it had become a considerable industry when, in the tenth century, the import of English wool began. With their great wealth and their trade-routes which stretched deep into Russia, the Vikings offered a splendid market for high-quality textiles, just at the time when effective government was bringing sufficient peace and stability to the land to make industrial development possible. During the eleventh, twelfth and thirteenth centuries a great cloth industry grew up and spread until the whole of what is now Belgium and north-east France had become the most highly industrialized part of a predominantly agricultural continent. With this concentration of industry the Rhine valley was closely linked. In the twelfth century Flemish merchants were trading along the Rhine; by the thirteenth the merchants of the Rhine valley themselves were dominating the international commerce of northern Europe and Flemish cloth was passing through their hands on its way to the new markets in central and southern Germany and in the Levant. In Cologne, the meeting-point of many trade-routes, flourishing textile and copper industries had grown up.

The new industrial centres exerted a powerful attraction on the peasantry – primarily no doubt on the surplus population, but also on those who wished to escape from the restrictions and exactions which harassed them on the manor, on those who were restless and eager for a change, on those also who happened to have exceptional enterprise and imagination. For life in those centres certainly offered to the common people opportunities and satisfactions such as they had never known on the land. Industry was concentrated in towns, and any serf who was received into a town shed his servile status and became free. Moreover it was far easier there, especially in the early stages of economic expansion, for a poor man to improve his position than it had ever been on the manor. A penniless immigrant with a flair for business might always end as a rich merchant. And even amongst the artisans, those who produced for the local market developed, in the craft-guilds, associations which fulfilled many of the functions which the village community and the kinship-group had fulfilled for peasants, and did so with considerably more profit. As social and economic horizons expanded, hardship and poverty and dependence ceased to appear the inescapable fate of common folk.

There were however many who merely acquired new wants without being able to satisfy them; and in them the spectacle of a wealth undreamt-of in earlier centuries provoked a bitter sense of frustration. In all the over-populated, relatively urbanized and industrialized areas there were many people living on the margin of society, in a state of chronic insecurity. There industry even at the best of times could never absorb the whole of the surplus population. Beggars crowded in every market-place and roamed in gangs through the streets of the towns and along the roads from town to town. Many became mercenaries, but in those days of short campaigns mercenaries were constantly being disbanded. The very word *Brabançons* came to signify the marauding bands of unemployed soldiers of fortune who were for ever coming down from Brabant and the neighbouring territories to devastate whole provinces of France. And even amongst artisans in employment many found themselves more defenceless than peasants on the manor.

It is of course true that medieval industry is not to be compared, either in degree of rationalization and impersonality or for sheer scale, with the giant enterprises which were to transform the social structure of Europe in the nineteenth century. But neither did it consist simply of small workshops in which the 'master', himself a man of modest means and no great ambition, exercised a benevolent patriarchal supervision over some three or four assistants and apprentices who together formed almost a family group. This familiar picture is valid only for the industries which produced for the local market. Industries which made goods for export, on the contrary, had their economic basis in a rather primitive form of uncontrolled capitalism. Notably in the great cloth industry it was merchant capitalists who provided the raw materials and who owned the finished product, which was sold in the international market. There the position even of skilled workers – the weavers and fullers – was precarious; though they had their guilds, these could not protect them as artisans working for the local market were protected. These men knew that at any moment a war or a slump might interrupt trade and that then they too would be thrown into the desperate mass of the unemployed; while the many unskilled workers, who were miserably paid, owned no equipment and had no guild organization, were wholly at the mercy of the market.

In addition to poverty as great as that of any peasant, the journeymen and casual labourers suffered disorientation such as could scarcely occur under the manorial regime. There was no immemorial body of custom which they could invoke in their defence, there was no shortage of labour to lend weight to their claims. Above all, they were not supported by any network of social relationships comparable to that which sustained a peasant. Although by modern standards the largest medieval towns seem small, there can be no doubt that in conglomerations of towns such as were to be found for instance in Flanders, in which each town had a population of from 20,000 to 50,000, the unfortunate could go under in a way which would not be possible in a village of perhaps fifty, perhaps a couple of hundred souls. And if in the upper strata of the urban population kinship-groups were still important, in the lower strata they dwindled away to the point of insignificance. The migrations from the over-populated country-side into the industrial centres began by disrupting and ended by destroying the large peasant families. Amongst the industrial population on the other hand kinship-groups of any considerable size hardly had a chance to form – partly because, given the high death-rate, that population had largely to be recruited anew each generation; and partly because poor families were unable to acquire more than a small amount of living-space in any one quarter.

Journeymen and unskilled workers, peasants without land or with too little land to support them, beggars and vagabonds, the unemployed and those threatened with unemployment, the many who for one reason or another could find no assured and recognized place – such people, living in a state of chronic frustration and anxiety, formed the most impulsive and unstable elements in medieval society. Any disturbing, frightening or exciting event – any kind of revolt or revolution, a summons to a crusade, an interregnum, a plague or a famine, anything in fact which disrupted the normal routine of social life – acted on these people with peculiar sharpness and called forth reactions of peculiar violence. And one way in which they attempted to deal with their common plight was to form a salvationist group under a messianic leader.

For amongst the surplus population living on the margin of society there was always a strong tendency to take as leader a layman, or maybe an apostate friar or monk, who imposed himself not simply as a holy man but as a prophet and saviour or even as a living god. On the strength of inspirations or revelations for which he claimed divine origin this leader would decree for his followers a communal mission of vast dimensions and world-shaking importance. The conviction of having such a mission, of being divinely appointed to carry out a prodigious task, provided the disoriented and the frustrated with new bearings and new hope. It gave them not simply a place in the world but a unique and resplendent place. A fraternity of this kind felt itself an elite, set infinitely apart from and above ordinary mortals, sharing in the extraordinary merits of its leader, sharing also in his miraculous powers. Moreover the mission which most attracted these masses from the neediest strata of the population was – naturally enough – a mission which was intended to culminate in a total transformation of society. In the eschatological phantasies which they had inherited from the distant past, the forgotten world of early Christianity, these people found a social myth most perfectly adapted to their needs.

This was the process which, after its first occurrence in the area between the Somme and the Rhine, was to recur in later centuries in southern and central Germany and, still later, in Holland and Westphalia. In each case it occurred under similar circumstances – when population was increasing, industrialization was getting under way, traditional social bonds were being weakened or shattered and the gap between rich and poor was becoming a chasm. Then in each of these areas in turn a collective sense of impotence and anxiety and envy suddenly discharged itself in a frantic urge to smite the ungodly – and by doing so to bring into being, out of suffering inflicted and suffering endured, that final Kingdom where the Saints, clustered around the great sheltering figure of their Messiah, were to enjoy ease and riches, security and power for all eternity.

The poor in the first crusades

The half-century that saw the messiahs Tanchelm of Antwerp and Eon of Brittany also saw the first outbreaks of what one may call, without reservation, the messianism of the poor. The context was provided by the first two crusades, in 1096 and 1146.

When Pope Urban II summoned the chivalry of Christendom to the Crusade, he released in the masses hopes and hatreds which were to express themselves in ways quite alien to the aims of the papal policy. The main object of Urban's famous appeal at Clermont, in 1095, was to provide Byzantium with the reinforcements it needed in order to drive the Seldjuk Turks from Asia Minor; for he hoped that in return the Eastern Church would acknowledge the supremacy of Rome, so that the unity of Christendom would be restored. In the second place he was concerned to indicate to the nobility, particularly of his native France, an alternative outlet for martial energies which were still constantly bringing devastation upon the land. The moment was appropriate, for the Council of Clermont had been largely concerned with the Truce of God, that ingenious device by which the Church had for half a century been trying to limit feudal warfare. In addition to clerics a large number of lesser nobles had accordingly come to Clermont; and it was primarily to these that, on the last day of the Council, the Pope addressed himself.

To those who would take part in the Crusade Urban offered impressive rewards. A knight who with pious intent took the Cross would earn a remission from temporal penalties for all his sins; if he died in battle he would earn remission of his sins. And there were to be material as well as spiritual rewards. Over-population was not confined to the peasantry; one of the reasons for the perpetual wars between nobles was a real shortage of land. Younger sons had often no patrimony at all and had no choice but to seek their fortune. According to one account Urban himself contrasted the actual indigence of many nobles with the prosperity which they would enjoy when they had conquered fine new fiefs in southern lands. Whether he did so or not, this was certainly a consideration which weighed with many crusaders. And nevertheless it is clear that already amongst the prelates and priests and nobles who heard Urban's appeal at Clermont something was at work which was not simply an expectation of individual gain, whether material or spiritual. As the assembly listened it was swept by emotions of overwhelming power. Thousands cried with one voice: 'Deus le volt!' – 'It is God's will!' Crowding around the

Pope and kneeling before him they begged leave to take part in the holy war. A cardinal fell on his knees and recited the *Confiteor* in the name of the whole multitude and as they echoed it after him many burst into tears and many were seized with convulsive trembling. For a brief moment there reigned in that predominantly aristocratic assembly an atmosphere of collective enthusiasm such as was to become normal in the contingents of common folk which were formed later.

For the appeal at Clermont was only the beginning of an agitation which was at once taken up by many preachers. The Crusade continued to be preached to the nobility by Urban himself, who spent several months travelling through France for the purpose, and by the bishops who had returned from Clermont to their dioceses. It was also preached to the common people by a number of *prophetae*, men who though not equipped with any official authorization had the prestige which always surrounded the miracle-working ascetic. The most celebrated of these was Peter the Hermit. Born near Amiens, he had passed a sternly ascetic life, first as a monk and then as a hermit. He went barefoot and never touched meat or wine. A small thin man with a long grey beard, he possessed a commanding presence and great eloquence; so that, according to one who knew him, his every word and act seemed half-divine. Over the masses he exercised an irresistible fascination. People flocked around him, struggling to pluck from the ass he rode on a single hair to treasure as a relic. Myths proliferated around his life-story. Before ever the Pope had spoken, it was said, Peter had been to Jerusalem. In the Church of the Holy Sepulchre Christ had appeared to him and had given him a letter commissioning him to summon the Crusade. Peter seems to have contributed to the myth by carrying the Heavenly Letter with him wherever he preached. His success as a propagandist was immense. As he passed through northern France an army of crusaders sprang into being. People hastened to sell their belongings to buy weapons and travelling-kit; then, having no longer any means of subsistence, they began to move off. In March, 1096 – four months before the official Crusade of the barons was ready – Peter crossed from French into German territory at the head of the horde which he had inspired. And meanwhile other hordes were forming around other leaders in northern France, in Flanders and along the Rhine.

The army which the Pope had envisaged was to have consisted of knights with their retainers, all of them trained in warfare and properly equipped; and most of the nobles who responded to the papal summons did in fact prepare themselves in a sober and realistic manner for the campaign. The hordes conjured up by the preachings of the *prophetae*, on the other hand, consisted of people whose lack of military qualifications was only equalled by their impetuosity. They had indeed no reason to delay and every reason to hurry. Almost all of them were poor; and they came from those overcrowded regions where the lot of the poor was perpetual insecurity. Moreover during the decade 1085–95 life had been much harder even than usual. Precisely in north-eastern France and western Germany there had been an almost unbroken series of floods, droughts and famines. Since 1089 the population had also been living in constant terror of a particularly unpleasant form of plague which would suddenly and without apparent cause strike at town or village, bringing an agonizing death to the majority of the inhabitants. The mass reactions to these calamities had been the usual ones: people had clustered in devotional and penitential groups around hermits and other holy men and had embarked on a collective quest for salvation. The sudden appearance of the *prophetae* preaching the Crusade gave these afflicted masses the chance to form salvationist groups on a much vaster scale and at the same time to escape from lands where life had become intolerable. Men and women alike hastened to join the new movement. Often whole families would move together, with the children and household chattels loaded on to carts. And as the hordes grew they were further swollen by all kinds of nondescript adventurers – by renegade monks, women disguised as men and many robbers and brigands.

To these hordes the Crusade meant something quite different from what it meant to the Pope. The *pauperes*, as the chroniclers call them, were not greatly interested in assisting the Christians of Byzantium, but they were passionately interested in reaching, capturing and occupying Jerusalem. The city which was the holiest city in the world for Christians had been in the hands of Moslems for some four and a half centuries. Although the possibility of recapturing it seems to have played little part in Urban's original plan, it was this prospect that intoxicated the masses of the poor. In their eyes the Crusade was an armed and militant pilgrimage, the greatest and most sublime of pilgrimages. For centuries a pilgrimage to the Holy Sepulchre had been regarded as a singularly efficacious form of penance and during the eleventh century such pilgrimages had been undertaken collectively: penitents tended to travel no longer singly or in small groups but in bands organized hierarchically under a leader. Sometimes – notably in 1033 and 1064 – mass pilgrimages had taken place, involving many thousands of people. In 1033 at least, the first to go had been the poor and amongst them there had been some who went with the intention of staying in Jerusalem until their death. In the Crusade too the poor, or many of them, had no thought of ever returning to their homes: they meant to take Jerusalem from the infidel and by settling in it turn it into a Christian city. Everyone who took part in the Crusade wore a cross sewn on to his outer garment – the first badge worn by an army in post-Classical times and the first step towards modern military uniforms; but whereas for the knights this cross was a symbol of Christian victory in a military expedition of limited duration, the poor thought rather of the sentence: 'Take up the Cross and follow me!' For them the Crusade was above all a collective *imitato Christi*, a mass sacrifice which was to be rewarded by a mass apotheosis at Jerusalem.

For the Jerusalem which obsessed their imagination was no mere earthly city but rather the symbol of a prodigious hope. It had been so ever since the messianic ideal of the Hebrews had first begun to take shape in the eighth century B.C. Already through the mouth of Isaiah the Lord had bidden the Hebrews:

Rejoice ye with Jerusalem, and be glad with her. . . . That ye may suck and be satisfied with the breasts of her consolations; that ye may milk out, and be delighted with the abundance of her glory. . . . Behold, I will extend peace to her like a river . . . then shall ye suck, ye shall be borne upon her sides, and be dandled upon her knees. As one whom his mother comforteth, so will I comfort you: and ye shall be comforted in Jerusalem.

In the prophecies of the post-exilic period and in the apocalypses the messianic kingdom is imagined as centred on a future Jerusalem which has been rebuilt in great magnificence. These ancient Jewish phantasies all went to reinforce the great emotional significance which Jerusalem would in any case have possessed for medieval Christians. When, a generation after the event, a monk composed the appeal which he imagined Urban to have made at Clermont, he made the Pope speak of the Holy City not simply as the place made for ever illustrious by the Advent, Passion and Ascension of Christ but also as 'the navel of the world, the land fruitful above all others, like another paradise of delights', 'the royal city placed in the centre of the world', now held captive, demanding help, yearning for liberation. Moreover even for theologians Jerusalem was also a 'figure' or symbol of the heavenly city 'like unto a stone most precious' which according to the Book of Revelation was to replace it at the end of time. No wonder that – as contemporaries noted – in the minds of simple folk the idea of the earthly Jerusalem became so confused with and transfused by that of the Heavenly Jerusalem that the Palestinian city seemed itself a miraculous realm, abounding both in spiritual and in material blessings. And no wonder that when the masses of the poor set off on their long pilgrimage the children cried out at every town and castle: 'Is that Jerusalem?' – while high in the heavens there was seen a mysterious city with vast multitudes hurrying towards it.

While in northern France, Flanders and the Rhine valley the poor formed themselves into autonomous bands, in that other densely populated, highly urbanized area, Provence, they streamed into the army of the Count, Raymond of Toulouse. As a result there developed in that army an exaltation as intense as that which prevailed in the hordes which followed the *prophetae*. Alike in north and south, the poor who went on the Crusade regarded themselves as the elite of the crusaders, a people chosen by God as the barons had not been chosen. When at a critical moment in the siege of Antioch St Andrew brought the glad tidings that the Holy Lance was buried in one of the churches in the town, it was to a poor Provençal peasant that he appeared. And when the peasant, conscious of his lowly status, hesitated to transmit the news to the noble leaders, the saint reassured him: 'God has chosen you (poor folk) from amongst all peoples, as ears of wheat are gathered from amidst a field of oats. For in merit and in grace you surpass all who have been before you and all who shall come after you, as much as gold surpasses silver.' Raymond of Aguilers, who tells the story, comes nearest of the chroniclers to sharing the outlook of the poor. It seems to him natural that when some of the poor are killed, miraculous crosses should be found on their shoulderblades; and when he speaks of the *plebs pauperum* it is always with a certain awe, as the Chosen of the Lord.

The self-exaltation of the poor emerges still more clearly from the curious stories, compounded of fact and legend, which were told of the people called 'Tafurs'. A large part – probably by far the larger part – of the People's Crusade perished on its journey across Europe; but enough survived to form in Syria and Palestine a corps of vagabonds – which is what the mysterious word 'Tafur' seems to have meant. Barefoot, shaggy, clad in ragged sackcloth, covered in sores and filth, living on roots and grass and also at times on the roasted corpses of their enemies, the Tafurs were such a ferocious band that any country they passed through was utterly devastated. Too poor to afford swords and lances, they wielded clubs weighted with lead, pointed sticks, knives, hatchets, shovels, hoes and catapults. When they charged into battle they gnashed their teeth as though they meant to eat their enemies alive as well as dead. The Moslems, though they faced the crusading barons fearlessly, were terrified of the Tafurs, whom they called 'no Franks, but living devils'. The Christian chroniclers themselves – clerics or knights whose main interest was in the doings of the princes – while admitting the effectiveness of the Tafurs in battle clearly regarded them with misgiving and embarrassment. Yet if one turns to a vernacular epic written from the standpoint of the poor one finds the Tafurs portrayed as a Holy People and 'worth far more than the knights'.

The Tafurs are shown as having a king, *le roi Tafur*. He is said to have been a Norman knight who had discarded horse, arms and armour in favour of sackcloth and a scythe. At least in the beginning he was an ascetic for whom poverty had all the mystical value which it was to possess for St Francis and his disciples. Periodically King Tafur would inspect his men. Any who were found to have money about them were expelled from the company and sent off to buy arms and join the professional army under the barons; while those who had with greatest conviction renounced all property were admitted to membership of the 'college' or inner circle of followers. It was precisely because of their poverty that the Tafurs believed themselves destined to take the Holy City: 'The poorest shall take it: this is a sign to show clearly that the Lord God does not care for presumptuous and faithless men.' Yet though the poor made a merit of their poverty, they were full of cupidity. Booty captured from the infidel was not felt to diminish their claims on divine favour but rather to prove how real that favour was. After a successful skirmish outside Antioch the Provençal poor 'gallop on horseback amongst the tents to show their companions how their poverty is at an end; others, dressed in two or three silken garments, praise God as the bestower of victory and of gifts'. As King Tafur leads the final assault on Jerusalem he cries: 'Where are the poor folk who want property? Let them come with me! ... For today with God's help I shall win enough to load many a mule!' And later when the Moslems carry their treasures round the walls of the captured city in an effort to lure the Christians out into the open, we are shown the Tafurs unable to hold back. 'Are we in prison?' cries the King; 'They bring treasure and we dare not take it! ... What do I care if I die, since I am doing what I want to do?' And calling on 'St Lazarus' – the Lazarus of the parable, of whom the poor in the Middle Ages made their patron saint – he leads his horde out of the city to catastrophe.

In each captured city the Tafurs looted everything they could lay hands on, raped the Moslem women and carried out indiscriminate massacres. The official leaders of the Crusade had no authority over them at all. When the Emir of Antioch protested about the cannibalism of the Tafurs, the princes could only admit apologetically: 'All of us together cannot tame King Tafur.' The barons seem in fact to have been somewhat frightened of the Tafurs and to have taken care to be well armed whenever they came near them. That no doubt was the truth of the matter; but in the stories which are told from the standpoint of the poor the great princes regard the Tafur king not so much with anxiety as with humility, even with reverence. We find King Tafur urging on the hesitant barons to attack Jerusalem: 'My lords, what are we doing? We are delaying overlong our assault on this city and this evil race. We are behaving like false pilgrims. If it rested with me and with the poor alone, the pagans would find us the worst neighbours they ever had!' The princes are so impressed that they ask him to lead the first attack; and when, covered with wounds, he is carried from the battle-field, they gather anxiously around him. But King Tafur is shown as something more than simply the mightiest of warriors. Often he appears in close association with a *propheta* – in one version it is Peter the Hermit, in another a fictitious bishop who bears that emblem which the poor had made their own, the Holy Lance. And he himself clearly possesses a supernatural quality which sets him above all princes. When – in the story as edited for the poor – Godfrey of Bouillon is to become King of Jerusalem, the barons choose King Tafur as 'the highest one' to perform the coronation. He performs it by giving Godfrey a branch of thorns in memory of the Crown of Thorns: and Godfrey does homage and swears to hold Jerusalem as a fief from King Tafur and God alone. And when the barons, feeling that they have endured enough, hasten back to their wives and their domains, King Tafur will not see Jerusalem abandoned but pledges himself to stay, with his army of poor, to defend the new king and his kingdom. In these purely imaginary incidents the beggar-king becomes the symbol of the immense, unreasoning hope which had carried the *plebs pauperum* through unspeakable hardships to the Holy City.

The realization of that hope demanded human sacrifice on a vast scale – not only the self-immolation of the crusaders but also the massacre of the infidel. Although Pope and princes might intend a campaign with limited objectives, in reality the campaign tended constantly to become what the common people wanted it to be: a war to exterminate 'the sons of whores', 'the race of Cain', as King Tafur called the Moslems. It was not unknown for crusaders to seize all the peasants of a certain area and offer them the choice of being either immediately converted to Christianity or immediately killed – 'having achieved which, our Franks returned full of joy'. The fall of Jerusalem was followed by a great massacre; except for the governor and his bodyguard, who managed to buy their lives and were escorted from the city, every Moslem – man, woman and child – was killed. In and around the Temple of Solomon 'the horses waded in blood up to their knees, nay up to the bridle. It was a just and wonderful judgement of God that the same place should receive the blood of those whose blasphemies it had so long carried up to God.' As for the Jews of Jerusalem, when they took refuge in their chief synagogue the building was set on fire and they were all burnt alive. Weeping with joy and singing songs of praise the crusaders marched in procession to the Church of the Holy Sepulchre. 'O new day, new day and exultation, new and everlasting gladness. . . . That day, famed through all centuries to come, turned all our sufferings and hardships into joy and exultation; that day, the confirmation of Christianity, the annihilation of paganism, the renewal of our faith!' But a handful of the infidel still survived: they had taken refuge on the roof of the mosque of al-Aqsa. The celebrated crusader Tancred had promised them their lives in exchange for a heavy ransom and had given them his banner as a safe-conduct. But Tancred could only watch with helpless fury while common soldiers scaled the wall of the mosque and beheaded every man and woman save those who threw themselves off the roof to their death.

If one bears these happenings in mind it seems natural enough that the first great massacre of European Jews should also have occurred during the First Crusade. The official crusading army, consisting of the barons and their retainers, had no part in this massacre, which was carried out entirely by the hordes which formed in the wake of the *prophetae*. As the Crusade came into being, observes one chronicler, 'peace was established very firmly on all sides and the Jews were at once attacked in the towns where they lived'. It is said that already at the very beginning of the crusading agitation Jewish communities in Rouen and other French towns were given the choice between conversion and massacre. But it was in the episcopal cities along the Rhine that the most violent attacks took place. Here, as along all the trade routes of western Europe, Jewish merchants had been settled for centuries; and because of their economic usefulness they had always enjoyed the special favour of the archbishops. But by the close of the eleventh century in all these cities tension between the townsmen and their ecclesiastical lords was already giving rise to a general social turbulence. It was an atmosphere which proved as favourable to the *prophetae* of the Crusade as it was shortly to prove to Tanchelm.

At the beginning of May, 1096, crusaders camping outside Speyer planned to attack the Jews in their synagogue on the Sabbath. In this they were foiled and they were only able to kill a dozen Jews in the streets. The Bishop lodged the rest in his castle and had some of the murderers punished. At Worms the Jews were less fortunate. Here too they turned for help to the Bishop and the well-to-do burghers, but these were unable to protect them when men from the People's Crusade arrived and led the townsfolk in an attack on the Jewish quarter. The synagogue was sacked, houses were looted and all their adult occupants who refused baptism were killed. As for the children, some were killed, others taken away to be baptised and brought up as Christians. Some Jews had taken shelter in the Bishop's castle and when that too was attacked the Bishop offered to baptise them and so save their lives; but the entire community preferred to commit suicide. In all, some eight hundred Jews are said to have perished at Worms.

At Mainz, where there lived the largest Jewish community in Germany, events took much the same course. There too the Jews were at first protected by the Archbishop, the chief lay lord and the richer burghers but in the end were forced by the crusaders, supported by the poorer townsfolk, to choose between baptism and death. The Archbishop and all his staff fled, in fear of their lives. More than a thousand Jews and Jewesses perished, either by suicide or at the hands of the crusaders. From the Rhine cities a band of crusaders moved to Trier. The Archbishop delivered a sermon demanding that the Jews be spared; but as a result he himself had to flee from the church. Here too, although some Jews accepted baptism, the great majority perished. The crusaders moved on to Metz, where they killed some more Jews, and then returned in mid-June to Cologne. The Jewish community had gone into hiding in neighbouring villages; but they were discovered by the crusaders and massacred in hundreds. Meanwhile other bands of crusaders, making their way eastwards, had imposed baptism by force on the communities at Regensburg and Prague. In all the number of Jews who perished in the months of May and June, 1096, is estimated at between four and eight thousand.

It was the beginning of a tradition. While in 1146 the Second Crusade was being prepared by King Louis VII and the French nobility, the populace in Normandy and Picardy killed Jews. Meanwhile a renegade monk called Rudolph made his way from Hainaut to the Rhine, where he summoned the masses to join in a People's Crusade and to make a start by killing the Jews. As at the time of the First Crusade, the common people were being driven to desperation by famine. Like every successful *propheta*, Rudolph was believed to perform miracles and to be favoured with divine revelations; and hungry crowds flocked to him. It was still the episcopal cities with their bitter internal conflicts – Cologne, Mainz, Worms, Speyer and also this time Strasbourg and, when the Crusade passed through it, Würzburg – that proved the most fertile ground for anti-Jewish agitation. From them the movement spread to many other towns in Germany and France. The Jews turned for protection, as they had done half a century earlier, to the bishops and prosperous burghers. These did what they could to help; but the *pauperes* were not to be so easily deterred. In many towns the populace was on the point of open insurrection and it seemed that another overwhelming catastrophe was about to descend on the Jews. At that point St Bernard intervened and, with the full weight of his prestige, insisted that the massacre must stop.

Even St Bernard, with all his extraordinary reputation as a holy man and a worker of miracles, was scarcely able to check the popular fury. When he confronted Rudolph at Mainz and, as an abbot, ordered him back to his monastery, the common people almost took up arms to protect their *propheta*. Thereafter, the massacre of Jews was to remain a normal feature of popular, as distinct from knightly, crusades; and it is clear enough why. Although the *pauperes* looted freely from the Jews they killed (as they did from the Moslems), booty was certainly not their main object. It is a Hebrew chronicle that records how during the Second Crusade the crusaders appealed to the Jews: 'Come to us, so that we become one single people'; and there seems no doubt that a Jew could always save both life and property by accepting baptism. On the other hand it was said that whoever killed a Jew who refused baptism had all his sins forgiven him; and there were those who felt unworthy to start on a crusade at all until they had killed at least one such. Some of the crusaders' own comments have been preserved: 'We have set out to march a long way to fight the enemies of God in the East, and behold, before our very eyes are his worst foes, the Jews. They must be dealt with first.' And again: 'You are the descendants of those who killed and hanged our God. Moreover (God) himself said: "The day will yet dawn when my children will come and avenge my blood." We are his children and it is our task to carry out his vengeance upon you, for you showed yourselves obstinate and blasphemous towards him. . . . (God) has abandoned you and has turned his radiance upon us and has made us his own.'

Here, unmistakably, speaks the same conviction which tried to turn the First Crusade into an annihilation of Islam.

4 The Saints Against the Hosts of Antichrist

Saviours in the Last Days

Scanty though the records are for this early period, they are sufficient to show that in the People's Crusades a great eschatological ferment was at work. For the *pauperes* certainly saw themselves as actors in the prodigious consummation towards which all things had been working since the beginning of time. On all sides they beheld the 'signs' which were to mark the beginning of the Last Days, and heard how 'the Last Trump proclaimed the coming of the righteous Judge'. Above all they seem to have been fascinated by the prophecy of the great Emperor who in the Last Days was to journey to Jerusalem; and they seem to have done all they could to persuade themselves that they were really being led by that mysterious monarch.

Originally, in the Greek prophecies which circulated in the East, the Last Emperor had been a Roman Emperor ruling from Constantinople. But when in the eighth century the *Pseudo-Methodius* was translated into Latin in Paris, new interpretations were called for. It was to be expected that as the Emperor of the Last Days took his place in the eschatological phantasies of the West he would cease to be a Byzantine. From the point of view of western Europe the Emperor at Constantinople was a very remote and shadowy figure. On the other hand the West was able to persuade itself that in Charlemagne's acquisition of the imperial title it had witnessed a resurrection of the Roman Empire. The gap left by the deposition of the last Emperor in the West, after remaining unfilled for more than three centuries, seemed to have been most magnificently filled when at St Peter's in Rome on Christmas Day of the year 800, Charles, King of the Franks and King of the Lombards, was crowned Emperor of the Romans. Thenceforth it was possible for the Emperor of the Last Days to be imagined as a western monarch and it remained so even though Charlemagne left no territorial empire behind him. Both in the part of Charlemagne's domains which became France and in that which became Germany men continued to dream of a great emperor who would arise in their midst and in whom the Sibylline prophecies would be fulfilled.

Towards the close of the eleventh century, as the idea of a crusade was taking shape, these phantasies acquired a new immediacy and urgency. A few years before the First Crusade we find Benzo, Bishop of Alba, foretelling that the reigning German King and Roman Emperor, Henry IV, would conquer Byzantium, defeat the infidel and march on Jerusalem. He would meet Antichrist there and would overthrow him; after which he would reign over a universal empire until the end of the world. Coming from a politically-minded prelate who was an ardent partisan of the Emperor in his struggle with the Papacy, such words should not perhaps be taken at their face value; but when shortly afterwards the *pauperes* gathered for the Crusade in an atmosphere of feverish excitement, the old Sibylline prophecies reappeared endowed with a startling dynamism. As a learned abbot disdainfully remarked, thanks to the activities of false prophets these people were full of stories about Charlemagne's having risen from the dead for the purpose of leading the Crusade.

A great mass of folklore had in fact been accumulating around the formidable figure of the first Carolingian. Charlemagne had come to be seen as above all the heroic champion of Christ, the tireless defender of Christendom against the armed might of Islam; and in the second half of the eleventh century it came to be almost universally believed that he had once led a crusade to Jerusalem, put the infidel there to flight and reinstated the Christians who had been expelled. More than one chronicler tells how the crusaders of 1096 travelled along the road which Charlemagne was supposed to have constructed on that occasion. Moreover it was also widely believed that Charlemagne had never died at all but was only sleeping, either in his vault at Aachen or inside some mountain, until the hour came for him to return to the world of men. It was easy enough for popular preachers, recruiting for the Crusade, to combine these tales with the Sibylline prophecies and to lead the common people to see in Charlemagne that great Emperor who was to shake off his slumber, overthrow the power of Islam and establish the age of bliss which was to precede the End. Did *Carolus redivivus* also become, at the hands of the *prophetae*, a beggar-king and patron of the poor, comparable with that King Tafur who, penniless, was yet 'the highest one' and had Jerusalem itself in his gift? We do not know; but the poor certainly were capable of transforming the sleeping emperor of the *Pseudo-Methodius* according to their own desires, into a saviour who would not only annihilate the infidel but also succour and raise up the lowly. They

72

did so often enough in later centuries and they may well have done so already at the time of the First Crusade.

The *pauperes* felt the Last Emperor to be so indispensable to the realization of their deepest hopes that they saw him not merely in the phantom of the risen Charlemagne but also at times in living men, the actual leaders of the Crusade. The gigantic messianic image was projected on to Godfrey of Bouillon, Duke of Lower Lorraine, on to that hard-headed politician, Raymond of Saint-Giles, Count of Toulouse, perhaps also on to that Norman knight who is said to have become King Tafur. Above all, it seems clear that the man who inspired the great massacres of Jews in the cities along the Rhine, Emico or Emmerich, Count of Leiningen, imposed himself on his followers as the Emperor of the Last Days. He was a feudal baron notorious for his ferocity but he claimed to have been led to take the Cross by visions and revelations sent by God. One day a messenger from Christ had come to him and set a sign upon his flesh – doubtless that traditional sign of divine election, the cross on or between the shoulder-blades, which it was believed had been borne by Charlemagne and would be borne also by the Last Emperor. Emico claimed that this mark was a token that Christ himself would lead him to victory and in due course set a crown upon his head; and this coronation was to take place in that part of southern Italy which was ruled by the Byzantine Emperor. What can all this mean but that this petty German lord was assuming the role which Bishop Benzo had tried in vain to impose upon the Emperor Henry – that he had decided to be the eschatological emperor who was to unite the Western and Eastern Empires and then make his way to Jerusalem? In reality Emico's expedition was inglorious enough. His horde of *pauperes* – Germans, Frenchmen, Flemings, Lorrainers – never reached Asia Minor at all but was routed and dispersed by the Hungarians; and he himself returned home alone. Nevertheless an aura of the supernatural always clung to Emico. Years after he was killed in 1117 he was supposed to be continuing some kind of existence in a mountain near Worms, from which he was seen to emerge from time to time in the midst of an armed band – a legend which strongly suggests that popular imagination had insisted on turning him too into a sleeping hero who must some day return.

As for the Second Crusade, there could be no doubt who was the most suitable candidate for the role of Last Emperor. Whereas no monarch had taken part in the First Crusade, when Pope Eugenius appealed for help for the hard-pressed kingdom of Jerusalem half a century later, Louis VII of France responded with enthusiasm. On Christmas Day 1145 the king took the crusader's vow at the royal abbey of Saint-Denis amidst scenes of great popular enthusiasm. Ever since the turn of the century there had been circulating new versions of the *Tiburtina* which told of a future King of France who was to reign over both the Western Empire and the Byzantine Empire and who in the end, as Emperor of the Last Days, would lay down his crown and robes at Golgotha. Naturally enough, when crusading enthusiasm once more gripped the populations of western Europe the prophecy was applied to Louis VII. At the same time as the *propheta* Rudolph was preaching the massacre of the Jews a strange and cryptic oracle, also put about by a *propheta*, was being eagerly studied. All that is clear about this utterance is that it promises Louis the cities of Constantinople and 'Babylon' and an empire in Asia Minor – and adds that when he has attained that much, his 'L' will be changed into 'C'. But these hints suffice to indicate a whole eschatological programme. Louis is to become Emperor of the East, reigning over Byzantium. Then he is to capture that 'Babylon' which in the Sibylline prophecies figured as the mystical capital of the infidel, the haunt of demons and birthplace of Antichrist – a sort of diabolic counterpart to the Holy City of Jerusalem. Finally, he is to become 'the king whose name shall be C' (as the *Tiburtina* has it) – in other words, that new or resurrected Constans who was to be the Emperor of the Last Days.

The influence of this oracle was very great. It seems that it was only by studying the Sibylline that St Bernard was persuaded to overcome his initial reluctance to preach the crusade – and but for that teaching there might have been no crusade. Moreover the oracle was studied not only in France but also in Germany, where the king, Conrad III, was but a reluctant crusader and no rival at all to Louis. Yet Louis himself, for all his crusading fervour, was not in the least disposed to have an eschatological role thrust upon him. And being a real and not an amateur king he was in any case involved willy-nilly in the political intrigues and rivalries which dogged this Crusade from the start. The result was that while the kings of France and Germany made their way to the ludicrous siege of Damascus the *pauperes* were left, harassed by massacre and famine, leaderless and bewildered, to pursue alone the fatal mirage of the Kingdom of the Saints.

The demonic hosts

The *pauperes* who took part in the People's Crusades saw their victims as well as their leaders in terms of the eschatology out of which they had made their social myth.

According to the Johannine and Sibylline traditions alike, before the Millennium could dawn misbelief had to be eliminated. In a sense the ideal of a wholly Christian world is of course as old as Christianity itself. Nevertheless Christianity has usually remained, as it was in its origin, a missionary religion which has insisted that the elimination of misbelievers must be achieved through their conversion. The messianic hordes which began to form in the eleventh and twelfth centuries, on the other hand, saw no reason at all why that elimination could not equally well be achieved by the physical annihilation of the unconverted. In the *Chanson de Roland*, the famous epic which is the most impressive literary embodiment of the spirit of the First Crusade, the new attitude is expressed quite unambiguously:

> The Emperor has taken Saragossa. A thousand Franks are sent to search thoroughly the town, the mosques and synagogues. With iron hammers and axes they smash the images and all the idols; henceforth there will be no place there for spells or sorceries. The King believes in God, he desires to serve him. His bishops bless the water and the heathen are brought to the baptistry. If any one of them resists Charlemagne, the King has him hanged or burnt to death or slain with the sword.

In the eyes of the crusading *pauperes* the smiting of the Moslems and the Jews was to be the first act in that final battle which – as already in the eschatological phantasies of the Jews and early Christians – was to culminate in the smiting of the Prince of Evil himself. Above these desperate hordes, as they moved about their work of massacre, there loomed the figure of Antichrist. The gigantic and terrifying shadow falls even across the pages of the chronicles. Antichrist is already born – at any moment Antichrist may set up his throne in the Temple at Jerusalem: even amongst the higher clergy there were some who spoke like this. And little as these phantasies had to do with the calculations of Pope Urban, they were attributed even to him by chroniclers struggling to describe the atmosphere in which the First Crusade was launched. It is the will of God – Urban is made to announce at Clermont – that through the labours of the crusaders Christianity shall flourish again at Jerusalem in these last times, so that when Antichrist begins his reign there – as he shortly must – he will find enough Christians to fight.

As the infidels were allotted their roles in the eschatological drama, popular imagination transformed them into demons. In the dark days of the ninth century, when Christendom really was gravely threatened by the victorious advance of Islam, a few clerics had sadly decided that Mohammed must have been the 'precursor' of a Saracen Antichrist and saw in Moslems in general the 'ministers' of Antichrist. Now, as Christendom launched its counter-offensive against an Islam which was already in retreat, popular epics portrayed Moslems as monsters with two sets of horns (front and back) and called them devils with no right to live. But if the Saracen (and his successor the Turk) long retained in the popular imagination a certain demonic quality, the Jew was an even more horrifying figure. Jews and Saracens were generally regarded as closely akin, if not identical; but since the Jews lived scattered through Christian Europe, they came to occupy by far the larger part in popular demonology. Moreover they occupied it for much longer – with consequences which have extended down the generations and which include the massacre of millions of European Jews in mid-twentieth century.

By the time they began to take on demonic attributes the Jews were far from being newcomers to western Europe. Following the disastrous struggle against Rome and the destruction of the Jewish nation in Palestine, mass emigrations and deportations had carried great numbers of Jews to France and the Rhine valley. Although they did not in these lands attain either the cultural eminence or the political influence which were theirs in Moslem-dominated Spain, their lot in the early Middle Ages was by no means a hard one. From the Carolingian period onwards there were Jewish merchants travelling to and fro between Europe and the Near East with luxury goods such as spices, incense and carved ivory; and there were also many Jewish artisans. There is no evidence to suggest that in those early centuries Jews were regarded by their Christian neighbours with any particular hatred or dread. On the contrary, social and economic relations between Jews and Christians were harmonious, personal friendships and commercial partnerships between them not uncommon. Culturally, the Jews went a long way in adapting themselves to the various countries they inhabited. Still, they remained Jews, they refused to be absorbed into the populations amonst which they lived; and this was to be decisive for the fate of their descendants.

This refusal to be assimilated, which has been repeated by so many generations of Jews since the first dispersals began in the sixth century B.C., is itself a very strange phenomenon. Save to some extent for the Gipsies, there seems to have been no other people which, scattered far and wide, possessing neither a nationality nor a territory of its own nor even any great ethnic homogeneity, has yet persisted indefinitely as a cultural entity. It is likely that the solution of this sociological puzzle is to be found in Jewish religion which not only – like Christianity and Islam – taught its adherents to regard themselves as the Chosen People of a single omnipotent God, but also taught them to regard the most overwhelming communal misfortunes – defeat, humiliation, dispersal – as so many tokens of divine favour, so many guarantees of future communal bliss. What made the Jews remain Jews was, it seems, their absolute conviction that the Diaspora was but a preliminary expiation of communal sin, a preparation for the coming of the Messiah and the return to a transfigured Holy Land – even though, after the final collapse of the Jewish state, they usually thought of that consummation as belonging to a remote and indefinite future. Moreover for the very purpose of ensuring the survival of the Jewish religion a body of ritual was elaborated which effectively prevented Jews from mixing with other people. Intermarriage with non-Jews was prohibited, eating with non-Jews made very difficult; even to read a non-Jewish book was an offence.

These circumstances were perhaps enough to explain why Jewry persisted through so many centuries of dispersion as a clearly recognizable community, bound together by an intense feeling of solidarity, somewhat aloof in its attitude to outsiders and jealously clinging to the tabus which had been designed for the very purpose of emphasizing and perpetuating its exclusiveness. On the other hand this self-preservative, self-isolating tendency cannot adequately account for the peculiarly intense and unremitting hatred which in Christendom (and only in Christendom) has been directed against Jewry above all other 'outgroups'. What accounts for that is the wholly phantastic image of the Jew which suddenly gripped the imagination of the new masses at the time of the first crusades.

Official Catholic teaching had prepared the way. The Church had always tended to regard the Synagogue as a dangerous influence and even as a potential rival and had never ceased to carry on a vigorous polemic against Judaism. For generations the laity had been accustomed to hear the Jews bitterly condemned from the pulpit – as perverse, stubborn and ungrateful because they refused to admit the divinity of Christ, as bearers also of a monstrous hereditary guilt for the murder of Christ. Moreover the eschatological tradition had long associated the Jews with Antichrist himself. Already in the second and third centuries theologians were foretelling that Antichrist would be a Jew of the tribe of Dan; and this idea became such a commonplace that in the Middle Ages it was accepted even by scholastics such as St Thomas Aquinas. Antichrist, it was held, would be born at Babylon; he would grow up in Palestine and would love the Jews above all peoples; he would rebuild the Temple for them and gather them together from their dispersion. The Jews for their part would be the most faithful followers of Antichrist, accepting him as the Messiah who was to restore the nation. And if some theologians looked forward to a general conversion of the Jews, others maintained that their blindness would endure to the end and that at the Last Judgement they would be sent, along with Antichrist himself, to suffer the torments of hell for all eternity. In the compendium of Antichrist-lore which Adso of Montier-en-Der produced in the tenth century and which remained the stock authority throughout the Middle Ages, Antichrist, while remaining a Jew of the tribe of Dan, has become still more uncanny and sinister. Now he is to be the offspring of a harlot and a worthless wretch and moreover at the moment of his conception the Devil is to enter the harlot's womb as a spirit, thereby ensuring that the child shall be the very incarnation of Evil. Later, his education in Palestine is to be carried out by sorcerers and magicians, who will initiate him into the black art and all iniquity.

When the old eschatological prophecies were taken up by the masses of the later Middle Ages all these phantasies were treated with deadly seriousness and elaborated into a weird mythology. For just as the human figure of Antichrist tended to merge into the wholly demonic figure of Satan, so the Jews tended to be seen as demons attendant on Satan. In drama and picture they were often shown as devils with the beard and horns of a goat, while in real life ecclesiastical and secular authorities alike tried to make them wear horns on their hats. Like other demons, they were imagined and portrayed in close association with creatures which symbolize lust and dirt – horned beasts, pigs, frogs, worms, snakes and scorpions. Conversely Satan himself was commonly given Jewish features and was referred to as 'the father of the Jews'. The populace was convinced that in the synagogue Jews worshipped Satan in the form of a cat or a toad, invoking his aid in making black magic. Like their supposed master, Jews were thought of as demons of destruction whose one object was the ruin of Christians and Christendom – 'dyables d'enfer, ennemys du genre humain', as they are called in French miracle-plays.

And if the power of the Jews seemed greater than ever, their evil-doing more outrageous, their sorceries more baleful, that was but one more sign that the End was indeed at hand. It was believed that in preparation for the final struggle Jews held secret, grotesque tournaments at which, as soldiers of Antichrist, they practised stabbing. Even the ten lost tribes of Israel, whom Commodianus had seen as the future army of Christ, became identified with those hosts of Antichrist, the peoples of Gog and Magog – peoples whom the *Pseudo-Methodius* described as living off human flesh, corpses, babes ripped from their mothers' wombs, and also off scorpions, serpents and all the most disgusting reptiles. Dramas were written showing how the Jewish demons would help Antichrist to conquer the world until, on the eve of the Second Coming and the beginning of the Millennium, Antichrist and Jews would be annihilated together amidst the rejoicings of the Christians. During the performance of such works armed force was needed to protect the Jewish quarter from the fury of the mob. Popes and Councils might insist that, although the Jews ought to be isolated and degraded until the day of their conversion, they must certainly not be killed – subtleties such as these made little impression on turbulent masses swept by eschatological hopes and fears and already, as they thought, embarked on the prodigious struggles of the Last Days.

Hatred of the Jews has so often been attributed to their role as money-lenders that it is worth emphasizing how slight the connection really was. The phantasy of the demonic Jew existed before the reality of the Jewish money-lender, whom indeed it helped to produce. As, in the age of the crusades, religious intolerance became more and more intense, the economic situation of the Jews rapidly deteriorated. At the Lateran Council of 1215 it was ruled that Jews should be debarred from all civil and military functions and from owning land; and these decisions were incorporated into Canon Law. As merchants too the Jews were at an ever greater disadvantage, for they could no longer travel without risk of being murdered. Besides, Christians themselves began to turn to commerce and they very quickly outstripped the Jews, who were debarred from the Hanseatic League and who could of course not compete with the Italian and Flemish cities. For the richer Jews money-lending was the one field of economic activity which remained open. As money-lenders they could remain in their homes, without undertaking dangerous journeys; and by keeping their wealth in a fluid state they might in an emergency be able to flee without losing it all. Moreover in the rapidly expanding economy of western Europe there was a constant and urgent demand for credit. The lending of money at interest – stigmatized as usury – was forbidden to Christians by Canon Law. The Jews, who were of course not subject to this prohibition, were encouraged and even compelled by the authorities to lend their money against securities and were commended for carrying out this necessary function.

Jewish money-lending was however of only transitory importance in medieval economic life. As capitalism developed Christians themselves with ever greater determination ignored the canonical ban on money-lending. Already by the middle of the twelfth century the capitalists of the Low Countries were making large loans at interest and the Italians were expert bankers. With these men the Jews could not compete. Cities, territorial lords, kings all taxed their Jews severely – often the Jewish contribution to the royal exchequer was ten times what their numbers warranted. Once again Jews found themselves at a hopeless disadvantage. Although individual Jewish money-lenders were able from time to time, especially in backward countries, to amass considerable fortunes, arbitrary levies soon reduced them to poverty again. And rich Jews were never numerous: most were what would nowadays be called lower-middle-class and many were downright poor. At the end of the Middle Ages there was very little Jewish wealth in northern Europe to share in the prodigious development which followed upon the discovery of the New World.

Ousted from high finance, some Jews turned to smallscale money-lending and pawnbroking. Here, certainly, were grounds for popular hatred. What had once been a flourishing Jewish culture had by that time turned into a terrorized society locked in perpetual warfare with the greater society around it; and it can be taken for granted that Jewish money-lenders often reacted to insecurity and persecution by deploying a ruthlessness of their own. But already long before that happened hatred of the Jews had become endemic in the European masses. And even later, when a mob set about killing Jews it never confined itself to the comparatively few money-lenders but killed every Jew it could lay hands on. On the other hand any Jew, money-lender or not, could escape massacre by submitting to baptism, for it was believed that baptism infallibly washed away his demonic nature.

Jews were not however the only ones to be killed. As we shall see in later chapters, the eschatologically inspired hordes of the poor soon turned on the clergy as well. And here again the killing was carried out in the belief that the victims were agents of Antichrist and Satan whose extermination was a prerequisite for the Millennium. If most people believed that Antichrist was to be born a Jew, there were many who believed that he would be the son of a bishop and a nun. Moreover Martin Luther was not (as is often supposed) the first to hit upon the idea that the Antichrist who sets up his throne in the Temple can be no other than the Pope at Rome and that the Church of Rome is therefore the Church of Satan. Amongst the eschatologically minded in the later Middle Ages the idea was already a commonplace. Even such a champion of the Church as St Bernard could come to believe, in his tense expectation of the final drama, that many of the clergy belonged to the hosts of Antichrist. And in the pronouncements of the *propheta* who was burnt as a heretic at Paris in 1209 similar ideas appear as an integral part of a doctrine which clearly drew heavily upon the Johannine and Sibylline traditions. This man, a cleric turned gold-smith, foretold that within five years the people would be con-sumed by famine, the kings would slay one another with the sword, the earth would open and swallow up the town-dwellers and finally fire would fall upon those members of Antichrist, the prelates of the Church. For, he insisted, the Pope was Antichrist, on account of the power he held; and the Babylon of the Apocalypse was really Rome. After that great purification the whole earth with all its kingdoms would be subject to the future King of France, Louis VIII – he was still Dauphin at the time – an eschatological monarch who would be possessed of the knowledge and power of the Scriptures and would reign for ever under the dispensation of the Holy Spirit.

Any millenarian movement was in fact almost compelled by the situation in which it found itself to see the clergy as a demonic fraternity. A group of laymen headed by a messianic leader and convinced that it was charged by God with the stupendous mission of preparing the way for the Millennium – such a group was bound to find in the institutionalized Church at best an intransigent opponent, at worst a ruthless persecutor. But was it not of the very nature of Antichrist that he should do everything in his power to hinder, by fraud and violence, the divinely ordained consummation? And what better means could he find than to disguise himself under the papal mantle and tiara and to deploy the massive power and authority of the Church against the Saints? But if that was so, how else could the Church of Antichrist be seen than as the Whore of Babylon, 'the woman drunken with the blood of the Saints', the Mother of Abominations 'with whom the kings of the earth have committed fornication, and the inhabitants of the earth have been made drunk with the wine of her fornica-tion'? And how else could the clergy of that Church be seen than as the many-headed Beast which served Antichrist and bore the Whore upon its back, which uttered blasphemies and warred against the Saints? The clergy as the Beast of the Apocalypse: what image could be more convincing to enthusiastic millenarians in whose eyes the life of the clergy was indeed nothing but bestiality, the *vita animalis*, an existence utterly given over to the World and the Flesh?

Was the medieval Church really sunk in such crass materialism? Or is the belief to that effect, which is still widespread today, an over-simplification comparable with that which equates medieval Jewry with medieval usury? It certainly cannot be denied that the Church which had done so much to shape medieval society was also very much part of that society. Already before the fall of the Western Empire the emperors, by endowing the Church with the wealth of the pagan temples, had made it the greatest landed proprietor in the world. This wealth, which enabled the Church to survive the great migrations and invasions relatively un-scathed, was increased century after century by legacies and offerings from princes and the rich. By Canon Law Church property was inalienable and so, despite depredations by lay magnates, it ended by becoming enormous. An organization so well endowed had of course many tempting appointments to offer; and noble families commonly obtained, by influence or even by purchase, comfortable benefices for their younger sons. Many of the bishops and abbots appointed in this way were simply politicians, courtiers or princes in ecclesiastical garb. Abbots turned their monasteries into luxurious establishments, while bishops built palaces with moats and turrets, in which they lived in the same magnificent style as other great feudal lords. It was not without cause that the common people complained of the clergy that 'they take no care at all of us, they live scandalous lives, they tread upon our heads. . . . The common people make everything and deliver everything and still cannot live without being for ever tormented and driven to ruin by the clergy. . . . The prelates are raging wolves . . .'

Moreover, at least from the thirteenth century onwards, the Papacy itself was decidedly worldly. Popes tended to be primarily statesmen and administrators. The greater circulation of money and the revival of trade enabled the Papacy to develop a fiscal system on a European scale, operated by an elaborate and highly trained bureaucracy. However energetically the Papacy might condemn 'usury', as it called the new capitalism, its own financial needs compelled it to make use of every means of raising money. Earlier than secular monarchs, popes employed the services of bankers. By such means the Papacy was enabled to fight purely political battles by purely political means and even to buy allies and wage wars. It was also able, as a great monarchy, to maintain a court of unparalleled splendour, at which intrigue and debauchery sometimes flourished as luxuriantly as at other courts. Throughout the higher ranks of the ecclesiastical hierarchy there was in fact a marked tendency to approximate to the normal way of life of the upper strata of lay society.

When the millenarians of the later Middle Ages talked of the worldliness of the Church they were certainly talking of something that existed; but it is no less significant that worldliness was all that they could see in the Church. What they did not see was that, however deeply it might be involved in secular society, the Church still represented a more humane and disinterested way of life – and not only by its teaching but also, even at its most worldly periods, by its practice. In an age which knew nothing of social services, monks and later friars cared for the poor and the sick as part of an unquestioned routine and without thought of earthly reward. In a continent harassed by feudal wars bishops did what they could, by preaching the Truce of God and the Peace of God, to limit the suffering and devastation. At all times great numbers of clergy led relatively austere lives and many even of the great prelates aimed at sanctity. And if the clergy were constantly slipping into a comfortable laxity – as any large body of human beings will always tend to do – they were never lacking some who possessed the will and the power to call a halt and at least attempt reform. The founding of the new monastic orders of the eleventh and twelfth centuries, the innovations of St Francis and St Dominic in the thirteenth century, the conciliar movement of the fifteenth century, even the 'evangelical' movement which was spreading on the very eve of the Reformation, are only a few examples out of many of the capacity of the medieval Church for facing up to its own shortcomings.

Judged by the norms of medieval Latin Christianity, which were accepted in principle by all alike, the record of the Church was in reality far from being wholly black. But it looked wholly black to millenarians who, at once terrified and enthralled by the imminence of the Second Coming, applied those norms with absolute intransigence and a total refusal to make allowances. The eschatologically inspired hordes sought leaders whom they could regard as purely spiritual beings, remote from material concerns and calculations, free from the needs and desires of the body. Such leaders could be seen as miracle-working saints, even as living gods. But by these standards an attitude of utter condemnation was the only possible one towards a clergy which, being human, abounded in human frailty. It was because of their inordinate expectations that eschatological movements could not – as the Church itself could and did – simply condemn certain specific abuses and criticize certain individual clerics, but had to see the whole clergy in all its doings as the militia of Antichrist, bound by its very nature to strive for the spiritual and material ruin of Christendom and striving all the more ferociously now that the End was at hand. In Lorch's engraving [Plate 2] it is a demonic cardinal, vomiting a bishop, who says: 'Take yourselves off, God and men: the Devil and I are masters.' And in Dürer's illustration to the sixth chapter of the Book of Revelation [Plate 3] not only a pope and a bishop but also ordinary priests and monks figure among those who on the Day of Wrath will call in vain on the mountains and rocks to fall on them and hide them from the face of the avenging Christ. Despite their date, what cries from these two apocalyptic drawings is still that same horrified denunciation of the Church of Antichrist which had first been uttered by the millenarian sects of the twelfth and thirteenth centuries.

Phantasy, anxiety and social myth

It has been remarked by psychoanalysts that in the world-view of medieval Christianity life tends to be seen as a mortal struggle waged by good fathers and good children against bad fathers and bad children. Certainly this pattern stands out with stark crudity in the phantasies of popular eschatology and the mass movements they inspired.

Already in the figure of the eschatological leader – the Emperor of the Last Days or the returning Christ – there are combined the phantastic images of the good father and the good son. For on the one hand the leader has – like the pharaoh and many another 'divine king' – all the attributes of an ideal father: he is perfectly wise, he is perfectly just, he protects the weak. But on the other hand he is also the son whose task it is to transform the world, the Messiah who is to establish a new heaven and a new earth and who can say of himself: 'Behold, I make all things new!' And both as father and as son this figure is colossal, superhuman, omnipotent. He is credited with such abundance of supernatural powers that it is imagined as streaming forth as light – that radiance which traditionally symbolizes the indwelling Spirit, which not only surrounds the risen Christ but was also attributed to the future Emperor Constans. Moreover being thus filled with the divine spirit the eschatological leader possesses unique miracle-working powers. His armies will be invariably and triumphantly victorious, his presence will make the earth yield prodigious crops, his reign will be an age of such perfect harmony as the old, corrupt world has never known.

This image was of course a purely phantastic one, in the sense that it bore no relation to the real nature and capacity of any human being who ever existed or ever could exist. It was nevertheless an image which could be projected on to a living man; and there were always men about who were more than willing to accept such a projection, who in fact passionately desired to be seen as infallible, wonder-working saviours. In the main such men came from the lower strata of the intelligentsia. They included many members of the lower clergy, priests who had left their parishes, monks who had fled from their monasteries, clerks in minor orders. They included also some laymen who, unlike the laity in general, had acquired a certain literacy – artisans chiefly, but also some administrative officials and even occasionally a nobleman whose ambitions were loftier than his status. And the secret of the ascendancy which they exercised never lay in their birth nor to any great extent in their education, but always in their personalities. Contemporary accounts of these messiahs of the poor commonly stress their eloquence, their commanding bearing and their personal magnetism. Above all one gets the impression that even if some of these men may perhaps have been conscious impostors, most of them really saw themselves as incarnate gods or at least as vessels of divinity, they really believed that through their coming all things would be made new. And this total conviction would communicate itself easily enough to the multitudes whose deepest desire was precisely for an eschatological saviour.

Those who attached themselves to such a saviour saw themselves as a holy people – and holy just because of their unqualified submission to the saviour and their unqualified devotion to the eschatological mission as defined by him. They were his good children and as a reward they shared in his supernatural power. It was not only that the leader deployed his power for their benefit – they themselves, so long as they clung to him, partook in that power and thereby became more than human, Saints who could neither fail or fall. They were the bright armies, 'clothed in white linen, white and clean'. Their final triumph was decreed from all eternity; and meanwhile their every deed, though it were robbery or rape or massacre, not only was guiltless but was a holy act.

But opposite the armies of the Saints, and scarcely less powerful than they, there appears a host of demonic fathers and sons. The two opposing hosts, each the negative of the other, are held together in a strange symmetrical pattern. As in the eschatological Messiah, so in the eschatological Enemy, Antichrist, the images of the son and the father are fused – only here of course the images are those of the bad son and the bad father. As 'the son of perdition' Antichrist is in every way a demonic counterpart to the Son of God. It was his birth that was to usher in the Last Days; men waited tensely for tidings of the mysterious and ominous nativity at Babylon. In his relation to God the Father Antichrist appears as a defiant and rebellious child, passionately concerned to frustrate the intentions of the father and even daring to usurp the father's place and to ape his authority. In his relation to human beings, on the other hand, Antichrist is a father scarcely to be distinguished from Satan himself: a protecting father to his devilish brood, but to the Saints an atrocious father, deceitful, masking evil intentions with fair words, a cunning tyrant who when crossed becomes a cruel and murderous persecutor. Like the messianic leader, Antichrist is filled with supernatural power which enables him to work miracles; but this power comes from Satan and is exhibited in the black arts which he exploits for the ruin of the Saints. Since his power is not that of the Spirit no radiance comes from him. On the contrary, like Satan he is a creature of darkness, he is the Beast who ascends out of the bottomless pit, he is an earthbound monster out of whose mouth come unclean frogs, scorpions and other familiar symbols of earth and dirt.

Everything which was projected on to the imaginary figure of Antichrist was also projected on to those 'outgroups' which were regarded as serving him. Even by orthodox theologians Jews were seen as wicked children who stubbornly denied the claims and affronted the majesty of God, the Father of all; and in the eyes of sectarians who saw the Pope as Antichrist the clergy too was bound to seem a traitorous brood in rebellion against their true father. But the Jew and the cleric could also themselves very easily be seen as father-figures. This is obvious enough in the case of the cleric, who after all is actually called 'Father' by the laity. If it is less obvious in the case of the Jew it is nevertheless a fact, for even today the Jew – the man who clings to the Old Testament and rejects the New, the member of the people into which Christ was born – is imagined by many Christians as typically an 'old Jew', a decrepit figure in old, wornout clothes.

Integrated into the eschatological phantasy, Jew and cleric alike became father-figures of a most terrifying kind. That monster of destructive rage and phallic power whom Melchior Lorch portrays wearing the triple tiara and carrying the keys and the papal cross was seen by millenarians in every 'false cleric'. As for the Jews, the belief that they murdered Christian children was so widespread and so firmly held that not all the protests of popes and bishops – and they were many – could ever eradicate it. If one examines the picture of Jews torturing and castrating a helpless and innocent boy [Plate 4], one appreciates with just how much fear and hate the phantastic figure of the bad father could be regarded. And the other stock accusation brought against Jews in medieval Europe – of flogging, stabbing and pulverizing the host – has a similar significance. For if from the point of view of a Jew an atrocity committed on the host would be meaningless, from the point of view of a medieval Christian it would be a repetition of the torturing and killing of Christ. Here too, then, the wicked (Jewish) father is imagined as assaulting the good son; and this interpretation is borne out by the many stories of how, in the middle of the tortured wafer, Christ appeared as a child, dripping blood and screaming.

To these demons in human form, the Jew and the 'false cleric', was attributed every quality which belonged to the Beast from the Abyss – not only his cruelty but also his grossness, his animality, his blackness and uncleanness. Jewry and clergy together formed the foul black host of the enemy which stood opposite the clean white army of the Saints – 'the children of God, that we are, poisonous worms, that you are', as a medieval rhymster put it. And the Saints knew that it was their task to wipe that foul black host off the face of the earth, for only an earth which had been so purified would be fit to carry the New Jerusalem, the shining Kingdom of the Saints.

The civilization of the later Middle Ages was always prone to demonize 'outgroups'; but at times of acute disorientation this tendency was especially marked. Hardship and distress did not in themselves produce this result. Poverty, wars and local famines were so much a part of normal life that they were taken for granted and could therefore be faced in a sober and realistic manner. But when a situation arose which was not only menacing but went altogether outside the normal run of experience, when people were confronted with hazards which were all the more frightening because they were unfamiliar – at such times a collective flight into the world of demonological phantasies could occur very easily. And if the threat was sufficiently overwhelming, the disorientation sufficiently widespread and acute, there could arise a mass delusion of the most explosive kind. Thus when the Black Death reached western Europe in 1348 it was at once concluded that some class of people must have introduced into the water-supply a poison concocted of spiders, frogs and lizards – all of them symbols of earth, dirt and the Devil – or else maybe of basilisk-flesh. As the plague continued and people grew more and more bewildered and desperate, suspicion swung now here, now there, lighting successively on the lepers, the poor, the rich, the clergy, before it came finally to rest on the Jews, who thereupon were almost exterminated.

But not all strata of society were equally exposed to traumatic and disorienting experiences. As we have seen, amongst the masses in the overpopulated, highly urbanized areas there were always many who lived in a state of chronic and inescapable insecurity, harassed not only by their economic helplessness and vulnerability but by the lack of the traditional social relationships on which, even at the worst of times, peasants had normally been able to depend.

These were the people who were most frequently hit by disasters and least able to cope with them. And these were the people who, when faced with overwhelming problems and tormented by intolerable anxieties, were prone to seek messianic leaders and to imagine themselves as warrior-Saints. The resulting phantasy could easily be integrated into the old eschatology derived from the Johannine and Sibylline traditions; and in this form it became a coherent social myth. The myth did not of course enable the helpless masses to overcome their dilemmas, and it often prompted them to courses' of action that proved downright suicidal. But it did hold their anxieties at bay, and it did make them feel both immensely important and immensely powerful. That gave it irresistible fascination.

So it came about that multitudes of people acted out with fierce energy a shared phantasy which, though delusional, yet brought them such intense emotional relief that they could live only through it, and were perfectly willing both to kill and to die for it. This phenomenon was to recur many times, in various parts of western and central Europe, between the twelfth and the sixteenth centuries.

5 In the Backwash of the Crusades

The Pseudo-Baldwin and the 'Master of Hungary'

The gigantic enterprise of the crusades long continued to provide the background for popular messianic movements. In the official crusades secular politics bulked ever larger. Already in the Third Crusade, which started on its way in 1189, the political interests of the secular states – the Empire and France and England – found open expression. And the Fourth Crusade, in the opening years of the thirteenth century, ended as a purely lay war waged for purely political ends – an expedition in which the commercial ambition of Venice combined with the territorial ambitions of French and German princes to bring about the capture of Constantinople and the conquest and partition of the Eastern Empire. In such a crusade there was no longer any room for the *pauperes* – they were not wanted and would not have been interested. But they had not abandoned the old ideal of the liberation and defence of the Holy City, nor the old eschatological hopes. On the contrary, now that the barons had given themselves up altogether to worldliness, the poor were even more convinced than before that they and they alone were the true instruments of the divine will, the true custodians of the eschatological mission.

In 1198 for the first time there seems to have appeared a *propheta* who summoned the poor to a crusade which should be theirs and theirs alone. Fulk of Neuilly was a typical ascetic miracle-worker whose immense popular prestige owed much to his supposed ability to heal the blind and the dumb. And what he envisaged would seem to have been nothing less than an independent army which would be as rigorously insistent on its poverty as, it was said, the horde of King Tafur had been. The crowds set in motion by Fulk perished miserably on the coast of Spain; but within a few years they were succeeded by the Children's Crusades. In 1212 armies of children set out to recapture the Holy City, one army from France and another, much larger, from the Rhine valley. Each was headed by a youth who believed himself chosen by God and who was regarded by his followers as a miracle-working saint. These thousands of children could be held back neither by entreaty nor by force; their faith was such that they were convinced the Mediterranean would dry up before them as the Red Sea had dried up before the Israelites. These crusades too ended disastrously, with almost all the children either drowned in the sea or starved to death or sold into slavery in Africa. Nevertheless these mass migrations had inaugurated a tradition; for more than a century autonomous crusades of the poor continued to occur from time to time, and with consequences which were no longer disastrous to themselves alone.

Meanwhile in Flanders and Hainaut the Fourth Crusade itself gave rise, indirectly and after an interval of a generation, to a movement which appealed strongly to the messianic hopes of the masses, even though its origin lay in a political intrigue. When the crusaders captured Constantinople in 1204 they installed Baldwin IX, Count of Flanders, as Emperor of Constantinople and suzerain of all the princes from the West who were now carving fiefs for themselves out of the territories of the Eastern Empire. Baldwin's state was however very vulnerable and within a year the Emperor was captured by the Bulgarians and put to death. At home Baldwin's daughter Joanna became Countess; but as she could not effectively oppose that resolute and able politician Philip Augustus of France her lands of Flanders and Hainaut fell under French domination. It was an unwelcome domination and on the death of Philip in 1223 it was only lack of a leader that prevented a general rising. At this point the age-old phantasy of the Sleeping Emperor reappeared in a form adapted to the hour. In virtue of his extraordinary history Baldwin had become in the popular imagination a figure of superhuman dimensions, a fabulous creature, half demon and half angel. Gradually a whole legend was elaborated. It was rumoured abroad that the Count was after all not dead but, having sinned greatly, was still discharging a penance imposed on him by the Pope. For many years he had been living in obscurity as a wandering beggar and hermit; but his expiation was now almost completed and he would very soon be returning in glory to free his land and people.

In 1224 a stranger passed through the country around Tournai, distributing largesse and announcing that Baldwin was about to return. A few months later there appeared between Tournai and Valenciennes a begging hermit, in appearance a typical *propheta*, of imposing stature, with long hair and flowing beard. He was traced to a nearby forest, where he was found to be living in a hut made of branches; and at once the rumour began to spread that he was no other than the missing Count. It has never been decided whether the hermit suggested this role for himself or simply accepted it when it was proposed to him. What is certain is that, having insisted on spending another year in the forest to complete his penance, he used the time to provide himself with counsellors and to organize a secret court. He was visited by the nobility; a nephew of Baldwin really believed that he recognized his uncle in him; the leaders of the Flemish resistance to France at least claimed to recognize him so that they could adopt him as their man. Fortified by this support the hermit announced that he was indeed Baldwin, returned home from the East after terrible sufferings. Great crowds streamed out from Valenciennes to see him and in April 1225 brought him back to the town on horseback, clad in a scarlet robe, amidst scenes of wild jubilation.

Accepted by most of the nobility and towns of Flanders and Hainaut, the hermit assumed sovereign powers. But when the Countess Joanna invited him to come to her court to be recognized and acclaimed, he refused to go. Instead, he prepared to establish his position by force; while Joanna on her side, having interviewed crusaders who had known her father, denounced the hermit as an impostor. The towns were in a turbulent mood, not only because they saw a chance to extend their liberties by throwing off the suzerainty of the King of France but because they really believed that their true lord had been restored to them. Now they rose in arms and deposed Joanna, who only narrowly escaped capture. Civil war broke out; and the hermit, at the head of a powerful force, devastated Hainaut from end to end, pillaging and destroying every centre of resistance and setting fire to churches crammed full with people. This was no ordinary war but (as a modern historian has described it) a war of religious exaltation, a crusade against the Countess Joanna – who was now detested not merely as the ally of France but as an undutiful and rebellious daughter. And the leader of the crusade was no ordinary commander but a holy prince, a being so revered that people kissed the scars which bore witness to his long martyrdom, fought for a hair of his head or a scrap of his clothing and drank his bathwater as an earlier generation had drunk Tanchelm's.

In May the hermit was crowned, probably at Valenciennes, as Count of Flanders and Hainaut and Emperor of Constantinople and Thessalonica, in a ceremony in which the splendours of western and of eastern ritual were combined. The new monarch at once created knights, distributed fiefs and benefices and largesse and set off on a state visit to his towns. Clad in imperial purple, borne in a litter or mounted on a noble palfrey, surrounded by the banners of his domains in the East and West and preceded by the cross which traditionally preceded the successors of Constantine – yet still wearing the long beard of a holy hermit and carrying the white wand of benevolence instead of a metal sceptre, he must indeed have seemed the messianic Emperor, come at last to fulfil the old Sibylline prophecies.

The popular enthusiasm was overwhelming. Headed by abbots and monks, long processions of townsmen and peasants came everywhere to meet him; towns such as Lille and Ghent and Bruges offered him not only their keys but money as well, praising God for a return so miraculous that it seemed a rebirth; people dropped on their knees as he passed by. As a contemporary observer significantly remarked: 'If God had come down to earth, he could not have been better received.' Yet the enthusiasm was not equally great in all classes. While the rich tended to look askance at the new sovereign, the poor were all convinced that it was indeed Baldwin who had appeared amongst them. Although modern historians have tended to ignore the fact, the original sources show clearly enough that it was the urban poor, and especially the workers in the great textile industry, who adopted the man as their messiah. According to the same observer, 'the poor folk, weavers and fullers, were his intimates, and the better-off and rich people got a bad deal everywhere. The poor folk said they would have gold and silver . . . and they called him Emperor.' The comment seems all the more significant when one realizes that in that year of 1225 Flanders and Hainaut were in the throes of an appalling famine, such as had not been seen for generations.

Politically the hermit had become a force to be reckoned with, for he had not only established his authority at home but was winning recognition abroad. Neighbouring princes sent ambassadors to his court and Henry III of England offered a treaty of alliance, directed of course against France. To all this the French king Louis VIII replied by concluding a treaty of alliance with the Countess Joanna, at the same time hinting that he himself might recognize the claims of the new ruler if the latter would visit him in person. The hermit accepted the invitation and made his way in magnificent state to the French court at Péronne. This turned out to be a fatal blunder. In conversation with Louis the hermit proved unable to recall things which the real Baldwin must certainly have known. Very soon he was identified as one Bertrand of Ray in Burgundy, a serf who had indeed taken part in the Fourth Crusade as a minstrel in the suite of his lord and who in later life had become notorious as a charlatan and impersonator.

Unmasked, the impostor lost his nerve and fled overnight from the court, while his suite of a hundred knights, hitherto his devoted partisans, dispersed in utter disillusionment. He might still have saved his life, for Louis had granted him a three-day grace in which to leave French territory; but instead of availing himself of this safeguard he made his way to his old headquarters at Valenciennes. His arrival threw the town into uproar. The rich burghers tried to arrest him but were prevented by the popular fury. Instead, some of the rich were themselves taken prisoner and held to ransom, while the rest fled from the town. The common people deposed the old administration and proclaimed a commune ← amidst scenes of hectic festivity. They also lodged their messiah in the town fortress and set about strengthening the town walls. And Valenciennes was indeed about to be besieged by the French when the pseudo-Baldwin again lost his nerve and fled, taking with him a large sum of money. Recognized and captured, he was paraded with great ignominy through the towns which had witnessed his triumph. In October he was hanged in the market-place at Lille, some seven months after he had first declared himself Count and Emperor.

Before his execution Bertrand of Ray described himself as a poor devil who had been led astray by the evil counsel of knights and burghers. But nothing could break the hold which he had obtained over the popular imagination. The towns had to beg forgiveness of the King of France, but at heart the common people remained true to their lost lord. Although the Countess Joanna ruled her dominions with prudence and courage, for many generations after her death she continued to be execrated as a parricide, while the figure of Baldwin, the Latin Emperor of the East who for a few weeks had appeared amongst the Flemish masses as their messiah, took his place (as Count Emico of Leiningen had taken his) amongst the sleeping monarchs who must one day return. Again in the words of the contemporary observer, 'at Valenciennes people await him as the Bretons await King Arthur'; one might add, as the common people everywhere had long awaited the resurrected Constans. Brief though the episode had been, it had inaugurated an epoch of social turbulence which was to continue for a century and a half.

In France messianic expectations centred on the Capetian dynasty, which during the twelfth and the thirteenth century came to enjoy a quasi-religious prestige of peculiar intensity. Already at the time of the Second Crusade Louis VII had been regarded by many as the Emperor of the Last Days. By the beginning of the thirteenth century the common people were at one with the king and his official apologists in claiming for the French monarchy an absolute primacy over all other monarchies. The King of France was anointed from the *sainte ampoule*, which had been brought by a dove from heaven; his standard was the oriflamme, which had also descended from heaven; he himself possessed miraculous powers, particularly as a curer of disease. Philip Augustus – whose very title was modelled on the *semper augustus* of the imperial title – saw himself as a second Charlemagne, appointed by God to be the leader of all Latin Christendom. On the day of the battle of Bouvines in 1214, which by smashing the coalition of England, Germany and Flanders went far towards gaining him that leadership, Philip actually assumed the role of priest-king and, like Charlemagne in the *Chanson de Roland*, blessed his army as a host which was fighting for the true faith.

In those same years there were sectarians in Paris who saw in the Dauphin, the future Louis VIII, a messiah who would reign for ever under the dispensation of the Holy Spirit over a united and purified world. If in the event Louis VIII distinguished himself by his shrewdness and determination rather than by any spiritual gifts, his successor was indeed a secular saint. Louis IX – St Louis – set a new standard for kings throughout Christendom. Together with his rigorous asceticism, the genuine solicitude which he extended to the humblest of his subjects earned him an extra-ordinary veneration. What miraculous happenings were expected, one wonders, when this radiant figure set off on the Seventh Crusade? Certainly when he was defeated at Mansura in 1250 and led into a captivity which was to last four years it was a terrible blow to all Christendom. The disillusionment was so great that many in France began to taunt the clergy, saying that after all Mohammed seemed to be stronger than Christ.

It was in response to this catastrophe that there sprang up the first of the anarchic movements known as the Crusades of the Shepherds. At Easter 1251 three men began to preach the crusade in Picardy and within a few days their summons had spread to Brabant, Flanders and Hainaut – lands beyond the frontiers of the French kingdom, but where the masses were still as hungry for a messiah as they had been in the days of Bertrand of Ray a genera-tion earlier. One of these men was a renegade monk called Jacob, who was said to have come from Hungary and was known as the 'Master of Hungary'. He was a thin, pale, bearded ascetic of some sixty years of age, a man of commanding bearing and able to speak with great eloquence in French, German and Latin. He claimed that the Virgin Mary, surrounded by a host of angels, had appeared to him and had given him a letter – which he always carried in his hand, as Peter the Hermit is said to have carried a similar document.

According to Jacob, this letter summoned all shepherds to help King Louis to free the Holy Sepulchre. God, he proclaimed, was displeased with the pride and ostentation of the French knights and had chosen the lowly to carry out his work. It was to shepherds that the glad tidings of the Nativity had first been made known and it was through shepherds that the Lord was now about to manifest his power and glory.

Shepherds and cowherds – young men, boys and girls alike – deserted their flocks and, without taking leave of their parents, gathered under the strange banners on which the miraculous visitation of the Virgin was portrayed. Before long thieves, prostitutes, outlaws, apostate monks and murderers joined them; and these elements provided the leaders. But many of these new-comers too dressed as shepherds and all alike became known as the *Pastoureaux*. Soon there was an army which – though the contemporary estimate of 60,000 need not be taken seriously – must certainly have numbered some thousands. It was divided into fifty companies; these marched separately, armed with pitchforks, hatchets, daggers, pikes carried aloft as they entered towns and villages, so as to intimidate the authorities. When they ran short of provisions they took what they needed by force; but much was given freely for – as emerges from many different accounts – people revered the *Pastoureaux* as holy men.

Soon the *Pastoureaux* were behaving exactly like the hordes which had followed Tanchelm and Eudes de l'Étoile. Surrounded by an armed guard, Jacob preached against the clergy, attacking the Mendicants as hypocrites and vagabonds, the Cistercians as lovers of land and property, the Premonstratensians as proud and gluttonous, the canons regular as half-secular fast-breakers; and his attacks on the Roman Curia knew no bounds. His followers were taught to regard the sacraments with contempt and to see in their own gatherings the sole embodiment of truth. For himself he claimed that he could not only see visions but could heal the sick – and people brought their sick to be touched by him. He declared that food and wine set before his men never grew less, but rather increased as they were eaten and drunk. He promised that when the crusaders arrived at the sea the water would roll back before them and they would march dryshod to the Holy Land. On the strength of his miraculous powers he arrogated to himself the right to grant absolution from every kind of sin. If a man and a woman amongst his followers wished to marry he would perform the ceremony; and if they wished to part he would divorce them with equal ease. He was said to have married eleven men to one woman – which rather suggests that he saw himself as a 'living

Christ' requiring 'Disciples' and a 'Virgin Mary'. And anyone who ventured to contradict him was at once struck down by the bodyguard. The murder of a priest was regarded as particularly praiseworthy; according to Jacob it could be atoned for by a drink of wine. It is not surprising that the clergy watched the spread of this movement with horror.

Jacob's army went first to Amiens, where it met with an enthusiastic reception. The burghers put their food and drink at the disposal of the crusaders, calling them the holiest of men. Jacob made such a favourable impression that they begged him to help himself to their belongings. Some knelt down before him 'as though he had been the Body of Christ'. After Amiens the army split up into two groups. One of these marched on Rouen, where it was able to disperse a synod which was meeting there under the Archbishop. The other group proceeded to Paris. There Jacob so fascinated the Queen Mother Blanche that she loaded him with presents and left him free to do whatever he would. Jacob now dressed as a bishop, preached in churches, sprinkled holy water after some strange rite of his own. Meanwhile the *Pastoureaux* in the city began to attack the clergy, putting many to the sword and drowning many in the Seine. The students of the University – who of course were also clerics, though in minor orders – would have been massacred if the bridge had not been closed in time.

When the *Pastoureaux* left Paris they moved in a number of bands, each under the leadership of a 'Master', who, as they passed through towns and villages, blessed the crowds. At Tours the crusaders again attacked the clergy, especially Dominican and Franciscan friars, whom they dragged and whipped through the streets. The Dominicans' church was looted, the Franciscan friary was attacked and broken into. The old contempt for sacraments administered by unworthy hands showed itself: the host was seized and, amidst insults, thrown on to the street. All this was done with the approval and support of the populace. At Orleans similar scenes occurred. Here the Bishop had the gates closed against the oncoming horde, but the burghers deliberately disobeyed him and admitted the *Pastoureaux* into the town. Jacob preached in public, and a scholar from the cathedral school who dared to oppose him was struck down with an axe. The *Pastoureaux* rushed to the houses where the priests and monks had hidden themselves, stormed them and burned many to the ground. Many clergy, including teachers at the University, and many burghers were struck down or drowned in the Loire. The remaining clergy were forced out of the town. When the *Pastoureaux* left the town the Bishop, enraged at the reception that had been accorded them, put Orleans under interdict. It was indeed the opinion of contemporaries that the *Pastoureaux* owed their prestige very largely to their habit of killing and despoiling priests. When the clergy tried to protest or resist they found no support amongst the populace. It is understandable that some clerics, observing the activities of the *Pastoureaux*, felt that the Church had never been in greater danger.

At Bourges the fortunes of the *Pastoureaux* began to change. Here too the burghers, disobeying their Archbishop, admitted as many of the horde as the town could hold; the rest remaining encamped outside. Jacob preached this time against the Jews and sent his men to destroy the Sacred Rolls. The crusaders also pillaged houses throughout the town, taking gold and silver where they found it and raping any woman they could lay hands on. If the clergy were not molested it was only because they remained in hiding. But by this time the Queen Mother had realized what sort of movement this was and had outlawed all those taking part in it. When this news reached Bourges many *Pastoureaux* deserted. At length, one day when Jacob was thundering against the laxity of the clergy and calling upon the townsfolk to turn against them, someone in the crowd dared to contradict him. Jacob rushed at the man with a sword and killed him; but this was too much for the burghers, who in their turn took up arms and chased the unruly visitors from the town.

Now it was the turn of the *Pastoureaux* to suffer violence. Jacob was pursued by mounted burghers and cut to pieces. Many of his followers were captured by the royal officials at Bourges and hanged. Bands of survivors made their way to Marseilles and to Aigues Mortes, where they hoped to embark for the Holy Land; but both towns had received warnings from Bourges and the *Pastoureaux* were caught and hanged. A final band reached Bordeaux but only to be met there by English forces under the Governor of Gascony, Simon de Montfort, and dispersed. Their leader, attempting to embark for the East, was recognized by some sailors and drowned. One of his lieutenants fled to England and having landed at Shoreham collected a following of some hundreds of peasants and shepherds. When the news of these happenings reached King Henry III he was sufficiently alarmed to issue instructions for the suppression of the movement to sheriffs throughout the kingdom. But very soon the whole movement disintegrated, even the apostle at Shoreham being torn to pieces by his own followers. Once everything was over rumours sprang up on all sides. It was said that the movement had been a plot of the Sultan's, who had paid Jacob to bring him Christian men and youths as slaves. Jacob and other leaders were said to have been Moslems who had won ascendency over Christians by means of black magic. But there were also those who believed that at the time of its suppression the movement of the *Pastoureaux* had broached only the first part of its programme. These people said that the leaders of the *Pastoureaux* had intended to massacre first all priests and monks, then all knights and nobles; and when all authority had been overthrown, to spread their teaching throughout the world.

The last crusades of the poor

The messianic movements of the masses were not only becoming more independent, they were becoming more frankly hostile to the rich and privileged. In this they reflected a real change in popular sentiment. Not that antagonism between rich and poor was anything new. Even under the old manorial system peasants would turn against their lord if his rule was tyrannical or capricious or contrary to the custom of the manor; local revolts were by no means unknown. Nevertheless it was only as the manorial system was disrupted by the development of a commercial and industrial economy that the upper classes of the laity became the target for a steady stream of resentful criticism.

Much of the hostility was directed against the merchant capitalists in the towns. These men were often very rich – forty capitalists might own half the wealth in a town as well as most of the land on which it was built. It is true that in the early stages in the growth of a town such men rendered great public services and that in some towns – Venice for instance – they continued to do so throughout the Middle Ages; but in many a town in the Low Countries and the Rhine valley they soon came to form a selfish oligarchy which was concerned solely with protecting its own interests. As the sole municipal authorities these capitalists were able to a large extent to determine wages and hours of work in industry, including the industries from which they drew their profits. Above all there was no traditional social bond, hallowed by immemorial custom, to unite the great capitalists even with the master artisans who worked more or less permanently for them, let alone with the casual labourers and unemployed. It was inevitable that the highly urbanized areas, where these opulent oligarchies lived in close proximity to a floating population of workers who were now overdriven, now unemployed, and always desperately poor, should witness the growth of a class hatred of great ferocity.

The old nobility was hated just as much as the urban patricians, with whom indeed they were often allied by marriage. The traditional function of the nobles as the armed defenders of an unarmed peasantry came to seem less necessary as the great invasions ceased and as private warfare was gradually restricted by the royal power. Moreover in the most highly urbanized areas the manorial system rapidly disintegrated. Standards of living which had seemed adequate even to a great landowner in earlier centuries appeared quite inadequate now that a revived commerce was filling the towns with luxuries. Landowners wanted to live at the new standard and usually they wanted to live in the towns; but they could not do so on the income derived from services and dues in kind, often fixed centuries earlier. Instead, they had to make money; and they could only make money by allowing their serfs first to purchase their liberty and then to pay cash rent for their holdings. Materially the peasants often benefited greatly from the change; but their attitude was determined rather by the snapping of a bond which, burdensome and oppressive though they had often found it, had yet possessed a certain paternal quality. As serfdom disappeared, material interest tended to become the sole criterion regulating the landowner's dealings with his peasants. And there were many individuals to whom the collapse of the manorial economy brought sheer disaster. When – as often happened – it became profitable for landowners to reduce the number of their tenants, they would evict them on any pretext they could find. The many peasants who were unable to keep their hold upon the land became rural proletarians. At the same time many small landowners, ruined by the effort to keep up a standard of living beyond their means, sank into the ranks of the dispossessed.

In this new world, where undreamed-of prosperity flourished side by side not only with great poverty but with great and unaccustomed insecurity, the protests of the poor were loud and frequent. They are preserved in documents of various kinds – in the proverbs which the poor themselves composed:

'The poor man works always, worries and labours and weeps, never laughing from his heart, while the rich man laughs and sings . . .'

– in the miracle plays which were perhaps the principal means of popular self-expression:

'. . . each man ought to have as much property as every other, and we have nothing we can call our own. The great lords have all the property and poor folk have nothing but suffering and adversity . . .'

and also in the most widely-read and influential satires:

'Magistrates, provosts, beadles, mayors – nearly all live by robbery. . . . They all batten on the poor, they all want to despoil

them, ... they pluck them alive. The stronger robs the weaker ...'
or again:

'I would like to strangle the nobles and the clergy, every one of them. ... Good working-men make the wheaten bread but they will never chew it; no, all they get is the siftings from the corn, and from good wine they get nothing but the dregs and from good cloth nothing but the chaff. Everything that is tasty and good goes to the nobles and the clergy ...'

On occasion this sullen, passive resentment would give place to a militant egalitarianism. As early as the 1180's a carpenter in central France was moved – as usual by a vision of the Virgin – to found a fraternity which would clear the land of a plague of disbanded mercenaries turned brigand. At first these 'crusaders of peace', as they called themselves, were a pious association comparable to the fraternities of church-builders; including people of all classes, sanctioned by bishops, pledged not to drink or gamble or swear. But by the time they had coped with the brigands, the *Caputiati* – so called from their white hooded uniform – had turned into a revolutionary movement of poor folk which proclaimed the equality of all men and insisted that all alike were entitled to the liberty which they had inherited from Adam and Eve. In the end the *Caputiati* became violent and began to kill nobles, until they were suppressed by armed force.

Although the monk who described these happenings might exclaim in horror at 'the frantic madness of the *Caputiati*', egalitarians such as these were always quick to invoke in their defence the teachings of the Church itself. For, however worldly its practice might often be, the Church never ceased to exalt poverty as one of the highest values and one of the chief means of attaining sanctity. For the professional holy men of the Church, the monks, poverty was supposed to be as obligatory as chastity and obedience. A century before St Francis, a religious virtuoso such as St Norbert could choose to wander through the world in rags. And surely such a glorification of poverty must imply a condemnation of wealth? Theologians of course denied the validity of this conclusion. St Thomas Aquinas reaffirmed the doctrine laid down by the Fathers: that men are assigned by Providence to different stations in life and that a rich man, though he ought indeed to give alms generously, ought also to keep enough to enable himself and his family to live in a manner appropriate to their station. But this did not prevent the needy masses from regarding the rich as damnable and damned. Had not Christ himself said to the rich young man: 'Sell all thou hast, and distribute unto the poor, and thou shalt have treasure in heaven.... For it is easier for a camel to go through a needle's eye than for a rich man to enter into the kingdom of God'? And had he not told of Dives, the rich man who 'was clothed in purple and fine linen, and fared sumptuously every day', and who for that very reason was cast into hell-fire while the beggar Lazarus reposed in the bosom of Father Abraham?

As soon as the rich layman shed his patriarchal function he became a subject for the same projections as the cleric and the Jew; that is to say, he came to be seen as a bad father and also as a bad son, and at the same time acquired a demonic quality. There are sermons which portray the rich as undutiful sons of Christ – hardhearted sons whose indifference to their father's sufferings would surely meet with dire chastisement. And in the fine Romanesque carving which decorates the porch of the abbey-church of St Pierre at Moissac, for instance, the rich man is shown as a bad, neglectful father. Here the whole story of Dives and Lazarus is portrayed with intense passion, from the banquet-scene where Lazarus is rejected by the bad patriarch Dives down to the point where Lazarus rejoices in Abraham's paternal care while Dives, weighed down by his money-bag, is being tormented by devils (Plate 5). But the deep emotional meaning which this story had for the masses is conveyed still more vividly by the figures in the bottom right-hand corner. These figures symbolize the masterpassions of Dives, *Avaritia* and *Luxuria*, his craving for gain and his craving for worldly pleasures; and the symbolic language is that of medieval demonology. Lust for gain is symbolized by a male devil, while the love of pleasure is symbolized by the Woman with the Snakes – a stock figure who was at once a visual embodiment of carnal desire and an earth demon – a denizen, in fact, of that dark world where dwelt Satan and the Beast of the Apocalypse and their companion snakes, scorpions and toads.

Moreover in innumerable commentaries on the Book of Revelation *Avaritia* and *Luxuria* are given as the marks of the servants of Antichrist; so that already in the orthodox view Dives, as portrayed at Moissac, is at only one remove from the demonic Jew and the demonic cleric. But if, in its efforts to secure the allegiance of the new masses, the Church could speak such language as this, what must have been the language of those heretics who spread their teachings amongst weavers in their workshops and hovels, or of those renegade priests whom St Bernard found, to his horror, sitting bearded and untonsured at the looms, alongside men and women weavers? For such people Dives belonged, quite simply, to the hosts of Antichrist. In the minds of the apocalyptic sectarians of the twelfth and thirteenth centuries the rich layman was already undergoing the metamorphosis which in course of time was to transform him into the Capitalist of twentieth-century propaganda: a being truly demonic in its destructiveness, its cruelty, its gross sensuality, its capacity to deceive and, above all, its near-omnipotence.

Set in this context, the last of the People's Crusades can be seen as first essays in a type of millenarianism which was new to medieval Europe and which aimed, however confusedly, at casting down the mighty and raising up the poor. By the first quarter of the fourteenth century crusading zeal was more than ever a monopoly of the very poor. The kingdom of Jerusalem had come to an end and Syria had been evacuated; the Papacy had exchanged the mystical aura of Rome for the security of Avignon; political power in each country was passing into the hands of hard-headed bureaucrats – only the restless masses between Somme and Rhine were still stirred by old eschatological phantasies which they now transfused with a bitter truculence. Very little was required to launch these people upon some wholly unrealistic attempt to turn their phantasies into realities. In 1309 Pope Clement V sent an expedition of the Knights Hospitallers to conquer Rhodes as a stronghold against the Turks; and the same year saw a very serious famine in Picardy, the Low Countries and along the lower part of the Rhine. The two circumstances together were quite sufficient to provoke another People's Crusade in that same area. Again armed columns appeared, consisting of miserably poor artisans and labourers with an admixture of nobles who had squandered their wealth (one recalls the many bankrupt landowners). These people begged and pillaged their way through the country, killing Jews but also storming the castles in which nobles sheltered those valuable sources of revenue. In the end they attacked the fortress of the Duke of Brabant, a vigorous opponent of all popular risings, who only three years before had routed an army of insurgent clothworkers and, it is said, buried its leaders alive. The Duke at once led an army against the crusaders and drove them off with heavy losses. But within a few years new hordes were gathering again.

This was indeed a time of great distress and great exaltation. While in 1315 a universal failure of crops was driving the poor to cannibalism, long processions of naked penitents cried to God for mercy and millenarian hopes flared high. In the midst of the famine there circulated a prophecy which foretold that, driven by hunger, the poor would in that very year rise in arms against the rich and powerful and would also overthrow the Church and a great monarchy. After much bloodshed a new age would dawn in which all men would be united in exalting one single Cross. It is not surprising that when in 1320 Philip V of France halfheartedly suggested yet another expedition to the Holy Land the idea was at once taken up by the desperate masses, even though it was wholly impracticable and was rejected out of hand by the Pope. This time it was an apostate monk and an unfrocked priest who began to preach the crusade in northern France, and to such good effect that a great movement sprang up 'as suddenly and unexpectedly as a whirlwind'. But here too a large part seems to have been played by *prophetae* who claimed to be divinely appointed saviours. Jewish chroniclers, drawing on a lost Spanish source, tell of a shepherd-boy who announced that a dove had appeared to him and, having changed into the Virgin, had bidden him summon a crusade and had promised it victory. And they also tell of a leader who claimed to be marked with that sign of divine election, the cross between the shoulder blades.

As in 1251, the first to respond were shepherds and swineherds, some of them mere children; and so this movement too became known as a Shepherds' Crusade. But once more, as the columns passed through the towns other elements joined them – male and female beggars, outlaws, bandits; and the resulting army soon became turbulent. Before long numbers of *Pastoureaux* were being arrested and imprisoned; but always the remainder, enthusiastically supported by the populace, would storm the prison and free their brethren. When they reached Paris these hordes terrified the city, breaking into the Châtelet, assaulting the Provost and finally, on a rumour that armed forces were to be brought out against them, drawing themselves up in battle formation in the fields of St Germain-des-Prés. As no force materialized to oppose them they left the capital and marched south until they entered the English territories in the south-west. The Jews had been expelled from the French kingdom in 1306 but here they were still to be found; and as the *Pastoureaux* marched they killed Jews and looted their property. The French king sent orders that the Jews should be protected but the populace, convinced that this massacre was holy work, did everything to help the crusaders. When the governor and the royal officials at Toulouse arrested many *Pastoureaux* the townsfolk stormed the prison and a great massacre of the Jews followed. At Albi the consuls closed the gates but the crusaders forced their way in, crying that they had come to kill the Jews, and were greeted by the populace with wild enthusiasm. In other towns the authorities themselves joined the townsfolk and the crusaders in the massacre. Throughout south-west France, from Bordeaux in the west to Albi in the east, almost every Jew was killed.

Gradually the *Pastoureaux* began to turn their attention to the clergy. As shepherds of God they started to attack priests as 'false shepherds who rob their herds'. It was said that they were planning a great expropriation of all property held by the secular clergy or by monasteries. A royal officer, the Seneschal of Carcassonne, tried to raise a force to resist them; but he had the greatest difficulty in doing so, for everywhere the common people refused to help. At the papal residence at Avignon there was great alarm, as the Curia expected the crusaders to bear down upon the city and dreaded the consequences. At length Pope John XXII excommunicated the *Pastoureaux* and called upon the Seneschal of Beaucaire to take the field against them; and these measures proved effective. People were forbidden, on pain of death, to give food to the would-be crusaders; towns began to close their gates; and many *Pastoureaux* perished miserably of hunger. Many were killed in battle at various points between Toulouse and Narbonne, or captured and hanged from trees in twenties and thirties. Pursuits and executions continued for some three months. The survivors split up into small groups and crossed the Pyrenees to kill more Jews, which they did until the son of the King of Aragon led a force against them and dispersed them. More than any earlier crusade, this one was felt while it lasted to threaten the whole existing structure of society. The *Pastoureaux* of 1320 struck terror into the hearts of all the rich and privileged.

Beyond this point it becomes increasingly difficult to trace the operation, in that northern area between Somme and Rhine, of the social myth which in one form or another had been fascinating the masses for more than two centuries. The war between 'the great' and 'the little', which had scarcely ceased in the Low Countries since the days of Bertrand of Ray, was now becoming ever more violent and ruthless. In 1325 the free and prosperous peasantry of Maritime Flanders, supported by the cloth workers of Bruges, refused to pay tithes and dues and took up arms against the landlords, ecclesiastical and lay. The result was a ferocious civil war which lasted until 1328, when the King of France intervened and defeated the rebels at Mount Cassel. From 1320 to 1380 the weavers in the three great centres of the cloth industry, Ghent, Bruges and Ypres, rose again and again in bloody insurrections which ended in bloody repression. Finally in 1379 the weavers of Ghent seized power and from their town succeeded in dominating all Flanders and even in overthrowing the rule of the Count. It was only after three years of war that they were defeated at Rosebeke, again by the French army. During those same years (1381–2) northern France – Paris, the towns of Picardy and Normandy, all the old haunts of the *Pastoureaux* – was witnessing a series of popular revolts provoked by severe taxation. The first objective of these people was always the tax-farmer's office, where they destroyed the files, looted the coffers and murdered the tax-farmers; their next, the Jewish quarter, where they also murdered and looted their fill. At Rouen they got as far as electing themselves a king, whom they exhibited in triumph and at whose orders they killed not only tax-collectors but also some of the more prosperous burghers. In Paris and Rouen alike the insurgents were inspired by the example of Ghent – 'Long live Ghent!' was their slogan. In both towns the revolt was crushed by the King and his army of nobles on their return from their victory over the Flemish weavers; but the poor from town and country united in bands which ravaged the land.

In the main these movements had severely limited and practical aims; what the rebels wanted was more money and more independence. Yet was there not still running through them some undercurrent of millenarian enthusiasm? It cannot be proved, though it is worth remarking that Henri Pirenne, who was pre-eminently qualified to judge, believed so. What is certain is, on the one hand, that at the height of the class-war – at Ypres in 1377, for instance – cloth workers were not only being hanged as rebels but were being sentenced by the Inquisition and burnt as heretics; and on the other hand, that some dissident clerics were preaching a millenarianism of a markedly revolutionary and egalitarian kind. One of these men, a Franciscan called John of Roquetaillade, who spent the last twenty years of his life in ecclesiastical prisons under constant threat of being burnt for his views, has left prophetic writings of great interest. In 1356, the year of the catastrophic defeat at Poitiers, when Free Companies were ravaging the countryside and that great outburst of peasant fury, the *Jacquerie*, was in the offing, he produced his *Vademecum in tribulationibus*. This celebrated work, which was translated into English, Catalan and Czech, shows very clearly how the old eschatological tradition had been adapted as a vehicle for the new radicalism.

The capture of the King at Poitiers, declared Roquetaillade, marks the beginning of a disastrous time for France, when the kingdom will be brought very low by defeat in war. Indeed, a time of troubles lies ahead for the whole of Christendom; for between 1360 and 1365 the lowly will rise against the great. In those years popular justice will rise up and cut down tyrants and nobles with a twice-sharpened sword; many princes and nobles and mighty ones will be cast down from their dignities and the vanity of their wealth; there will be unbelievable affliction amongst the nobles; and the great ones will be robbed, they who by their depredations bring such suffering upon the people. The man who can find a faithful servant and companion in those days can count himself fortunate indeed. Then tempests, floods and plagues will kill off the greater part of mankind, wiping out hardened sinners and preparing the way for the renewal of the earth. A Western Antichrist will appear in Rome, while an Eastern Antichrist will spread his false doctrines from Jerusalem; the latter will find his following amongst the Jews, who will persecute the Christians, destroying churches and altars. Saracens and Tatars will ravage Italy and Spain, Hungary and Poland and parts of Germany. Rulers and peoples, outraged by the luxury, wealth and pride of the clergy, will combine to strip the Church of all its property. Destitution and massacre will be the chastisements of the clergy and particularly of the Franciscans; but thereafter the Church and particularly the Franciscans, purified by suffering and living in absolute poverty, as Christ and the Apostles were believed to have lived, will rise to new life and spread their influence throughout the world. By 1367 the time of troubles will be at an end. A great reformer, *reparator orbis*, will become Pope and at the same time the King of France will, against all custom, be elected Roman Emperor. Pope and King-Emperor acting together will expel the Saracens and Tatars from Europe; they will convert all Moslems, Jews and Tatars, reconcile the schismatic Greeks to the Church of Rome and wipe all heresy from the face of the earth. The King of France will become conqueror and ruler of the whole world, in west and east and south; his kingdom will be more worthy of honour than any the world has known, for it will include all kingdoms that have ever existed in Asia, Africa or Europe. Yet this ever-victorious descendant of Charlemagne will be 'the very poor husband of the universal Church' and the holiest monarch since the beginning of time. And although both Pope and Emperor must die within a decade, the reign of peace which they establish will last a thousand years, until the End.

Prophecies of a 'Second Charlemagne' who would become Emperor, conquer the world and make the last journey to the Holy Sepulchre continued to appear in France throughout the fourteenth and fifteenth and into the sixteenth century. But these later prophecies had all the quality of political propaganda produced to serve dynastic ends, and none of the quality of revolutionary myths. The centre of eschatological excitement had in fact shifted away from France and the Low Countries. As the struggle against the English invaders became more desperate the devotion of the common people of France became ever more concentrated on the actual monarch as the symbol of the national will to survival and independence, until the place once occupied by millenarian *prophetae* could be taken only by a St Joan. The France which emerged from the great effort of reconstruction which followed the Hundred Years War was a monarchy centralized to the point of despotism, controlled by a royal army and civil service; a land moreover where the towns had lost every scrap of autonomy. In such a state there was little opening for popular movements of any kind. But above all the concentrations of surplus population which had existed for so long in the area between Somme and Rhine existed no more. Picardy, Flanders, Hainaut, Brabant no longer made up the most densely populated and highly industrialized area in northern Europe. By the end of the fourteenth century a number of factors – class-war, international war, emigration, the shortage of English wool and increased competition from the Italian towns – had reduced the cloth industry to ruin and population was falling steeply.

Very different was the situation in Germany. There the royal power had been declining ever since the beginning of the thirteenth century and the nation had been disintegrating into a welter of petty principalities, at the same time as industry and commerce had been expanding and population increasing. And it was Germany which became the scene of a new series of messianic movements.

6 The Emperor Frederick as Messiah

Joachite prophecy and Frederick II

In the course of the thirteenth century yet another kind of eschatology appeared alongside the eschatologies derived from the Book of Revelation and the Sibylline Oracles – alongside them at first, but soon blending with them. The inventor of the new prophetic system, which was to be the most influential one known to Europe until the appearance of Marxism, was Joachim of Fiore (1145–1202). After many years spent in brooding over the Scriptures this Calabrian abbot and hermit received, some time between 1190 and 1195, an inspiration which seemed to reveal in them a concealed meaning of unique predictive value.

The idea that the Scriptures possessed a concealed meaning was far from new; traditional methods of exegesis had always given a large place to allegorical interpretations. What was new was the idea that these methods could be applied not simply for moral or dogmatic purposes but as a means of understanding and forecasting the development of history. Joachim was convinced that he had found a key which, when applied to the events and personages of the Old and New Testaments and especially of the Book of Revelation, enabled him to perceive in history a pattern and a meaning and to prophesy in detail its future stages. For in his exegeses of the Scriptures Joachim elaborated an interpretation of history as an ascent through three successive ages, each of them presided over by one of the Persons of the Trinity. The first age was the Age of the Father or of the Law; the second age was the Age of the Son or of the Gospel; the third age would be the Age of the Spirit and that would be to its predecessors as broad daylight compared with starlight and the dawn, as high summer compared with winter and spring. If the first age had been one of fear and servitude and the second age one of faith and filial submission, the third age would be one of love, joy and freedom, when the knowledge of God would be revealed directly in the hearts of all men. The Age of the Spirit was to be the sabbath or resting-time of mankind. Then the world would be one vast monastery, in which all men would be contemplative monks rapt in mystical ecstasy and united in singing the praises of God. And this new version of the Kingdom of the Saints would endure until the Last Judgement.

Joachim was not consciously unorthodox and he had no desire to subvert the Church. It was with the encouragement of no less than three popes that he wrote down the revelations with which he had been favoured. And nevertheless his thought had implications which were potentially dangerous to the structure of orthodox medieval theology. His idea of the third age could not really be reconciled with the Augustinian view that the Kingdom of God had been realized, so far as it ever could be realized on this earth, at the moment when the Church came into being, and that there never would be any Millennium but this. However mindful Joachim might be of the doctrines and claims and interests of the Church, he had in effect propounded a new type of millenarianism – and moreover a type which later generations were to elaborate first in an anti-ecclesiastical and later in a frankly secular sense.

For the long-term, indirect influence of Joachim's speculations can be traced right down to the present day, and most clearly in certain 'philosophies of history' of which the Church emphatically disapproves. Horrified though the unworldly mystic would have been to see it happen, it is unmistakably the Joachite phantasy of the three ages that reappeared in, for instance, the theories of historical evolution expounded by the German Idealist philosophers Lessing, Schelling, Fichte and to some extent Hegel; in Auguste Comte's idea of history as an ascent from the theological through the metaphysical up to the scientific phase; and again in the Marxian dialectic of the three stages of primitive communism, class society and a final communism which is to be the realm of freedom and in which the state will have withered away. And it is no less true – if even more paradoxical – that the phrase 'the Third Reich', first coined in 1923 by the publicist Moeller van den Bruck and later adopted as a name for that 'new order' which was supposed to last a thousand years, would have had but little emotional significance if the phantasy of a third and most glorious dispensation had not, over the centuries, entered into the common stock of European social mythology.

What impressed the men of the thirteenth century was above all Joachim's account of how and when the world was to undergo its final transformation. In the Joachite view of history each age must be preceded by a period of incubation. The incubation of the first age had lasted from Adam to Abraham, that of the second from Elijah to Christ; as for the third age, its incubation had begun with St Benedict and was nearing its close by the time Joachim composed his works. According to St Matthew forty-two generations lay between Abraham and Christ; and as the Old Testament was a model for all later happenings the period between the birth of Christ and the fulfilment of the third age must also last forty-two generations. Taking a generation as thirty years Joachim was able to place the culmination of human history between the years 1200 and 1260. Meanwhile however the way must be made straight; and this was to be achieved by a new order of monks who would preach the new gospel throughout the world. From amongst them there would come twelve patriarchs who would convert the Jews, and one supreme teacher, *novus dux*, who would lead all mankind away from the love of earthly things and towards the love of the things of the spirit. During the three and a half years immediately preceding the fulfilment of the third dispensation Antichrist would have his reign. He would be a secular king who would chastise the corrupt and worldly Church until in its present form it was utterly destroyed. After the overthrow of this Antichrist the Age of the Spirit would come in its fulness.

How explosive this doctrine was became apparent when it was appropriated by the rigorist wing of the Franciscan Order. Joachim's ideal of a totally unworldly monastic order came very near to being realized in the confraternity which, within a few years of the prophet's death, began to form around the *poverello* of Assisi. Later, as the confraternity developed into a great Order, concessions had to be made to the demands of every-day reality; the Order penetrated into the universities, it sought and wielded influence, it acquired property. But many Franciscans refused to accept these innovations and clung to the old ideal of absolute poverty. These men – the Franciscan Spirituals – formed a minority party, at first within the Order, later outside it. By the middle of the century they had disinterred Joachim's prophecies (which hitherto had attracted little attention) and were editing them and producing commentaries upon them. They were also forging prophecies which they successfully fathered upon Joachim and which became far better known and more influential than Joachim's own writings. In these works the Spirituals adapted the Joachite eschatology in such a way that they themselves could be seen as the new order which, replacing the Church of Rome, was to lead mankind into the glories of the Age of the Spirit. The vicissitudes of pseudo-Joachite prophecies in southern Europe lie beyond the scope of the present study; another volume would be required to describe how on the fringes of the Spiritual party still more extreme groups sprang up until, around such figures as Fra Dolcino and Rienzo, there flourished a millenarianism as revolutionary and as militant as any to be found in the North. But though composed in Italy, the pseudo-Joachite prophecies influenced developments in Germany as well. It was largely thanks to them that the role of chastiser of the Church in the Last Days came to be assigned in the popular imagination to the Emperor Frederick II.

Already at the beginning of his career, and long before the Joachites began to concern themselves with him, Frederick was the object of eschatological expectations. All that the French had expected of the Capetians, the Germans expected of him. No sooner had Frederick I (Barbarossa) perished on the Third Crusade in 1190 than there began to appear in Germany prophecies which told of a future Frederick, who as Emperor of the Last Days would complete the unfinished work; an eschatological saviour who by liberating the Holy Sepulchre would prepare the way for the Second Coming and the Millennium. When, thirty years later, the imperial crown was bestowed on Frederick II, who was Barbarossa's grandson, these prophecies were confidently applied to him. So for the first time the image of the Emperor of the Last Days was attached to the actual ruler of the territorial complex, centring on Germany but embracing also Burgundy and most of Italy, which had come to be known in the West as the Roman (and latterly as the Holy Roman) Empire.

There was much in Frederick's life and personality to foster the growth of a messianic myth. He was a most brilliant figure, whose versatility and intelligence, licentiousness and cruelty combined to fascinate his contemporaries. Moreover he did in fact go on a crusade in 1229 and was even able to recapture Jerusalem and crown himself king of that city. Above all, he was repeatedly embroiled in conflicts of extraordinary bitterness with the Papacy. Christendom was treated to the spectacle of the Emperor, several times excommunicated as a heretic, perjurer and blasphemer, threatening in return to strip the Church of that wealth which, he proclaimed, was the source of its corruption. All this helped to fit him for the role of chastiser of the clergy in the Last Days; and the pseudo-Joachite *Commentary on Jeremiah*, which was written in the 1240's, did in fact foretell that Frederick would so persecute the Church that in the year 1260 it would be utterly overthrown. To the Italian Spirituals this chastisement of the clergy, though fully deserved and an indispensable prologue to the Third Age, was still devilish work. To them the Emperor was the Beast of the Apocalypse and the Holy Roman Empire was Babylon – instruments of Satan and themselves doomed to be annihilated in their turn. But it was possible to see the imperial opponent of the Papacy in quite another light. In Germany Frederick continued to be regarded as a saviour, but as a saviour whose role now included the chastisement of the Church; a figure in whom the Emperor of the Last Days merged into the *novus dux* of Joachite prophecy.

In its efforts to bring Frederick back to obedience the Holy See placed the whole of Germany under the interdict – which meant that indispensable sacraments could no longer be administered and implied, according to current beliefs, that anyone dying at that time would inevitably be damned. By 1248 the populous Duchy of Swabia, which belonged to the imperial domain and was particularly firm in its support of the Hohenstauffen, was being visited by wandering preachers who were declaring publicly that the clergy were so sunk in sin that they had in any case forfeited the power to administer valid sacraments. As for Pope Innocent IV, his life was so evil that no interdict imposed by him could have the slightest weight. Truth was preserved by the wandering preachers themselves and they alone were empowered by God to absolve from sin. The Pope and the bishops were downright heretics and should be ignored; on the other hand people ought to pray for the Emperor Frederick and his son Conrad, for these were righteous and indeed perfect. While this propaganda was being disseminated in the town of Hall the artisans rose in revolt and expelled not only the clergy but also many of the rich patricians. The fact is of some interest, for it is certain that popular imagination, which in Flanders not long before had made Baldwin, Emperor of Constantinople, into a saviour of the poor, was now – however inappropriately – doing the same to the Emperor Frederick.

A Joachite manifesto which was produced in Swabia at this very time by one Brother Arnold, a dissident Dominican, expresses this phantasy very clearly. Like the Joachite prophecies in Italy, this work looks forward to 1260 as the apocalyptic year which will see the fulfilment of the Third Age. But before then Brother Arnold will call upon Christ in the name of the poor to judge Pope and hierarchy; and Christ will respond, he will appear on earth to pronounce his judgement. The Pope will stand revealed as Antichrist, the clergy as limbs of Antichrist. Christ will condemn them utterly not only for their immorality and worldliness and their abuse of the interdict but also – and chiefly – for exploiting and oppressing the poor. Through Arnold and his associates the will of God finds expression; and it is their task to carry out that will by depriving the Church of Rome of its authority and assuming that authority themselves, as holy men who live and will continue to live in absolute poverty. As for the great wealth of the Church, that will be confiscated and distributed to the poor – who in the eyes of Arnold, self-styled 'advocate of the poor', are the only true Christians. And this great social revolution will be carried out under the auspices of the Emperor Frederick, who according to Arnold had already had the programme laid before him and had promised his support.

The social radicalism of these phantasies – so utterly different from the rarefied spirituality of Joachim's own prophecies – appealed strongly to the poor. Perhaps it might even have stimulated a widespread revolutionary movement but for the fact that in 1250 Frederick suddenly died, a decade before he was to have assumed his eschatological role. His death was a catastrophic blow both to the German Joachites, whom it deprived of their saviour, and to the Italian Joachites, whom it deprived of their Antichrist. But soon it was being rumoured that the Emperor was still alive; he had been driven overseas by the Pope or else, on the advice of an astrologer, he had gone voluntarily; or maybe he was carrying out a long penance as a pilgrim or hermit. But there were also current theories of a more supernatural kind. In southern Italy and Sicily, where Frederick had spent most of his life, a cryptic Sibylline phrase was heard: 'Vivit et non vivit'; and a monk saw the Emperor enter into the bowels of Etna while a fiery army of knights descended into the hissing sea. If to the monk this meant that Frederick had gone down to hell, many Sicilians put another construction on the matter. Etna had long been regarded as an abode of departed heroes, including King Arthur himself; when Frederick took his place among these he became a Sleeping Emperor who would one day return as saviour. And when the critical time arrived he did in fact reappear: for a couple of years after 1260 an impostor dwelling on the slopes of Etna was able to attract a numerous following. It is true that in Sicily the phantasy of a resurrected Frederick soon lost its appeal; but it was to enthrall generation after generation of Germans, just as the phantasy of a resurrected Charlemagne, *Carolus redivivus*, enthralled the French.

The resurrection of Frederick

Thirty-four years after his death Frederick II underwent a resurrection very similar to that which had once befallen Baldwin, Count of Flanders. Under the year 1284 a chronicler tells of a former hermit near Worms who had been claiming to be the Emperor, and about the same time another tells of a similar personage who had been escorted into Lübeck amidst great popular enthusiasm. In both cases the pseudo-Frederick had vanished as soon as he seemed likely to be unmasked. Was it the same man who in 1284 succeeded in establishing himself in royal state in the Rhine valley? Perhaps not, for this last seems to have been not so much an impostor as a megalomaniac who really believed himself to be Frederick. Driven from Cologne as a madman, he met with an excellent reception at the neighbouring town of Neuss, which happened to be at loggerheads with the Archbishop of Cologne; and there he set up court. Just like Bertrand of Ray, this man described how he had spent long years as a pilgrim, carrying out a penance for the sins of his earlier life; though at times, exploiting the legends which had already gathered round the dead Frederick, he claimed to have been dwelling in the depth of the earth. The news of his coming spread far afield; in Italy it created such a stir that several towns sent ambassadors to Neuss to look into the matter, while the Joachites leaped to the conclusion that at long last Frederick really was assuming his proper role of Antichrist.

Conditions in Germany were favourable to such a resurrection. Ever since the beginning of the century the central government in Germany had been becoming ever weaker and the kingdom had been disintegrating into a welter of semi-independent principalities – a process which was exactly the reverse of that taking place in France. Although Frederick had done nothing to arrest this disintegration and had always been far more interested in Italy and Sicily than in Germany, his strong and colourful personality had nevertheless provided a focus for German loyalty. His death was followed by the Great Interregnum, a period of a generation during which no king was even able to attain general recognition in Germany. The country passed into a turmoil such as France had experienced two centuries earlier, with feuds and private wars raging on all sides. This state of affairs continued even after Rudolph, the first Habsburg monarch, was elected German King in 1273. The princes, having once tasted the joys of independence, were determined not to give them up; which meant that the King had to be kept weak. As soon as there was a pretender who claimed to be Frederick II several of the greatest princes hastened to accord him official recognition, not because they believed him but because they wished to embarrass Rudolph. By this time, moreover, there was in Germany a flourishing urban civilization. Precisely during the Interregnum manufacture and trade had made great progress in the self-governing towns; but although these towns preserved a more orderly and prosperous life than existed anywhere else in Germany, they were riven by social conflicts. In the Rhine towns there were more artisans living insecure and needy existences than there had ever been. What contributed most to the success of the pseudo-Frederick was certainly the fact that the urban poor were still clinging to messianic expectations concerning the Emperor Frederick II. The monarch of Neuss appeared as above all the friend of the poor; and he found his publicists amongst *prophetae* whom the chronicles label as heretics.

In the end, intoxicated by success, the pseudo-Frederick overreached himself. Moving southwards, he announced his intention of holding an imperial diet at Frankfort and summoned King Rudolph to appear before him so that, as Emperor, he could grant him the Kingdom of Germany. Rudolph's answer was to march against the pretender and to besiege the town of Wetzlar where he had taken refuge. The town was divided, as Valenciennes had been divided in the case of the pseudo-Baldwin; now as then the common people were ready to take up arms to defend their emperor. Nevertheless, the man was handed over to Rudolph, or handed himself over; and after trial he was burnt at the stake. The method of execution is significant, for burning was used not in cases of political insurrection but only in cases of sorcery or heresy; which confirms what the chronicles also indicate – that this man was a fanatic who regarded himself not merely as the real Frederick II but as an eschatological saviour sent by God to chastise the clergy and to establish his rule over the whole world. It seems too that to the very end the pseudo-Frederick was utterly convinced that he would rise again within a couple of days, that he promised his followers to do so and that they believed him. And in sober fact he was at once replaced by a similar personage, this time in the Low Countries, who claimed that three days after being burnt he had risen from the dead – and who in his turn was executed at Utrecht.

Folklore now began to accumulate around the figure of the pseudo-Frederick just as it had accumulated around the figure of Frederick himself. The execution at Wetzlar had served only to increase the reputation of the Emperor as a superhuman and immortal being. It was reported that amongst the ashes at the stake no bones had been found but only a little bean; and people at once concluded that this must mean that the Emperor had been rescued from the flames by divine providence, that he was still alive, that he must one day return. This conviction persisted for generation after generation. In the middle of the fourteenth century it was still being said that Frederick must infallibly return, though he were cut into a thousand pieces or – surely a reference to Wetzlar – though he were burnt to ashes; for such was God's unalterable decree. Strange and picturesque legends were elaborated.

That fabulous oriental monarch Prester John had provided the Emperor with an asbestos robe, a magic ring which enabled him to disappear, a magic drink which kept him for ever young. Often the Emperor, in the guise of a pilgrim, would appear to peasants and confide in them that the time would yet come when he would take his rightful place at the head of the Empire.

In the course of the fourteenth century all the eschatological hopes which the medieval masses had ever managed to squeeze out of the Sibylline and Johannine prophecies became concentrated, in Germany, on the future, resurrected Frederick:

In all countries a hard time sets in. A feud flares up between the two heads of Christendom, a fierce struggle begins. Many a mother must mourn her child, men and women alike must suffer. Rapine and arson go hand in hand, everyone is at everyone else's throat, everyone harms everyone else in his person and his belongings, there is nobody but has cause to lament. But when suffering has reached such a pitch that nobody can allay it, then there appears by God's will the Emperor Frederick, so noble and so gentle. . . . Full of courage, men and women at once stream together for the journey overseas. The Kingdom of God is promised to them. They come in crowds, each hurrying ahead of the other. . . . Peace reigns in all the land, fortresses threaten no longer, there is no need to fear force any more. Nobody opposes the crusade to the withered tree. When the Emperor hangs his shield upon it, the tree puts forth leaf and blossom. The Holy Sepulchre is freed, from now on no sword need be drawn on its behalf. The noble Emperor restores the same law for all men. . . . All heathen realms do homage to the Emperor. He overthrows the power of the Jews, though not by force of arms; their might is broken for ever and they submit without struggle. Of the domination of the clergy almost nothing remains. The high-born prince dissolves the monasteries altogether, he gives the nuns to be wedded; I tell you, they must grow wine and corn for us!

By the middle of the fourteenth century Germany had become what it was to remain down to the sixteenth century: a mass of warring principalities, a perpetual chaos in the midst of which the Emperor was altogether helpless. At the same time the towns of southern and central Germany had replaced the towns of the Low Countries as the main centres of mercantile capitalism north of the Alps; and the social conflicts within them had reached a fierce intensity. While the prosperous guilds fought the patricians and one another, amongst the poor there smouldered a deadly hatred of all the rich. One finds a chronicler of Magdeburg warning the well-to-do burghers that 'one must not let the common people have their way too much, as has been done of late. They should be kept firmly under control; for there is an old hatred between rich and poor. The poor hate everyone with any possessions and are more ready to harm the rich than the rich are to harm the poor.' The point of view of the poor now found in German literature an expression as violent as it had found a century earlier in French. The poet Suchenwirt, for instance, describes how hungry men, leaving their pale and emaciated wives and children in their hovels, crowd together in the narrow streets, armed with improvised weapons and full of a desperate courage:

'The coffers of the rich are full, those of the poor are empty. The poor man's belly is hollow. . . . Hack down the rich man's door! We're going to dine with him. It's better to be cut down, all of us, than die of hunger, we'd rather risk our lives bravely than perish in this way . . .'

It was to be expected that in such a society the future Frederick would take on ever more clearly the aspect of the great social revolutionary, the messiah of the poor. In 1348, after a lapse of just a century, the prophecies of Arnold and the Swabian preachers recur in a still more emphatic form in the popular expectations noted by the monk John of Winterthur: 'As soon as he has risen from the dead and stands once more at the height of his power, he will marry poor women and maidens to rich men, and *vice versa*. . . . He will see to it that everything that has been stolen from minors and orphans and widows is returned to them, and that full justice is done to everyone.' Moreover – and the image is taken straight from a pseudo-Joachite prophecy – 'he will persecute the clergy so fiercely that if they have no other means of hiding their tonsures they will cover them with cow-dung . . .'

John of Winterthur hastens to dissociate himself from these alarming beliefs. It is, he remarks, sheer madness to think that the Emperor-heretic can ever return; it is (again the shadow of Wetzlar!) contrary to Catholic faith that a man who has been burnt at the stake can ever again wield sovereign power. The monk had good reason to be emphatic; for what might be called the dogma of the Second Coming of Frederick was regarded as a most dangerous heresy. This was still true a century later, and two centuries after the days of Frederick himself. 'From the Emperor Frederick, the heretic,' wrote a chronicler in 1434, 'a new heresy arose which some Christians still hold to in secret; they believe absolutely that the Emperor Frederick is still alive and will remain alive until the end of the world, and that there has been and shall be no proper Emperor but he. . . . The Devil invented this folly, so as to mislead these heretics and certain simple folk . . .' How seriously the clergy took this heresy and how alert they were to detect it is shown by the curious story of a Greek philosopher who ventured in 1469 to divulge in Rome the conviction which he had derived from long study of the Greek Sibyllines – which was that the Last Emperor would shortly be converting all peoples to Christianity. In this as in other Byzantine prophecies the coming of the Last Emperor in no way implied a massacre of the clergy or social upheavals of any kind. But this was so inconceivable to the ecclesiastical authorities in Rome that they imprisoned the unfortunate man and confiscated his belongings.

Manifestos for a future Frederick

For the fifteenth century and the early years of the sixteenth century the myth of the future Frederick has no longer to be pieced together from occasional reports of hostile witnesses. At this point it emerges into full daylight; for now, after an interval of some two or three centuries, Brother Arnold's manifesto was followed by several much more detailed manifestos.

The earliest of these works, the Latin tract known as *Gamaleon*, which was produced either in 1409 or in 1439, tells of a future German Emperor who is to overthrow the French monarchy and the Papacy. When he has accomplished his mission France will be remembered no more, the Hungarians and the Slavs will have been subjugated and reduced to complete dependence, Jewry will have been crushed for ever; while the Germans will be exalted above all peoples. The Church of Rome will have been expropriated and all its clergy killed. In place of the pope a German patriarch will preside from Mainz over a new church, but a church subordinate to the Emperor, 'the eagle from the eagle's race', a new Frederick whose wings will stretch from sea to sea and to the very limits of the earth. And those will be the Last Days before the Second Coming and the Judgement.

About 1439 there was produced a far more influential work, the so-called *Reformation of Sigismund*. The origin of this work seems to have lain in a Latin programme prepared by a priest called Frederick of Lantnaw for submission to the General Council of Basle, which from 1431 onwards had been struggling to inaugurate a reform of the Church. But the German *Reformation of Sigismund* is far more than a mere translation of that programme. The author – who may have been Frederick of Lantnaw himself but was more probably a lay friend of his – deals with the reform of the Empire as fully as with that of the Church. He was clearly familiar with the conditions of life in the towns of southern Germany and appears as the spokesman above all of the urban poor – not of the skilled artisans organized in guilds but of the unorganized workers, the poorest and least privileged stratum of the urban population. The *Reformation of Sigismund* demands the suppression of the monopolistic guilds and the great trading companies; it advocates an egalitarian order in which wages, prices and taxes will be fixed to serve the interests of the poor. At the same time wherever serfdom still survives in the country it must be abolished; and as in olden times the towns must open their gates to former serfs.

Thus far the programme is, if not immediately practicable, at least inspired by an empirical rather than a millenarian approach. But the book ends with a curious messianic prophecy which the author puts into the mouth of the Emperor Sigismund, who had only recently died after being himself for some years a subject of messianic expectations. Sigismund is made to tell how the voice of God bade him prepare the way for a priest-king who was to be no other than Frederick of Lantnaw and who, as Emperor Frederick, would reveal himself as a monarch of unparalleled might and majesty. Any moment now Frederick's standard and that of the Empire would be set up, with the Cross between them; and then every prince and lord and every city would have to declare for Frederick, on pain of forfeiting property and freedom. Sigismund goes on to describe how he sought for this Frederick of Lantnaw until he found him at the Council of Basle, in a priest whose poverty was equal to that of Christ. He had given him a robe and entrusted him with the government of all Christendom. For this Frederick will reign over a dominion which will reach from sea to sea and none will be able to withstand him. He will tread all trouble and wrong-doing underfoot, he will destroy the wicked and consume them by fire – and by the wicked are meant those corrupted by money, simoniac prelates and avaricious merchants. Under his rule the common people will rejoice to find justice established and all their desires of soul and body satisfied.

Far longer, more detailed and more truculent than the *Reformation of Sigismund* is the *Book of a Hundred Chapters*, by an anonymous publicist who lived in Upper Alsace or the Breisgau and who is generally known as 'the Revolutionary of the Upper Rhine'. This elderly fanatic was thoroughly familiar with the enormous mass of medieval apocalyptic literature and drew freely on it for the purpose of elaborating an apocalyptic programme of his own. Written in German in the opening years of the sixteenth century, his treatise is the last and most comprehensive expression of the popular eschatology of the Middle Ages.

In a foreword the Revolutionary specifies the source of his inspiration. In true medieval fashion, it was a communication from the Almighty, conveyed by the Archangel Michael. God was so angered by the sins of mankind that he had intended to visit it with the most fearful catastrophes. Only at the very last moment he had suspended the sentence of doom so that people might have one more chance to mend their ways. To this end God desired a certain pious person – naturally it is the author himself – to organize an association of pious laymen. Only those born in wedlock and who were themselves married and had always been monogamous would be eligible for membership (the author's preoccupation with adultery is obsessive). Members would wear a yellow cross as their badge. From the start they would enjoy the active support of St Michael; and before long they would be gathered together under the leadership of the Emperor Frederick, 'the Emperor from the Black Forest' – a prodigious figure who recalls not only the Emperor of the Last Days but also the Messiah of Judeo-Christian apocalyptic and particularly the Book of Revelation. 'He will reign for a thousand years. . . . The heavens will be opened up to his people. . . . He will come in a garment white as snow, with white hair, and his throne will be as fire, and a thousand times a thousand and ten times a hundred thousand shall serve him, for he will execute justice.' And again: 'The King will come on a white horse and will have a bow in his hand, and a crown shall be given him by God so that he shall have power to compel the whole world; he will have a great sword in his hand and will strike many down . . .' At the same time this saviour will establish a messianic kingdom for the benefit of his followers, in which their every need, spiritual and material, will be amply supplied. He will be able to say of himself: 'I am the beginning of the new government and will give of the living water to those who thirst; he who follows me shall have enough. I will be his God . . .' He will distribute abundance of bread and barley and wine and oil at a low price. Clearly in this phantasy the Emperor from the Black Forest and the returning Christ have merged together to form one single messiah. This makes it all the more striking when the publicist lets slip, as he does from time to time, that he expected this messiah to be no other than himself.

However, the route to the Millennium leads through massacre and terror. God's aim is a world free from sin. If sin continues to flourish, divine punishment will surely be visited upon the world; whereas if sin is once abolished, then the world will be ready for the Kingdom of the Saints. The most urgent task of the Brethren of the Yellow Cross is therefore to eliminate sin, which in effect means to eliminate sinners. The Brotherhood is portrayed as a crusading host led by an elite – the author calls it 'a new chivalry' –

which in turn is subordinate to the eschatological Emperor himself. And the object of the crusade is to enable the Emperor 'to smash Babylon in the name of God ... and bring the whole world under his own rule, so that there shall be one shepherd, one sheepfold and one faith throughout the whole world'. To achieve that end assassination is wholly legitimate: 'Whoever strikes a wicked man for his evildoing, for instance for blasphemy – if he beats him to death he shall be called a servant of God; for everyone is in duty bound to punish wickedness.' In particular the Revolutionary calls for the assassination of the reigning Emperor, Maximilian, for whom he had an overwhelming hatred. But beyond these preliminary murders lies the day when the new Emperor from the Black Forest, together with the Brotherhood, will 'control the whole world from West to East by force of arms' – an age of ubiquitous and incessant terror, in which the hopeful prophecy was to be amply justified: 'Soon we will drink blood for wine!'

The Revolutionary leaves no doubt as to who these crusading brethren are to be: they will be the common people, the poor. As for the dwellers in Babylon, the sinners who must be destroyed – they are the devotees of *Luxuria* and *Avaritia*, of dancing and fine clothes and fornication, they are 'the great men, both in the Church and amongst the laity'. And as so often, it is the rich, well-fed, loose-living clergy who are the chief enemy. The fanatical layman never tires of portraying – and in the most lurid possible colours – the chastisement which the coming Emperor, that is he himself, will inflict on those children of Satan, the friars and monks and nuns. In particular, he rages against priests who break their vow of chastity and set up households. Such priests, he cries, should be strangled or burnt alive, or else driven with their concubines into the hands of the Turks; their children – true children of Antichrist – should be left to starve. But indeed the whole clergy must be annihilated: 'Go on hitting them', cries the Messiah to his army, 'from the Pope right down to the little students! Kill every one of them!' He forsees that 2,300 clerics will be killed each day and that this massacre will continue for four and a half years. And this is not the end, for scarcely less abominable than the clerics are the 'usurers' who flourish in the towns. Alongside the simoniac prelates drawing fat prebends from taxes and tithes the Revolutionary sees a swarm of money-lenders mercilessly extracting exorbitant interest from the poor, of merchants busily contriving price rings, of shopkeepers for ever overcharging and giving short measure – and attendant upon all these a swarm of unscrupulous lawyers eagerly justifying every injustice. All these alike are to be massacred; assisted by those who are referred to now as 'the pious Christians', now as 'the common people', the Emperor from the Black Forest is to burn all usurers and hang all lawyers.

The possibility of profit was just as alluring in the society of the later Middle Ages as it has proved in every other society where it has existed at all; and there is no doubt that the abuses of which the Revolutionary complained were real enough. But this cannot account for the most characteristic feature of this particular piece of social criticism, which is its eschatological tone. The Revolutionary is utterly convinced that God has ordered the great massacre of clergy and 'usurers' in order to remove such abuses for ever, the holocaust is to be an indispensable purification of the world on the eve of the Millennium. And one fact about the Millennium which emerges with great clarity is that it is to be strongly anti-capitalist. Church property is to be secularized and used by the Emperor for the benefit of the community as a whole and the poor in particular. All income derived either from landed property or from trade is to be confiscated – which amounts to an abolition of the principalities and an expropriation of all the rich. Rents, taxes, dues of every kind are to be imposed by the Emperor alone. But beyond these immediate reforms – sweeping as they are – the Revolutionary looks forward to a far more drastic transformation of society, to a state where private property will be abolished altogether and all things will be held in common: 'What a lot of harm springs from self-seeking! . . . It is necessary therefore that all property shall become one single property, then there will indeed be one shepherd and one sheepfold.'

Would human beings prove altruistic enough for such a system, or would there be reactionaries who would disturb the general harmony by clinging to *Luxuria* and *Avaritia*? The Revolutionary at least does not shirk the question. Once a year, he declares, the Emperor will issue a decree for the purpose of unmasking sin – usury and lechery above all; urging people to inform against sinners but also – and on this he lays great weight – to come forward and voluntarily confess their own sins. An official tribunal will be set up in each parish and sinners, moved above all by an irresistible inner compulsion, will appear before it to be judged *in camera*. The judges must punish all sin 'with cruel severity' – for what is mercy towards sinners but a crime against the community as a whole? If therefore a first offence may perhaps be rewarded by a mere flogging, the position of a sinner who appears before the tribunal in three different years is grave indeed. 'If a person will not stop sinning he is better out of the world than in it': therefore he is to be executed forthwith by certain secret messengers of unquestionable piety. The Revolutionary revels in describing the various ways in which these executions are to be carried out – by burning, stoning, strangling, burying alive. Nothing, he insists, will do more to establish and protect the new order of equality and communal ownership than this new type of justice.

As we shall see, others before this sixteenth-century phantast had imagined an egalitarian social order, and moreover had thought of it as being imposed and maintained by force. But in one respect the Revolutionary of the Upper Rhine was truly original – nobody before him had combined such devotion to the principal of communal or public ownership with such megalomaniac nationalism. This man was convinced that in the remote past the Germans had in reality 'lived together like brothers on the earth', holding all things in common. The destruction of that happy order had been the work first of the Romans and then of the Church of Rome. It was Roman Law and Canon Law which had introduced the distinction between Mine and Thine and which had thereby undermined the sentiment of fraternity and opened the way to envy and hate. Behind this curious idea lay a whole philosophy of history. The Old Testament was dismissed as valueless; for from the time of the Creation onwards it was not the Jews but the Germans who were the Chosen People. Adam and all his descendants down to Japhet, including all the Patriarchs, were Germans speaking German; other languages – Hebrew among them – came into existence only at the Tower of Babel. It was Japhet and his kin who first came to Europe, bringing their language with them. They had chosen to settle in Alsace, the heart of Europe; and the capital of the Empire which they founded was at Trier. This ancient German Empire was a vast one, for it covered the whole of Europe – Alexander the Great could be claimed as a German national hero. And it was the most perfect of empires, a true earthly Paradise, for it was governed according to a legal code, known as the Statutes of Trier, in which the principles of fraternity, equality and communal ownership were enshrined. It was in these Statutes, and not in the Decalogue invented by the charlatan Moses, that God had expressed his commandments to mankind – for which reason the Revolutionary thoughtfully appended a copy of them to his work.

Very different was the history of the Latin peoples. These wretched breeds were not descended from Japhet and were not numbered amongst the original inhabitants of Europe. Their homeland lay in Asia Minor, where they had been defeated in battle by the warriors of Trier and whence they had been brought to act as the serfs of their conquerors. The French – a peculiarly detestable lot – ought therefore by rights to be a subject people, ruled by the Germans. As for the Italians, they were descended from serfs who had been banished over the Alps for offences against the Statutes of Trier; whence the fact, which the publicist had no difficulty in establishing, that Roman history consisted of an almost uninterrupted series of defeats. These Latin peoples were the source of all wickedness – a poisoned source which had gradually polluted the whole sea. Roman Law, the Papacy, the French, the Republic of Venice were so many aspects of an immense, age-old conspiracy against the German way of life.

Fortunately the time was at hand when the power of evil was to be broken for ever. When the great leader from the Black Forest seized power as Emperor Frederick he would not only cleanse German life from the Latin corruption and bring back the Golden Age based on the Statutes of Trier – he would also restore Germany to the position of supremacy which God intended for her. 'Daniel's dream', that old apocalypse which had brought such inspiration to the Jews during the Maccabean revolt, was subjected by the Revolutionary to yet another reinterpretation. Now the four successive empires turn out to be France, England, Spain and Italy. Enraged by the overweening pride of these nations the Emperor will conquer them all – the Revolutionary claimed already to have discovered by means of alchemy the new explosives which the undertaking would demand. 'By his cruelty he will instil fear into the peoples'; thereby establishing the Germans as the fifth and greatest empire, which shall not pass away. Next the Emperor, returning from his western campaigns, will utterly defeat the Turks who have penetrated into Europe. Pressing east at the head of a vast army drawn from many peoples he will carry out the task traditionally assigned to the Last Emperor. The Holy Land will be conquered for Christendom and 'the society of Mohammedans' will be utterly overthrown. The infidel will be baptised 'and those that will not accept baptism are no Christians nor people of the Holy Scriptures, so they are to be killed, then they will be baptised in their blood'. After all this the Emperor will rule supreme over the whole world, receiving homage and tribute from thirty-two kings.

It is worth remarking that the Christianity which was to be imposed so vigorously is scarcely recognizable as such. According to the Revolutionary the first Christians were the citizens of the Trier Empire and the God whom they worshipped was the same as Jupiter; his holy day was Thursday, not Sunday; as emissaries to the Germans he sent not angels but spirits who dwelt in the Alsatian mountains. The teachings of the historical Christ were directed only to Jews, not to Germans. The proper religion for Germans was still that which had prevailed in the Golden Age of Trier and this was the religion which the Emperor Frederick was to reinstate. When that happened – and here the Revolutionary draws heavily on *Gamaleon* – the spiritual centre of the world would be not Rome but Mainz, where a patriarch would preside in place of the vanished pope. But this patriarch would be no pope but wholly dependent on the Emperor who would appoint and could if need be depose him. It was the Emperor – the Revolutionary himself, triumphant and glorified – who was to stand at the centre of the future religion, who would be 'the supreme priest' and whom 'one must recognize as an earthly God'. The future Empire was indeed to be nothing less than a quasi-religious community united in adoration and dread of a messiah who was the incarnation of the German spirit. This is what the Revolutionary had in mind when he cried, jubilantly: 'The Germans once held the whole world in their hands and they will do so again, and with more power than ever.'

In these phantasies the crude nationalism of a half-educated intellectual erupted into the tradition of popular eschatology. The result is almost uncannily similar to the phantasies which were the core of National-Socialist 'ideology'. One has only to turn back to the tracts – already almost forgotten – of such pundits as Rosenberg and Darré to be immediately struck by the resemblance. There is the same belief in a primitive German culture in which the divine will was once realized and which throughout history has been the source of all good – which was later undermined by a conspiracy of capitalists, inferior, non-Germanic peoples and the Church of Rome – and which must now be restored by a new aristocracy, of humble birth but truly German in soul, under a God-sent saviour who is at once a political leader and a new Christ. It is all there – and so were the offensives in West and East – the terror wielded both as an instrument of policy and for its own sake – the biggest massacres in history – in fact everything except the final consummation of the world-empire which, in Hitler's words, was to last a thousand years.

The *Book of a Hundred Chapters* was not printed at the time (nor has it ever been). There is nothing to suggest that the anonymous Revolutionary played any significant part in the social movements of his day. His importance lies not in any influence he exerted but in the influences which he underwent and registered. For even if some of the details may have been born of his own private meditations, in its broad outline the phantasy which he expounds is simply an elaboration of the traditional prophecy of a future Frederick who would be the messiah of the poor. And there can be no doubt that in one form or another that prophecy continued to fascinate and excite the common people of Germany, peasants and artisans alike, until well into the sixteenth century. In one Emperor after another – Sigismund, Frederick III, Maximilian, Charles V – the people contrived to see a reincarnation (in the most literal sense of the word) of Frederick II. And when these monarchs failed to play the eschatological role expected of them the popular imagination continued to dwell on a purely fictitious emperor, a Frederick who would arise from the midst of the poor – 'of lowly descent' as the Revolutionary puts it – to oust the actual monarch and reign in his stead.

It would no doubt be easy to exaggerate the part played by such expectations in the movements of resistance and revolt which punctuate German history during the first quarter of the sixteenth century. The attitude of the peasantry, in particular, was usually realistic enough. Even when peasants looked beyond their immediate grievances and demanded a general reform of the social and political structure of the Empire, their programme tended to be a limited and tolerably practicable one. Nevertheless in the series of risings known as the *Bundschuh* (of which more will be said in a later chapter) phantasies akin to those in the *Book of a Hundred Chapters* certainly did play some part. Writing in 1510 the Revolutionary of the Upper Rhine had forecast the apocalyptic year for 1515; and when a *Bundschuh* rising broke out in that same area in 1513 its declared aim was nothing less than 'to help righteousness and get rid of blasphemers' and finally to recover the Holy Sepulchre. And some of those who took part in that rising even managed to persuade themselves that the Emperor Maximilian was favourable to their cause – even though at present he was compelled to keep his sympathy secret.

7   An Elite of Self-immolating Redeemers

The genesis of the flagellant movement

The practice of self-flagellation seems to have been unknown in Europe until it was adopted by the hermits in the monastic communities of Camaldoli and Fonte Avellana early in the eleventh century. Once invented, the new form of penance spread rapidly until it had become not only a normal feature of monastic life throughout Latin Christendom but the commonest of all penitential techniques – so much so in fact that the very meaning of the term *disciplina* was restricted to 'scourge'. What it could mean to those who practised it is vividly shown in the description which a fourteenth-century friar has left of his own experience. One winter's night this man

shut himself up in his cell and stripped himself naked ... and took his scourge with the sharp spikes, and beat himself on the body and on the arms and on the legs, till blood poured off him as from a man who has been cupped. One of the spikes on the scourge was bent crooked, like a hook, and whatever flesh it caught it tore off. He beat himself so hard that the scourge broke into three bits and the points flew against the wall. He stood there bleeding and gazed at himself. It was such a wretched sight that he was reminded in many ways of the appearance of the beloved Christ, when he was fearfully beaten. Out of pity for himself he began to weep bitterly. And he knelt down, naked and covered in blood, in the frosty air, and prayed to God to wipe out his sins from before his gentle eyes.

Medieval self-flagellation was a grim torture which people inflicted on themselves in the hope of inducing a judging and punishing God to put away his rod, to forgive them their sins, to spare them the greater chastisements which would otherwise be theirs in this life and the next. Yet beyond mere forgiveness lay another, still more intoxicating prospect. If even an orthodox friar could see in his own bleeding body an image of the body of Christ, it is not surprising that laymen who became flagellants and then escaped from ecclesiastical supervision should often have felt themselves to be charged with a redemptive mission which would secure not only their own salvation but that of all mankind. Like the crusading *pauperes* before them, heretical flagellant sects saw their penance as a collective *imitatio Christi* possessing a unique, eschatological value.

It was in the crowded Italian cities that organized flagellant processions appeared for the first time. The movement was launched in 1260 by a hermit of Perugia and spread southwards to Rome and northwards to the Lombard cities with such rapidity that to contemporaries it appeared a sudden epidemic of remorse. Led usually by priests, masses of men, youths and boys marched day and night, with banners and burning candles, from town to town. And each time they came to a town they would arrange themselves in groups before the church and flog themselves for hours on end. The impact which this public penance made upon the general population was great. Criminals confessed, robbers restored their loot and usurers the interest on their loans, enemies were reconciled and feuds forgotten. Even the two warring parties which were dividing Italy, the Guelphs or supporters of the Pope and the Ghibellines or supporters of the Emperor, for a moment lost some of their intransigence. Whole towns became involved in the movement – at Reggio the chief magistrate, the bishop and all the guilds took part. As the processions moved along they constantly increased in size, until they were many thousand strong. But if at times people of all classes would join in, it was the poor who persevered; so that in the latter stages of the movement they alone remained.

The circumstances under which this first outbreak of mass self-flagellation occurred are significant. Even by medieval standards, conditions in Italy at that moment were exceptionally hard. In 1258 there had been famine, in 1259 a serious outbreak of plague. Above all, incessant warfare between Guelph and Ghibelline had reduced the country to a state of the utmost misery and insecurity. The situation of the Guelph towns was particularly desperate, for their cause had just suffered a heavy blow when the Florentines were defeated at Montaperto, with fearful slaughter, by the Tuscan Ghibellines. Frederick II's son Manfred seemed well on the way to establishing his sway over the whole of Italy. It was not for nothing that the flagellant movement started in a Guelph city and flourished most amongst Guelphs. Yet all these afflictions were felt to be but a prelude to a final and overwhelming catastrophe. A chronicler remarked that during the flagellant processions people behaved as though they feared that as a punishment for their sins God was about to destroy them all by earthquake and by fire from on high. It was in a world which seemed poised on the brink of the abyss that these penitents cried out, as they beat themselves and threw themselves upon their faces: 'Holy Virgin take pity on us! Beg Jesus Christ to spare us!' and : 'Mercy, mercy! Peace, peace!' – calling ceaselessly, we are told, until the fields and mountains seemed to echo with their prayers and musical instruments fell silent and love-songs died away.

But what these flagellants were striving to wrest from God was more than mere relief from present trouble. That year of 1260 was the apocalyptic year in which, according to the pseudo-Joachite prophecies, the Third Age was due to reach its fulfilment. Amidst famine, plague and war multitudes of Italians were impatiently awaiting the dawning of the Age of the Holy Spirit, the age in which all men would live in peace, observing voluntary poverty, rapt in contemplative bliss. As month after month passed by, these millenarian expectations became ever more tense until, towards the end of the year, they took on a desperate and hysterical quality and men began to clutch at straws. By September even the battle of Montaperto could be given an eschatological importance. When yet a further six weeks had passed and November had begun the flagellants appeared; and the chronicler Salimbene of Parma, who was himself a Joachite, tells how eager people were to see in these woeful processions the beginning of the great consummation.

In Italy the mass flagellant movement soon died of disillusionment; but in 1261–2 it crossed the Alps and reappeared in the towns of south Germany and the Rhine. The leaders seem still to have been Italians but as they passed through the German towns the inhabitants flocked in hundreds to form new processions. Doubtless the movement had possessed an organization already in Italy but it is at this point that chroniclers begin to notice one. These German flagellants possessed rituals and songs; they had even devised a uniform. Moreover the leaders proved to be in possession of a Heavenly Letter such as had once been carried by Peter the Hermit and again – only a few years back – by the 'Master of Hungary'; and in this instance the text has been preserved. A marble tablet shining with supernatural light – the letter stated – had recently descended upon the altar of the Church of the Holy Sepulchre at Jerusalem, in the presence of a multitude of the faithful. An angel had appeared beside it and had read out the message which God himself had inscribed on it. It was a message fraught with eschatological meaning, abounding in phrases taken from that famous piece of apocalyptic, attributed to Christ, which tells of the miseries and abominations which are to precede the Second Coming. For God was angry with human beings for their pride and ostentation, their blasphemies and adulteries, their neglect of the Sabbath and the Friday fast, their practice of usury – in fact for all those sins which were commonly regarded as in a special sense the sins of Dives. Already he had punished mankind by sending earthquakes and fire, drought and floods, famine and pestilence, and wars and invasions in which the Saracens and other pagans had devastated the lands of Christendom. In the end, outraged by the obstinacy with which men clung to their evil ways, he had decided to kill every living thing on earth. But the Virgin and the angels had fallen at his feet and implored him to grant mankind one last chance. Moved by these appeals, God promised that if people would even now mend their ways, abandoning the practice of usury and adultery and blasphemy, the land would flourish, the earth would bring forth fruit in abundance. At this news the faithful at Jerusalem had begun to seek desperately for some means of curing mankind of its fatal propensity to sin. At length the angel had appeared a second time to bid them go on a flagellant procession of $33\frac{1}{2}$ days, in memory of the number of years which, according to a traditional calculation, were spent by Christ on earth. So – the letter concluded – the movement had come into being: launched in the first place by the King of Sicily (is this Frederick II again, one wonders, as Saviour in the Last Days?), the great pilgrimage had now reached Germany. And any priest who in his worldliness omitted to pass on the divine message to his congregation would be infallibly and eternally damned.

One cannot but be reminded of that other Heavenly Letter by which, two and a half centuries later, the Revolutionary of the Upper Rhine was to try to call into being his anti-ecclesiastical Brotherhood of the Yellow Cross. And whereas the Italian flagellants had always been firmly controlled by the clergy, the German flagellants did in fact quickly turn against the Church. Germans were as familiar as Italians with the pseudo-Joachite prophecies and expected just as much of the apocalyptic year 1260; but they tended to be far more bitter against the clergy and far more uncompromising in their rejection of Rome. Only a few years had passed since the Swabian millenarian Brother Arnold had declared that he and his followers were the holy community which in 1260 would take over all authority from the Church of Antichrist. And if in the interval Frederick II had died and the Great Interregnum had begun, that only intensified the longing amongst the German masses for a millennial Kingdom of the Saints. The movement ended by becoming the monopoly of the poor, of weavers, cobblers, smiths and the like; and as it did so it turned into a conspiracy against the clergy. The flagellants began to claim that they were able to achieve salvation by their own merits and without the aid of the Church; even that the very act of taking part in one of their own processions absolved a man from all sin. Soon archbishops and bishops were busily excommunicating and expelling these dangerous penitents, with secular princes such as the Duke of Bavaria helping in the work of repression.

In Germany and southern Europe alike flagellant groups continued to exist for two centuries and more after their first appearance, but their status and function in the two zones differed greatly. In Italy and southern France flagellant communities flourished openly in every important town. They were generally severely orthodox in their religious opinions and enjoyed the recognition of both ecclesiastical and secular authorities. In Germany, on the other hand, such communities were suspected always of heretical and often of revolutionary tendencies, and not without good reason. The movement which had been suppressed in 1262 continued to exist underground. In 1296, when towns on the Rhine were experiencing the worst famine for eighty years, uniformed, hymn-singing flagellants suddenly appeared there. And when the greatest flagellant movement of all time swept through Germany in 1348–9 it too turned out to possess rituals and songs and even the very same Heavenly Letter, scarcely modified at all – which seems to prove that some at least of its leaders must have come from a clandestine movement and been able to draw upon an esoteric tradition.

The outbreak of 1348–9 was precipitated by the Black Death. This epidemic of bubonic fever seems to have had its origin in India and to have been carried overland to the Black Sea and thence by shipping to the Mediterranean. Early in 1348 it was raging in the ports of Italy and southern France. From the coasts of western Europe it travelled slowly along the trade routes until it had reached every country except Poland, which established a quarantine at its frontiers, and Bohemia, which was protected by mountains. In each area the epidemic lasted from four to six months. In the crowded towns the plague flourished exceedingly, overwhelming all efforts to check it; corpses lay unburied in the churchyards. It seems certain that in terms of the rate of mortality this plague was incomparably the greatest catastrophe that has befallen western Europe in the last thousand years – far greater than the two World Wars of the present century together. Responsible modern authorities estimate that in 1348–9 about a third of the population perished.

The plague was interpreted, in normal medieval fashion, as a divine chastisement for the transgressions of a sinful world. The flagellant processions were in part an attempt to divert the chastisement; and a new paragraph was added to the Heavenly Letter to stress this point. It was the rumour and foreboding of plague, rather than the experience of it, that brought the processions into being; usually they had disappeared well before the plague itself arrived. From Hungary, where it seems to have started late in 1348, the movement spread westwards to flourish above all in the towns of central and southern Germany and finally of the Rhine valley, whence it radiated on the one hand into Westphalia and on the other into Brabant, Hainaut and Flanders – and France, until it was checked by the king. From the Low Countries a contingent took ship for London, where it performed in front of St Paul's; but in England the movement found no followers.

Considering the manner in which it operated the movement spread rapidly. In March, for instance, it had reached Bohemia, in April Magdeburg and Lübeck, in May Würzburg and Augsburg, in June Strasbourg and Constance, in July Flanders. Nevertheless it did not move in a steady sweep. The main streams were full of minor currents, cross-currents and eddies. The flagellants proceeded in bands varying in size from fifty to 500 or more. At Strasbourg a new band arrived each week for half a year. About a thousand burghers are said to have joined them and moved off, some up, some down the river. At Tournai a new band arrived every few days from mid-August to the beginning of October. In the first two weeks of the period bands arrived there from Bruges, Ghent, Sluys, Dordrecht and Liége; then Tournai itself joined in and sent off a band in the direction of Soissons. To conceive the movement as a whole one must picture a number of regions passing one after another into a state of emotional agitation which would remain in full force for some three months and then gradually subside. In the East, where the movement began, it was over by the middle of the year. In central and southern Germany it began to wane soon afterwards. In the Low Countries and northern France it lasted till late autumn. The number of men who took part at one stage or another must have been great. Figures are hard to come by; but it is reliably reported that a single monastery in the Low Countries which became a place of pilgrimage for the flagellants had to provide food for 2,500 in half a year and that the flagellants arriving at Tournai in two and a half months numbered 5,300. It is also said – though perhaps with some exaggeration – that when Erfurt refused to open its gates to the flagellants, some 3,000 encamped outside the walls.

What made of this mass self-flagellation something more than an epidemic, something which can properly be called a movement, was the way in which it was organized. Save at the last stage, in the Low Countries, this organization was singularly uniform. The flagellants had their collective names; they called themselves Cross-bearers, or Flagellant Brethren, or – like the crusaders of 1309 – Brethren of the Cross. Like their precursors in 1262 – and for that matter like the crusaders – they wore a uniform; in this case a white robe with a red cross before and behind and a hat or hood similarly marked. Each band of flagellants was commanded by a leader, who had – significantly – to be a layman. This 'Master' or 'Father', as he was called, heard the confessions of the members and – as the clergy noted with horror – imposed penances and granted absolution, both during the public flagellations and in private. Each member had to swear absolute obedience to his Master for the duration of the procession. And that duration too was fixed: except for some short local processions in the Low Countries, which were organized by the Church, it was always the mystic $33\frac{1}{2}$ days. During that period the flagellants were subject to a rigorous discipline. They were not allowed to bath or shave or change their clothes or sleep in soft beds. If they were offered hospitality they could wash their hands only when kneeling on the floor as a token of humility. They were not allowed to speak to one another without the Master's permission. Above all they were forbidden to have any dealings with women. They had to avoid their wives; in the houses where they lodged they could not be served at table by women. If a flagellant spoke a single word to a woman he had to kneel down before the Master, who would beat him, saying: 'Arise by the honour of pure martyrdom, and henceforth guard yourself against sin!'

When they came to a town the flagellants would make their way to a church, form a circle in front of it, take off their clothes and shoes and put on a sort of skirt reaching from the waist to the feet. Then there would begin a rite which, despite certain local variations, was remarkably standardized. The penitents marched round in a circle and one by one threw themselves on their faces and lay motionless, with outstretched arms, in the form of a crucifix. Those behind stepped over the prostrate body, striking it gently with their scourges as they passed. Men with heavy sins to redeem lay in positions which symbolized their transgressions; and over these men the Master himself stepped, beating them with his scourge and repeating his formula of absolution: 'Arise, by the honour of pure martyrdom . . .'

When the last man had lain down all rose to their feet and the flagellation began. The men beat themselves rhythmically with leather scourges armed with iron spikes, singing hymns meanwhile in celebration of Christ's Passion and of the glories of the Virgin. Three men standing in the centre of the circle led the singing. At certain passages – three times in each hymn – all would fall down 'as though struck by lightning' and lie with outstretched arms, sobbing and praying. The Master walked amongst them, bidding them pray to God to have mercy on all sinners. After a while the men stood up, lifted their arms towards heaven and sang; then they recommenced their flagellation. If by any chance a woman or a priest entered the circle the whole flagellation became invalid and had to be repeated from the beginning. Each day two complete flagellations were performed in public; and each night a third was performed in the privacy of the bedroom. The flagellants did their work with such thoroughness that often the spikes of the scourge stuck in the flesh and had to be wrenched out. Their blood spurted on to the walls and their bodies turned to swollen masses of blue flesh.

The mass of the population was very favourably disposed towards the flagellants. Wherever the penitents went great crowds flocked to watch and listen. The solemn rites, the fearful beatings, the hymns – perhaps the only ones which had yet been heard in a language understandable to the masses – and, as culmination, the reading of the Heavenly Letter produced an overwhelming effect, so that the whole audience would be swept by sobbing and groaning. Nobody questioned the authenticity of the Letter. The flagellants were regarded as they regarded themselves – not simply as penitents who were atoning for their own sins but as martyrs who were taking upon themselves the sins of the world and thereby averting the plague and, indeed, the annihilation of mankind. It became a privilege to welcome and assist such people. When a flagellant procession approached a town the bells were rung and when the flagellation was over the inhabitants hastened to invite the participants to their houses. People were glad to contribute towards the cost of the candles and flags; even the urban authorities drew freely upon public funds.

It was the story of the *Pastoureaux* over again. As at all times since civilization had begun to revive and material wealth to increase, the urban masses were dissatisfied with a clergy in whom – with whatever justice – they could see nothing but worldliness. Samples of the criticisms which were rife in those days of the middle of the fourteenth century have been preserved in the utterances of clerics themselves. One says:

Simony had penetrated so deep and become so firmly established that all secular and regular clerics, whether of high or middle or low rank, bought and sold ecclesiastical offices shamelessly and even publicly, without being reproved by anyone, let alone punished. It seemed as though the Lord, instead of driving the buyers and sellers from the Temple, had rather shut them up inside it; as though simony must be held not heretical but churchly and Catholic and holy. Prebends, parsonages, dignities, parish churches, chapels, curacies and altars were sold for money or exchanged for women and concubines, or staked and lost and won in a game of dice. Everyone's rank and career depended only on money and influence or other considerations of profit. Even abbeys, priories, guardianships, preceptorships, lectureships and other positions, even the least important, were purchased from prelates or the Roman Curia by incapable, raw, ignorant, young, inexperienced men with whatever they could collect, whether by theft or by other means; or else they grabbed them in some other way. Hence it comes that it is not now easy to find amongst the secular or regular clergy persons who can be respected, although that used to be quite common. Look at the abbots, priors, guardians, Masters, lecturers, provosts and canons, and sigh! Look at their life and example, conduct and teaching, and at the dangerous situation of those in their charge, and tremble! Take pity on us, O Lord, Father of Mercy, for we have sinned grievously before you!

'How contemptible has the Church become!' cries another cleric. 'The pastors of the Church feed themselves instead of their flocks; the flocks they shear, or rather they flay them; they behave not like pastors but like wolves! All beauty has left the Church of God, from crown to heel there is no healthy spot on her!'

The precise extent to which such complaints were justified is irrelevant. What is certain is that laymen could not easily find amongst the clergy what they so desperately needed – religious virtuosos whose asceticism seemed to guarantee their miracle-working powers. The flagellants, on the other hand, seemed to be just such virtuosos. They themselves claimed that through their flagellations they were not only absolved from all sin and assured of heaven but were empowered to drive out devils, to heal the sick, even to raise the dead. There were flagellants who claimed to eat and drink with Christ and to converse with the Virgin; at least one claimed to have risen from the dead. All these claims were eagerly accepted by the populace. People not only brought their sick to be healed by these holy men, they dipped cloths in the flowing blood and treasured them as sacred relics. Men and women alike begged to be allowed to press these cloths to their eyes. On one occasion a dead child was carried round the circle during the flagellation in the hope that he would be resurrected. Wherever the flagellants appeared in Germany the common people, especially in the centres of industry and trade, turned to them as to men of God and at the same time began to curse the clergy. And this presented the flagellants with the opportunity for which many of them had been waiting.

Revolutionary flagellants

It was only in limited areas of the Low Countries that the flagellant movement of 1349 was effectively controlled by the clergy. In other parts of the Low Countries and all over Germany it ended as a militant and bloodthirsty pursuit of the Millennium.

The moment was most propitious to such a development, for eschatological expectations were more than usually widespread and intense. It is no coincidence that it was in these years that the most famous of the German Antichrist-plays were composed and performed. Already in 1348 people were interpreting earthquakes in Carinthia and Italy as those 'messianic woes' which were to usher in the Last Days; and even if one were not expressly told so, one would have assumed that the uniquely appalling catastrophe of the Black Death would be interpreted in the same sense. In fact the experience of overwhelming insecurity, disorientation and anxiety had the effect – as so often – of raising eschatological excitement amongst the masses to fever-pitch. The flagellant processions took their place in the world-shattering, world-transforming drama of the Last Days which was now unfolding in all its terror and exaltation:

'Plague ruled the common people and overthrew many,

'The earth quaked. The people of the Jews is burnt,

'A strange multitude of half-naked men beat themselves.'

And beyond these tribulations there lay, of course, the Millennium. Multitudes were living in expectation of the coming of a warrior-messiah, such as was later to fascinate the Revolutionary of the Upper Rhine. Precisely under the year 1348 John of Winterthur notes how generally and eagerly the common people were expecting a resurrected Emperor Frederick who would massacre the clergy and compel the rich to wed the poor. It was also for that year of 1348 that a certain 'great astrologer' was supposed to have forecast not only the plague but also the advent of an emperor who would scatter and judge the Pope and his cardinals, overthrow the King of France and establish his own dominion over all countries.

Many of the flagellants themselves certainly lived in a world of millenarian phantasy. A contemporary chronicler reports that the processions of 1349, each lasting $33\frac{1}{2}$ days, were regarded as merely a beginning; the movement as a whole was intended to last $33\frac{1}{2}$

years, by which time Christendom was to have been saved. An enquiry into the beliefs of the flagellants at Breslau likewise revealed millennial preoccupations. There the penitents were telling how the existing orders of monks and friars would pass through great tribulations, until after seventeen years (half the total period of transition!) they would be replaced by a new monastic order which would last until the End. This of course is a prophecy in the Joachite tradition; and it is worth recalling at this point the reappearance of the Heavenly Letter, which had itself been handed down from 1260, the apocalyptic year of Joachite prophecy. It was not for nothing that such a document had become the manifesto of the flagellant movement; for it is certain that when flagellants talked of a new monastic order of unique holiness they were referring to themselves alone. These people really saw themselves as a holy people, an army of Saints. It was not simply that they called themselves Cross-bearers and Brethren of the Cross and during their self-inflicted tortures sang of Christ's Passion – they often went much further, claiming that Christ himself had shown them his bleeding wounds and bidden them go out and beat themselves. Some even said openly that no shedding of blood could be compared with theirs save that at the Crucifixion, that their blood blended with that of Christ, that both had the same redemptive power.

As might be expected, the development of these phantasies corresponded to a change in the social composition of the flagellant processions. The movement always consisted in the main of peasants and artisans; but whereas at first nobles and rich burghers also took part, latterly these dropped out and the tone of the movement came to be set more by a mass of new recruits from the margins of society – vagabonds, bankrupts, outlaws and criminals of all kinds. At the same time leadership passed into the hands of a number of *prophetae*, who seem to have consisted largely of dissident or apostate clerics. When the Pope finally decided to issue a Bull against the flagellants he made it plain that he regarded the majority as simple folk who had been led astray by heretics who themselves knew very well what they were doing. He added that these heretics included numbers of monks and friars and that such men must be arrested without fail. A chronicler of the Low Countries also expressed the view that the movement was organized, with the object of destroying clergy and Church, by apostate monks in Germany. And three years after the movement had disappeared from view the Archbishop of Cologne was still threatening excommunication to deacons and subordinate clerics who had taken part in it, unless they could produce witnesses to swear to their innocence. What lay behind such accusations is shown by the happenings at Breslau – a city where, as we have seen, the flagellants openly avowed their Joachite beliefs. There the leader is known to have been a deacon who incited his followers to attack the clergy and who ended by being burnt as a heretic.

As the flagellant movement turned into a messianic mass movement its behaviour came to resemble that of its forerunners, the People's Crusades. The German flagellants in particular ended as uncompromising enemies of the Church who not only condemned the clergy but utterly repudiated the clergy's claim to supernatural authority. They denied that the sacrament of the Eucharist had any meaning; and when the host was elevated they refused to show it reverence. They made a practice of interrupting church services, saying that their own ceremonies and hymns alone had value. They set themselves above pope and clergy, on the grounds that whereas ecclesiastics could point only to the Bible and to tradition as the sources of their authority, they themselves had been taught directly by the Holy Spirit which had sent them out across the world. The flagellants absolutely refused to hear criticism from any cleric; on the contrary – just like the 'Master of Hungary' – they declared that any priest who contradicted them should be dragged from his pulpit and burnt at the stake. When two Dominicans ventured to dispute with a flagellant band they were stoned, one being killed and the other escaping only by flight; and similar incidents occurred elsewhere. At times flagellants would urge the populace on to stone the clergy. Anyone, including any member of their own fraternity, who tried to moderate their fury against the Church did so at his peril. The Pope complained that whenever they had the chance these penitents appropriated ecclesiastical property for their own fraternity; and a French chronicler said that the flagellant movement aimed at utterly destroying the Church, taking over its wealth and killing all the clergy. There is no reason to think that either was exaggerating.

As usual the Jews suffered along with the clergy and on a far greater scale. In the great massacre of European Jewry which accompanied the Black Death – the greatest before the present century – the flagellants played an important part. The first killings were carried out spontaneously by a populace convinced that the Jews had caused the plague by poisoning the wells. They had come to an end by March 1349; perhaps because by that time people had noticed that the plague was attacking Jews as much as Christians and was not sparing areas where all Jews had already been killed. Four months later a second wave of massacre was launched by the propaganda of the flagellants. Wherever the authorities had so far protected the Jews, these hordes now demanded their massacre. When in July 1349, flagellants entered Frankfort they rushed straight to the Jewish quarter, where the townsfolk joined them in exterminating the entire community. The town authorities were so perturbed by the incident that they drove the penitents from the town and reinforced the gates to prevent their return. A month later massacres took place simultaneously at Mainz and at Cologne. During a flagellant ceremony at Mainz the crowd of spectators suddenly ran amok and fell upon the Jews, with the result that the largest community in Germany was annihilated. At Cologne a flagellant band which had for some time been encamped outside entered the town and collected a great crowd of 'those who had nothing to lose'. Against the wish of the town council and the rich burghers this horde attacked the Jews and killed many of them. At Brussels too it was the approach of the flagellants, coupled with the rumour of well-poisoning, that launched the massacre in which the whole community of 600 Jews was killed, despite the efforts of the Duke of Brabant to protect it. Through large areas of the Low Countries the flagellants, aided by the masses of the poor, burnt and drowned all the Jews they could find, 'because they thought to please God in that way'.

The sources are scanty and it is impossible to say how many such massacres were led or instigated by the flagellants during the second half of 1349; but they must have been numerous. The Jews themselves came to regard the flagellants as their worst enemies; while the Pope gave as one of his chief complaints against the flagellants that 'most of them or their followers, beneath an appearance of piety, set their hands to cruel and impious works, shedding the blood of Jews, whom Christian piety accepts and sustains'. This at least is certain, that by the time the flagellants had finished the work which the panic of 1348 had begun there were very few Jews left in Germany or the Low Countries. The massacres of 1348–9 completed the deterioration in the position of the Jews which had begun in 1096. Throughout the remainder of the Middle Ages the Jewish communities in Germany remained small and poor and, moreover, condemned to the segregation of the ghetto.

Did the flagellants also intend to overthrow that other traditional Enemy, the one personified by Dives? Did they, like other eschatologically inspired hordes, aim at exterminating the rich and privileged? The Pope accused them of robbing and killing laymen as well as clerics and Jews, while a chronicler specifies that it was the well-to-do whom they assaulted. Certainly these hordes did in the end – like the *Pastoureaux* – come to be feared by the 'great'. In France Philip V forbade public self-flagellation on pain of death and was thus able to prevent the movement from penetrating further than Picardy. In Germany some towns, such as Erfurt, closed their gates against the flagellant hordes, while others, such as Aachen and Nuremberg, promised death to any flagellant found within their walls. What these urban authorities feared emerges clearly enough from the story of the smaller flagellant movement which accompanied a fresh outbreak of plague in 1400. In that year flagellants were imprisoned at Visé on the Maas, resisted by the town of Tongeren and suppressed at Ghent by the Count of Flanders. When a flagellant band approached Maastricht the well-to-do burghers tried to close the gates against it, but the proletarian cloth-fullers rose and overthrew the magistracy and its supporters, admitted the penitents and then, fortified by the presence of these holy men, closed the gates against the overlord of the town, the Bishop of Liége.

By the second half of 1349 the flagellant movement had become a force as anarchic as the two great risings of the *Pastoureaux* and had mobilized against itself the same coalition of ecclesiastical and secular powers. Princes and bishops in areas disturbed by the flagellants turned to the Sorbonne for advice. The Sorbonne referred the matter to the Pope at Avignon but also sent him one of its doctors, the Flemish monk Jean du Fayt, who had studied the movement in his homeland. When the plague had first reached southern France, in May of the preceding year, Clement VI had himself instituted public flagellations in which vast numbers of both sexes had taken part. Later he had realized the danger of such performances; a band of flagellants which arrived at Avignon from Basle met with a rebuke. Now du Fayt's report evoked an immediate response; in October, 1349, the Pope issued a Bull against the flagellants. After summarizing their doctrinal vagaries and their offences against the clergy and the Jews the Bull pointed out that these people were already ignoring the secular authorities and added that if they were not opposed now they might soon be beyond opposing. The 'sect' was therefore to be suppressed; the 'masters of error' who had elaborated its doctrines were to be arrested and dealt with, if necessary by burning. The Bull was dispatched to the archbishops in Germany, Poland, France, England and Sweden, and was followed by letters to the kings of France and England. The University of Paris too now pronounced its formal condemnation; and clerics hastened to write tracts against the flagellants.

The effect of the Bull was immediate. Archbishops and bishops throughout Germany and the Low Countries forbade all further flagellant processions. Many parish priests, chaplains and canons were unfrocked and excommunicated, and made their way to Avignon to seek absolution. The secular authorities co-operated enthusiastically in repressing the movement. Those towns which were still being frequented by flagellants took steps to remove them. We hear of flagellants being beheaded at the order of a count and of many in Westphalia being hanged. At the behest of the Archbishop the urban authorities in the See of Trier set about executing flagellants and nearly exterminated them. Under pressure of persecution almost all the penitents quickly abandoned their movement – 'vanishing', as one chronicler puts it, 'as suddenly as they had come, like night phantoms or mocking ghosts'. Some literally tore off their uniforms and fled. In the following year – which happened to be a Holy Year – many were doing penance by being beaten, this time by clerics, before the High Altar of St Peter's at Rome. Nevertheless the movement lingered on here and there. The town of Tournai found it necessary to renew its prohibitions periodically up to 1351, the Bishop of Utrecht was still pursuing flagellants in 1353, the Archbishop of Cologne had to deal with them in 1353 and again in 1357. Thereafter no more is heard of the flagellants in those western areas.

Set in the context of medieval popular eschatology the story of the flagellant movement of 1349 provokes one obvious query: was there, somewhere in Germany, some self-appointed messiah who was trying by means of the flagellant movement to bring about a state of affairs in which he could publicly assume the role of eschatological saviour? Unfortunately the available sources provide no answer. One can only point to a smaller flagellant movement which had appeared in Italy a few years earlier and which had also escaped from ecclesiastical control. In that instance the leader is known to have been a layman, Domenico Savi of Ascoli, who, after spending many years as a hermit, claimed to have become the Son of God; for which he was burnt as a heretic. That of course does not establish the existence in 1349 of a similar figure in Germany; it merely makes it seem more probable. On the other hand there is abundant information concerning a flagellant messiah called Konrad Schmid – a true counterpart of the Italian heresiarch and at the same time a pseudo-Frederick – who in the 1360s headed the movement which under pressure of persecution had turned into a clandestine sect in the towns of central and southern Germany. The story of this man and his followers is worth examining in some detail.

The secret flagellants of Thuringia

A layman who was sufficiently literate to steep himself in apocalyptic prophecies in a monastery library, Konrad Schmid was also thoroughly familiar with the traditional, more or less esoteric lore of the earlier flagellant movements. In many respects his doctrine was simply that of the penitents of 1348–9. For his followers self-flagellation was, as it had been then, a collective *imitatio Christi*, a redemptive sacrifice which alone protected the world from final, overwhelming catastrophe, and by virtue of which they themselves became a holy elite. For them too it was a matter of course to reject the Church of Rome and all its works, to ridicule the Eucharist, to call churches dens of thieves and to denounce the clergy as blood-sucking charlatans whose true nature stood revealed in the Beast of the Apocalypse. Even in repudiating the authority of the secular powers as well, in insisting that the Emperor had no more claim than the Pope on their submission and that all laws without exception were annulled for them, these sectarians merely confirm what could be surmised already from the behaviour of their predecessors. In other respects however Schmid's teachings are most illuminating; for in them the messianic faith which had always been implicit in the flagellant movement in Germany is proclaimed with the greatest possible emphasis.

According to these teachings the prophecies of Isaiah which were regarded traditionally as foretelling the coming of Christ really referred to the coming of Schmid, who was now the sole bearer of the true religion. From this it would seem that when Schmid's Catholic adversaries said that he believed himself to be God, they were speaking the sober truth. At the same time the flagellant leader assumed the title of King of Thuringia. Nowhere else, perhaps, had the flagellant movement of 1348–9 flourished quite as vigorously as in the large area of central Germany which at that time was known as Thuringia. No town or village had remained unaffected; the flagellants had become so popular and powerful that they had openly incited the common people to stone the clergy; the town of Erfurt had closed it gates in panic while hordes of flagellants encamped outside. Yet in assuming the style of King of Thuringia Schmid was not simply recognizing a region which was particularly favourable to his apostolate; Thuringia was also a region which had played a unique part in building up the body of folklore concerning the future Emperor Frederick.

From 1314 to 1323 Thuringia had been ruled by a grandson of Frederick II, the Margrave Frederick the Undaunted. There was at that time a faction which saw this man as a natural heir to the imperial dignity and disseminated propaganda urging his claims; while in the eyes of the common people he became an eschatological figure. It was widely believed that he bore the miraculous birthmark – the luminous gold cross between the shoulder-blades – which was the predestined sign of the Emperor of the Last Days; and he was expected to carry out the final chastisement of the clergy. After his death the figure of Frederick the Undaunted merged into that of his maternal grandfather, the Emperor. The Thuringians began to tell of a mysterious Frederick who was sleeping in the Kyffhäuser mountain and who one day would return in glory to dominate the world from his Kingdom of Thuringia. Thus in claiming to be King of Thuringia Konrad Schmid was claiming to be the Frederick of eschatological prophecy. This is what he meant when he set himself up in opposition to the ruling Margrave, declaring that he himself had far greater exploits to his credit; and the common people did in fact call him Emperor Frederick. As at once the resurrected Frederick and incarnate God, this heresiarch was already acting out the role which a century and a half later was to obsess the imagination of the Revolutionary of the Upper Rhine.

In order to be received into the sect a would-be member had to make a general confession to Schmid, undergo flagellation at his hands and take an oath of absolute obedience to him. From that moment onwards the only obligation which he recognized was total submission to the messiah. Schmid taught his followers that their salvation depended on their attitude towards himself. If they were not 'as soft and yielding as silk' in his hands, if they showed the slightest striving after independence, they would be handed over to the Devil to be tortured both physically and mentally. He was their god and they must pray to him, addressing him as 'Our Father'.

Those who were faithful to Schmid had their reward. They could rejoice in the certain knowledge that in and through them human history was attaining its true end. They saw the flagellants of 1349 as standing in the same relationship to them as John the Baptist to Christ. Indeed Christ himself was no more than their precursor; for, granted that he had pointed the true way to salvation by enduring flagellation, it was only those who beat themselves who could claim to pursue that way to the end. Now the Christian dispensation was supplanted by a higher dispensation (one recognizes the familiar Joachite pattern) and of that dispensation the followers of Konrad Schmid were the only bearers. Just as Christ had changed water into wine, so they had replaced baptism with water by baptism with blood. God had indeed kept the best wine for last – it was nothing else than the blood shed by the flagellants.

These people were convinced that as they beat themselves an angel named – surprisingly – Venus watched over them. Their skins all red with blood seemed garments for a wedding-feast, the skirts which they wore during flagellation they called robes of innocence. How the Prophets would have rejoiced to be alive at this moment and share in these holy beatings! As for King David, he had actually foreseen this bliss and had been driven to despair by the knowledge that he could never live to join the sect. Even so he and his wife had beaten themselves nightly, as a way of participating in these works which were pleasing to God above all others. Yet all this was but a foretaste of the joy to come – of the millennial Kingdom which would shortly appear and in which, grouped around their Emperor-god, the flagellants would form an angelic choir and would be called sons of princes. Meanwhile, consumed by impatience, many members of the sect sold all their belongings and refused to work, so that they quickly sank into abject poverty.

As in 1348–9, flagellant propaganda was still greatly assisted by the plague. Smaller but decidedly alarming outbreaks continued to occur every few years, giving rise each time to a fresh wave of panic. It may well have been the particularly severe epidemic of 1368 which inspired Schmid to announce that the Last Judgement would be held and the Millennium begin in the following year. But by that time the Inquisition had begun to take an interest in the proliferation of heretical groups in Thuringia. An outstandingly energetic inquisitor was sent to deal with the situation and there were many executions. There are grounds for believing that Konrad Schmid was one of the seven heretics who were burnt in 1368 at Nordhausen, a bare fifteen miles from the Kyffhäuser mountain from which, as the resurrected Frederick, he was supposed to have emerged.

Once more the ecclesiastical authorities set about stamping out the flagellant movement in Germany. In 1370 the Bishop of Würzburg forbade flagellation in his diocese and two years later the Pope was encouraging the Inquisition in Germany to deal promptly with any flagellants it could lay hands on. But still the movement continued underground. In 1391–2 new flagellant groups were found among the peasants and artisans around Heidelberg; and the inquisitor who dealt with them thought it best to proceed immediately to Schmid's old headquarters in Thuringia. There he found that plague was raging and Jews were being slaughtered; and without difficulty he discovered a group of heretical flagellants at Erfurt. The leaders of the group were burnt, on others penances were imposed; while the rest simply fled.

The years around 1400 were an unhappy and troubled time for all Christendom. The Ottoman Turks were advancing in the Balkans and in 1396 inflicted an annihilating defeat on the crusading army which the West sent against them. More disturbing even than this external threat was the disunity springing from the Great Schism which divided the Church between two rival popes, each of whom claimed the obedience of all Christendom and denounced the other as a heretic. It was a period of profound and widespread disorientation which – as so often – proved a great stimulus to eschatological excitement. In 1396 the Dominican St Vincent Ferrer had a vision of the approaching Last Days and, convinced that Antichrist was on the point of beginning his reign, began to lead flagellant processions through Spain, southern France and Italy. In 1399 an Italian peasant was favoured with an apocalyptic vision which resulted in the formation of a flagellant movement which swept all Italy. Even in those southern lands, where such movements had generally remained under ecclesiastical control, they could at times escape from it. When a great flagellant procession from the Lombard towns descended on Rome the Pope had their leader arrested and burnt; and a procession of some hundreds of Lombard artisans which, led by one of Ferrer's disciples, entered the same city with the intention of waging war on Antichrist must also have been most disquieting to the Curia. It was sad experience which led that eminent and prudent divine, Charlier de Gerson, to direct from the Council of Constance in 1417 a most earnest appeal to Ferrer to stop encouraging tendencies so dangerous to the Church.

But it was still in and around Thuringia that heretical flagellants were most numerous. These people too were convinced that they were living in the Last Days; and it was in terms of traditional popular eschatology that they interpreted the life and death of the founder Konrad Schmid. The Book of Revelation told of two 'witnesses' who were to preach against Antichrist and be killed by him and then be miraculously resurrected; and popular eschatology had identified these witnesses as Elijah and Enoch, the two personages in the Old Testament who were 'translated' to heaven without undergoing death in the body. It was as Elijah and Enoch, reincarnated in the Last Days as the witnesses, that the flagellants now saw Schmid and his closest associate, who had perished with him; while Antichrist was of course the Church of Rome. But the sectarians were also convinced that Schmid would return yet again, this time to overthrow Antichrist and preside over the Last

Judgement. Precisely because the return of Elijah and Enoch lay already in the past, they expected this Second Coming at every moment; and there can be little doubt that it was as the Last Emperor as well as the Son of Man that they expected Schmid to appear. Early in the fifteenth century a chronicler of Thuringia noted how vigorously the 'secret heresy' concerning the sleeping Frederick was flourishing there – how firmly simple folk were persuaded that the Emperor really did appear from time to time among men and how confidently they were awaiting his return as the Emperor of the Last Days; and it was surely no coincidence that it was in the towns around the Kyffhäuser that the clandestine flagellant movement persisted. For the rest, these secret flagellants were still very conscious of their link with their predecessors. They had preserved the rites of the movement of 1349 and were still defending their practices by appealing to the Heavenly Letter. They had also preserved Schmid's doctrine in all its purity, handing it from parents to children with such fidelity that after a century it had scarcely changed at all. They formed in fact a tightly organized community, into which newborn babies were baptised by being beaten until they bled.

Traditionally proceedings against heretics were instituted and carried out by the Church; the intervention of the secular authorities being limited to carrying out the sentences imposed. It is all the more significant that, so far as can be gathered, it was always the local territorial princes who took the initiative in pursuing the Thuringian flagellants. In prosecuting these people, who were indeed social revolutionaries as much as they were heretics, the role of the Inquisition was at best a secondary one. This was already the case when in 1414–16 a large flagellant community was unearthed in the town of Sangerhausen. After mass trials held by inquisitors and secular judges acting together the leader and two disciples were burnt as impenitent heretics. The rest recanted and were released; but when the inquisitor had left the area the princes of the neighbouring territories seized every flagellant they could find. Eighty or ninety flagellants were burnt in 1414 and, it seems, 300 on a single day in 1416 – certainly a startling expression of the fear which this movement inspired in 'the great'. Even that failed to put a stop to the movement. A generation later, in 1446, a dozen flagellants were discovered at Nordhausen, the town where Schmid himself had probably been burnt. In this case, too, even those who recanted were burnt – a course of action which could only have been adopted by the secular authorities without sanction from the Church; it is probably not irrelevant that the one victim whose trade is known was a weaver. In 1454, again, a couple of dozen flagellants, men and women, were burnt at Sonderhausen; and it was as late as the 1480s that the last (so far as is known) of the secret flagellants were tried and burnt – again at the instigation of the local prince.

If thereafter no more is heard of the sect, it is still of some interest that the district where it had flourished most was the district which was to witness the exploits of Thomas Müntzer. The village where, in 1488 or 1489, that *propheta* of the Peasants' War was born lies within a few miles of Nordhausen, and so does the scene of the massacre which overwhelmed his peasant army.

8 An Elite of Amoral Supermen (i)

The heresy of the Free Spirit

Compared with the vast amount which has been written about the heresy variously known as Catharist, Albigensian and Neo-Manichean, the literature on the heresy of the Free Spirit or of Spiritual Liberty is scanty indeed. This is not altogether surprising; for whereas the Catharist *perfecti* dominated the religious life of a large part of southern France for half a century or more, until their power was broken by a crusade which changed the history of France, the story of the adepts of the Free Spirit is less obviously dramatic. Nevertheless in the social – as distinct from the purely political – history of western Europe the heresy of the Free Spirit played a more important part than Catharism. The area over which it extended was, by medieval standards, a vast one. In the fourteenth century when a man in Moravia wished to join one of its communities he was led across Europe until he was introduced to one at Cologne; while women adepts would make their way from Cologne to a community in the depths of Silesia, 400 miles away. A century later a band of adepts from Picardy exercised an appreciable influence on the Taborite revolution in Bohemia. And this movement had an extraordinary capacity for survival; for, constantly harassed by persecution, it persisted as a recognizable tradition for some five centuries.

The heresy of the Free Spirit therefore demands a place in any survey of revolutionary eschatology – and that is still true even though its adherents were not social revolutionaries and did not find their followers amongst the turbulent masses of the urban poor. They were in fact gnostics intent upon their own individual salvation; but the gnosis at which they arrived was a quasi-mystical anarchism – an affirmation of freedom so reckless and unqualified that it amounted to a total denial of every kind of restraint and limitation. These people could be regarded as remote precursors of Bakunin and of Nietzsche – or rather of that bohemian intelligentsia which during the last half-century has been living from ideas once expressed by Bakunin and Nietzsche in their wilder moments. But extreme individualists of that kind can easily turn into social revolutionaries – and effective ones at that – if a potentially revolutionary situation arises. Nietzsche's Superman, in however vulgarized a form, certainly obsessed the imagination of many of the 'armed bohemians' who made the National-Socialist revolution; and many a present-day exponent of world revolution owes more to Bakunin than to Marx. In the later Middle Ages it was the adepts of the Free Spirit who conserved, as part of their creed of total emancipation, the only thoroughly revolutionary social doctrine that existed. And it was from their midst that doctrinaires emerged to inspire the most ambitious essay in total social revolution which medieval Europe was ever to witness.

The heresy of the Free Spirit has long been regarded as one of the most perplexing and mysterious phenomena in medieval history and its nature has been much debated by historians. It has often been suggested that no such movement existed at all outside the polemics of ecclesiastics whose one concern was to defame and discredit every venture in dissent. But these doubts could exist only because no attempt was ever made to use all the sources available. Hostile sources – the reports of inquisitorial interrogations, the warnings and condemnations uttered by popes and bishops, the polemical dissertations of theologians, the revelations of disillusioned followers – are not really (as has often been believed) the only sources which exist. As the clergy repeatedly noted with consternation, the adepts of the Free Spirit produced an abundant doctrinal literature of their own. Although these works were constantly being seized and destroyed by the Inquisition, three items are available for study. Two of these have been available for many years: a tract called *Schwester Katrei* ('Sister Catherine'), which was written in the fourteenth century in the Alemannic dialect of Middle High German and was protected by being ascribed – quite wrongly – to the great Dominican mystic Meister Eckhart; and a list of 'articles of faith' in Latin, which was discovered in a hermit's cell near the Rhine in the fifteenth century, but which is certainly far older than that. The third item is a long mystical text called *Le Mirouer des simples ames* ('The mirror of simple souls'). Previously attributed to an obscure orthodox mystic, this text has now been identified by Professor Romana Guarnieri as the work of a celebrated adept of the Free Spirit, Marguerite Porete. Marguerite was burned as a heretic in 1310; and her book turns out to have been a key document in the history of the Free Spirit and its persecution.

There may well be other such texts still awaiting discovery. Meanwhile what is already available goes far to show that the accounts which Catholics gave of the heresy of the Free Spirit were substantially correct. And it can be supplemented by other evidence, from a later period. During and after the English Civil War accusations were brought against certain sectarians, known to their enemies as Ranters, which were repetitions of the accusations brought in earlier centuries against the adepts of the Free Spirit. Like those of the medieval heretics, the writings of the Ranters were condemned to be burnt; but a few copies have survived and these works can be compared with the accusations. Until samples of it were reprinted in the first edition of the present study, this material was practically ignored by historians of the Free Spirit; yet it is highly relevant. The samples given in the Appendix to this book cover the whole range of the cult of the Free Spirit, from its most spiritual to its crudest forms; and they prove conclusively that in the seventeenth century there did indeed exist a movement closely resembling that which emerges, in outline, from the less complete medieval sources.

Historically the heresy of the Free Spirit can be regarded as an aberrant form of the mysticism which flourished so vigorously in Western Christendom from the eleventh century onwards. Orthodox and heretical mysticism alike sprang from a craving for immediate apprehension of and communion with God; both alike stressed the value of intuitive and particularly of ecstatic experiences; and both alike were enormously stimulated by the rediscovery of Neo-Platonic philosophy, from which they took the greater part of their conceptual apparatus. There however the resemblance ends. The Catholic mystics lived their experiences within a tradition sanctioned and perpetuated by a great institutionalized church; and when – as often happened – they criticized that church, their aim was to regenerate it. The adepts of the Free Spirit on the other hand were intensely subjective, acknowledging no authority at all save their own experiences. In their eyes the Church was at best an obstacle to salvation, at worst a tyrannical enemy – in any case an outworn institution which must now be replaced by their own community, seen as a vessel for the Holy Spirit.

The core of the heresy of the Free Spirit lay in the adept's attitude towards himself: he believed that he had attained a perfection so absolute that he was incapable of sin. Although the practical consequences of this belief could vary, one possible consequence was certainly antinomianism or the repudiation of moral norms. The 'perfect man' could always draw the conclusion that it was permissible for him, even incumbent on him, to do whatever was commonly regarded as forbidden. In a Christian civilization, which attached particular value to chastity and regarded sexual intercourse outside marriage as particularly sinful, such antinomianism most commonly took the form of promiscuity on principle. Accusations of promiscuity were of course often brought by one religious community against another; it was a stock technique of polemic in the medieval as in the early Church. But when they are directed against the adepts of the Free Spirit these accusations take on a different ring. What emerges then is an entirely convincing picture of an eroticism which, far from springing from a carefree sensuality, possessed above all a symbolic value as a sign of spiritual emancipation – which incidentally is the value which 'free love' has often possessed in our own times.

Within the area of Western Christendom, the heresy of the Free Spirit cannot be identified with any certainty before the beginning of the thirteenth century. On the other hand, analogous cults did flourish before that time both in the area of Eastern Christendom and in Moslem Spain. Almost from its beginnings, the Armenian Church had to cope with the mystical sect known as the Euchites or Messalians, which flourished in the area around Edessa as early as the fourth century. The Euchites were wandering 'holy men' who lived by begging; and they cultivated a self-exaltation that often amounted to self-deification, and an antinomianism that often expressed itself in anarchic eroticism.

Towards the close of the twelfth century various Spanish cities, and notably Seville, witnessed the activities of mystical brotherhoods of Moslems. These people, who were known as Sufis, were 'holy beggars' who wandered in groups through the streets and squares, dressed in patched and particoloured robes. The novices amongst them were schooled in humiliation and self-abnegation: they had to dress in rags, to keep their eyes fixed on the ground, to eat revolting foodstuffs; and they owed blind obedience to the master of the group. But once they emerged from their noviciate, these Sufis entered a realm of total freedom. Disclaiming book-learning and theological subtleties, they rejoiced in direct knowledge of God – indeed, they felt themselves united with the divine essence in a most intimate union. And this in turn liberated them from all restraints. Every impulse was experienced as a divine command; now they could surround themselves with worldly possessions, now they could live in luxury – and now, too, they could lie or steal or fornicate without qualms of conscience. For since inwardly the soul was wholly absorbed into God, external acts were of no account.

It is likely that Sufism, as it developed from the ninth century onwards, itself owed much to certain Christian mystical sects in the East. In turn it seems to have assisted the growth of the mysticism of the Free Spirit in Christian Europe. Certainly every one of the features that characterized Sufiism in twelfth-century Spain – even to such details as the particoloured robes – were to be noted as typical of the adepts of the Free Spirit a century or two later.

In any case, around 1200 the cult of the Free Spirit began to emerge as an identifiable heresy in Western Christendom.

The Amaurians

Early in the thirteenth century the doctrine of the Free Spirit was elaborated into an all-embracing theological and philosophical system. This was the work of a most interesting group, consisting of men who had been trained at the greatest school of orthodox theology in Western Christendom, the University of Paris. The fullest account has been given by a German chronicler, the prior of the abbey of Heisterbach. 'In the city of Paris,' he writes, 'that fount of all knowledge and well of the divine writings, the Devil by persuasion instilled a perverse understanding into several learned men.' They were fourteen in number and all of them clerics – parish priests, chaplains, deacons and acolytes from Paris and its environs and from such towns as Poitiers, Lorris near Orleans, Troyes. 'Men great in knowledge and understanding,' laments the same chronicler, and in the main the description seems justified: nine of the fourteen had studied theology in Paris and two are mentioned as being sexagenarians. Their leader was a certain William, also a cleric and trained in theology, but known as *Aurifex* – which has resulted in his being regarded as a goldsmith but may have meant that he was a philosophical alchemist: the dormant magical powers of the soul, which it was the ambition of such alchemists to awake, were often symbolized by gold.

Owing partly to the indiscretion of this William and partly to espionage organized by the Bishop of Paris, the heretics were detected and rounded up. Interrogated at a synod held under the Archbishop of Sens, three recanted and were sentenced to life imprisonment but the remainder publicly professed their heretical beliefs and were accordingly burnt. Even at the moment of death they gave no sign of repentance. The chronicler's comment can still conjure up the atmosphere of that moment: 'As they were being led to punishment such a furious storm arose that nobody doubted that the air was being stirred up by the beings who had seduced these men, now about to die, into their great error. That night the man who had been their chief knocked at the door of a certain woman recluse. Too late he confessed his error and declared that he was now an important guest in hell and condemned to eternal fires.'

The philosophical master of these sectarians had been Amaury of Bène, a brilliant lecturer in logic and theology at the University of Paris. This man had at one time enjoyed great prestige and the patronage of the royal court; a number of eminent persons, including the Dauphin, had been his friends and had been impressed by his ideas. But in the end, denounced for teaching erroneous doctrine, he was condemned by the Pope and forced to make a public recantation. This experience broke Amaury's spirit; he took to his bed and shortly afterwards – in 1206 or 1207 – he died. When some two or three years later the heretical sect was unearthed the clergy at once proclaimed Amaury's responsibility and labelled the heretics 'Almaricans' or 'Amaurians'. Already before their execution a tract *Contra Amaurianos* was circulating. A few years later, in 1215, Robert of Courçon, the cardinal and papal legate who was entrusted with drawing up statutes for the University, was careful to forbid all study of 'the summary of the doctrine of the heretic Amaury'. And at the Lateran Council of the same year Innocent III uttered his judgement in a Bull: 'We reprove and condemn the most perverse dogma of the impious Amaury, whose mind was so blinded by the Father of Lies that his doctrine is to be considered not so much heretical as insane.' At the same time that the sectarians were burnt Amaury's bones were exhumed and transferred to unconsecrated ground.

All that is known for certain of Amaury's own doctrine is that it was a mystical pantheism which owed much to the Neo-Platonic tradition and particularly to the most distinguished exposition of Neo-Platonism that had been made in western Europe, the *De divisione Naturae* of Johannes Scotus Erigena. This book, which was already three and a half centuries old, had never been condemned as heretical before; but the use which Amaury had made of it resulted in its being condemned by the Council of Sens in 1225. Suspicion also fell upon the Arabian summaries of and commentaries on Aristotle which were just beginning to appear in Latin translation in Paris. The synod which condemned the Amaurians also condemned these works and Robert of Courçon introduced precautions against study of them into the university statutes of 1215. It is a curious fact that on his first appearance in Europe the intellectual giant who was to supply the framework for orthodox medieval philosophy was banned on suspicion of having inspired Amaury of Bène. But there is little in any of these metaphysical speculations to account for the explosive doctrine which was discovered in 1209. And it will always be doubtful to what extent

Amaury was in fact responsible for the doctrine of the Amaurians.

Amaury was a professional philosopher; the Amaurians, for all their university education, had quite different interests. They were *prophetae*, concerned not with abstract ideas but with working upon the turbulent emotions of the lay world. And it was as true of them as of other *prophetae* that they imposed themselves as holy men, gifted with miraculous powers. 'Outwardly,' remarks one of their enemies, 'in face and speech, they are pious-seeming'; and it was certainly for that reason that their teachings were so eagerly accepted. Moreover like most 'apostolic' preachers they operated in the great commercial centres. Their chief stronghold seems to have been Troyes in Champagne, then a most important town on the route from Flanders to Lyons. At Troyes a knight who seems to have been a follower of the Amaurians was caught and burnt in 1220; and at Lyons echoes of the heresy lingered on as late as 1225. The spy who penetrated into the sect found himself wandering with a number of missionaries across the whole County of Champagne – and Champagne, like Flanders, was a land where a series of strong rulers had, by imposing peace, enabled population to grow and trade and industry to develop. A flourishing cloth industry existed there; it was there that the trade-routes from the Mediterranean to Germany and from Flanders to central and eastern Europe intersected; by the thirteenth century the great fairs of Champagne had become major centres of trade. In this populous, urbanized area the missionaries went from one secret meeting to another, where they would go into trances and see visions. They would preach on texts from the Scriptures and give them a heretical interpretation; and so, we are told, seduce a great multitude of innocent people. The sect even produced a literature of its own, suitable for use by the laity. The synod of Paris condemned, along with the esoteric Aristotle, several purely popular works of theology, all of them in the vernacular.

The Amaurians kept their master's pantheism but gave it a strongly emotional content. The synod found that they spoke the language of pantheism on occasion, professing that 'all things are One, because whatever is, is God.' But what is more striking is the conclusion which one of the three ringleaders drew from that general proposition: 'He dared to affirm that, in so far as he was, he could neither be consumed by fire nor tormented by torture, for he said that, in so far as he was, he was God.' One can detect the Neo-Platonism; but certainly such strength, in a man on trial for his life, is not to be derived from mere pantheistic speculation. And in fact its source lay elsewhere – in the mysticism of the Free Spirit. When the Amaurians claimed that 'each one of them was

Christ and Holy Spirit', they meant all that Tanchelm had meant. They were convinced that what Christian theology regards as the unique miracle of the Incarnation was now being repeated in each one of them.

Indeed they believed that the Incarnation as it had taken place in Christ was now being surpassed. For these French *prophetae* had arrived at an interpretation of history which had striking similarities with that of Joachim of Fiore – even though they drew very different consequences from it and even though, at that early date, they can hardly have known much about the doctrine which lay buried in the manuscripts of the Calabrian abbot. Like Joachim, the Amaurians saw history as divided into three ages, corresponding to the three Persons of the Trinity; but unlike him, they believed that each age had its appropriate Incarnation. From the beginning of the world until the birth of Christ the Father had acted alone; and he had been incarnated in Abraham, perhaps in the other Patriarchs of the Old Testament as well. The age since the Nativity had been the Age of the Son. But now there was beginning the Age of the Holy Spirit, which would last to the end of the world. That age was to be marked by the last and greatest Incarnation. It was the turn of the Spirit to take on flesh and the Amaurians were the first men in whom it had done so – the first 'Spirituals', as they called themselves.

The Amaurians did not expect to remain the only living gods on the face of the earth, but rather that they would lead all mankind into its perfection. Through them the Holy Spirit would speak to the world; but as a result of its utterances the Incarnation would become ever more general, until soon it would be universal. Under the guidance of the 'Spirituals' the world was entering on its supreme epoch, in which every man would be, and know himself to be, divine. 'Within five years,' they foretold, 'all men will be Spirituals, so that each will be able to say: "I am the Holy Spirit" and "Before Abraham was, I am"; just as Christ was able to say: "I am the Son of God" and "Before Abraham was, I am."' Yet this did not mean that in Amaurian eschatology the Kingdom was no longer reserved for an elite of Saints. The minds of these obscure intellectuals were steeped in the traditional messianic phantasies which were current amongst the masses. William the Goldsmith foretold that within those same five years of transition the world would pass through a series of catastrophies – the familiar 'messianic woes' – in which the majority of mankind were to perish, some killed off by wars and famines, others swallowed into the abysses of the earth, others again consumed by fire from on high; which makes it clear enough that only a 'saving remnant' was expected to survive to taste the joys of divinity. Moreover amongst the Amaurians the phantasy of the Age of the Spirit did not, any more than it did amongst the German Joachites, oust the older phantasies centred on the Last Emperor. The five years of tribulation were to culminate in the overthrow of Antichrist and his hosts, who were no other than the Pope and the Church of Rome. Thereafter all kingdoms would be under the domination of the King of France – the reigning king, Philip Augustus, at first, but later Amaury's friend and patron the Dauphin, who would never die but would rule for ever in the Age of the Spirit. And 'to the King of the French twelve loaves shall be given' – meaning (one may suppose) that Louis VIII was to be a second Christ who – just like Tanchelm and the 'Master of Hungary' – would preside over a privy council or sacred college of twelve, modelled on the twelve Disciples.

The Amaurians were believed – probably correctly – to be mystical antinomians. The Abbot of St Victor near Paris – the monastery which at that time was leading all Western Christendom in the theory and practice of mysticism – thought it necessary to warn his monks against these dangerous results of aberrant mysticism – 'lest this city, fount of learning, be polluted by this plague'. 'There are profane novelties,' he cried, 'which are being introduced by certain men, disciples of Epicurus rather than of Christ. With most dangerous deceit they strive secretly to persuade people that sinners shall not be punished, saying that sin is nothing, so that nobody shall be punished by God for sin. And if outwardly, in face and speech, they are pious-seeming, the worth of that piety is denied inwardly, in their minds and in their secret schemes. But the supreme madness and the most impudent falsehood is that such men should not fear nor blush to say that they are God. O what boundless folly, what abominable presumption, that an adulterer, a male concubine, one weighed down with infamy, a vessel of iniquity, should be called God!' And here, as so often, self-exaltation expressed itself above all in total promiscuity: 'they committed rapes and adulteries and other acts which give pleasure to the body. And to the women with whom they sinned, and to the simple people whom they deceived, they promised that sins would not be punished.' It was a protest which was to be voiced again and again, and with good cause, during the following centuries.

The sociology of the Free Spirit

It is true of all the great heretical movements of the later Middle Ages that they can be understood only in the context of the cult of voluntary poverty. When from the twelfth century onwards there appeared a wealth previously unheard-of in western Europe, most of those who could, revelled in the new opportunities for luxury and display. But there were always some who saw in the new enjoyments so many temptations of the Devil and who felt impelled to renounce all property, power and privilege and to descend into the poverty-stricken masses. And since the contrast between wealth and poverty was far more striking in the towns than on the manor, it was in the towns that voluntary destitution acquired its special significance.

The craving for renunciation was not confined to any one class. It was felt sometimes in the merchant class, which of all classes was drawing the greatest material benefits from the new conditions; the two most celebrated converts to voluntary poverty – Peter Waldo, founder of the heretical sect of Waldensians, and St Francis – both came from this class. The lower ranks of the secular clergy, which were recruited from the lower strata of society, were also perturbed. Many a priest, in protest against the pomp and worldliness of the great prelates, abandoned his parish in order to pursue a life of total poverty. Many clerks in minor orders – intellectuals often of considerable education – felt a similar urge. And there is no doubt that, just as peasants and artisans could join a crusade or a flagellant procession, so they could sometimes exchange their normal poverty, which was unavoidable, for a more extreme destitution which was voluntary and was therefore felt to be meritorious. In contemporary descriptions of the voluntarily poor there are many references to weavers; and if in the twelfth century these people were often ascetics who in their quest for poverty had become workers in the one industry which was sufficiently developed to employ casual labour, from the thirteenth century onwards they certainly included genuine artisans.

The voluntarily poor formed a mobile, restless intelligentsia, members of which were constantly travelling along the trade-routes from town to town, operating mostly underground and finding an audience and a following amongst all the disoriented and anxious elements in urban society. They saw themselves as the only true imitators of the Apostles and indeed of Christ; they called their way of life 'apostolic'; and up to the middle of the twelfth century it was for this reason, rather than on account of any peculiar theological doctrines, that they were sometimes condemned as heretics. But from the second half of the twelfth century onwards these multitudes of itinerant 'holy beggars' of both sexes showed themselves ready to assimilate any and every heretical doctrine that there was. If many became Cathars, Waldensians or Joachites, there were also some who became adepts and propagators of the heresy of the Free Spirit. Already about 1230, in Tanchelm's old domain of Antwerp, a certain Willem Cornelis was demonstrating how easy it was to combine the antinomianism that was so characteristic of that heresy with the cult of poverty, voluntary or not so voluntary. For this man, who had himself resigned an ecclesiastical benefice in order to follow the 'apostolic' life, was declaring that whereas monks were utterly damned for not observing perfect poverty, poverty properly observed abolished every sin; from which it followed that the poor could, for instance, fornicate without sin – and Cornelis himself is said to have been 'wholly given up to lust'. Twenty and more years later the ecclesiastical authorities were still trying to extirpate such ideas from amongst the populace of Antwerp. By then people were maintaining that all the rich, being corrupted by *Avaritia*, were infallibly damned; that even to possess a change of clothing was an obstacle to salvation; that to invite a rich man to dinner was a mortal sin; that it was right to take from the rich in order to give to the poor; but that the poor, on the other hand, were necessarily in a state of grace which carnal indulgence could in no way impair.

Early in the thirteenth century the great Mendicant Orders, the Franciscan and the Dominican, came into being and began to do with the encouragement of the Church much that 'apostolic' heretics were doing in opposition to the Church. An elite joined these Orders and as wandering preachers, practising poverty and every kind of self-abnegation, won the devotion of the urban masses. At the same time vast numbers of townspeople joined the Franciscan and Dominican Third Orders and while living in society as laymen rivalled the regular friars in asceticism. By sanctioning the Mendicant Orders the Church was able for a time to control and use the emotional energies which had been threatening its security; but already by the middle of the century this method of canalization was becoming less efficient. The Orders lost much of their primitive ardour, their asceticism became less intransigent, their prestige dropped accordingly; and once more the Church found itself confronted with autonomous groups of the voluntary poor. In southern Europe various hyper-ascetic groups split off from the main body of Franciscans and turned against the Church; the north of Italy and the south of France, where formerly the Cathars had flourished, became the homes of the Franciscan 'Spirituals' and the *Fraticelli*. Northern Europe, on the other hand, saw a great revival of the Free Spirit.

The heresy of the Free Spirit, after being held in check for half a century, began to spread rapidly again towards the close of the thirteenth century. From then onwards until the close of the Middle Ages it was disseminated by men who were commonly called Beghards and who formed an unofficial lay counterpart to the Mendicant Orders. They too were mendicants – indeed it is probably from their name that the English words 'beg' and 'beggar' derive. They frequented towns and ranged through the streets in noisy groups, shouting for alms and crying their characteristic begging-cry: 'Bread for God's sake!' They wore costumes rather like those of the friars, yet specially designed to differ from these in certain details. Sometimes the robe was red, sometimes it was split from the waist down; to emphasize the profession of poverty the hood was small and covered with patches. The Beghards were an ill-defined and restless fraternity – running about the world, we are told, like vagabond monks. At the slightest disturbance they were up and away, splitting up into small groups, migrating from mountain to mountain like some strange sparrows. These self-appointed 'holy beggars' were full of contempt for the easy-going monks and friars, fond of interrupting church services, impatient of ecclesiastical discipline. They preached much, without authorization but with considerable popular success. They held no particular heretical doctrine in common, but by the beginning of the fourteenth century the ecclesiastical authorities realized that amongst them were a number of missionaries of the Free Spirit.

Superficially the heretical Beghards or (as they came to be called in the fourteenth century) the Brethren of the Free Spirit seemed no less ascetic than the 'apostolic' heretics of earlier generations. Some settled near towns and lived as hermits, on the offerings which their admirers brought them. In at least one case, at Cologne, a community of heretical Beghards occupied a 'House of Voluntary Poverty' and lived on the alms which they could collect on the streets. More often such people led the same wandering, property-less, homeless life as other Beghards. Some of them had no fixed abode at all, would carry nothing on their persons, refused to enter any house and insisted on staying in the street to eat whatever food was given them. And – again like the rest of the 'voluntarily poor' – they included people of very varied social antecedents. If we hear of Brethren of the Free Spirit who were artisans by origin, we hear of others who came from prosperous and well-established families and of others still – as in all messianic movements – who came from the less privileged strata of the intelligentsia: former monks and priests and clerks in minor orders. But all alike seem to have been literate and articulate: again and again we find the clergy who had to combat these people dismayed by the subtlety and eloquence of their teaching and by the skill with which they handled abstruse theological concepts.

Like any other *propheta*, an adept of the Free Spirit owed his ascendancy to his reputation for asceticism – regarded as a guarantee of miracle-working powers – and partly to personal qualities of eloquence and bearing. But the following which he sought was different from that of other *prophetae*. He appealed not to the uprooted and disoriented poor but to people who had other but less compelling reasons to feel disoriented and frustrated – to women, and particularly to unmarried women and widows in the upper strata of urban society. Owing partly to the perpetual wars and feuds and partly to the celibacy of that very large section of the male population which made up the regular and secular clergy, the number of women always far exceeded the number of possible husbands. In the peasant and artisan classes spinsters and widows were absorbed by industry and agriculture, in the aristocracy they could always become nuns. To women born into the families of prosperous merchants, on the other hand, medieval society offered no recognized role save marriage. It is not surprising that spinsters and widows in that class – with no need to work, with not even household duties to perform, occupying no definite status and enjoying no social esteem – often longed as intensely as the masses of the poor for some saviour, some holy man with whose help they would attain a superiority as absolute as their present abasement.

At all times women such as these played a large part in the heretical movement of the Free Spirit. Already of the Amaurians we are told that they worked as unauthorized spiritual directors 'in the houses of widows'. When they were arrested a large number of female followers whom they had 'corrupted and deceived' were also brought to Paris for interrogation. In later generations, and right down to the close of the Middle Ages, the movement owed much to the women known as Beguines – women of the towns, and often from well-to-do families, who dedicated themselves to a religious life whilst continuing to live in the world. During the thirteenth century Beguines became very numerous in the area which is now Belgium, in northern France, in the Rhine valley – Cologne had two thousand Beguines – and in Bavaria and in central German towns such as Magdeburg. As a sign of their status these women adopted a religious dress – a hooded robe of grey or black wool and a veil; but there was no single way of life which was common to them all. Some of them lived lives which, save for a general religious orientation, differed little from those of other women; they lived with their families, or enjoyed private incomes, or supported themselves by work. Others lived unattached lives as wandering mendicants: true female counterparts to the Beghards. Most Beguines, however, formed themselves into unofficial religious communities, living together in a house or group of houses.

To the Church this widespread women's movement presented much the same problem as the kindred 'apostolic' movement amongst the men. Already in the second half of the thirteenth century mendicant Beguines, who begged either on their own behalf or on behalf of some community, attracted the suspicion of the ecclesiastical authorities. Along with their counterparts the Beghards they were condemned by a council of the See of Mainz in 1259; and the condemnation was repeated in 1310. These councils excommunicated the 'holy beggars' who in behaviour and dress set themselves apart from other Christians, and ordered that if they refused to mend their ways they should be expelled from every parish. At the same time the orthodoxy of the Beguines began to be called in question. In the Rhine valley monks were forbidden to speak to a Beguine except in a church or in the presence of witnesses; for a monk to enter a house of Beguines was punishable by excommunication. Reports on abuses in the Church submitted in preparation for the Ecumenical Council at Lyons in 1274 included several complaints against the Beguines. A Franciscan of Tournai reported that, though untrained in theology, the Beguines rejoiced in new and oversubtle ideas. They had translated Scripture into French and interpreted its mysteries, on which they discoursed irreverently in their meetings and on the streets. Vernacular Bibles, full of errors and heresies, were available to the public at Paris. An east German bishop complained that these women were idle, gossiping vagabonds who refused obedience to men under the pretext that God was best served in freedom.

The Beguines had no positive heretical intentions but they did have a passionate desire for the most intense forms of mystical experience. This desire was of course shared by many nuns; only for Beguines mysticism held temptations against which nuns were usually protected. Beguines lacked the discipline of a regular order; and at the same time they received no adequate supervision from the secular clergy, who had scant sympathy for this new-fangled and audacious religiosity. It is true that the friars were better able to guide the emotional energies of these women so that they served and did not threaten the Church; and in the first half of the fourteenth century almost all the Beguines were affiliated to the Franciscan and Dominican Third Orders. But the friars never succeeded in mastering the whole movement. Precisely amongst the most ascetic Beguines there were some who admitted as their spiritual directors not friars but Brethren of the Free Spirit.

By 1320 persecution had driven the movement of the Free Spirit underground; and thereafter the heretical Beghards seem to have done less begging and to have relied rather on a conspiratorial understanding which they were able to develop with certain of the Beguine communities. When a missionary of the Free Spirit approached such a community he was immediately taken in and given shelter and food. Under an oath of secrecy the news was sent to other sympathetically disposed communities that the 'angel of the divine word' had arrived and was waiting in hiding. From all sides Beguines streamed to hear the holy man. The Beghard would preach his mystical doctrine, wrapped up in elaborate phrases – 'unbelievably subtle words,' says one chronicler, 'and as sublime, spiritual and metaphysical as the German tongue can manage'. The Beguines, entranced, would declare him 'a man who had great likeness to God and great familiarity with him'. It was in this way and in this milieu that the doctrine was preserved and developed. The Millennium of the Free Spirit had become an invisible empire, held together by the emotional bonds – which of course were often erotic bonds – between men and women.

9   An Elite of Amoral Supermen (ii)

The spread of the movement

From the time of the Amaurians and Willem Cornelis onwards it is possible to follow the spread of the heresy of the Free Spirit across vast areas of Europe.

It seems that adepts of the Free Spirit were active along the Upper Rhine about 1215 and that some were burnt at Strasbourg. In 1240 the famous schoolman Albertus Magnus met with adepts at Cologne; and there are indications that they were busy in the dioceses of Trier in the 1270's. In 1307 a provincial synod of Cologne, summoned by the Archbishop for that purpose, tried to clear the city of the mendicant Beghards and Beguines who were teaching the doctrine of the Free Spirit. These efforts were unsuccessful and the Franciscans of Cologne still had cause to regard these heretics as serious rivals. And meanwhile the Free Spirit was spreading deeper into the German territories. About 1270 two red-robed Beghards were carrying on secret propaganda in the area around Nördlingen in Bavaria, which was not at that time a remote district but lay on the Brenner route and on the route from France to the East. Some of the male and female converts of these men were detected and interrogated and the heretical articles which they professed were submitted to Albertus Magnus for expert examination and refutation. But the heresy had found a new home and it was to flourish long in the Bavarian towns.

By the beginning of the fourteenth century it had also found a home in northern France; for a learned Beguine from Hainaut called Marguerite Porete was disseminating it in the dioceses of Cambrai, Châlons and Paris. She wrote a work of mystical theology: it was the *Mirouer des simples ames*, now rediscovered by Professor Guarnieri. At the time the book was condemned by the Bishop of Cambrai and publicly burned at Valenciennes; but Marguerite produced another copy and, despite several warnings, insisted on showing it to 'Beghards and other simple people'. She led a wandering, penniless life, accompanied by a Beghard who believed that he was divinely ordained as 'guardian angel' to the voluntary poor. In the end both fell into the hands of the Inquisition at Paris. During eighteen months' imprisonment Marguerite steadfastly refused to purchase absolution by recantation. In 1310 her book was condemned by a committee of theologians; and she herself was excommunicated and sentenced to death by burning. This woman seems to have had many followers, for some months after her death Clement V was bidding the inquisition at Langres to proceed with vigour against the heretics who were multiplying there so rapidly that they were becoming a grave danger to the faith. Her book was even introduced into England by someone in the suite of Philippa of Hainaut when she arrived as the bride of Edward III, in 1327 – a further instance of the appeal which the Free Spirit exercised in the upper strata of society.

By the time that Marguerite was executed the Free Spirit was causing serious concern to the Church. The Ecumenical Council held under Clement V at Vienne on the Rhône in 1311–12 made a long and careful examination of the 'errors of the Beghards'; one of their main sources being, as we now realize, Marguerite's *Mirouer des simples ames*. In the Bull *Ad nostrum* the doctrine of the Free Spirit was analysed and condemned; bishops and inquisitors were instructed to observe the lives and conversation of Beghards and Beguines and to proceed against any who were found to hold unorthodox views. These instructions were supplemented by a further Bull, *Cum de quibusdam*, which aimed at ensuring that in future all Beguines would live in communities under proper ecclesiastical supervision. This however was an extremely confused pronouncement and one of its effects was to start a persecution of quite harmless and orthodox Beguine communities. It was not long before the Pope himself was trying, largely in vain, to protect the many virtuous women in the Rhine towns who were being made to suffer for the transgressions of the Brethren of the Free Spirit. The confusion and the persecution were to last for more than a century.

The Beghards and Beguines who really were Brethren of the Free Spirit were of course persecuted as well. In 1317 the Bishop of Strasbourg, having received many complaints about heresy in his diocese, set up a commission of enquiry; and he was soon able to send a pastoral letter to his clergy based on its findings. The 'Little Brothers and Sisters of the Free Spirit' – vulgarly known as the 'Beghards and "Swestrones" of Bread for God's Sake' – were forbidden on pain of excommunication to wear their peculiar costumes; and the populace was forbidden, also on pain of excommunication, to give alms to people so attired. Houses in which heretical meetings were held were declared confiscated for the use of the poor. The heretical literature was to be surrendered and the begging-cry of 'bread for God's sake' abandoned. The Bishop did everything possible to ensure that these instructions were carried out. He made a visitation of his diocese and, finding everywhere signs of heresy, organized the first regular episcopal inquisition on German soil. This inquisition persecuted the heretics relentlessly. Some heretical Beghards fled into neighbouring dioceses but even there the Bishop of Strasbourg pursued them. He wrote to his fellow-bishops in the See of Mainz to warn them of the danger which threatened their dioceses and urge them to follow his own example. Yet the man was no blind fanatic, for he also wrote to the Pope in the interests of those Beguines who were being wrongfully persecuted.

The next attack on the Brethren of the Free Spirit was made in their traditional domain, Cologne. Their old enemy, the Archbishop – the same who had summoned the provincial synod of 1307 – summoned another in 1322 to deal with their unceasing propaganda. By that time the movement had become clandestine. The heretics of Cologne had found a remarkable leader in a certain Walter, who came from Holland and who had already been active as a missionary at Mainz. This man was a preacher of great eloquence and persuasiveness; and he wrote various tracts in German which circulated secretly amongst his followers. In the end he was caught; and having refused under the worst tortures to betray his associates or to recant he was burnt. According to one source Walter was an apostate priest, and the head of a large secret group which was captured by a ruse in 1325 or 1327. As many as fifty Brethren of the Free Spirit are said to have been executed on that occasion, some by burning and some by drowning in the Rhine.

Despite all persecution the Free Spirit persisted at Cologne and along the Rhine. In 1335 a community of heretical Beghards was found to have been living in a House of Voluntary Poverty at Cologne for thirty years or more. In 1339 three heretical Beghards were caught at Constance after a lifetime spent in initiating women into the lore of the Free Spirit. In 1353 Pope Innocent VI was so alarmed by the renewed activity of the heretical Beghards that he appointed the first papal inquisitor in Germany and ordered the secular authorities to assist this man and to put their prisons at his disposal. In 1356 an adept who had come from Bavaria to the Rhine valley was arrested for teaching the Free Spirit and was burnt at Speyer. A year later the Archbishop of Cologne was again complaining that heretics were so numerous that they might well contaminate the whole of his flock. In the last decade of the century an important heresiarch, Nicholas of Basle, won a following along almost the whole length of the Rhine from Constance to Cologne. Followers of his were burnt at Heidelberg and Cologne; and he himself, after several times defeating the efforts of the inquisitors to convict him, was caught at Vienna and burnt. But the Free Spirit survived along the Rhine. An adept was burnt at Mainz in 1458; and in the closing years of the century the Strasbourg satirist Sebastian Brant was still writing of the heresy as of a familiar phenomenon.

In Bavaria, too, the heresy which had first appeared in 1270 had a long history. By about 1330, it seems, it had travelled across Bavaria and reached the frontiers of the Kingdom of Bohemia and the Duchy of Austria. By the middle of the century missionaries of the Free Spirit were very active amongst the Bavarian Beguine communities. In 1342 a secret association of heretical Beghards was discovered in the diocese of Würzburg. In 1377 a synod of Regensburg still found cause to complain of the prevalence of beliefs associated with the Free Spirit; and four years later a Brother of the Free Spirit was captured and tried in the neighbouring diocese of Eichstätt. About 1400 an inquisitor gave an account of some Brethren of the Free Spirit who were living in a community of voluntary poverty at Cham, near Regensburg. Throughout the fifteenth century the Free Spirit seems to have lingered on in Bavaria. In the middle of the century a synod of Würzburg was repeating the old prohibitions on wandering, preaching Beghards, and the Bishop of Eichstätt was pronouncing excommunication on the heretical Beghards, commonly called 'of voluntary poverty', who were still begging their way through the country. Such bans were frequently repeated down to the end of the century.

The stages by which the Free Spirit penetrated eastwards across the territories of the Empire are unknown but in 1322 a heretical community of Beguines was discovered as far east as Schweidnitz in Silesia. These women were living in a House of Voluntary Poverty which closely resembled the men's house found at Cologne three years later and which – again like the men's house – was already some thirty years old. The house at Schweidnitz was only one of a number of houses which made up a clandestine organization; through the heretical Beghards who passed through these parts it kept in contact with similar groups as far afield as Breslau, Prague, Leipzig, Erfurt and Mainz. In central Germany the area between Erfurt and Magdeburg became an important centre of the Free Spirit. Beguines were known there almost as early as anywhere – it was in 1235 that the most famous of all Beguines, Matilda of Magdeburg, entered her community – and wandering Beghards already attracted the attention of the synod of Magdeburg in 1261.

In the book about her own mystical experiences which Matilda wrote between 1265 and 1277 she utters warnings against the Brethren of the Free Spirit. But the records are scanty; and the earliest clear trace of the Free Spirit in central Germany dates only from 1335, when a scribe who had been influenced by the doctrine of the Free Spirit was arrested and, having refused the plea of lunacy, burnt at Erfurt. The following year three Beguines 'of the lofty Spirit' were arrested at Magdeburg but recanted and were released.

In the second half of the fourteenth century the Brethren of the Free Spirit in central Germany were intimately associated with the flagellant sect founded by Konrad Schmid; and the two sects reinforced one another so effectively that the area came to be regarded by the authorities as the most dangerous stronghold of heresy in German territory. Towards 1370, when a truce occurred in the perennial struggle between Pope and Emperor, Walter Kerlinger, the chaplain and friend of the Emperor Charles IV, was appointed by Urban V inquisitor for Germany and granted vast privileges by the Emperor. It was upon central Germany that this man concentrated his efforts. In 1368 he conducted at Erfurt the trial of a leading Brother of the Free Spirit and soon afterwards he captured a group of more than forty heretics, male and female, at Nordhausen; Konrad Schmid seems to have been amongst the seven whom he burnt. Very soon Erfurt and Magdeburg were clear of heretical Beghards and Beguines. But when the Emperor announced that Kerlinger had exterminated all heresy in central Germany he was being unduly optimistic. As we have seen, a clandestine flagellant sect persisted there for another century; and it can hardly be a coincidence that as late as 1551 a sect called the Blood Friends, which showed all the essential characteristics of the Free Spirit, was discovered within thirty miles of Erfurt.

In 1372 Urban's successor Gregory XI observed that heretics who had fled from central Germany were taking refuge in the Rhine valley and the Low Countries and in the extreme north of Germany; and he urged the Emperor to ensure that the secular authorities in those areas should co-operate with the inquisitors in tracking down the fugitives. The Free Spirit does in fact seem to have reached north Germany by the end of the fourteenth century. About 1402 two 'apostles' were burnt in the Hansa towns of Lübeck and Wismar. If nothing else is known of the Brethren of the Free Spirit in the Baltic towns – whether because they really were few or because the Inquisition seldom pursued them so far – it is certain that in the Low Countries they remained numerous. In the late fourteenth century Holland was regarded, along with

Brabant and the Rhine valley, as an area where the heresy had struck particularly deep roots. When the preacher Gerhard Groot founded the religious but non-monastic community of the Brethren of Common Life – to which Thomas à Kempis was to give such lustre – one of his objects was to provide an outlet within the limits of orthodoxy for needs which had been seeking satisfaction in the heretical communities of the Free Spirit.

In Brabant the famous mystic, Ruusbroec 'the Admirable', saw much of the Brethren of the Free Spirit. A woman called Heilwijch Blomart (commonly known as Bloemardinne), the daughter of a rich merchant, won enormous prestige in Brussels as a living saint. Her following seems to have ranged from the highest circles of the aristocracy to the common people. It is said that when she died, in 1335, a silver chair she was accustomed to sit on was accepted as a legacy by a duchess, while crowds of cripples came to touch her body in the hope of miraculous cure. Bloemardinne taught some kind of mystical doctrine; and even if this did not originally amount to a manifestation of the Free Spirit, it became so in the hands of her disciples after her death. The struggle against these people inspired Ruusbroec's earliest writings, between 1335 and 1340, and among them his masterpiece, *The Spiritual Marriage*. He continued to attack the Brethren of the Free Spirit in book after book right up to his death in 1381, at the age of 88; and the accounts of the heretical mystics given by this mystic are amongst the most detailed and penetrating which we possess.

Brussels continued to harbour Brethren of the Free Spirit. In 1410 the Bishop of Cambrai appointed two inquisitors to extirpate what was still called 'Bloemardinne's heresy'; but they found themselves helpless in the face of the popular enthusiasm. Songs were sung after them in the streets and attempts were even made upon their lives. They were however able to unearth a particular heretical group; and in 1411 the bishop examined a monk named William of Hildernissen who was suspected of being one of its leaders. He was a man of noble birth who had had a successful career as a lecturer in theology in the Rhine valley and the Low Countries and had twice been prior of a friary. The degree of his complicity was not clear and he was sentenced only to some years of penance and reclusion. The enquiry revealed the existence of a secret community calling itself *Homines intelligentiae*; '*intelligentia*' being, in the terminology of medieval mysticism, that highest faculty of the soul, which makes mystical ecstasy possible. The community had been founded as a result of a revelation experienced by a certain Aegidius de Leeuwe, or Sanghers (latinized as Cantor), a layman who was descended from a distinguished Flemish family and who was already dead by the time of the investigation. The *Homines intelligentiae* included a number of women; and it is significant that William had to make a public recantation in the district of Brussels inhabited by the Beguines.

The activities of the Brethren of the Free Spirit in the Low Countries cannot be separated from their activities in the Rhine valley; as we have seen, Beghards passed backwards and forwards across this whole area. The same happened between the Low Countries and northern France; and in 1365 Pope Urban V thought it necessary to comment on the activities of French Beghards. The bishops and inquisititors were warned that these men were still, under a mask of holiness, disseminating their errors amongst simple people, and the Bishop of Paris was provided with full particulars of their way of life and the places where they were to be found. In 1372 certain male and female heretics who called themselves 'the Society of the Poor', but who were popularly known by the obscene nickname of Turlupins, were captured at Paris. Their leader was also a woman, Jeanne Dabenton. She was burnt; and so were the body of her male assistant, who had died in prison, and the writings and peculiar costumes of her followers. Nothing is known of the teachings of this group, but the name 'Turlupin' was normally given only to the Brethren of the Free Spirit. Certainly the Free Spirit was attracting attention in northern France at the end of the fourteenth and the beginning of the fifteenth centuries. Charlier de Gerson, the Chancellor of the University of Paris, was well qualified to judge, for he combined great intelligence and wide experience with a keen sympathy with mysticism. In a whole series of works written between 1395 and 1425 Gerson considers and condemns the false mysticism of the Turlupins and Beghards and Beguines who held the heresy of 'the Spirit of Liberty'. The beliefs and customs which he attributed to the French heretics are indistinguishable from those of their German counterparts. And indeed it was from Lille and Tournai that a band of forty enthusiasts in 1418 carried the doctrine of the Free Spirit right across Europe, to introduce it into a Bohemia on the brink of revolution and civil war – with consequences which will be considered in a later chapter.

A century later, in the midst of the turmoil of the Reformation, the Low Countries and northern France witnessed the spread of a doctrine which was called Spiritual Liberty but which in all essentials was still the old doctrine of the Free Spirit – and as horrifying to the Reformers as it was to their Catholic opponents. In 1525 an illiterate young slater of Antwerp called Loy Pruystinck, who had found a following amongst artisans and apprentices such as cloth-croppers and hosiers, sent a couple of emissaries to Wittenberg to meet Martin Luther. It was the very year when the Peasants' War was shaking the whole structure of German society and when Luther himself was raging against the millenarian *propheta* of the peasants, Thomas Müntzer. Luther was sufficiently impressed and shocked by his visitors to send a letter to the Lutheran party in Antwerp, warning them against the false prophet in their midst. But if Luther's warning and the vigilance of the Catholic Inquisition together impeded the growth of the movement, they could not permanently prevent it. A severe outbreak of plague in Antwerp in 1530 brought many new disciples. Amongst the poor Pruystinck's prestige was such that, it is said, they dropped on their knees at his approach; and the sect included many from the margins of society – thieves, prostitutes and beggars. But wealthy merchants and even the jeweller of the French king Francis I were to be found amongst the followers who contributed funds. All these people, however diverse their social status, were expected to fraternize and to embrace one another in public; while Pruystinck himself, as though to symbolize at once his vocation of poverty and his claim to a supreme dignity, dressed in robes cut as rags but also sewn with jewels. The sect had spread widely not only in Antwerp but all over Brabant and Flanders by the time that, in 1544, the secular authorities set about crushing it. In the end Pruystinck was burnt to death on a slow fire and five of his disciples were beheaded, while others fled to England.

If the little that is known of Pruystinck's doctrine hardly confirms the charges of antinomianism which were brought against him and his followers, the sect of Quintinists certainly does seem to have inherited all the anarchism of the medieval Brethren of the Free Spirit. The career of the tailor Quintin, who founded it, extended over almost exactly the same period as that of Pruystinck. A native of Hainaut, he too was first heard of in 1525, at Lille; a decade later, along with another tailor and an apostate priest, he had moved to Paris. There Calvin found these 'Quintinists' or 'Spiritual Libertines', as he called them, at work amongst the adherents of the reformed religion. He engaged them in public disputation and in 1539 denounced them in the revised version of his *Institutes of the Christian Religion.* Meanwhile the German Reformer Bucer, having met Spiritual Libertines at Strasbourg and observed their clandestine propaganda, wrote to Queen Marguerite of Navarre – who was keenly interested in mysticism – warning her not to be deceived by these people. The warning was much to the point, for in 1543 Quintin and three of his associates did in fact manage to find themselves places as domestic servants in the suite of the Queen, who accepted them as Christian mystics. Two years later Calvin himself was writing to Marguerite to enlighten her concerning the true nature of her *protégés*; and Quintin at least seems to have been dismissed from the court, for in 1547 he was back in his homeland. As a result of his attempt to seduce a number of respectable ladies of Tournai, he was discovered, tried and burnt.

Meanwhile the propaganda which Quintin and his disciples had been carrying on by means of clandestine preaching and of pamphlets had converted many in Tournai and Valenciennes – Calvin puts their number at 10,000! To counter these activities, the French Protestant community in Strasbourg sent one of their ministers to Tournai, where however he was caught by the Catholic authorities and burnt. More effective was the polemic which Calvin continued to conduct against the sect. In 1545 he produced his treatise *Contre la secte phantastique et furieuse des Libertins qui se nomment Spirituels*; and when in 1550 a former Franciscan who became the *protégé* of the good ladies of Rouen wrote in defence of the sect and its faith both Calvin and his collaborator Farel produced tracts in reply. The heresy then disappeared – or at least went underground – in those regions which for so long had been its stronghold; and this happened at the very same time as it finally collapsed in its other great stronghold in central Germany.

The above survey will suffice to show that the cult of the Free Spirit extended over a very wide area; but that is not the whole story. For reasons indicated in the Introduction, southern Europe is barely touched upon in this book; but in fact the Free Spirit flourished at various times both in Italy and in Spain. In 1307, at the very time when Marguerite Porete was active in northern France, one Bentivenga da Gubbio was proselytizing amongst the nuns of Umbria; he even tried to convert St Claro of Montefalco to the Free Spirit or – as it was called in Italy – the Spirit of Freedom. And later in the fourteenth century there are further references to the heresy as flourishing in Umbria and Tuscany – often, as in the north, in combination with the cult of voluntary poverty. By the 1340's Italian and Latin translations of Marguerite Porete's book were circulating in Italy; St Bernardino of Siena warned against them, while at Padua the ecclesiastical authorities exerted themselves to prevent their falling into the hands of monks. And in the following century, while Calvin was battling against the Spiritual Libertines in France, very similar doctrines were flourishing in Spain, amongst the mystics known as the Alumbrados.

To pursue these developments further lies outside the scope of this book. On the other hand, the brief reappearance of the Free Spirit in Cromwell's England can be studied in detail in the documents given in the Appendix.

The way to self-deification

The adepts of the Free Spirit did not form a single church but rather a number of likeminded groups, each with its own particular practices, rites and articles of belief; and the links between the various groups were often tenuous. But these people did keep in touch with one another; and the Free Spirit was at all times clearly recognizable as a quasi-religion with a single basic *corpus* of doctrine which was handed down from generation to generation. It is in the fourteenth century that this doctrine first emerges into full view; and the features which it showed then were to remain almost unmodified throughout the history of the movement.

The metaphysical framework was provided by Neo-Platonism; but all the efforts which had been made, from Pseudo-Dionysius and Erigena onwards, to adapt Neo-Platonism to Christian beliefs were discounted. The pantheism of Plotinus, so far from being slurred over, was emphasized. The Brethren of the Free Spirit did not hesitate to say: 'God is all that is', 'God is in every stone and in each limb of the human body as surely as in the Eucharistic bread', 'Every created thing is divine.' At the same time they took over Plotinus' own interpretation of this pantheism. It was the eternal essence of things, not their existence in time, that was truly God; whatever had a separate, transitory existence had emanated from God, but no longer was God. On the other hand whatever existed was bound to yearn for its Divine Origin and to strive to find its way back into that Origin; and at the end of time everything would in fact be reabsorbed into God. No emanation would remain, nothing would exist in separateness, there would no longer be anything capable of knowing, wishing, acting. All that would be left would be one single Essence, changeless, inactive: one all-embracing 'Blessedness'. Even the Persons of the Trinity, the Brethren of the Free Spirit insisted, would be submerged in that undifferentiated One. At the end of time, God really would be all.

Even now reabsorption was the fate of the human soul as soon as the body was dead. On the death of the body the soul disappeared into its Divine Origin like a drop of water which has been taken from a jug and then dropped back into it again, or like a drop of wine in the sea. This doctrine amounted of course to an assurance of a universal, though impersonal, salvation; and the more consistent of the Brethren of the Free Spirit did in fact hold that heaven and hell were merely states of the soul in this world and that there was no afterlife of punishment or reward. To have the Holy Spirit incarnated in oneself and to receive the revelation which that brought – that was to rise from the dead and to possess heaven. A man who had knowledge of the God within himself carried his own heaven about with him. One had only to recognize one's own divinity and one was resurrected as a Spiritual, a denizen of heaven on earth. To be ignorant of one's own divinity, on the other hand, was mortal sin, indeed it was the only sin. That was the meaning of hell; and that too was something which one carried with one in this life.

Plotinus had held that human beings could even experience something of this reabsorption before the death of the body. It was possible for the soul to escape from its sensual bonds and from its awareness of itself and to sink for a moment, motionless and unconscious, into the One. This was the aspect of Neo-Platonism which appealed to the Brethren of the Free Spirit. Although the Free Spirit has been traditionally known as 'the pantheistic heresy', many of the heretics showed little interest in or understanding of pantheist metaphysics. What they all had in common was a certain attitude to the human soul. 'The soul,' said one woman, 'is so vast that all the saints and angels would not fill it, so beautiful that the beauty of the saints and angels cannot approach it. It fills all things.' For the Brethren of the Free Spirit the soul was not merely destined to be reabsorbed into God on the death of the body; in its essence it had itself been divine from all eternity and was still potentially divine even whilst inhabiting a human body. In the words of the heretical treatise which was found in the hermit's cell near the Rhine: 'The divine essence is my essence and my essence is the divine essence. . . . From eternity man was God in God. . . . From eternity the soul of man was in God and is God. . . . Man was not begotten, but was from eternity wholly unbegettable; and as he could not be begotten, so he is wholly immortal.' It is in the light of this that one must interpret the recurring assertion of the heretics: 'Every rational creature is in its nature blessed.'

In practice however the Brethren of the Free Spirit were as convinced as any other sectarians that the highest spiritual privileges were reserved for their own fraternity. They divided humanity into two groups – the majority, the 'crude in spirit', who failed to develop their divine potentialities, and themselves, who were the 'subtle in spirit'. And they claimed that that total and permanent absorption into God which was possible for other mortals only after death, and which would be possible for the universe only at the end of time, was attained by the 'subtle in spirit' already during their lifetime on earth. This was far more than Plotinus had ever suggested. The heart of the heresy was in fact not a philosophical idea at all but an aspiration; it was a passionate desire of certain human beings to surpass the condition of humanity and to become God. The clergy who observed the heretics had no doubts on the matter. These men and women, they complained, set themselves above the saints, the angels, the Virgin and even Christ Himself. 'They say they are God by nature, without any distinction,' commented the Bishop of Strasbourg, 'they believe that all divine perfections are in them, that they are eternal and in eternity.' Ruusbroek makes his heretical opponent voice the highest possible claims:

It is the same with me as with Christ in every way and without any exception. Just like him, I am eternal life and wisdom, born of the Father in my divine nature; just like him, too, I am born in time and after the way of human beings; and so I am one with him, God and man. All that God has given him he has given me too, and to the same extent. .... Christ was sent into the active life to serve me, so that he could live and die for me; whereas I am sent into the contemplative life, which is far higher. .... If Christ had lived longer he would have attained the contemplative life which I have attained. All the honour which is given to Christ is really given to me and to all those who have attained this higher life. .... When his body is elevated at the altar during the sacrament, it is I who am lifted up; where his body is borne I am borne; for I am one flesh and blood with him, a single Person whom none can divide.

These accounts have often been regarded as polemical exaggerations, yet they are certainly quite objective. Many instances have been recorded of heretics saying that the Virgin and Christ had stopped short of the perfection required of the 'subtle in spirit'. And the adepts of the Free Spirit have themselves left very full accounts of their experiences. First came a period during which the novice practised various techniques, ranging from self-abnegation and self-torture to the cultivation of absolute passivity and indifference, designed to include the desired psychic condition. Then, after a training which might last for years, came the reward. 'The Spirit of Freedom or the Free Spirit,' said one adept, 'is attained when one is wholly transformed into God. This union is so complete that neither the Virgin Mary nor the angels are able to distinguish between man and God. In it one is restored to one's original state, before one flowed out of the Deity. One is illumined by that essential light beside which all created light is darkness and obfuscation. One can be, according to one's wish, Father or Son or Holy Spirit.' Such claims were in no way exceptional amongst the Brethren of the Free Spirit. An inmate of the House of Voluntary Poverty at Cologne affirmed that he was 'wholly liquefied in Eternity', united with God so that the angels could not distinguish between God and him. An inmate of the house at Schweidnitz insisted that she was God even as God himself was God; just like Christ, she was inseparable from God. The hermit's treatise says much the same: 'The perfect man is God. ... Because such a man is God, the Holy Spirit takes its essential being from him as though from God. ... The perfect man is more than a created being. ... He has attained that most intimate union which Christ had with the Father. ... He is God and man.' But it is the heretical tract known as *Schwester Katrei* that gives the fullest account of all. After a whole series of ecstasies in which her soul 'soared up' but after a time fell back again, Sister Catherine experiences one great ecstasy which releases her altogether from the limitations of human existence. She calls out to her confessor – himself clearly a Brother of the Free Spirit: 'Rejoice with me, I have become God!' 'Praise be to God!' he answers. 'Now leave all people, withdraw again into your state of oneness, for so you shall remain God.' The woman falls into a deep trance, from which she emerges with the assurance: 'I am made eternal in my eternal blessedness. Christ has made me his equal and I can never lose that condition.'

Such experiences differ vastly from the *unio mystica* as it was recognized and approved by the Church; for the *unio mystica* was a momentary illumination, granted only occasionally, perhaps but once in a lifetime. Whatever energies it might release and whatever assurance it might bestow, the human being who experienced it did not thereby shed his human condition; it was as an ordinary mortal that he had to live out his life on earth. The adept of the Free Spirit, on the other hand, felt himself to be utterly transformed; he had not merely been united with God, he was identical with God and would remain so for ever. And even this is an understatement, for often an adept would claim to have surpassed God. The women of Schweidnitz claimed that their souls had by their own efforts attained a perfection greater than they had possessed when they first emanated from God, and greater than God ever intended them to possess. They claimed to have such command over the Holy Trinity that they could 'ride it as in a saddle'. The Swabian heretics of 1270 said that they had mounted up above God and, reaching the very pinnacle of divinity, abandoned God. Often the adept would affirm that he or she 'had no longer any need of God'.

Naturally enough, the attainment of divinity implied the acquisition of prodigious miracle-working powers. Some of the Brethren of the Free Spirit believed that they had received the gift of prophecy, that they knew all things in heaven and earth, that they could perform miracles – cross water dryshod, walk a yard above the ground. But for most of them such claims were too petty, for they felt themselves to be quite literally omnipotent. 'They say,' remarked the Bishop of Strasbourg, 'that they created all things, that they created more than God.' The mystic Ruusbroec makes his heretical counterpart speak as follows:

When I dwelt in my original being and in my eternal essence there was no God for me. What I was I wished to be, and what I wished to be I was. It is by my own free will that I have emerged and become what I am. If I wished I need not have become anything and I would not now be a creature. For God can know, wish, do nothing without me. With God I have created myself and I have created all things, and it is my hand that supports heaven and earth and all creatures. . . . Without me nothing exists.

Once more any doubts one might feel about these accounts are dispelled by the heretics themselves. 'When God created all things I created all things with him. . . . I am more than God,' said one woman at Schweidnitz. And the hermit's treatise summarizes in a phrase the fusion of absolute passivity with absolute creative power: 'The perfect man is the motionless Cause.'

The doctrine of mystical anarchism

From the standpoint of depth-psychology it could be said that all mystics start their psychic adventure with a profound introversion, in the course of which they live through as adults a reactivation of the distorting phantasies of infancy. Thereafter, however, two courses are possible. It can happen that a mystic emerges from his or her experience of introversion – like a patient from a successful psychoanalysis – as a more integrated personality, with a widened range of sympathy and freer from illusions about himself and his fellow human beings. But it can also happen that the mystic introjects the gigantic parental images in their omnipotent, most aggressive and wanton aspects and emerges as a nihilistic megalomaniac. This last was the case with many adepts of the Free Spirit.

In this connection it is instructive to glance at the strange figure of Jean-Antoine Boullan (1824–93), who founded a sect which is said to have had at one time some 600,000 members, chiefly in eastern Europe. This man regarded himself as 'the sword of God', charged with the task of cleansing the earth of that impurity, the Church of Rome, and of saving mankind in the Last Days. He pronounced furious judgements on the clergy, whom he regarded as his persecutors. Himself wildly impulsive in his sexual behaviour, he taught his followers to practise a 'mystical marriage', which enabled them to indulge in sexual promiscuity without 'original sin'. He had a great taste for luxurious living; and in order to obtain money he hoodwinked the credulous by means of supposed supernatural revelations. At the same time much of the money he procured he distributed again to the poor. In all his doings he behaved like a typical if belated adept of the Free Spirit. Now psychiatric and graphological studies of Boullan, published in 1948, show him as a typical paranoiac, obsessed by delusions of grandeur and of persecution; intelligent, audacious, full of vitality and initiative; a personality driven by frantic and insatiable cravings, to gratify which he would deploy now the subtlest technique of dissimulation, now a ruthlessness which would trample underfoot anyone weaker than himself. It is an interpretation which fits perfectly with all that we know of the medieval Brethren of the Free Spirit and of their successors the Spiritual Libertines.

In a sketch written about 1330 in the chief stronghold of the heresy, Cologne, the Catholic mystic Suso evokes with admirable terseness those qualities in the Free Spirit which made it essentially anarchic. He describes how on a bright Sunday, as he was sitting lost in meditation, an incorporeal image appeared to his spirit. Suso addresses the image: 'Whence have you come?' The image answers: 'I come from nowhere.' – 'Tell me, what are you?' – 'I am not.' – 'What do you wish?' – 'I do not wish.' – 'This is a miracle! Tell me, what is your name?' – 'I am called Nameless Wildness.' 'Where does your insight lead to?' – 'Into untrammelled freedom.' – 'Tell me, what do you call untrammelled freedom?' – 'When a man lives according to all his caprices without distinguishing between God and himself, and without looking before or after . . .'

What distinguished the adepts of the Free Spirit from all other medieval sectarians was, precisely, their total amoralism. For them the proof of salvation was to know nothing of conscience or remorse. Innumerable pronouncements of theirs bear witness to this attitude: 'He who attributes to himself anything that he does, and does not attribute it all to God, is in ignorance, which is hell. ... Nothing in a man's works is his own.' And again: 'He who recognizes that God does all things in him, he shall not sin. For he must not attribute to himself, but to God, all that he does.' – 'A man who has a conscience is himself Devil and hell and purgatory, tormenting himself. He who is free in spirit escapes from all these things.' – 'Nothing is sin except what is thought of as sin.' – 'One can be so united with God that whatever one may do one cannot sin.' – 'I belong to the Liberty of Nature, and all that my nature desires I satisfy. . . . I am a natural man.' – 'The free man is quite right to do whatever gives him pleasure.' These sayings are typical and their implication is unmistakable. Every act performed by a member of this elite was felt to be performed 'not in time but in eternity'; it possessed a vast mystical significance and its value was infinite. This was the secret wisdom which one adept revealed to a somewhat perplexed inquisitor with the assurance that it was 'drawn from the innermost depths of the Divine Abyss' and worth far more than all the gold in the municipal treasury of Erfurt. 'It would be better,' he added, 'that the whole world should be destroyed and perish utterly than that a "free man" should refrain from one act to which his nature moves him.'

After twenty-two years of penance Heinrich Suso received a command from God to throw away his scourge and other instruments of torture and to abandon asceticism for ever. The new adept of the Free Spirit went much further than that. Reborn into a state where conscience ceased to operate and sin was abolished, he felt like some infinitely privileged aristocrat. The strength which had been consumed in the ascetic exercises of the noviciate had now to be restored. Vigils were at an end, it was right to sleep in a soft bed. There was no more fasting; henceforth the body must be nourished on the finest meats and wines, and to feast was of greater spiritual value than to partake of the Eucharist. A golden goblet was now a more appropriate gift than a crust of bread. The outward bearing and appearance of the heretic also changed. Sometimes the cowl of the Beghard or Beguine continued to be worn, but nothing more is heard of patched or scanty clothing. At Schweidnitz the adepts helped themselves to whatever clothes the novice brought with her, and wore fine dresses beneath their hooded robes. As soon as Sister Catherine 'became God' she was told by her confessor to put on a 'soft shift' and 'noble clothes', and sometimes the Brethren of the Free Spirit did in fact dress as nobles. In the Middle Ages, when dress was normally a clear and reliable guide to social status, such behaviour naturally caused confusion and resentment. 'They have no uniform,' complains one cleric. 'Sometimes they dress in a costly and dissolute fashion, sometimes most miserably, all according to the time and place. Believing themselves to be impeccable, they really think that for them every kind of dress is permissible.' By adopting noble robes in place of the beggar's rags a heretic symbolized his transformation from the 'lowest of mortals' into a member of an elite which believed itself entitled to dominate the world.

For it should not be thought that the adepts of the Free Spirit lived in a state of more or less permanent seclusion and contemplation. They moved about the world and had dealings with other people. These dealings were however of a peculair kind, for the capacity to 'become God' certainly did lead to a rejection of all normal social relations. The social doctrine of the Free Spirit has been little understood; yet the texts are there to illustrate it and they are unanimous. There exists a description, written in mid-fourteenth century and probably based on direct observation, of a Beguine reciting her catechism to the heretical Beghard who is her spiritual director:

When a man has truly reached the great and high knowledge he is no longer bound to observe any law or any command, for he has become one with God. God created all things to serve such a person, and all that God ever created is the property of such a man. . . . He shall take from all creatures as much as his nature desires and craves, and shall have no scruples of conscience about it, for all created things are his property. . . . A man whom all heaven serves, all people and creatures are indeed obliged to serve and to obey; and if any disobeys, it alone is guilty.

The surviving heretical literature confirms all this. Of 'the perfect man who is both God and man' the hermit's treatise says: 'All things that exist belong to him.' *Schwester Katrei* sets the social doctrine of the Free Spirit against its Neo-Platonic background. All things, the argument runs, use others: the deer uses grass, the fish water, the bird air. So the person who has 'become God' must use all created things; for by doing so, he or she 'drives all things up to their first Origin'. The advice which Sister Catherine receives immediately after her apotheosis is conceived in the same terms: 'You shall order all created beings to serve you according to your will, for the glory of God. . . . You shall bear all things up to God. If you want to use all created beings, you have the right to do so; for every creature that you use, you drive up into its Origin.'

As in the earliest days of the movement, one expression of this attitude was still a promiscuous and mystically coloured eroticism. According to one adept, just as cattle were created for the use of human beings, so women were created to be used by the Brethren of the Free Spirit. Indeed by such intimacy a woman became chaster than before, so that if she had previously lost her virginity she now regained it. From the Swabian heretics in the thirteenth century down to the Ranters in the seventeenth the same view is expressed again and again: for the 'subtle in spirit' sexual intercourse cannot under any circumstances be sinful. And it was held that one of the surest marks of the 'subtle in spirit' was, precisely, the ability to indulge in promiscuity without fear of God or qualms of conscience. Some adepts attributed a transcendental, quasi-mystical value to the sexual act itself, when it was performed by such as they. The *Homines intelligentiae* called the act 'the delight of Paradise' and 'the acclivity' (which was the term used for the ascent to mystical ecstasy); and the Thuringian 'Blood Friends' of 1550 regarded it as a sacrament, which they called 'Christerie'. For all alike adultery possessed a symbolic value as an affirmation of emancipation. As the Ranter Clarkson put it, 'till acted that so-called sin, thou art not delivered from the power of sin'.

In this context the Adam-cult which is frequently found amongst the adepts of the Free Spirit becomes perfectly comprehensible. One can probably discount the chroniclers' claim that this cult involved communal sexual orgies. From the days of the early Church onwards such tales have been told for the purpose of discrediting minority groups and there is nothing in the extant documents to suggest that even when told of adepts of the Free Spirit they were justified. On the other hand the adepts did at times practise ritual nakedness, just as they did at times indulge in sexual promiscuity; and there is no doubt that in both cases they were asserting – as one inquisitor put it – that they were restored to the state of innocence which had existed before the Fall. That acute commentator Charlier de Gerson saw the connection perfectly clearly. He noted that the 'Turlupins' were often naked together, saying that one ought not to blush at anything that was natural. To be naked and unashamed, like Adam and Eve, they regarded as an essential part of the state of perfection on earth; and they called this 'the state of innocence'. Similarly the leader of the *Homines intelligentiae* claimed to have a special way of performing the sexual act which was that practised by Adam and Eve in the Garden of Eden. The same man set himself up as the Saviour whose mission it was to inaugurate the Third and Last Age; and he was certainly not the only adept to fuse these originally disparate phantasies. In 1381 an adept at Eichstätt proclaimed himself as a Second Adam who, replacing Christ, was establishing the Third and Last Age in the form of an earthly Paradise which would last until it was bodily lifted up to heaven. The Spiritual Libertines whom Calvin denounced declared that they had found the way back to the state enjoyed by Adam before he had tasted of the knowledge of good and evil – and also that they were living in the Last Days, in which the Christian dispensation was to be replaced by a new and higher one. In fact one can already recognize in this medieval heresy that blend of millenarianism and primitivism which has become one of the commoner forms of modern romanticism. In the Adam-cult the lost Paradise was recreated and at the same time the advent of the Millennium was affirmed. Primitive innocence and blessedness were restored to the world by living gods in whom Creation was felt to have attained its perfection and to be transcended.

If the bliss of the new Paradise was enjoyed to the full only by the adepts, certain others could at least taste of it. Below the adepts, the 'living gods', there existed a more numerous class of men and women who were fully initiated into the secret of the Free Spirit. These people were themselves ecstatics, but they had not been through the decisive experience which transformed a human being into God. Instead, they enjoyed a vicarious super-humanity through their special relationship with the adept. What that relationship was is clear enough. After 'becoming God', a new adept began to seek contact with pious souls who wished to 'attain perfection'. From these he exacted an oath of blind obedience, which was made on bended knees. This oath was regarded as annulling all vows previously made, including those of marriage. It was of such men and women that Charlier de Gerson said they gave a promise of absolute obedience to a human being and received in return an assurance that they could do no sin. These were the people who formed and made up the rank-and-file of the movement of the Free Spirit.

The relationship that existed between adept and disciple is strikingly illustrated in the confession of the renegade monk Martin of Mainz, who was tried at Cologne in 1393 and burnt as an impenitent heretic. This man, who had been disseminating the heresy of the Free Spirit in the Rhine valley, was a disciple of the celebrated heresiarch Nicholas of Basle, who claimed to be a new Christ. In Martin's view there was only one path to salvation and that lay through making an act of absolute submission to his master. That act was a terrible experience; but once it was made it brought immense privileges. For Nicholas was the sole true source of understanding and authority. He could interpret the Gospels as not even the Apostles had been able to interpret them, and if a Master of Theology wished to progress spiritually he had but to put the Scriptures on one side and make the act of sub-mission. Nicholas alone had the right to ordain a priest. With his sanction one could preach and celebrate Mass. Because it lacked that sanction the whole Catholic hierarchy was unable to perform one valid act. But above all, if one followed Nicholas' orders one would not sin. One could commit fornication or murder without a qualm if he ordered it. The only sin would be to disobey or deny him. At the moment when one made the act of submission to him one 'entered the state of primal innocence'.

Between the closed community of the Free Spirit and the mass of unredeemed humanity lay an immeasurable and impassable gulf. Of an ordinary mortal the adepts 'took no account, no more than of a horse'; in their eyes mankind in general existed only to be exploited by themselves, 'the mortified Elect'. Hence the blithe dishonesty which, century after century, was noted as being peculiarly characteristic of these above all other sectarians. Calvin still observed that it was one of the main articles of their faith that an adept must simulate whatever role would gain him most influence. And there is no doubt that these people really did develop an extraordinary skill in lying and pretence, which they deployed not only to protect themselves against their enemies the clergy but to worm their way into the favour of simple souls.

Curiously enough, it was the same conviction of their infinite superiority which first turned the adepts of the Free Spirit into bearers of a revolutionary social doctrine. By the fourteenth century some of them at least had decided that the state of innocence could take no cognisance of the institution of private property. In 1317 the Bishop of Strasbourg commented: 'They believe that all things are common, whence they conclude that theft is lawful for them.' It was in fact quite normal for an adept to regard all things as his property. The point was made clearly enough by Johann Hartmann, an adept who was captured at Erfurt at the same time as the flagellant messiah Konrad Schmid: 'The truly free man is king and lord of all creatures. All things belong to him, and he has the right to use whatever pleases him. If anyone tries to prevent him, the free man may kill him and take his goods.' John of Brünn, an adept who lived in the House of Voluntary Poverty at Cologne, was even more explicit. God, he said, was 'free' and had therefore created all things 'in common'. In practice this meant that all things were there to be shared amongst the 'free in spirit'. If anyone possessed an abundance of food, he explained, that was so that he might minister to the needs of the Brethren of the Free Spirit. An adept of the Free Spirit was free to eat in a tavern and then refuse to pay; if the tavern-keeper asked for money he should be beaten. Food given free to an adept was 'transmitted to Eternity'. This view was generally held amongst the Brethren of the Free Spirit; and what was said of food was said equally of money. Whatever money was spent by an adept of the Free Spirit was 'transmitted to Eternity', or to 'the supreme degree of poverty'. According to John of Brünn, if an adept found money on the road, that was a sign that God wished him to spend it with his brethren. He had therefore to keep it for that purpose, even if its owner claimed it and tried to take it back by violence. If the owner or even the adept himself was killed in the struggle, that was no matter; for a soul returned to its Origin. But if the money was surrendered the adept would have retreated 'from the eternal to the temporal'. When, as an act of charity, an adept helped a sick man, he would ask for alms; and if they were refused he was free to take money by force, and need have no scruple even if the man died of hunger as a result. Cheating, theft, robbery with violence were all justified. John admitted having committed them all and said that they were normal amongst some two hundred Beghards of his acquaintance; and there is evidence that these were in fact common practices amongst the Brethren of the Free Spirit. 'Whatever the eye sees and covets, let the hand grasp it', was one of their sayings.

This attitude persisted right down to the sixteenth and seventeenth centuries. The Spiritual Libertines are described by Calvin as holding that nobody should possess anything of his own but that each should take whatever he could lay hands on. If all this had been merely a justification of theft it would have been of little importance, for professional thieves need no doctrine and other people would have been unmoved. But in fact what the adepts of the Free Spirit had to say about private property had far wider implications. 'Give, give, give, give up your houses, horses, goods, lands, give up, account nothing your own, have all things common . . .' The cry of the Ranter Abiezer Coppe echoes the cry of John of Brünn three centuries earlier: 'All things which God created are common!' The full force of these phrases becomes apparent when they are recognized as carrying on a particular tradition of social criticism which was not only very radical but – as we shall see – was already very old.

The above account of the self-deification and mystical anarchism of the adepts of the Free Spirit was written several years before the text of Marguerite Porete's *Mirouer des simples ames* was published by Professor Guarnieri. As this is the only complete work by a medieval adept known to have survived, some account of it is called for, even at the risk of a certain repetitiveness.

The book is obviously an esoteric work; as the author herself says, its language is not intended to be understood by those crude mortals who live according to the dictates of reason. It was written as a manual of instruction, to be read aloud to groups of would-be adepts of the Free Spirit; and its theme is the ascent of the soul towards total freedom.

The soul progresses through seven stages. The first three are devoted to ascetic self-denial and obedience; after which, in the fourth stage, the soul attains a condition of exultation, in which it is blinded by the radiant light of Love. But though the soul may believe that it has already attained union with God, it is still only at the beginning of its ascent. In the fifth stage it recognizes its own sinfulness, and the immense gulf that still separates it from that perfect goodness which is God; and at that point God, in an overwhelming flood of love and light, sweeps it into himself, so that the soul's will becomes at one with the divine will.

So far, nothing distinguishes this ascent from that known to orthodox mystics. But at the sixth stage divergence begins: the soul is annihilated in the Deity, to the point that nothing exists any more save God. Now the soul sees nothing but itself, which is God; while God sees his divine majesty in that soul. This total identification of the soul with God lies quite outside the experience of Catholic mystics; and so does the seventh and last stage of the ascent, where the soul rejoices permanently, while still on this earth, in the glory and blessedness which orthodox theology reserves for heaven.

This deification of the soul is possible because the soul has existed in God from all eternity. The soul is one with God, as the flame is one with the fire; it comes from God and returns to God as a drop of water comes from and returns to the sea. Indeed God is everything that is; so that in being annihilated in God the soul is reintegrated into its true and original being.

It is also reintegrated into that primal state of innocence enjoyed by Adam before the Fall. Thereby it is liberated from the consequences of Original Sin and becomes sinless. Moreover it becomes incapable of sin; for 'this soul has no will but the will of God, who makes it will what it ought to will.' And this in turn means that it is free to do whatever pleases it. The adepts therefore 'do nothing but what pleases them; or if they do, they deprive themselves of peace, freedom and nobility. For the soul is not perfected until it does what it pleases, and is not reproached for taking its pleasure.' Since Love, i.e. God, has taken up residence in the soul, he takes charge of all things and all deeds; so the soul can experience no unease and no remorse. Whatever external acts are done, they are the work of God, operating in the soul.

Exalted beyond the limits of humanity, the soul passes into a state of total indifference, in which it cares for nothing – not for other human beings, not even for God. It does not even care about its own salvation: 'Such souls cannot see themselves as good or evil, they are not conscious of themselves, they cannot judge whether they are converted or perverted.' To concern oneself with such matters would be to fall back into self-will and to lose one's freedom.

Since salvation has become a matter of indifference, the aids to salvation offered or recommended by Christ are also matters of indifference. Neither the sacraments, nor preaching, nor asceticism, nor meditation have any value; and the intercession of the Virgin and the saints has become meaningless. Indeed, the deified soul has no need even of God himself. Once the absolute stillness of the divine Oneness has been reached, neither knowledge nor praise nor even the love of God exist any more. 'At the highest point of being, God himself is abandoned by himself in himself'; meaning that the God of Christianity is left behind, in favour of the God of pantheistic ecstasy.

And towards terrestrial matters, too, the deified soul feels only profound indifference. 'This soul feels no pain for any sin it may ever have committed, nor for the suffering which God suffered for that soul, nor for the sin and pain in which its neighbours still remain.' 'The thoughts of such souls are so divine that they never concern themselves with past things or things that have been created.' At the same time, such souls are free to use all created things for their own purposes: 'Why should such souls have qualms about taking what they need, when necessity demands it? That would be a lack of innocence and a hindrance to that peace in which the soul rests from all things.... Such souls use all things that are made and created, and which nature requires, with such peace of mind as they use the earth they walk on.'

All in all, then, Marguerite Porete's book confirms our view of the Free Spirit; an interpretation which originally had to be constructed step by step from a variety of more or less defective sources is shown to have been substantially correct. As Marguerite repeatedly stresses, she is addressing an elite only – those whom she calls 'the great Church', as distinct from 'the little Church' which is the institutionalized Church of Rome. But to this elite she does indeed preach a doctrine of self-deification and of mystical anarchism.

Only on two points does Marguerite's teaching differ from that attributed to, say, Johann Hartmann or John of Brünn or Calvin's Spiritual Libertines. Marguerite nowhere suggests that the deified soul – or as we would say, the adept of the Free Spirit – would or should indulge in what were commonly regarded as sins, such as theft or sexual promiscuity; and save by implication she says nothing, either, about community of goods. There is nothing surprising in this. If one examines the Ranter material in the Appendix to the present book one finds that while all these writers shared much the same mystical doctrine, they differed in the practical conclusions which they drew from it.

The following chapters will in any case show what revolutionary and anarchic potentialities were contained in some aspects of the doctrine of the Free Spirit.

10 The Egalitarian State of Nature

In the thought of Antiquity

Like the other phantasies which have gone to make up the revolutionary eschatology of Europe, egalitarian and communistic phantasies can be traced back to the ancient world. It was from the Greeks and Romans that medieval Europe inherited the notion of the 'State of Nature' as a state of affairs in which all men were equal in status and wealth and in which nobody was oppressed or exploited by anyone else; a state of affairs characterized by universal good faith and brotherly love and also, sometimes, by total community of property and even of spouses.

In both Greek and Latin literature the State of Nature is represented as having existed on earth in some long-lost Golden Age or 'Reign of Saturn'. The version of the myth in Ovid's *Metamorphoses* was to be repeatedly echoed in later literature and to exercise considerable influence upon communistic speculation during the Middle Ages. According to Ovid, at the beginning of human history, in that first Golden Age before Saturn had been deposed by Jupiter, 'men used to cultivate good faith and virtue spontaneously, without laws. Punishment and fear did not exist, nor were threatening phrases to be read from fixed bronze tablets. . . . Earth herself, untroubled and untouched by the hoe, unwounded by any ploughshare, used to give all things of her own accord . . .' But the day was to come when 'shame and truth and good faith fled away; and in their place came deceit and guilt and plots and violence and the wicked lust for possession. . . . And the wary surveyor marked out with long boundary-lines the earth which hitherto had been a common possession like the sunshine and the breezes. . . . Now pernicious iron was produced, and gold that is still more pernicious than iron; and these produced war. . . . Men live from plunder . . .'

Saturn was sometimes shown – by Virgil, for instance – as taking refuge in Italy after his deposition from the Olympian throne and as establishing a local Golden Age on Italian soil. A contemporary of Ovid's whose work was also very familiar to medieval scholars, the historian Gnaeus Pompeius Trogus, gives an illuminating account of that blessed reign and of the annual festival by which it was commemorated:

The first inhabitants of Italy were Aborigines. Their king, Saturn, is said to have been so just that under his rule nobody was a slave and nobody had any private property either; but all things were held by all in common and without division, as though there were one single inheritance for all men. In memory of that example it was decreed that during the Saturnalia all should be given equal rights, so that at banquets slaves sit down with their masters, without any discrimination.

As presented by the satirist Lucian, in the second century A.D., the import of the myth is still more emphatically egalitarian. Addressing the god of the Golden Age Lucian remarks:

Now I hear poets tell that in the old days, when you were king, things were otherwise in this world; earth bearing its fruits for men without being sown or ploughed – for each man a meal all prepared, and more than enough of it; rivers flowing with wine, and others with milk, and others again with honey. And most important of all, they say that at that time people themselves were of gold; poverty never approached them. Whereas we are hardly even men of lead, but rather of some still meaner metal; most of us eating our crust of bread in the sweat of our brow; forever saddled with poverty and want and helplessness, crying out 'Alas!' and 'Oh, what a fate!' – that is how we poor men live. And believe me, all this would be less galling to us if only we did not see the rich enjoying such a good time – with so much gold and silver in their coffers, and so many garments and slaves and carriages and estates and farms; having such abundance of all these things, and then not deigning even to cast a glance at us, the many, let alone share anything with us.

The egalitarian State of Nature provided a theme for philosophical speculation as well as for *belles-lettres*; and it was in philosophical even more than in literary guise that the notion was to influence medieval political theory. Already in the third century B.C. the Greek Stoics were vigorously affirming that all men were brothers and moreover that all were by nature free and equal. The founder of the Old Stoa, Zeno himself, seems to have inaugurated his teaching by describing an ideal world-society in which men would live like a vast flock of sheep in a single, communal pasturage. Differences of race and of political loyalty, perhaps also of status and of individual temperament were to disappear and all men were to be united in total community of feeling and will. Moreover Stoic religion, which derived largely from Chaldean astrology and centred on the worship of the heavenly bodies, soon allotted a position of unique importance to the sun-god, who was celebrated as pre-eminently generous, benevolent and above all equitable. In the universal diffusion of light by the sun some Stoics saw the supreme example of social justice and even of community of goods – an idea which soon became and long remained a commonplace in the rhetoric of egalitarianism.

Two works which seem to have been written under strong Stoic influence – one probably in the second century B.C. and the other probably in the second century A.D. – illustrate most vividly the kind of egalitarian phantasy which the ancient world was to bequeath to the Middle Ages. The earlier of the two is a description of the Isles of the Blessed which survives only in the summary given by the Greek historian Diodorus Siculus in his *Historical Library* – in which form it was edited and translated as a separate work dozens of times during the Renaissance. The seven islands are dedicated to the sun and are inhabited by the Heliopolitans, or sun-men. Each day throughout the year the sun passes immediately over the islands, with the result that the days are always exactly as long as the nights, the climate is invariably perfect and the season invariably summer, abounding in fruit and flowers. The population of each island is divided into four tribes, each 400 strong. All citizens have the same perfectly healthy constitution and the same perfectly beautiful features. Each takes his turn to perform every necessary task as hunter or fisherman or in the service of the state. All land, livestock and tools are thus used in turn by every citizen and therefore belong to nobody in particular. Marriage is unknown and sexual promiscuity complete; the tribe is responsible for bringing up the children, and this is done in such a way that mothers cannot recognize their own. The consequent lack of heirs removes any cause for competition or rivalry; and the Law of Nature, operating in undistorted souls, produces amongst these people a complete and unfailing concord. And indeed in so equitable an order dissension is inconceivable. Even in their expectation of life the Heliopolitans are all equal, for all die voluntarily and peacefully while at the height of their powers, at the age of 150.

The other work too is known only through extracts preserved by a later writer. Clement of Alexandria, in the course of attacking the Gnostic heresies which he saw proliferating around him, gave considerable attention to some sectarians whom he called Carpocratians and to whose founder he attributed a Greek treatise called *On Justice*. Recent research makes it seem improbable that Gnostics were responsible for the treatise. There is however no reason to doubt either that the treatise itself existed or that Clement's quotations from it are accurate. Once again one finds a doctrine of absolute egalitarianism supported by the example of the impartially beneficent sun. For according to this treatise, God's justice is 'community in equality'. The heavens envelop the earth equally on all sides and night displays all stars equally. By God's decree the sun shines with the same splendour for rich and poor, for the ruler and his people, for the ignorant and the wise, for men and women, for free men and slaves, for animals of all kinds, good and bad alike: none can take more than his share of light or rob his neighbour of it. God has also bestowed the gift of sight on all alike, without distinction or discrimination, to be enjoyed in equality and community. And he has seen to it that the sun shall produce food for all animals alike; food too is to be enjoyed by all equally and in common.

In these ways God has established beyond all question what he means by justice. And it was originally his will that the same principle should apply to all things – to the earth and its fruits and to goods of every kind. God made the vine and grain and all other fruits for the benefit of all; and at first they offered themselves freely to every sparrow and to every passer-by. But man-made laws have undermined the divine law and destroyed the communal order in which it was expressed. It was these human laws which created the distinction between Mine and Thine, so that things which by right belong to all can now no longer be enjoyed in common. And it was this violation of community and equality which gave rise to theft and to all crime. Moreover God intended men and women to mate as freely as animals still do; in this sphere too community and equality have been ordained by divine justice and destroyed by human beings themselves.

In contrast with some of the Greeks, the Roman Stoics – as might be expected – had no interest in making propaganda for egalitarianism; but even they agreed that once, in a Golden Age long ago, men had lived together in a state of equality. The most comprehensive version of their teaching on the subject is given by Seneca in a number of passages, of which the following is a fair example:

[Those were] happy times, when the bounties of nature were there to be used indiscriminately by all, before avarice and the craving for luxury brought division amongst men, so that they turned from fellowship to robbing one another. . . . Indeed there is no condition of mankind that anybody would value more; and if God were to allow one to make earthly beings and to lay down customs for the peoples, one would attempt nothing else than what is told of that age when 'no labourers ploughed up the soil, nobody was allowed to mark out or divide the ground; when men put everything into a common store, and the earth bore all things more freely because none demanded it.' What could be happier than that race of men? All that nature produced they enjoyed in common. So nature sufficed as the mother and guardian of all men, and all were secure in the possession of the public wealth. Why should I not call that the richest race of men, where there was no poor man to be found? But Avarice invaded that best of possible arrangements and, while aiming at appropriating things and claiming them for herself, ended by making all things the property of others and reducing herself from infinite wealth to penury. Avarice caused poverty and, by desiring many things, forfeited all. Now Avarice may strive to get back what she has lost, she may add fields to fields, drive out her neighbour by money or by force, expand her estates until they are the size of provinces, pretend that long travelling through her lands is the same as owning them – no extension of boundaries leads back to what we have forsaken. When we have done everything, we shall possess much; but once we possessed the whole world. The very earth was more fertile when unploughed, and ample for the needs of peoples who did not snatch it from one another. Whatever nature brought forth, the pleasure which men took in finding it was no greater than their pleasure in showing others what they had found. Nobody could have either more or less than anybody else; all things were shared out by common agreement. The stronger had not yet got his hands on the weaker; the miser had not yet, by hiding away his wealth, denied others the very necessities of life. Each took as much care of his neighbour as of himself ...

But – and this was central to his whole argument – Seneca was convinced that the old egalitarian order was not only lost but necessarily lost. As time passed, men had become vicious; and once that happened, institutions such as private property, coercive government, differentiation of status, even slavery were not only inevitable but also needful; not only consequences of but also remedies for the corruption of human nature. And it was in this form, and saddled with these qualifications, that the notion of the primal egalitarian State of Nature was adopted by the Fathers and incorporated into the political theory of the Church.

In patristic and medieval thought

At least by the third century A.D. Christian doctrine had assimilated from the extraordinarily influential philosophy of Stoicism the notion of an egalitarian State of Nature which was irrecoverably lost. And although it was hardly possible to talk of social and economic organization of the Garden of Eden, orthodox theologians nevertheless managed to use the Graeco-Roman myth to illustrate the dogma of the Fall.

At the centre of this theory of society stands the distinction between the State of Nature, which was based on Natural Law and expressed directly the divine intention, and the conventional state, which has grown out of and is sanctioned by custom. It was agreed by most of the later Fathers that inequality, slavery, coercive government and even private property had no part in the original intention of God and had come into being only as a result of the Fall. Once the Fall had taken place, on the other hand, a development began which made such institutions indispensable. Corrupted by Original Sin, human nature demanded restraints which would not be found in an egalitarian order; inequalities of wealth, status and power were thus not only consequences of but also remedies for sin. The only recommendations which could be authorized by such a view were recommendations directed towards individuals and dealing solely with problems of personal conduct. That a master ought to behave fairly and reasonably towards his slave, who is as dear to God as he is himself; that the rich have a moral obligation to give alms liberally; that a rich man who uses his wealth for evil purposes forfeits his right to it – such were the practical conclusions which were drawn, within the limits of orthodoxy, from the doctrine of the primal egalitarian State of Nature. They were important conclusions and they influenced life in Christendom in many ways; but they neither produced nor were intended to produce a society without rich and poor, let alone without private property.

And nevertheless it was above all the teaching of the Church which perpetuated the idea that the 'natural' society was an egalitarian one. Many of the Fathers elaborated at great length the theme of the primitive equality of human nature, and they did so particularly in their discussions of the institution of slavery. The Church accepted slavery and urged upon slaves the duty of obedience and submission even to harsh masters; but that did not prevent, for instance, the influential fourth-century theologian known as 'Ambrosiaster' from reminding masters in their turn that God made not slaves and free men, but all men free. In St Augustine's *City of God* the same point is made with the utmost clarity:

This the order of nature has prescribed and thus God has created man. For he said: 'Let them have dominion over the fish of the seas, and over the fowl of the air, and over every creeping thing that creepeth upon the earth.' Having made man in his own image, a rational being, he meant him to be lord only over irrational beings; not man set over man, but man set over beasts. . . . The first cause of servitude is sin, by which man is subjected to man by the bonds of his condition. . . . But by that nature in which God formerly created man nobody is slave either to man or to sin.

Despite the fact that the Church itself came to have vast numbers of serfs, the view expressed by St Augustine remained the orthodox one throughout the Middle Ages. It was also to be the judgement of the secular feudal lawyers. The opinion of the famous French jurist Beaumanoir, in the thirteenth century, can be taken as representing the normal opinion of medieval thinkers: 'Although there now exist several estates of men, it is true that in the beginning all were free and of the same freedom; for everyone knows that we are all descended from one father and one mother ...'

Most curious is the way in which Catholic doctrine incorporated and conserved the idea that all things on earth ought to belong to all human beings communally. In the third century we find the stock phrases of the Stoics being repeated by St Cyprian. God's gifts, he points out, are given to all mankind. The day brings light to all, the sun shines upon all, the rain falls and the wind blows for all, the splendour of the stars and the moon are common property. Such is the impartial beneficence of God; and a man who would imitate God's justice should share all his belongings with his fellow-Christians. By the second half of the fourth century this view had won wide acceptance amongst Christian writers. We find St Zeno of Verona repeating the comparison, which had become a commonplace: ideally all goods ought to be in common 'like the day, the sun, the night, the rain, being born and dying – things which divine justice bestows equally on all mankind without distinction of persons'. More striking still are certain pronouncements of the great Bishop of Milan, St Ambrose, in which the tradition once formulated by Seneca finds most vigorous expression: 'Nature has poured forth all things for all men, to be held in common. For God commanded all things to be produced so that food should be common to all, and that the earth should be a common possession of all. Nature, therefore, created a common right, but use and habit created private right ...' In support of this view Ambrose cites, as though they were wholly concordant authorities, the Stoics and the Book of Genesis. And elsewhere he remarks: 'The Lord God specially wanted this earth to be the common possession of all, and to provide fruits for all; but avarice produced the rights of property.'

A passage glorifying the communistic state of nature, including free love, is to be found even in Gratian's *Decretum*, the treatise which became the basic text for the study of Canon Law in all universities and which forms the first part of the *Corpus juris canonici*. The story of how it came to be there is surely one of the strangest in the history of ideas. Pope Clement I, one of the earliest bishops of Rome, who flourished towards the end of the first century, came to be regarded after his death as a pupil of

St Peter himself. The prestige which this brought to his name resulted in a great amount of apocryphal literature being fathered upon him. One of these works purported to be a narrative written by Clement to St James, describing his travels with St Peter and culminating in his 'recognition' of his parents and brothers, from whom he had been separated since childhood. Probably first written in Syria about 265 A.D., the work was given its present form about a century later. In the *Recognitions of Clement* as we possess them the father of Clement appears as a pagan with whom Peter and Clement debate and whom they finally convert. In the course of the argument the father quotes the following opinions, which he attributes to 'Greek philosophers' – correctly enough, if only he had not then tried to father them on to Plato:

For the use of all things that are in this world ought to have been common to all men, but through injustice one man says this is his, and another says that is his, and so division is created amongst mortals. In short, a very wise Greek, knowing these things to be so, says that all things should be in common amongst friends. And unquestionably amongst 'all things' spouses are included. He also says, just as the air cannot be divided up, nor the splendour of the sun, so the other things which are given in this world to be held in common by all ought not to be divided up, but really ought to be held in common.

Some five centuries later this passage acquired an entirely new significance. About 850 A.D. the French monk known as Pseudo-Isidore (because he fathered his works upon Isidore, Archbishop of Seville) was producing spurious decretals and canons for the celebrated collection now known as the False Decretals. The collection opens with five 'Epistles of Pope Clement', all of them apocryphal and three of them forged by Pseudo-Isidore himself. In the fifth epistle, which is addressed to St James and the Christians of Jerusalem, Pseudo-Isidore included the passage quoted above – no longer however as the saying of a pagan but as expressing the views of Pope Clement himself. And the Pope is made to reinforce the argument by quoting *Acts* iv on the first Christian community at Jerusalem:

And the multitude of them that believed were of one heart and of one soul: neither said any of them that aught of the things which he possessed was his own; but they had all things common. ... Neither was there any among them that lacked: for as many as were possessors of lands and houses sold them, and brought the prices of the things that were sold, and laid them down at the apostles' feet: and distribution was made unto every man according to his need.

It was in this hybrid form, half Christian and half Stoic, that the argument was encountered by the founder of the science of Canon Law. When, about 1150, Gratian came to make his great compilation, he never questioned – any more than his contemporaries did – the genuineness of the decretals of Pseudo-Isidore. The Fifth Epistle of Clement, with its strange affirmation of anarcho-communism, was included in the *Decretum* and thereby acquired an authority which it was to keep until the sixteenth century, when it was discredited along with the rest of the False Decretals. Gratian, it is true, attaches to the document certain comments which tend to restrict its scope; but elsewhere in the *Decretum* he makes its arguments (save in the matter of free love) unreservedly his own. And in the later Middle Ages it became a commonplace amongst canonists and scholastics that in the first state of society, which had also been the best state, there had been no such thing as private property because all things had belonged to all people.

About 1270 the egalitarian State of Nature was presented, for the first time since Antiquity, in a work of literature. Jean de Meun, a layman of enquiring mind, living in the middle of the Latin Quarter of Paris, profoundly influenced by current debates in the University, thoroughly versed also in Latin literature, dealt with the matter at some length in his vast poem the *Roman de la Rose*. No other vernacular work in the whole of medieval literature was so popular – some 200 manuscript copies in French still survive and there were numerous translations. It was through the *Roman de la Rose* that a social theory which so far had been familiar only to learned clerics became accessible to large numbers of the laity. Jean de Meun's description of the Golden Age and the decline therefrom is a sociological essay which is both serious and popular – a foretaste, some five centuries in advance, of the second part of Rousseau's *Discours sur l'inégalité* and, like that work, itself a document of great interest to the student of social myths.

'Once upon a time, in the days of our first fathers and mothers,' writes the poet, 'as the writings of the Ancients bear witness, people loved one another with a delicate and honest love, and not out of covetousness and lust for gain. Kindness reigned in the world.' In those days tastes were simple, people nourished themselves from fruit and nuts and herbs, they drank only water, they dressed in the skins of beasts, they knew nothing of agriculture, they lived in caves. Yet there was no hardship, for the earth gave freely all the food they needed. Lovers embraced on beds of flowers, beneath curtains of leaves (for this writer free love was an important part of the primal bliss). 'There they danced and disported themselves in sweet idleness, simple quiet people who cared for nothing but to live joyously and in all friendship with one another. No king or prince had yet, like a criminal, snatched up what belonged to others. All were equals and had no private property of their own. They knew well the maxim that love and authority never yet dwelt companionably together. . . . And so, my friend, the Ancients kept one another company, free from any bond or constraint, peacefully, decently; and they would not have given up their liberty for all the gold in Arabia and in Phrygia . . .'

Unfortunately this happy state of affairs was brought to an end by the appearance of an army of vices – Deceit, Pride, Covetousness, Envy and the rest. Their first act was to set Poverty and her son Larceny loose upon the earth, which so far had known nothing of them. Next

these demons, mad with rage and envy at seeing human beings happy, invaded the whole earth, sowing discord, chicanery, disagreements and lawsuits, quarrels, disputes, wars, slanders, hatred and rancour. As they were infatuated with gold, they had the earth fleeced, they dragged from her bowels the hidden treasures, metals and precious stones. For Avarice and Covetousness have lodged in the human heart the passion for acquiring wealth. Covetousness makes money and Avarice locks it away – unhappy creature that she is, and she will never spend it but will leave it to her heirs and executors to manage and guard, if no mischance befalls it first.

As soon as mankind became the prey of that band, it abandoned its first way of life. Men never paused from doing evil; they became false and began to cheat; they fastened on properties, they divided the very soil and in doing so they drew boundaries, and often in settling these boundaries they fought and snatched whatever they could from one another; the strongest got the biggest shares . . .

In the end the anarchy became so intolerable that men had to elect someone to restore and keep order. They chose 'a big villein, the biggest-boned, the most strapping, the strongest they could find; and they made him prince and lord'. But he needed help and so taxes and dues were instituted to pay for the apparatus of coercion; it was the beginning of the royal power. Money was coined, weapons were manufactured –

and at the same time men fortified cities and castles and built great palaces covered with sculpture, for those who held these riches were much afraid lest they should be taken from them, either by stealth or by force. Then they were much more to be pitied, those unhappy men, for they never knew any security again, from the day when, out of greed, they took for themselves what had previously been common to all, as are the air and the sun.

Such were the egalitarian and communistic ideals which were acknowledged by very many thoughtful souls in medieval Europe.

And it cannot be said that no attempt at all was made to translate them into reality. The Church itself consistently maintained that a communal life in voluntary poverty was 'the more perfect way'; only insisting that in a corrupt world, labouring under the consequences of the Fall, this was an ideal which could and should be pursued only by an elite. Amongst the clergy this attitude found an institutionalized expression in the orders of monks and friars. It was an attitude which appealed also to many of the laity, especially when commerce revived, new wealth appeared and an urban civilization grew up. From the eleventh century onwards there were to be found in all the more developed and populous parts of Europe groups of laymen living in quasi-monastic communities, holding all property in common; sometimes with, sometimes without the sanction of the Church. For all such communities a model was provided by the description in *Acts* iv of the first Christian community at Jerusalem. This example – which, as we have seen, was cited already by Pseudo-Isidore in the forged Epistle of Clement – acquired immense prestige; for it was nowhere appreciated how far St Luke had allowed his imagination to overrule his sense of historical fact.

But to imitate this imaginary version of the primitive Church was not yet to restore, or even attempt to restore, the lost Golden Age of all humanity which had been portrayed for the ancient world by Seneca and for medieval Europe by Jean de Meun. And even the heretical sects which flourished from the twelfth century onwards were on the whole less concerned with social and economic 'levelling' than has sometimes been asserted; neither the Cathars nor the Waldensians, for instance, showed much interest in the matter. Until almost the end of the fourteenth century it would seem to have been only a few obscure sectarians, such as some of the adepts of the Free Spirit, who tried to call the egalitarian State of Nature out of the depths of the past and to project it into the future. But however few might undertake it, this attempt to recreate the Golden Age was not without importance. It produced a doctrine which became a revolutionary myth as soon as it was presented to the turbulent poor and fused with the phantasies of popular eschatology.

Marginalia to the English Peasants' Revolt

When did people cease to think of a society without distinctions of status or wealth simply as a Golden Age irrecoverably lost in the distant past, and begin to think of it instead as preordained for the immediate future? So far as can be judged from the available sources, this new social myth came into being in the turbulent years around 1380. Perhaps it first took shape in the towns of Flanders and northern France, which were swept at that time by a wave of insurrectionary violence; but though that has sometimes been suggested, it has yet to be proved. When on the other hand one examines, in the chronicles dealing with the English Peasants' Revolt of 1381, the pronouncements attributed to the celebrated John Ball one finds the myth – unexpectedly but unmistakably – just below the surface.

Not that most of the insurgents were appreciably influenced by that myth. Most of the peasants and the urban artisans who supported them seem to have been almost exclusively concerned with limited and realistic objectives. By that time the bond between a lord and his peasants had lost whatever paternal character it may once have possessed; and peasants saw no reason why they should render heavy dues and services to a lord who was no longer their protector. Moreover since the Black Death there had been a chronic shortage of labour, from which the common people had benefited greatly but still less than they would have liked. Peasants and artisans alike had long chafed under the legal restrictions – notably those embodied in the Statute of Labourers – that prevented them from exploiting to the full the strength of their economic position. The discontent generated by these standing grievances was further exacerbated by the mismanagement of the French war and the levying of a peculiarly onerous poll-tax. And yet, however resentful and angry the common people might feel, when the revolt broke out its aims were still severely practical. The charter of liberty granted by the king at Mile End (and later annulled) reflects those aims accurately enough: to secure the commutation of manorial dues for cash rents, the replacement of villeinage by wage-labour, the removal of restrictions on free buying and selling. In that programme there is nothing at all to hint at any impending miraculous restoration of an egalitarian State of Nature. But that is not to say that no such phantasy was entertained anywhere amongst the insurgents.

In a celebrated passage Froissart gives what is supposed to be a typical sermon of John Ball's:

And if we are all descended from one father and one mother, Adam and Eve, how can the lords say or prove that they are more lords than we are - save that they make us dig and till the ground so that they can squander what we produce? They are clad in velvet and satin, set off with squirrel fur, while we are dressed in poor cloth. They have wines and spices and fine bread, and we have only rye and spoilt flour and straw, and only water to drink. They have beautiful residences and manors, while we have the trouble and the work, always in the fields under rain and snow. But it is from us and our labour that everything comes with which they maintain their pomp.

For this state of affairs the preacher prescribes a drastic remedy: 'Good folk, things cannot go well in England nor ever shall until all things are in common and there is neither villein nor noble, but all of us are of one condition.'

The English chronicler Thomas Walsingham, the monk of St Albans, also gives a report of the sermon which Ball is said to have preached to the rebel host at Blackheath on a text which was already then a traditional proverb and which has remained famous to this day:

> When Adam delved and Eve span,
> Who was then a gentleman?

According to Walsingham, Ball's argument was that in the beginning all human beings had been created free and equal. It was evil men who, by unjust oppression, had first introduced serfdom, against the will of God. But now was a time given by God when the common people could, if they only would, cast off the yoke they had borne so long and win the freedom they had always yearned for. Therefore they should be of good heart and conduct themselves like the wise husbandman in the Scriptures who gathered the wheat into his barn, but uprooted and burnt the tares which had almost choked the good grain; for harvest-time was come. The tares were the great lords, the judges and the lawyers. All these must be exterminated, and so must everyone else who might be dangerous to the community in the future. Then, once the great ones had been cut off, men would all enjoy equal freedom, rank and power.

Although there is no way of knowing whether sermons such as these really were delivered by John Ball, there is every reason to believe that the teaching which they enshrine was indeed being disseminated at the time of the revolt. The doctrine of the primal egalitarian State of Nature was certainly familiar enough in England. In the *Dialogue of Dives and Pauper*, which was written in the first decade of the fourteenth century, we read that 'by the lawe of kynde (i.e. Nature) and by Goddes lawe all thynge is common'; and the point is hammered home by reference to the stock authorities, the spurious Fifth Epistle of Clement and *Acts* iv. Perfectly orthodox preachers invoked St Ambrose to the same effect: 'In commune to all, rich and poore, the earth was made. Why will ye ritch chalenge proper right herein? Kinde knoweth no riches, that bringeth forth al men poore . . .' In academic guise the same idea was even mooted by Wyclif in the treatise *De civili dominio* which he composed at Oxford in 1374. There it was argued that for the unrighteous to hold lordship was mere usurpation, contrary to the first principles of law and incompatible with the divine purpose; whereas the righteous man, who renounced lordship for Christ's sake, obtained in exchange complete lordship of the universe, such as had not been enjoyed even by our First Parents before the Fall. And Wyclif went on to produce his own variation on the theme which had been developed by so many scholastics since the days of Gratian:

Firstly, that all good things of God ought to be in common. The proof of this is as follows: Every man ought to be in state of grace; if he is in a state of grace he is lord of the world and all that it contains; therefore every man ought to be lord of the whole world. But, because of the multitudes of men, this will not happen unless they all hold all things in common: therefore all things ought to be in common.

Wyclif of course never intended this theory to be applied in practice to secular society. He uttered it once and once only, and that time in Latin; and even then he qualified it by adding that in practical life the righteous must acquiesce in inequalities and injustices and leave the unrighteous in possession of their wealth and power. If in his attacks on the wealth and worldliness of the clergy Wyclif was in deadly earnest, these comments of his on the communal ownership of all things were little more than an exercise in formal logic. Nevertheless when abstracted from their scholastic context and stripped of their qualifying clauses those same comments were barely distinguishable from the mystical anarchism of the Free

Spirit. It would be surprising if amongst the swarm of students of all sorts and classes who congregated at Oxford there had been none who snatched at such ideas and scattered them abroad, simplified into propagandist slogans. And indeed Langland, writing on the morrow of the great revolt, has told in *Piers Plowman* how speculations concerning the State of Nature penetrated from the universities to the common people, and with what effect:

> Envy heard this; and bade friars go to school,
> And learn Logic and Law, and also Contemplation,
> And preach to men of Plato, and prove it by Seneca,
> That all things under heaven ought to be in common.
> He lies, as I live, who to the unlearned so preaches,
> For God made to men a law, and Moses taught it:
> Thou shalt not covet any thing that is thy neighbour's.

Yet in all its long history the phantasy of the egalitarian State of Nature had never acted as a dynamic social myth; and it would not have done so now if it had not been reinforced by social criticism of a more personal and passionate kind. In his fascinating survey of medieval sermons the late Professor G. R. Owst has shown how even the most orthodox preachers, though they castigated the sins of all classes of the community, yet reserved their most virulent criticism for the rich and powerful. Particularly significant is the interpretation of the Last Judgement as the day of vengeance of the poor – an interpretation which, developed and elaborated from the thirteenth century onwards, was given masterly expression by the Chancellor of Cambridge, John Bromyard, in his guide for preachers. The following extract from Owst's summary and translation will give some idea of the emotional power of Bromyard's argument:

On the left, before the supreme Judge's throne, stand 'the harsh lords, who plundered the people of God with grievous fines, amercements and exactions, . . . the wicked ecclesiastics, who failed to nourish the poor with the goods of Christ and His poor as they should have done, the usurers and false merchants . . . who deceived Christ's members . . .'. Among the righteous, on the right hand, are many who have been 'afflicted, spoiled and overwhelmed by the aforesaid evil-doers'. Then the oppressed bring a fearful indictment against their oppressors, in the divine presence.

And with boldness will they be able to put their plaint before God and seek justice, speaking with Christ the judge, and reciting each in turn the injury from which they specially suffered. . . . 'Our labours and goods . . . they took away, to satiate their greed. They afflicted us with hunger and labours, that they might live delicately upon our labours and our goods. We have laboured and lived so hard a life that scarce for half a year had we a good sufficiency, scarce nothing save bread and bran and water. Nay, rather, what is worse, we died of hunger. And they were served with three or four courses out of our goods, which they took from us. ... We hungered and thirsted and were afflicted with cold and nakedness. And those robbers yonder gave not our own goods to us when we were in want, neither did they feed or clothe us out of them. But their hounds and horses and apes, the rich, the powerful, the abounding, the gluttons, the drunkards and their prostitutes they fed and clothed with them, and allowed us to languish in want ...

'O just God, mighty judge, the game was not fairly divided between them and us. Their satiety was our famine; their merriment was our wretchedness; their jousts and tournaments were our torments. ... Their feasts, delectations, pomps, vanities, excesses and superfluities were our fastings, penalties, wants, calamities and spoliation. The love-ditties and laughter of their dances were our mockery, our groanings and remonstrations. They used to sing – "Well enough! Well enough!" – and we groaned, saying– "Woe to us! Woe to us!"...' *It is easier for a camel to pass thru the eye of a needle, than for a richman to pass thru the Gates of Heaven.*

'Without a doubt,' adds Bromyard, 'the just Judge will do justice to those clamouring thus.' Terrible as is the indictment of the wronged, terrible likewise will be the fate of the oppressors: 'Many who here on earth are called nobles shall blush in deepest shame at that Judgement-seat...'

Needless to say the purpose of such a sermon was not to incite to social revolt. When addressed to the rich it was intended as an exhortation to deal justly and mercifully with the poor and to be liberal in giving alms; when addressed to the poor it was intended not to arouse but on the contrary to pacify and console. Nevertheless this portrayal of the Day of Judgement presents the whole complaint of the lowly against 'the great' – and presents it, moreover, as part of a great eschatological drama. All that was required in order to turn such a prophecy into revolutionary propaganda of the most explosive kind was to bring the Day of Judgement nearer – to show it not as happening in some remote and indefinite future but as already at hand. And this is precisely what is done in the sermon which Walsingham attributes to John Ball. To appreciate the full significance of that sermon one has only to recall the scriptural context of the parable of the wheat and the tares – a context which, one may be sure, would have leaped to the mind of any medieval audience. For as interpreted by Christ to the Disciples the parable is an eschatological prophecy, dealing with the prodigious convulsions of the Last Days:

He that soweth the good seed is the Son of Man; the field is the world; the good seed are the children of the kingdom; but the tares are the children of the wicked one; the enemy that sowed them is the devil; the harvest is the end of the world; and the reapers are the angels.

As therefore the tares are gathered and burned in the fire; so shall it be in the end of this world. The Son of Man shall send forth his angels, and they shall gather out of his kingdom <u>all things that offend</u>, and them which do iniquity; and shall cast them into a furnace of fire; there shall be wailing and gnashing of teeth. Then shall the righteous shine forth as the sun in the kingdom of their Father. Who has ears to hear, let him hear.

By proclaiming that this prophecy is now on the point of fulfilment, that the harvest-time appointed by God has come at last, the sermon in effect summons the common people, as the children of the Kingdom, to carry out the annihilation of the demonic powers which was to usher in the Millennium. And in those cryptic rhymes attributed to Ball – but which, no less than the sermons, should be regarded rather as of uncertain authorship – the symbolism used in *Piers Plowman* is adapted to convey the same revolutionary message. Here too one can recognize the same eager expectation of a final battle between the poor, seen as the hosts of God, and their oppressors, seen as the hosts of Satan. By that battle the world will be cleansed of sin and especially of those sins, such as *Avaritia* and *Luxuria*, traditionally attributed to the rich; 'truth set under a lock' will be liberated; 'true love that was so good' will be restored to the world. It is the dawn of the Millennium, but of a Millennium which is to be not only that Kingdom of the Saints foretold in traditional eschatology but also a recreation of the primal egalitarian State of Nature, a second Golden Age. And the rhymes too insist that this is appointed to happen now, at this very moment: 'God give redress, for now is time.'

It has generally been held that the three great peasant risings of the fourteenth century – the rising in Maritime Flanders between 1323 and 1328, the *Jacquerie* of 1358 and the English rising of 1381 – were all of them directed solely towards limited aims of a social and political nature. In reality this would seem to be less true of the English revolt than of its precursors on the Continent. Even though here too the majority of the insurgents were simply moved by specific grievances to demand specific reforms, it seems certain that millenarian hopes and aspirations were not altogether lacking. And from a sociological point of view this is in no way surprising. In the English revolt an exceptionally large part was played by members of the lower clergy and especially by apostates and irregulars of the type of John Ball; and, as we have seen, such men were always eager to assume the role of divinely inspired prophets, charged with the mission of guiding mankind through the preordained convulsions of the Last Days. At the same time it is a peculiarity of this revolt that it was almost as much an urban as a rural one. Impelled, it would seem, by their faith in the benevolence and omnipotence of the King, the peasants of Kent and Essex marched on London; but when they arrived there the populace of the city also arose, prevented the gates being shut against the oncoming hordes and then joined forces with the rebels. And this certainly modified the character of the revolt.

It was no doubt with good reason that Froissart remarked that Ball's most enthusiastic followers were to be found amongst Londoners 'envious of the rich and the nobility'. By that date there existed in London an underworld such as had long existed in the towns of France and Germany and the Low Countries: journeymen who were excluded from the guilds and at the same time were forbidden to form organizations of their own; unskilled workers, worn-out soldiers and deserters; a surplus population of beggars and unemployed – in fact a whole urban underworld living in great misery and perpetually on the verge of starvation, and constantly swollen by the flight of villeins from the country-side. In such a milieu, where fanatical *prophetae* mixed with the disoriented and desperate poor on the very margin of society, an upheaval which was in any case shaking the whole social structure of the country was bound to make itself felt with cataclysmic force and to produce repercussions of the utmost violence. There it must really have seemed that all things were being made new, that all social norms were dissolving and all barriers collapsing. Indeed it may be tentatively suggested that millenarian expectations may have lain behind several of the more surprising by-products of the revolt: the burning of the palace of the Savoy and the destruction of all its treasures by Londoners who would take nothing what-soever for themselves; the more obviously impracticable of the demands presented to the King at Smithfield; perhaps also Jack Straw's admission (always assuming that he really made it) that in the end the magnates and all the clergy save some of the Mendicants were to have been killed off.

Certainly it was a situation in which it must have been easy enough to proclaim and to believe that the path lay wide open to an egalitarian, even a communistic Millennium. And it was just such a situation that was to arise again, and on a far vaster scale, when some forty years later the Hussite revolution broke out in Bohemia.

The Taborite Apocalypse

Although overwhelmingly Slavonic in ethnic composition and in language, the Bohemian state had for many centuries been included within the sphere of western rather than of eastern European civilization. Its Christianity was Latin, not Greek; and politically it formed part of the Holy Roman Empire. A Bohemian monarchy existed without interruption from about 1200 onwards; in the second half of the fourteenth century the King of Bohemia wore also the German and then the imperial crown. At that time Bohemia was both the premier electorate in the Empire and the seat of the premier university – that of Prague, founded in 1348–9; and it effectively dominated both the political and the cultural life of central Europe. This position was lost in the first years of the fifteenth century, when the Bohemian King Wenceslas IV was deposed from the imperial throne and the University, from being international, became purely Czech. But in those same years Bohemia became the centre of a religious movement of such explosive force that it profoundly disturbed the whole of Europe for several decades.

There was no part of Europe in which the usual criticisms could be brought against the Church with greater conviction than in Bohemia. The wealth of the Church there was enormous – one half of all the land was ecclesiastical property; many of the clergy, and especially of the great prelates, lived decidedly worldly lives; while the Curia was constantly interfering in the internal affairs of the country and was also extracting from it very great financial profits. Moreover here the customary bitterness of the laity against the clergy was powerfully reinforced by national sentiment. Ever since the twelfth century there had been in Bohemia a substantial minority group of German descent, speaking German and resolutely preserving its German character; and these people were particularly numerous amongst the higher clergy. The grievances of the Czechs against the clergy fused with their grievances against an alien minority.

In the 1360's an ascetic reformer called John Milíč of Kroměříž won enormous influence in Prague. He was much concerned with Antichrist, whom he imagined at first as an individual but later as corruption within the Church itself. The fact that the Church was manifestly corrupt meant that the reign of Antichrist had already begun, and that meant that the End was at hand. But in preparation for the End Antichrist must be overthrown – meaning that the clergy must learn to live in poverty; while the laity, for their part, must turn away from 'usury'. Even more influential than Milíč was his disciple Matthew of Janov, who was active around 1390. He too was preoccupied with the idea of Antichrist, interpreted metaphorically as meaning all those who put love of self and the world before the love of Christ. And even more than Milíč, he was impressed by the overwhelming power of Antichrist; in his eyes the present time was wholly dominated by Antichrist – the worldliness of priests and monks, and above all the scandal of the Great Schism, were proof of it. Of course Christ's final triumph was assured; but it was the task of all true Christians to prepare for it. This they could do partly by returning to the precepts enunciated in the Bible and partly by daily communion. The Eucharist, Matthew insisted, was the Christian's indispensable spiritual food; and it should be as fully and frequently available to laymen as it was to priests. The body of Antichrist comprised false priests above all – and why should those members of Antichrist enjoy more of the most intimate contact with Christ than most Christians? In Matthew of Janov's mind the Eucharist received, for the first time, the central place that it was later to have for the Hussite movement as a whole.

The demand for reform initiated by John Milíč and Matthew of Janov was carried on by other preachers and was further stimulated by the teaching and example of Wyclif, whose works were known in Bohemia from 1380 onwards. At the turn of the century it was taken up by John Hus – himself an ardent admirer of Wyclif – who voiced it so effectively that the significance of the movement ceased to be merely local and became as wide as Latin Christendom. Like his predecessors, Hus was a popular preacher whose favourite theme was the corruption and worldliness of the clergy. But an unusual combination of gifts made him at once the Rector of the University, the spiritual leader of the common people and an influential figure at the court; and this gave his protests great weight. He also carried his protests further than any of his predecessors; for when Pope John XXIII* sent emissaries to Prague to preach a 'crusade' against his political enemy, the King of Naples, and to grant indulgences to those who contributed money to the cause, Hus revolted against the papal commands. Like Wyclif before him, he proclaimed that when papal decrees ran counter to the law of Christ as expressed in the Scriptures, the faithful ought not to obey them; and he launched against the sale of indulgences a campaign which roused nation-wide excitement.

Never an extremist or a rebel, Hus offended simply by refusing

* John XXIII (1410–1415) is not recognized as a legitimate pope; which is why the late Pope John was likewise John XXIII.

blind obedience to his ecclesiastical superiors; but that was enough to cost him his life. Excommunicated in 1412, he was summoned in 1414 to appear before the Ecumenical Council then sitting at Constance; and, unwisely relying on a safeconduct from the Emperor Sigismund, he complied with the summons. His intention was to persuade the Council by argument that the Church was truly in need of fundamental reform. In the event he was arrested and, on his refusal to recant, burnt as a heretic. The core of his 'heresy' was his claim that the Papacy was not a divine but a human institution, that not the pope but Christ was the true head of the Church, and that an unworthy pope should be deposed. Ironically enough, the Council which condemned him had itself just deposed Pope John XXIII for simony, murder, sodomy and fornication.

The news of Hus's execution turned the unrest in Bohemia into a national reformation. For the first time – and a full century before Luther – a nation challenged the authority of the Church as represented by pope and council. During the years 1415–18 reform was established throughout Bohemia, with the approval and support of the major Czech barons and of King Wenceslas. In effect the existing Church hierarchy was largely replaced by a national church which was no longer controlled from Rome but was under the patronage of the secular powers of Bohemia. At the same time, at the urging of a former follower of Hus, Jakoubek of Stříbro, it was decided that henceforth laymen should receive Holy Communion in both kinds instead of – as had become customary during the later Middle Ages – receiving the bread only.

These were far-reaching changes, but they in themselves did not amount to a formal break with the Church of Rome; on the contrary, they were conceived as reforms for which it was hoped to win the Church as a whole. If Rome, or the Council of Constance, had concurred in this programme, the Czech nobility, the Masters of the University, and many of the common people would have been satisfied; but it was not to be. In 1419 King Wenceslas, under pressure from the Emperor Sigismund (his brother) and from Pope Martin V, reversed his policy and abandoned the Hussite cause. Hussite propaganda was restricted, and even utraquism (as communion in both kinds was called) was regarded with disfavour. In the part of Prague known as the New City the common people, inspired by a former monk and ardent Hussite called John Zelivský, became increasingly restive; and when, in July 1419, Wenceslas removed all Hussite councillors from the government of the New City, the populace rose, stormed the town-hall and threw the new councillors from the windows.

This unsuccessful attempt to suppress the Hussite movement greatly strengthened the radical tendencies within that movement. For from the start the movement had included people whose aims went far beyond those of the nobility or of the Masters of the University. The great majority of these radicals belonged to the lower social strata; they included weavers and other cloth-workers, tailors, brewers, smiths – in fact manual workers in many trades. The part played by these people was so striking that Catholic polemicists could even pretend that the whole Hussite movement had from the very beginning been financed by the artisan guilds. It would have been truer to say that the general upheaval in Bohemia encouraged social unrest amongst the artisans; and this was particularly the case in Prague.

Economically quite well situated, the artisans in the capital were excluded from all influence on a municipal administration which was entirely in the hands of the great patrician families – mostly violently anti-Hussite and many of them German. This situation was suddenly transformed by the rising of July 1419. The success of the insurrection enormously increased the power of the guilds and gave them effective control of the administration. The artisans expelled large numbers of Catholics, appropriating their houses and property and many of their offices and privileges. Moreover the monasteries were expropriated and much of their wealth passed to the City of Prague; and this too, though indirectly, benefited the artisans. Although the New City was no more egalitarian under the rule of the guilds than it had been under that of the patricians, the very fact that it was controlled by artisans made it a centre of radical influence.

But if it was the guilds that organized and directed the radical movement in Prague, the rank-and-file were largely drawn not from the skilled artisans but from the lowest strata of the population – the heterogeneous mass of journeymen, unskilled workers, indentured servants, beggars, prostitutes and criminals. Even at the height of its prosperity in the fourteenth century the capital had had a large population of extremely poor slum-dwellers; and the thirty or forty years preceding the Hussite revolution had seen both a great increase in the numbers of such people and a great deterioration in their condition. By that time Bohemia was suffering from over-population; and as always the surplus population drifted from the rural areas into the towns and particularly into the capital. But Bohemia had no export industry capable of absorbing these people, so that many of them merely went to swell the numbers of unemployed. And even those who found some kind of unskilled work were still in a desperate situation; for while wages remained at the level of about 1380, the value of the currency was undermined by inflation and prices rose relentlessly. By 1420 the great majority of the population of Prague, which was between 30,000 and 40,000, seem to have been living – or dying – on starvation wages. The radical wing of the Hussite movement was largely recruited from this harassed proletariat.

Radicalism also found massive support amongst the peasantry. The bulk of the rural population had long been dependent on the lords, ecclesiastical or lay, who owned the land. But – largely thanks to the system of land-tenure which had been introduced by the German colonists and which had spread amongst the Czech peasantry – the dependence of the peasant upon his lord was by no means absolute. Rents and dues were precisely fixed; tenancies were hereditary and therefore provided much security; yet sometimes tenancies could be sold by the tenants, so that many peasants enjoyed a certain freedom of movement. The increase in the royal power in the fourteenth century further impeded exploitation of the common people by the nobility; in 1356 a law gave dependent peasants the right to sue their lords in the territorial law-courts. The nobles chafed under these restrictions; and by the beginning of the fifteenth century a determined effort was being made to deprive the peasants of their traditional rights and to force them into a position of total dependence. By manipulation of the law many peasants were gradually being deprived of their right to bequeath their holdings to their heirs, while they themselves were being bound more firmly to the soil and their dues and services increased. It seems that by the time of the Hussite upheaval the Bohemian peasantry was uneasily aware that its position was threatened. Moreover in the countryside too there existed a stratum with nothing to lose: landless labourers, farm hands and many members of that surplus population which could be accommodated neither in towns nor on the land. All these people were more than ready to support any movement which seemed likely to bring succour and relief.

From 1419 onwards the radical wing of the Hussite movement began to split off from the more conservative wing and to develop along lines of its own. Faced with the new, persecutory policy of King Wenceslas, a number of radical priests began to organize congregations outside the parish system, on various hilltops in south Bohemia. There they gave communion in both kinds and preached against the abuses of the Church of Rome. The new congregations soon turned into permanent settlements where life was lived in conscious imitation of the original Christian community as portrayed in the New Testament; together these communities formed an embryonic society which was wholly outside the feudal order and which attempted to regulate its affairs on the basis of brotherly love instead of force. The most important of these settlements was on a hill near Bechyně castle, on the River Lužnica. Most significantly, the spot was renamed 'Mount Tabor'; for, according to a tradition going back to the fourth century, Tabor was the name of the mountain where Christ had foretold his Second Coming (Mark xiii), where he had ascended to heaven and where he was expected to reappear in majesty. And soon this name, with all its eschatological undertones, was attached to the radical Hussites themselves; already to their contemporaries they were known as Taborites, as they are to historians today.

A unified programme of the Taborites hardly existed, for their aspirations were manifold and confused. These people were moved by an animosity which was national and social as well as religious. The fact that most of the prosperous merchants in the towns were not only staunch Catholics but were also Germans, the widespread though erroneous belief that feudalism and serfdom were peculiarly German institutions – these things meant that the Taborites were even more fervently anti-German than the Utraquists (as the more moderate Hussites were called). But above all they absolutely rejected the Church of Rome. Whereas the Utraquists clung in most respects to traditional Catholic doctrine, the Taborites affirmed the right of every individual, layman as well as priest, to interpret the Scriptures according to his lights. Many Taborites rejected the dogma of purgatory, dismissed prayers and masses for the dead as vain superstitions, saw nothing to venerate in the relics or images of saints, treated many rites of the Church with contempt. They also refused to take oaths and protested against the institution of capital punishment. Most important of all, they insisted that nothing need by regarded as an article of faith that was not expressly affirmed by Holy Writ.

All this recalls the heretics of earlier centuries and particularly those Bible-studying sectarians the Waldensians or Vaudois, who had indeed been very active amongst the poorer classes in Bohemia. But there had also long existed in Bohemia, as in other parts of Europe, a millenarian tendency which was as remote from the sober dissent of the Waldensians as it was from Catholic orthodoxy. In the days of the Black Death and the mass flagellant processions the Roman tribune and *propheta* Rienzo had foretold at Prague that an age of peace, harmony and justice, a true paradisiacal order, was about to be inaugurated. John Milíč and the reformers who succeeded him lived in constant expectation of the Second Coming; while towards the close of the fourteenth century there appeared in Bohemia millenarian sectarians who were influenced by the doctrine of the Free Spirit. Millennial expectations were powerfully reinforced by some forty *Pikarti* who arrived in Prague from abroad in 1418. It is possible that *Pikarti* merely meant Beghards, but more probable that it meant Picards, and that these people were fugitives from the persecution which was raging at that time at Lille and Tournai. In any case they seem to have had close relations with those adepts of the Free Spirit, the *Homines intelligentiae* of Brussels. They bitterly denounced the prelates who, unmindful of Christ's injunction of absolute poverty, exploited the poor so as to be able to live in luxury and debauchery. They held that they themselves, on the other hand, were vessels of the Holy Spirit and possessed of a knowledge of truth as complete as that of the Apostles, if not of Christ. And since they believed the Church of Rome to be the Whore of Babylon and the Pope to be Antichrist, it is clear that they felt themselves to be living on the eve of the Millennium or maybe – like the *Homines intelligentiae* – of the Third and Last Age.

At first the Waldensian tendency was dominant amongst the Taborites. During the greater part of 1419 the Taborites aimed at a national reformation which, unlike the original Hussite reformation, would involve a total break with Rome. The religious life, and therefore to some extent the social life, of Bohemia was to be brought into accord with the Waldensian ideal of apostolic poverty and moral purity. In October and again in November Taborites from all over Bohemia congregated in Prague, where the radical leaders tried to win the Hussite magistrates and University Masters for their programme. Naturally they were unsuccessful; and they soon found themselves confronted with a far more ruthless opposition than they had bargained for. King Wenceslas had died in August, from shock at the killing of the councillors; and the great Hussite nobles joined with their Catholic colleagues to secure the succession for Wenceslas's brother, the Emperor Sigismund – and also to frustrate the plans of the radicals. Soon the Prague magistrates threw their weight on the conservative side. All were agreed that utraquist communion should be preserved – but they were also agreed, most emphatically, that the Taborites must be suppressed. For a period of several months, starting in November 1419, Taborites throughout Bohemia were isolated from the national movement and were exposed to a savage persecution aiming at their extermination. At the same time, as was to be expected, apocalyptic and millenarian phantasies took on a new dynamism.

A number of former priests, led by one Martin Huska – also known as Loquis because of his extraordinary eloquence – began to preach openly of the coming of the great consummation; announcing that the time had come when all evil must be abolished in preparation for the Millennium. Between the 10 and 14 February 1420, they prophesied, every town and village would be destroyed by fire, like Sodom. Throughout Christendom the wrath of God would overtake everyone who did not at once flee to 'the mountains' – which were defined as the five towns in Bohemia that had become Taborite strongholds. The message was heard, and in the lowest social strata it roused great enthusiasm. Multitudes of poor folk sold their belongings and, moving to these towns with their wives and children, threw their money at the feet of the preachers.

These people saw themselves as entering on the final struggle against Antichrist and his hosts. This emerges quite clearly from an open letter distributed at that time: 'There are five of these cities, which will not enter into agreements with the Antichrist or surrender to him.' And a contemporary Taborite song also makes the point: 'Faithful ones, rejoice in God! Give him honour and praise, that he has pleased to preserve us and graciously liberate us from the evil Antichrist and his cunning army. . .' In the very afflictions descending on them the millenarians recognized the long-expected 'messianic woes'; and the conviction gave them a new militancy. No longer content to await the destruction of the godless by a miracle, the preachers called upon the faithful to carry out the necessary purification of the earth themselves. One of them, a graduate of Prague University called John Capek, wrote a tract which is said to have been 'fuller of blood than a pond is of water' and in which he demonstrated, with the help of quotations from the Old Testament, that it was the inescapable duty of the Elect to kill in the name of the Lord. This work served as a polemical armoury for other preachers, who used its arguments to urge their hearers on to massacre. No pity, they declared, must be shown towards sinners, for all sinners were enemies of Christ. 'Accursed be the man who withholds his sword from shedding the blood of the enemies of Christ. Every believer must wash his hands in that blood.' The preachers themselves joined eagerly in the killing, for 'every priest may lawfully pursue, wound and kill sinners.'

The sins which were to be punished by death included those old bugbears of the poor, *Avaritia* and *Luxuria*; but also, and above all, they included every opposition to the will of 'the men of the Divine Law'. In the eyes of the radical Taborites all their opponents were sinners and must be exterminated. And the evidence for this bloodthirstiness does not, by any means, all come from hostile sources. Peter Chelčicky, a Taborite who declined to abandon his pacific, Waldensian outlook, noted and lamented the change that

1. *The Story of Antichrist.* On the left, Antichrist preaching at the inspiration of the Devil, while on the right the 'two witnesses' Enoch and Elijah preach against him. Above, Antichrist, supported by demons, trying to fly and thereby show that he is God, while an archangel prepares to strike him down.

2. *The Pope as Antichrist: Melchior Lorch*. In this horrific picture, dedicated to Luther, the Pope is shown with the tail and other animal attributes of Satan, while the frogs issuing from his mouth (along with other reptiles) recall the description of Antichrist in Revelation 16. 13. One of the captions also equates the figure with the Wild Man. As Dr Bernheimer has shown in his study, the Wild Man of medieval demonology was a monster of erotic and destructive power – an earth spirit originally of the family of Pan, the fauns, satyrs and centaurs, but transformed into a terrifying demon. Lorch has given his Wild Man a papal cross which is also a tree-trunk such as was carried by the centaurs – which in turn was a phallic symbol.

3. *The Day of Wrath: Albrecht Durer.* An illustration to Revelation
6. 9–16: ' . . . I saw under the altar the souls of them that were slain
for the word of God, and for the testimony which they held . . . And
lo, there was a great earthquake; and the sun became black as sackcloth
of hair, and the moon became as blood; and the stars of heaven fell
unto the earth . . . And the kings of the earth, and the great men, and
the rich men, and the chief captains, and the mighty men, and every
bond man, and every free man, hid themselves in the dens and in the
rocks of the mountains; and said to the mountains and rocks, Fall on
us, and hide us from the face of him that sitteth on the throne, and from
the wrath of the Lamb.'

4. A medieval version of the ritual murder of a Christian boy by Jews. A striking example of the projection on to the Jews of the phantastic image of the torturing and castrating father.

5. *Dives and Laʒarus. Above:* Dives feasts while Lazarus dies at his gates and the soul of Lazarus is borne by an angel to Abraham's bosom. *Centre:* Dives dies and, weighed down by his money-bag, is thrust down by demons into hell.

Below, right: Avaritia, symbolised by a devil, and *Luxuria*, symbolised by the Woman with the Snakes.

6. (a) *A flagellant procession*, 1349.

6. (b) *A burning of Jews*, 1349.

7. *The Drummer of Niklashausen.* The Drummer, prompted by the hermit or Beghard, propounds his teachings, which are then taken up by the pilgrims. Resting against the church are the giant candles carried by the peasants on their march to Würzburg.

8. *The Ranters as imagined by their contemporaries.* This crude but curious woodcut seems to show that smoking ranked alongside 'free love' as an expression of antinomianism.

Text within the engraving:

IOHAN · VA · LEIDEN · EY · KONINCK · DER · WEDERDOPER ·
THO · MONSTER · WA   ERHAFTICH · CÖTER ·

HÆC · FACIES · HIC · CVLTVS · ERAT · CV̄ · SEPTRA · TENE ·
REX · ανα βαω̃ τιsὥν · SED · BREVE · TĒPVS · EGO ·
HENRICVS · ALDEGREVER · SVXATIĒ · FACIEBAT ·
· ANNO · M · D · ꞏ XXXVI ·
GOTTES · MACHT · IST · MYN · CRACHT ·

9. *John of Leyden as King: Heinrich Aldegrever.* This fine engraving is believed to have been made from life some time after the fall of Münster, at the Bishop's request. The orb with the two swords symbolises Bockelson's claim to universal dominion, both spiritual and secular. 'God's power is my strength' was one of Bockelson's mottoes.

had come over so many of his colleagues. Satan, he observed, had seduced them into regarding themselves as angels who must purify Christ's world of all scandals and who were destined to judge the world; on the strength of which they 'committed many killings and impoverished many people'. A Latin tract written by one of the millenarians themselves is still extant, and it confirms all this: 'The just ... will now rejoice, seeing vengeance and washing their hands in the blood of the sinners.' But the most extreme amongst the Taborites went still further and maintained that anyone, of whatever status, who did not actively help them in 'liberating the truth' and destroying sinners was himself a member of the hosts of Satan and Antichrist and therefore fit only for annihilation. For the hour of vengeance had come, when the imitation of Christ meant no longer an imitation of his mercy but only of his rage, cruelty and vengefulness. As 'avenging angels of God and warriors of Christ' the Elect must kill all, without exception, who did not belong to their community.

Millennarian excitement was encouraged by the development of the political situation. In March 1420 the truce between the moderate Hussites and the Emperor Sigismund was terminated and a Catholic army, international in composition but predominantly German and Magyar, invaded Bohemia. The Czechs for their part never accepted Sigismund as their king; in effect, if not in law, the country embarked on an Interregnum which was to last until 1436. It also embarked on a war in which, under the leadership of a military commander of genius, John Žižka, it was to fight off the invaders in battle after battle. Žižka was a Taborite, and it was the Taborites who bore the brunt of the struggle. At least in the early stages, the more extreme amongst them never doubted that they were living through 'the consummation of time, the extermination of all evils'.

And beyond the extermination of all evils lay the Millennium. These people were utterly convinced that while the earth was being cleansed of sinners Christ would descend 'in glory and great power'. Then would come the 'messianic banquet', which would be held in the holy mountains of the Taborites; after which Christ would take over the regal office in the place of the unworthy Emperor Sigismund. He would rule over the millennial realm in which the Saints would 'shine like the sun in the kingdom of their Father'; 'living, radiant as the sun, quite without stain', they would rejoice for ever in a state of innocence like that of the angels or of Adam and Eve before the Fall. And this Millennium was to be at the same time the Third and Last Age of the pseudo-Joachite prophecies. In that realm no sacraments would be needed to ensure salvation; the book-learning of the clergy would be revealed as vanity; the Church itself would disappear. There nobody would experience physical want or suffering; women would conceive without intercourse and bear children without pain; sickness and death would be unknown. And there the Saints would live together in a community of love and peace, subject to no law and free from all coercion: denizens of a new Paradise which – as we shall see – was also to be a recreation of the egalitarian State of Nature.

Anarcho-communism in Bohemia

If in the main Taborite eschatology derives from the Johannine and Joachite prophecies, some of its features certainly recall the myth of the Golden Age. This is particularly striking when one comes to examine the social organization of the Taborite Millennium. It is impossible to say what influence may have been exerted here by the fame of John Ball, by the teachings of the Picard immigrants or by those of native adepts of the Free Spirit. Explosive ideas lay in any case ready to hand in the traditional literature of the Czechs. It was not simply that, like other countries, Bohemia was familiar with the phantasy of an anarcho-communistic State of Nature – in Bohemia that phantasy had taken on a peculiar national significance. Already some three centuries earlier the first Bohemian historian, Cosmas of Prague, had imagined and portrayed the first people ever to settle in Bohemia as living in a state of total community:

Like the radiance of the sun, or the wetness of the water, so the ploughed fields and the pastures, yea even the very marriages, were all in common. . . . For after the fashion of animals they entered on matings for a single night. . . . Nor did anyone know how to say 'Mine', but, as in the monastic life, they called whatever they had 'Ours', with tongue and heart and in their deeds. There were no bolts to their shacks, they did not shut their doors against the needy, because there existed neither thief nor robber nor poor man. . . . But alas! they exchange prosperity for its opposite, and communal for private property . . . because the passion for possessing burns in them more fiercely than the fires of Etna . . .

Later chroniclers had perpetuated these ideas amongst the learned. Still more significant was the appearance of the same phantasy early in the fourteenth century in the *Czech Rhymed Chronicle*, a vernacular work which was to remain extremely popular right down to the close of the Middle Ages and which in many ways foreshadowed the Taborite storm. For there the long-lost blissful community of the earliest Czechs is portrayed with propagandist intent, in a context of virulent attacks upon the commercial, and German, civilization of the towns – very much as, a couple of centuries later, the Revolutionary of the Upper Rhine was to contrast the supposed communal life of the earliest Germans with the wicked usurious ways introduced by the Romans. How deeply these phantasies coloured the social and historical outlook of the Czechs is shown by the fact that when the fourteenth-century legal code known as the *Majestas Carolini* was rendered into the vernacular, even that solemn document was made to say not only that originally, and for a long time, all things had been held in common, but also that that custom had been the right one.

As the extreme Taborites understood it, the Millennium was to be characterized by a return of the lost anarcho-communist order. Taxes, dues, rents were to be abolished and so was private property of all kinds. There was to be no human authority of any sort: 'All shall live together as brothers, none shall be subject to another.' 'The Lord shall reign, and the Kingdom shall be handed over to the people of the earth.' And since the Millennium was to be a classless society, it was to be expected that the preparatory massacres would take the form of a class-war against 'the great' – of a final assault, in fact, upon that old ally of Antichrist, Dives. The Taborites were quite explicit on the point: 'All lords, nobles and knights shall be cut down and exterminated in the forests like outlaws.' Yet, as had been the case in other lands in earlier centuries, it was above all the rich town-dweller, the merchant or the absentee landowner, rather than the old-style feudal lord, who was seen as Dives. And it was this urban Dives whom the radical Taborites were most eager to destroy, just as it was the towns that they proposed to burn to the ground, so that no believer should ever enter one again. Prague, the stronghold of the supporters of Sigismund, was an object of special detestation; and by calling the city Babylon the Taborites showed clearly enough the meaning that they attached to its impending doom. For Babylon, birthplace of Antichrist and demonic counterpart of Jerusalem, was traditionally regarded as the embodiment of *Luxuria* and *Avaritia*; and this is how the Book of Revelation foretells its fall:

How much she hath glorified herself, and lived deliciously, so much torment and sorrow give her. . . . Therefore shall her plagues come in one day, death, and mourning, and famine; and she shall be utterly burned with fire: for strong is the Lord God who judgeth her. And the kings of the earth, who have committed fornication and lived deliciously with her, shall bewail her, and lament for her, when they shall see the smoke of her burning, standing afar off for the fear of her torment, saying, Alas, alas, that great city Babylon, that mighty city! for in one hour is thy judgement come. And the merchants of the earth shall weep and mourn over her; for no man buyeth their merchandise any more...

After which the warrior-Christ appears in the heavens at the head of the army of angels, to make war upon Antichrist and to establish the Millennium on earth.

Once the great purification had been carried out and the state of total community had been recreated on Bohemian soil, the Saints must go forth to conquer and dominate the rest of the world. For they were 'the army sent through all the world to carry the plagues of vengeance and to inflict revenge upon the nations and their cities and towns, and judgement upon every people that shall resist them'. Thereafter 'kings shall serve them, and any nation that will not serve them shall be destroyed'; – 'the Sons of God shall tread on the necks of kings and all realms under heaven shall be given unto them'. It was a most potent social myth, and one to which some of the extremists clung for many years and through the most discouraging experiences. The Second Coming might be indefinitely delayed, the traditional social order might remain unchanged, every real chance of an egalitarian revolution might disappear – still these phantasies lingered on. As late as 1434 we find a speaker at a Taborite assembly declaring that, however unfavourable the circumstances might be at present, the moment would soon come when the Elect must arise and exterminate their enemies – the lords in the first place, and then any of their own people who were of doubtful loyalty or usefulness. That done, with Bohemia fully in their control, they must proceed at whatever cost in bloodshed to conquer first the neighbouring and then all other territories: 'For that is what the Romans did, and in that way they came to dominate the whole world.'

In practice the plan to establish a world-wide anarcho-communistic order met with very limited success. Early in 1420 communal chests were set up at certain centres, under the control of Taborite priests; and thousands of peasants and artisans throughout Bohemia and Moravia sold all their belongings and paid the proceeds into these chests. These people broke utterly with their past lives – often they even burnt their homesteads to the ground. Many of them joined the Taborite armies to lead, as propertyless nomadic warriors of Christ, a life strangely like that of the *plebs pauperum* of the crusades. But there were also many who settled in towns which happened to be Taborite strongholds and formed what were intended to be completely egalitarian communities, held together by brotherly love alone and knowing nothing of Mine or Thine.

The first of these communities was formed, at the beginning of 1420, at Písek in south Bohemia. The next came into being in February 1420, shortly after Christ had failed to return to earth as predicted. A force of Taborites and peasants, led by Taborite priests, captured the town of Ústí on the River Lužnica; and after a few days they moved to a nearby promontory which, jutting into the river, formed a natural fortress. All this was in the neighbourhood of the hill which, the year before, had been named Mount Tabor; and now the fortress was renamed Tabor also. In March the military commander John Žižka abandoned his headquarters at Plžen and moved to Tabor, with all the Plžen Taborites. The local feudal lords were quickly defeated in a series of sorties and the whole neighbourhood came under the domination of Tabor. During 1420 and 1421 Tabor and Písek were the two main strongholds of the Taborite movement; but it was Tabor that became the home of the most radical and millenarian wing of the movement. Dominated at first by the very poor, it set about inaugurating the new Golden Age: 'As Mine and Thine do not exist at Tabor, but all possession is communal, so all people must always hold everything in common, and nobody must possess anything of his own; whoever owns private property commits a mortal sin.'

Unfortunately for their social experiment, the Taborite revolutionaries were so preoccupied with common ownership that they altogether ignored the need to produce. They even seemed to have believed that, like Adam and Eve in Paradise, the denizens of the new ideal communities would be exempted from all need to work. But if it is not surprising that this early essay in applied communism was short-lived, the way in which it ended still deserves some attention. The adepts of the Free Spirit commonly regarded themselves as entitled to steal and rob; and now very similar expedients, but on a far bigger scale, were adopted by these Taborite communities. When the funds in the communal chests were exhausted the radicals declared that, as 'men of the Law of God', they were entitled to take whatever belonged to the enemies of God – meaning at first the clergy and the nobility and the rich in general, but soon anyone who was not a Taborite. Thenceforth, alongside or in combination with the major campaigns waged under Žižka, many campaigns occurred which were simply robbers' raids. As the more moderate Taborites complained at their synod, 'many communities never think of earning their own living by the work of their hands but are only willing to live on other people's property and to undertake unjust campaigns for the sole purpose of robbing'. Even while they abominated the luxurious ways of the rich, many of the radical Taborites – just like some adepts of the Free Spirit – made themselves garments of truly regal magnificence, which they wore under their tunics.

The local peasantry suffered much. Of the peasants who owed allegiance to the Taborite regime it was only a minority who sold their belongings and joined the body of the Elect. In the spring of 1420, in the first flush of revolutionary enthusiasm, the Taborites proclaimed the abolition of all feudal bonds, dues and services; and multitudes of peasants accordingly hastened to place themselves under the protection of the new regime. Within half a year they had good cause to regret their decision. By October 1420, the Taborites were driven by their own economic plight to set about collecting dues from the peasants in the territories which they controlled; and not long afterwards the dues were greatly increased, so that many peasants found themselves worse off than they had been under their former lords.

Again it is a synod of the moderate Taborites which has left the most striking description. 'Almost all the communities,' the synod complained, 'harass the common people of the neighbourhood in quite inhuman fashion, oppress them like tyrants and pagans and extort rent pitilessly even from the truest believers – and that although some of these people are of the same faith as themselves, are exposed to the same dangers of war along with them and are cruelly ill-treated and robbed by the enemy.' The plight of these peasants, caught between the warring armies, was indeed a wretched one. As the fortunes of war swung now one way, now another, they had to pay dues now to the Taborites and now to their old feudal lords. Moreover they were constantly being penalized by both sides for having (however unwillingly) collaborated with the enemy; by the Taborites for being 'the allies of tyrants' and by the Catholics for being 'the friends of heretics'. While they were under the domination of the Taborites they were treated by their so-called brethren as the most abject serfs. Dues would be extracted by 'the men of the Law of God' with such threats as: 'If you disobey, we will with God's help compel you, by every means and especially by fire, to carry out our command.' Though the Taborites had challenged the feudal order with an effectiveness hitherto undreamed-of, it is doubtful how much the Bohemian peasantry benefited. Certainly by the time the war was over the peasantry was weaker and the nobility stronger than before. Serfdom of a most onerous kind could then be imposed easily enough.

Even within Tabor itself the anarcho-communistic experiment

had soon to be abandoned. However reluctant the experimenters were to do any work, they could not live without it; and soon the artisans were organizing themselves in a system of crafts very similar to that existing in other Bohemian towns. Above all, from March 1420 onwards the Taborites were involved in the national war against the invading armies; for several months they actually helped the non-Taborite Hussites of Prague in the defence of the capital. Not even a Taborite army could function without a hierarchy of command; and in the event Žižka, who was neither an egalitarian nor a millenarian, saw to it that the positions of command were reserved for men who, like himself, came from the lower nobility. All this tended to dampen the fire of the Taborite priests; and by the time they returned to Tabor, in September, they were less concerned with the Millennium than with electing a 'bishop' to supervise them and to administer their funds. Yet the pursuit of the New Golden Age was not abandoned without a struggle. While more and more Taborites prepared to adjust themselves to the exigencies of economics, of war and of a social stratification which gave no signs of collapsing, a minority responded by developing new forms of millenarian faith.

The preacher Martin Húska, partly inspired by the immigrant *Pikarti*, developed a Eucharistic doctrine which represented a total break with the usual Taborite ideas. Žižka and many other Taborites shared with the Utraquists of Prague a profound reverence for the Eucharist as the very body and blood of Christ; when they went into battle a chalice on a pole was carried in front, as a standard. Húska on the other hand rejected transsubstantiation and propagated instead a communion service which had primarily the significance of a love-feast – and of a rehearsal for the 'messianic banquet' which the returning Christ was to hold with his elect. For spreading such ideas abroad he was burned to death in August 1421.

These ideas spread to Tabor itself. Early in 1421 some hundreds of radicals, to whom the name of *Pikarti* was also given, were busy there under the leadership of a priest called Peter Kániš. They caused much dissension, until in February they left the town or were expelled from it. Most of them simply shared Húska's ideas about the Eucharist, but amongst them there were some extremists – perhaps as many as 200 – who held the doctrine of the Free Spirit in its most militant form. These were the people who were to become famous in history under the name of Bohemian Adamites. They held that God dwelt in the Saints of the Last Days, that is, in themselves; and that that made them superior to Christ, who by dying had shown himself to be merely human.

They accordingly dispensed with the Bible, the Creed and all book-learning, contenting themselves with a prayer which ran: 'Our Father who art in us, illumine us, thy will be done ...' They maintained that heaven and hell had no existence save in the righteous and the unrighteous respectively; and concluded that they, being righteous, would live for ever as denizens of the earthly Millennium.

Žižka interrupted a campaign to deal with the Adamites. In April 1421 he captured some seventy-five of them, including Peter Kániš, and had them burnt as heretics; some strode laughing into the flames. The survivors found a new leader in a peasant, or possibly a blacksmith, whom they called both Adam and Moses; he was supposed to be entrusted with the government of the world. There seems also to have been a woman who claimed to be the Virgin Mary. For the rest, these Adamites are said – just like the adepts of the Free Spirit – to have lived in a state of community so unconditional that not only did nobody possess anything of his own but that exclusive marriage was regarded as a sin. Whereas the Taborites in general were strictly monogamous, in this sect free love seems to have been the rule. On the strength of Christ's remark about harlots and publicans, the Adamites declared that the chaste were unworthy to enter their messianic Kingdom. On the other hand no couple could have sexual intercourse without the consent of 'Adam-Moses', who would bless them saying: 'Go, be fruitful and multiply and replenish the earth.' The sect was much given to naked ritual dances held around a fire and accompanied by hymn-singing. Indeed these people seem to have spent much of their time naked, ignoring heat and cold and claiming to be in the state of innocence enjoyed by Adam and Eve before the Fall.

When Žižka was pursuing the *Pikarti*, these ultra-anarchists took refuge on an island in the River Nezarka, between Vesely (Weseli) and Jindřichuv Hradec (Neuhaus). Like other Taborites, the Adamites regarded themselves as avenging angels, whose mission it was to wield the sword throughout the world until all the unclean had been cut down. Blood, they declared, must flood the world to the height of a horse's head; and despite their small number they did their best to achieve this aim. From their island stronghold they constantly made nocturnal sorties – which they called a Holy War – against neighbouring villages; and in these expeditions their communistic principles and their lust for destruction both found expression. The Adamites, who had no possessions of their own, seized everything they could lay hands on. At the same time they set the villages on fire and cut down or burnt alive every man, woman and child whom they could find; this too they justified with a quotation from the Scriptures: 'And at midnight there was a cry made – Behold, the bridegroom cometh . . .' Priests, whom they called incarnate devils, they slaughtered with particular enthusiasm.

In the end Žižka sent a force of 400 trained soldiers under one of his senior officers to put a stop to the disorder. Unperturbed, 'Adam-Moses' declared that the enemy would be stricken with blindness on the battle-field, so that a whole host would be utterly helpless; whereas the Saints, if they stood steadfastly by him, would be invulnerable. His followers believed him and, barricaded on their island, defended themselves with furious energy and courage, killing many of the attackers. On 21 October 1421, they were at last overwhelmed and exterminated. One man only was spared on Žižka's orders, so that he might give a full account of the doctrines and practices of the group. His testimony was duly recorded and submitted for the consideration of the Utraquist Faculty of Theology at Prague. He himself was then burnt and his ashes were sunk in the river – a precaution which strongly suggests that he was no other than the messianic leader, 'Adam-Moses'.

By that time social revolution in Bohemia was already bulking less large amongst the aims of the Taborite movement. In the following year a counter-revolution put an end to the ascendancy of the artisans in Prague; and thereafter, though talk of revolution might continue, effective power came to lie increasingly with the nobility. But beyond the frontiers the teaching and example of the Bohemian revolutionaries continued to work upon the discontented poor. 'The Bohemians,' says a hostile chronicler, 'now became so strong and mighty, and so arrogant, that they were feared on all sides and all honest folk were terrified lest the roguery and disorder should spread to other peoples and turn against all who were decent and law-abiding, and against the rich. For it was the very thing for the poor who did not want to work, yet were insolent and pleasure-loving. There were many such in all countries, coarse and worthless people who encouraged the Bohemians in their heresy and unbelief as much as ever they could; and when they dared not do so openly, they did it secretly. . . . So the Bohemians had many secret supporters amongst the rough folk. . . . They used to argue with the priests, saying that everyone should share his property with everyone else. This would have pleased many worthless fellows and could very well have come to pass.'

Everywhere the rich and privileged, clerics and laymen alike, were obsessed by the fear that the spread of Taborite influence would result in a revolution which would overthrow the whole social order. Taborite propaganda aiming at the overthrow not only of the clergy but of the nobility penetrated to France and even to Spain; and it found many sympathetic readers. When peasants in Burgundy and around Lyons rose against their ecclesiastical and secular overlords, the French clergy at once attributed the revolts to the influence of Taborite pamphlets; and they may well have been right. But it was in Germany that the Taborites had most chance to exert influence, for in 1430 their armies penetrated as far as Leipzig, Bamberg and Nuremberg; and it was in Germany that anxiety was keenest. When at Mainz, Bremen, Constance, Weimar and Stettin the guilds rose against the patricians, the disorders were blamed on the Taborites. In 1431 the patricians of Ulm called upon the towns allied with them to join together in a new crusade against Hussite Bohemia. They pointed out that there were in Germany revolutionary elements which had much in common with the Taborites. It would be all too easy for the rebellion of the poor to spread from Bohemia into Germany; and if it did, the patricians in the towns would be amongst the chief sufferers. The General Council of Basle, meeting in the same year, also expressed its concern lest the common people in Germany should enter into an alliance with the Taborites and begin to seize Church property.

Such fears may have been exaggerated and premature; but it was to be proved several times in the course of the next hundred years that they were not altogether unfounded.

12 The Egalitarian Millennium (ii)

The Drummer of Niklashausen

In 1434 the Taborite army was defeated and almost annihilated in the battle of Lipan, by an army not of foreign Catholics but of Bohemian Utraquists; and from then onwards the strength of the Taborite wing of the Hussite movement rapidly declined. After the town of Tabor itself was taken over by the Utraquists in 1452, a coherent Taborite tradition survived only in the sect known as the Bohemian or Moravian Brethren – and there only in a purely religious form, pacifist, unrevolutionary and apolitical. Nevertheless an underground current of militant millenarianism must have continued in Bohemia. In the 1450's or early 1460's two brothers belonging to a rich and noble family, Janko and Livin of Wirsberg, began to disseminate eschatological prophecies to which both the Johannine and the Joachite traditions contributed.

At the centre of this doctrine stood a messiah who was referred to as the Anointed Saviour and who was expected to inaugurate the Third and Last Age. The brothers asserted that this man, not Christ, was the Messiah prophesied in the Old Testament, the true Son of Man who was to appear in glory at the end of history. He was endowed with insight such as had been granted to no other man; he had beheld the Trinity and the Divine Essence; his understanding of the hidden meaning of the Scriptures made all previous interpreters seem, by comparison, blind or drunk. And it was his mission to save not simply mankind but God himself; for God had been suffering because of the sins of men ever since the world began, and now he was calling daily to the Anointed Saviour to release him from his anguish. But such a task could not of course be carried out without much bloodshed; and so the new messiah would begin by slaying Antichrist – the Pope – and would go on to destroy all the clergy, as ministers of Antichrist, save only the Mendicant Orders. In the end he would turn upon all who resisted him in any way, and to such good effect that – as prophesied in the Book of Revelation – a mere 14,000 would survive. This 'saving remnant' would be united in a single faith, a spiritual church without an external cult; and over them all the Anointed Saviour would reign at once as Roman Emperor and as God (*sicut Caesar imperator et Deus*).

The massacre itself was to be carried out with the aid of bands of mercenaries – a curious idea, and not without significance. At that time territories bordering on Bohemia were in fact being devastated by demobilized Bohemian mercenaries who had preserved enough of Taborite ways to call themselves 'Brethren' and their fortified camp 'Tabor'. Although these people were no zealots but merely brigands, to enthusiastic souls in Bohemia – such as the Wirsberg brothers – they could easily appear as true successors to the revolutionary millenarians of 1420. Certainly the new order which was to emerge from the massacre was intended to have egalitarian traits: the clergy who survived – the Mendicants – were to hold no property at all; the nobles were to abandon their castles and to live in towns like ordinary burghers. Contemporaries were indeed particularly struck by the fact that, disseminated in the vernacular, the doctrine encouraged the populace 'to rise in seditious rebellion against its spiritual and secular superiors'; and they did not hesitate to compare it with the doctrine of the *Pikarti* – 'who used to be in Bohemia ... and wanted to make an earthly Paradise there'.

The begetter of the doctrine seems to have been not one of the Wirsberg brothers themselves but a Franciscan who had broken away from his community and who believed that he himself was the Anointed Saviour. The brothers were completely dominated by this personage and were happy to regard themselves as his emissaries and heralds; Janko even saw himself as a new John the Baptist and adopted the name of John out of the East. From their headquarters at Eger (Cheb), at the westernmost extremity of Bohemia, they distributed their master's prophecies far and wide, both amongst the laity and amongst Franciscans of 'Spiritual' and Joachite tendency. They claimed to have so many supporters in Germany that, if they were all united, they could deal with any prince. This was certainly a gross exaggeration; yet it is interesting to note that when the doctrine penetrated to Erfurt – at that time a large city with extreme contrasts of wealth and poverty – the professor who was the intellectual leader of the University felt called upon to compose and read a paper against it.

The preordained year for the advent of the Anointed Saviour was 1467; but what would have happened then can never be known, for in the preceding year the ecclesiastical authorities, led by the papal legate, decided that it was high time that the movement was suppressed. Janko of Wirsberg seems to have fled – his fate is unknown – but Livin, having avoided the stake by recanting his errors, was confined in the prison of the Bishop of Regensburg, where after a couple of years he died. Meanwhile the town of Eger was busily defending itself, in letters to its sister cities of the Empire and even to the Pope, against the accusation of being a hotbed of heresy.

If in Bohemia itself there was less and less scope for such movements, in Germany conditions were singularly propitious for the reception of Taborite influences. Those defects in the structure of the state which for generations had been causing disarray amongst the common people were still making themselves felt, and more powerfully than ever. The dignity and authority of the imperial office continued to dwindle, Germany continued to disintegrate into a jumble of principalities. During the second half of the fifteenth century the prestige of the Emperor sank particularly low. Frederick III had at first, because of his name, been the focus of the wildest millennial expectations; but in the course of a reign which lasted from 1452 to 1493 he proved a singularly ineffective monarch. His deposition was prevented only by the lack of any suitable rival and latterly his very existence was almost forgotten by his subjects. The vacuum at the centre of the state produced a chronic and widespread anxiety – an anxiety which found expression in the folklore of 'the future Frederick' but which could also vent itself in sudden waves of eschatological excitement. Amongst its commonest manifestations were mass pilgrimages, reminiscent of the popular crusades and the flagellant processions of earlier times, and no less liable to escape from ecclesiastical control.

The German territories bordering on Bohemia offered a particularly favourable field for Taborite propaganda. The centuries-old heretical tradition of the Bavarian towns persisted throughout the fifteenth century. In the middle of the century the Bishop of Eichstätt still found it necessary to threaten with excommunication flagellants who were beating themselves in front of the churches and Beghards 'of voluntary poverty' who were wandering begging through the land and who believed themselves to have attained perfection. This ban was repeated from time to time right down to the end of the century. At Würzburg too a synod in the middle of the century repeated the old prohibition on wandering, preaching Beghards. In such an environment the radical Taborite tradition could continue to make itself felt long after it had died out in its homeland. It throve all the better because nowhere was the clergy more given to *Luxuria* and *Avaritia* than in Bavaria. Innumerable episcopal complaints bear witness to the debauchery of the lower clergy, many of whom devoted themselves to drink and gaming and did not hesitate to take their mistresses with them even to synods. And the bishops themselves often did little enough to win the devotion of their flocks.

The situation was particularly explosive in the territories of the Prince-Bishop of Würzburg. For generations the bishops had been at loggerheads with the burghers of Würzburg; and the fact that at the beginning of the fifteenth century the burghers were decisively defeated did not put an end to the tension. Moreover the bishops during the first half of the century were wildly extravagant and could pay their debts only by levying ever heavier taxes. By 1474 the taxes had become so exorbitant that one of the Bishop's officials, comparing the local peasantry to a team of horses drawing a heavy wagon, remarked that if a single egg were added to that wagon the horses would no longer be able to pull it. To a laity which had learnt from generations of heretical preachers that the clergy ought to live in total poverty, this heavy burden of taxation was bound to appear particularly monstrous. This was not altered by the fact that the Bishop at that time, Rudolph of Scherenberg, was both able and responsible. In the city and diocese of Würzburg it was no longer possible in the 1470's for the bishop, whatever his personal qualities, to be regarded by the laity and especially by the poor as anything but an exploiter.

In 1476 there began at Niklashausen, a small village in the valley of the Tauber, not far from Würzburg, a movement which could almost be called a new People's Crusade. Much that had occurred during the earlier crusades in France and the Low Countries and the Rhine valley was now repeated in southern Germany; but this time the messianic Kingdom was no Heavenly Jerusalem but the State of Nature, as it had been pictured by John Ball and the radical Taborites. The messiah of the movement was a young man called Hans Böhm – a name which suggests either that he was of Bohemian descent or else that in the popular mind he was associated with Hussite teachings. He was a shepherd and, in his spare time, a popular entertainer, drumming and piping in hostelries and in the market-place – whence the nickname, by which he is still known, of Drummer (or Piper) of Niklashausen. It happened that one day this lad heard tell of the Italian Franciscan Giovanni di Capistrano who a generation earlier had gone through Germany preaching repentance, urging his hearers to put away their fine clothes and to burn all dice and playing-cards. Shortly afterwards, in the middle of Lent, the shepherd burnt his drum before the parish church of Niklashausen and began to preach to the people.

Exactly like that other shepherd lad who is said to have launched the Shepherds' Crusade in 1320, Böhm declared that the

Virgin Mary had appeared to him surrounded by a heavenly radiance and had given him a message of prodigious importance. Instead of summoning people to dance, Böhm was to edify them with the pure Word of God. He was to explain how divine Providence had favoured Niklashausen above all places. In the parish church of Niklashausen there stood a statue of the Virgin to which miraculous powers were attributed and which had long attracted pilgrims. Now – the Virgin had declared – this spot had become the salvation of the world. The message went on in terms strongly reminiscent of the Heavenly Letters used by the flagellants in 1260 and again in 1348. God had intended to punish mankind most grievously; the Virgin had interceded and God had agreed to withhold punishment; but now men must go in their multitudes on pilgrimage to the Virgin of Niklashausen or else punishment would after all descend upon the world. From Niklashausen, and from there alone, the Virgin would bestow her blessings upon all lands; in the Tauber valley alone, and not at Rome or anywhere else, was to be found divine grace. Whoever made the pilgrimage would be absolved from all his sins; whoever died there would go immediately to heaven.

The former shepherd was a simple man but now he was suddenly able to command astonishing eloquence. On Sundays and feastdays crowds streamed to hear him. Soon he was following the course which has been followed by so many *prophetae* from Tanchelm onwards. At first he merely preached repentance: women were to throw away their golden necklaces and gay kerchiefs, men were to wear less colourful costumes and less pointed shoes. But before long the *propheta* was claiming for himself miraculous powers as startling as those which at first he had attributed to the Virgin. That God had not sent a frost to kill off all corn and vines was, he proclaimed, due to his prayers alone. Moreover he swore that he could lead any soul out of hell with his own hand.

Although Böhm had begun to preach with the consent of the parish priest it was to be expected that he would end by turning against the clergy. With the utmost violence he voiced the traditional accusations of *Avaritia* and *Luxuria*. It would, he said, be easier to make a Christian out of a Jew than out of a priest. God had long been outraged by the behaviour of the clergy; now he would tolerate it no longer. The day of reckoning was at hand, when the clergy would be happy to cover up their tonsures to escape from their pursuers (one recognizes the old pseudo-Joachite prophecy which John of Winterthur had found to be so popular in 1348); for to kill a cleric would then be seen as a most meritorious act. God had withdrawn his strength from the clergy and there would soon be no priests or monks left on earth. Even now, he added threateningly, they would be ill-advised to burn him as a heretic. A fearful punishment awaited them if they did, for it was they themselves who were the real heretics.

Böhm did not stop at general criticisms and vague threats. He called upon his hearers to refuse all payment of taxes and tithes. Henceforth, he cried, priests should be made to give up their many benefices and live from meal to meal on what people chose to give them. The appeal of this familiar teaching was just as great as it had always been. Trithemius, the celebrated Abbot of Sponheim, commented: 'What would the layman like better than to see clergy and priesthood robbed of all their privileges and rights, their tithes and revenues? For the common people is by nature hungry for novelties and ever eager to shake off its master's yoke.' And the Primate of Germany, the Archbishop of Mainz, saw in the *propheta* of Niklashausen a force which might inflict irreparable damage upon the Church.

In the end Böhm emerged as a social revolutionary, proclaiming the imminence of the egalitarian Millennium based on Natural Law. In the coming Kingdom the use of wood, water and pasturage, the right to fish and hunt would be freely enjoyed by all, as they had been in olden times. Tributes of all kinds would be abolished for ever. No rent or services would be owed to any lord, no taxes or duties to any prince. Distinctions of rank and status would cease to exist and nobody would have authority over anybody else. All would live together as brothers, everyone enjoying the same liberties and doing the same amount of work as everyone else. 'Princes, ecclesiastical and secular alike, and counts and knights should only possess as much as common folk, then everyone would have enough. The time will have to come when princes and lords will work for their daily bread.' And Böhm extended his attack beyond the local lords and princes to the very summit of society. 'The Emperor is a scoundrel and the Pope is useless. It is the Emperor who gives the princes and counts and knights the right to levy taxes on the common people. Alas, poor devils that you are!'

No doubt Böhm's teaching appealed in different ways to different sections of the population. The demand for the overthrow of all rulers, great and small, probably appealed particularly to the urban poor; we know that townsfolk did in fact come to Niklashausen, not only from Würzburg but from all over southern and central Germany. On the other hand in demanding that wood, water, pasturage, fishing and hunting should be free to all men, Böhm was voicing a very general aspiration of the peasants. The

German peasants believed that these rights had in fact been theirs in olden time, until usurped by the nobility; this was one of the wrongs which they were always expecting the future 'Emperor Frederick' to undo. But above all it was the prestige of the preacher himself, as a miraculous being sent by God, which drew the tens of thousands into the Tauber valley. The common people, peasants and artisans alike, saw in him a supernatural protector and leader, such as the 'Emperor Frederick' was to have been: a saviour who could bestow on them individually the fulness of divine grace and who would lead them collectively into an earthly Paradise.

News of the wonderful happenings at Niklashausen passed rapidly from village to village in the neighbourhood and was carried further afield, too, by messengers who went out in all directions. Soon vast hordes of common folk of all ages and both sexes, and including whole families, were streaming towards Niklashausen. Not only the surrounding country but all parts of southern and central Germany were in commotion, from the Alps to the Rhineland and to Thuringia. Artisans deserted their workshops and peasants their fields, shepherds and shepherdesses abandoned their flocks and hastened – often still in the same clothes and carrying their picks and hammers and scythes – to hear and adore him who was now known as 'the Holy Youth'. These people greeted one another only as 'Brother' or 'Sister' and these greetings acquired the significance of a rallying-cry. Amongst the multitudes of simple, wildly excited folk there circulated fantastic rumours. What the *plebs pauperum* had believed of Jerusalem these people believed of Niklashausen. There Paradise had literally descended upon the earth; and infinite riches were lying ready to be gathered by the faithful, who would share them out amongst themselves in brotherly love. Meanwhile the hordes – like the *Pastoureaux* and the flagellants before them – advanced in long columns, bearing banners and singing songs of their own composition. Of these songs one became particularly popular:

> To God in Heaven we complain
> *Kyrie eleison*
> That the priests cannot be slain
> *Kyrie eleison*

As the pilgrims arrived at Niklashausen they placed offerings before the statue of the Virgin. But an even intenser devotion was given to the *propheta* himself. Before him the pilgrims dropped on the knees, crying: 'O Man of God, sent from Heaven, take pity on us!' They crowded about him so closely by day and night that he was scarcely able to eat or sleep and was often in danger of being crushed to death. Articles of his clothing were seized and cut into minute pieces; and whoever could acquire one of these treasured it as a relic of inestimable worth, 'as though it were hay from the manger of Bethlehem'. Before long it was reported that he had, by a laying-on of hands, cured people who had been blind or dumb from birth; that he had raised the dead; and that he had made a spring gush from a rock.

The returning multitudes of pilgrims were constantly replaced by new multitudes. Chroniclers talk of thirty, forty, even seventy thousand gathered together on a single day at Niklashausen; and though these figures are absurd, the concourse must certainly have been very great. A vast camp sprang up around the little village; tents were set up in which tradesmen, artisans and cooks catered for the travellers' needs. From time to time Böhm would mount a tub, or appear at an upper window, or even climb a tree, to preach his revolutionary doctrine to the crowds.

The pilgrimages began towards the end of March 1474. By June the authorities, ecclesiastical and secular alike, decided that Böhm's propaganda was a serious menace to the social order and must be dealt with. First the Town Council of Nuremberg forbade the inhabitants of that city to go on pilgrimage to Niklashausen. Next vigorous measures were taken at Würzburg, the city most directly affected. Perturbed at the great number of strangers who were pouring through the town, the Council closed as many of the gates as possible, bade its citizens look to their arms and armour, and did what it could to stop wild talk. In the end the Prince-Bishop set about breaking the power of the *propheta*. At the diet which he summoned it was decided that Böhm was to be arrested.

According to his Catholic enemies Böhm now tried to organize a revolt. He is said at the end of a sermon delivered on 7 July to have told the men amongst his hearers that on the following Sunday they were to come armed, and without women and children; for, at the Virgin's bidding, he had some serious things to say to them. What is certain is that on the night of Saturday 12th a squad of horsemen sent by the Bishop descended on Niklashausen, seized Böhm and carried him off to Würzburg. In the darkness the pilgrims were unable to protect their *propheta*; but next day a peasant took up the prophetic role, declaring that the Holy Trinity had appeared to him and had given him a message for the assembled pilgrims. They were to march boldly to the castle at Würzburg where Böhm was imprisoned. As they approached it the walls would crumble like those of Jericho, the gates would open of their own accord and the Holy Youth would emerge triumphantly from captivity. This communication at once convinced the pilgrims. Bearing hundreds of giant candles taken from the church at Niklashausen but almost no weapons, some thousands of men, women and children marched through the night until they arrived at dawn beneath the castle walls.

The Bishop and Town Council did what they could to avoid violence. They sent an emissary to reason with the pilgrims but he was driven off with stones. A second emissary was more successful: the many pilgrims who were subjects of the Bishop deserted and went peacefully to their homes. The rest stood firm, insisting that the Holy Youth must be released or else, with the miraculous help of the Virgin, they would release him by force. A few cannon-shots were fired over their heads, but the fact that nobody was hurt only strengthened their belief that the Virgin was protecting them; and they tried to storm the town, shouting their saviour's name. This time shots were fired in earnest and followed by a cavalry-charge. Some forty pilgrims were killed and the rest at once fled in helpless panic.

Support for Böhm was so strong that even after this overwhelming victory the Bishop and Town Council could not feel secure. The burghers of Würzburg were warned to expect a second and more formidable attack; but it was also feared that within the city itself there were many who were only waiting for a chance to join forces with the pilgrim host. The Bishop accordingly asked the neighbouring lords to hold themselves ready to come to his help in case of need. But before any fresh disturbances could occur Böhm had been tried by an ecclesiastical court and found guilty of heresy and sorcery. Two of his peasant disciples – one of them being the visionary who had tried to organize his rescue – were beheaded; and he himself was burnt at the stake, singing hymns to the Virgin as he perished. During the execution the spectators kept far away from the stake; the common people expecting a miracle from Heaven which would save the Holy Youth and scatter the flames amongst his persecutors, the Bishop and his clergy expecting some diabolical intervention. Afterwards – as with the pseudo-Frederick of Neuss two centuries before – the ashes were thrown into the river, lest followers of the *propheta* should treasure them as relics; but even then some of these people scraped the earth from around the foot of the stake and treasured that.

Everything possible was done to destroy all trace of Böhm and his works. The offerings left at the church of Niklashausen, which must have been considerable, were confiscated and shared between the Archbishop of Mainz, the Bishop of Würzburg and the count in whose territory the church stood. In all the affected areas of Germany archbishops, princes and town councils joined in forbidding any further pilgrimages to the shrine. Nevertheless pilgrims continued to arrive particularly from the diocese of Würzburg, and they still continued to arrive after they were threatened with excommunication and the church had been closed and placed under an interdict. In the end, at the beginning of 1477, the church was demolished by order of the Archbishop of Mainz. But for many years the spot had its secret visitors, especially by night.

There is no doubt that the Holy Youth of Niklashausen had been exploited by men who were far shrewder than he. It is known that certain local lords tried to use the popular excitement to weaken their overlord, the Bishop of Würzburg, with whom they had for some years been at loggerheads. These were the men who headed the nocturnal march on Würzburg; one of them had later, by way of penance, to hand over much of his land to the cathedral chapter. But more important than these political intriguers were two personages who lurk in the shadowy background of the story and but for whom the whole mass pilgrimage might perhaps never have taken place.

Again one is reminded of the *Pastoureaux* rising of 1320. On that occasion, too, the simple shepherd-boy saw a vision of the Virgin and received a message from her. But it was only when an apostate monk and an unfrocked priest had given him their support and organized the necessary propaganda that a mass movement sprang into being; and it was under the leadership of these men that the movement became a revolutionary one. Böhm too was a simple shepherd-boy; we are told that from earliest youth he had been regarded as half-witted, that until he began to preach he had never been able to form a coherent sentence, and that to his dying day he remained ignorant of the Lord's Prayer. That he was nevertheless able to throw vast areas of Germany into commotion was due to the backing which he received. The parish priest of Niklashausen was quick to realize that a few miracles could attract large offerings to his hitherto obscure shrine; and accordingly – as he himself later admitted – he invented miracles and attributed them to the Holy Youth. But the major part was played by a hermit who had for some time been living in a cave nearby and who had acquired a great reputation for holiness.

This hermit seems to have exercised a total domination over Böhm, intimidating and inspiring him. Even the vision of the Virgin was said by some to have been a trick devised by him to deceive the young shepherd. It was also said that when Böhm addressed the crowds from a window the hermit stood behind him and prompted him – as he is shown to be doing in the wood-cut from Schedel's Chronicle (Plate 7). Even if the story is fanciful, it probably indicates well enough what the relationship between the two men really was. Certainly it adds to the interest of the names which the ecclesiastical authorities applied to the hermit – who fled when the Holy Youth was arrested, but was caught soon afterwards. They called him a Beghard, a native of Bohemia and a Hussite. Although the evidence cannot be called conclusive, it seems reasonably certain that it was the hermit who turned the religious pilgrimage into a revolutionary movement. In the quiet Tauber valley he must have seen the future centre of a millennial Kingdom in which the primal egalitarian order was to be restored. And perhaps modern historians have been too hasty in rejecting, as an obvious slander, the story that when Böhm was arrested he was found stark naked in a tavern, preaching wondrous things. After all, was that not the very way in which the Bohemian Adamites had represented, symbolically, the return of the State of Nature to a corrupted world?

Egalitarian millenarianism had now effectively penetrated into Germany; and more was to be heard of it during the next half-century. The *Reformation of Sigismund*, after existing as an almost forgotten manuscript for some forty years, appeared for the first time as a printed book within a couple of years of Böhm's execution and was reprinted in 1480, 1484, 1490 and 1494. Originally written just after the collapse of Taborite power in Bohemia, the work was itself an example of the attraction of Taborite ideals. Despite its relatively moderate programme, it too summoned the poor to take up the sword and enforce their rights under the leadership of the priest-king Frederick. In a far more violent form the same theme reappears in that *Book of a Hundred Chapters* which was produced by the Revolutionary of the Upper Rhine in the opening years of the sixteenth century. What that strange prophecy foretells at such enormous length is, after all, precisely what had been tersely indicated by John Ball and by the radical Taborites: that after one last bloody struggle against the hosts of Antichrist perfect justice would be re-established on earth and all men would be equals and brothers, perhaps even holding all things in common. And these phantasies were not confined to books; also in the neighbourhood of the Upper Rhine there appeared conspiratorial movements which were dedicated to translating them into reality. These were the movements which were known collectively as the *Bundschuh* – a term meaning a peasant's clog and having the same significance as the term *sans-culotte* during the French Revolution. The leader of the *Bundschuh* was a peasant called Joss Fritz and many of the rank-and-file were also peasants. But the urban poor, disbanded mercenaries, beggars and the like are known to have played a large part in the movement; and that no doubt is what gave it its peculiar character. For there were many other peasant risings in southern Germany in those years and they all aimed merely at limited reforms; only the *Bundschuh* aimed at the Millennium. Like the outbreak at Niklashausen, the *Bundschuh* rising which occurred in the diocese of Speyer in 1502 was provoked in a general sense by the failure of the latest attempt to restore the disintegrating structure of the Empire, and more immediately by the excessive taxes levied by an insolvent Prince-Bishop; but its object was nothing less than a social revolution of the most thorough-going kind. All authority was to be overthrown, all dues and taxes abolished, all ecclesiastical property distributed amongst the people; and all woods, waters and pastures were to become communal property. The flag of the movement showed Christ crucified with on one side a praying peasant, on the other the peasant clog, above it the slogan:'Nothing but God's justice!' It was planned to capture the town of Bruchsal, which included the palace of the Prince-Bishop; and from there the movement was to spread like wildfire through the length and breadth of Germany, bringing freedom to the peasants and town-dwellers who supported it, but death to everyone else. And although this plot was betrayed and the movement crushed, Joss Fritz survived to organize similar risings in 1513 and 1517, where yet again one finds the familiar blend of phantasies: on the one hand of exterminating all the rich and powerful and establishing an egalitarian order, on the other hand of 'getting rid of blasphemers', of being led by the Emperor, even of recovering the Holy Sepulchre. Indeed the image of the *Bundschuh* came to possess such prodigious significance that it was popularly believed that the original capture of Jerusalem had been achieved by peasants fighting under that sign.

And meanwhile in a different part of Germany – Thuringia, always so fertile in millenarian myths and movements – Thomas Müntzer was embarking on the stormy career which was to end by making him too into a prophet of the egalitarian Millennium, and one whose fame has endured to the present day.

Thomas Müntzer

Thomas Müntzer was born in Stolberg in Thuringia in 1488 or 1489. He was born not – as has often been stated – to poverty but to modest comfort; and his father was not hanged by a feudal tyrant but died in bed in the fulness of years. When he first comes clearly into view, in his early thirties, Müntzer appears neither as a victim nor as an enemy of social injustice but rather as an 'eternal student', extraordinarily learned and intensely intellectual. After becoming a university graduate and then a priest he led a restless, wandering life, always choosing places where he could hope to further his studies. Profoundly versed in the Scriptures, he learned Greek and Hebrew, read patristic and scholastic theology and philosophy, immersed himself also in the writings of the German mystics. Yet he never was a pure scholar; and his voracious reading was carried on in a desperate attempt to solve a personal problem. For Müntzer at that time was a troubled soul, full of doubts about the truth of Christianity and even about the existence of God but obstinately struggling after certainty – in fact in that labile condition which so often ends in a conversion.

Martin Luther, who was some five or six years older than Müntzer, was just then emerging as the most formidable opponent that the Church of Rome had ever known and also – if only incidentally and transitorily – as the effective leader of the German nation. In 1517 he nailed the famous theses against the sale of indulgences on to the church door at Wittenberg, in 1519 he questioned in public disputation the supremacy of the Pope, in 1520 he published – and was excommunicated for publishing – the three treatises which launched the German Reformation. Although it was to be many years before there appeared Evangelical churches organized on a territorial basis, there now existed a recognizable Lutheran party; and many of the clergy joined it, even while the majority clung firmly to 'the old religion'. It was as a follower of Luther that Müntzer first broke away from Catholic orthodoxy; and all the deeds that have made him famous were done in the midst of the great religious earthquake which first cracked and at length destroyed the massive structure of the medieval Church. Yet he himself abandoned Luther almost as soon as he had found him; and it was in ever fiercer opposition to Luther that he worked out and proclaimed his own doctrine.

What Müntzer needed if he was to become a new man, sure of himself and of his aim in life, was not indeed to be found in Luther's doctrine of justification by faith alone. It was to be found, rather, in the militant and bloodthirsty millenarianism that was unfolded to him when in 1520 he took up a ministry in the town of Zwickau and came in contact with a weaver called Niklas Storch. Zwickau lies close to the Bohemian border, Storch himself had been in Bohemia and it was essentially the old Taborite doctrines that were revived in Storch's teaching. He proclaimed that now, as in the days of the Apostles, God was communicating directly with his Elect; and the reason for this was that the Last Days were at hand. First the Turks must conquer the world and Antichrist must rule over it; but then – and it would be very soon – the Elect would rise up and annihilate all the godless, so that the Second Coming could take place and the Millennium begin. What most appealed to Müntzer in this programme was the war of extermination which the righteous were to wage against the unrighteous. Abandoning Luther, he now thought and talked only of the Book of Revelation and of such incidents in the Old Testament as Elijah's slaughter of the priests of Baal, Jehu's slaying of the sons of Ahab and Jael's assassination of the sleeping Sisera. Contemporaries noted and lamented the change that had come over him, the lust for blood which at times expressed itself in sheer raving.

By force of arms the Elect must prepare the way for the Millennium; but who were the Elect? In Müntzer's view they were those who had received the Holy Spirit or, as he usually called it, 'the living Christ'. In his writings, as in those of the Spiritual Libertines, a clear distinction is established between the historical Christ and the 'living' or 'inner' or 'spiritual' Christ who is imagined as being born in the individual soul; and it is the latter who possesses redemptive power. Yet in one respect the historical Christ retains great significance: by submitting to crucifixion he had pointed the way to salvation. For he who would be saved must indeed suffer most direly, he must indeed be purged of all self-will and freed from everything that binds him to the world and to created beings. First he must voluntarily subject himself to an ascetic preparation and then, when he has become fit and worthy to receive them, God will impose further and unutterable sufferings upon him. These last afflictions, which Müntzer calls 'the Cross', may include sickness and poverty and persecution, all of which must be borne in patience – but above all they will include intense mental agonies, weariness with the world, weariness with oneself, loss of hope, despair, terror. Only when this point has been reached, when the soul has been stripped utterly naked, can direct communication with God take place. This was of course traditional doctrine, such as had been held by many Catholic mystics of the Middle Ages; but when Müntzer comes to speak of the outcome he follows another and less orthodox tradition. For according to him when once 'the living Christ' enters into the soul it is for evermore; and the man so favoured becomes a vessel of the Holy Spirit – Müntzer even speaks of his 'becoming God'. Endowed with perfect insight into the divine will and living in perfect conformity with it, such a man is incontestably qualified to discharge the divinely appointed eschatological mission; and that is precisely what Müntzer claimed for himself. It was not for nothing that this *propheta* had been born within a few miles of Nordhausen, the centre of that underground movement in which the doctrine of the Free Spirit blended with that of the flagellants. The scourge might be cast away – the underlying phantasy was still the same.

As soon as Storch had enabled him to find himself Müntzer changed his way of life, abandoning reading and the pursuit of learning, condemning the Humanists who abounded amongst Luther's followers, ceaselessly propagating his eschatological faith amongst the poor. Since the middle of the preceding century silver-mines had been opened up at Zwickau and had turned the town into an important industrial centre, three times the size of Dresden. From all over southern and central Germany labourers streamed to the mines, with the result that there was a chronic surplus of man-power. Moreover the uncontrolled exploitation of the silver resulted in an inflation which reduced all the industrial workers, including those in the old-established weaving industry, to near-penury. A few months after he arrived in Zwickau Müntzer became a preacher at the very church where the weavers had their special altar; and he used the pulpit to utter fierce denunciations not only of the local Franciscans, who were generally unpopular, but also of the preacher – a friend of Luther's – who enjoyed the favour of the well-to-do burghers. Before long the whole town was divided into two hostile camps and the antagonism between them was becoming so sharp that violent disorders seemed imminent.

In April 1521, the Town Council intervened and dismissed the turbulent newcomer; whereupon a large number of the populace, under Storch's leadership, rose in revolt. The rising was put down and many arrests were made – including, significantly enough, more than fifty weavers. As for Müntzer, he betook himself into Bohemia, apparently in the hope that even at that late date he would find some Taborite groups there. In Prague he preached with the help of an interpreter; and he also published in German, Czech and Latin a manifesto announcing the foundation in Bohemia of a new church which was to consist solely of the Elect and which would therefore be directly inspired by God. His own role he now defined in terms of that same eschatological parable of the wheat and the tares which had been invoked during the English Peasants' Revolt: 'Harvest-time is here, so God himself has hired me for his harvest. I have sharpened my scythe, for my thoughts are most strongly fixed on the truth, and my lips, hands, skin, hair, soul, body, life curse the unbelievers.'

Müntzer's appeal to the Bohemians was, naturally enough, a failure; and he was expelled from Prague. For the next couple of years he wandered from place to place in central Germany, in great poverty but sustained by a now unshakable confidence in his prophetic mission. He no longer used his academic degrees but signed himself 'Christ's messenger'. His very hardships assumed in his eyes a messianic value: 'Let my sufferings be a model for you. Let the tares all puff themselves up as much as ever they like, they will still have to go under the flail along with the pure wheat. The living God is sharpening his scythe in me, so that later I can cut down the red poppies and the blue cornflowers.' His wanderings came to an end when, in 1523, he was invited to take up a cure at the small Thuringian town of Allstedt. There he married, created the first liturgy in the German language, translated Latin hymns into the vernacular and established a reputation as a preacher which extended throughout central Germany. Peasants from the surrounding countryside, above all some hundreds of miners from the Mansfeld copper-mines, came regularly to hear him. Together with the artisans of Allstedt these people provided him with a following which he set about turning into a revolutionary organization, the 'League of the Elect'. This league, consisting in the main of uneducated people, was Müntzer's answer to the university, which had always been the centre of Luther's influence. Now spiritual illumination was to oust the learning of the scribes; Allstedt was to replace Wittenberg and become the centre of a new Reformation which was to be both total and final and which was to usher in the Millennium.

Before long Müntzer became involved in conflicts with the civil authority, so that the two princes of Saxony – the Elector Frederick the Wise and his brother Duke John – began to observe his doings with a mixture of curiosity and alarm. In July 1524, Duke John, who had himself abandoned the traditional Catholic faith and become a follower of Luther, came to Allstedt and, by way of finding out what kind of man Müntzer was, ordered him to preach him a sermon. Müntzer did so, taking his text from that fountain-head of the apocalyptic tradition, the Book of Daniel; and the sermon, which he very soon had printed, gives the clearest possible conspectus of his eschatological beliefs. The last of the world-empires is approaching its end; now the world is nothing but the Devil's empire, where those serpents, the clergy, and those eels, the secular rulers and lords, pollute one another in a squirming heap. It is high time indeed that the Saxon princes chose whether to be servants of God or of the Devil. If it is to be the former, their duty is clear:

Drive Christ's enemies out from amongst the Elect, for you are the instruments for that purpose. Dearly beloved brethren, don't put up any shallow pretence that God's might will do it without your laying on with the sword, otherwise your sword might rust in its scabbard. . . . Christ is your master. So don't let them live any longer, the evil-doers who turn us away from God. For a godless man has no right to live if he hinders the godly.

Priests, monks and godless rulers must all perish; and the preacher insists:

The sword is necessary to exterminate them. And so that it shall be done honestly and properly, our dear fathers the princes must do it, who confess Christ with us. But if they don't do it, the sword shall be taken from them. . . . If they resist, let them be slaughtered without mercy. . . . At the harvest-time one must pluck the weeds out of God's vineyard. . . . But the angels who are sharpening their sickles for that work are no other than the earnest servants of God. . . . For the ungodly have no right to live, save what the Elect choose to allow them . . .

Müntzer however admits that the princes cannot carry out these tasks effectively unless they are informed of God's purposes; and that they cannot attain for themselves, since they are still too far from God. Therefore, he concludes, they must have at their court a priest who by self-abnegation and self-mortification has fitted himself to interpret their dreams and visions, just as Daniel did at the court of Nebuchadnezzar. And the Biblical allusions which accompany this recommendation show clearly enough that he saw himself as the inspired prophet who was to replace Luther in the favour of the princes, as Daniel replaced the unillumined scribes. In this way he reckoned to acquire such influence over the rulers of the land that he would be able to direct them in making the necessary preparations for the Millennium.

How Müntzer pictured the Millennium has been much debated and cannot indeed be easily decided. To judge by his writings he certainly showed far less interest in the nature of the future society than in the mass extermination which was supposed to precede it. Nor does he seem to have shown much interest in improving the material lot of the peasants amongst whom he lived. A couple of days after delivering his sermon to the princes we find him writing to his followers at Sangerhausen that they must obey their lord in all temporal matters. If the lord is not satisfied with the services and rents which he is at present receiving, they must be prepared to let him have all their worldly goods; only if he interferes in matters of spiritual well-being – notably by forbidding them to go to Allstedt to listen to Müntzer – they must cry aloud for all the world to hear. And even when Müntzer talks of the League of the

Elect his attitude is the same. He tries to persuade the Elector's agent at Allstedt to join the league, and in these terms:

If knaves and rogues should also join for the purpose of misusing the league, one must hand them over to their tyrants or else, according to the nature of the case, pass judgement on them oneself. Particularly as regards rendering the prescribed services, it must be clearly laid down in the league that members are not to think that they are thereby exempted from giving anything to their tyrants . . . lest certain wicked men should think that we have combined in order to further material ends.

Yet all this does not – as has sometimes been suggested – necessarily mean that Müntzer cannot have imagined his Millennium as egalitarian, even as communistic. It could equally well mean that he regarded the existing order as irremediable until the catastrophes of the Last Days had run their course, and at the same time took it for granted that once that had happened the primal State of Nature would automatically be restored. Such phantasies, which had never lost their fascination since the days of the Taborites, are known to have been familiar in the circles in which Müntzer moved. According to a fairly reliable source Müntzer's first teacher, the weaver Niklas Storch, held views on these matters which are hardly to be distinguished from those of the Brethren of the Free Spirit; maintaining that God makes all men alike naked and so sends them into the world, that they may be all of the same rank and may share all things equally amongst them. Again, Müntzer knew the young Humanist Ulrich Hugwald; and Hugwald had written a work prophesying that mankind would return 'to Christ, to Nature, to Paradise', which he defined as a state without war or want or luxury and in which every man would share all things as with his brethren. Moreover on the grounds that a peasant's life was nearest to that which God had appointed for Adam and Eve, Hugwald ended by turning himself into a peasant; and so did the Humanist Karlstadt, who was a close associate and even a disciple of Müntzer's. At a less sophisticated level, a simple member of the League of the Elect remarked that he had understood its programme to mean 'that they should be brothers and love one another like brothers'.

As for Müntzer himself, when he writes of the Law of God he certainly seems to equate it with that original and absolute Natural Law which was supposed to have known no distinctions of property or status. This impression is strengthened by the *Histori Thomä Müntzers* – admittedly a tendentious work, but one which was written while Müntzer's story was still very fresh in people's memory and which in general shows a high standard of factual accuracy. According to this account Müntzer, at least in the last months of his life, taught that there should be neither kings nor lords and also, on the strength of a misunderstanding of *Acts* iv, that all things should be held in common. Taken together, these facts certainly suggest that the confession which the *propheta* made just before his death was probably accurate enough, even though it was extracted by torture. For what he confessed was that the basic principle of his league was that all things are common to all men; that its aim was a state of affairs in which all would be equal and each would receive according to his need; and that it was prepared to execute any prince or lord who stood in the way of its plans. In this programme there is after all nothing that was not also laid down, under no duress at all, in the programme which the Revolutionary of the Upper Rhine drew up for his imaginary Brotherhood of the Yellow Cross.

When Müntzer delivered his sermon before Duke John he clearly hoped that the princes of Saxony could be won over to the cause; and when, a few days later, followers of his were expelled by their lords – notably by the Count of Mansfeld – and came as refugees to Allstedt, he called on the princes to avenge them. But the princes made no move and this transformed his attitude. In the last week of July he preached a sermon in which he proclaimed that the time was at hand when all tyrants would be overthrown and the messianic Kingdom would begin. This in itself would no doubt have sufficed to alarm the princes; but in any case Luther now wrote his *Letter to the Princes of Saxony*, pointing out how dangerous Müntzer's agitation was becoming. As a result Müntzer was summoned to Weimar to explain himself before Duke John. Although even then he was merely told to refrain from making any more provocative pronouncements until the matter had been considered by the Elector, this was enough to set him on the road to revolution.

In the pamphlet which he now produced, *The explicit unmasking of the false belief of the faithless world*, Müntzer makes it plain that the princes are unfit to play any part at all in bringing about the Millennium – 'for they have spent their lives in bestial eating and drinking, from their youth onwards they have been brought up most delicately, in all their life they have never had a bad day and they neither wish nor intend to accept one.' Indeed it is the princes and the lords and all the rich and powerful who, by stubbornly maintaining the existing social order, prevent not only themselves but others also from attaining the true faith: 'The powerful, self-willed unbelievers must be put down from their seats because they hinder the holy, genuine Christian faith in themselves and in the whole world, when it is trying to emerge in all its true, original force.' Abetted by venal scribes – such as Luther – 'the great do everything in their power to keep the common people from perceiving the truth'. Bound together 'like toadspawn' by their common interest in financial profit, they so harass the poor with their usury and taxes that these have no time left in which to study and follow the Law of God. Yet, Müntzer argues, all this is no reason for despair – on the contrary, the very excesses of the tyranny which now oppresses the world are a sure sign that the great consummation is indeed at hand. It is precisely because God is sending his light into the world that 'certain (lords) are only now really beginning to hamper and harass, to shear and shave their people, to threaten all Christendom and shamefully and most cruelly to torture and kill their own folk and strangers too.'

Müntzer had reached the point which had been reached by earlier *prophetae* during the English Peasants' Revolt and the Hussite Revolution. For him too it was now the poor who were potentially the Elect, charged with the mission of inaugurating the egalitarian Millennium. Free from the temptations of *Avaritia* and *Luxuria*, the poor had at least a chance of reaching that indifference to the goods of this world which would qualify them to receive the apocalyptic message. It was therefore the poor who, while the rich and mighty were being cut down like weeds in the last great harvest, would emerge as the one true church: 'Then must what is great yield to what is small. Ah, if the poor, downtrodden peasants knew that, it would be a great help to them.' And nevertheless – Münster insisted – so far not even the poor were fit to enter into their appointed glory. First they too must be broken of such worldly desires and frivolous pastimes as they had, so that they should with sighs and prayers recognize their abject condition and at the same time their need for a new, God-sent leader. 'If the holy church is to be renewed through the bitter truth, a servant of God must stand forth in the spirit of Elijah ... and set things in motion. In truth, many of them will have to be roused, so that with the greatest possible zeal and with passionate earnestness they may sweep Christendom clean of ungodly rulers.' Just as Müntzer had previously offered his services to the princes as a new Daniel, so he now proposed himself for the office of divinely inspired leader of the people.

The explicit unmasking was followed at no great interval by another and more virulent pamphlet, directed specifically against Luther and accordingly entitled *The most amply called-for defence and answer to the unspiritual soft-living flesh at Wittenberg.* It was with good cause that Luther and Müntzer had by this time come to regard one another as deadly enemies. Just as much as Müntzer, Luther performed all his deeds in the conviction that the Last Days were at hand. But in his view the sole enemy was the Papacy, in which he saw Antichrist, the false prophet; and it was by the dissemination of the true Gospel that the Papacy would be overcome. When that task had been accomplished Christ would return to pass sentence of eternal damnation upon the pope and his followers and to found a Kingdom – but a Kingdom which would not be of this world. In the context of such an eschatology armed revolt was bound to seem irrelevant, because bodily death inflicted by men was as nothing in comparison with the sentence of damnation imposed by God. And armed revolt was also bound to seem pernicious, partly because it would shatter the social order which allowed the Word to be disseminated and still more because it would discredit that Reformation which to Luther was incomparably the most important thing in the world. It was therefore to be expected that Luther would do his utmost to counteract Müntzer's influence. On the other hand it is not surprising that Müntzer for his part saw in Luther an eschatological figure, the Beast of the Apocalypse and the Whore of Babylon. And in fact the very title of his pamphlet is an allusion to the apocalyptic passage in the Epistle of Jude which tells how the Lord with ten thousands of his Saints will execute judgement upon the ungodly – 'mockers in the last time', as they are called there, seeking their own advantage by fawning upon the great; men of the flesh and 'having not the spirit'.

It is in attacking Luther in *The most amply called-for defence* that Müntzer formulates most coherently his doctrine of social revolution. Whearas Luther dedicated his tract to the Elector and to Duke John, Müntzer dedicates his reply to Christ as King of kings and Duke of all believers – and makes it plain that by Christ he means the spirit of Christ as experienced by himself and his followers. And he gives his reason: the princes – those 'godless rascals' as he now calls them – have forfeited all claim to honour, obedience and dominion, which henceforth belong to the Elect alone. It is still true that 'the will of God and his work must be carried out in their entirety by the observation of the Law' – but this is no task for the ungodly. When the ungodly take upon themselves the task of suppressing sin they use the Law as a means of exterminating the Elect. More specifically, Müntzer maintains that in the hands of 'the great' the Law of God becomes simply a device for protecting property – meaning the property which they themselves have appropriated. In a bitter attack on Luther he exclaims: 'The wretched flatterer is silent ... about the origin of all theft. . . . Look, the seed-grounds of usury and theft and robbery are our lords and princes, they take all creatures as their property: the fish in the water, the birds in the air, the plants on the ground have all got to be theirs.' And he refers to the passage in *Isaiah*: 'Woe unto them that join house to house, that lay field to field, till there be no place . . .' These robbers use the Law to forbid others to rob: 'They publish God's commandments amongst the poor and say, "God has commanded, thou shalt not steal." . . . They oppress all people, and shear and shave the poor ploughman and everything that lives – yet if (the ploughman) commits the slightest offence, he must hang.' Luther's greatest crime is that he justifies these injustices. Müntzer, on the other hand, proclaims the right and duty of the Elect, who are to be found amongst the common people, to wield the sword for the extermination of the ungodly, who include all 'the great'. 'You wily fox,' he cries to Luther, 'by your lies you have made sad the heart of the righteous man, whom God has not saddened, and thereby you have strengthened the power of the ungodly scoundrels, so that they shall continue in their old ways. Therefore things will go with you as with a fox when it is caught. The people will become free and God alone means to be Lord over them.'

Ironically enough, the princes whom Müntzer had chiefly in mind – the Elector Frederick and Duke John – were alone amongst the German princes in being extremely tolerant. Profoundly disoriented in the midst of the vast upheaval inaugurated by Luther and of which their territories remained the centre, they were filled with misgivings about their own rights and status. Duke John listened without protest to Müntzer's provocative sermon, the Elector was known to have remarked that if God would have it so government must pass into the hands of the common man; and in dealing with the revolutionary *propheta* of Allstedt both brothers showed equal uncertainty. It was more as a gesture of defiance than out of serious concern for his safety that Müntzer, a week after his hearing at Weimar, broke parole, climbed by night over the town wall of Allstedt and made his way to the free imperial city of Mühlhausen.

This relatively large Thuringian town had already been in a state of intermittent turbulence for over a year. A former monk called Heinrich Pfeiffer was leading the poorer burghers in their struggle to wrest political control from the oligarchy which so far monopolized it. And half the population of the town – a larger proportion, so far as is known, than in any other German town at that time – consisted of paupers, who in times of crisis always showed themselves ready for radical social experiments. Here

Müntzer found a small but enthusiastic following. Obsessed as always by the impending destruction of the ungodly, he had a red crucifix and a naked sword carried in front of him when, at the head of an armed band, he patrolled the streets of the town. Yet when open revolt broke out it was quickly suppressed and Müntzer, expelled once more, resumed his wanderings. At Nuremberg he managed to publish his two revolutionary tracts; but these were at once confiscated by the Town Council and Müntzer had to leave that town too. After some weeks of wandering which took him as far as the borders of Switzerland he was called back to Mühlhausen, where Pfeiffer had succeeded in re-establishing himself and which was once more in a state of revolutionary ferment. In March 1525, the existing Town Council was overthrown and a new one, elected by the burghers, installed in its place. But Müntzer does not seem to have played any great part in these happenings; what enabled him to show himself as a revolutionary in action was less the revolution at Mühlhausen than the outbreak of the Peasants' War.

The causes of the German Peasants' War have been and will no doubt continue to be a subject of controversy, but there are a few general comments that can be made with some confidence. It is at least certain that the background of this rising resembled that of the English Peasants' Revolt rather than that of the *Jacquerie*. The well-being of the German peasantry was greater than it had ever been; and particularly the peasants who everywhere took the initiative in the insurrection, so far from being driven on by sheer misery and desperation, belonged to a rising and self-confident class. They were people whose position was improving both socially and economically and who for that very reason were impatient of the obstacles which stood in the way of further advance. It is therefore not surprising that in their efforts to remove these obstacles the peasants showed themselves not at all eschatologically minded but, on the contrary, politically minded in the sense that they thought in terms of real situations and realizable possibilities. The most that a peasant community ever sought under the leadership of its own peasant aristocracy was local self-government; and the first stage of the movement, from March 1525 to the beginning of May, consisted simply of a series of local struggles in which a great number of communities really did extract from their immediate lords, ecclesiastical or lay, concessions giving them greater autonomy. And this was achieved not by bloodshed but by an intensification of the tough, hard-headed bargaining which the peasantry had been conducting for generations.

Underlying the rising there was however a deeper conflict. With the progressive collapse of the royal power the German state had disintegrated into a welter of discordant and often warring feudal authorities. But by 1525 this condition of near-anarchy was approaching its end, for the great territorial princes were busily creating their absolutist principalities. The peasantry saw its traditional way of life disrupted and its inherited rights threatened by the development of states of this new type. It resented the additional taxes, the substitution of Roman Law for 'custom', the interference of the centralized administration in local affairs; and it fought back. The princes for their part realized clearly enough that the peasantry stood in the way of their plans for state-building; and they realized also that the peasant insurrection offered them a splendid chance to assert and consolidate their authority. It was the princes – or rather, a particular group of princes – who saw to it that the rising ended catastrophically, in a series of battles, or massacres, in which perhaps 100,000 peasants perished. And it was the princely dynasties which gained from the reduction alike of the peasantry, the lower nobility and the ecclesiastical foundations to a condition of helpless dependence that was to last for centuries.

The part played by Thomas Müntzer in the Peasants' War as a whole can easily be, and often has been, exaggerated. The main theatres of the struggle were the areas where the development of the new states had gone furthest. These areas all lay in southern and western Germany, which had already seen many peasant risings in the years before 1525; and there Müntzer seems to have had no influence at all. In Thuringia however the situation was a peculiar one, for there had been no previous peasant revolts and there was little sign of an impending revolt even in 1525. The insurrection came in fact very late and moreover took a curiously anarchic form. Whereas in the south and west the peasants had conducted themselves in an orderly and disciplined fashion, in Thuringia they formed small, unorganized bands which scoured the countryside, looting and burning monasteries and convents. And it may well be that these outbreaks were encouraged, if not caused, by the agitation which Müntzer had been conducting.

The hard core of Müntzer's following still consisted in the League of the Elect. Some of his former congregation at Allstedt joined him at Mühlhausen and no doubt helped him in building up a new organization. Above all he continued to rely on the workers in the copper-mines at Mansfeld, who had joined the league in their hundreds. Such people – often recruited from abroad, often migrants, often exposed to unemployment and every kind of insecurity – were as notoriously prone to revolutionary excitement as the weavers and were correspondingly dreaded by the authorities. That he was able to command such a following naturally gave Müntzer a great reputation as a revolutionary leader; so that, if in Mühlhausen itself he never rivalled Pfeiffer in influence, in the context of the peasant insurrection he loomed far larger. Although – as their written demands for reform clearly show – not even the Thuringian peasants shared Müntzer's millenarian phantasies, they certainly looked up to him as the one famous, learned and pious man who had unreservedly thrown in his lot with theirs. There has been much disagreement about the extent to which Müntzer can rightly be called the leader of the Thuringian peasants in their 'war'; but one thing seems certain, and that is that they had no other leader.

In April 1525 Müntzer set up in his church at Mühlhausen a white banner bearing a rainbow as a symbol of God's covenant, and announced that he would shortly be marching out under this standard at the head of two thousand 'strangers' – obviously real or imaginary members of his league. At the end of the month he and Pfeiffer did in fact take part in a marauding expedition in the course of which a number of monasteries and convents were destroyed; but this was not yet, by any means, the apocalyptic struggle of which he dreamed. In a letter which he sent to his followers at Allstedt one recognizes the tone which had once been attributed to John Ball – except that one now hears it directly instead of merely by report:

I tell you, if you will not suffer for God's sake, then you must be the Devil's martyrs. So take care! Don't be so disheartened, supine, don't fawn upon the perverse visionaries, the godless scoundrels! Start and fight the Lord's fight! It's high time. Keep all your brethren to it, so that they don't mock the divine testimony, otherwise they must all be destroyed. All Germany, France and Italy are on the alert. The Master wants to have sport, so the scoundrels must go through it. The peasants in Klettgau and Hegau and in the Black Forest have risen, 3,000 strong, and the crowd is getting bigger all the time. My only fear is that the foolish fellows will let themselves be taken in by some treacherous agreement, simply because they haven't yet seen the harm of it.

If there are but three of you who, trusting in God, seek only his name and honour, you will not fear a hundred thousand.

Now go at them, and at them, and at them! It is time. The scoundrels are as dispirited as dogs. . . . It is very, very necessary, beyond measure necessary. . . . Take no notice of the lamentations of the godless! They will beg you in such a friendly way, and whine and cry like children. Don't be moved to pity. . . . Stir people up in villages and towns, and most of all the miners and other good fellows who will be good at the job. We must sleep no more! ... Get this letter to the miners! ...

At them, at them, while the fire is hot! Don't let your sword get cold! Don't let it go lame! Hammer cling, clang on Nimrod's anvil! Throw their tower to the ground! So long as they are alive you will never shake off the fear of men. One can't speak to you about God so long as they are reigning over you. At them, at them, while you have daylight! God goes ahead of you, so follow, follow! ...

This letter shows clearly enough in what phantasies Müntzer was living. For Nimrod was supposed to have built the Tower of Babel, which in turn was identified with Babylon; and he was popularly regarded not only as the first builder of cities but as the originator of private property and class-distinctions – in fact as the destroyer of the primal egalitarian State of Nature. And to his summons to cast down Nimrod and his tower Müntzer adds a whole series of references to apocalyptic prophecies in the Bible: the prophecy of the messianic kingdom in *Ezekiel* xxxiv, Christ's prophecy of his Second Coming as given in *Matthew* xxiv, the prophecy of the Day of Wrath in *Revelation* vi, and of course 'Daniel's dream'. All this shows how completely, even at this last stage of Müntzer's career, the assumptions on which he worked and the terms in which he thought were still prescribed by the eschatological tradition. It is indeed of some interest that at that same time the man who had been his model was himself assuming the role of eschatological saviour. For, expelled from Zwickau, Niklas Storch had built up a new following, in which apostate monks mixed with weavers and other artisans, and had organized it around a core of twelve 'apostles' and seventy-two 'disciples'. And when the Peasants' War broke out he was claiming to have received a promise from on high to the effect that within four years he would be able to oust the present godless rulers, to rule over the whole world and to bestow the kingdoms of the earth upon his followers.

At the same time as Müntzer and Storch were preparing the way for the Millennium, Luther for his part was composing his ferocious pamphlet *Against the thievish, murderous gangs of the peasants*. This work did much to rouse the princes of central Germany, who hitherto had shown far less resolution than those in the south and west, to oppose the revolt. The old Elector Frederick, who had shown most unwillingness to act against the peasants, died on 4 May and was succeeded by his brother John. The new Elector joined with other princes in appealing for help to the Landgrave Philip of Hesse – a young man scarcely twenty years of age, but one who had already earned a considerable reputation as a military commander and who moreover had just put down a rising in his own territories. The Landgrave at once marched into Thuringia and headed for Mühlhausen, in which the princes were agreed in seeing the source of the whole Thuringian insurrection. As for the peasants, some 8,000 of them had at last formed themselves into an army at Frankenhausen. This town lay so close to Müntzer's headquarters at Mühlhausen, and so close also to the castle of his old enemy, Ernest of Mansfeld, that it seems probable that the choice was inspired by the *propheta* himself. Certainly the peasants now turned to Müntzer as to a saviour, begging him to take his place amongst them; and they did not call in vain. While Pfeiffer, who was opposed to intervention, stayed in Mühlhausen, Müntzer set out at the head of some 300 of his most devoted and fanatical supporters. The number is significant, for 300 was the size of the force with which Gideon overthrew the Midianites. In *The explicit unmasking* Müntzer invoked the example of Gideon and in the most violent of his letters he added 'with the sword of Gideon' to his signature – just as a generation later the leader of the Blood Friends, likewise centred on Mühlhausen, was also to proclaim his mission as the extermination of the ungodly with the sword of Gideon. Müntzer arrived at the peasants' camp on 11th May and at once made his influence felt. He ordered the peasants in the neighbouring villages to join the army and threatened that if they failed to do so he would have them brought in by force. He sent an urgent appeal to the town of Erfurt for reinforcements and he also sent threatening letters to the enemy. To his particular enemy, Count Ernest of Mansfeld, he wrote: 'Say, you wretched, shabby bag of worms, who made you a prince over the people whom God has purchased with his precious blood? ... By God's mighty power you are delivered up to destruction. If you do not humble yourself before the lowly, you will be saddled with everlasting infamy in the eyes of all Christendom and will become the Devil's martyr.' But all was in vain; Erfurt either could not or would not respond and the enemy was not to be so easily intimidated.

In his conduct of operations Philip of Hesse showed the most complete contempt for the military skill of the peasants; and the outcome fully justified the risks he took. By 15th May his forces, now strengthened by those of other princes, had occupied a strong position on a hill overlooking the peasant army. Although numerically somewhat inferior, the army of the princes had ample artillery, whereas the peasants had very little, and some 2,000 cavalry, whereas the peasants had none. A battle fought under such circumstances could have only one possible result; but the princes nevertheless offered terms, promising the peasants their lives on condition that they handed over Müntzer and his immediate following. The offer was probably made in good faith, for in dealing with the insurrection in his own territories the Landgrave, while demanding submission, had also avoided unnecessary bloodshed. And the offer would probably have been accepted but for the intervention of Müntzer himself.

According to the account in the *Histori* – which seems plausible enough – the *propheta* made a passionate speech in which he declared that God had spoken to him and had promised victory; that he himself would catch the enemy cannon-balls in the sleeves of his cloak; and that in the end God would transform heaven and earth rather than allow his people to perish. The effect of this speech was heightened by the appearance of a rainbow which, as the symbol on Müntzer's banner, was of course interpreted as a token of divine favour. Müntzer's immediate followers at least seem to have been confident that some tremendous miracle was about to take place; and being organized as well as fanatical they were no doubt able to dominate the confused and amorphous mass of peasantry.

Meanwhile the princes, receiving no satisfactory reply to their offer, grew impatient and gave the order to fire the cannon. The peasants had made no preparations to use what artillery they had nor even to escape. Indeed they were still singing 'Come, Holy Spirit' – as though expecting the Second Coming at that very moment – when the first and only salvo was fired. The effect was immediate and catastrophic: the peasants broke ranks and fled in panic, while the enemy cavalry ran them down and slaughtered them in hundreds. For the loss of half a dozen men the army of the princes dispersed the peasants and captured Frankenhausen, killing some 5,000 in the process. A few days later Mühlhausen surrendered without a struggle; and as punishment for the part which it was believed to have played the town was made to pay heavy fines and reparations and was deprived of its status as a free city of the Empire. As for Müntzer, he had escaped from the battle-field but was soon found hiding in a cellar at Frankenhausen. Handed over to Ernest of Mansfeld, he was tortured and made a confession concerning his League of the Elect; after which he was beheaded in the camp of the princes, along with Pfeiffer, on 27 May 1525. Storch, who seems also to have played some part in the rising, died as a fugitive in the same year.

Müntzer's historical role was however by no means finished. It is natural enough that in the Anabaptist movement which spread far and wide during the years following the Peasants' War his memory should have been venerated, even though he had never called himself an Anabaptist. More curious is the resurrection and apotheosis which he has undergone during the past hundred years. From Engels down to the Communist historians of today – Russian as well as German – Marxists have inflated Müntzer into a giant symbol, a prodigious hero in the history of the 'class war'. This is a naïve view, and one which non-Marxist historians have countered easily enough by pointing to the essentially mystical nature of Müntzer's preoccupations, his general indifference to the material welfare of the poor. Yet it may be suggested that this point too can be over-emphasized. Müntzer was a *propheta* obsessed by eschatological phantasies which he attempted to translate into reality by exploiting social discontent. Perhaps after all it is a sound instinct that has led Marxists to claim him for their own.

Anabaptism and social unrest

The Lutheran Reformation was accompanied by certain phenomena which, though they appalled Luther and his associates, were so natural as to appear in retrospect inevitable. As against the authority of the Church of Rome the Reformers appealed to the text of the Bible. But once men took to reading the Bible for themselves they began to interpret it for themselves; and their interpretations did not always accord with those of the Reformers. Wherever Luther's influence extended the priest lost much of his traditional prestige as a mediator between the layman and God and an indispensable spiritual guide. But once the layman began to feel that he himself stood face to face with God and to rely for guidance on his individual conscience, it was inevitable that some laymen should claim divine promptings which ran as much counter to the new as to the old orthodoxy.

Above all, the Lutheran Reformation heightened for a time the intense and widespread excitement which had helped to produce it. This result was inevitable once the Reformation challenged the validity and authority of the one church which had hitherto existed in the West. Hitherto people had accepted – and on the whole unquestioningly – the coherent interpretation of the universe and of man's nature expounded by the Church of Rome. Catholic doctrine had provided an unchanging landscape within which all Christians had been accustomed to orient themselves, just as Catholic ecclesiastic organization had provided a system of authority on which they had been accustomed to depend. The very criticism which was for ever being directed against lax and worldly clerics, the very outcry evoked by the Great Schism, go to show how much people demanded of the Church. For many centuries the Church of Rome, whatever its failings, had been fulfilling a very important normative function in European society. Luther's onslaught, precisely because it was so effective, seriously disturbed that function. As as result it produced, along with a sense of liberation, a sense of disorientation which was just as widespread.

Moreover the Lutheran Reformation could not itself master all the anxieties which it had released in the population. Partly because of the content of his doctrine of salvation, partly because of his alliance with the established secular powers, Luther failed to hold the allegiance of great multitudes of the common people. Amongst the perturbed, disoriented masses there grew up, in opposition to both Lutheranism and Roman Catholicism, the movement to which its opponents gave the name of Anabaptism – in many ways a successor to the medieval sects, but far larger than they.

Anabaptism was not a homogeneous movement and it never was centrally organized. There existed some forty independent sects of Anabaptists, each grouped around a leader who claimed to be a divinely inspired prophet or apostle; and these sects – clandestine, constantly threatened with extermination, scattered throughout the length and breadth of the German-speaking lands – developed along the separate lines which the various leaders set. Nevertheless certain tendencies were common to the movement as a whole. In general the Anabaptists attached relatively little importance either to theological speculations or to formal religious observances. In place of such practices as church-going they set a meticulous, literal observance of the precepts which they thought they found in the New Testament. In place of theology they cultivated the Bible – which however they were apt to interpret in the light of the direct inspirations which they believed they received from God. Their values were primarily ethical; for them religion was above all a matter of active brotherly love. Their communities were modelled on what they supposed to have been the practice of the early Church and were intended to realize the ethical ideal propounded by Christ.

It was their social attitudes that were most characteristic of the Anabaptists. These sectarians tended to be uneasy about private property and to accept community of goods as an ideal. If in most of the groups little attempt was made to introduce common ownership, Anabaptists certainly did take seriously the obligations of charitable dealing and generous mutual aid. On the other hand Anabaptist communities often showed a marked exclusiveness. Within each group there was great solidarity; but the attitude to society at large tended to be one of rejection. In particular, Anabaptists regarded the state with suspicion, as an institution which, though no doubt necessary for the unrighteous, was unnecessary for true Christians, meaning themselves. Though they were willing to comply with many of the state's demands, they refused to let it invade the realm of faith and conscience; and in general they preferred to minimize their dealings with it. Most

Anabaptists refused to hold an official position in the state, or to invoke the authority of the state against a fellow Anabaptist, or to take up arms on behalf of the state. The attitude towards private persons who were not Anabaptists was equally aloof; Anabaptists commonly avoided all social intercourse outside their own community. These people regarded themselves as the only Elect and their communities as being alone under the immediate guidance of God: small islands of righteousness in an ocean of iniquity. Even Luther granted that a Roman Catholic could be saved; but for the Anabaptists Lutherans and Catholics alike were worse than Turks, true ministers of Antichrist. The practice of rebaptism, from which Anabaptism received its name, was above all a means of expressing symbolically this voluntary separation from the unredeemed world. But even amongst Anabaptists themselves the same obsession with exclusive election prevailed; and the history of the movement is punctuated by schisms.

The movement spread from Switzerland into Germany in the years following the Peasants' War. Most Anabaptists were peaceful folk who in practice were quite willing, except in matters of conscience and belief, to respect the authority of the state. Certainly the majority had no idea of social revolution. But the rank-and-file were recruited almost entirely from peasants and artisans; and after the Peasants' War the authorities were desperately afraid of these classes. Even the most peaceful Anabaptists were therefore ferociously persecuted and many thousands of them were killed. This persecution in the end created the very danger it was intended to forestall. It was not only that the Anabaptists were confirmed in their hostility to the state and the established order – they interpreted their sufferings in apocalyptic terms, as the last great onslaught of Satan and Antichrist against the Saints, as those 'messianic woes' which were to usher in the Millennium. Many Anabaptists became obsessed by imaginings of a day of reckoning when they themselves would arise to overthrow the mighty and, under a Christ who had returned at last, establish a Millennium on earth. The situation within Anabaptism now resembled that which had existed within the heretical movement of earlier centuries. The bulk of the Anabaptist movement continued the tradition of peaceful and austere dissent which in earlier centuries had been represented by the Waldensians. But alongside it there was growing up an Anabaptism of another kind, in which the equally ancient tradition of militant millenarianism was finding a new expression.

The first propagandist of this new Anabaptism was an itinerant bookbinder called Hans Hut – a former follower and disciple of Müntzer's and like him a native of Thuringia. This man claimed to be a prophet sent by God to announce that at Whitsuntide, 1528, Christ would return to earth and place the two-edged sword of justice in the hands of the rebaptised Saints. The Saints would hold judgement on the priests and pastors for their false teachings and, above all, on the great ones of the earth for their persecutions; kings and nobles would be cast into chains. Finally Christ was to establish a Millennium which, it seems, was to be characterized by free love and community of goods. Hut was captured in 1527 and imprisoned at Augsburg, where he died, or was killed, in prison; but not before he had made some converts in the towns of southern Germany.

In the professions of faith of Hut's followers one recognizes the doctrines of John Ball and the radical Taborites, repeated almost word for word: 'Christ will give the sword and revenge to them, the Anabaptists, to punish all sins, stamp out all governments; communize all property and slay those who do not permit themselves to be rebaptised.' And again: 'The government does not treat the poor people properly and burdens them too heavily. When God gives them revenge they want to punish and wipe out the evil . . .' And if Hut himself expected all this to take place only when Christ 'came on the clouds', not all his disciples were so patient: at Esslingen on the Neckar Anabaptists seem in 1528 to have planned to set up the Kingdom of God by force of arms. Amongst these militant millenarians the ideal of communal ownership clearly possessed a revolutionary significance; and it was no doubt with some justification that the town authorities at Nuremberg warned those at Ulm that Anabaptists were aiming at overthrowing the established order and abolishing private property. It is true that in south Germany revolutionary Anabaptism remained a small and ineffective force and that it was crushed out of existence by 1530. But a few years later it was to reappear elsewhere, in Holland and the extreme north-west of Germany, and this time with results which gripped the attention of Europe.

North-west Germany at the beginning of the sixteenth century consisted in the main of a number of petty ecclesiastical states, each with a prince-bishop as its sovereign. Usually such a state was torn by fierce social conflicts. The government of the state was in the hands of the prince-bishop and of the chapter of the diocese, which elected him and to a large extent controlled his policy. The members of the chapter were recruited solely from the local aristocracy – a coat of arms with at least four quarterings was commonly an indispensable qualification – and they often chose one of their own number as bishop. This group of aristocratic clerics was subject to no control by any higher authority; in the regional diet they were powerfully represented and could always rely on the support of the knighthood. They therefore tended to govern solely in the interest of their own class and of the clergy of the diocese. In an ecclesiastical state the clergy were not only very numerous – in the bishopric of Münster there were some thirty ecclesiastical centres, including four monasteries, seven convents, ten churches, a cathedral and of course the chapter itself – but also highly privileged. Members of the chapter enjoyed rich prebends and canonries. The monks were permitted to carry on secular trades and handicrafts. Above all, the clergy as a whole were almost entirely exempt from taxation.

But the power of the clerico-aristocratic stratum in an ecclesiastical state seldom extended very effectively to the capital city. In these states as elsewhere the development of commerce and a money economy had given an ever greater importance to the towns. The state governments were in constant need of money; and by the usual method of bargaining over taxes the towns had gradually won concessions and privileges for themselves. In the largest and most important of the ecclesiastical states, the bishopric of Münster, this was particularly true. From the beginning of the fourteenth century the town of Münster had enjoyed a large measure of self-government and the power of the bishop – who seldom resided there – had been much restricted.

That did not of course mean that the populations of the towns were satisfied with the concessions they had obtained. The bishop and chapter commonly enjoyed no religious prestige whatsoever and this is not surprising, since they lived luxurious and purely secular lives; often, as in Münster in the 1530's, the bishop was simply a secular lord who had not even been ordained. Moreover the taxes imposed by the prince-bishop were commonly heavy and the whole burden fell on the laity, who benefited least from the administration. In addition, an ecclesiastical state had to pay vast sums to the Roman Curia each time a new bishop was elected; Münster did so three times between 1498 and 1522. It is not surprising that the immunity of the clergy from taxation was bitterly resented. Tradesmen and artisans also objected to the competition of monks who engaged in commerce and industry and who, having no families to maintain, no military service to perform or provide, and no guild regulations to observe, had every advantage on their side.

By the sixteenth century the centre of resistance to the power of bishop and chapter usually lay not in the town council, which had become a staid and relatively conservative body, but in the guilds. This was certainly the case in Münster. As the town, in the course of the fifteenth century, became an important commercial centre and a member of the Hanseatic League, the guilds obtained great political power. Organized in one great guild, which in the sixteenth century contained no less than sixteen separate guilds, they could at a suitable opportunity rouse and lead the whole population against the clergy. One such opportunity was offered by the Peasants' War. It is a striking fact that when the revolutionary excitement which spread from the south of Germany reached the north-west, it was neither the peasantry nor the towns in the secular states which rose in revolt, but solely the capitals of the ecclesiastical states: Osnabrück, Utrecht, Paderborn and Münster. In Münster the guilds led an attack on a monastery which had entered into commercial competition with them and they also demanded a general restriction of the privileges of the clergy; and the chapter was forced to make very considerable concessions.

On that occasion the triumph of the guilds was shortlived, at Münster as in all its sister towns. As soon as the princes had defeated the peasants in the south, the chapters in the northern bishoprics were able to regain whatever power they had lost. They promptly withdrew all concessions, crushed every attempt at reform and did all they could to humiliate the rebellious towns. By 1530 the old system of government was re-established in all the ecclesiastical states. Nevertheless it was far less secure than it had ever been, for the townsmen now resented the ascendancy of clergy and nobles more bitterly than ever before. They had felt their own strength and waited impatiently for a suitable occasion to deploy it again. Moreover their situation in these years was a desperate one. In 1529 an outbreak of the Black Death devastated Westphalia and at the same time the crops failed; between 1529 and 1530 the price of rye almost trebled. Finally in 1530 an extraordinary tax was levied to finance resistance to the Turkish invasion of the eastern territories of the Empire. There is evidence that in the early 1530's the distress in north-west Germany was altogether exceptional. It was to be expected that in one or other of the ecclesiastical states there would be new disorders; and when in 1530 the Bishop of Münster tried to sell his bishopric to the Bishop of Paderborn and Osnabrück and thereby alienated his allies in the Chapter, the disorders commenced.

In 1531 an eloquent young chaplain called Bernt Rothmann – a blacksmith's son whose remarkable gifts had won him a university education – began to attract vast congregations in the town of Münster. Very soon he became a Lutheran and put himself at the head of a movement, which in its origins reached back to 1525, to bring the town into the Lutheran fold. He found support in the guilds and an influential ally in a rich cloth-merchant and patrician called Bernt Knipperdollinck. The movement, at once Protestant and democratic, was furthered by the resignation of one bishop and the death of his successor. In 1532 the guilds, supported by the populace, were masters of the town and were able to force the Council to install Lutheran preachers in all churches. The new bishop was unable to make the town abandon its faith and early in 1533 he recognized Münster officially as a Lutheran town.

It was not to remain so for long. In the neighbouring Duchy of Julich-Cleves Anabaptist preachers had for some years enjoyed a freedom of propaganda such as existed hardly anywhere else; but in 1532 they were expelled and a number of them sought refuge in Münster. In the course of 1533 more Anabaptists arrived, this time from the Netherlands. These were followers of Melchior Hoffmann, a celebrated visionary who – a true successor to the itinerant *prophetae* of the Middle Ages – had wandered far and wide through Europe preaching the imminence of the Second Coming and the Millennium. About 1529 Hoffmann had joined the Anabaptist movement and during the following year a new wing of the movement, profoundly influenced by his ideas, had developed above all in the northern provinces of the Netherlands. According to Hoffmann the Millennium was to begin, after a period of 'messianic woes' and many signs and wonders, in the year 1533, which was supposed to be the fifteenth centenary of the death of Christ. And in 1533 the millenarian phantasy which Hoffmann's followers brought with them into Münster rapidly turned into a mass obsession, dominating the whole life of the poorer classes in the town.

Meanwhile Rothmann had abandoned his Lutheran faith and had brought all his eloquence and prestige to the service of Anabaptism; and in his preaching an old tradition took on new life. In 1524 that old source of anarcho-communistic doctrine, the spurious Fifth Epistle of Clement, had been printed at Basle. In 1531 the Humanist Sebastian Franck had summarized it in a lively, colloquial German which found many readers; and he had also added his own comments:

Shortly after that, Nimrod began to rule and then whoever could manage it got the better of the other. And they started dividing the world up and squabbling about property. Then Mine and Thine began. In the end people became so wild, they were just like wild beasts. Each wanted to be finer and better than the other, in fact wanted to be his master. Yet God had made all things common, as today still we can enjoy air, fire, rain and sun in common, and whatever else some thieving, tyrannical man cannot get hold of and keep for himself.

This was the theme which was now taken up by Rothmann. By October 1533, he was holding up the supposed communism of the primitive Church as the ideal for a truly Christian community. In sermons and tracts he declared that the true believers ought to model their lives minutely upon the lives of the first Christians and that this involved holding all things in common.

As in earlier centuries this teaching appealed in different ways at different social levels. There were capitalists who suddenly renounced usury and cancelled all debts that were owing to them; there were many well-to-do people who resolved to live as loving brethren, holding all property in common, forswearing all luxuries, giving away all superfluities to the poor. But at the same time the news of this preaching spread far and wide amongst the propertyless, the uprooted and the failures. 'And so they came,' remarks one observer, 'the Dutch and the Frisians and scoundrels from all parts, who had never settled anywhere: they flocked to Münster and collected there.' Other sources refer to 'fugitives, exiles, criminals' and to

people who, having run through the fortunes of their parents, were earning nothing by their own industry; ... who, having learnt from their earliest years to live in idleness, had saddled themselves with debts; who hated the clergy not for what was told of their religion but for what was told of their wealth, and who themselves pretended to practise community of goods like the Apostles – until, growing weary of poverty, they thought of plundering and robbing the clergy and the richer burghers.

It is no coincidence that these phrases recall those once applied to the hordes of *Pastoureaux*. By the sixteenth century social conditions in the northern Netherlands had become very similar to those which had existed in Flanders, Hainaut and Picardy some two centuries earlier. While the population in these old centres had been declining, in Holland (as in southern Germany) it had been rising. As the cloth industry of Flanders had collapsed, that of Holland had leaped ahead; the most important centre of the industry was now Leyden. It was Holland which now contained the greatest concentration of insecure and harassed workers. Moreover the situation of these workers seems to have been worse than for some centuries previously. The new capitalist industry was to a great extent a rural industry, in which the artisans worked in their own homes on materials supplied by capitalists; and under this system the guilds could no longer effectively operate. There is evidence to suggest that the unemployed and the unorganized were both more numerous and more desperate than in earlier centuries. It was amongst such people that Anabaptism flourished in its most militant and crudely millenarian form; and it was such people who now streamed into Münster.

The more prosperous burghers of Münster were, naturally enough, much perturbed. If most of them had rejoiced at the defeat of the Bishop and Chapter and the victory of the Lutheran cause, a powerful Anabaptist movement supported by a mass of unemployed and desperate foreigners held obvious and grave dangers for all of them alike. In the face of this threat Lutherans and Roman Catholics closed their ranks. Towards the end of the year the Council several times tried to silence or expel Rothmann but, secure in the devotion of his followers, he was always able to defy it. The other Anabaptist preachers were indeed expelled and replaced by Lutherans; but before long they returned and the Lutherans were hounded from the churches. Week by week excitement in the town increased until, in the first days of 1534, the men arrived who were to direct it towards a specific aim.

Melchior Hoffmann, who believed that the Millennium would dawn in Strasbourg, had been arrested in that town and imprisoned inside a cage in a tower; and there he spent the rest of his days. The prophetic mantle descended on a Dutch Anabaptist, the baker Jan Matthys (Matthyszoon) of Haarlem. This change of leadership changed the whole tone of the movement. Hoffmann was a man of peace who had taught his followers to await the coming of the Millennium in quiet confidence, avoiding all violence. Matthys on the other hand was a revolutionary leader who taught that the righteous must themselves take up the sword and actively prepare the way for the Millennium by wielding it against the unrighteous. It had, he proclaimed, been revealed to him that he and his followers were called to cleanse the earth of the ungodly. In this teaching the spirit of the *Pikarti*, of Thomas Müntzer and Hans Hut rose to new life.

From the Netherlands Matthys sent out to the various Anabaptist communities apostles who believed that the Holy Spirit had descended upon them as upon the original Apostles at Pentecost. In each town that they visited they baptised great numbers of adults and appointed 'bishops' with the power to baptise. Then they moved on, while from the newly converted town new apostles set out on similar missions. In the first days of 1534 two apostles reached Münster, where their arrival at once produced a veritable contagion of enthusiasm. Rothmann and the other Anabaptist preachers were rebaptised; and they were followed by many nuns and well-to-do laywomen and in the end by a large part of the population. It is said that within a week the number of baptisms reached 1,400.

The first apostles moved on but they were replaced by two more; and these – most significantly – were at first taken to be Enoch and Elijah, those prophets who according to traditional eschatology were to return to earth as the two 'witnesses' against Antichrist and whose appearance was to herald the Second Coming. One of the newcomers was Jan Bockelson (Bockelszoon, Beukelsz), better known as John of Leyden, a young man of twenty-five who had been converted and baptised by Matthys only a couple of months before and who was to achieve in Münster a fame which has lasted to the present day. For here as so often – as in the case of the 'Master of Hungary' and many another in the Middle Ages and indeed at all times – the messianic leader was to be the stranger, the man from the periphery. It was Bockelson, at first together with his master and later alone, who was to give to Anabaptism in Münster a fierce militancy such as it possessed nowhere else and who was to stimulate an outbreak of revolutionary millenarianism even more startling than that at Tabor a century before.

Münster as the New Jerusalem

During February 1534, the power of the Anabaptists in Münster increased rapidly. Bockelson had at once established relations with the leader of the guilds and patron of the Anabaptists, the cloth-merchant Knipperdollinck, whose daughter he was shortly to marry. On 8 February these two men ran wildly through the streets, summoning all people to repent of their sins. No more was needed to release a flood of hysteria, especially amongst the women Anabaptists, who from the first had been Rothmann's most enthusiastic followers and whose numbers had latterly been swollen by the many nuns who had broken out of their convents, put on secular attire and undergone rebaptism. These women now began to see apocalyptic visions in the streets, and of such intensity that they would throw themselves on the ground, screaming, writhing and foaming at the mouth. It was in this atmosphere, charged with supernatural expectations, that the Anabaptists made their first armed rising and occupied the Town Hall and market-place. They were still only a minority and could certainly have been defeated if the Lutheran majority had been willing to use the armed force at its disposal. But the Anabaptists had their sympa-thizers on the Council; and the outcome of the rising was the official recognition of the principle of liberty of conscience.

The Anabaptists thus won legal recognition for their already large and powerful community. Many well-to-do Lutherans, alarmed at the prospect of ever-increasing pressure from their opponents, withdrew from the town with all their movable belongings. The majority of the remaining population was Anabaptist; and messengers and manifestos were sent out urging the Anabaptists in nearby towns to come with their families to Münster. The rest of the earth, it was announced, was doomed to be destroyed before Easter; but Münster would be saved and would become the New Jerusalem. Food, clothes, money and accommodation would be ready for the immigrants on their arrival, but they were to bring arms. The summons met with a vigorous response. From as far afield as Frisia and Brabant Anabaptists streamed to Münster, until the number of newcomers exceeded that of the Lutheran emigrants. As a result, in the annual election for the Town Council on 23 February an overwhelmingly Anabaptist body was elected, with Knipperdollinck as one of the two burgomasters. On the following days monasteries and churches were looted and in a nocturnal orgy of iconoclasm the sculptures and paintings and books of the cathedral were destroyed.

Meanwhile Jan Matthys himself had arrived, a tall, gaunt figure with a long, black beard; and together with Bockelson he quickly dominated the town. Rothmann and the other local Anabaptist preachers could not compete for popular support with the 'Dutch prophets' and were soon being borne along by a wild movement which they no longer had any power to influence, let alone to resist. They functioned merely as obedient propagandists for a regime in which all effective power was concentrated in the hands of Matthys and Bockelson. The regime was a theocracy, in which the divinely inspired community had swallowed up the state. And the God whom that theocracy was supposed to serve was God the Father – that jealous and exacting Father of overwhelming power who had dominated the imagination of so many earlier millenarians. It was the Father, not the Son, whom Matthys and Bockelson encouraged their followers to invoke. And it was in order that the Children of God might serve the Father in unity that they resolved to create a 'New Jerusalem purified of all uncleanness'. To achieve this pure and uncontaminated community Matthys advocated the execution of all remaining Lutherans and Roman Catholics; but Knipperdollinck having pointed out that this would turn the whole outside world against the town, it was decided merely to expel them.

On the morning of 27 February armed bands, urged on by Matthys in prophetic frenzy, rushed through the streets calling: 'Get out, you godless ones, and never come back, you enemies of the Father!' In bitter cold, in the midst of a wild snowstorm, multitudes of the 'godless' were driven from the town by Anabaptists who rained blows upon them and laughed at their afflictions. These people included old people and invalids, small children and pregnant women and women who had just given birth. Mostly they came from the more prosperous part of the population; but they were forced to leave behind all their belongings and money and spare clothes, even their food was taken from them and they were reduced to begging through the countryside for food and shelter. As for the Lutherans and Roman Catholics who remained in the town, they were rebaptised in the market-place. The ceremony lasted three days; and once it was finished it became a capital offence to be unbaptised. By the morning of 3 March there were no 'misbelievers' left in Münster; the town was inhabited solely by the Children of God. These people, who addressed one another as 'Brother' and 'Sister', believed that they would be able to live without sin, in a community bound together by love alone.

In eliminating the Lutheran and Roman Catholic elements from the population the prophets were moved not only by fanaticism but also by the knowledge that Münster was about to be besieged. Though the Bishop had reluctantly granted official recognition to the Lutheran community he was not prepared to do the same for the Anabaptists. At every stage he had attempted to halt the progress of Anabaptism; and as soon as, under the leadership of the prophets, Anabaptism became a militant movement he prepared to crush it by force. When the Anabaptists first took up arms and occupied the market-place he hastened to the town with troops; but on that occasion the Council refused him help. During the following weeks he set about raising an army of mercenaries. The neighbouring towns and principalities contributed arms, ammunition and supplies, and some – though grudgingly and inadequately – also contributed mercenaries. When therefore the Anabaptists claimed in their propaganda that they were simply defending themselves against Roman Catholic aggression they were no doubt perfectly sincere. What is certain is that the expulsion of the Lutherans and Roman Catholics precipitated the opening of hostilities. On the following day, 28 February, earthworks were thrown up around the town and the siege began.

The rank-and-file of the Anabaptists were much surprised to find themselves suddenly at war; but under the vigorous leadership of Knipperdollinck they soon recovered their self-confidence and responded courageously to the threat. Officers were appointed, regular watches were organized for day and night, a fire service was created, dugouts and trenches were constructed for the cannons, huge earthworks rose behind the town-gates. To each man, woman and youth some definite duty was allotted. Very soon sorties were being made against the besieging troops and skirmishes were taking place outside the walls. At the same time a social revolution was being inaugurated under the direction of Jan Matthys. His first step was to confiscate the property of the emigrants. All IOUs, account books and contracts found in their houses were destroyed. All clothing, bedding, furniture, hardware, weapons and stocks of food were removed and placed in central depots. After praying for three days Matthys announced the names of seven 'deacons' who had been chosen by God to administer these stores. The poor were encouraged to apply to them and received commodities according to their needs.

However popular these measures may have been with the beneficiaries, the fact that they were carried out at the bidding of a foreigner, a newcomer to the town, aroused resentment; and a blacksmith spoke out against Matthys. The *propheta* at once had him arrested and taken to the market-place. The whole population was also summoned there; and Matthys, surrounded by a body-guard, made a speech in which he declared that the Lord was outraged at the slandering of his prophet and would take vengeance on the whole community unless this godless smith was cut off from the body of the Chosen People. The few eminent citizens who protested against the illegality of the proceedings were themselves thrown into prison and Matthys first stabbed and then shot the smith. The crowd was warned to profit by this example and dutifully sang a hymn before it dispersed.

The terror had begun and it was in an atmosphere of terror that Matthys proceeded to carry into effect the communism which had already hovered for so many months, a splendid millennial vision, in the imagination of the Anabaptists. A propaganda campaign was launched by Matthys, Rothmann and the other preachers. It was announced that true Christians should possess no money of their own but should hold all money in common; from which it followed that all money, and also all gold and silver ornaments, must be handed over. At first this order met with opposition; some Anabaptists buried their money. Matthys responded by intensifying the terror. The men and women who had been baptised only at the time of the expulsions were collected together and informed that unless the Father chose to forgive them they must perish by the swords of the righteous. They were then locked inside a church, where they were kept in uncertainty for many hours until they were utterly demoralized. At length Matthys entered the church with a band of armed men. His victims crawled towards him on their knees, imploring him, as the favourite of the Father, to intercede for them. This he did or pretended to do; and in the end informed the terrified wretches that he had won their pardon and that the Father was pleased to receive them into the community of the righteous. After this exercise in intimidation Matthys could feel much easier about the state of morale in the New Jerusalem.

Propaganda against the private ownership of money continued for weeks on end, accompanied both by the most seductive blandishments and by the most appalling threats. The surrender of money was made a test of true Christianity. Those who failed to comply were declared fit for extermination and it seems that some executions did take place. After two months of unremitting pressure the private ownership of money was effectively abolished. From then on money was used only for public purposes involving dealings with the outside world – for hiring mercenaries, buying supplies and distributing propaganda. Artisans within the town, on the other hand, received their wages not in cash but in kind; and it would seem that they were paid no longer by private employers but by the theocratic government.

Steps were also taken to establish communal ownership of commodities. At each town-gate there was set up a communal dining-hall where the men who were on duty on the walls dined together, to an accompaniment of readings from the Old Testament. Each of the halls was in charge of one of the deacons appointed by Matthys. The deacon was responsible for providing the rations; and the way in which he did this was by visiting private houses, listing the foodstuffs he found there and requisitioning them as required. Again, accommodation had to be found for the multitude of immigrants. At first it was considered sufficient to allocate to them the monasteries and the houses belonging to Lutherans or Roman Catholics; but later the exclusive possession of accommodation came to be regarded as sinful and the doors of all houses had to be left open day and night.

All these measures were of course favoured by the conditions of the siege. Nevertheless it is certainly mistaken to suggest – as has sometimes been done – that 'communism' at Münster amounted to no more than requisitioning to meet the needs of war. The abolition of private ownership of money, the restriction of private ownership of food and shelter were seen as first steps towards a state in which – as Rothmann put it – everything would belong to everybody and the distinction between Mine and Thine would disappear; or – as Bockelson later expressed it – 'all things were to be in common, there was to be no private property and nobody was to do any more work, but simply trust in God.' Rothmann after all had been holding up community of goods as an ideal for the elite long before the siege was thought of; now, in the service of the 'Dutch prophets', he demanded that the same ideal be translated into a social institution and accepted by all alike. The familiar blend of millenarianism and primitivism emerges quite clearly from the following passage in the propaganda pamphlet which he produced in October 1534, for distribution to the Anabaptist communities in other towns:

Amongst us God – to whom be eternal praise and thanks – has restored community, as it was in the beginning and as befits the Saints of God. We hope too that amongst us community is as vigorous and glorious, and is by God's grace observed with as pure a heart, as at any time before. For not only have we put all our belongings into a common pool under the care of deacons, and live from it according to our needs: we praise God through Christ with one heart and mind and are eager to help one another with every kind of service. And accordingly, everything which has served the purposes of selfseeking and private property, such as buying and selling, working for money, taking interest and practising usury – even at the expense of unbelievers – or eating and drinking the sweat of the poor (that is, making one's own people and fellow-creatures work so that one can grow fat) and indeed everything which offends against love – all such things are abolished amongst us by the power of love and community. And knowing that God now desires to abolish such abominations, we would die rather than turn to them. We know that such sacrifices are pleasing to the Lord. And indeed no Christian or Saint can satisfy God if he does not live in such community or at least desire with all his heart to live in it.

The appeal of the new social order was by no means wholly idealistic. Already the year before, swarms of homeless and propertyless people had been attracted to Münster by the prospect of social revolution. But now the revolution was taking place; and the propaganda which the leaders sent out to other towns was sometimes couched in purely social terms and aimed specifically at the poorest classes. 'The poorest amongst us, who used to be despised as beggars,' runs one letter, 'now go about dressed as finely as the highest and most distinguished. ... By God's grace they have become as rich as the burgomasters and the richest in the town.' There is no doubt that the poorest classes over a wide area did indeed look towards the New Jerusalem with a mixture of sympathy, hope and awe. From Antwerp a scholar could write to Erasmus of Rotterdam: 'We in these parts are living in wretched anxiety because of the way the revolt of the Anabaptists has flared up. For it really did spring up like fire. There is, I think, scarcely a village or town where the torch is not glowing in secret. They preach community of goods, with the result that all those who have nothing come flocking.' How seriously the authorities took the threat is shown by the repressive measures which they adopted. Anabaptism was made a capital offence not only throughout the diocese of Münster but in the neighbouring principalities, the Duchy of Cleves and the Archbishopric of Cologne. Squads of horsemen patrolled the roads and arrested all suspects. During the months of the siege countless men and women in the towns were beheaded, drowned, burnt or broken on the wheel.

Supported by and constantly appealing to the semi-literate, the social revolution in Münster was uncompromisingly anti-intellectual. The Anabaptists boasted of their innocence of book-learning and declared that it was the unlearned who had been chosen by God to redeem the world. When they sacked the cathedral they took particular delight in defiling, tearing up and burning the books and manuscripts of its old library. Finally, in the middle of March, Matthys banned all books save the Bible. All other works, even those in private ownership, had to be brought to the cathedral-square and thrown upon a great bonfire. This act symbolized a complete break with the past, a total rejection above all of the intellectual legacy of earlier generations. In particular it deprived the inhabitants of Münster of all access to theological speculations from the Fathers onwards and thereby assured the Anabaptist leaders of a monopoly in the interpretation of the Scriptures.

By the end of March Matthys had established an absolute dictatorship; but a few days later he was dead. At Easter he received what he believed to be a divine command to make a sortie at the head of a mere handful of men. He went out convinced that with the Father's aid this handful would drive off the besieging army and liberate the town; instead of which he and his companions were literally cut to pieces. This event gave an opening to Matthys's young disciple Jan Bockelson, who so far had played no great part but who was in every way fitted to seize such a chance and use it to the full. He himself had every reason to hunger after some stupendous compensation for the humiliations and failures which he had experienced in his life. Born out of wedlock, as the son of a Dutch village mayor and a woman serf from Westphalia, he had received sufficient education to acquire a smattering of book-learning. Yet it was as an apprentice tailor that he had started his career, and when he tried to set up as a merchant on his own account he was soon ruined. On the other hand he possessed remarkable gifts which were only waiting to be deployed. Endowed with extraordinarily good looks and an irresistible eloquence, he had from youth onwards revelled in writing, producing and acting plays. In Münster he was able to shape real life into a play, with himself as its hero and all Europe for an audience. The denizens of the New Jerusalem were fascinated by him and gave him at first even greater devotion than they had given to Matthys.

In exploiting this devotion Bockelson showed himself more of a politician than Matthys. He had much shrewdness; he knew how to arouse enthusiasm in the masses and how to use it for his purposes when it was aroused. On the other hand it seems certain that he was himself easily moved to quasi-mystical enthusiasm. When a deserter who had returned to the town as a spy declared that he had been brought there by angels, Bockelson believed him and at once took him into his confidence. Moreover he himself claimed frequent revelations and it would be rash to assume that this was all conscious fabrication. When, face to face with death, he declared that he had always sought God's glory, he may not have been lying. In fact – like many another *propheta* from Tanchelm onwards – Bockelson seems to have been a megalomaniac, whose behaviour cannot be adequately interpreted either simply as sincere fanaticism or simply as calculating hypocrisy. This much at least is certain: it was no commonplace personality that could induce a little town of some 10,000 inhabitants, of whom only 1,500 were capable of bearing arms, to hold out against a coalition of principalities, and through appalling hardships, for well over a year.

Bockelson's first important act was – characteristically – at once a religious and a political one. Early in May he ran naked through the town in a frenzy and then fell into a silent ecstasy which lasted three days. When speech returned to him he called the population together and announced that God had revealed to him that the old constitution of the town, being the work of men, must be replaced by a new one which would be the work of God. The burgomasters and Council were deprived of their functions. In their place Bockelson set himself and – on the model of Ancient Israel – twelve Elders. It is an indication of his political shrewdness that the Elders included some of the deposed councillors, representatives of the guilds, a member of the local aristocracy and some of the immigrants from the Netherlands. This new government was given authority in all matters, public and private, spiritual and material, and power of life and death over all inhabitants of the town. A new legal code was drawn up, aimed partly at carrying still further the process of socialization and partly at imposing a severely puritanical morality. A strict direction of labour was introduced. Artisans who were not conscripted for military service became public employees, working for the community as a whole without monetary reward – an arrangement which of course deprived the guilds of their traditional functions and quickly led to their disappearance. At the same time the new code made capital offences not only of murder and theft but also of lying, slander, avarice and quarrelling. But above all it was an absolutely authoritarian code; death was to be the punishment for every kind of insubordination – of the young against their parents, of a wife against her husband, of anyone against God and God's representatives, the government of Münster. These last provisions could not possibly have been literally enforced but did provide the prophet with an instrument of intimidation. To ensure that it should be an effective instrument Knipperdollinck was appointed executioner and given the Sword of Justice and an armed bodyguard.

Sexual behaviour was at first regulated as strictly as all other aspects of life. The only form of sexual relationship permitted was marriage between two Anabaptists. Adultery and fornication – which were held to include marriage with one of the 'godless' – were capital offences. This was in keeping with the Anabaptist tradition; like the Waldensians in earlier centuries the Anabaptist in general observed a stricter code of sexual morality than most of their contemporaries. This order came to an abrupt end, however, when Bockelson decided to establish polygamy. That such an undertaking was possible at all was due to the fact that many of the emigrants had left their womenfolk behind in the town, so that there were now at least three times as many women of marriageable age as there were men. On the other hand there is no evidence to support the view that Bockelson's intention was to provide protectors for otherwise defenceless women. Nothing of the kind was ever suggested by the Anabaptists themselves. The path along which Bockelson now led the Anabaptists in Münster was in fact that which in earlier centuries had been trodden by the Brethren of the Free Spirit and by the Adamites. To the assembled preachers and Elders he explained how God had revealed to him that the Biblical precept to 'increase and multiply' must be taken as a divine commandment. The Patriarchs of Israel had given a good example; the polygamy which they had practised must be restored in the New Jerusalem. Bockelson argued for days on end and finally threatened dissenters with the wrath of God; after which the preachers went out obediently to expound the new doctrine in the cathedral-square.

Like community of goods, polygamy met with resistance when it was first introduced. There was an armed rising during which Bockelson, Knipperdollinck and the preachers were thrown into prison; but the rebels, being only a small minority, were soon defeated and some fifty of them were put to death. During the following days others who ventured to criticize the new doctrine were also executed; and by August polygamy was established. Bockelson, who had left a wife in Leyden, began by marrying the beautiful young widow of Matthys, Diever or Divara, and before long he had a harem of fifteen wives. The preachers and then almost the whole male population followed his example and began to hunt for new wives. As for the women, though there were many who welcomed the institution of polygamy there were many others for whom it was a great tyranny. A law was made by which all women under a certain age had to marry, whether they wanted to or not. Since there were very few unmarried men this meant that very many women were legally obliged to accept the role of second or third or fourth wife. Moreover since all marriages with the 'godless' were declared invalid the wives of emigrants were forced to be unfaithful to their husbands. Refusal to comply with the new law was made a capital offence and some women were in fact executed. On the other hand many of the established wives at once began to quarrel with the strange women who had suddenly entered their households. This too was made a capital offence and resulted in more executions; but no amount of severity could enforce domestic harmony. In the end divorce had to be permitted and this in turn changed polygamy into something not very different from free love. The religious ceremony of marriage was dispensed with and marriages were contracted and dissolved with great facility. Even if much in the hostile accounts which we possess is discounted as exaggeration, it seems certain that norms of sexual behaviour in the Kingdom of the Saints traversed the whole arc from a rigorous puritanism to near-promiscuity.

The reorganizing of society in Münster did not distract Bockelson from defending the town against the enemy outside. It is true that for many months that enemy was not a very formidable one. The Bishop found great difficulty in waging effective warfare. The help he received from his allies, Cleves and Cologne, was given grudgingly and was never sufficient and he had constantly to appeal for more money and troops. Drawn from the same social strata as the majority of the Anabaptists, his mercenaries were always ready to sympathize with the besieged population; and the fact that their pay arrived very irregularly made them still more unreliable, especially as Bockelson shrewdly – and in flat contradiction to his communistic theory – offered them regular pay. Leaflets which the Anabaptists fired into the enemy camp produced the desired effect. During June some 200 mercenaries went over to the Anabaptists, whilst others simply deserted and returned to their homes.

By comparison with the besiegers the garrison was a disciplined military force. This was in the main a personal achievement of Bockelson's. Unlike Matthys he did not – for all his extravagance – lose sight of the material realities of warfare; and he must have been a very competent organizer. When the town was bombarded in preparation for an attack, the women worked all night to repair the damaged walls. When the mercenaries tried to take the town by storm they were received not only with cannon-shot but with stones, boiling water and flaming pitch. On the other hand when the besiegers made a sortie they threw the mercenaries into such disorder that they were able to spike many of the guns. Within the town discipline was strictly enforced. Everyone was allotted an essential task, as artisan or in the maintenance and repair of the fortifications. The guards on the walls were regularly inspected by the Elders, day and night. When some mercenaries who had come over got drunk and created a disturbance in a tavern, they were shot. On one occasion the Bishop tried to copy Bockelson's technique and had pamphlets fired over the walls promising that if the town surrendered there would be a general amnesty. Bockelson at once made it a capital offence to read such pamphlets.

Bockelson's prestige was at its highest when, at the end of August 1534, a major attack was beaten off so effectively that the Bishop found himself abruptly deserted both by his vassals and by the mercenaries. Bockelson would have done well to organize a sortie which might perhaps have captured the Bishop's camp; but instead he used the opportunity to have himself proclaimed king.

The messianic reign of John of Leyden

It was not as an ordinary king but as a Messiah of the Last Days that Bockelson imposed himself. In order to do so he invoked yet another divine revelation – in which he may or may not have believed – and in a manner even more dramatic than usual. At the beginning of September one Dusentschur, a goldsmith from a neighbouring town, set up as a new prophet. One day, in the main square, this man declared that the Heavenly Father had revealed to him that Bockelson was to be king of the whole world, holding dominion over all kings, princes and great ones of the earth. He was to inherit the sceptre and throne of his forefather David and was to keep them until God should reclaim the kingdom from him. Thereupon Dusentschur took the Sword of Justice from the Elders and presented it to Bockelson, anointed him and proclaimed him King of the New Jerusalem. Bockelson fell on his face and, protesting his unworthiness, called on the Father for guidance in his new task. Then he addressed the assembled populace, saying: 'In like manner was David, a humble shepherd, anointed by the prophet, at God's command, as King of Israel. God often acts in this way; and whoever resists the will of God calls down God's wrath upon himself. Now I am given power over all nations of the earth, and the right to use the sword to the confusion of the wicked and in defence of the righteous. So let none in this town stain himself with crime or resist the will of God, or else he shall without delay be put to death with the sword.' A murmur of protest rose from the crowd and Bockelson continued: 'Shame on you, that you murmur against the ordinance of the Heavenly Father! Though you were all to join together to oppose me, I shall still reign, despite you, not only over this town but over the whole world, for the Father will have it so; and my kingdom which begins now shall endure and know no downfall!' After this the people dispersed in silence to their homes. For the next three days the preachers delivered one sermon after another, explaining that the Messiah foretold by the Prophets in the Old Testament was none other than Bockelson.

The new king did everything possible to emphasize the unique significance of his accession. The streets and gates in the town were given new names; Sundays and feastdays were abolished and the days of the week were renamed on an alphabetical system; even the names of new-born children were chosen by the king according to a special system. Although money had no function in Münster a new, purely ornamental coinage was created. Gold and silver coins were minted, with inscriptions summarizing the whole millennial phantasy which gave the kingdom its meaning. 'The Word has become Flesh and dwells in us.' – 'One King over all. One God, one Faith, one Baptism.' A special emblem was devised to symbolize Bockelson's claim to absolute spiritual and temporal dominion over the whole world: a globe, representing the world, pierced by the two swords (of which hitherto pope and emperor had each borne one) and surmounted by a cross inscribed with the words: 'One king of righteousness over all.' The king himself wore this emblem, modelled in gold, hanging by a gold chain from his neck. His attendants wore it as a badge on their sleeves; and it was accepted in Münster as the emblem of the new state.

The new king dressed in magnificent robes and wore rings, chains and spurs made from the finest metal by the most skilful craftsmen in the town. Gentlemen-at-arms and a whole train of officers of the court were appointed. Whenever the king appeared in public he was accompanied by his suite, also splendidly dressed.

Divara, who as Bockelson's chief wife was proclaimed queen, also had her suite and held court like her husband. The lesser wives, none of whom was older than twenty, were subject to Divara and had to obey her commands; but even they were provided with beautiful clothes. It was a luxurious court of some 200 that flourished in the requisitioned mansions by the cathedral.

In the market-place a throne was erected; draped with cloth of gold it towered above the surrounding benches which were allotted to the royal councillors and the preachers. Sometimes the king would come there to sit in judgement or to witness the proclamation of new ordinances. Heralded by a fanfare, he would arrive on horseback, wearing his crown and carrying his sceptre. In front of him marched officers of the court, behind him came Knipperdollinck, who was now chief minister, Rothmann, who was now the royal orator, and a long line of ministers, courtiers and servants. The royal bodyguard accompanied and protected the whole procession and formed a cordon around the square while the king occupied his throne. On either side of the throne stood a page, one holding a copy of the Old Testament – to show that the king was the successor of David and endowed with authority to interpret anew the Word of God – the other holding a naked sword.

While the king elaborated this magnificent style of life for himself, his wives and friends, he imposed on the mass of the people a rigorous austerity. People had already surrendered their gold and silver and had submitted to a requisitioning of accommodation and food; now the prophet Dusentschur suddenly announced that it had been revealed to him that the Father abominated all superfluity in dress. Clothing and bedding were therefore severely rationed; and at the king's command all 'surplus' had to be handed over on pain of death. Every house was searched and eighty-three wagonloads of 'surplus' clothing and bedding were collected. Some at least of this seems to have been distributed to the immigrants from Holland and Frisia and to the mercenaries who came over from the besieging army; but that was no consolation to the ordinary citizens of Münster, who were more impressed by the contrast between their own privations and the boundless luxury of the royal court.

Bockelson realized that even his great prestige would not by itself secure the acquiescence of the unprivileged in the new regime; and he used various techniques to hold the masses in subjection. In language worthy of any adept of the Free Spirit he explained that pomp and luxury were permissible for him because he was wholly dead to the world and the flesh. At the same time he assured the common people that before long they too would be in the same situation, sitting on silver chairs and eating at silver tables, yet holding such things as cheap as mud and stones. And in general millennial prophecies and promises, such as had already kept the town in a state of excitement for over a year, were now uttered more and more frequently and with ever greater intensity. In October Rothmann produced his pamphlet *Restitution* and in December his *Announcement of Vengeance*; and these documents show clearly enough how the inhabitants of Münster were encouraged to regard their role and destiny.

In these works the phantasy of the Three Ages appeared in a new form. The First Age was the age of sin and lasted until the Flood; the Second Age was the age of persecution and the Cross and had lasted down to the present; the Third Age was to be the age of the vengeance and triumph of the Saints. Christ, it was explained, had once tried to restore the sinful world to truth, but with no lasting success; within a century that attempt had been invalidated by the Catholic Church. There had followed fourteen centuries of decline and desolation, during which Christendom lay helpless in a Babylonian Captivity. But now the time of tribulation was at an end. Christ was about to return; and in preparation for his Coming he had already established his kingdom in the town of Münster and had set over it the new David, Jan Bockelson. In that kingdom already all prophecies of the Old Testament had been realized and surpassed and the restoration of all things had been accomplished. From that kingdom God's People must go forth, wielding the Sword of Justice, to enlarge the kingdom until it should include the whole world: 'One sheep-fold, one flock, one King.' It was their sacred task to purify the world of evil in preparation for the Second Coming: 'The glory of all the Saints is to wreak vengeance. . . . Revenge without mercy must be taken of all who are not marked with the Sign (of the Anabaptists).' Only when that great killing was accomplished would Christ return, to hold judgement and to proclaim glory for all his Saints. Then indeed there would appear a new heaven and a new earth, in which the Saints – or Children of God – freed from their long servitude to the unrighteous, would live without weeping and sighing. In that realm there would no longer be any princes or lords, and all goods would be held in common. Gold and silver and precious jewels would no longer serve the vanity of the rich, but only the glory of the Children of God, for these would have inherited the earth.

These promises were supplemented and illustrated by spectacular stunts. In October the prophet Dusentschur suddenly announced that the Trumpet of the Lord would sound thrice and that at the third blast all the inhabitants of the town must foregather at Mount Sion, *alias* the cathedral-square. The men were to come armed but they were to bring their women and children too. Together the Children of God would march out of the town. They would be endowed with supernatural strength, so that five of them could kill a hundred of the enemy and ten could kill a thousand; the enemy would flee before them. So they would march victoriously to the Promised Land; and the Lord would see to it that they suffered neither hunger, thirst nor fatigue on the journey. The trumpets did indeed sound, but they were blown by Dusentschur himself, at fortnightly intervals. Failure to obey the prophet would have been suicidal; so when the third blast sounded everyone, even women with new-born babies, came to the meeting-place. The king came also, in armour and on horseback, wearing his crown and surrounded by his court. Officers were appointed to lead the army of the Lord. But at the last moment the expedition was suddenly cancelled. The king announced that he had wished merely to test the loyalty of his people; now, fully satisfied, he invited everyone to a banquet. Each man sat down with his wives and a banquet was held under the benevolent supervision of the king and queen. It ended with the celebration of a communion, in which small loaves and portions of wine were distributed by the king and queen and the royal councillors, while the preachers expounded the meaning of this sacrament. Then it was time for king and court to dine. After dinner the king, acting on a sudden illumination, sent for a captured mercenary from the prison and beheaded him.

Terror, long a familiar feature of life in the New Jerusalem, was intensified during Bockelson's reign. Within a few days of his proclamation of the monarchy Dusentschur proclaimed that it had been revealed to him that in future all who persisted in sinning against the recognized truth must be brought before the king and sentenced to death. They would be extirpated from the Chosen People, their very memory would be blotted out, their souls would find no mercy beyond the grave. Within a couple of days executions began. The first victims were women: one was beheaded for denying her husband his marital rights, another for bigamy – for the practice of polygamy was of course entirely a male prerogative – and a third for insulting a preacher and mocking his doctrine. These sentences may have afforded the new king a sadistic gratification and they certainly served to reinforce the domination of the male over the female Saints. But the terror had wider purposes than these; it was above all a political weapon wielded by a foreign despot against the native population. Bockelson was careful to build up his bodyguard out of immigrants. These men, who either had no possessions or had left them to come to Münster, were Bockelson's creatures and stood or fell with him. So long as they served him they were secure in the enjoyment of enormous privileges. Clad in magnificent robes, they could lord it over the ill-clad citizens. They also knew that, if hunger came, they would be the last to suffer from it. One of the king's first acts was to requisition all riding horses and turn his bodyguard into a mounted squadron. This squadron drilled in public; and the populace was quick to recognize in it an armed force which could be employed against an internal enemy as well as against the enemy outside the walls.

For the besieged community as a whole the establishment of the monarchy was in every way disastrous. While Bockelson and the other leaders were absorbed in setting up the royal court and in increasing and securing their own privileges they missed the most favourable moment for a decisive break-out. The Bishop recovered from his defeat and within a few weeks the town was again encircled; by the time Dusentschur summoned the population to march out of the town such an undertaking would have been suicidal. Bockelson no doubt realized this perfectly well; for while he continued to talk of going forth to conquer the world he sent out propaganda to the Anabaptists in other towns with the object of rousing them to relieve Münster. At the end of the great banquet on Mount Sion Dusentschur received yet another revelation, as the result of which he and twenty-six preachers set out as 'apostles' to neighbouring towns. Confident that any town which refused to welcome them would immediately be engulfed into hell, they behaved with great assurance and preached their doctrine publicly. At first they had some success; but the authorities intervened energetically and before long the 'apostles' were executed along with many local Anabaptists who had welcomed them.

When Bockelson learned the fate of his 'apostles' he abandoned open in favour of clandestine agitation. It seems that much of the confiscated gold and silver was smuggled out of Münster and an attempt was made to raise an army of mercenaries in Westphalia, the Netherlands and Switzerland. Little seems to have come of this plan; but at the same time thousands of copies of Rothmann's pamphlets were smuggled out and distributed in Holland and Frisia and this propaganda produced a considerable effect. Mass risings of Anabaptists were planned. In January 1535, a thousand armed Anabaptists assembled in the province of Groningen under the leadership of a prophet who called himself Christ, the Son of God.

These men intended to march towards Münster in the belief that Bockelson would come to meet them and that the enemy would flee at his approach. In the event they were defeated and scattered by the troops of the Duke of Gelderland. In March some 800 Anabaptists captured a monastery in West Frisia and held it against a force of mercenaries under the Imperial Stadtholder until, after heavy bombardment and repeated assaults, they were exterminated. At the same time three ships full of Anabaptists were stopped on their way up the river Ijsel and sunk with all their occupants. In March too an Anabaptist at Minden put himself at the head of the poorest section of the population and attempted to establish a communistic New Jerusalem after the model of Münster. This rising was dealt with by the Town Council, which threatened to use cannon; but as late as May an emissary from Münster was able to lead a rising in Amsterdam, which captured the Town Hall and was put down only after bitter fighting. The aim of all these insurrections was the one appointed by Bockelson; and it was still the identical aim which had inspired so many millenarian movements ever since the days of the *Pastoureaux*: 'To kill all monks and priests and all rulers that there are in the world; for our king alone is the rightful ruler.' And there is no doubt that the Anabaptist risings of the early months of 1535 would have been even more serious than they were if the plans, along with many of the names of the conspirators and the location of the munition dumps, had not been betrayed to the authorities already at the beginning of January. They are in any case a further proof of the devotion which the New Jerusalem could call forth amongst the Anabaptists and the common people of north-west Germany and the Netherlands.

Meanwhile the Bishop on his side intensified his efforts to reduce the town. At the end of 1534 representatives of the states of the Upper and Lower Rhine, meeting at Koblenz, agreed to supply the troops, equipment and finance required to make the siege really effective. Münster was encircled by trenches and blockhouses and by a double line of infantry and cavalry. It was thus for the first time completely cut off from the outside world. When, at an Imperial Diet held in April at Worms, all the states of the Empire undertook to contribute funds for the prosecution of the siege, the town was irrevocably doomed. The besiegers no longer needed to take the town by storm. Instead, they concentrated on starving the population to death; and in this they were largely successful. The blockade began in January 1535, and almost at once a shortage of foodstuffs made itself felt. At the king's command all houses were again visited by the deacons and the last scraps of food requisitioned; and all the horses were killed. It seems that much of this food was reserved for the royal court, which is said at all times to have eaten well and to have possessed sufficient stocks of meat, corn, wine and beer for half a year. Although this was later denied by both Bockelson and Knipperdollinck, on the balance the evidence would seem to be against them. Certainly the rations which were distributed to the populace were soon exhausted and by April famine was raging in the town. Every animal – dog, cat, mouse, rat, hedgehog – was killed and eaten and people began to consume grass and moss, old shoes and the whitewash on the walls, the bodies of the dead.

Enthroned over this nightmare kingdom Bockelson deployed with ever greater extravagance his old techniques of domination. He proclaimed that it had been revealed to him that the people would be saved by Easter; if they were not, he should be burnt in the market-place. When no deliverance came he explained that he had spoken only of a spiritual salvation. He promised that, rather than let his children starve, the Father would change the cobblestones to bread; many believed him and wept bitterly to find that stone remained stone. True to his first love, the stage, he devised ever more and more fantastic amusements for his subjects. On one occasion the starving population was summoned to take part in three days of dancing, racing and athletics; for such was the will of God. Dramatic performances were staged in the cathedral: an obscene parody of the Mass, a social morality based on the story of Dives and Lazarus. But meanwhile famine was doing its work; death from starvation became so common that the bodies had to be thrown into great communal graves. At last, in May, when most of the inhabitants had tasted no bread for eight weeks, the king agreed that those who wished should leave the town. Even then he cursed the fugitives, promising them that the reward of their infidelity would be everlasting damnation. Their earthly fate was indeed fearful enough. The able-bodied men were at once put to the sword; as for the women and old men and children, the Bishop feared – not unreasonably – that if they passed through his lines they would stir up trouble in the rear and accordingly refused to allow them past the blockhouses. These people therefore lingered on for five long weeks in the no-man's-land before the town walls, begging the mercenaries to kill them, crawling about and eating grass like animals and dying in such numbers that the ground was littered with corpses. In the end the Bishop, having consulted his allies, removed the survivors, executed those who were held to be convinced Anabaptists and banished the rest to remote villages in the diocese.

Again and again the besiegers fired leaflets into the town offering an amnesty and safeconduct to the inhabitants if only they would hand over the king and his court. Everything possible was done to encourage a revolt against the king. By this time the common people would gladly have acted on these suggestions if they had been able, but they were utterly helpless. It was during these last, most desperate weeks of the siege that Bockelson displayed to the full his mastery of the technique of terror. At the beginning of May the town was divided for administrative purposes into twelve sections and over each section there was placed a royal officer with the title of Duke and an armed force of twenty-four men. These 'dukes' were chosen from amongst the foreign immigrants and were mostly simple artisans. Bockelson promised them that, when the town was relieved and the Millennium dawned, they should all be real dukes, ruling over vast areas of the Empire, which he had already specified.

Perhaps the 'dukes' believed their king; but in case any of them had doubts they were forbidden ever to leave their sections or to meet one another. They proved loyal enough and exercised against the common people a ruthless terror. To preclude any possibility of organized opposition, meetings of even a few individuals were strictly forbidden. Any man who was found to be plotting to leave the town, or to have helped anyone else to leave, or to have criticized the king or his policy, was at once beheaded. These executions were mostly carried out by the king himself, who declared that he would gladly do the same to every king and prince. Sometimes the body was quartered and the sections nailed up in prominent places as a warning. By mid-June such performances were taking place almost daily.

Rather than surrender the town Bockelson would doubtless have let the entire population starve to death; but in the event the siege was brought abruptly to a close. Two men escaped by night from the town and indicated to the besiegers certain weak spots in the defences. On the night of 24 June 1535 the besiegers launched a surprise attack and penetrated into the town. After some hours of desperate fighting the last two or three hundred surviving Anabaptists accepted an offer of safeconduct, laid down their arms and dispersed to their homes, only to be killed one by one and almost to the last man in a massacre which lasted several days.

All the leaders of Anabaptism in Münster perished. Rothmann is believed to have died fighting. The queen Divara, having refused to renounce her faith, was beheaded. As for Bockelson, at the Bishop's command he was for some time led about on a chain and exhibited like a performing bear. In January 1536 he was brought to Münster; and there he, Knipperdollinck and another leading Anabaptist were publicly tortured to death with red-hot irons. Throughout their agony the ex-king uttered no sound and made no movement. After the execution the three bodies were suspended from a church-tower in the middle of the town, in cages which are still to be seen there today. Meanwhile those who had fled or had been driven from Anabaptist Münster had returned. The clergy were restored to their offices, the city became once more officially Catholic and to forestall any further attempts at autonomy the fortifications were razed to the ground.

In its original, pacific form, Anabaptism has survived to the present day in such communities as the Mennonites, the Brethren and the Hutterian Brethren; and it has also influenced the Baptists and the Quakers. As for militant Anabaptism, the movement which after so many others had taken up the struggle to establish the Millennium by force – that rapidly declined. At first it seemed as if a new leader in the tradition of Matthys and Bockelson had been found in Johann Batenburg; but he was executed in 1537. A generation later, in 1567, a cobbler called Jan Willemsen collected round him some 300 militants, some of them survivors from the days of Münster, and set up another New Jerusalem in Westphalia, this time in the area around Wesel and Cleves. These Saints too practised polygamy – Willemsen himself, as the messiah, had twenty-one wives – and by way of justifying their practices they had Rothmann's *Restitution* secretly reprinted. Moreover the mystical anarchism of the Free Spirit provided these people, as it had once provided the Bohemian Adamites, with a communal code. Claiming that all things rightly belonged to them, they formed themselves into a robber-band which attacked the residences of nobles and priests and ended by practising sheer terrorism. In all this episode lasted a dozen years, until the messiah and his followers were captured and executed.

With the burning of Willemsen at Cleves in 1580 the story which opened with Emico of Leiningen and 'King Tafur', Tanchelm and Eon, can conveniently be brought to a close.

Conclusion

How did the movements we have been considering stand in relation to other social movements?

They occurred in a world where peasant revolts and urban insurrections were very common and moreover were often successful. It frequently happened that the tough, shrewd rebelliousness of the common people stood them in excellent stead, compelling concessions, bringing solid gains in prosperity and privilege. In the age-old laborious struggle against oppression and exploitation the peasants and artisans of medieval Europe played no ignoble part. But the movements described in this book are in no way typical of the efforts which the poor made to improve their lot. *Prophetae* would construct their apocalyptic lore out of the most varied materials – the Book of Daniel, the Book of Revelation, the Sibylline Oracles, the speculations of Joachim of Fiore, the doctrine of the Egalitarian State of Nature – all of them elaborated and reinterpreted and vulgarized. That lore would be purveyed to the poor – and the result would be something which was at once a revolutionary movement and an outburst of quasi-religious salvationism.

It is characteristic of this kind of movement that its aims and premises are boundless. A social struggle is seen not as a struggle for specific, limited objectives, but as an event of unique importance, different in kind from all other struggles known to history, a cataclysm from which the world is to emerge totally transformed and redeemed. This is the essence of the recurrent phenomenon – or, if one will, the persistent tradition – that we have called 'revolutionary millenarianism'.

As we have seen again and again in the course of this book, revolutionary millenarianism flourishes only in certain specific social situations. In the Middle Ages the people for whom it had most appeal were neither peasants firmly integrated in the life of village and manor nor artisans firmly integrated in their guilds. The lot of such people might at times be one of poverty and oppression, and at other times be one of relative prosperity and independence; they might revolt or they might accept their situation; but they were not, on the whole, prone to follow some inspired *propheta* in a hectic pursuit of the Millennium. These *prophetae* found their following, rather, where there existed an unorganized, atomized population, rural or urban or both. This was as true of Flanders and northern France in the twelfth and thirteenth centuries as of Holland and Westphalia in the sixteenth; and recent researches have shown it to have been equally true of the Bohemia of the early fifteenth century. Revolutionary millenarianism drew its strength from a population living on the margin of society – peasants without land or with too little land even for subsistence; journeymen and unskilled workers living under the continuous threat of unemployment; beggars and vagabonds – in fact from the amorphous mass of people who were not simply poor but who could find no assured and recognized place in society at all. These people lacked the material and emotional support afforded by traditional social groups; their kinship-groups had disintegrated and they were not effectively organized in village communities or in guilds; for them there existed no regular, institutionalized methods of voicing their grievances or pressing their claims. Instead they waited for a *propheta* to bind them together in a group of their own.

Because these people found themselves in such an exposed and defenceless position they were liable to react very sharply to any disruption of the normal, familiar, pattern of life. Again and again one finds that a particular outbreak of revolutionary millenarianism took place against a background of disaster: the plagues that preluded the First Crusade and the flagellant movements of 1260, 1348–9, 1391 and 1400; the famines that preluded the First and Second Crusades and the popular crusading movements of 1309–20, the flagellant movement of 1296, the movements around Eon and the pseudo-Baldwin; the spectacular rise in prices that preluded the revolution at Münster. The greatest wave of millenarian excitement, one which swept through the whole of society, was precipitated by the most universal natural disaster of the Middle Ages, the Black Death; and here again it was in the lower social strata that the excitement lasted longest and that it expressed itself in violence and massacre.

But the rootless poor were not only shaken by those specific calamities or upheavals that directly affected their material lot – they were also peculiarly sensitive to the less dramatic but equally relentless processes which, generation after generation, gradually disrupted the framework of authority within which medieval life had for a time been contained. The one authority which was universal, embracing with its prescriptions and demands the lives of all individuals, was that of the Church; but the authority of the Church was not unquestioned. A civilization which regarded asceticism as the surest sign of grace was bound to doubt the value and validity of a Church which was manifestly infected with *Luxuria* and *Avaritia*. Again and again during the second half of the Middle Ages worldliness amongst the clergy resulted in disaffection amongst the laity – and that disaffection naturally extended to the poor. It was inevitable that many of those whose lives were condemned to hardship and insecurity should doubt whether ostentatious prelates and easy-going priests could really help them towards salvation. But if these people were alienated from the Church, they also suffered from their alienation. How much they needed the Church is shown by the enthusiasm with which they welcomed every sign of ascetic reform and the eagerness with which they would accept, even adore, any genuine ascetic. To be uncertain of the consolation and guidance and mediation of the Church aggravated their sense of helplessness and increased their desperation. It is because of these emotional needs of the poor that the militant social movements we have considered were at the same time surrogates for the Church – salvationist groups led by miracle-working ascetics.

Almost as much as to the Church, supernatural authority pertained to the national monarchy. Medieval kingship was still to a large extent a sacred kingship; the monarch was the representative of the powers that govern the cosmos, an incarnation of the moral law and the divine intention, a guarantor of the order and rightness of the world. And here again it was the poor who most needed such a figure. When we first meet the *pauperes*, in the First Crusade, they are already creating prodigious monarchs out of their own imagination: a resurrected Charlemagne, an Emico of Leiningen made emperor, a King Tafur. And to the poor any prolonged interruption or manifest failure of the royal power brought intense anguish from which they struggled to escape. It was 'the poor, weavers and fullers' of Flanders who refused to accept the death in captivity of Count Baldwin IX and who became the most devoted followers of the pseudo-Baldwin, Emperor of Constantinople. The first hordes of *Pastoureaux*, in 1251, were inspired by the prospect of rescuing Louis IX from Saracen captivity. And later, whereas in France revolutionary millenarianism waned as the prestige of the monarchy increased, in Germany the long decline of the imperial office fostered the cult of the saviour of the poor in the Last Days, the resurrected or future Frederick. The last emperor to possess all the aura of sacred kingship was Frederick II; and with his death and the fatal disruption known as the Great Interregnum there appeared amongst the common people in Germany an anxiety that was to persist for centuries. The career of the pseudo-Frederick of Neuss in the thirteenth century, the imperial lore that grew up around the flagellant leader Konrad Schmid in the fourteenth and fifteenth centuries, the prophecies and pretensions of the Revolutionary of the Upper Rhine in the sixteenth century – these things bear witness both to an enduring disarray and to the wild millenarianism that throve upon it.

When, finally, one comes to consider the anarcho-communistic millenarian groups which flourished around the close of the Middle Ages, one fact is immediately obvious: it was always in the midst of some much wider revolt or revolution that a group of this kind emerged into daylight. This is equally the case with John Ball and his followers in the English peasants' revolt of 1381; with the extremists during the early stages of the Hussite revolution in Bohemia in 1419–21; and with Thomas Müntzer and his 'League of the Elect' in the German peasants' revolt of 1525. And it is true, also, of the radical Anabaptists at Münster – for the establishment of their New Jerusalem came at the end of a whole series of revolts, not only at Münster but throughout the ecclesiastical states of north-west Germany. In each of these instances the mass insurrection itself was directed towards limited and realistic aims – yet in each instance the climate of mass insurrection fostered a special kind of millenarian group. As social tensions mounted and the revolt became nation-wide, there would appear, somewhere on the radical fringe, a *propheta* with his following of paupers, intent on turning this one particular upheaval into the apocalyptic battle, the final purification of the world.

Like the millenarian movements themselves, the *propheta* evolved over the centuries. Whereas Tanchelm and Eon claimed to be living gods, and Emico of Leiningen, the pseudo-Baldwin and the various pseudo-Fredericks claimed to be Emperors of the Last Days, men such as John Ball, Martin Húska, Thomas Müntzer, even Jan Matthys and Jan Bockelson were content to be precursors and prophets of the returning Christ. Nevertheless certain generalizations can be made about the *propheta* as a social type. Unlike the leaders of the great popular risings, who were usually peasants or artisans, *prophetae* were seldom manual workers or even former manual workers. Sometimes they were petty nobles; sometimes they were simply impostors; but more usually they were intellectuals or half-intellectuals – the former priest turned freelance preacher was the commonest type of all. And what all these men shared was a familiarity with the world of apocalyptic and millenarian prophecy. Moreover, whenever the career of one of them can be traced, it turns out that he was obsessed with eschatological phantasies long *before* it occurred to him, in the midst of some great social upheaval, to turn to the poor as possible followers.

Usually a *propheta* possessed a further qualification: a personal magnetism which enabled him to claim, with some show of plausibility, a special role in bringing history to its appointed consummation. And this claim on the part of the *propheta* deeply influenced the group that formed around him. For what the *propheta* offered his followers was not simply a chance to improve their lot and to escape from pressing anxieties – it was also, and above all, the prospect of carrying out a divinely ordained mission of stupendous, unique importance. This phantasy performed a real function for them, both as an escape from their isolated and atomized condition and as an emotional compensation for their abject status; so it quickly came to enthrall them in their turn. And what emerged then was a new group – a restlessly dynamic and utterly ruthless group which, obsessed by the apocalyptic phantasy and filled with the conviction of its own infallibility, set itself infinitely above the rest of humanity and recognized no claims save that of its own supposed mission. And finally this group might – though it did not always – succeed in imposing its leadership on the great mass of the disoriented, the perplexed and the frightened.

The story told in this book ended some four centuries ago, but it is not without relevance to our own times. The present writer has shown in another work* how closely the Nazi phantasy of a world-wide Jewish conspiracy of destruction is related to the phantasies that inspired Emico of Leiningen and the Master of Hungary; and how mass disorientation and insecurity have fostered the demonization of the Jew in this as in much earlier centuries. The parallels and indeed the continuity are incontestable.

But one may also reflect on the left-wing revolutions and revolutionary movements of this century. For, just like medieval artisans integrated in their guilds, industrial workers in technologically advanced societies have shown themselves very eager to improve their own conditions; their aim has been the eminently practical one of securing a larger share of economic prosperity or social privilege or political power, or any combination of these. But emotionally charged phantasies of a final, apocalyptic struggle or an egalitarian Millennium have had much less attraction for them. Those who are fascinated by such ideas are, on the one hand, the populations of certain technologically backward societies which are not only overpopulated and desperately poor but also involved in a problematic transition to the modern world, and are corres-

* *Warrant for Genocide: the myth of the Jewish world conspiracy and the Protocols of the Elders of Zion*, London and New York, 1967.

pondingly dislocated and disoriented; and, on the other hand, certain politically marginal elements in technologically advanced societies – chiefly young or unemployed workers and a small minority of intellectuals and students.

One can indeed discern two quite distinct and contrasting tendencies. On the one hand working people have in certain parts of the world been able to improve their lot out of all recognition, through the agency of trade unions, co-operatives and parliamentary parties. On the other hand during the half-century since 1917 there has been a constant repetition, and on an ever-increasing scale, of the socio-psychological process which once joined the Taborite priests or Thomas Müntzer with the most disoriented and desperate of the poor, in phantasies of a final, exterminatory struggle against 'the great ones'; and of a perfect world from which self-seeking would be for ever banished.

And if one looks in a somewhat different direction, one can even find an up-to-date version of that alternative route to the Millennium, the cult of the Free Spirit. For the ideal of a total emancipation of the individual from society, even from external reality itself – the ideal, if one will, of self-divinization – which some nowadays try to realize with the help of psychedelic drugs, can be recognized already in that deviant form of medieval mysticism.

The old religious idiom has been replaced by a secular one, and this tends to obscure what otherwise would be obvious. For it is the simple truth that, stripped of their original supernatural sanction, revolutionary millenarianism and mystical anarchism are with us still.

Appendix: The Free Spirit in Cromwell's England: the Ranters and their Literature*

It has often been maintained that we can know nothing of the real beliefs of the Brethren of the Free Spirit or the Spiritual Libertines, since our information comes from their enemies. Did the adepts really regard themselves as divine beings? Did they really hold that they could commit murder, robbery, fornication without sin? Or were they not, rather, simply experimenting in that passive kind of mysticism which was later to be known as Quietism? And are the scandalous tales told of them merely conscious or unconscious slanders?

The evidence produced in Chapters 8 and 9 of the present study should go far to dispel such doubts. Still, it is true that the accusations brought against these sectarians cannot be checked in detail against their own writings. To find such corroboration it is necessary to look at the brief but hectic revival of the 'Free Spirit' which took place in England during and after the Civil War. Like those of their predecessors, the writings of the English adepts – who were known as Ranters – were ordered to be burnt. But it is much harder to destroy a whole edition of a printed work than a few manuscripts; and stray copies of the Ranter tracts have survived. These works, which have not previously been reprinted, turn out to be of great interest. Viewed as historical documents, they establish beyond all doubt that the 'Free Spirit' really was exactly what it was said to be: a system of self-exaltation often amounting to self-deification; a pursuit of a total emancipation which in practice could result in antinomianism and particularly in an anarchic eroticism; often also a revolutionary social doctrine which denounced the institution of private property and aimed at its abolition. But the interest of the Ranter literature is not only historical. If the stylistic idiosyncrasies of Abiezer Coppe are

---

*Reprinted *verbatim* from the 1957 edition. Since then, confirmatory evidence about the Free Spirit has become available, with Professor Guarnieri's publication of Marguerite Porete's book in 1961 and 1965; see above, the end of Chapter 9.

sufficiently vigorous and colourful to earn him an honourable place in the gallery of literary eccentrics, Joseph Salmon surely deserves recognition as a writer of real poetic power.

Thanks to all the work which has been done on the religious and social life of Cromwell's England, there is no lack of information concerning the milieu in which the Ranters flourished. It is well known that during and after the Civil War religious excitement ran high both in the Army and amongst civilians and that neither the Episcopalian nor the Presbyterian Church was able to canalize the flood of lay religiosity. Many felt that the time had come when God was pouring out his spirit upon all flesh. Ecstasies were everyday occurrences, prophecies were uttered on all hands, millennial hopes were rife throughout the population. Cromwell himself, especially before he came to power, was moved by such hopes; and thousands of soldiers in the New Model Army and thousands of artisans in London and other towns lived in daily expectation that through the violence of civil war the Kingdom of the Saints would be established on English soil and that Christ would descend to reign over it.

Excitement was most intense during the period of political instability and uncertainty which followed the execution of the King and lasted until the establishment of the Protectorate. In 1649–50 Gerrard Winstanley was moved by supernatural illuminations to found the celebrated community of 'Diggers' near Cobham in Surrey. Convinced that the old world was 'running up like parchment in the fire, and wearing away', Winstanley attempted to restore mankind to its 'Virgin-state', a primitivist Millennium in which private property, class distinctions and human authority would have no place. At the same time groups of religious enthusiasts multiplied exceedingly. As one pamphleteer remarked in 1651, 'it is no new work of Satan to sow Heresies, and breede Heretickes, but they never came up so thick as in these latter times: They were wont to peep up by one and one, but now they sprout out by huddles and clusters (like locusts out of the bottomlesse pit). They now come thronging upon us in swarmes, as the Caterpillers of Aegypt.' The heresy which this writer had particularly in mind was that of the Ranters. These people, who were also known as 'high attainers' and 'high professors', became very numerous about 1650. Some were to be found in the Army – one hears of officers being cashiered and publicly whipped and of a soldier being whipped through the City of London 'for ranting'. There were also groups of Ranters scattered throughout the country. Above all they abounded in London, where they numbered many thousands.

The first Quakers – George Fox, James Nayler and their followers – often came into contact with the Ranters. Hostile observers, such as Episcopalians or Presbyterians, sometimes came near to identifying Quakers with Ranters; for both alike discarded the outward forms of religion and saw true religion only in the 'indwelling spirit' in the individual soul. The Quakers themselves, however, regarded the Ranters as erring souls to be converted. George Fox has a curious passage on his first meeting with Ranters, in prison at Coventry in 1649. He writes:

When I came into the jail, where the prisoners were, a great power of darkness struck at me, and I sat still, having my spirit gathered into the love of God. At last these prisoners began to rant, and vapour, and blaspheme, at which my soul was greatly grieved. They said they were God; but that we could not bear such things. . . . Then seeing they said they were God, I asked them, if they knew whether it would rain tomorrow? they said they could not tell. I told them, God could tell. . . . After I had reproved them for their blasphemous expressions, I went away; for I perceived they were Ranters.

Fox saw a good deal of the Ranters in 1654–5 – though by that time their influence was rapidly diminishing. At a joint meeting of Baptists, Quakers and Ranters at Swannington in Leicestershire he found that the Ranters 'were very rude, and stirred up the rude people against us. We sent to the Ranters to come forth, and try their God. Abundance of them came, who were very rude, and sung, and whistled, and danced; but the Lord's power so confounded them, that many of them came to be convinced.' At a similar meeting at Reading Fox again confounded the Ranters. When he was in prison at Charing Cross he was visited by Ranters, who shocked him by calling for drink and tobacco. In his description of this incident the traditional dogmas of the Free Spirit appear in the form of slogans: 'One of them cried "all is ours" and another said "all is well."' That time too Fox was able to bring dismay upon these people. As late as 1663 he had occasion to lament that the Ranters had converted two Quakers, one of whom 'ran quite out and was disowned by Friends', though the other 'was recovered, and afterwards became serviceable'. It is certain that many Ranters became Quakers; and some contemporaries were convinced that only the Friends could possibly have mastered what Winstanley himself called 'the Rantering power . . . a devouring beast'. In 1652 one Justice Hotham said to Fox that 'if God had not raised up this principle of light and life, which (Fox) preached, the nation had been overrun with Ranterism, and all the justices in the nation could not have stopped it with all their laws; because (said he) they would have said as we said, and done as we commanded, and yet have kept their own principle still. But this principle of truth, said he, overthrows their principle, and the root and ground thereof . . .' And it is a fact that as the Quaker movement grew the Ranter movement shrank, until by the end of the Protectorate it was no longer of any importance.

In this Appendix materials relevant to the Ranters are grouped as follows:

1. The Ranters described by their contemporaries.
2. Extracts from the writings of the Ranters.

1. The Ranters described by their Contemporaries

(i) That doctrines associated with the Free Spirit were becoming known in England by 1646 is shown by the second (enlarged) edition of Thomas Edwards's *Gangraena, or a Catalogue and Discovery of Many of the Errours, Heresies, Blasphemies and pernicious Practices of the Sectaries of this time, vented and acted in England in these four last years*, 1646, pp. 21 sq. Although Edwards was a Presbyterian and a bitter opponent of all Independents, there are no grounds for doubting the accuracy of this account:

. . . Every creature in the first estate of creation was God, and every creature is God, every creature that hath life and breath being an efflux from God, and shall return into God again, be swallowed up in him as a drop is in the ocean. . . . A man baptized with the holy Ghost, knows all things even as God knows all things, which point is a deep mystery and great ocean, where there is no casting anchor, nor sounding the bottome. . . . That if a man by the spirit knew himself to be in a state of grace, though he did commit murther or drunkennesse, God did see no sin in him. . . . All the earth is the Saints, and there ought to be a community of goods, and the Saints should share in the Lands and Estates of Gentlemen, and rich men. . . . That God the Father did reign under the Law, God the Son under the Gospel, and now God the Father and God the Son are making over the Kingdom to God the holy Ghost, and he shall reign and be poured out upon all flesh. . . . That there shall be a generall restauration, wherein all men shall be reconciled to God and saved, only those who now beleeve and are Saints before this restauration shall be in a higher condition then those that do not beleeve . . .

I could relate also other errours, that have been reported to me and others by honest understanding men, to have been vented (and 'tis likely enough they may be true) as that . . . if a man were strongly moved by the spirit to kill, to commit adultery &c and upon praying against it again and again it continued, and yet was still strongly pressed, he should do it . . .

(ii) The eminent Puritan divine Richard Baxter, an essentially serious and responsible writer, recorded his recollections of the Ranters in his autobiography, *Reliquiae Baxterianae*, 1696, pp. 76–7:

... the Ranters ... made it their Business ... to set up the Light of Nature, under the Name of *Christ in Men*, and to dishonour and cry down the Church, the Scripture, the present Ministry, and our Worship and Ordinances; and call'd men to hearken to Christ within them: But withal, they conjoyned a Cursed Doctrine of *Libertinism*, which brought them to all abominable filthiness of Life: They taught ... that God regardeth not the Actions of the Outward Man, but of the Heart; and that to the Pure all things are Pure, (even things forbidden): And so as allowed by God, they spoke most hideous Words of Blasphemy, and many of them committed Whoredoms commonly: Insomuch that a Matron of great Note for Godliness and Sobriety, being perverted by them, turned so shameless a Whore, that she was Carted in the streets of London.

There could never a Sect arise in the World, that was a lowder Warning to Professors of Religion to be *humble, fearful, cautelous*, and *watchful*: Never could the World be told more lowdly, whither the Spiritual Pride of ungrounded Novices in Religion tendeth; and whither Professors of Strictness in Religion may be carried in the Stream of Sects and Fashions. I have seen my self Letters written from Abbington, where among both Soldiers and People, this Contagion did then prevail, full of horrid Oaths and Curses and Blasphemy, not fit to be repeated by the Tongue or Pen of Man; and this all uttered as the Effect of Knowledge, and a part of their Religion, in a Fanatick Strain, and fathered on the Spirit of God.

(iii) A singularly vigorous account of Ranter doctrine is contained in a sermon on *Revelation* xii, 3 and 2 *Corinthians* xi, 14 preached by the Episcopalian Edward Hyde, D.D.: *A Wonder and yet no Wonder: a great Red Dragon in Heaven*, 1651, pp. 24, 35 sq.:

Lastly, The Dragon in Heaven, is the Dragon in a pretended, perfect immediate, and high enjoyment of God in the Spirit, Allegorizing the Scripture, and so denying the letter thereof...

Say some, nothing is unclean to us, no not sin; we can commit any sin, for we esteem not any thing to be unclean, but those that do, to those it is sin. ... We are pure, say they, and so all things are pure to us, adultery, fornication, etc. we are not defiled, but beleeving, and so all things are pure to us, but those that beleeve not their minds and consciences are defiled. ... God doth all things. ... If he does all things, then he doth sin, he acts sin, there is not any thing that is but he doth it, wickednesse is that he doth. ... If God be all things, then he is sin and wickednesse; and if he be all things, then he is this Dog, this Tobacco-pipe, he is me, and I am him, as I have heard some say ...

That they are very God, infinite and Almighty as the very God is; that they are in Honour, Excellency, Majesty and Power equally and the same with the true God; That the eternal Majesty dwells in them, and nowhere else; That there is no such thing as the Holiness and Righteousness of God; That unrighteousness in them, and the acts of uncleanness, prophane swearing, drunkenness, and the like filthiness and brutishness, are not unholy and forbidden in the Word; That these acts in them and others are approved of by God, and that such acts and the persons that commit them, are like God: That the acts of denying and blaspheming God, or the Holiness and Righteousness of God; That the acts of cursing God, swearing prophanely and falsly by his Name, and the acts of lying, stealing, cozening and defrauding others; the acts of murther, adultery, incest, fornication, unclean Sodomy drunkenness [*sic*], filthy and lascizious [*sic*] speaking, are not things in themselves shameful, wicked, sinful, impious, abominable and detestable in any person: That the acts of adultery, drunkenness, swearing, and the like open wickedness, are in their own nature as holy and righteous as the duties of prayer, and giving of thanks; That whatsoever is acted by them, whether whoredom, adultery, drunkenness, and the like, may be committed without sin; and that such acts are acted by the true God, or by the Majesty of God, and by the Eternity that is in them: That Heaven and all happiness consist in the acting of those things which are sin and wickedness; That those are most perfect, and like to God and Eternity, which do commit the greatest sins without least remorse or shame; That there is no such thing really and truly as unrighteousness and sin, but as a man or woman judgeth thereof; and that there is neither Heaven nor Hell, neither Salvation nor Damnation, and that these are one and the same thing and that there is not any distinction between them, or between light and darkness; That Reason is God; That we shall not have peace and quietness in our spirits, till we come to this liberty of whoring, swearing and the like: That man is deified; That the spirit after a man is dead goes into a Dog or Cat; That God beleeves in God; That all the women in the world are but one womans husband in unity [*sic*]; so that one man may be with all the women in the world, for they are her husband in unity etc. [*sic*].

(iv) Many polemical tracts were devoted solely to the Ranters. One of these, the work of a man who calls himself 'an eye and ear witness', makes by its tone and its careful organization an impression of entire trustworthiness: John Holland's *Smoke of the Bottomlesse Pit or, A More true and fuller Discovery of the Doctrine of those men which call themselves Ranters: or, The Mad Crew*, 1651 (6 pp.):

A word to the Christian Reader
... to publish to the world, the more and worse than Atheistical blasphemies of these men, not with any intent (the Lord knoweth) to make their persons odious unto any, much lesse to stir up any to persecute them barely for their judgements; for when I consider what

the Scripture saith, I find it is not Gods method to deal with Spiritual enemies with carnal weapons ...

... concerning God

They maintain that God is essentially in every creature, and that there is as much of God in one creature, as in another, though he doth not manifest himself so much in one as in another: I saw this expression in a Book of theirs, that the essence of God was as much in the Ivie leaf, as in the most glorious Angel; I heard another say, that the essence of God was in that board, as much as it was in heaven; he then laying his hand on a Deal board. They all say there is no other God but what is in them, and also in the whole Creation, and that men ought to pray and seek to no other God but what was in them.

The titles they give God are these: They call him the *Being*, the *Fulnesse*, the *Great motion*, *Reason*, the *Immensity*: I heard a man swear that if there was any God at all he was one. I said to him that God knew all things, and was able to do whatsoever he pleased, but you cannot, therefore you are not God, but a blasphemer: Another made answer, he was not The G o d, but he was God, because God was in him and in every creature in the world ...

... concerning the Spirit

They all affirme that there is but one spirit in the world, and those names of good spirit, and bad spirit, are meere imaginations and scarcrowes to feare men withall, that they are taught and are onely under teaching of this spirit, and that all other teachings either by Scripture or otherwise are of no use to them. There was one of them said in my hearing that he need not read the Scripture, nor heare Sermons, for the Father, the Son, and the Spirit were all three in him; and this he said he could prove, but his best arguments were of no force in my opinion ...

... concerning marriage

They say that for one man to be tyed to one woman, or one woman to one man, is a fruit of the curse; but they say, we are freed from the curse; therefore it is our liberty to make use of whom we please: ... this opinion they infer from these words of the Lord to Eve, *Thy desire shall be to thy husband.*

... concerning the Commandements of God

They say that all the Commandements of God, both in the Old and New Testaments, are fruits of the curse, and that all men being freed from the curse, are also free from the Commandments. Others say, that all the Commandments are to bring men up to live in God, and God in them; and they say that we are living in God, and God in us, therefore we are above all Commands whatsoever and further they say Gods will is our will, and our will is Gods will; and they say Gods will is his law, for sometimes he commands men to kill, to steale, and to

293

lye; and at other times he commands the contrary, hereon they infer that we living in God, and God in us, why may we not do the like? and if it be a sin to kil, to steale, to lye, God is the author; for say they, it is his will these things should be done, and it is by his power thay are done . . .

. . . concerning heaven and earth [*sic*]

They teach that there is neither heaven nor hell but what is in man, and that those men that do see God to be in all things, and his will to be done by all men, though they do never so wickedly, and not apprehend any wrath to be in God, and can quietly without any check of Conscience commit any sin as we call it, and can see themselves to be above all Ordinances, and all Commands, and [*sic*] that these men are in heaven, and heaven is in them; but those men that cannot see and beleeve these things are in hell, and hell in them. I saw a Letter that one of them writ to a friend of his, but it never came to his hand, and at the bottom of the Letter he writ thus, *From Heaven and Hell, or from Detford in the first yeare of my reconciliation to my selfe.* . . .

Postscript

Reader, I have not followed that orderly method I might have done, but have written the judgements of these men, in a confused manner, but I do professe in the presence of the Lord, who is the searcher of all hearts, I have done them no wrong in the matter of their judgement, except it be in forbearing to repeat their bloody swearing and cursing, and for this offence I hope those that truly feare God will excuse me. Farewell.

(v) The subjectivity of the Ranters seems sometimes to have led to an extraordinary impulsiveness. Samuel Fisher, Baptist and later Quaker, has some picturesque comments on their volatility in *Baby-Baptism meer Babism; or an Answer to Nobody in Five Words, to Everybody who finds himself concerned in it*, 1653, p. 516:

. . . thou hast left off to read [the Scripture], diswading others also from the reading of it, as unprofitable, as no other then the writings and inventions of men, to keep the world in awe, so that it cannot come to enjoy that liberty (alias licence for lewdnesse and fleshly lusts, which thou promisest, and pleadest for) and that makes thee to be such a weather cock, such a well without water, such a wandring star as thou art, such a cloud tost to and fro with a tempest, because thou hast no steady rule to steer by, no whither goest thou to talke with, or to take heed to, to recall, or to fix thee to any one point, but only the whistling, multifarious fancies, and foolish figments of thy own aiery brain, and unconstant spirit.

(vi) Parliament showed itself much concerned at the spread of the doctrines of the Free Spirit. There are indications of this concern as early as 1648. At length, on 14 June 1650, the Rump appointed a committee 'to consider of a Way for Suppression of the obscene, licentious and impious Practices, used by Persons, under Pretence of Liberty, Religion, or otherwise'. A week later the committee reported on 'the several abominable Practices of a Sect called Ranters', and was instructed to prepare a Bill 'for suppressing and punishing these abominable Opinions and Practices'. On 24 June, 5 July, 12 July and 19 July the House debated the resulting Bill and on 9 August passed it. The following November the committee was revived to consider fresh information about Ranters in Ely and Dorsetshire.

The relevant passages from the Act of 9 August 1650, for the 'Punishment of Atheistical, Blasphemous and Execrable Opinions' (H. Scobell, *A Collection of Acts and Ordinances* . . ., 1658, Part II, pp. 124–6), run as follows:

. . . finding to their great grief and astonishment, that there are divers men and women who have lately discovered themselves to be most monstrous in their Opinions, and loose in all wicked and abominable Practises hereafter mentioned, not onely to the notorious corrupting and disordering, but even to the dissolution of all Humane Society, who do deny the necessity of Civil and Moral Righteousness among Men; The Parliament . . . Enact and Ordain . . . That all and every person and persons (not distempered with sickness, or distracted in brain) who shall presume avowedly in words to profess, or shall by writing proceed to affirm and maintain him or her self, or any other meer Creature, to be very God, or to be Infinite or Almighty, or in Honor, Excellency, Majesty and Power to be equal, and the same with the true God, or that the true God, or the Eternal Majesty dwells in the Creature and no where else; or whosoever shall deny the Holiness and Righteousness of God, or shall presume as aforesaid to profess, That Unrighteousness in persons, or the acts of Uncleanness, Prophane Swearing, Drunkenness, and the like Filthiness and Brutishness, are not unholy and forbidden in the Word of God, or that these acts in any person, or the persons for committing them, are approved of by God, or that such acts, or such persons in those things are like unto God: Or whosoever shall presume as aforesaid to profess, That these acts of Denying and Blaspheming God, or the Holiness or Righteousness of God; or the acts of cursing God, or of Swearing prophanely or falsly by the Name of God, or the acts of Lying, Stealing, Cousening and Defrauding others; or the acts of Murther, Adultery, Incest, Fornication, Uncleanness, Sodomy, Drunkenness, filthy and lascivious Speaking, are not things in themselves shameful, wicked, sinful, impious, abominable and detestable in any person, or to be practised or done by any person or persons: Or shall as aforesaid profess, That the acts of Adultery, Drunkenness, Swearing and the like open wickedness, are in their own nature as Holy and Righteous as the Duties of Prayer, Preaching or giving of Thanks to God: Or whosoever shall avowedly as aforesaid profess, That whatsoever is acted by them (whether Whoredom, Adultery, Drunkenness or the like open Wickedness) may be committed without sin; or that such acts are acted by the true God, or by the Majesty of God, or the Eternity that is in them; That Heaven and all happiness consists in the acting of those things which are Sin and Wickedness; or that such men or women are most perfect, or like to God or Eternity, which do commit the greatest Sins with least remorse or sense; or that there is no such thing really and truly as Unrighteousness, Unholiness or Sin, but as a man or woman judgeth thereof; or that there is neither Heaven nor Hell, neither Salvation nor Damnation, or that those are one and the same thing, and that there is not any distinction or difference truly between them: All and every person or persons so avowedly professing, maintaining or publishing as aforesaid, the aforesaid Atheistical, Blasphemous or Execrable Opinions, or any of them, upon complaint and proof made of the same in any the cases aforesaid ... or Confession of the said persons, the party so convicted or confessing, shall be ... committed to Prison or to the House of Correction, for the space of six moneths ...

The Act also defines the punishment for a second offence as banishment; and the punishment for refusing to accept banishment, or for returning from banishment without special Licence of Parliament, as death.

(vii) Faced with persecution, many Ranters seem to have adopted a secret language and to have carried on a wary and clandestine propaganda, exactly like the heretical Beghards and Beguines before them. After listening to the 'recantation sermon' preached by the Ranter Abiezer Coppe at Burford in September 1651, John Tickell, Minister of Abingdon, commented on these tactics in *The Bottomles Pit Smoaking in Familisme ... together with some breef notes on AB. COPPS Recantation Sermon (as 'twere) ...*, 1651, pp. 37–40:

[They] use to speak one thinge and mean another. ... They will say and unsay in one breath. ... Before the late Act against *Raunters*, they spake boldly, now they dare not. ... Since the pretence of the conversion of severall of them to the way of truth, they have a *generall straine* of Clothing their corrupt notions with sound words, especially such Scripture expressions as will beare a generall sence, as for Instance. They will tell you that Christ was *Crucified* at Jerusalem, ... but in what sence? abominably corrupt, as a type and figure of the true death of Christ in them (as they pretend). ... It seems to me, from what I have knowne of them, they will put themselves on all expressions, wayes and windings, to keep themselves from being *known*, but to their *owne*: you shall not know where to find them, so as to fasten on them, but their own shall know their meaning, and so may you when you have once got their *Key*. ... You shall find it, for a never failing observation, they will first insinuate an interest in your affections, and then corrupt your judgements. They will smile upon you, and cut your throate: use melting words, *Honnysweet*, smoothe as oyle, but full of poyson . . .

(viii) Many of the accounts of the Ranters give the impression of journalistic sallies of the most fanciful and scurrilous kind; such are to be found in *The Ranters Religion or, A faithfull and infallible Narrative of their damnable and diabolical opinions, with their destestable lives and actions. With a true discovery of some of their late prodigious pranks, and unparalleled deportments* . . . Published by Authority (December) 1650 (8 pp.); in G. Roulston's *The Ranters Bible, or, Seven several Religions by them held and maintained* (December) 1650 (6 pp.); in *The Routing of the Ranters* (November) 1650, and (belatedly, in 1706) in C. Gildon's *The Post-Boy robb'd of his Mail* (second edition), Letter LXVI, pp. 426–9. The recurrent accounts of communal 'adamitic' orgies, for instance, are not confirmed in any way even by the very frank confessions of the Ranters. Of all this material the only item which is perhaps worth preserving is the description of a female Ranter in *The Routing of the Ranters* – and that more for its picturesqueness than for its reliability:

. . . she speaks highly in commendation of those husbands that give liberty to their wives, and will freely give consent that she should associate her self with any other of her fellow creatures, which she shall make choice of; she commends the Organ, Viol, Symbal and Tonges in Charterhouse-Lane to be heavenly musick [;] she tosseth her glasses freely, and concludeth there is no heaven but the pleasures she injoyeth on earth, she is very familiar at the first sight, and danceth the Canaries at the sound of a hornpipe.

One Ranter feast has however been described by hostile critics in detail and with complete trustworthiness. *The Arraignment and Tryall with a Declaration of the Ranters* . . . published according to order, 1650 (6 pp.); *Strange Newes From the Old-bayly or The Proofs, Examinations, Declarations, Indictments and Conviction of the Ranters, at the Sessions of Gaole-Delivery, held in the Old Bayly, the 18, 19 and 20 of this instant January* . . . , 1651 (6 pp.); *The Ranters Ranting: with The apprehending, examinations and confession* . . . , 1650 (6 pp.), all deal with a group of eight Ranters arrested in London on 1 November 1650. Some of the names are known: John Collins, T. Shakespear ('a warrener'), Thomas Reeve, Thomas Wiberton, M. Waddleworth ('a glover'). The Ranters met at a tavern, the *David and Harp* in Moor Lane, in the parish of Giles Cripplegate. The host of the tavern was Middleton. His wife, 'who long before was suspected to be of the Ranting crew', entertained the company (presumably she was the same Mrs Mary Middleton to whom Clarkson in his confession refers as his mistress). Other women were also present. The Ranters sang blasphemous songs to the tune of the Psalms. The neighbours informed the police, who sent an *agent provocateur*. This man carefully observed the behaviour of the Ranters. He found that they addressed one another as 'Fellow-creature' – a form of address which was undoubtedly normal amongst Ranters, especially between men and women. They swore a good deal and, although there was certainly no promiscuous orgy, one of the men did display himself in an indecent manner. Later the Ranters sat down to eat together, and it is clear that the meal possessed for them the significance of a pantheistic Eucharist. 'One of them took (a piece of beef) in his hand, tearing it asunder said to the other, This is the flesh of Christ, take and eat.' When they were arrested one of them took a candle and began to hunt about the room, saying 'that he sought for his sins but there were none, and that which they thought so great unto him, was so small, that he could not see it'. This is the language of mystical antinomianism; and that these people did indeed attach a quasi-mystical value to their acts is shown by their slogan or code-word 'Ram me, damn me!' When asked they said that 'Ram' meant God; but the full significance of the expression becomes plain only when one sets it alongside certain phrases in the writings of the Ranters: 'I was . . . consumed, damned, rammed and sunke into nothing, into the bowels of the still Eternity (my mothers wombe)' (Coppe); and again: 'Now it is damm'd and ramm'd into its only Center, there to dwell eternal in the bosom of its only Father: This, and only this, is the damnation so much terrifying the Creature in its dark apprehension . . .' (Clarkson).

Seven of these Ranters appeared next morning before Sir John Wolaston, who sent them to Bridewell to beat hemp. Collins and Reeve also appeared in the following January at the Old Bailey to answer charges under the Act of 9 August 1650, for the suppressing of 'atheistical, blasphemous and execrable opinions'. They were sentenced to six months' imprisonment.

(ix) Humphrey Ellis in *Pseudochristus; Or, A true and faithful Relation of the Grand Impostures, Horrid Blasphemies, Abominable Practises, Gross Deceits; Lately spread abroad and acted in the County of Southampton . . .* , 1650 (62 pp.), gives a detailed account of the case of William Franklin and Mary Gadbury, who seem to have been true successors to those 'Christs' and 'Mothers of God' who headed the medieval groups of the Free Spirit. Ellis, who was a minister at Winchester, is a wholly reliable source. He describes, as he says, 'things done among ourselves, and that very lately, that they are fresh in the memories of most persons hereabout'. Much he observed at first hand; and he had access to the confessions made by the sectarians when they were examined in court.

William Franklin, a native of Andover, lived for many years in London as a ropemaker. He was a respectable married man and a Congregationalist who was 'esteemed by the godly as an eminent Saint, as a choyce Professor of godliness'. But misfortunes befell him. His family was struck by plague, he himself was afflicted by illness and for a time in 1646 by some mental disorder. It was under the influence of this disorder that he first horrified his fellow-Congregationalists by declaring himself to be God and Christ. After a short time he recovered and professed repentance. Thereafter his everyday bearing did not give an impression of insanity. He developed 'a cautious wary manner of expressing himself'; and he seemed to Ellis to be fully responsible for his actions. On the other hand he soon abandoned his co-religionists and, claiming revelations and the gift of prophecy, began to associate with Ranters.

Franklin, who was now about forty years of age, rejected his wife and began to live with other women. Chief amongst these was one Mary Gadbury, a woman of thirty who had long since been deserted by her husband and who earned her keep in London by selling 'trinkets for gentlewomen'. As soon as she met Franklin, Mary Gadbury began to see visions and hear voices. The purport of her mystical revelations was that 'there shall be No King, but the King of Kings, and Lord of Lords. . . . The Saints shall judge the Earth, and the World shall confess and say, This is the City of the Lord. . . . I will send my Son in the person of a man, who shall rule over the Nations, and they shall see him face to face, eye to eye.' The ecstatic woman was easily convinced by Franklin that he was the promised Christ; and she began to spread the glad tidings amongst her neighbours. Under Franklin's influence she felt that she must follow Christ in the path of voluntary poverty. She accordingly sold everything she possessed, gave the money to feed the hungry and clothe the naked, and followed Franklin – 'embracing him . . . as her Lord and Christ'.

Persuaded that the Lord had destroyed Franklin's former body and thereby severed the links that bound him to wife and children, Mary Gadbury began to lie with him nightly – although she insisted that she 'companied with him' only as a 'spiritual man'. When a minister asked her whether she was not ashamed of her cohabitation with Franklin she replied that 'Adam and Eve in innocency were naked, and were not ashamed; but sin brought shame into the world: but when they come to be in Christ, it is taken away!' In all this the Adam-cult of the medieval heresy is clearly recognizable. One is not surprised that the woman also began to call herself the 'Bride of the Lamb', 'the Spouse of Christ', 'the Mother of Christ', and 'the Woman clothed with the Sun', and that she even claimed to be herself 'equal to God'.

In 1649 the couple received a divine commission to go to Hampshire – a convincing sign of their sincerity, since this was the one part of the country in which Franklin was known and was sure to be recognized. In the seventeenth century voluntary poverty was no longer practicable as a consistent way of life and Franklin had to return frequently to London to earn money. During his absences Mary Gadbury carried on unremitting propaganda on his behalf. Her sole authorities were her own revelations, but these were expounded in Biblical phrases. Her success was considerable: 'many both in Town and Countrey were some shaken, some wholly seduced by these her deceits.' Franklin himself, moreover, had that curious eloquence which was so characteristic of heresiarchs of the Free Spirit, being 'very plausible in his speech, that might easily insinuate it self into the mindes of the simple. . . . He would oftentimes alledg Scripture in his discourse, and speak much in the language of it, but very strangely abusing, perverting, wresting it from the true sense thereof by his Allegorical fancies.' Ellis makes the same comment on the activities of his pair as the clerics of Antwerp had made on Tanchelm's movement five centuries earlier: in these things the Devil was transforming himself into an Angel of Light.

Millenarian expectations, says Ellis, were rife at that moment; and the living god and goddess soon found believers. One enthusiastic convert was the wife of a Minister Woodward. Before long the couple were living in the minister's house and soon after that the minister himself was won over. 'Now,' says Ellis, 'doth this poysonous infection begin amaine to spread it selfe, having gotten many, and these also very active persons, to be the Preachers, Spreaders, and publishers of it abroad to the people . . . they perswade others to imbrace and entertain also, that . . . this Franklin is the Son of God, the Christ, the Messiah.' The disciples were allotted particular roles: one was John the Baptist, 'sent forth to tell that Christ was come upon the earth', another was a destroying angel 'sent forth to curse the earth', yet another was a healing angel, charged with healing those whom his companion had cursed. From beneath these Biblical trappings there emerges, unmistakably, the religion of the Free Spirit. One finds Mary Gadbury, for instance, demanding white linen from her hostess Mrs Woodward, saying that God had bidden her make a white robe for herself, 'for he had made her pure'. One finds a soldier watching for these supernatural beings to perform miracles, and still professing absolute pantheism. And one finds the 'destroying angel' himself denying all antagonism between God and Devil, affirming that 'all things came by nature', and claiming to be himself 'the God of Light and the God himself'.

Franklin and his chief followers were arrested and tried at Winchester in January 1650. At first they bore themselves very confidently, denying nothing. Asked for their names and habitations they insisted that they had none 'according to the flesh', since they were wholly spiritual. Their ages they reckoned from their first meetings with Franklin, 'as if they had been but then born'. Franklin maintained, and his disciples agreed, that he was literally Christ. At the prospect of Bridewell, however, Franklin's courage failed. He recanted; and his disciples, furious, immediately abandoned him. In March the prisoners appeared at the Assize of the Western Circuit. All the men were sentenced to imprisonment until they should give security for their good behaviour; and all were immediately released on bail except Franklin himself, who was unable to give such security. Mary Gadbury was sent to Bridewell to receive whippings for some weeks.

(x) The anarcho-communistic attitudes which had so often, in one form or another, been associated with the Free Spirit, persisted amongst the Ranters. Richard Hickock, in *A Testimony against the People call'd Ranters and their Pleads*, 1659 (8 pp.), makes the Ranters say, 'Cast in thy Lot among us, let us all have one Purse.' Moreover it seems that in December 1650, when many Ranters were beginning to desert the movement, a 'Ranters' Parliament' was held in London, near Southampton House; and eight dissident Ranters (who give their names) have left, in *The Ranters Declaration . . . published by M. Stubs, a late fellow-Ranter*, 1650 (6 pp.), a report of the proceedings which throws considerable light both on the social composition and on the social doctrine of the movement:

... many queries were propounded, in behalf of the poor of their fraternity; desiring to know how they should be maintained notwithstanding the falling off of many hundreds of the great ones. To which answer was made, That they should borrow money, and never pay it again; and that they should not only make use of a Man's Wife, but of his Estate, Goods and Chattels also, for all things were common: But alas! this *Engine* would not prove effectual; for many of the poorer sort conceiving this stratagem no wayes feasible, brake forth into a great agony, cursing all those who had so deluded them, and utterly detested against them; so that of 300 there present, not above 150 returned with

Satans visage, the rest, having a great change, by Gods divine mercy, wrought in them ... are converted ... and now live civilly in their respective places and Habitations ...

There are other indications that on becoming Ranters working folk abandoned their normal occupations and lived on charity; and *The Ranters Religion* remarks: 'That idlenesse is the mother of all mischiefe was never so evidently proved, as by the ... Ranters, a People so dronish, that the whole course of their lives is but one continued Scene of Sottishness ...'

(xi) The Ranters provided the theme for a satirical comedy by 'S. S. Gent' (i.e. Samuel Sheppard): *The Joviall Crew, or, The Devill turn'd Ranter: Being a Character of The roaring Ranters of these Times*, 1651. Most of their more obvious traits are caricatured in this production. Their 'communism', for instance, moves them to announce:

> ... our women are all in common.
> We drink quite drunk together, share our Oaths,
> If one man's cloak be rent, all tear their Cloaths.

Members of the 'jovial crew' come from many different classes; they include a Scholar (sometime an Episcopalian), a Painter, an Apothecary, a Tailor, a Soldier, and a Gentleman. These men go to a tavern to 'drink sweet Wine and strong Tobacco, till we become immortall.' Two ladies, wives of respectable citizens, join the party; and an orgy is beginning when all are arrested and taken to Bridewell to be whipped.

In one scene the Ranters, dancing, sing in chorus:

> Come away, make no delay, of mirth we are no scanters,
> Dance and sing all in a Ring, for we are Jovial Ranters

> > Let fearfull souls refuse their bowls,
> > And tremble for to tipple:
> > Let moon-men fear to *domineere*,
> > And halt before a Cripple.

> Come away etc.

> > No hell we dread when we are dead,
> > No Gorgon nor no Fury:
> > And while we live, wee'l drink and ****
> > In spight of judge and jury.

> > Come on my Boys, receive your joys,
> > And take your fill of pleasure,
> > Shoot for shoot, away let's doo't,
> > But we must have our measure.

All lie down, as in a swown,
To have a pleasing vision.
And then rise with bared thighs,
Who'd fear such sweet incision?

About, about, ye Joviall rout,
Dance antick like Hob-gobblins;
Drink and roar, and swear and whore,
But yet no brawls or squoblings.

2. Extracts from the Writings of the Ranters

Four Ranters are known to have written books, and despite the
best efforts of the authorities copies of most of these books survive.
They fill in, as it were by analogy, the gap left by the destruction
of the medieval literature of the Free Spirit.

(i) Jacob Bauthumley, or Bottomley, wrote *The Light and Dark
sides of God, Or a plain and brief Discourse of The light side (God,
Heaven and Earth) The dark side (Devill, Sin, and Hell). As also of
the Resurrection and Scripture . . .*, 1650 (84 pp.). He was in the
Army at the time and was punished for writing this work by
being burned through the tongue. In 1654–5 he appeared at joint
meetings of the Quakers and Ranters in Leicestershire. Bauthumley
represents Ranterism at its most academic and refined. Though his
teachings could easily be used to justify moral anarchism, one can
accept his assurance that he wrote 'not to countenance any unseemly act or evill in any man'. One imagines that the teachings of
Amaury of Bène bore the same relation to those of the Amaurians
as did Bauthumley's teachings to those of Ranters such as Laurence
Clarkson and Abiezer Coppe. The following extracts, though
short compared with the work as a whole, are representative:

Concerning God

O God, what shall I say thou art, when thou canst not be named?
what shall I speak of thee, when in speaking of thee, I speak nothing
but contradiction? For if I say I see thee, it is nothing but thy seeing of
thy selfe; for there is nothing in me capable of seeing thee but thy self:
If I say I know thee, that is no other but the knowledge of thy self;
for I am rather known of thee, then know thee: If I say I love thee, it is
nothing so, for there is nothing in me can love thee but thy self; and
therefore thou dost but love thy self: My seeking of thee is no other but
thy seeking of thy selfe: My delighting enjoying thee, is no other but
thy delighting in thy self, and enjoying of thy selfe after a most
unconceivable manner.

... thou being the life and substance of all Creatures, they speak and move, yea live in thee; and whatever any Creature is, it is that as it is in thee. ... Lord whither shall I go from thy presence? for it is thy presence and Being, that is the substance and Being of all Creatures and things; and fills Heaven and Earth, and all other places ...

Nay, I see that God is in all Creatures, Man and Beast, Fish and Fowle, and every green thing, from the highest Cedar to the Ivey on the wall; and that God is the life and being of them all, and that God doth really dwell, and if you will personally; if he may admit so low an expression in them all, and hath his Being no where else out of the Creatures ...

Did men see that God was in them, and framing all their thoughts, and working all their works, and that he was with them in all conditions: what carnall spirit would reach out to that by an outward way, which spiritually is in him, and which he stands really possest of? and which divine wisdom sees the best, and that things can be no otherwise with him. ... [Formerly I] thought that my sins or holy walking did cause [God] to alter his purpose of good or evill to me.

But now I cannot looke upon any condition or action, but methinks there appears a sweet concurrance of the supreame will in it nothing comes short of it, or goes beyond it, nor any man shall doe or be any thing, but what shall fall in a sweet compliance with it; it being the wombe wherein all things are conceived, and in which all creatures were formed and brought fourth [*sic*].

... As all things were let out of God: so shall they all give up their Being, life and happiness into God again ... though the Clothing dissolve, and come to nothing, yet the inward man still lives; though the shadow dies, yet the soule or substance which is God, lives to all eternity. Further, to me it is cleare, that there is nothing that partakes of the divine nature, or is of God, but it is God. The reason is, because there are no distinctions in God, he being one individed [*sic*] essence: ... I cannot see ... that [God] is capable of any degrees of more or lesse, or that he loves one man more than another, or hates one man more then another ... I cannot see that there is love and hatred in God, or any such passions: that which admits of degrees is not perfect.

... And God loves the Being of all Creatures, yea, all men are alike to him, and have received lively impressions of the divine nature, though they be not so gloriously and purely manifested in some as in others, some live in the light side of God, and some in the dark side; But in respect of God, light and darkness are all one to him; for there is nothing contrary to God, but onely to our apprehension. ...

Bauthumley rejects the Trinity and concludes this section.

I do not apprehend that God was onely manifest in the flesh of Christ, or the man called Christ; but that he as really and substantially dwells in the flesh of other men and Creatures, as well as in the man Christ.

Concerning Heaven

... then men are in Heaven, or Heaven in men, when God appears in his glorious and pure manifestations of himself, in Love and Grace, in Peace and rest in the Spirit ...

... I find that where God dwells, and is come, and hath taken men up, and wrapt them up into the Spirit; there is a new Heaven and a new Earth, and all the Heaven I look ever to enjoy is to have my earthly and dark apprehensions of God to cease, and to live no other life then what Christ spiritually lives in me.

Concerning Sinne

... though men act in darknesse, yet God is there vailing his glory, and so they must needs sin; for sin is properly the dark side of God which is a meere privation of light.

Further, we must consider, that God gives not any Law or Rule out of himselfe, or beyond his own glory ... sin it self doth as well fall in compliance with the glory of God, as well as that which we call grace and goodnesse; for *sinne abounds that grace may abound much more* ...

And whereas some may say, then men may live as they list, because God is the same, and all tends to his glory, if we sin, or if we do well:

I answer them in the words of the Apostle: Men should not sin because grace abounds; but yet if they do sin, that shall turn to the prayse of God, as well as when they do wel. And so the wrath of man praises God as well as his love and meekness, and God glorified in the one as well as the other. And however this may seeme to countenance that God is the Authour of sin, and wills sin; yet to me it is plain, that there is nothing that hath a Being but God, and sin being a nullity, God cannot be the Authour of it, and sof alls not within the decree of God; ...

Further, I see that the reason why we cal some men wicked and some godly, is not any thing in the men; but as the divine Being appeares more gloriously in one then in another: so we say, the one is a Saint and godly, and the other is wicked and profane; and yet the one acts as he is carried forth by the Supreme power, and so doth the other: And if there be any difference it is not in respect of the creature, of what it is, or doth; for the same divine Being, is in the one as well as the other; but onely it doth not manifest it self in the one as the other ...

[God's] will is his power, and his power is his will: and by the self same act that he wills things, by the selfe same act he doth things: and it is our weaknesse otherwise to apprehend; for God being one and intire, admitting of no distinction or division in himself, he admits of no variations, but all things are as that supreme will acts, and brings them forth; And I see according to the Councell of his will they did no more that crucified Christ, then they that did imbrace him.

These things I write, not to countenance any unseemly act or evill in any man; ...

Concerning Hell

... I was continually suffering the torment of Hell, and tossed up and down, being condemned of my self ... And this is that I found til

God appeared spiritually, and shewed me that he was all the glory and happiness himself, and that flesh was nothing. . . . God . . . brought me into the glorious liberty of the Sons of God, whereas I was before in bondage to sin, law, an accusing Conscience which is Hell . . .

[The soul] came immediately from God, and is no other but of God, and if I may say further without offence, it is God; for that which is of God is God, because God cannot be divided. . . .

. . . how this soule, as men speak of, should be impure and sinfull, I know not; for how flesh should defile a spirit I cannot imagine . . .

The truth is, there is nothing lives to all eternity but God: every thing below God perisheth and comes to nothing: and as all things had their subsistence and Being in God, before they were ever manifested in the world of Creatures: so in the end, whatsover is of God, or God in the world at the end of it, they shall all be rapt up into God againe. And so as God from all eternity lived in himself and all things in him: so when he shall cease to live in flesh and creatures, he will then live in himself unto all eternity, and will gloriously triumph over Sin, Hell and death; and all Creatures shall give up their Power and Glory unto God backe againe, from whence it Originally came, and so God shall be all.

(ii) Amongst the Ranters whom George Fox found in the prison at Coventry in 1649 was one Joseph Salmon who 'not long after this . . . put forth a paper, or book of recantation; upon which they were set at liberty'. From 1650 Salmon was for some years a minister in Kent, preaching frequently in Rochester Cathedral. At various stages of his life he wrote a number of works. One of these, it seems, was a Ranter tract called *Divinity anatomised*, which appears to be lost. The following extracts, which reveal a very considerable poetic talent, are taken from a recantation called *Heights in Depths and Depths in Heights, or Truth no less Secretly than Sweetly sparkling out of its Glory from under a Cloud of Obloquie* . . . *Together with a sincere abdication of certain Tenents, either formerly vented by him, or now charged upon him*, 1651 (54 pp.).

. . . It is not long since wherein that eminent appearance of light, which dawned out of its glory upon my Spirit, and from thence gave a sweet and powerfull reflexe upon the World, did shroud it selfe under a most sable and enigmaticall cloud of darknesse, and withdrew for a season, behinde the dark Canopies of Earth and Flesh; in which state the Hemispheare of my spirit was so bespread with obscurity, that I knew not whither I walked, or what I did.

Thus was I led into paths that I had not known, and turned from a King into a Beast, and fed upon huskes for a season. After a while posting most furiously in a burning zeal towards an unattainable end: my manner of walking being adjudged by those in power contrary to the peace and civill order of the Commonwealth I was justly apprehended as an offender . . .

I suffered above halfe a years imprisonment under the notion of a blaspheamer; which through want of air, and many other conveniences, became very irksome and tedious to my outward man . . .

Salmon records how he repented, recanted and was released.

I now am made to speak, because I am almost weary of speaking, and to informe the world that silence hath taken hold of my spirit. The thunderstrokes of the Almighty have to purpose uttered their voices in me, heaven and earth have trembled at their dreadfull sounds: the Alarm being over, ther's silence now in heaven; for how long I know not.

I lie quietly secure in the Lord while I see the whole world consuming in the fire of envie one against another. I heare much noyse about me, but it serves onely to deafen me into the still slumbers of Divine rest. The formall world is much affrighted, and every form is up in Arms to proclaim open wars against it selfe: The Almighty power is dashing one thing against another, and confounding that which he hath formerly faced with the glory of his own presence: Hee setteth up and casteth down, and who shal say, *What doest thou*? Come then, O my soule, enter thou into my Chamber, shut thy doores about thee, hide thy selfe in silence for a season till the indignation bee blown over.

. . . We seem to live in the State of variety, wherein we are not truely living, but onely in appearance: in Unity is our life: in one we are, from one divided, we are no longer.

While we perambulate variety, we walk but as so many Ghosts or Shadows in it, that [*sic*] it self being but the Umbrage of the Unity.

To descend from the oneness or Eternity, into the multiplicity, is to lose ourselves in an endlesse Labyrinth.

To ascend from variety into uniformity, is to contract our scattered spirits into their original center and to finde our selves where we were, before we were . . .

Ob. How then shall a man attaine to a oneness, and communion with this inaccessible glory?

Sol. Seeing there is no way probable for us, (by our most lofty aspires) to interesse our selves in that.

We must patiently expect its seasonable descension upon us; whose nature it is to consume us into it selfe, and to melt us into the same nature and likenes;

And truly till this come, and thus manifest it selfe, all that man doe to acquire satisfaction, does but multiply his sorrow upon his head, and augment cares upon his spirit . . .

Salmon gives an account of his spiritual adventures:

I presently set forth for heaven, the whole powers and faculties of my soule being infinitely ingaged thereunto. . . . I now forsooke my owne kindred and my fathers house . . .

He became a Presbyterian, an Independent, a Baptist and in the end a mystic:

I appeared to my selfe as one confounded into the abyss of eternitie, nonentitized into the being of beings ...

He became a Ranter:

Being thus clouded from the presence of the Lord, I was violently posted through most dark paths, where I ever and anon stumbled and fell into the snare of open terror and profaneness,, led and hurried, (by what power let the wise judg) in a principle of mad Zeal, to tear and rend the very appearances of God, which I had formerly cherished in my brest.

Delighting my selfe in nothing but in that which rendèrd me most vile and ugly in the sight of all men, and glorying in nought, but my own shame ...

I was indeed full sick of wrath, a vial of wrath was given me to drink ...

Well – drink I must, but mark the riddle.

'Twas given me, that I might drink, I drank, that I might stumble, I stumbled, that I might fall; I fell, and through my fall was made happy.

It is strange to think, how the hidden and secret presence of God in me, did silently rejoyce while flesh was thus manifested;

I had a sweet rest and refuge in the Lord, even while my flesh was frying and scorching in the flames of ireful fury.

I was ark'd up in the eternal bosome, while the flesh was tumbling in the foaming surges of its own vanity: ...

... and this I know is a riddle to many, which none but the true Nazarite can expound; and til he is pleased to unfold it, it pleases me it should lie dark.

But to conclude –

Thus have I been forc't into the strange paths of obscurity, driven up and down in a tempestuous storm of wrath, and split upon the rocks of dreadful astonishment; All the waves and billows of the Almighty have gone over me.

I am now at rest in the silent deeps of eternity, sunk into the abyss of silence, and (having shot this perilous gulf) am safely arrived into the bosome of love; the land of rest.

I sometimes hear from the world, which I have now forsaken; I see its Diurnals are fraught with the tydings of the same clamor, strife, and contention, which abounded in it when I left it; I give it the hearing, and that's all ...

My great desire (and that wherein I most delight) is to see and say nothing.

I have run round the world of variety, and am now centered in eternity; that is the womb out of which I was taken, and to which my desires are now reduced ...

Every thing beares a constant and greedy motion towards the center;

and when once we are wearied of the prolixity of variety, wee resolve into silence, where we are as if we had never been ...

God is one simple, single, uncompounded glory: nothing lives in him or flows from him, but what is his pure individual self.

Unity is the Father, the Author and begetter of all things; or (if you will) the Grandmother in whose intrinsecal womb, variety lies occult, till time orderly brings it forth ...

(iii) Laurence Clarkson or Claxton (1615–67) was a native of Preston. Brought up in the Church of England, in youth he showed Puritan leanings; dancing on the Sabbath he regarded with particular horror. He became a Presbyterian and then an Independent. As an Antinomian (in the theological sense which the word then possessed) he became a 'parish priest' in Norfolk. Thereafter he led a wandering life. In 1644 he became an Anabaptist and the following year he was imprisoned for 'dipping'. Up to the end of 1648 he followed another of the major religious tendencies of the time, that of the Seekers. During this period he was an itinerant preacher in Kent and minister of two more parishes, in Hertfordshire and Lincolnshire. He also began to write religious tracts. Of this period he says: 'There was few of the clergy able to reach me in Doctrine or Prayer; yet notwithstanding, not being an University man, I was very often turned out of employment.' He was therefore constantly in financial straits. He became a preacher to an Army regiment, then tried to find a parish in London. Finally, early in 1649, he turned Ranter. He soon became notorious as leader of a particularly licentious group calling itself 'My One Flesh'. The committee appointed by the Rump to investigate Ranterism gave much thought to Clarkson's 'impious and blasphemous' book, *A Single Eye*. On 27 September 1650, the House sentenced the author to a month's imprisonment, to be followed by banishment. The book was burned at Westminster and the Exchange by the public hangman. All copies were ordered to be handed in for burning but a few escaped this fate. The sentence of banishment was never carried out. On his release from prison Clarkson resumed his wandering life, now as an astrologer. In 1658 he joined a sect of extreme ascetics, the Muggletonians, and thereafter wrote several tracts on their behalf. He died as a debtor in Ludgate gaol. His last book was an autobiography, which casts much light on the way of life of the Ranters: *The Lost sheep found: or, The Prodigal returned to his Fathers house, after many a sad and weary Journey through many Religious Countryes ... Written by Laur. Claxton, the onely true converted Messenger of Christ Jesus, Creator of Heaven and Earth*, 1660 (64 pp.). The following extracts from this work describe Clarkson's entry into the community of Ranters, and some of its consequences:

... I Quartered in a private-house, who was a former friend of mine, asked me if I heard not of a people called *My one flesh?* I said no, what was their opinion, and how should I speak with any of them? Then she [*sic*] directed me to *Giles Calvert*, ... so coming to *Calvert*, and making enquiry after such a people, he was afraid I came to betray them, but exchanging a few words in the height of my language, he was much affected, and satisfied I was a friend of theirs, so he writ me a Note to Mr *Brush*, and the effect thereof was, the bearer hereof is a man of the greatest light I ever yet heard speak, and for ought I know instead of receiving of him you may receive an *Angel*, so to Mr *Brush* I went, and presented this Note, which he perused, so bid me come in, and told me if I had come a little sooner, I might have seen Mr *Copp*, who then had lately appeared in a most dreadful manner; so there being *Mary Lake*, we had some discourse, but nothing to what was in me, however they told me, if next Sunday I would come to Mr *Melis* in *Trinity-Lane*, there would that day some friends meet. Now observe at this time my judgment was this, that there was no man could be free'd from sin, till he had acted that so called sin, as no sin, this a certain time had been burning within me, yet durst not reveal it to any, in that I thought none was able to receive it, and a great desire I had to make trial, whether I should be troubled or satisfied therein; so that ... I took my progress into the *Wilderness*, and according to the day appointed I found Mr *Brush*, Mr *Rawlinson*, Mr *Goldsmith*, with *Mary Lake*, and some four more: now *Mary Lake* was the chief speaker, which in her discourse was something agreeable, but not so high as was in me experienced, and what I then knew with boldness declared, in so much that *Mary Lake* being blind, asked who that was that spoke? *Brush* said the man that *Giles Calvert* sent to us, so with many more words I affirmed that there was no sin, but as man esteemed it sin, and therefore none can be free from sin, till in purity it be acted as no sin, for I judged that pure to me, which to a dark understanding was impure, for to the pure all things, yea all acts were pure: thus making the Scripture a writing of wax, I pleaded the words of *Paul, That I know, and am perswaded by the Lord Jesus, that there was nothing unclean, but as man esteemed it,* unfolding that was intended all acts, as well as meats and drinks, and therefore till you can lie with all women as one woman, and not judge it sin, you can do nothing but sin: now in Scripture I found a perfection spoken of, so that I understood no man could attain perfection but this way, at which Mr *Rawlinson* was much taken, and *Sarah Kullin* being then present, did invite me to make trial of what I had expressed, so as I take it, after we parted, she invited me to Mr *Wats* in *Rood-lane*, where was one or two more like her self, and as I take it, lay with me that night: now against next sunday it was noised abroad what a rare man of knowledge was to speak at Mr *Brushes*; at which day there was a great company of men and women, both young and old, and so from day to day increased, that now I had choice of what before I aspired after, insomuch that it came to our Officers ears; but having got my pay I left them, and lodged in *Rood-lane*; where I had Clients many, that I was not able to answer all desires, yet none knew our actions but our selves; however I was careful with whom I had to do. This lustful principle encreased so much, that the Lord Mayor with his Officers came at midnight to take me, but knowing thereof, he was prevented. . . . I was moved to write to the world what my Principle was, so brought to publick view a Book called *The Single Eye*, so that men and women came from many parts to see my face, and hear my knowledge in these things, being restless till they were made free, as then we called it. Now I being as they said, Captain of the Rant, I had most of the principle women came to my lodging for knowledge, which then was called The Head-Quarters. Now in the height of this ranting, I was made still careful for moneys for my Wife, onely my body was given to other women: so our Company encreasing, I wanted for nothing that heart could desire, but at last it became a trade so common, that all the froth and scum broke forth into the height of this wickedness, yea began to be a publick reproach, that I broke up my Quarters, and went into the countrey to my Wife, where I had by the way disciples plenty, . . . Major *Rainsborough*, and Doctor *Barker* . . . Mr *Walis* of *Elford*, so there I met them, where was no small pleasure and delight in praising of a God that was an infinite nothing, what great and glorious things the Lord had done, in bringing us out of bondage, to the perfect liberty of the sons of God, and yet then the very notion of my heart was to all manner of theft, cheat, wrong, or injury that privately could be acted, though in tongue I professed the contrary, not considering I brake the Law in all points (murther excepted:) and the ground of this my judgement was, God had made all things good, so nothing evil but as man judged it; for I apprehended there was no such thing as theft, cheat, or a lie, but as man made it so: for if the creature had brought this world into [no] propriety, as *Mine* and *Thine*, there had been no such title as theft, cheat, or a lie; for the prevention hereof *Everard* and *Gerrard Winstanley* did dig up the Commons, that so all might have to live of themselves, then there had been no need of defrauding, but unity one with another. . . . This I conceived, as I knew not what I was before I came into being, so for ever after I should know nothing after this my being was dissolved; but even as a stream from the Ocean was distinct in it self while it was a stream, but when returned to the Ocean, was therein swallowed and become one with the Ocean; so the spirit of man while in the body, was distinct from God, but when death came it returned to God, and so became one with God, yea God it self; yet notwithstanding this, I had sometimes a relenting light in my soul, fearing this should not be so, as indeed it was contrary; but however, then a cup of Wine would wash away this doubt . . .

Clarkson goes on to describe how in the end he was arrested in a tavern in Bishopsgate and imprisoned at Whitehall. He was supposed to pay for the military guard set over him; but Ranterism had its sympathizers in the Army: 'Some being of my principle, they would guard me for nothing, and a Captain of theirs would give me moneys.' When examined by the committee of the House he equivocated and lied – by his own account – exactly after the manner described by Tickell in *The Bottomless Pit*.

(iv) The full title of Clarkson's Ranter tract is *A Single Eye All Light, no Darkness; or Light and Darkness One ... This Revealed in L. C. one of the UNIVERSALITY. Imprinted at London, in the Yeer that the POWERS of Heaven and Earth Was, Is, and Shall be Shaken, yea Damned, till they be no more for EVER*, printed by Giles Calvert, 1650 (16 pp.). This work establishes beyond all possibility of doubt that some Ranters really did teach the total amoralism which medieval ecclesiastics ascribed to the Brethren of the Free Spirit:

> Behold, the King of glory now is come
> T' reduce God, and Devil to their Doom;
> For both of them are servants unto Me
> That lives, and rules in perfect Majesty: ...
> Fie then for shame, look not above the Skies
> For God, or Heaven; for here your Treasure lies
> Even in these Forms, *Eternal Will* will reigne.
> Through him are all things, onely One, not Twain:
> Sure he's the Fountain from which every thing
> Both good and ill (so term'd) appears to spring ...

Having experience that his Majesty, the Being and Operation of all things, appeareth in and to the Creature under a two-fold Form or Visage, by which that becometh real with the Creature, which is but a shadow with this Infinite Being ...

And therefore it is the cry of his Majesty is not fulfilled and obeyed, but by Churches, Saints, and Devils opposed and contemned: So that rare it is to find the Creature that is awaked out of his deep sleep, that hath shaked off the covering, so that he can from the clear Appearance of God say, the vail is taken away, and that he believeth the Truth as it is in his Majesty ...

... if Reason were admitted, and thereby Scripture interpreted, then should they observe in [*sic*] that Act they call Honesty, to be Adultry, and that Act so called Adultry, to have as much honesty as the other, for with God they are but one, and that one Act holy, just, and good as God; This to me by Reason is confirmed, and by Scripture declared, *That to the pure all things are pure*: So that for my part I know nothing unclean to me, no more than it is of it self, and therefore what Act soever I do, is acted by that Majesty in me. ... So that I weigh not how I am judged, in that I judge not my self. So to conclude, the censures of Scripture, Churches, Saints, and Devils, are no more to me than the cuting [*sic*] off of a Dogs neck,   Vale.

Isiah, 42.16. I will make Darkness Light before them.

. . . now is the time come, now is the day that God will plunder them of their Idols, that God will enlighten their dark understandings, as in my Text, *God will make darkness light before them.*

. . . now doth the time draw neer that the sayings in this Text shall appear in the unfoldings of the Spirit, *I will make darkness light before them.*

Being now arrived at the wished Haven, all the difficulty will be how to unload the Vessel fraughted with such hidden pearls, how to make merchandise of them, how to unfold this Subject to your capacity, how to give you the mind of God, in such terms as God appears in you.

. . . you may read Light and Darkness are both alike to God. So then it appeareth but a darkness in the Creatures apprehension, so but an imagined darkness; for saith the Text, *God is light, and in him no darkness.* So that you see, whatsoever or howsoever it is called darkness in Scripture, yet it is none with God.

Clarkson answers those who attribute sinful acts, such as the Crucifixion, to the Devil, or else to the 'wicked inventions' of men:

Being now surrounded with the black Regiment, whose Commander is the Devil, and the whole legion consisting of the imaginations of the whole Creation, I have no way to escape this Camp and bottomlesse gulf, but by breaking through the Bulwark and strong hold fortified against me.

So that being armed with a weapon of Majesty, I doubt not but that God in me shall cast down those strong holds and imaginations, yea every thing that exalteth it self against the Power of the most high . . .

. . . I must tell you . . . that as all Powers are of God, so all acts, of what nature soever are produced by this Power, yea this Power of God: so that all those acts arising from the Power, are as Pure as the Power, and the Power as Pure as God.

So from hence it comes, there is no act whatsoever, that is impure in God, or sinful with or before God . . .

As I have said, so I say again, that those acts, or what act soever, so far as by thee is esteemed or imagined to be sinfull, is not in God, nor from God, yet still, as I said, all acts that be are from God, yea as pure as God.

. . . sin hath its conception only in the imagination; therefore; so long as the act was in God, or nakedly produced by God, it was holy as God: but after there is an appearance in thee, or apprehension to thee, that this act is good, or that act is evil, then hast thou with *Adam* eat of the forbidden Tree, of the Tree of knowledge of good and evil, then hast thou tasted of that fruit, which is not in God; for saith the Text, *Out of the mouth of the most High proceedeth not evil, and good*: good but not evil; for God is good, and good is God: therefore it was he made all things good: yea that which by you is imagined evil, he made good: so that thou apprehending that from God which is not in God doth of all his Creatures most abuse God, in making God the author of that which is not in God, (to wit) Sin. But to the matter in hand, Thou hast heard all acts that are, had their being and birth from God, yea acted by God, to be plain those acts by thee called Swearing, Drunkenesse, Adultery, and Theft, &c. These acts simply as acts, were produced by the Power of God, yea, perfected by the Wisdom of God.

What said I, a Swearer, a Drunkard, an Adulterer, a Theef, had these the power and wisdom of God, to Swear, Drink, Whore, and Steal? . . . Well Friends, although the appearance of God in me be as terrible to you, as it were to *Moses* in the mount, yet notwithstanding, that what I have seen and heard, I do not in the least tremble, but rejoyce, that I have this opportunity to declare it unto you; however it may be received by you.

. . . as I said before, so I say again, the very title Sin, it is only a name without substance, hath no being in God, nor in the Creature, but only by imagination; and therefore it is said, *the imaginations of your hearts are evil continually*. It is not the body, nor the life, but the imagination only, and that not at a time, or times, but continually. Herein sin admitting of no form in itself, is created a form in the estimation of the Creature . . .

. . . Consider what act soever, yea though it be the act of Swearing, Drunkennesse, Adultery and Theft; yet these acts simply, yea nakedly, as acts are nothing distinct from the act of Prayer and Prayses. Why dost thou wonder? why art thou angry? they are all one in themselves; no more holynesse, no more puritie in the one then the other.

But once the Creature esteemeth one act Adultery, the other honesty, the one pure, the other impure; yet to that man that so esteemeth one act unclean, to him it is unclean: (as saith the History) there is nothing unclean of it self, but . . . to him that esteemeth it unclean: yea again and again it is recorded that to the pure all things, yea all things are pure, but to the defiled, all things are defiled . . .

No matter what Scripture, Saints, or Churches say, if that within thee do not condemn thee, thou shalt not be condemned; for saith the History, *Out of thine own mouth*, not anothers, *will I judge thee*: Therefore, remember that if thou judge not thy self, let thy life be what it will, yea act what thou canst, yet if thou judge not thy self, thou shalt not be judged; For, *I came not into the World to condemn, but to save the World*. But if the reproach and slander of Saints and Churches do cause thee to question thy self, then art thou ready to say within what they report without, I am guilty of what they accuse me: So that true is the saying, *O Adam*, thy destruction is of thy self . . .

. . . the Lord declared that those filthy abominable works of darkness (by thee so apprehended) shall be destroyed and damned; But how, or where shall they be damned? that is in the sayings of this Text, *I will make darkness light*: Oh that this were purely minded, then thou wouldst see that sin must not be thrown out, but cast within, there being in the Vat, it is dyed of the same colour of the liquor; as Saffron converts milk into its own colour, so doth the fountain of light convert sin, hell, and devil into its own nature and light as it self; *I will make rough Waies smooth*: Now it is damm'd and ramm'd into its only Center, there to dwell eternal in the bosom of its only Father: This, and only this, is the damnation so much terrifying the Creature in its dark apprehension ...

Of the resurrection of the body Clarkson says:

> ... thy body consisting of flesh and bone, is made of the dust of the earth, therefore when thy body is reduced to its center, then (and not till then) is thy body alive, perfected in its happiness; ... that place called heaven, would become a hell to the Body, for after laid in the grave, it is buried in its heaven, glory, and happiness, where it shall rot and consume into its own nature for ever and ever ...

So that in light I declare, that the corrupt senses must put on incorruption, thy mortal apprehension must put on immortality, that whereas before thou wast alive to five, and dead to one, now thou shalt be dead to five, and alive to one, that lovely pure one who beholds nothing but purity, wheresoever it goeth, and whatsoever it doth, all is sweet and lovely; let it be under what title soever, thou art risen from title to act, from act to power, from power to his name, and that only one name, pure and undefiled; so that now thou art of purer eys than to behold any iniquity, so that Devil is God, Hell is Heaven, Sin Holiness, Damnation Salvation, this and only this is the first Resurrection.

Yet here is no lodging, no safe inhabiting, in that thou art yet on the borders of Ægypt, not only with *Moses* on Mount Hermon, only verbally, not practically, so short of the second Resurrection which is the life and power what thou saw, for till thou be delivered of that thou wast risen to, thou canst not say, *Death, where is thy sting? Grave, where is thy victory?*

Wonder not at me, for without Act, without Birth, no powerful deliverance, not only the Talkers, but the Doers; not only your Spirit, but your Body must be a living and acceptable Sacrifice; therefore till acted that so called Sin, thou art not delivered from the power of sin, but ready upon all Alarums to tremble and fear the reproach of thy body.

... I say, till flesh be made Spirit, and Spirit flesh, so not two, but one, thou art in perfect bondage: for without vail, I declare that whosoever doth attempt to act from flesh, in flesh, to flesh, hath, is, and will commit Adultery: but to bring this to a period, for my part, till I acted that, so called sin, I could not predominate over sin; so that now whatsoever I act, is not in relation to the Title, to the Flesh, but that Eternity in me; So that with me, all Creatures are but one creature, and this is my form, the Representative of the whole Creation: So that see what I can, act what I will, all is but one most sweet and lovely. Therefore my deer ones consider, that without act, no life; without life, no perfection; and without perfection, no eternal peace and freedom indeed, in power, which is the everlasting Majesty, ruling, conquering, and damning all into its self, without end, for ever.

(v) The most celebrated of the Ranters, Abiezer Coppe (1619–72), was born and grew up at Warwick. It is interesting to note that this future adept of the Free Spirit was in adolescence obsessed by a conviction of his sinfulness. A prey to neurotic anxiety, he kept a daily register of his sins. He fasted much, imposed vigils and humiliations on himself. Of this period he says: 'In my evening and midnight prayer ... I did constantly ... (with grief of soul, sighs and groans, and frequently with tears) confess over my sins. ... Tears were my drink: dust and ashes my meat. And sack-cloth my clothing. Zeal, Devotion, and exceeding strictness of life and conversation, my life.' He 'set a strict guard', watching every word, action, thought. He had an almost obsessive urge to swear and curse; but by such methods he was able – he claims – to avoid all swearing for twenty-seven years.

In 1636 Coppe went up to Oxford as a 'poor scholar' – at first as a Servitor at All Souls and soon afterwards as a Postmaster at Merton. It is said – it is impossible to judge how truly – that by this time his morals were less strict and that he would often overnight 'entertain a wanton Housewife in his Chamber'. The outbreak of the Civil War interrupted his career at Oxford and he left the University without taking a degree. Like Laurence Clarkson he was for some time a Presbyterian and later became an Anabaptist minister. In this capacity he was very active in Oxfordshire, Warwickshire and part of Worcestershire, 'dipping', it is said, some 7,000 persons, and officiating as preacher to a garrison. For these activities he was, about 1646, imprisoned at Coventry.

Other misfortunes were perhaps brought upon Coppe by the growing eccentricity of his religious life. He says that his father and mother forsook him, that his wife turned from him in loathing, that his reputation was ruined, and that his house was set on fire. These events in turn prepared the way for his conversion to Ranterism, which took place in 1649. Coppe adopted the usual Neo-Platonic pantheism of the Free Spirit, holding that God 'is in Heaven, Earth, Sea, Hell ... filleth all things, all places ... is All in All', and that 'all things are returning to their Original.' He seems also to have adopted Adamitic ways. ''Twas usual with him,' says Wood in *Athenae Oxonienses*, 'to preach stark naked many blasphemies and unheard-of Villanies in the Daytime, and in the Night to drink and lye with a Wenche, that had been also his hearer, stark naked.' It was no doubt for such conduct that he was imprisoned for fourteen weeks at Warwick. Later he seems – to judge by Clarkson's reference to him – to have belonged to the group of Ranters around Giles Calvert who called themselves 'My One Flesh'. Coppe was commonly listed together with Clarkson as a leader of the orgiastic Ranters; and he seems on occasion, when acting as a missionary for Ranterism, to have employed arguments from Clarkson's *Single Eye*.

Coppe was the leader of the drinking, smoking Ranters who appeared in George Fox's prison at Charing Cross. He seems indeed to have been much addicted to drunkenness. But above all, once he turned Ranter he indulged his long-suppressed craving to curse and swear. Richard Baxter asks with horror how it came that, as followers of this man, 'men and women professing the zealous fear of God, should . . . be brought to place their Religion in revelling, roaring, drinking, whoring, open full-mouthed swearing ordinarily by the Wounds and Blood of God, and the fearfullest cursing that hath been heard'. We hear of Coppe cursing for an hour on end in the pulpit of a London church, and swearing at the hostess of a tavern so fearsomely 'that she trembled and quaked for some hours after.' Disciples of his were put in the stocks at Stratford for their swearing.

It was as a Ranter in 1649 that Coppe produced his only noteworthy writings: *Some Sweet Sips of some Spirituall Wine*, *A Fiery Flying Roll* and (bound and issued together with this last) *A Second Fiery Flying Roule*. The two *Rolls* resulted in his arrest in January 1650. He was imprisoned at Coventry (for a second time) and then at Newgate. Parliament issued an order that the *Rolls*, as containing 'many horrid Blasphemies, and damnable and detestable Opinions', be seized by mayors, sheriffs and justices of the peace throughout the Commonwealth and burnt by the public hangman; and that copies be publicly burnt at Westminster, the Exchange, and Southwark. The Act of 9 August 1650 against 'atheistical, blasphemous and execrable opinions' (quoted above) was largely occasioned by Coppe's works. Finally the committee of Parliament which in September 1650 examined Clarkson shortly afterwards examined Coppe. During the interrogation the prisoner feigned madness, 'throwing nut-shells and other things about the room' and talking to himself.

In Newgate Coppe received many visitors, and by 'smooth arguments' converted not a few to Ranterism. In the end, however, the strain of imprisonment began to tell. At the beginning of 1651 he issued from prison a *Remonstrance of the sincere and zealous*

Protestation of Abiezer Coppe, against the Blasphemous and Execrable Opinions recited in the Act of Aug. 10 1650 (6 pp.). This was followed some five months later by a full recantation, *Copps Return to the wayes of Truth ... and the Wings of the Fiery flying Roll clipt,* &c. (28 pp.). In this Coppe attributes his imprisonment to 'some strange actions and carriages ... some difficult, dark, hard, strange, harsh and almost unheard-of words, and expressions' of his. Of his Ranting he says:

The terrible, notable day of the Lord stole upon me unawares, like a thiefe in the night. ... And the cup of the Lords right hand, was put into mine hand. And it was filled brim full of intoxicating wine, and I drank it off, even the dregs thereof. Whereupon being mad drunk, I so strangely spake, and acted I knew not what. To the amazement of some. To the sore perplexity of others. And to the great grief of others. And till that cup passed from me, I knew not what I spake or did.

Now that 'his Understanding was returned unto him', he begged that the 'Wings of the Fiery flying Roll be clipt ... and let it be thrown headlong into its own place, the Lake of fire and brimston, and the great Abyss from whence it came'. As a result of this petition to Parliament and the Council of State Coppe was released, after a year and a half of prison. In September he preached at Burford the recantation sermon which called forth the suspicious comments of John Tickell (quoted above). Thereafter Coppe's life was unadventurous. After the Restoration he practised physic at Barnes, under the name of Dr Higham, until his death.

Baxter, who had spoken with Coppe, was certain that he was no madman; and Coppe's writings make an impression of eccentricity rather than of any truly psychotic condition. Always strongly individual, sometimes almost incoherent, they possess an undeniable verbal vitality. For understanding the religion of the Free Spirit they are of the very greatest value. More clearly than any other source, these tracts show how the extravagant and anarchic behaviour of the adepts of the Free Spirit flowed from and was nourished by their quasi-mystical and ecstatic experiences. They throw much light, too, on the 'social doctrine' of the Free Spirit. We find Coppe affirming that all things belong, or ought to belong, to the Lord alone, and utterly condemning the institution of private property. The urge to apostolic poverty and public self-abasement, normally regarded as characteristically medieval, can be seen here at work in seventeenth-century England. We can also observe in these writings how easily such a rejection of private property can merge with a hatred of the rich, and so – as on the Continent in earlier centuries – give rise to an intransigent social radicalism.

Coppe's most significant work is undoubtedly the one for which he suffered imprisonment: *A Fiery Flying Roll: A Word from the Lord to all the Great Ones of the Earth, whom this may concerne: Being the last WARNING PIECE at the dreadful day of JUDGE-MENT. For now the Lord is come to* 1) *Informe* 2) *Advise and warne* 3) *Charge* 4) *Judge and sentence the Great Ones. As also most compassionately informing, and most lovingly and pathetically advising and warning London. With a terrible Word, and fatall Blow from the Lord, upon the Gathered CHURCHES. And all by his Most Excellent MAJESTY, dwelling in, and shining through AUXILIUM PATRIS, alias, Coppe. With another FLYING ROLL ensuing (to all the Inhabitants of the Earth). Imprinted at London, in the beginning of that notable day, wherein the secrets of all hearts are laid open; and wherein the worst and foulest of villanies, are discovered, under the best and fairest outsides.* 1649 (15 pp. and 22 pp.).

The Preface

An inlet into the Land of Promise, the new *Hierusalem*, and a gate into the ensuing Discourse, worthy of serious consideration.

My Deare One.

All or None.

Every one under the Sunne.

Mine own.

My most Excellent Majesty (in me) hath strangely and variously transformed this forme.

And behold, by mine owne Almightinesse (in me) I have been changed in a moment, in the twinkling of an eye, at the sound of the Trump.

And now the Lord is descended from Heaven, with a shout, with the voyce of the Arch-angell, and with the Trump of God.

And the sea, the earth, yea all things are now giving up their dead. And all things that ever were, are, or shall be visible . . . are the Grave wherein the King of Glory (the eternall, invisible Almightinesse,) hath lain as it were dead and buried.

But behold, behold, he is now risen with a witnesse, to save *Zion* with vengeance, or to confound and plague all things into himself; who by his mighty Angell is proclaiming (with a loud voyce) That Sin and Transgression is finished and ended; and everlasting righteous-nesse brought in; and the everlasting Gospell preaching; Which ever-lasting Gospell is brought in with most terrible earth-quakes, and heaven-quakes, and with signes and wonders following.

And it hath pleased my most Excellent Majesty, (who is universall love, and whose service is perfect freedome) to set this forme (the Writer of this Roll) as no small signe and wonder in fleshly *Israel*, as you may partly see in the ensuing Discourse.

And now (my deare ones!) every one under the Sun, I will onely point at the gate, thorow which I was led into that new City, new *Hierusalem*, and to the Spirits of just men, made perfect, and to God the Judge of all.

First, all my strength, my forces were utterly routed, my house I dwelt in fired; my father and mother forsook me, the wife of my bosome loathed me, mine old name was rotted, perished; and I was utterly plagued, consumed, damned, rammed, and sunke into nothing, into the bowels of the still Eternity (my mothers wombe) out of which I came naked, and whetherto I returned again naked. And lying a while there, rapt up in silence, at length (the body or outward forme being awake all this while) I heard with my outward eare (to my apprehension) a most terrible thunderclap, and after that a second. And upon the second thunder-clap, which was exceeding terrible, I saw a great body of light, like the light of the Sun, and red as fire, in the forme of a drum (as it were) whereupon with exceeding trembling and amazement on the flesh, and with joy unspeakable in the spirit, I clapt my hands, and cryed out, *Amen, Halelujah, Halelujah, Amen*. And so lay trembling, sweating and smoaking (for the space of half an houre) at length with a loud voyce I (inwardly) cryed out, Lord, what wilt thou do with me; my most excellent majesty and eternall glory (in me) answered & sayd, Fear not, I will take thee up into mine everlasting Kingdom. But thou shalt (first) drink a bitter cup, a bitter cup, a bitter cup; whereupon (being filled with exceeding amazement) I was throwne into the belly of hell (and take what you can of it in these expressions, though the matter is beyond expression) I was among all the Devils in hell, even in their most hideous hew.

And under all this terrour, and amazement, there was a little spark of transcendent, transplendent, unspeakable glory, which survived, and sustained it self, triumphing, exulting, and exalting itself above all the Fiends. And confounding the very blacknesse of darknesse (you must take it in these tearmes, for it is infinitely beyond expression). Upon this the life was taken out of the body (for a season) and it was thus resembled, as if a man with a great brush dipt in whiting, should with one stroke wipe out, or sweep off a picture upon a wall, &c. after a while, breath and life was returned into the form againe; whereupon I saw various streames of light (in the night) which appeared to the outward eye; and immediately I saw three hearts . . . of exceeding brightnesse; and immediately an innumerable company of hearts, filling each corner of the room where I was. And methoughts there was variety and distinction, as if there had been severall hearts, and yet most strangely and unexpressibly complicated or folded up in unity. I clearly saw distinction, diversity, variety, and as clearly saw all swallowed up into unity. And it hath been my song many times since, within and without, unity, universality, universality, unity, Eternall Majesty, &c. And at this vision, a most strong, glorious voyce uttered these words, *The spirits of just men made perfect*, the spirits &c. with whom I had as absolut, cleare, full communion, and in a two fold more familiar way, then ever I had outwardly with my dearest friends, and nearest relations. The visions and revelations of God, and the strong hand of eternall invisible almightinesse, was stretched out upon me, within me, for the space of foure dayes and nights, without intermission.

The time would faile if I would tell you all, but it is not the good will and pleasure of my most excellent Majesty in me, to declare any more (as yet) then thus much further: That amongst those various voyces that were then uttered within, these were some, *Blood, blood, Where, where? upon the hypocriticall holy heart,* &c. Another thus, *Vengeance, vengeance, vengeance,* Plagues, *plagues, upon the inhabitants of the earth; Fire, fire, fire, Sword, sword,* &c, *upon all that bow not down to eternall Majesty, universall love; I'le recover, recover, my wooll, my flax, my money. Declare, declare, feare thou not the faces of any; I am (in thee) a munition of Rocks,* &c.

Go up to *London,* to *London,* that great City, write, write, write. And behold I writ, and lo a hand was sent to me, and a roll of a book was therein, which this fleshly hand would have put wings to, before the time. Whereupon it was snatcht out of my hand, & the Roll thrust into my mouth; and I eat it up, and filled my bowels with it, (Eze. 2. 8. &c cha. 3.1,2,3.) where it was as bitter as worm wood; and it lay broiling, and burning in my stomack, till I brought it forth in this forme.

And now I send it flying to thee, with my heart, And all
Per AUXILIUM PATRIS

From the first *Fiery Flying Roll,* Chapter I:

Thus saith the Lord, *I inform you, that I overturn, overturn, overturn.* And as the Bishops, *Charles,* and the Lords, have had their turn, overturn, so your turn shall be next (ye surviving great ones) by what Name or Title soever dignified or distinguished, who ever you are, that oppose me, the Eternall God, who am UNIVERSALL Love, and whose service is perfect freedome, and pure Libertinisme . . .

And now thus saith the Lord:

Though you can as little endure the word LEVELLING, as could the late slaine or dead *Charles* (your forerunner, who is gone before you –) and had as live heare the Devill named, as heare of the Levellers (Men-Levellers) which is, and who (indeed) are but shadowes of most terrible, yet great and glorious good things to come.

Behold, behold, behold, I the eternall God, the Lord of Hosts, who am that mighty Leveller, am comming (yea even at the doores) to Levell in good earnest, to Levell to some purpose, to Levell with a witnesse, to Levell the Hills with the Valleyes, and to lay the Mountaines low.

High Mountaines! lofty Cedars! its high time for you to enter into the Rocks, and to hide you in the dust, for feare of the Lord, and for the glory of his Majesty. For the lofty looks of man shall be humbled, and the haughtinesse of men shall be bowed downe, and the Lord ALONE shall be exalted in that day . . .

Hills! Mountains! Cedars! Mighty men! Your breath is in your nostrils.

Those that have admired, adored, idolized, magnified, set you up, fought for you, ventured goods, and good name; limbe and life for you, shall cease from you.

You shall not (at all) be accounted of (not one of you) ye sturdy Oake[s] who bowe not downe before eternall Majesty : Universall Love, whose service is perfect freedome, and who hath put down the mighty (remember, remember, your fore-runner) and who is putting down the mighty from their seats; and exalting them of low degree ...

And the Prime levelling, is laying low the Mountaines, and levelling the Hils in man.

But this is not all.

For lo I come (saith the Lord) with a vengeance, to levell also your Honour, Riches, &c to staine the pride of all your glory, and to bring into contempt all the Honourable (both persons and things) upon the earth, Isa. 23.9.

For this Honour, Nobility, Gentility, Propriety, Superfluity, &c. hath (without contradiction) been the Father of hellish horrid pride, arrogance, haughtinesse, loftinesse, murder, malice, of all manner of wickednesse and impiety; yea the cause of all the blood that ever hath been shed, from the blood of the righteous *Abell*, to the blood of the last Levellers that were shot to death. *And now (as I live saith the Lord) I am come to make inquisition for blood; for murder and pride, &c.*

I see the root of it all. *The Axe is laid to the root of the Tree* (by the Eternall God, *My Self*, saith the Lord) *I will hew it down.* And as I live, I will plague your Honour, Pompe, Greatness, Superfluity, and confound it into parity, equality, community; that the neck of horrid pride, murder, malice, and tyranny, &c. may be chopt off at one blow. And that my selfe, the Eternall God, who am Universall Love, may fill the Earth with universall love, universall peace, and perfect freedome; which can never be by humane sword or strength accomplished ...

Chapter II:

Thus saith the Lord: Be wise now therefore, O ye Rulers, &c. Be instructed, &c. Kisse the Sunne, &c. Yea, kisse Beggers, Prisoners, warme them, feed them, cloathe them, money them, relieve them, release them, take them into your houses, don't serve them as gods, without doore, &c.

Owne them, they are flesh of your flesh, youre owne brethren, your owne Sisters, every whit as good (and if I should stand in competition with you) in some degrees better then your selves.

Once more, I say, own them; they are your self, make them one with you, or else go howling into hell; howle for the miseries that are comming upon you, howle.

The very shadow of levelling, sword-levelling, man-levelling, frighted you, (and who, like your selves, can blame you, because it shook your Kingdome?) but now the substantiality of levelling is coming.

The Eternall God, the mighty Leveller is comming, yea come, even at the door; and what will you do in that day . . .

Mine eares are filled brim full with cryes of poore prisoners, Newgate, Ludgate cryes (of late) are seldome out of mine eares. Those dolefull cryes, Bread, bread, bread for the Lords sake, pierce mine eares, and heart, I can no longer forebeare.

Werefore high you apace to all prisons in the Kingdome,

Bow before those poore, nasty, lousie, ragged wretches, say to them, your humble servants, Sirs, (without a complement) we let you go free, and serve you, &c.

Do this or (as I live saith the Lord) thine eyes (at least) shall be boared out, and thou carried captive into a strange Land.

. . . Loose the bands of wickednesse, undo the heavy burdens, let the oppressed go free, and breake every yoake. Deale thy bread to the hungry, and bring the poore that are cast out (both of houses and Synagogues) to thy house. Cover the naked: Hide not thy self from thine owne flesh, from a creeple, a rogue, a begger, he's thine owne flesh. From a Whoremonger, a thief, &c. he's flesh of thy flesh, and his theft, and whoredome is flesh of thy flesh also, thine owne flesh. Thou maist have ten times more of each within thee, then he that acts outwardly in either, Remember, turn not away thine eyes from thine OWN FLESH.

Give over, give over thy midnight mischief.

Let branding with the letter B. alone.*

Be no longer so horridly, hellishly, impudently, arrogantly wicked, as to judge what is sinne, what not, what evill, and what not, what blasphemy, and what not.

For thou and all thy reverend Divines, so called (who Divine for Tythes, hire, and money, and serve the Lord Jesus Christ for their owne bellyes) are ignorant of this one thing.

That sinne and transgression is finisht, its a meere riddle, that they, with all their humane learning can never reade.

Neither can they understand what pure honour is wrapt up in the Kings Motto, *Honi Soit qui Mal y Pense*. Evill to him that evill thinks.

Some there are (who are accounted the off scouring of all things) who are Noble Knights of the Garter. Since which – they could see no evill, thinke no evill, doe no evill, know no evill.

ALL is Religion that they speak, and honour that they do.

But all you that eat of the Tree of Knowledge of Good and Evill, and have not your Evill eye Pickt out, you call Good Evill, and Evill Good; Light Darknesse, and Darknesse Light; Truth Blasphemy, and Blasphemy Truth.

And you are at this time of your Father the Devill, and of your brother the Pharisee, who still say of Christ (who is now alive) say we not well that he hath a Devill.

*For 'Blasphemer'.

Take heed, take heed, take heed.

Filthy blinde Sodomites called Angels men, they seeing no further then the formes of men.

There are Angels (now) come downe from Heaven, in the shapes and formes of men, who are fully of the vengeance of the Lord; and are to poure out the plagues of God upon the Earth, and to torment the Inhabitants thereof.

Some of these Angels I have been acquainted withall.

And I have looked upon them as Devils, accounting them Devils incarnate, and have run from place to place, to hide my self from them, shunning their company; and have been utterly ashamed when I have been seen with them.

But for my labour; I have been plagued and tormented beyond expression. So that now I had rather behold one of these Angels pouring out the plagues of God, cursing; and teaching others to curse bitterly.

And had rather heare a mighty Angell (in man) swearing a full-mouthed Oath; and see the spirit of *Nehemiah* (in any forme of man, or woman) running upon an uncleane Jew (a pretended Saint) and tearing the haire of his head like a mad man, cursing, and making others fall a swearing, then heare a zealous Presbyterian, Independent, or spirituall Notionist, pray, preach, or exercise.

Well! To the pure all things are pure. God hath so cleared cursing, swearing, in some, that that which goes for swearing and cursing in them, is more glorious then praying and preaching in others.

And what God hath cleansed, call not thou uncleane.

And if *Peter* prove a great transgressor of the Law, by doing that which was as odious as killing a man; if he at length (though he be loath at first) eat that which was common and unclean &c. (I give but a hint) blame him not, much lesse lift up a finger against, or plant a hellish Ordinance – against him, least thou be plagued, and damned too, for thy zeale, blinde Religion, and fleshly holinesse, which now stinks above ground, though formerly it had a good savour.

But O thou holy, zealous, devout, righteous, religious one (who-ever thou art) that seest evill, or any thing uncleane; do thou sweare, if thou darest, if it be but (I'faith) I'le throw thee to Hell for it (saith the Lord) and laugh at thy destruction.

While Angels (in the forme of men) shall sweare, Heart, Blood, Wounds, and by the Eternall God, &c. in profound purity, and in high Honour, and Majesty.

From the second *Fiery Flying Roll*, Chapter II:

(Thus saith the Lord,)

I say (once more) deliver, deliver, my money which thou hast . . . to poor creeples, lazars, yea to rogues, thieves, whores, and cut-purses, who are flesh of thy flesh, and every whit as good as thy self in mine eye, who are ready to starve in plaguy Gaols, and nasty dungeons, or els by my selfe, saith the Lord, I will torment thee day and night, inwardly, or outwardly, or both waies, my little finger shall shortly be heavier on thee, especially on thee thou holy, righteous, religious *Appropriator*, then my loynes were on *Pharaoh* and the Egyptians in time of old; you shall weep and howl for the miseries that are suddenly coming upon you; for your riches are corrupted, &c. and whilst impropriated, appropriated the plague of God is in them.

The plague of God is in your purses, barns, houses, horses, murrain will take your hogs, (O ye fat swine of the earth) who shall shortly go to the knife, and be hung up i'th roof, except – blasting, mill-dew, locusts, caterpillars, yea fire your houses and goods, take your corn and fruit, the moth your garments, and the rot your sheep, did you not see my hand, this last year, stretched out?

You did not see.

My hand is stretched out still.

Your gold and silver, though you can't see it, is cankered, the rust of them is a witnesse against you, and suddainly, because by the eternall God, my self, its the dreadful day of Judgement, saith the Lord, shall eat your flesh as it were fire, *Jam.* 5. 1 to 7.

The rust of your silver, I say, shall eat your flesh as it were fire ...

... give, give, give, give up, give up your houses, horses, goods, gold, Lands, give up, account nothing your own, have ALL THINGS common, or els the plague of God will rot and consume all that you have.

By God, by my self, saith the Lord, its true.

Come! give all to the poore and follow me, and you shall have treasure in heaven.

Chapter III:

A strange, yet most true story; under which is couched that Lion, whose roaring shall make all the beasts of the field tremble, and all the Kingdoms of the earth quake ...

Follow me, who, last Lords day Septem. 30. 1649. met him in open field, a most strange deformed man, clad with patcht clouts: who looking wishly on me, mine eye pittied him; and my heart, or the day of the Lord, which burned as an oven in me, set my tongue on flame to speak to him, as followeth.

How now friend, art thou poore?

He answered, yea Master very poore.

Whereupon my bowels trembled within me, and quivering fell upon the worm-eaten chest, (my corps I mean) that I could not hold a joynt still.

And my great love within me, (who is the great God within that chest, or corps) was burning hot toward him; and made the lock-hole of the chest, to wit, the mouth of the corps, again to open: Thus.

Art poor?

Yea, very poor, said he.

Whereupon the strange woman who flattereth with her lips, and is subtill of heart, said within me,

It's a poor wretch, give him two-pence.

But my EXCELLENCY and MAJESTY (in me) scorn'd her words, confounded her language; and kickt her out of his presence.

But immediately the WEL-FAVOURED HARLOT (whom I carried not upon my horse behind me) but who rose up in me, said:

'Its a poor wretch give him 6d. and that's enough for a Squire or Knight, to give to one poor body.

'Besides (saith the holy Scripturian Whore) hee's worse then an Infidell that provides not for his own Family.

'True love begins at home, &c.

'Thou, and thy Family are fed, as the young ravens strangely, though thou hast been a constant Preacher, yet thou hast abhorred both tythes and hire; and thou knowest not aforehand who will give thee the worth of a penny.

'Have a care of the main chance.'

And thus she flattereth with her lips, and her words being smoother then oile; and her lips dropping as the honey comb, I was fired to hasten my hand into my pocket; and pulling out a shilling, said to the poor wretch, give me six pence, heer's a shilling for thee.

He answered, I cannot, I have never a penny.

Whereupon I said, I would fain have given thee something if thou couldst have changed my money.

Then saith he, God blesse you.

Whereupon with much reluctancy, with much love, and with amazement (of the right stamp) I turned my horse head from him, riding away. But a while after I was turned back (being advised by my Demilance)* to wish him cal for six pence, which I would leave at the next Town at ones house, which I thought he might know (*Saphira* like) keeping back part.

But (as God judged me) I, as she, was struck down dead.

And behold the plague of God fell into my pocket, and the rust of my silver rose up in judgement against me, and consumed my flesh as with fire: so that I, and my money perisht with me.

I being cast into that lake of fire and brimstone.

And all the money I had about me to a penny (though I thought through the instigation of my *quondam Mistris* to have reserved some, having rode about 8 miles, not eating one mouthfull of bread that day, and had drunk but one small draught of drink; and had between 8 or 9 miles more to ride, ere I came to my journeys end: my horse being lame, the waies dirty, it raining all the way, and I not knowing what extraordinary occasion I might have for money.) Yet (I say) the rust of my silver did so rise up in judgement against me, and burnt my flesh like fire: and the 5. of *James* thundered such an alarm in mine ears, that I was fain to cast all I had into the hands of him, whose visage was more marr'd then any mans that I ever saw.

This is a true story, most true in the history.

Its true also in the mystery.

*Probably a misprint for 'Delilah'; cf. below, p. 329, 'my Delilah'.

And there are deep ones coucht under it, for its a shadow of various, glorious (though strange) good things to come.

Wel! to return — after I had thrown my rusty canker'd money into the poor wretches hands, I rode away from him, being filled with trembling, joy, and amazement, feeling the sparkles of a great glory arising up from under these ashes.

After this, I was made (by that divine power which dwelleth in this Ark, or chest) to turn my horse head — whereupon I beheld this poor deformed wretch, looking earnestly after me: and upon that, was made to put off my hat, and bow to him seven times, and was (at that strange posture) filled with trembling and amazement, some sparkles of glory arising up also from under this; as also from under these ashes, yet I rode back once more to the poor wretch, saying, because I am a King, I have done this, but you need not tell any one.

The day's our own.

This was done on the last LORDS DAY, Septem. 30. in the year 1649. which is the year of the Lords recompences for Zion, and the day of his vengeance, the dreadfull day of Judgement. But I have done (for the present) with this story, for it is the later end of the year 1649.

Chapter V:

The Authors strange and lofty carriage towards great ones, and his most lowly carriage towards Beggars, Rogues and Gypseys: together with a large declaration what glory shall rise up from under all this ashes ...

And because I am found of those that sought me not.

And because some say, wilt thou not tell us what these things are to us, that thou dost so?

Wherefore waving my charging so many Coaches, so many hundreds of men and women of the greater rank, in the open streets, with my hand stretched out, my hat cock't up, staring on them as if I would look thorough them, gnashing with my teeth at some of them, and day and night with a huge loud voice proclaiming the day of the Lord throughout London and Southwark, and leaving divers other exploits, &c. It is my good will and pleasure (only) to single out the former story with its Parallels.

(*Viz.*) in clipping, hugging, imbracing, kissing a poore deformed wretch in London, who had no more nose on his face, then I have on the back of my hand, (but only two little holes in the place where the nose uses to stand.)

And no more eyes to be seen then on the back of my hand, and afterwards running back to him in a strange manner, with my money giving it to him, to the joy of some, to the afrightment and wonderment of other Spectators.

As also in falling down flat upon the ground before rogues, beggars, cripples, halt, maimed, blind, &c. kissing the feet of many, rising up againe, and giving them money, &c. Besides that notorious businesse with the Gypseys and Gaolbirds (mine own brethren and sisters, flesh of my flesh, and as good as the greatest Lord in England) at the prison in Southwark neer S. *Georges* Church.

Now that which rises up from under all this heap of ashes, will fire both heaven and earth; the one's ashamed, and blushes already, the other reels to and fro, like a drunken man.

Wherefore thus saith the Lord, Hear O heavens, and hearken O earth, Ile overturne, overturne, overturne, I am now staining the pride of all glory, and bringing into contempt all the honourable of the earth, *Isa.* 23. 9. not only honourable persons, (who shall come down with a vengeance, if they bow not to universall love the eternall God, whose service is perfect freedome) but honorable things, as Elderships, Pastorships, Fellowships, Churches, Ordinances, Prayers, &c. Holinesses, Righteousnesses, Religions of all sorts, of the highest strains; yea, Mysterians, and Spirituallists, who scorne carnall Ordinances, &c.

I am about my act, my strange act, my worke, my strange work, that whosoever hears of it, both his ears shall tingle.

I am confounding, plaguing, tormenting nice, demure, barren *Mical*, with *Davids* unseemly carriage, by skipping, leaping, dancing, like one of the fools, vile, base fellowes, shamelessely, basely, and un-covered too, before handmaids, –

... It's meat and drink to an Angel (who knows none evill, no sin) to sweare a full mouth'd oath, *Rev.* 10.6. It's joy to *Nehemiah* to come in like a mad-man, and pluck folkes hair off their heds, and curse like a devil – and make them swear by God – *Nehem.* 13. Do thou O holy man (who knowest evill) lift up thy finger against a Jew, a Church-member, cal thy brother fool, and wish a peace-cods* on him; or swear I faith, if thou dar'st, if thou dost, thou shalt howl in hell for it, and I will laugh at thy calamity, &c.

... Hear one word more (whom it hitteth it hitteth) give over thy base nasty stinking, formall grace before meat, and after meat (I call it so, though thou hast rebaptized it –) give over thy stinking family duties, and thy Gospell Ordinances as thou callest them; for under them all there lies snapping, snarling, biting, besides covetousnesse, horrid hypocrisie, envy, malice, evill surmising.

Give over, give over, or if nothing els will do it, I'l at a time, when thou least of all thinkest of it, make thine own child, the fruit of thy loines, in whom thy soul delighted, lie with a whore – before thine eyes: That that plaguy holinesse and righteousnesse of thine might be confounded by that base thing. And thou be plagued back again into thy mothers womb, the womb of eternity: That thou maist become a little child, and let the mother *Eternity*, *Almightinesse*, who is univer-sall love, and whose service is perfect freedome, dresse thee, and un-dresse thee, swadle, unswadle, bind, loose, lay thee down, take thee up, &c.

... And to such a little child, undressing is as good as dressing, foul cloaths, as good as fair cloaths – he knows no evil, &c. – And shall see

*For 'peasecod' (=peapod): a mock imprecation.

evill no more, – but he must first lose all his righteousnesse, every bit of his holinesse, and every crum of his Religion, and be plagued, and confounded (by base things) into nothing.

By base things which God and I have chosen.

And yet I shew you a more excellent way, when you have past this. . . . In a word, my plaguy, filthy, nasty holinesse hath been confounded by base things. And then (behold I shew you a mystery, and put forth a riddle to you) by base things, base things so called have been confounded also; and thereby have I been confounded into eternall Majesty, unspeakable glory, my life, my self.

Ther's my riddle, but because neither all the Lords of the Philistins, no nor my Delilah her self can read it,

I'l read it my self, I'l (only) hint it thus.

Kisses are numbered amongst transgressors – base things – well! by base hellish swearing, and cursing, (as I have accounted it in the time of my fleshly holinesse) and by base impudent kisses (as I then accounted them) my plaguy holinesse hath been confounded, and thrown into the lake of fire and brimstone.

And then again, by wanton kisses, kissing hath been confounded; and externall kisses, have been made the fiery chariots, to mount me swiftly into the bosom of him whom my soul loves, (his excellent Majesty, the King of glory.)

Where I have been, where I have been, where I have been, hug'd, imbrac't, and kist with the kisses of his mouth, whose loves are better than wine, and have been utterly overcome therewith, beyond expression, beyond admiration.

Again, Lust is numbered amongst transgressors – a base thing –

Now faire objects attract Spectators eyes.

And beauty is the father of lust or love.

Well! I have gone along the streets impregnant with that child (lust) which a particular beauty had begot: but coming to the place, where I expected to have been delivered, I have providentially met there a company of devills in appearance, though Angels with golden vialls, in reality, powring out full vialls, of such odious abominable words, that are not lawfull to be uttered.

Words enough to deafen the ears of plaguy holinesse. And such horrid abominable actions, the sight whereof were enough to put out holy mans eyes, and to strike him stark dead, &c.

These base things (I say) words and actions, have confounded and plagued to death, the child in the womb that I was big of.

And by, and through these BASE things (as upon the wings of the wind) have I been carried up into the arms of my love, which is invisible glory, eternall Majesty, purity it self, unspotted beauty, even that beauty which maketh all other beauty but meer uglinesse, when set against it, &c.

Yea, could you imagine that the quintessence of all visible beauty, should be extracted and made up into one huge beauty, it would appear to be meer deformity to that beauty, which through BASE things I have been lifted up into.

Which transcendent, unspeakable, unspotted beauty, is my crown and joy, my life and love: and though I have chosen, and cannot be without BASE things, to confound some in mercy, some in judgment, Though also I have concubines without number, which I cannot be without, yet this is my spouse, my love, my dove, my fair one.

Chapter VI:

Again, thus saith the Lord, I in thee, who am eternall Majesty, bowed down thy form, to deformity.

And I in thee, who am durable riches, commanded thy perishable silver to the poore, &c.

Thus saith the Lord,

Kings, Princes, Lords, great ones, must bow to the poorest Peasants; rich men must stoop to poor rogues, or else they'l rue for it . . .

Well! we must all bow, and bow, &c. And MEUM must be converted. . . . It is but yet a very little while; and you shall not say that ought that you possesse is your own, &c. . . .

It's but yet a little while, and the strongest, yea, the seemingly purest propriety, which may mostly plead priviledge and Preorogative from Scripture, and carnall reason; shall be confounded and plagued into community and universality. And ther's a most glorious design in it: and equality, community, and universall love; shall be in request to the utter confounding of abominable pride, murther, hypocrisie, tyranny and oppression, &c. . . .

Chapter VII:

. . . Howl, howl, ye nobles, howl honourable, howl ye rich men for the miseries that are coming upon you.

For our parts, we that hear the APOSTLE preach, will also have all things common; neither will we call any thing that we have our own.

Do you (if you please) till the plague of God rot and consume what you have.

We will not, wee'l eat our bread together in singlenesse of heart, wee'l break bread from house to house.

Notes and Bibliography

The following Notes and Bibliography indicate the original sources and modern works which have supplied historical material for the present study. In the Notes sources are cited whenever possible under the name of the author, otherwise under an abbreviated title or the name of the editor. References are to items and editions given in the Bibliography. Where necessary the abbreviations OS, MW, have been used to indicate whether the item appears under Original Sources or under Modern Works.

Items specified in the Appendix or in the Notes thereto are not repeated in the Bibliography.

An asterisk before an item in the Bibliography denotes that it has become available since the original version of this book was written, and has been taken into account in the revision.

It was not in general practicable to include the works on sociology, anthropology, psychology or politics which in one way or another have influenced the general argument. But a selection of recent works on millenarian and messianic movements in the world is given as a third part of the Bibliography.

Notes

1 The Tradition of Apocalyptic Prophecy

Jewish and early Christian apocalyptic

Page

19   Later Middle Ages: for lack of better ones, the term 'Middle Ages' has been used here for the period between, approximately, the fall of the Roman Empire in the West and the Reformation; and the term 'later Middle Ages' in a rather broad sense, for the period from *c.* 1100 to the Reformation.

For general surveys of the Judeo-Christian tradition of millenarian and messianic prophecy: Case, Döllinger (MW), Gry, Hübscher, Hundeshagen, Nigg (1); of the development of Hebrew religion: Oesterley and Robinson, and of that of Hebrew and Jewish eschatology in particular: MacCulloch (1), pp. 376–81.

The possible connexion between Persian (Mazdean) and Judeo-Christian eschatology and apocalyptic is still a matter of debate amongst experts. For contrasting views: Söderblom, pp. 270–320, and Cumont, pp. 64–96; while more recently Cumont's arguments in favour of such a connexion have been accepted by Eliade, p. 126, and rejected by Vulliaud, p. 33.

21   'shall be diverse . . .': Daniel vii, 23.

'came with the clouds . . .': ibid., 13–14, 27.

Jewish apocalyptic: Of course by no means all Jewish apocalypses are concerned with phantasies of this kind.

22   On the development of Hebrew and Jewish phantasies of the Messiah: Klausner; but cf., for their pre-exilic origins, Johnson.

Ezra-Apocalypse, XI–XIII, pp. 608–19.

Baruch-Apocalypse, XXXIX–XL, p. 501; LXXII–LXXIV, p. 518; XXIX, pp. 497–8.

23   Josephus, Book VI, Chap. V (vol. II, p. 108).

On Jewish pseudo-messiahs: Hyamson.

'For the Son of Man . . .': Matthew xvi, 27–28 (=Luke ix, 27). Cf. Matthew x, 23.

On the two eras: Vulliaud, pp. 45 sq.

For a prophecy of the Second Coming, attributed to Christ, but which is altogether in the tradition of Jewish apocalyptic: Mark xiii (=Matthew xxiv, Luke xxi); it seems to date from the 50s. On the vogue of *Baruch* amongst Christians: Charles, vol. II, p. 470.

24–25   Revelation xiii, 1, 7–8, 11, 13, 14; xix, 11, 14–15, 19–21; xx, 4; xxi, 1–5, 10–11.

'Spirit of Truth': John xv, 26; xvi, 13.

26   Tertullian, cols. 355–6.

'shortly': Revelation xxii, 6; and cf. ibid., 7, 20.

'until all should . . .': 2 Peter iii, 9.

Justin Martyr, cap. lxxx, cols. 664–8.

27 Papias, cols. 1258–9. This fragment is preserved in Irenaeus, cols. 1213–14. Cf. *Baruch-Apocalypse*, XXIX, p. 498.
Irenaeus, lib. V, cap. xxxii–xxxiv. The passage quoted is at col. 1210.

28 Lactantius (2), cols. 1090–2. The passage is condensed from Lactantius (1) (*Divinae Institutiones*), lib. VII, cap. xx, xxiv, xxvi; see esp. cap. xxiv, cols. 808–811.
Commodianus (1), pp. 53–61; and (2), pp. 175–80. The fifth century is now regarded as a more probable date for Commodianus than the third; cf. *Oxford Classical Dictionary*, 1949, p. 222.

29 Gog and Magog: These peoples continued to figure in apocalyptic literature throughout the Middle Ages; cf. Bousset (2), pp. 113–31, and Peuckert, pp. 164–71. Originally believed to be living in the far North, they were later placed behind the Caucasus and could therefore easily be equated with the hordes which periodically came out of central Asia. For the origin of the idea see Ezekiel xxxviii–xxxix and Revelation xx, 8–9.

The apocalyptic tradition in medieval Europe

Augustine, lib. XX, cap. vi–xvii (vol. II, pp. 458–84).
On the suppression of the chapters in Irenaeus: Gry, p. 74; and in PL, Note to col. 1210 of Irenaeus.

30 On the Jewish and early Christian Sibyllines: Lanchester. For a recent and convenient edition of these 'oracles': Kurfess (OS). Book VIII was the most important for the development of the Sibylline tradition in medieval Europe.
The standard work on the phantasy of the eschatological Emperor during the Middle Ages is still Kampers (1). See also Bernheim, pp. 63–109; Dempf, pp. 255–6. Kampers (2) deals chiefly with pre-Christian versions of the saviour-king.

31 For the Latin text of the *Tiburtina*: see *Tiburtina*, and Sackur (both OS). This version dates from about 1047. For a bibliographical list of the numerous revisions of the *Tiburtina* known to the Middle Ages: Hübscher, pp. 213–14.

32 For the Latin text of the *Pseudo-Methodius*: see *Pseudo-Methodius*, and Sackur. This translation was made by a Syrian or Greek monk at St Germain-des-Prés in the eighth century.

33 On the influence of the medieval Sibyllines: Kurfess, p. 347, remarks that save for the Bible and the works of the Fathers there was scarcely a writing which had such universal influence during the Middle Ages as the *Pseudo-Methodius*.
For a detailed analysis of the Antichrist symbol: Bousset (1), pp. 142–89.
'shall exalt himself . . .': Daniel xi, 36.
'speak great words . . .': Daniel vii, 25.
St Paul: 2 Thessalonians ii, 4, 9; and cf. Revelation xiii, 13–14.

34 'And it was given . . .': Revelation xiii, 7.
'waxed great . . .': Daniel viii, 10.
For the two Beasts: Revelation xi, xii, xiii.
Hildegard (1), col. 713. Vision XI as a whole is an excellent source for medieval Antichrist lore.

35 On the influence of eschatology upon political judgements in the Middle Ages: Bernheim, pp. 69–101.
On the dynastic exploitation of Sibylline prophecies: Kampers (1), *passim*.

334

On medieval expectations of Antichrist: Wadstein, pp. 81–158, and Preuss, esp. p. 21.

2 The Tradition of Religious Dissent

The ideal of the apostolic life

37 Recent bibliographies for medieval religious dissent, or 'heresy' are: Grundmann (6); Kulcsár.
38 St Benedict of Nursia, p. 110 (cap. xlviii).
Acts ii.44 and iv.32.
On lay preachers from the eighth to the twelfth centuries: Russell (2).
39 Henry (often, but on insufficient grounds, called 'of Lausanne') is the subject of an abundant literature. For a good recent summary: Russell (2), pp. 68–74.
40 To appreciate the continuity of the tradition of wandering preachers see, e.g., Russell (2), Grundmann (4) and (5), Leff and Williams.

Some early messiahs

41 St Gregory of Tours, p. 437 (lib. X, cap. xxv).
42 'there shall be famines ...': Matthew xxiv, 7 and 24; cf. Mark xiii, 22.
For Aldebert: Synod of Rome, 745, pp. 108–18. For recent accounts: Russell (1) and, more briefly, Russell (2), pp. 102–8.
44 Major contemporary sources for Eon or Eudes are *Sigeberti Continuatio Gemblacensis*, p. 389; *Chronicum Britannicum*, p. 558; and Synod of Rheims, 1157, pp. 771 sq. William of Newburgh, pp. 97–8 (lib. I, cap. XIX) is partly based on the first two of these. See also *Sigeberti Continuatio Praemonstratensis*, p. 454; *Annales Cameracenses*, p. 517; *Annales Casinenses*, p. 310; *Annales Parchenses*, p. 605; and Otto of Freising, p. 81. For a recent account: Russell (2), pp. 118–23.
'like flies ...': William of Newburgh, loc. cit.
45 On Eon's following: Otto of Freising, loc. cit.; William of Newburgh, loc. cit. On the famine: *Continuatio Gemblacensis*, loc. cit.; and cf. Alphandéry and Dupront, p. 166.
For the pseudo-Baldwin see below, Chapter 5.
46 'Per *eum* ...': *Continuatio Praemonstratensis*, loc. cit.
47 On Tanchelm's mission to the Holy See: Pirenne (2) and De Smet.
For the principal sources on Tanchelm see OS under Chapter of Utrecht and *Vita S. Norberti A*. (The account in *Vita S. Norberti B* is more scurrilous and less reliable.) Of modern writers Janssen (1867) and Essen (1912) accepted these early accounts as substantially accurate; but more recent writers, such as Philippen (1934), Mohr (1954) and De Smet (1961) have tried to discredit them and to present Tanchelm as simply a Gregorian reformer, grossly maligned. More recently still, Russell (2), adopts much the same standpoint as the present work.
48 For the monk Henry see above, pp. 39–40.
49 Werner and Erbstösser pp. 265–6, and Werner (2), pp. 385–93, suggest that Tanchelm modelled his behaviour on a tradition, still familiar in the twelfth century, concerning Simon Magus. Simon's group of followers is supposed to have consisted of a number of men and one woman, who represented wisdom (the Gnostic Sophia). The hypothesis is interesting,

but perhaps over-ingenious: the 'Master of Hungary' (Chapter 5) and the leader of the Bohemian Adamites (Chapter 11) also had 'Marys'; and their model was surely Jesus rather than Simon Magus.

50 'many massacres': *Continuatio Praemonstratensis*, p. 449.
Lost biography of St Norbert: Potthast, vol. II, p. 1494.
For documents concerning Norbert's foundations: Fredericq (OS), vol. I, pp. 24–5 and vol. II, pp. 3–6. Cf. Philippen, pp. 256–69.

51 Weber (2), p. 278 (my translation). On the general characteristics of salvationist religion amongst the underprivileged see Weber (1), pp. 245–8; and (2), pp. 267, 276–82, 296–7. For colonial and ex-colonial territories see Bibliography, part 3, on millenarian and messianic movements.
Sundkler, p. 114. (Bibliography, 3).

52 On Shembe: ibid., p. 278.
Messiah and ruler: ibid., pp. 115, 288.

3 The Messianism of the Disoriented Poor

The impact of rapid social change

56 On peasant kinship-groups: Bloch (2), pp. 163–70, and (3), pp. 190–220; Thalamas, pp. 157–8.

59 On the insecurity of workers in the cloth industry: Carus-Wilson, p. 387. On the disintegration of kinship-groups: Bloch (3), p. 217; Dupré Theseider, p. 58; Weber (2), pp. 527–31; and in Italy: Tamassia, pp. 112–14.

The poor in the first crusades

61 For a recent and concise account of the political background and the launching of the First Crusade: Runciman (2), vol. I, pp. 93–109. Other reliable accounts in: Chalandon; Grousset, vol. I; Röhricht (4); Sybel; more briefly in Stevenson; and in great detail in the monumental work edited by Setton and Baldwin (esp. Chap. VIII, by F. Duncalf).
Urban on indigence and future prosperity: Robert the Monk, p. 728.

62 On the religious inspiration of the knightly crusade: Rousset (1) and (2). On the other hand the fullest account of the popular movements accompanying the First and Second Crusades, and of the phantasies that inspired them, is that of Alphandéry and Dupront.
On Peter the Hermit and the preaching to the people: Hagenmeyer, esp. pp. 127–51; Alphandéry and Dupront, pp. 69–71.
Peter's acts seem half-divine: Guibert of Nogent (1), p. 142.

63 For the list of catastrophes, 1085–95: Wolff, pp. 108–9. The famine of 1095 is described by Guibert (1), p. 141. Many chroniclers mention the plague, the so-called 'mal des ardents' or 'St Anthony's fire'; e.g. Bernold of Constance, p. 459; *Chron. S. Andreae*, p. 542; Ekkehard of Aura (1), pp. 105–9 (cap. viii) and (2), p. 207; Sigebert of Gembloux, pp. 366–7.
For examples of the new devotional groups: Alphandéry and Dupront, vol. I, pp. 48–9.
On the social composition of the People's Crusade: Baudri of Dol, col. 1070; Bernold, p. 464; Fulcher of Chartres, p. 385; Guibert (1), p. 142.

Urban ignores Jerusalem: in the account of the Clermont appeal given by Fulcher, the earliest and most reliable source, Jerusalem is not mentioned. On the pilgrimage of 1033: Radulph Glaber, col. 680; and on that of 1064: *Annales Altahenses maiores*, pp. 815 sq.

64 On the People's Crusade as an *imitatio Christi*, cf. Erdmann (2), pp. 318–19.

'Rejoice ye . . .': Isaiah lxvi, 10–13.

'the navel of the world . . .': Robert the Monk, p. 729.

On the descent of the Heavenly Jerusalem: Revelation xxi, 1–5, 10–11. For the interpretation of the earthly as a symbol of the heavenly city: Röhricht (1), p. 376, Note 76; Alphandéry and Dupront, I, p. 22; Konrad,

65 (2). On the confusion of the two by the *pauperes*: Ekkehard (1), p. 301 (cap. xxxiv); the city in the sky: ibid., p. 117 (cap. x); the children: Guibert (1), p. 142.

On the sense of election amongst the *pauperes*: cf. Alphandéry (5), pp. 59 sq.

'God has chosen . . .': Raymond of Aguilers, p. 254.

For the miraculous crosses: ibid., p. 272.

On the Tafurs: Guibert (1), p. 242; *Conquête de Jérusalem, passim*, and esp. pp. 65 sq.; *Chanson d'Antioche*, vol. II, *passim*, and esp. pp. 254–5. The original versions of both these vernacular epics were composed at the beginning of the twelfth century. The only extant versions are those revised by Graindor of Douai in the early thirteenth century; but the passages concerning the Tafurs do not give the impression of having been much edited. It has often been held that both epics were written by one Richard the Pilgrim, but it seems most improbable that the same author could have written both. The *Conquête de Jérusalem* portrays the crusade from the standpoint of the poor. It is valuable as a guide to the psychology rather than to the external history of the People's Crusade in the East; and what it tells of the Tafurs is their legend. The *Chanson d'Antioche* gives a soberer, less flattering and no doubt factually more accurate account of the Tafurs. For a good recent account: Sumberg.

On the word 'Tafur': *Trudannes*, which Guibert, p. 242, gives as an equivalent of *Tafurs*, is a variant of *trutani*, 'vagrants', 'vagabonds', 'beggars'.

66 'no Franks . . .': *Chanson d'Antioche*, p. 5. Cf. ibid., pp. 254–5, 294–5; and *Conquête de Jérusalem*, p. 230.

'worth far more . . .': *Conquête*, p. 194. In the *Conquête*, p. 72, the *pauperes* of the Provençal army appear in close association with the Tafurs and are described in very similar terms.

On the cult of poverty amongst the Tafurs: Guibert, p. 242.

'The poorest shall take it. . .': *Conquête*, pp. 163.

The Provençal poor 'gallop on horseback . . ': Raymond of Aguilers, p. 249.

'Where are the poor folk . . .': *Conquête*, pp. 165–6. Cf. *Anonymi Gesta Francorum*, pp. 204–5.

67 For the sortie from Jerusalem: *Conquête*, pp. 243–53.

For the princes' view of the Tafurs: *Chanson*, pp. 6–7.

King Tafur urges the barons: *Conquête*, pp. 64–7; is carried from the field: ibid., pp. 82–3; crowns Godfrey: ibid., pp. 191–3; pledges himself to stay at Jerusalem: ibid., pp. 193–5.

For a forced conversion of peasants: *Anonymi Gesta*, pp. 162–4.

68 'the horses waded in blood . . .': Raymond, p. 300.

The Jews of Jerusalem burnt: Ibn al-Qalānisī, p. 48.

'O new day ...': Raymond, loc. cit. Cf. Du Cange (MW) on the sense of *exanitio*.

For the massacre on the roof: *Anonymi Gesta*, pp. 204–6. Cf. *Conquête*, pp. 178–9.

First great massacre of European Jews: There had been some attacks on Jews in Spain at the time of the 'crusade' against the Moslems there in 1064; but they were on a far smaller scale. For a modern account of the massacres which accompanied the First and Second Crusades: Parkes, pp. 61–89.

'peace was established ...': Sigebert of Gembloux, p. 367. On the massacres in France: Guibert (2), p. 240; Richard of Poitiers, pp. 411–12.

69   On the happenings at Speyer and Worms: Anonymous of Mainz-Darmstadt, pp. 171–2; Eliezer bar Nathan, pp. 154–6; Salomo bar Simeon, p. 84; Bernold of Constance, pp. 464–5. For critical examinations of the Hebrew sources: Elbogen; Porgès; Sonne.

For Mainz: Anonymous of Mainz-Darmstadt, pp. 178–80; Eliezer, pp. 157–8; Salomo, pp. 87–91; Albert of Aix, p. 292; Annalista Saxo, p. 729.

For Trier: Salomo, pp. 131 sq.; *Gesta Treverorum, Continuatio I*, pp. 182, 190.

For Metz: Salomo, p. 137.

For Cologne: Eliezer, pp. 160–63; Salomo, pp. 116 sq.

For Regensburg: Salomo, p. 137.

For Prague: Cosmas of Prague, p. 164.

On the monk Rudolph: Ephraim bar Jacob, pp. 187 sq.; Otto of Freising, pp. 58–9; *Annales Herbipolenses*, p. 3; *Annales Rodenses*, pp. 718–19 (a contemporary source, and one which favours Rudolph as against St Bernard); *Annales S. Jacobi Leodiensis minores*, p. 641. For Bernard's own comments: Bernard (3) and (4). For a modern account: Setton and Baldwin, pp. 472–3 (by V. G. Berry).

70   'Come to us ...': Joseph ha-Cohen, p. 24.

Jew-killing earns forgiveness of sins: Anonymous of Mainz-Darmstadt, p. 170.

'We have set out ...': Guibert (2), p. 240; Richard of Poitiers, p. 411.

'Jesus said ...': Salomo, pp. 88–9.

4 The Saints Against the Hosts of Antichrist

Saviours in the Last Days

71   On the 'signs' and 'the Last Trump': Ekkehard of Aura (1), pp. 54–6 (cap. ii). The 'signs' are those listed in the prophecy of the Parousia in Mark xiii.

Adso, monk and later abbot of Montier-en-Der, produced his treatise at the request of Gerberga, wife of Louis IV (d'Outremer). For a recent study of his work and influence: Konrad, R. (1).

The Last Emperor becomes a western monarch: Kampers (1), pp. 30–39.

72   Benzo of Alba: pp. 605, 617, 623.

On Sibylline prophecies in the First Crusade: Erdmann (1), p. 413, and (2), pp. 276–8; Heisig, *passim*.

On Charlemagne resurrected: Ekkehard (1), pp. 120–21 (cap. xi).

On Charlemagne as pilgrim and crusader: Benedict, monk of St Andrew on Mount Soracte, writing in the second half of the tenth century, tells (cols. 32–6) of a mass pilgrimage to Jerusalem, headed by Charlemagne; but this seems to have contributed little to the growth of the legend. It is only at the time of the First Crusade that we meet the story of an armed crusade led by Charlemagne; notably in the *Descriptio* (OS), which was forged by the monks of Saint-Denis to explain the presence in their abbey of the Crown of Thorns and other relics (the relevant passage is at p. 108). On the dissemination of this legend and its employment as propaganda for the crusades: Rauschen, pp. 141–7. Of the chronicles of the First Crusade the *Anonymi Gesta Francorum*, p. 4, and the appeal attributed to Urban by Robert the Monk, p. 728, refer to Charlemagne's supposed route.

On the sleeping Charlemagne: Heisig, pp. 52 sq.; Kampers (1), p. 58. The sleeping hero, biding his time in cave or mountain, was a common figure in medieval as in other folklore. Belief in the continued existence and future return of King Arthur was particularly widespread and intense; and as for Frederick II Hohenstauffen, see Chap. 6 of the present study.

73   On leaders of the crusade who were seen as the Last Emperor: Alphandéry and Dupront, vol. I, pp. 75, 112, 131; Alphandéry (4), pp. 3–8.

On the cross on the shoulder-blades: Grauert (2), esp. pp. 709–19.

On Emico and his revelations: Salomo bar Simeon, p. 92; Annalista Saxo, p. 729; Ekkehard (1), p. 126 (cap. xii).

On Emico's horde and its fate: Albert of Aix, pp. 293–5; Ekkehard (1), pp. 128–31 (cap. xii). Albert, though often unreliable, is doubtless correct in saying that almost all of Emico's horde proceeded on foot; other chroniclers give the same impression.

For Emico in the mountain: Ekkehard (2), p. 261. On Emico's death in battle while defending Mainz against the Duke of Swabia: Otto of Freising, p. 29.

74   New versions of the *Tiburtina*: Kampers (1), pp. 53–4, describes how the prophecy was revised in the late eleventh and early twelfth centuries so as to make it refer now to the French, now to the German kings.

For the text of the oracle: Otto of Freising, pp. 10–11; and cf. *Annales S. Jacobi Leodiensis minores*, p. 641. The text is preserved also in other chronicles; see Kampers (1), p. 192, Note 32, and (1A), Appendix I, pp. 204–5. On the survival of the name Constans: ibid., pp. 206–7. For the influence of the oracle on St Bernard: Radcke, pp. 115 sq.

The oracle in Germany: Otto says it was studied 'in the Gauls'. But for him, as a learned man, the term 'Gaul' included much territory which by the twelfth century was German. Thus he refers, p. 58, to the *propheta* Rudolph as being active 'in those parts of Gaul which touch the Rhine'. When he means France he tends to speak of 'occidentalis Gallia'.

The demonic hosts

75   On the popular idea of the crusade as a Holy War, and the contrast which this presented with the papal intentions: Erdmann (2), pp. 264–73, 321. Already the Pisan invasion of Moslem-held Sicily in 1087 was seen as a Holy War. A poem written to celebrate its success shows St Michael sounding the Trump as for the battle against the Dragon, and St Peter displaying the Cross, to encourage the burghers in an attack which ends in the slaughter of every single infidel, man, woman and child; see Schneider (OS), poem 25, esp. lines 33–40.

'The Emperor has taken . . .': *Chanson de Roland*, lines 3660–70 (p. 304).

Antichrist already born: According to St Bernard (2), Tanchelm's opponent St Norbert believed this; and so, three centuries later, did St Vincent Ferrer.

Urban on Antichrist: Guibert of Nogent (1), p. 138.

Bernard on Antichrist and Saracens: Bernard (3).

Antichrist and the infidel: Like the idea of an individual Antichrist, the idea of the hosts of Antichrist developed out of Jewish eschatological phantasies which existed before Christianity; cf. Rigaux, esp. p. 402.

76   For Moslems as 'ministers' of Antichrist: Eulogius, col. 748 sq.; Alvarus of Cordova, cols. 535–6.

For Moslems as demons: *Aliscans*, lines 71–3, 1058–61.

On the identification of Jews with Saracens: Bulard, pp. 225 sq. Bulard proves from iconographical evidence that Saracens were even believed to have taken part, along with Jews, in the Crucifixion.

On the social and economic situation of the Jews in the Middle Ages: Baron, Caro, vol. II; Kisch; Parkes; Roth.

77   Antichrist a Jew: For an early example of this belief see Irenaeus, col. 1205. The choice of the tribe of Dan was determined by Genesis xlix, 16–17.

78   For a typical example of the anti-Jewish version of the Antichrist legend: Hippolytus (attrib.), esp. cols. 920, 925, 928, 944. The modern *Protocols of Zion*, which have exerted such enormous influence, derive directly from the Antichrist legend. They first appeared in 1905, in a Russian volume which has as its major theme the imminent imposition of the reign of Antichrist through his Jewish agents: see Cohn (MW).

Adso on Antichrist: Adso, pp. 106–7. In a popular rhyme (quoted in Wadstein, p. 129, Note 3) incest is added to the picture:

> Un paillard Juif abominable
>
> Connaîtra charnellement sa propre fille.

On the Jew in medieval demonology: Trachtenberg.

For animals as symbols of Jewry see e.g. the frontispiece to Trachtenberg; for the scorpion in particular: Bulard.

On black magic in the synagogue, see the extract from the *Chanson de Roland* quoted at the beginning of this section.

Jews believed to hold tournaments: Burdach (4).

79   *Pseudo-Methodius*, p. 92.

On Jews in Antichrist dramas: Trachtenberg, pp. 36–40.

On papal policy cf. Trachtenberg, p. 161: '*Constitutio pro Judeis*, expressly forbidding violence, was endorsed by successive popes ten times from its issue in 1120 to 1250.'

On the *role* of Jews as money-lenders see works listed above under p. 76. That Jews in the Rhineland were not yet given to money-lending at the time of the First Crusade seems reasonably certain; see Caro, vol. I, pp. 211–25, and vol. II, pp. 110, 192 sq.; Graetz, vol. VI, p. 402.

80   On the part allocated to pope and clergy in the demonology of various dissident sects and movements: Benz, pp. 307–14, 366–8; Peuckert, pp. 112 sq.; Preuss, pp. 44 sq.

Antichrist the son of a bishop and a nun: Adso in PL, col. 1292.

For St Bernard's view of the clergy: Radcke, pp. 15–17, 102.

81   On the *propheta* of 1209: Caesarius of Heisterbach, pp. 304–7.

For the Whore of Babylon: Revelation xvii, 6, 2; and for the Beast: Revelation xiii, 17.

On the clergy seen as the Beast: Benz, pp. 330–31.
82 'they take no care . . .': Jean le Fèvre, bk. iii, lines 602 sq. (pp. 176 sq.).

Phantasy, anxiety and social myth

85 'clothed in white linen . . .': Revelation xix, 14.
Antichrist as the bad son and the bad father: In an essay published as early as 1912 Ernest Jones analysed the medieval image of Satan in terms of images of the bad father and the bad son. The essay is included as Chap. VI in the work specified in the Bibliography.

86 For the frogs: Revelation xvi, 13; and cf. Lorch's picture of Satan-Antichrist (Plate 2), where scorpions are added to the frogs.
Jews murder Christian children: The charge was revived in the Third Reich. Pictures of rabbis sucking blood from an 'Aryan' child abounded in the official newspaper *Der Stürmer*, which indeed devoted a whole issue (1 May 1934) to the subject; cf. Trachtenberg, p. 243.

87 'the children of God . . .': quoted in Trachtenberg, p. 42.

5 In the Backwash of the Crusades

The pseudo-Baldwin and the 'Master of Hungary'

89 On Fulk of Neuilly: Reinerus, p. 654. For a full modern account: Alphandéry and Dupront, vol. II, pp. 45–64. On the Children's Crusades: see Hecker, Appendix, pp. 346–53, and Runciman (2), vol. III, pp. 139–44, for concise summaries; Alphandéry (3) and Alphandéry and Dupront, vol. II, pp. 115–48 for fuller accounts which deal with the underlying phantasies; and cf. the critical examination of sources by Munro, esp. p. 520.

90 Baldwin seen as superhuman: Cahour, p. 82. Cahour's is the fullest modern account of the pseudo-Baldwin. For a briefer summary: Kervyn de Lettenhove (1). The present account is based mainly on Mouskes (OS), vol. II, lines 24463–25325.

91 On the war against the Countess Joanna: Alberic of Trois-Fontaines, p. 794; Baldwin of Ninove, p. 541; *Chronicon S. Medardi Suessionensis*, p. 722; Mouskes, lines 24839–43. Cf. Cahour, p. 168.
On reverence shown to the pseudo-Baldwin: Mouskes, lines 25117 sq.

92 'If God had come . . .': ibid., lines 24851–5.
'the poor folk . . .': ibid., lines 24741–8; and cf. ibid., lines 24771–2.
The social aspect of the movement emerges not only from the account of Mouskes but also from Latin chronicles (some of them admittedly rather late) such as *Chronicon Andrensis monasterii*, p. 579; *Chronicon Turonense*, pp. 307–9; and John of Ypres, p. 609.
For the treaties: Henry III in Rymer, vol. I, p. 177; the Countess in *Gesta Ludovici VIII*, pp. 308–9.

93 On the rising at Valenciennes: Mouskes, lines 25019 sq.
'at Valenciennes people await him . . .': ibid., lines 25201 sq.; cf. ibid., lines 24627–30. Several chroniclers describe the hermit as being the true Count; e.g. Paris, vol. III, pp. 90–91. But modern historians are united in regarding the episode as an imposture.
On the primacy of the French monarchy: Bloch (1), p. 237.

94 On the pretensions of Philip Augustus: *Giraldus Cambrensis*, pp. 292 sq. Cf. Folz, pp. 277–9.

On the sectarians at Paris: *Caesarius of Heisterbach*, pp. 304–7.

Mohammed stronger than Christ: *Salimbene*, p. 445.

The story of the Shepherds' Crusade of 1251 is told in a letter written at the time by a Franciscan of Paris to Adam Marsh and other Franciscans of Oxford, given in *Annales monasterii de Burton*, pp. 290–93; in the *Chroniques de Saint-Denis*, pp. 115–16; by Paris, vol. V, pp. 246–54; by Primat, pp. 8–10; by William of Nangis (1), p. 383, and (2), vol. I, pp. 207–8, 435–6. (William draws largely on Primat.) The present account is based mainly on these sources. The sources specified below are those which bring confirmation or additional information on particular points. For modern summaries: Berger, pp. 393–401; Röhricht (3).

On the 'Master of Hungary': *Chronica minor auctore minorita Erphordiensi*, p. 200; *Chronicon S. Martini Turonensis, Continuatio*, p. 476; *Flores temporum, Imperatores*, p. 241.

95 On the formation, composition and organization of the horde: Baldwin of Avesnes (attrib.), p. 169; *Chron. min. auct. minorita Erphordiensi*, loc. cit.; *Chronica universalis Mettensis*, p. 522; *Chronique anonyme des Rois de France*, p. 83; Gui (1), p. 697; John of Columna, pp. 123–4; Wykes, p. 100.

The *Pastoureaux* take food by force: *Annales monasterii de Waverleia*, p. 344; Richerus, p. 311.

Their contempt for sacraments and clergy: *Chron. univ. Mettensis*, loc. cit.

96 The *Pastoureaux* at Rouen: *Chronicon S. Catharinae de Monte Rotomagi*, pp. 401–2; *Chronicon S. Laudi Rotomagensis*, pp. 395–6; *Chronicon Rotomagense*, p. 339; *Visitationes Odonis Rigaudi*, p. 575.

At Paris, Tours, Orleans: *Annales monasterii de Oseneia*, p. 100; *Chron. univ. Mettensis*, loc. cit.; John of Columna, p. 124; John of Tayster, p. 589; Thomas of Chantimpré, p. 140.

97 Prestige from killing priests: *Chronicon Normanniae*, p. 214; Gui (1), loc. cit.

The Church in danger: Thomas of Chantimpré, loc. cit.

For the instructions of Henry III: Berger, p. 401, Note 1.

The *Pastoureaux* as Moslems: Baldwin of Ninove, p. 544.

98 On the ultimate aims ascribed to the *Pastoureaux* see the comments at the end of the letter to Adam Marsh.

The last crusades of the poor

98 On the situation in the Flemish towns in the thirteenth and fourteenth centuries Professor Carus-Wilson has recently remarked that 'the conflicts of capital and labour reached an intensity and a violence never since equalled even in the *Hochkapitalismus* of modern Europe. ... By this time the craftsmen (in the cloth industry) had everywhere fallen into dependence upon the entrepreneur' (Carus-Wilson, p. 399). On the relationship between capitalists and proletariat see also Bezold (3); Heer, pp. 469–71; Peuckert, p. 240.

On the change in the situation of the peasants: Nabholz, pp. 493 sq., 503.

99 'The poor man works ...': Tobler (OS), proverb 52.

'each man ought to have ...': quoted by Trachtenberg, p. 221.

'Magistrates, provosts ...': Jean de Meun, lines 11540–49.

100 'I would like ...': *Renart le Contrefait*, lines 25505 sq.

On the *Caputiati*: *Chronicon anonymi Laudunensis canonici*, pp. 705–6 (whence the quotation on 'frantic madness'); Robert of Auxerre, p. 251; and for the early stages of the movement: Robert of Torigny (see under Sigebert of Gembloux), p. 534.

'Sell all thou hast . . .': Luke xviii, 22–5.

101 Dives and Lazarus: Luke xvi, 19 sq.

For the rich as bad sons of Christ: Alphandéry and Dupront, vol. II, p. 197.

On the woman with the snakes: Bernheimer, p. 33; and cf. Heer, pp. 456–60.

On heretics working amongst weavers: Eckbert of Schönau, cols. 13–14; Bernard (1), col. 761.

102 On the People's Crusade of 1309: *Annales Austriacarum, Continuatio Florianensis*, pp. 752–3; *Annales Colbazenses*, p. 717; *Annales Gandenses*, p. 596; *Annales Lubicenses*, p. 421; *Annales S. Blasii Brunsvicenses*, p. 825; *Annales Tielenses*, p. 26; *Chronicon Elwacense*, p. 39; *Gesta abbatum Trudonensium*, p. 412; Gui (2), p. 67; John of Winterthur, p. 58; *Continuatio Brabantina* (see under Martin of Troppau), p. 262; Muisis, p. 175; Ptolomy of Lucca, p. 34; William of Egmont, p. 577. See also: Heidelberger, pp. 44–5.

Famines: The list of famines in Curschmann, pp. 82–5, reveals an illuminating fact: major famines occurred in the Low Countries and along the lower Rhine in 1225 (year of the pseudo-Baldwin), 1296 (year of flagellant processions: see Chap. V) and 1309 (year of a People's Crusade); and none are recorded for the intervening periods, long though these were.

On the famine of 1315: Lucas.

On the prophecy: William of Nangis, *Continuatio III*, vol. II, pp. 179–80.

103 On the Shepherds' Crusade of 1320: Gui (3), pp. 161–3; John, canon of St Victor, pp. 128–30 (written about 1322); William of Nangis, *Continuatio II*, vol. II, pp. 25–8 (probably copied from John of St Victor). For modern summaries: Devic and Vaissète, pp. 402–6; Graetz, vol. VII, pp. 277 sq.; Alphandéry and Dupront, vol. II, pp. 257–64. The Jewish chroniclers Usque (writing in Portuguese) and Ibn Verga (writing in Hebrew) tell the story some two centuries after the event, and with much obscurity and confusion. But, drawing on a lost Spanish source, both give valuable particulars not only about the 'saviours' but also about the massacres of Jews in southern France and in Spain: Usque, vol. III, pp. xvi sq.; Ibn Verga, pp. 4–6. Joseph ha-Cohen, pp. 46–7, copies Usque; cf. Loeb, pp. 218–20. Massacres in particular localities have been studied by: Kahn, p. 268; and Miret y Sans.

104 For the Pope's letter see John xxii.

On the class-war in the Low Countries: Pirenne (1).

On revolts in Paris and Rouen: Levasseur, p. 510.

105 A cloth-worker burnt at Ypres: document in Espinas and Pirenne (OS), p. 790.

The most accessible edition of the *Vademecum* is still that specified in the Bibliography under John of Roquetaillade, though the text is defective. Of the twenty *Intentiones* into which the work is divided, No. V prophesies social revolt. On John of Roquetaillade himself: Bignami-Odier. The social prophecy quoted there (pp. 32–3) as possibly originating in a lost work of Roquetaillade would be even more interesting than the *Vademecum* if it were genuine; but internal evidence strongly suggests that it is a fake, of much later date.

106 Of the later prophecies the most celebrated is that produced by the hermit Telesphorus of Cosenza in 1386. Dedicated to the Doge of Genoa, it aimed at bringing Genoa under French rule.

6 The Emperor Frederick as Messiah

Joachite prophecy and Frederick II

108 On Joachim of Fiore: Grundmann (1) and (3); Bloomfield. For an exhaustive bibliography to 1954: Russo.

109 On Joachite influence on modern 'philosophies of history': Löwith, pp. 158–9 and Appendix I; Taubes, pp. 90–94; Voegelin, pp. 110–21 *et passim*.

On the Joachite undertones in the phrase 'the Third Reich': Kestenberg-Gladstein, pp. 245, 283.

110 Forty-two generations: Matthew i, 17.

On Joachism in southern Europe: Benz; and more briefly: Hübscher, pp. 107–32; Morghen, pp. 287 sq. See also the account of contemporary attitudes to Rienzo in Burdach (1), pp. 5–53, *passim* and esp. pp. 1–23.

On the idea of the Angel-Pope, which played a large part in Italian Joachism: Baethgen. The French *propheta* John of Roquetaillade, mentioned in the preceding chapter, was in many respects a Joachite, though a belated one.

111 On the penetration of Joachism into northern Europe: Bloomfield and Reeves. For the influence of Joachism on the idea of the Last Emperor: Reeves (2).

Frederick II as Emperor of the Last Days: Kampers (1), pp. 76–7, 154–5.
On Frederick II, see the essays collected in Wolf, G.

112 On the preachers in Swabia: Albert of Stade, pp. 371–2. For a modern account of this movement or sect: Völter; and cf. Bloomfield and Reeves, pp. 791–2; Lempp; Schultheiss, pp. 19–20; Weller, pp. 146 sq.

For the text of the manifesto: Arnold, Dominican (OS); cf. Bloomfield and Reeves, loc. cit.; Bossert, pp. 179–81; Völter.

113 On the monk at Etna: Thomas of Eccleston, p. 568. Cf. Kampers (1), pp. 83–7, which also quotes sources for the belief in the resurrected Frederick in Sicily and Italy. At Tivoli, which being at perpetual loggerheads with Rome naturally adhered to the 'imperial' cause, Frederick's death was mourned in terms taken from the *Tiburtina*; see Hampe, esp. the Latin manifesto at pp. 18–20.

The resurrection of Frederick

113 For the pseudo-Frederick near Worms: *Annales Colmarienses maiores*, p. 211; at Lübeck: *Detmar-Chronik*, p. 367.

114 Principal sources for the story of the pseudo-Frederick of Neuss: Ellenhard of Strasbourg (2), pp. 125–6; *Vita Henrici II archiepiscopi (Treverensis) altera*, pp. 462–3. For an account which is factually less reliable but which shows how the story was reshaped in popular imagination see Ottokar's *Reimchronik*, lines 32324 sq. (pp. 423 sq.). Ottokar, an ex-minstrel writing between 1305 and 1320, seems to have drawn on a version which, circulating amongst the common people in Austria and strongly coloured by pseudo-Joachite ideas, accepted the monarch of

Neuss as the real Frederick II. For modern accounts: Meyer (Victor); Schultheiss, pp. 23–47; Voigt, pp. 145 sq.; Winkelmann.

The pseudo-Frederick a pilgrim: *Continuatio Anglica* (see under Martin of Troppau), p. 252. For his claim to have dwelt underground, see his letter given in the Note to the *Vita Henrici*, p. 462.

For reactions in Italy: Salimbene, p. 537.

German princes recognize the pretender: *Magdeburger Schöppenchronik*, p. 170.

115 On the pseudo-Frederick as the messiah of the urban poor: Schultheiss, p. 170; Voigt, p. 148.

The pseudo-Frederick promises to rise again: Ottokar, p. 426.

On the execution at Utrecht: *Annales Blandinienses*, p. 33.

The Emperor rescued from the flames: Ottokar, p. 427.

God has decreed his return: John of Winterthur, p. 280.

116 The Emperor and Prester John: Oswald der Schreiber, pp. 1012 sq. and esp. p. 1027.

On the belief in a future emperor-saviour (usually imagined as a resurrected Frederick) in Germany from the fourteenth to the sixteenth centuries: Bezold (4); Döllinger (MW), pp. 317 sq.; Kampers (1), pp. 100 sq.; Peuckert, pp 213–43, 606–29; Rosenkranz; Schultheiss; Wadstein, pp. 261 sq.

'In all countries . . .': Regenbogen. Cf. Oswald der Schreiber, loc. cit.

'one must not let . . .': *Magdeburger Schöppenchronik*, p. 313.

117 Suchenwirt: quoted in Bezold (3), p. 60.

John of Winterthur, p. 280. The *motif* of the hidden tonsures occurs already in the thirteenth-century pseudo-Joachite tract *Oraculum Cyrilli*. It was to become very popular in Germany; cf. Peuckert, p. 189.

'From the Emperor Frederick . . .': Rothe, p. 426. Cf. his comments (p. 466) on the pseudo-Frederick of Neuss and the many 'who have joined his heresy'.

On the Greek philosopher: Döllinger (MW), pp. 285–6.

Manifestos for a future Frederick

118 *Gamaleon*: For the Latin version: Wolf (OS), pp. 720 sq. (which contains most of it, in the form of a sermon supposed to have been delivered in 1409 or 1439); and Lazius (OS), H 2 (*b*)–H 3 (which contains the ending, under the title *Vaticinia de Invictissimo Caesare nostro Carolo V*). This version is summarized in Bezold (4), pp. 573 sq. For a vernacular German version: Reifferscheid (OS), Document 9. Cf. Döllinger (MW), pp. 349 sq.; Rosenkranz, pp. 516–17.

Reformation of Sigismund: see *Reformation Kaiser Sigmunds* (OS). On this work: Dohna; Bezold (3), pp. 70 sq., and (4), pp. 587 sq.; Peuckert, pp. 198 sq., 220 sq. On the vexed question of authorship see also Beer's introduction, pp. 71–4.

For 'Sigismund's prophecy': *Reformation Kaiser Sigmunds*, pp. 138–43.

119 *Book of a Hundred Chapters*: This work, which survives in a single enormous manuscript at Colmar, has never been edited. The present account is based on the lengthy analysis in Haupt (8) (MW). Cf. Doren, pp. 160 sq.; Franz, pp. 114–15; Peuckert, pp. 224–7.

120 'He will reign . . .'; 'The King will come . . .'; 'I am the beginning . . .': Haupt (8), pp. 202–3.

Abundance of bread, etc.: cf. Revelation vi, 6. Abundance and cheapness of bread, wine and oil are also characteristic of the reign of the future Constans as described in the *Tiburtina*.

The Revolutionary is himself the Messiah: Haupt (8), p. 209.

121 'to smash Babylon . . .': ibid., p. 202; and cf. pp. 163, 208 sq.

'Whoever strikes . . .', and the call to assassinate Maximilian: ibid., pp. 211–12.

'control the whole world . . .': ibid., p. 215.

'Soon we will drink . . .': ibid., p. 212; cf. p. 109.

'the great men . . .': ibid., p. 210.

'Go on hitting . . .': ibid., p. 212; cf. p. 179.

122 For the massacre of 'usurers' and lawyers: ibid., p. 201; cf. pp. 134, 166.

'What a lot of harm . . .': ibid., p. 168, Note 1; cf. pp. 167–72.

'If a person . . .', and comments on the new type of justice: ibid., pp. 164–6.

123 Oh the ancient German Empire: ibid., pp. 141–5.

On the Latin peoples: ibid., pp. 146–9.

124 On Germany's future destiny: ibid., pp. 156 sq., 200.

'and those that will not accept . . .': ibid., p. 201.

125 Christ taught Jews only: ibid., p. 188.

On patriarch and Emperor: ibid., pp. 156–9.

'The German's once held . . .': ibid., p. 157.

126 On the persistence of phantasies about the reincarnated Frederick: Peuckert, pp. 606 sq.

On the *Bundschuh* of 1513: Schreiber (MW). The millenarian elements in its programme emerge from Documents 20 (p. 89) and 22 (p. 92). Cf. Haupt (8), p. 200, Note 3; Peuckert, p. 625.

7 An Elite of Self-immolating Redeemers

The genesis of the flagellant movement

127 On the beginnings of self-flagellation in Europe: Förstemann, p. 7; Zöckler, p. 36. For the practice at Camaldoli and Fonte Avellana: Damian (1), cols. 415–17, and (2), col. 1002.

The friar: Suso (1), p. 43.

128 The present account of the Italian processions is based on: *Annales S. Justinae Patavini*, p. 179.

For modern accounts of the medieval flagellant movements: Förstemann, which for almost a century and a half was the most comprehensive account, has now been replaced by the symposium published at Perugia to mark the sixth centenary of the first outbreak; see *Il Movimento dei Disciplinati* (MW). Other valuable accounts: Fredericq (1) (MW); Hahn, vol. II, pp. 537 sq.; Haupt (1), (5) and esp. (11); Hübner, esp. pp. 6–60; Lea (MW), pp. 381 sq.; Lechner; Pfannenschmid; Werunsky, pp. 291 sq. For bibliography also: Röhricht (2).

129 The world about to be destroyed: *Annales S. Justinae*, loc. cit. Salimbene, p. 466.

On the movement of 1261–2 north of the Alps: *Chronicon rhythmicum Austriacarum*, p. 363; *Annales Mellicenses*, Continuations: *Mellicensis*, p. 509, *Zwetlensis III*, p. 656; *Sancrucensis II*, p. 645; *Annales Austriacarum, Continuatio Praedicatorum Vindobonensium*, p. 728; Ellenhard (1), pp. 102 sq. (on the processions at Strasbourg); Henry of Heimburg,

p. 714; Hermann of Altaha, p. 402. The movement also reached Bohemia and Poland: *Annales capituli Cracoviensis*, p. 601; Basko of Poznan, p. 74; Pulkava of Radenin, vol. III, p. 232.

On the debt of the German to the Italian movement: Hübner, pp. 33–92. For the text of the Heavenly Letter: Closener, pp. 111 sq. The context there is the movement of 1348–9, but internal evidence shows the letter to date from 1262; cf. Hübner, pp. 54 sq.; Pfannenschmid, pp. 155 sq.

The apocalyptic prophecy attributed to Christ: Mark xiii (=Matthew xxiv, Luke xxi).

130 On the social composition of the German movement: *Chronicon rhythmicum Austriacarum*, p. 363. Baszko of Poznan even refers to the flagellants as 'secta rusticorum'. Cf. Hübner, pp. 19–20.

On the flagellants' claims to salvation: Siegfried of Balnhusin, p. 705. The account in Pulkava, loc. cit., is of much later date and doubtful reliability.

131 On the repression in Germany: e.g. *Annales Veterocellenses*, p. 43.

On the flagellants of 1296: Closener, p. 104; and Note 5 thereto. For the famine see above, note to p. 102.

On the Black Death: Ziegler, which now replaces Coulton, Nohl. For Germany in particular: Hoeniger.

132 The flagellants precede the plague: *Kalendarium Zwetlense*, p. 692; *Annales Austriacorum, Continuato Claustroneoburgensis V*, p. 736. Both these sources expressly state that the flagellants were already active in Austria before the plague arrived.

For the progress of the plague across Europe: Lechner, pp. 443 sq.; but cf. Hübner, pp. 12–13.

On the flagellants in England: Robert of Avesbury, pp. 407–8.

For Strasbourg: Closener, pp. 105 sq.

For Tournai: Muisis, pp. 349, 354–5.

Statistics for the Low Countries: *Breve chronicon Flandriae*, p. 26; Muisis, pp. 354–5; and for Erfurt: *Chronicon S. Petri vulgo Sampetrinum Erfurtense*, p. 180.

133 The present account of the organization, rules and rituals of the flagellants is based on: du Fayt, pp. 703 sq.; Henry of Herford, p. 281; Hugh of Reutlingen, pp. 21 sq.; Matthew of Neuenburg, pp. 265–7; Muisis, pp. 355 sq.; Twinger, vol. IX, pp. 105 sq.

134 The ceremony invalidated by woman or priest: Gilles van der Hoye, p. 342; du Fayt, p. 704; vernacular chronicle in Fredericq (OS), vol. III, p. 15.

For the text of the hymns: Hübner.

'Simony had penetrated ...': Henry of Herford, p. 268.

135 'How contemptible ...': John of Winterthur, p. 278. The year is 1348. For the flagellants as saviours: Boendaele, vol. I, p. 590; Closener, p. 119; Fredericq (OS), loc. cit. and p. 18; Henry of Diessenhofen, p. 73; *Magdeburger Schöppenchronik*, p. 206.

People curse the clergy: Closener, loc. cit.; *Magdeburger Schöppenchronik*, loc. cit.; Muisis, p. 350; Taube of Selbach, p. 77.

Revolutionary flagellants

136 On the earthquakes as 'messianic woes': see Hübner, p. 30, Note 2, for sources.

For the eschatological interpretation of the Black Death: *Detmar-Chronik*, p. 522.

'Plague ruled . . .': quoted in Latin in Hübner, p. 31, where the source is also given.

John of Winterthur, p. 280.

For the great 'astrologer': Michael de Leone, p. 474.

For the intended duration (33½ years): Closener, p. 120.

137 For the enquiry at Breslau see the extracts from the *Quaestio* in Hübner, pp. 22, 24 (Note 1), 29, 47 (Note 2), 204 (Note 1).

The flagellants compare themselves with Christ: Boendaele, vol. I, p. 590; William of Nangis, Continuation III, vol. II, p. 218; chronicle in Fredericq (OS), vol. III, p. 18.

On the social composition of the processions: *Breve chronicon Flandriae*, p. 23; Henry of Herford, p. 282; Hugh of Reutlingen, pp. 51–2; Kervyn de Lettenhove (OS), pp. 30–31; Matthew of Neuenburg, p. 266; Tilemann Ehlen of Wolfhagen, pp. 32–3; also sources in Fredericq (OS), vol. II, p. 136, and in Kervyn de Lettenhove (2) (MW), vol. III, p. 353.

On clerics as *prophetae*: *Chronicon comitum Flandrensium*, p. 226; Closener, p. 118; *Gesta abbatum Trudonensium*, p. 432; and cf. the fourth version of Froissart, quoted in Fredericq (OS), vol. II, p. 131.

For the Bull: Clement VI, pp. 471–2.

The chronicler of the Low Countries: *Gesta abbatum Trudonensium*, loc. cit.

For the Archbishop of Cologne: Synod of Cologne, 1353, p. 471.

138 For Breslau: Klose (MW), p. 190.

On the anti-ecclesiastical attitude and acts of the flagellants: *Chron. comitum Flandrensium*, loc. cit.; *Magdeburger Schöppenchronik*, p 206; *Chron. S. Petri vulgo Sampetrinum*, p. 181; Closener, pp. 115, 119; *Detmar-Chronik*, p. 520; Henry of Herford, pp. 281–2; le Bel, vol. I, p. 225; chronicle in Fredericq (OS), vol. III, p. 18.

For the Pope's complaint: Clement VI, p. 471.

The French chronicler: le Bel, loc. cit.

For a modern study of the accusation of well-poisoning: Wickersheimer; and of the ensuing massacres: Graetz, vol. VII, pp. 360–84; Werunsky, pp. 239 sq.

139 On the happenings at Frankfort: *Annales Francofurtani*, p. 395; Camentz, p. 434; Matthew of Neuenburg, p. 264. Cf. Kracauer (MW), pp. 35 sq.

For Mainz: Henry of Diessenhofen, p. 70; Matthew of Neuenburg, pp. 264–5; Taube of Selbach, pp. 92–3. Cf. Graetz, vol. VII, p. 375; Schaab, pp. 87 sq.

For Cologne: *Annales Agrippenses*, p. 738; *Detmar-Chronik*, p. 275; *Gesta abbatum Trudonensium*, p. 432; Lacomblet, vol. III, p. 391, no. 489 (23 September 1350) (whence the quotation); *Notae Colonienses*, p. 365; Ennen and Eckertz, vol. IV, nos. 314, 385. Cf. Weyden (MW), pp. 186 sq.

For Brussels: Muisis, pp. 342–3.

On the massacres in the Low Countries: Boendaele, vol. I, pp. 588–93; du Fayt, pp. 705–7; Low German translation of Jan van der Beke in Fredericq (OS), vol. I, pp. 196–7.

'most of them . . .': Clement VI, p. 471.

The flagellants attack laymen: ibid.; and *Detmar-Chronik*, p. 275. Cf. Werunsky, pp. 300 sq.

140 Philip V bans flagellation: Muisis, p. 361; and sources in Fredericq (OS), vol. III, pp. 20–21, 116–17, and in Kervyn de Lettenhove (2) (MW), vol. III, p. 358.

Towns resist the flagellants: Erfurt: *Chron. S. Petri vulgo Sampetrinum*,

p. 180; Aachen: Haagen (MW), vol. I, p. 277; Nuremberg: Lochner (MW), p. 36.

On the flagellants of 1400: Zantfliet, p. 358.

Flagellants at Avignon: *Breve chronicon Flandriae*, p. 14; Matthew of Neuenburg, p. 267, Note 2.

For du Fayt's report, see du Fayt (OS); and cf. Fredericq (2) (MW).

On the action of the University of Paris: William of Nangis, Continuation III, vol. II, p. 217; Egasse du Boulay (OS), vol. IV, p. 314.

141 The movement suppressed by ecclesiastical authorities: Andrew of Regensburg, p. 2112; Benessius Krabice of Weitmühl, p. 516; Closener, p. 120; Francis of Prague, p. 599; Froissart, vol. IV, p. 100; *Magdeburger Schöppenchronik*, p. 206.

On the movement suppressed by secular authorities: *Annales breves Solmenses*, p. 449; Tilemann Ehlen, p. 33; and sources in Fredericq (OS), vol. II, pp. 112–18.

'vanishing as suddenly . . .': Henry of Herford, p. 282.

On the penance in St Peter's: *Magdeburger Schöppenchronik*, p. 219.

For later prohibitions: the Low Countries and particularly Tournai: Fredericq (1) (MW); Utrecht: Synod of Utrecht, 1353; Cologne: Synods of Cologne, 1353 and 1357, pp. 471, 485–6.

On the Italian movement: Duplessis d'Argentré (OS), pp. 336–7.

The secret flagellants of Thuringia

142 The present account of Schmid and the secret flagellants of Thuringia is based on documents printed in Stumpf (MW) and in Förstemann, Appendix II. For Documents 2 and 3 in Stumpf, which summarize the leader's own opinions, see also Schmid (1) and (2) (both OS). For a modern account of Schmid: Haupt (12); and of the history of the sect: Förstemann, pp. 159–81; Haupt (5), pp. 117 sq., and (11).

On the flagellants of 1348–9 in Thuringia: *Chron. S. Petri vulgo Sampetrinum*, p. 180.

On Thuringia as the centre of the Frederick-cult: Grauert (1); Kampers (1), pp. 97–109.

143 For Frederick the Undaunted as an eschatological figure: Peter of Zittau, pp. 424 sq.; and cf. Grauert (2), pp. 703 sq.

144 On the recurrence of the plague: Haupt (5), p. 118, Note.

For the executions at Nordhausen: Körner (OS), col. 1113.

The Pope encourages the Inquisition: Gregory XI (1).

On the group at Erfurt: Trithemius (1), vol. II, p. 296.

145 On the flagellant movements in southern Europe from 1396 onwards: Förstemann, pp. 104 sq.

On the flagellants at Rome: Wadding, vol. X, pp. 33–4; and cf. Wadstein, p. 89.

Charlier de Gerson: Gerson (4), p. 658, and (5), pp. 660–64.

For the doctrines of the Thuringian flagellants in the fifteenth century: Stumpf, Documents 4, 5 (= Reifferscheid, Documents 5, 6); for emendations and additions to the second document, from another manuscript: Haupt (5). Also Förstemann, document in Appendix II, pp. 278–91.

146 The fifteenth-century Thuringian chronicler: Rothe, p. 426.

On the repression of 1414–16: Körner, p. 1206. Cf., on the preponderant part played by secular authorities in these persecutions: Flade, pp. 80–82.

On the flagellants at Nordhausen, 1446: Förstemann, loc. cit., and pp. 173 sq.

At Sonderhausen, 1454; Stumpf, document 5; Haupt (5).

147 For the last trials of flagellants: Förstemann, pp. 180 sq. In 1468 a monk of Erfurt wrote a tract against the flagellants: see John of Hagen (OS).

8 An Elite of Amoral Supermen (i)

The heresy of the Free Spirit

148 By far the most comprehensive account of the heresy of the Free Spirit is now that in Guarnieri (2); published in 1965, it replaces Mosheim (2) (1790) and Jundt (1875). For briefer accounts published in the last few years: Guarnieri (1); and, down to the fifteenth century only, Leff, vol. I, pp. 308–407. The account in Erbstösser and Werner ignores the established facts, in favour of an *a priori* pseudo-Marxist thesis.

The name 'Free Spirit' was taken from 2 Corinthians iii, 17: 'Where the Spirit of the Lord is, there is liberty.'

149 The existence of the heresy of the Free Spirit was queried for instance by the eminent ecclesiastical historian Karl Müller; cf. Müller (1), p. 612, and (2), *passim*. For an effective reply to Müller (2) see Niesel.

Schwester Katrei: All extant versions contain large interpolations of orthodox Catholic theology. A fair idea of the original can be gained by using together the two published versions; see Pfeiffer, Birlinger (both (OS), and cf. Simon (MW).

For the list of 'articles of faith': Preger (2) (OS).

For the *Mirouer des simples ames* see Porete, Marguerite (OS).

The accuracy of Catholic accounts of the Free Spirit is also borne out by the documents concerning a very similar, though much smaller, movement which existed in Italy during the fourteenth century. They are published in Oliger (MW).

150 On orthodox medieval mysticism: Leclercq, Vandenbroucke and Bouyer. On the relationship between orthodox and heretical mysticism, especially in Germany: Leff, vol. II, pp. 259–94.

151 In the first edition of this book I gave grounds for thinking that the Free Spirit was known in the West already in the twelfth century; but further weighing of the evidence leaves me doubtful.

On the Euchites: Runciman (1), esp. pp. 21–5, 28–9; Guarnieri (2), pp. 272–3.

On the Sufi: Guarnieri (1), pp. 367–70; Guarnieri (2) cols. 1249–50.

The Amaurians

152 For modern accounts of the Amaurian sect: Aegerter, pp. 59 sq.; Alphandéry (1); Delacroix, pp. 34–52; Gilson, pp. 382–4; Hahn, vol. III, pp. 176 sq.; Jundt, pp. 20 sq.; Preger (1), pp. 166 sq.; and works specified below.

The German chronicler: Caesarius of Heisterbach, vol. I, pp. 304–7. The list of individual sectarians given by Caesarius is confirmed by the decree of condemnation; see Synod of Paris, 1209.

153 For the story of Amaury: William the Breton, pp. 230–31. Cf. Hauréau, pp. 83 sq. On Amaury's eminent associates: *Chronicon universale anonymi*

Laudunensis; and Hostiensis (Henry of Susa, Henricus de Bartholomaels) as quoted in Capelle (MW), p. 94.

On Amaury's responsibility: *Chronica de Mailros*, p. 109.

For the tract *Contra Amaurianos*: Garnier of Rochefort (attrib.).

Robert of Courçon: in Denifle and Chatelain (OS), vol. I, p. 79.

Innocent III: in *Concilium Lateranense IV*, cap. ii, p. 986.

On Amaury's own doctrine see, in addition to Caesarius and Hostiensis: Martin of Troppau, pp. 393 sq. Martin, who was chaplain to five popes, died in 1278. His account was adopted in the fifteenth century by Gerson; see Gerson (8), p. 394, (10), p. 1242. Both Martin and Hostiensis may however simply have attributed to Amaury opinions which they found in Erigena. On Amaury and Erigena see Jourdain – whose argument however could not now be maintained in its entirety: the Amaurians were certainly disciples of Amaury, even if errant ones, and not of David of Dinant.

154 'Outwardly, in face and speech ...': John, Abbot of St Victor.

For the heresy at Troyes: Caesarius, p. 307; at Lyons: Stephen of Bourbon, p. 294.

For the proselytism of the Amaurians: Caesarius, p. 306; *Chronica de Mailros*, loc. cit.; *Haereses sectatorum Amalrici*.

On the doctrine of the Amaurians: Caesarius; Garnier of Rochefort; *Haereses sectatorum*; John, Abbot of St Victor; and the report on the interrogation of the arrested clerics (see Alverny (MW)), which confirms the accuracy of *Haereses sectatorum*. For modern reconstructions of the doctrine: Capelle; Grundmann (2), pp. 355 sq.; Pra.

'He dared to affirm that ...': *Haereses sectatorum*.

'each one of them was Christ ...': Caesarius, p. 305.

155 On the theory of successive incarnations: *Haereses sectatorum*; Garnier of Rochefort, p. 30.

The Holy Spirit speaks through the Amaurians: Caesarius, p. 305.

'Within five years ...': Garnier of Rochefort, p. 51.

On the messianic phantasies of the Amaurians: Caesarius, pp. 305–6.

156 For the sermon of the Abbot of St Victor: John, Abbot of St Victor.

'They committed rapes ...': William the Breton, vol. I, p. 232.

The sociology of the Free Spirit

157 The sociological significance of the cult of voluntary poverty has long been a subject of controversy. In interpreting voluntary poverty as specifically a movement of the oppressed, some Marxist scholars have certainly distorted the facts. Grundmann (2) deals effectively with such over-simplifications, see esp. pp. 28 sq., 157 sq., 188 sq., 351. Nevertheless the unavoidably poor, particularly urban artisans, played a larger part in the movement, both inside and outside the Church, than Professor Grundmann suggests.

158 For Willem Cornelis: Thomas of Chantimpré, p. 432.

For antinomianism and the cult of poverty at Antwerp *c.* 1250: document in Fredericq (OS), vol. I, pp. 119–20; and cf. McDonnell, pp. 489–90.

On the female mystic Hadewijch, who also flourished at Antwerp around 1230, and for the Italian Jacopone of Todi, see Guarnieri (1) pp. 362–3, and Guarnieri (2) cols. 1243, 1247.

159 On the derivation of 'beg' and 'beggar' see the Oxford English Dictionary.

On the dress and public behaviour of Beghards: *Annales Basileenses*, p. 197; John of Dürbheim (1), pp. 259–60; Pelayo, vol. II, lib. ii, article 51, para. K; Wasmod of Homburg; Wattenbach (1) (OS). Pelayo, articles 51 and 52, deals at length with the way of life of Beghards, including Brethren of the Free Spirit.

The growing uneasiness with which the clergy viewed Beghards is shown in the decrees of several synods; e.g. (all OS): Synod of Mainz, 1259, p. 997; Magdeburg, 1261, p. 777; Trier, 1277, p. 27 (the date 1227 is an error); Trier, 1310, p. 247; Mainz, 1310, p. 297.

On the way of life of the Brethren of the Free Spirit see, in addition to Pelayo: Schmidt (2) (OS), pp. 224–33; Wattenbach (1) and (2) (both OS).

On artisans as Brethren of the Free Spirit: Conrad of Megenberg; Pelayo (the most relevant passage is quoted in Mosheim (2), p. 290). Evidence for the participation of apostate clerics and of men and women of prosperous families is abundant; and the attempt by Erbströsser and Werner to represent the entire movement as plebeian is misguided.

160 On the position of middle-class widows and spinsters: Power, pp. 413, 433.

On the Amaurians 'in the houses of widows': *Chron. de Mailros*, p. 109, where they are called 'Papelardi'; and *Chron. regia Coloniensis, Continuatio II*, p. 15, where they are called 'Beggini'. On the significance of these appellations: Grundmann (2), pp. 373 sq.; and cf. ibid., pp. 366 sq. For the arrest of the female followers: William the Breton, p. 233.

On the Beguines: Neumann; McDonnell; and for a brief summary: Haupt (9).

161 Monks forbidden to have dealings with Beguines: Synod of Mainz, 1261, p. 1089.

The Franciscan of Tournai: Simon of Tournai, pp. 33 sq.

The East German Bishop: Bruno of Olmütz, p. 27.

On the attitude of the secular clergy: Grundmann (2), pp. 378–84. On the assimilation of Beguines by the Mendicant Orders: ibid., pp. 199–318.

162 The reception given by a Beguine community to an adept of the Free Spirit is described by Conrad of Megenberg.

'Unbelievably subtle words . . .': Nider, lib. III, cap. v, p. 45.

'A man who had great likeness . . .': Ulanowski (OS), p. 248.

9 An Elite of Amoral Supermen (ii)

The spread of the movement

163 For the spread of the Free Spirit along the Upper Rhine: Hartmann (OS), p. 235. Sources for the executions at Strasbourg: in Duplessis d'Argentré, vol. I, p. 316.

For Albertus Magnus: Nider, lib. III, cap. v, p. 45.

For the diocese of Trier: Synod of Trier, 1277, p. 27.

For Cologne: Henry of Virnenburg; Wadding, vol. VI, pp. 108–9; and cf. Mosheim (2), pp. 232–3.

On the two Beghards at Nördlingen: *Annales Basileenses*, p. 194; and cf. Grundmann (2), pp. 404 sq. For the heretical articles see Albertus Magnus (OS). The manuscripts of Albert's analysis known to Preger and Haupt are both only copies. Nider, writing about 1435, claims (loc. cit.) that he saw the original list in Albert's own notebook; but that is lost. Preger gives as well another list of 29 articles, from an independent source but dealing with the same outbreak of heresy in the Swabian Ries; see Preger (1) (OS). For reconstruction of the doctrine presented by these sources: Delacroix, pp. 60–68; Grundmann (2), pp. 401–31; Preger (1) (MW), pp. 207–12.

163–164 For Marguerite Porete: William of Nangis, *Continuatio II*, vol. I, pp. 379–80; *Grandes chroniques de France*, vol. V, p. 188; Jean des Preis, pp. 141–2. For the condemnation of her book: Langlois (OS). For the sentence passed upon her: Lea (OS). For the letter of Clement V: ibid., p. 578, Note. See also Guarnieri (1), pp. 388–9, 408–13, and on the fate of the book in England, p. 434.

164 On the Council of Vienne: Müller (Ewald), esp. Appendix B. For the Bulls see Clement V.
On ecclesiastical persecution of Beguines: McDonnell, pp. 505–74.
Pastoral letter of the Bishop of Strasbourg: John of Dürbheim (1).

165 On the episcopal inquisition: Lea (MW), p. 370.
Bishop of Strasbourg to Bishop of Worms: John of Dürbheim (2); and for his letter to the Pope: Baluze (1) (OS), vol. III, pp. 353–6.
For the heresiarch Walter: Trithemius (1), vol. II, p. 155; and cf. Mosheim (2), pp. 270 sq.
For the capture and execution of the secret group: John of Viktring, vol. II, pp. 129–30; John of Winterthur, p. 116; William of Egmont, pp. 643–4 (the last being a contemporary source).
For the House of Voluntary Poverty at Cologne: Wattenbach (1) (OS); and cf. *Gesta Baldevvini Treverensis archiepiscopi*, p. 144.
For the three Beghards at Constance: John of Winterthur, pp. 248–50; and cf. Mosheim (2), pp. 301–5.
Papal inquisitor appointed: see Innocent VI.
For the adept at Speyer: Nauclerus, pp. 898 sq.; Trithemius (1), pp. 231 sq. See also Haupt (1), p. 8.
For Cologne in 1357: Synod of Cologne, 1357, pp. 482–3.

166 For Nicholas of Basle: Nider, lib. III, cap. ii, p. 40; and the sentence passed on one of his followers, as given in Schmidt (1) (OS), pp. 66–9, and emended in Haupt (4), p. 509. The general argument of Schmidt's book on Nicholas has long since been refuted. For a modern account of Nicholas: Strauch.
For the execution at Mainz: Ritter (OS).
Sebastian Brant: *De singularitate quorundam fatuorum additio*, in Brant (OS), pp. 119–21.
The Free Spirit reaches Bohemia and Austria: John of Viktring, vol. II, p. 130.
The Free Spirit amongst Bavarian Beguines: Conrad of Megenberg.
In the diocese of Würzburg: Haupt (1), pp. 6 sq., quoting from *Monumenta Boica*, vol. XL, pp. 415–21.
For the synod of Regensburg, 1377: Haupt (2), p. 488, quoting from *Monumenta Boica*, vol. XV, p. 612.
For the trial at Eichstätt: ibid., pp. 490 sq.
For the community at Cham: *Errores bechardorum et begutarum*, and Haupt (7).
On measures against Beghards in Bavaria during the fifteenth century: Haupt (2); Lea (MW), pp. 412–13.
For the community at Schweidnitz: Ulanowski (OS).
Synod of Magdeburg, 1261, p. 777.

Matilda of Magdeburg, p. 260.

167 For the scribe at Erfurt: *Gesta archiepiscoporum Magdeburgensium Continuatio I*, p. 434.

For the three Beguines at Magdeburg: ibid., p. 435; and *Erphurdianus Antiquitatum Variloquus*, pp. 134–5.

On the appointment and powers of Kerlinger: Urban V (1); Charles IV (1) and (2). The date of the Bull is however 1368 and not, as given by Mosheim, 1367.

For the repression at Erfurt: Wattenbach (1) (OS); and Nordhausen: Körner, p. 1113.

Erfurt and Magdeburg clear: *Gesta archiepiscoporum Magdeburgensium Continuatio I*, p. 441.

On the Thuringian sect of *c.* 1550: Hochhut, pp. 182–96; Wappler, pp. 189–206.

The Pope's appeal: Gregory XI (2).

Executions at Lübeck and Wismar: Körner, pp. 1185–6.

168 On Groot's struggle against the heresy: Groot (OS), pp. 24–48; and cf. Preger (2) (MW), pp. 24–6.

For Bloemardinne: Bogaert (OS), p. 286. The literature on Bloemardinne is abundant, but adds nothing to the information supplied by Bogaert, who wrote after Ruusbroec's death. However, Bogaert claimed to have his information from a companion of Ruusbroec, John of Schoonhoven; and most historians accept his account as accurate.

Ruusbroec publicly ridiculed: Latomus (MW), p. 85.

Ruusbroec's attacks on the Brethren of the Free Spirit will be found in the works listed in the Bibliography, as follows: Ruusbroec (1), pp. 52–5, (2), pp. 228–37, (3), p. 105, (4), pp. 191–2, 209–11, (5), pp. 278–82, 297–8, (6), pp. 39–52. Ironically, twenty years after his death Ruusbroec himself was accused of heresy, by Gerson; see Combes, *passim*.

On the appointment of inquisitors in 1410: Latomus, p. 84.

For the *Homines intelligentiae*: *Errores sectae hominum intelligentiae*; and cf. Altmeyer, pp. 82–3.

169 For the Bull of 1365: Urban V (2).

On the Turlupins: Gaguin, lib. IX, p. 89; Baronius and Raynaldus, vol. XXVI, p. 240. See also Du Cange, under 'Turlupini'. On the probable origin of the name: Spitzer.

Gerson's comments will be found in the works listed in the Bibliography, as follows: Gerson (1), p. 19, (2), p. 55, (3), p. 114, (6), pp. 306–7, (7), p. 369, (9), p. 866, (11), p. 1435. One of the sources of his information was a book of 'almost incredible subtlety' which he attributed to one 'Mary of Valenciennes'. It is now clear that the book was the *Mirouer des simple ames* of Marguerite Porete; cf. Guarnieri (1), pp. 461–2.

It has commonly been held that certain sectarians who emigrated from France to Savoy in the 1370's, and others who were executed at Douai in 1420, were Brethren of the Free Spirit; but the original sources do not bear this out. For a detailed examination of the evidence in the Douai case: Beuzart.

On Pruystinck and his followers: Frederichs (OS); Luther (3). For modern accounts: Frederichs (1) and (2) (both MW); Rembert, pp. 165 sq.

170 For Calvin's first attacks on the Spiritual Libertines, in 1539 and 1544: Calvin (1), pp. 300–301, 350–51, and (2), pp. 53–4.

For the warnings to Margaret of Navarre: Bucer; Calvin (3).

171 On Quintin's end: Calvin (5), cols. 361–2.

The estimate of 10,000 is at col. 163 of Calvin (4), which is the most important of his treatises against the sect.

For the replies to the former Franciscan: Calvin (5); Farel.

For the modern accounts of the Spiritual Libertines: Jundt, pp. 122 sq.; Niesel; and more briefly: Lefranc, pp. 112–13; Saulnier, pp. 246–9. There seem no adequate grounds for believing that the various tracts which have sometimes been attributed to members of the sect really were by them. Some of these works have in fact been identified as simply French translations from the Low German of the Anabaptist David Joris; see Bainton, p. 35.

The way to self-deification

172 Grundmann (7) shows that the inquisitors made the Free Spirit look far more of a uniform 'sect' than it really was. Nevertheless a coherent tradition of speculation and practice did exist. It can be traced also in southern Europe. On the Free Spirit, or the Spirit of Freedom, in Italy: De Stefano, pp. 327–44; Oliger; Guarnieri (1), pp. 404–97. See also the suggestive comments in Burdach (1), p. 588. For Spain, see references in Guarnieri (1), pp. 483–4.

'God is all . . .': John of Dürbheim (1), p. 256.

'God is in every stone . . .': *Errores sectae hominum intelligentiae*, p. 287.

'Every created thing . . .': Albertus Magnus, articles 76, 77.

For the same ideas amongst the Spiritual Libertines of the sixteenth century: Calvin (4), cols. 178–9; Farel, p. 263.

On the doctrine of the final, all-embracing 'Blessedness': Ruusbroec (3), p. 105, (4), p. 191, (5), p. 278 (where the absorption of the Persons of the Trinity is specifically mentioned).

The soul as a drop of liquid: Ruusbroec (6), p. 41; cf. John of Dürbheim (1), pp. 257–8; Calvin (4), cols. 221, 224.

173 No afterlife: Ruusbroec (3), *loc. cit.*; John of Dürbheim (1), *loc. cit.*; and cf. Pfeiffer (OS), p. 453.

The meaning of hell: Caesarius of Heisterbach, p. 304.

'The soul is so vast . . .': Ulanowski (OS), p. 247.

On the divinity of the soul: Albertus Magnus, articles 7, 95, 96; Ruusbroec (6), p. 43.

'The divine essence . . .': Preger (2) (OS).

'Every rational creature . . .': ibid.

174 The adepts set themselves above the saints, etc.: Albertus Magnus, articles 22, 31, 39, 70, 74, 93; Preger (1) (OS), article 1; John of Dürbheim (1), pp. 256–7; Ritter (1) (OS), p. 156.

'They say they are God . . .': John of Dürbheim (1), p. 256; cf. Calvin (4), col. 158.

'It is the same with me . . .': Ruusbroec (6), pp. 44–5.

The Virgin and Christ fail to reach perfection: e.g. Wattenbach (2) (OS), pp. 540–41.

On the training undergone by novices see e.g. Ulanowski; *Schwester Katrei* (esp. Birlinger, pp. 20 sq.; Pfeiffer, pp. 456 sq.); Wattenbach (1), pp. 30 sq.; *Errores bechardorum*. Ecclesiastical critics of the movement were also struck by the severity of the training; e.g. Ruusbroec (1), (2), and (3).

'The Spirit of Freedom ...': Wattenbach (2), p. 540. This quotation is not *verbatim* but is made up of replies given to several questions put by the inquisitor.

175 'wholly liquefied in Eternity ...': ibid., (1), p. 533.
The inmate at Schweidnitz: Ulanowski, p. 241.
'The perfect man is God ...': Preger (2) (OS).
Schwester Katrei: Birlinger, pp. 23–4.
For the claims of the adepts at Schweidnitz: Ulanowski, pp. 249, 242; and of the Swabian adepts: Albertus Magnus, articles 19, 70; Preger (1) (OS), article 30.
'had no longer any need of God': Albertus Magnus, articles 11, 74.

176 Adepts believe they possess miraculous powers: e.g. Gilles the Cantor according to *Errores sectae*; the hermit in the *Buch von den zwei Mannen* (Schmidt (2) (OS)); Hermann Küchener in Haupt (1).
'They say that they created ...': John of Dürbheim (1), p. 256.
'When I dwelt ...': Ruusbroec (6), pp. 42–3.
'When God created ...': Ulanowski, p. 243.
'The perfect man ...': Preger (2) (OS).

The doctrine of mystical anarchism

177 On Boullan: Bruno de Jésus-Marie.
Suso (2), pp. 352–7.
'He who attributes ...': Garnier of Rochefort, p. 12.
'He who recognizes ...': ibid., p. 9.
'A man who has a conscience ...': Wattenbach (1), pp. 532–3.

178 'Nothing is sin ...': Albertus Magnus, article 61.
'One can be so united ...': Preger (1) (OS), article 4. Cf. Albertus Magnus, articles 21, 24, 94. For the same beliefs amongst the Spiritual Libertines: Calvin (1), cols. 350–51, (4), cols. 155, 183–5, 201, 204–9, (5), cols. 356, 361; Farel, pp. 4–5, 23–5, 27, 263, 277–8, 456–7; and amongst the Thuringian 'Blood-friends': Hochhut (MW), pp. 185–8.
'I belong to the Liberty ...': Wattenbach (1), p. 533.
'The free man ...': Wattenbach (2), p. 540, where the revelation to the inquisitor is also to be found.
'It would be better ...': ibid., p. 539.
The adept must restore his strength: Wattenbach (1), p. 532; Schmidt (2) (OS); Nider, lib. III, cap. v, p. 45; Albertus Magnus, articles 44, 52 (and in Haupt's emendations: article 25 A); Preger (1) (OS), article 27.
The spiritual value of feasting is emphasized by Bertold of Rohrbach, the adept who was burnt at Speyer in 1356; for sources see above, Note to p. 171.
For the comment on the golden goblet: Wattenbach (2), p. 539.
Fine dresses at Schweidnitz: Ulanowski, p. 252.
Sister Catherine (Schwester Katrei): Birlinger, p. 31.
'They have no uniform ...': Nider, lib. III, cap. v.

179 'When a man ...': Schmidt (2) (OS).
'All things that exist ...': Preger (OS).
Schwester Katrei: Pfeiffer, p. 458; Birlinger, p. 31.
Virginity regained: Wattenbach (2), p. 541.

180 On promiscuity without qualms of conscience: Calvin (4), cols. 184, 212–14; Hochhut, pp. 189–94; Preger (1) (OS), article 11; *Errores sectae*, p. 283. Henry of Virnenburg accused the heretics of holding that fornica-

tion was no sin. The Beguines at Schweidnitz and the Beghards with whom they associated maintained that to resist sexual advances was the sign of a 'crude spirit'.

'The delight of Paradise', 'the acclivity': *Errores sectae*, p. 282. Cf. Nider, lib. III, cap. v; Calvin, col. 184.

'Christerie': Hochhut, pp. 183–5; Wappler, pp. 189–92.

'till acted ...': see Appendix, p. 352.

For the inquisitor's comment on primal innocence: *Errores bechardorum*.

For Gerson's comments: Gerson (7), pp. 306–7.

The Garden of Eden: *Errores sectae*, p. 282.

For the adept at Eichstätt: Haupt (2), pp. 490 sq.

For the Spiritual Libertines on Adam and the Last Days: Pocque (OS). Antoine Pocque, or Pocquet, was one of the leaders of the sect. In this tract, which is preserved only in the long quotations given by Calvin, the millenarian and quasi-mystical aspects of the doctrine emerge very clearly. The antinomian consequences are not stated as explicitly as in some of the English sources given in the Appendix to the present study; but cf. Calvin (4), col. 200, on the meaning which the sect attached on the notion of Adam and the state of innocence. For a comprehensive survey of the evidence concerning the Adam cult: Guarnieri (1), pp. 428–32.

181 The oath of obedience figures in e.g. Schmidt (2), Ulanowski, Wattenbach (1) (all OS).
       For Gerson's comment: Gerson (3), p. 114.
       The confession of Martin of Mainz: Schmidt (1) (OS).

182 'took no account ...': Calvin (4), p. 158.
       Calvin on simulation: ibid., pp. 170–71; Farel, pp. 87–8.
       'They believe that all things ...': John of Dürbheim (1), p. 257.
       'The truly free man ...': Wattenbach (2), p. 539.

183 John of Brünn: Wattenbach (1), pp. 532–5.
       For Calvin's comments: Calvin (4), cols. 184, 214–20.
       'Give, give, give ...': see Appendix, p. 325.

184 'this soul has no will ...': Guarnieri (1), p. 531.
       'do nothing but what pleases them ...': ibid., p. 591.

185 'Such souls cannot see themselves ...': ibid., p. 527.
       'At the highest point ...': ibid., p. 594.
       'This soul feels no pain ...': ibid., p. 537.
       'The thoughts of such souls ...': ibid., p. 537.
       'Why should such souls ...': ibid., p. 538.

10 The Egalitarian State of Nature

In the thought of Antiquity

187 A fine collection of texts illustrating Greek and Roman notions of the State of Nature will be found in Lovejoy and Boas.
       Ovid, lib. I, lines 90–112, and esp. 135–6.

188 'The first inhabitants ...': Trogus, lib. XLIII, cap. i.
       'Now I hear poets ...': Lucian, Letter I.
       On the egalitarianism of the Greek Stoics: Bidez, esp. pp. 27–35.

189 Diodorus Siculus, Book II, cap. lv–lx (vol. I, pp. 167–72).
       For the treatise *On Justice*: Clement of Alexandria, vol. VIII, cols. 1104–13 (Book III, chap. ii). For modern summaries: Adler, pp. 78 sq.;

Walter (G.), pp. 231 sq. (which however contains some errors). The traditional view, shared by these writers, has been that the treatise was the work of one Epiphanes, supposed founder of a sect of 'Carpocratians'; but this would seem to have been conclusively disproved by Kraft.

190–1 'Those were happy times . . .': Seneca, Epistola XC.

191 The egalitarian order irrecoverably lost: It is true that the Stoics, with their cyclical view of cosmic history, expected the Golden Age to recur – but only in the next cycle or *annus magnus*, and after a conflagration which was to annihilate the whole existing universe, including all souls.

In patristic and medieval thought

192 On the contrast between the State of Nature and the conventional state: Carlyle, vol. I, pp. 132–46; vol. II, pp. 136 sq.; vol. V, pp. 441–2: Troeltsch, vol. I, pp. 152–4. The texts and commentaries in Boas illustrate the various ways in which the State of Nature was imagined by the Fathers and during the Middle Ages.

'Ambrosiaster', col. 439.

'This is the order of nature . . .': Augustine, vol. II, pp. 428–9 (lib. XIX, cap. xv).

193 'Although there now exist . . .': Beaumanoir, p. 235, para. 1453.

Cyprian, cols. 620–21 (para. 25).

'like the day . . .': Zeno, col. 287.

'Nature has poured forth . . .': Ambrose (2), col. 62.

'The Lord God specially wanted . . .': Ambrose (1), col. 1303. Cf. Lovejoy (MW). What practical consequences Ambrose drew from this doctrine is far from clear. If, as Professor Lovejoy points out, he recommended almsgiving on an immense scale as a way of reducing economic inequalities, he also maintained that poverty, hunger and pain are so many aids towards a blessed life. (Ambrose (1), Book II, Chap. V.)

Gratian's *Decretum, pars secunda, causa XII, quaestio i*, cap. ii (cols. 882–3).

194 'For the use . . .': *Recognitiones*, cols. 1422–3 (lib. X, cap. v).

Pseudo-Isidore: *Decretales Pseudo-Isidorianae*, p. 65 (cap. lxxxii).

Acts iv, 32, 34–5.

195 Gratian adopts the argument of the Fifth Epistle: *Decretum, pars prima, distinctio VIII, Gratianus*.

The communistic State of Nature becomes a commonplace: cf. Bezold (2), pp. 18 sq.; Carlyle, vol. II, pp. 41 sq.

195–6 'Once upon a time . . .': Jean de Meun, lines 8356–8452.

196 'And so, my friend . . .': ibid., lines 9493–8.

On the process of degeneration: ibid., lines 9561–98.

'a big villein . . .': ibid., lines 9609–61.

197 On the attitude of the sects to property: Troeltsch, vol. I, pp. 344–5.

11 The Egalitarian Millennium (i)

Marginalia to the English Peasants' Revolt

198 On the insurrections in Flanders and northern France, see pp. 104–5 and Note thereto.

For the English Peasants' Revolt the standard works are still Oman, Petit-Dutaillis (2) and above all Réville with Petit-Dutaillis (1). For a more recent account: Lindsay and Groves. Important articles: Kriehn, Wilkinson. See also the relevant chapters in Hugenholtz, Steel, Trevelyan; and Burdach (2), pp. 171–203.

For the story of John Ball: Froissart, vol. X, pp. 94–7; Walsingham, pp. 32–4; and cf. *Anonimalle Chronicle*, pp. 137–8.

199 'And if we are all . . .': Froissart, vol. X, pp. 95–7.
Walsingham, pp. 32–3. Cf. Gower's version, at p. 41 (lib. I, cap. ix).

200 'by the lawe of kynde . . .': *Dialogue of Dives and Pauper*, The seventh precepte, Chap. IV, cols. 3–4.
'In commune to all . . .': Master Wimbledon, quoted in Owst (MW), p. 305.
Wyclif, Book I, Divisions i and ii, and esp. chaps. 3, 5, 6, 9, 10, 14.
'Firstly, that all good things . . .': Wyclif, p. 96.
On the popularization of Wyclif's comments: Hugenholtz, p. 212; Trevelyan, p. 198; and cf. Jusserand, pp. 159 sq.

201 'Envy heard this . . .': Langland, vol. I, pp. 594–5 (B Text, Passus XX, lines 271 sq.; C Text, Passus XXIII, lines 273 sq.). Cf. vol. II, p. 283, Note 277.

201–2 Owst, pp. 287 sq. The translation and summary of Bromyard are at pp. 300 sq.

203 'He that soweth . . .': Matthew xiii, 37–43.
For the text of the rhymes: Knighton, Continuation, vol. II, pp. 139–40; Walsingham, pp. 33–4.
On the part played by the lower clergy see, e.g., Calendar of the Close Rolls, Richard II, vol. II, p. 17; and cf. Hugenholtz, pp. 252–3. On the other hand it would seem that, contrary to a commonly accepted view, the rising was fomented neither by the friars nor by Wyclif's Poor Preachers; cf. Steel, p. 66.

204 On Richard II as 'thaumaturgic king': Hugenholtz, esp. pp. 175–9.
Froissart on Ball's following in London: vol. X, p. 97; and cf. Knighton, Continuation, vol. II, p. 132. On the part played in the revolt by Londoners in general: Hugenholtz, p. 111; Wilkinson, esp. pp. 12–20; and by the London poor in particular: Lindsay and Groves, pp. 112–14, 135; Oman, pp. 17, 68; and cf. Workman, vol. II, pp. 234–5.
For the burning of the Savoy: Monk of Westminster, p. 2; Walsingham, vol. I, p. 457.
For the Smithfield demands: *Anonimalle Chronicle*, p. 147.
For Jack Straw's confession: Walsingham, pp. 9–10. The authenticity of the confession has often been called in question.

The Taborite apocalypse

205 Huss and the Hussite movement have long been favourite subjects for Czech and also for Austrian and German historians. For a full bibliography up to the mid-1950s: Heymann; and for a shorter list of the principal works to that date: Betts, Notes to pp. 490–91. The standard general history in English is now that by Heymann; while useful summaries will be found in Leff, vol. II, and, amongst older works, Lützow, and Krofta (1), (2) and (3). The Communist regime in Czechoslovakia has fostered studies in this field from a Marxist point of view; relevant works are: Graus, Maček. Important recent studies from a sociological (but not Marxist) point of view are Seibt (1) and (2). Concerning the Taborite wing of the movement, scholarship has taken a considerable step forward

with Kaminsky (1), (2) and (3), published between 1956 and 1962; these papers make admirable use of recent Czech research without falling into Marxist oversimplifications. In German, Bezold (1) and Palacký, especially parts 1, 2 of vol. III, though inevitably dated, are still valuable. Kautsky's well-known account, which used to be the standard Marxist version, is quite unreliable.

205–6 On the teachings of Hus, his forerunners and associates: De Vooght; Leff, vol. II, pp. 610–85; and Molnár (1) and (2).

207 On the deposition of John XXIII: Leff, vol. II, p. 650.

208 On the role ascribed to the guilds: Andrew of Bömischbrod, p. 339; *Litera de Civitate Pragensi*, pp. 312–13. Cf. Bezold (1), p. 36.
On social stratification in the towns: Heymann, pp. 46–8; Maček, pp. 28–9.
On the urban poor: Graus, pp. 33–70.
On over-population: ibid., pp. 112–18.

209 On the inflation: ibid., p. 84, and Appendix I, pp. 174–95.
On the condition of the peasantry: Bezold (1), pp. 55 sq.; but cf. Heymann, pp. 42–4, who holds that for a large part of the peasantry conditions were still good.
On the rural proletariat: Maček, pp. 32, 68 sq.

210 On the founding of Tabor: Kaminsky (1).
On millenial expectations in Bohemia in the fourteenth century: Burdach (2), pp. 116, 133.

211 The *Pikarti*: There has been much controversy concerning the identity and opinions of these immigrants. The conclusions of Bartoš are still convincing; see Bartoš (3). But see also Holinka, pp. 168 sq; Kaminsky (2), pp. 69–70, Notes 77–81; and Kaminsky (3), pp. 174, Notes 23 and 24.

212 For the apocalyptic prophecy: *Tractatus contra errores* (*Picardorum*), articles 33–7. (This and all subsequent references to the articles follow the numbering in Döllinger's edition.) See also below, Notes to pp. 213–14.
The most comprehensive source for apocalyptic and millenarian beliefs of the Taborites is a list of articles of faith compiled in 1420 from the Taborite literature and statements. The list exists in various Czech and Latin versions; for a discussion of their relationship, and of the authenticity of the list, see Kaminsky (2), pp. 67–8, Note 54. A Czech version is given in Maček (1), pp. 57–66. There is no doubt that the list, which contains both Waldensian and millenarian items, is a reliable guide. Many of the articles are paralleled in extant Taborite texts; and when the articles were submitted to the Taborite preachers on the occasion known as 'the disputation at Zmrzlik's house' in Prague, on 10 December 1420, they were accepted by them as substantially correct.
'There are five ...': quoted in Kaminsky (2) p. 48.
'Faithful ones ...': quoted in Kaminsky (2), p. 47.
No pity towards sinners: *Tractatus*, article 29.
'Accursed be the man ...': ibid., article 31.
'every priest ...': ibid., article 32.

213 For Chelšicky's comments: Kaminsky, (2), p. 51.
'The just ...': quoted in Kaminsky (2), p. 68, Note 57.
The neutral as the Satanic hosts: *Tractatus*, article 39.
The imitation of Christ in the hour of vengeance: ibid., article 30.
'the consummation of time ...': ibid., article 25.
Christ descends 'in glory and great power': Taborite letter, quoted in

Kaminsky (3), p. 178.
'shine like the sun . . .': ibid.
214 On the millennial realm: *Tractatus*, articles 42, 43, 44, 50, 51, 53; and
cf. Lawrence of Březová, pp. 400–401; *Staří letopisové čeští*, p. 478.

Anarcho-communism in Bohemia

214 Cosmas of Prague, pp. 8–9 (lib. I, cap. iii).
Czech Rhymed Chronicle: *Rýmovaná kronika česká, p.* 8.
215 *Majestas Carolini*, para. 2, p. 68.
Taxes shall cease: *Tractatus*, article 46; cf. Lawrence of Březová, p. 400.
'All shall live . . .': *Staří letopisové*, p. 478.
'The Lord shall reign . . .': *Tractatus*, article 47.
'All lords, nobles . . .': Jan Příbam, quoted in Palacký, vol. III, part 2,
p. 190.
Towns to be destroyed; Prague as Babylon: Lawrence of Březová, pp.
349, 399–400; *Tractatus*, articles 33, 34, 35. Cf. Bezold (1), p. 50.
215–16 Revelation xviii, 7–11.
216 'the army sent . . .': *Tractatus*, article 38.
'kings shall serve . . .': Lawrence of Březová, p. 406.
'the Sons of God shall tread . . .': ibid., p. 400.
For the transactions of the Taborite assembly of 1434: Charlier (OS),
pp. 529 sq.
On the founding of the Taborite communities: Maček, pp. 76–8;
Palacký, vol. III, part I, pp. 394, 417; part 2, p. 60.
217 'As Mine and Thine . . .': *Articuli et errores Taboritarum*, p. 220. Cf.
Invectiva contra Hussitas, p. 627; Pulkava of Radenin, Continuation, vol.
IV, p. 136; and the quotation from Windecke given in Bezold (1), p. 44,
Note 1.
Property to be taken from the enemies of God: Lawrence of Březová,
p. 400; *Tractatus*, article 40.
'many communities never think . . .': *Sollicitudo sacerdotum Thaboriensium*, pp. 486–7. Cf. Andrew of Böhmischbrod, p. 334; Lawrence of
Březová, pp. 391, 395; *Tractatus*, articles 39, 40, 41.
218 On the fate of the peasantry: Bezold (1), pp. 59–63; Kaminsky (2), p. 62
and p. 70, Note 88.
'Almost all the communities . . .': *Sollicitudo sacerdotum Thaboriensium*,
p. 484. Cf. *Invectiva contra Hussitas*, pp. 628–9.
219 On Hůska's eucharistic doctrine: Kaminsky (3), pp. 174–8.
On the *Pikarti*: Bartoš (1) and (2); Palacký, vol. III, part 2, pp. 228–9;
and for the political and military grounds for their persecution: Chalupný.
The most reliable source for the Bohemian Adamites is in Lawrence of
Březová, pp. 500–501 (in Czech, with German translation at pp. 501–505);
this includes the confession forwarded to the University of Prague. Other
sources are: Aeneas Silvius, cap. xli, *De Adamiticis haereticis* (p. 109); and
addenda to *Staří letopisové*, pp. 476–9 (in Czech). For modern accounts
in English: Heymann, pp. 261–3; in Czech: Bartoš (1), pp. 101–2, 103;
in German: Büttner and Werner, which replaces earlier German accounts
such as Dobrowský, pp. 318 sq. and Svátek, pp. 100 sq. The attempt of
the eighteenth-century historian Beausobre to discredit the whole story
of the Adamites is of historical interest only; he did not know the confession in Lawrence of Březová. Modern scholars as dissimilar as

Kaminsky and Werner are at one in accepting the contemporary accounts as substantially accurate.

220 The ruler Adam: cf. Burdach (3), pp. 158–61 on Adam as king of the world in its state of primal innocence.
Christ's remark about harlots and publicans: Matthew xxi, 31.

221 'And at midnight . . .': Matthew xxv, 6.
'The Bohemians now became . . .': *Klingenberger Chronik*, p. 198.

222 On Taborite propaganda abroad: Palacký, vol. III, part 2, pp. 498–9.
On expressions of anxiety in Germany: Haupt (6), pp. 274–8.

12 The Egalitarian Millennium (ii)

The Drummer of Niklashausen

223 On the Wirsberg brothers and their doctrine: *Annales Mellicenses, Continuatio Mellicensis*, p. 521; Glassberger, pp. 422–6 (which includes letters from the Papal Legate at Breslau with a list of heretical articles); Jobst of Einsiedeln; Ritter (2) (OS) (also a list of heretical articles). The present account is based on these sources, supplemented by Schiff (2), which in addition draws upon an unpublished manuscript at Munich and some material first published in 1882 by H. Gradl. For briefer accounts: Haupt (13); Preuss, pp. 46–7.

224 On the mercenaries: Schiff, p. 785.
'to rise in seditious rebellion . . .': Dorsten (OS), pp. 277–8 (article 10 *ad fin.*); and cf. Kestenberg-Gladstein, Note 190, p. 294.
'who used to be in Bohemia . . .': Jobst of Einsiedeln, p. 281.
On Erfurt and the professor (Dorsten): Kestenberg-Gladstein, pp. 257 sq.

225 On popular eschatology in Germany in the fifteenth century: Peuckert, esp. pp. 152 sq.; and more briefly: Rohr.
Bans on flagellants at Eichstätt: Haupt (2), p. 493.
Ban on Beghards at Würzburg: Lea (MW), pp. 412–13.

226 The remark about the team of horses is quoted in Franz, p. 81.
The present account of Hans Böhm and the happenings at Niklashausen is based in the main on four sources. The accounts of the chroniclers Fries, pp. 852–4; Stolle, pp. 380–83; Trithemius (1), vol. II, pp. 486–91; and the report submitted to the Bishop of Würzburg by an agent who had listened to Böhm's preaching (*Handell Hannssen Behem*: Barack (OS), Document 3). These sources are not mentioned again below except to identify a quotation or for some other special reason. Original sources which bring additional information are mostly to be found in Barack (OS), and are here indicated by the numeral which they bear in that collection. The one source in Reuss (OS) which is not to be found in Barack is a contemporary vernacular poem on the episode; it adds nothing of importance. For modern accounts: Barack (MW); Franz, pp. 78–92; Gothein, pp. 10–25; Peuckert, pp. 263–96; Schäffler; Thoma.

228 'What would the layman . . .': Trithemius, p. 488.
The Archbishop of Mainz: Document 7.
'Princes, ecclesiastical and secular . . .': Document 3.
'The Emperor is a scoundrel . . .': ibid.
The urban poor attracted: cf. Peuckert, pp. 268, 283.
On the 'original rights' claimed by the peasants: ibid., pp. 254–9.

229 'To God in Heaven . . .': Widman (OS), pp. 216 sq.

230 For Böhm as miracle-worker: Document 4.

The estimates of the numbers of pilgrims are taken from Trithemius, Fries and Stolle, respectively.

The Town Council of Nuremberg: Document 6; and cf. Documents 9, 10.

The diet decides on Böhm's arrest: ibid., Document 8.

For Böhm's call to arms: ibid., Document 19. This document, a letter from the Bishop of Würzburg to the Duke of Saxony, was written six weeks after the supposed event; and Franz, Gothein and Thoma are at one in distrusting it.

231 On the dispersal of the pilgrims: Document 11; Stolle.
For the misgivings at Würzburg: Document 15; Trithemius, p. 490.
The Bishop asks for support: Document 12.

232 Bans on further pilgrimages: Documents 14, 16, 17, 18.
Pilgrims continue to arrive: Documents 20, 21, 22, 23.
The church under an interdict: Document 25.
The church demolished: Document 27.
On the part played by the local lords: Barack, p. 42; Peuckert, p. 284.
Land forfeited: Document 26.
Böhm regarded as half-witted: Stolle, p. 380; as unable to form a sentence: Trithemius, p. 486; as ignorant of the Lord's Prayer: Document 15.
On the part played by the parish priest: Document 4.
On the hermit: Documents 4, 10.
The vision a trick: Document 4; Fries, p. 853.
The hermit prompts Böhm: Trimethius, p. 486.

233 The hermit a Beghard: Document 4; a native of Bohemia: Document 10; and cf. Barack (MW), pp. 37 sq.
Böhm found naked: Stolle, p. 381.

234 On the *Bundschuh* at Speyer, 1502. Franz, pp. 108–9
On the later *Bundschuh* risings: ibid., pp. 124–30; Haupt (8), p. 200, Note 3; Peuckert, p. 625; and cf. document in Schreiber, p. 93.
Jerusalem captured under the sign of the *Bundschuh*: Franz, p. 93.

Thomas Müntzer

234 Works on Thomas Müntzer are numerous. A good number of writers, following in the footsteps of Engels (*Der deutsche Bauernkrieg* (1850)) and of Kautsky, pp. 104 sq., have regarded Müntzer (whether approvingly or not) as primarily a social revolutionary. Some of the resulting works are mere *vies romancées*; among those which have some claim to scholarship one may instance Franz, pp. 408–46; Merx; Walter (L.-G.); and two recent studies from a Communist standpoint: Meusel, a popular work but with a useful appendix of documents edited by H. Kamnitzer; and Smirin, a massive treatise. In general the most original and serious contributions have been made by scholars who have seen in Müntzer primarily a theologian and mystic: in German, Boehmer, Holl, Lohmann; in English, Carew Hunt, Williams. Particularly relevant to the interpretation advanced in the present study are the recent researches of Hinrichs and some of the observations of Heyer. As for original sources, the volume edited by Brandt (see Brandt; and Müntzer (both OS)) includes, in modernized spelling, all Müntzer's pamphlets and a useful selection of extracts from other contemporary sources. Unless otherwise stated, the indications given below refer to this comprehensive and convenient edition; while *Briefwechsel* refers to the edition of Müntzer's correspond-

ence by Boehmer and Kirn (see Müntzer (OS)). A critical edition of the last three of Müntzer's pamphlets, in the original spelling, will be found in *Thomas Müntzers politische Schriften*, ed. Hinrichs. Concerning a further pamphlet, commonly attributed to Müntzer's disciple Hans Hut but which may be by Müntzer himself, see Rupp.

On Müntzer's early years see Boehmer (1) and (2), where various time-honoured legends were first demolished.

235 On Storch: Bachmann.

236 Müntzer's blood-thirstiness was noted by the Reformer Johannes Agricola early in 1521; see *Briefwechsel*, p. 21.

For Müntzer's ascetic and mystical doctrine see in particular Müntzer (1) and (2); and cf. Holl, Lohmann.

Müntzer on 'becoming God': Förstemann (C.E.) (OS), p. 241.

237 Natusius, pp. 147 sq., remarks that Müntzer may have owed something to the tradition represented by the flagellants in Thuringia.

On the social conflicts at Zwickau see the introduction to Brandt, p. 5.

On the rising at Zwickau: Bachmann, p. 13.

The Prague manifesto: Four versions, in German, Czech and Latin, are given in *Briefwechsel*, pp. 139–59.

'Harvest-time is here . . .': ibid., p. 150 (second German version).

238 'Let my sufferings . . .': *Briefwechsel*, p. 40.

The sermon: Müntzer (3). The traditional belief that it was preached before the Elector and Duke John is incorrect; it was preached before Duke John and his son. Cf. Hinrichs (MW), p. 5, Note 1.

The Devil's empire: Müntzer (3), p. 158.

239 'Drive Christ's enemies . . .': ibid., p. 160.

'The sword is necessary . . .': ibid., pp. 161–2.

Müntzer sees himself as the new Daniel: Hinrichs, pp. 59–64; Lohmann, pp. 62–3; and cf. Heyer, p. 94.

Müntzer's letter to his followers at Sangerhausen: *Briefwechsel*, pp. 61–3.

240 'If knaves and rogues . . .': *Briefwechsel*, p. 76.

Storch on community of goods: Brandt (2); and on the reliability of this account see Brandt's note, pp. 224–5.

On Hugwald: Schiff (1), pp. 82–5.

Karlstadt becomes a peasant: Peuckert, p. 250.

'that they should be brothers . . .': Confession of Klaus Rautenzweig, in Opel (OS), p. 211; and cf. Hinrichs, p. 22.

On Müntzer's 'communistic' idea of the Law of God: Hinrichs, pp. 174 sq.

Histori Thomä Müntzers: Brandt (1); and see Brand't note, p. 223. The account of Müntzer's teaching is at pp. 41–2.

241 Müntzer's confession: Brandt (5).

For the events immediately following Müntzer's sermon before Duke John: Hinrichs, pp. 65 sq.

Luther's letter: Luther (1).

The explicit unmasking . . .: Müntzer (4).

'for they have spent . . .': Müntzer (4), p. 178.

'The powerful, self-willed unbelievers . . .': ibid., pp. 170–71.

242 'certain (lords) are only now . . .': ibid., p. 171.

'Then must what is great . . .': ibid., p. 177.

The poor not yet fit: ibid., p. 178.

'If the holy church . . .': ibid., p. 178.

The most amply called-for defence . . .: Müntzer (5).

Müntzer's and Luther's eschatology contrasted: cf. Hinrichs, pp. 147 sq.

243 On Müntzer's view of Luther as an eschatological figure: ibid., pp. 170 sq.
Epistle of Jude, 14–19. The allusion is all the more obvious because where (in verse 19) the English has 'sensual', the German has '*fleischlich*'.
'the will of God . . .': Müntzer (5), p. 191.

243–4 'The wretched flatterer . . .': ibid., p. 192.

244 'Woe unto them . . .': Isaiah v, 8.
'They publish . . .': Müntzer (5), p. 192.
'You wily fox . . .': ibid., p. 201.
For the Elector's remark on the common man: Hinrichs, p. 8.
On the crucifix and the sword, and their meaning: Boehmer (1), p. 17.
On social conflicts at Mühlhausen: Franz, pp. 408 sq.

245 On Müntzer's wanderings in southern Germany: Schiff (1); Carew Hunt, vol. CXXVII, pp. 239–45.
For a fair sample of divergent views on the causes of the German Peasants' War see Franz, Peuckert, Smirin, Waas. The interpretation tentatively advanced here would not be accepted by Marxist historians; but even Professor Smirin (p. 271) grants the essential point, which is that Müntzer's ultimate aim would have been quite incomprehensible to the great mass of the peasantry.

246 For the peculiarities of the war in Thuringia: Franz, pp. 434 sq.
On the situation of the copper-miners: Andreas, pp. 309–10.
Müntzer's part in the Peasants' War: As examples of disagreement one may instance the accounts in Bemmann, Boehmer (2) and Jordan, which come near to denying Müntzer all influence; in Franz, where Müntzer is shown as the sole author of the war in Thuringia; and in the works of Marxists such as Smirin, where Müntzer is presented as the ideologist of a radical tendency which, though shared only by a minority, manifested itself with great vigour and far beyond the confines of Thuringia.

247 For the banner: Kamnitzer (OS), p. 308; and cf. Boehmer (1), p. 17.
For the 2,000 'strangers': report of Berlepsch, mayor of Langensalza, quoted in Carew Hunt, vol. CCXXVII, p. 248, Note 184.

247–8 'I tell you . . .': Brandt (3); and in the original spelling: *Briefwechsel*, pp. 109–11.

248 For the symbolic meaning of Nimrod see the passage from Sebastian Franck quoted in Chapter 13 of the present study, p. 258.
On Storch's new activities: Meyer (Christian) (2), pp. 120–22.
Against the thievish, murderous gangs . . .: Luther (2).

249 On the battle at Frankenhausen, its prologue and epilogue: Baerwald, Jordan, and more briefly, Carew Hunt, vol. CXXVII, pp. 253–63.
Gideon: Judges vii, 6 sq.
Müntzer orders the peasants to join: cf. Baerwald, p. 37.
'Say, you wretched . . .': Brandt (4), p. 78.

250 The *Histori*: Brandt (1), pp. 45, 48.
On the surrender and fate of Mühlhausen: Carew Hunt, vol. CXXVII, p. 262.
For Müntzer's execution: Brandt (1), p. 50.
For Storch's death: Meyer (Christian) (2), p. 122.

13 The Egalitarian Millennium (iii)

Anabaptism and social unrest

252 The connection between Anabaptism and the medieval sects is emphasized by e.g. Erkbam; and by Knox, pp. 122 sq.

Since the first edition of this book the study of Anabaptism has advanced greatly; though very little has had to be changed in this account of the revolutionary wing of the movement, and of the Münster Anabaptists. The comprehensive and exhaustive study by Williams (1962) replaces Smithson's history as the standard work (the much earlier accounts of Bax, Heath and Newman are of purely historiographical interest). The great *Mennonite Encyclopedia* in four volumes (completed in 1959) is a splendid work of reference; while Hillerbrand (1962) is an indispensable bibliographical guide. On the aspects of Anabaptism most relevant to the present study Heyer, and the introduction to Detmer and Krumbholtz, retain their relevance.

253 On the economic doctrines of the Anabaptists: Klassen.

254 On Hans Hut: Meyer (Christian) (1); Zschäbitz, pp. 30–64; and Stayer (1). On Hut and Müntzer: Rupp.

255 'Christ will give ...', 'The government does not ...': quoted in Stayer (1), pp. 184–5.

On Anabaptist activity at Esslingen and Nuremberg: Keller, p. 46.

On the contrast between the southern and northern forms of Anabaptism: Stupperich, p. 13.

For brief accounts of the constitutional history of the ecclesiastical states and particularly of Münster: Keller, pp. 56–76; Köhler, pp. 539 sq.

257 Münster from 1531 onwards: The principal original sources for the history of the New Jerusalem at Münster are Kerssenbroch (in Latin) and Gresbeck (in Low German). As a boy of fifteen Kerssenbroch witnessed the beginnings of the revolution. He also became a distinguished scholar; and when in the 1570s he came to write his history he made use of a great number of documents from the time of the revolution, many of which are no longer extant. Although a strong partisan of the Catholic cause, Kerssenbroch was on the whole conscientious in his handling of his materials. Gresbeck, a joiner by trade, was in Münster throughout the siege and writes as an eyewitness who lived amongst the common people. He too was a Catholic and hostile to Anabaptism; but when he writes of what he himself heard or saw he is convincing. Other valuable sources are the reports and confessions collected in Cornelius and in Niesert (both OS); Anabaptist pamphlets, particularly those by Rothmann; and some of the pamphlets written by outside observers. As for Dorp's contemporary *Historia*, everything valuable that it contains was taken over by Kerssenbroch. For detailed criticism of sources see Cornelius's edition of Gresbeck and Detmer's edition of Kerssenbroch (Detmer (1) (MW)); and for bibliography: Bahlmann. Extracts from the original sources, translated into modern German and arranged in a coherent sequence, are given in Löffler (OS). For modern accounts: Apart from general studies of Anabaptism such as those listed above, there exist a number of works devoted solely to Münster. For shorter and more recent accounts: Horsch (in English); Blanke (in German). For a brief survey of recent research and of remaining problems: Stupperich. Older accounts in English include Janssen (Johannes) (translated from German); Pearson.

For studies with special reference to the communistic regime: Ritschl; Schubert. Despite all the attention which the New Jerusalem at Münster has received, its significance has generally been underestimated. This is because it has been viewed in isolation or as a mere excrescence from Anabaptism, instead of as a particularly vigorous expression of the age-old tradition of revolutionary millenarianism.

On the period of Rothmann's ascendancy: Keller, pp. 74–133; and on Rothmann: Detmer (2), vol. II.

258 On Knipperdollinck: Cornelius (4).

On Hoffman: Kawerau.

'Shortly after that . . .': Franck, p. 6A. Cf. Schubert, esp. p. 48.

259 Rothmann preaches community of goods: Rothmann (1), pp. 70–71; Kerssenbroch, pp. 419–20. Cf. Detmer (2), vol. II, pp. 154 sq.; Schubert, pp. 3 sq. About the same time the Spiritual Libertines were also invoking Acts iv to justify community of goods: see Calvin (4), col. 216.

'And so they came . . .': Gresbeck, p. 6.

'fugitives, exiles, criminals. . .': Bishop of Münster to the Imperial Diet, quoted in Keller, p. 195, Note 1.

'people who had run . . .': Kerssenbroch, p. 334.

260 On Matthys, in addition to the historical works listed above: Cornelius (5) (MW).

261 Enoch and Elijah: Kerssenbroch, p. 477.

For special studies of Bockelson: Detmer (2), vol. I; and more briefly: Cornelius (3) (MW). Cf. Keller, pp. 207–8.

Münster as the New Jerusalem

For the performance on 8 February: Kerssenbroch, p. 484.

On the women Anabaptists: ibid., pp. 472, 481–2, 499–500.

On the armed rising and its outcome: ibid., p. 505.

262 For the manifestos: Niesert (3) (OS), pp. 157–9; and the leaflet reprinted in Harting (MW), p. 78.

On the mass immigration: Kerssenbroch, p. 509.

On the iconoclasm: ibid., p. 521.

Only the Father invoked: ibid., p. 500.

All non-Anabaptists to be expelled: ibid., pp. 532–3.

263 The refugees reduced to beggary: ibid., pp. 534 sq.; Gresbeck, pp. 19 sq.; and the Bishop of Münster to the regional diet, quoted in Keller, pp. 198–9.

On the new community of love: Cornelius (8) (OS), p. 456.

The Anabaptists claim to act in self-defence: ibid., p. 445.

264 For the organization of the defence: Kerssenbroch, pp. 553 sq.

Matthys inaugurates social revolution: ibid., pp. 557 sq.

On the protest and execution of the blacksmith: ibid., pp. 559 sq.

The terror is intensified: ibid., pp. 561–4.

Private ownership of money abolished: ibid., p. 561; Gresbeck, p. 32; Ramert (attrib.), p. 246. For the attribution to Ramert of *Die Ordnung der Wiedertäufer* see Ritschl (MW), p. 5.

265 On the requisitioning of food: Gresbeck, p. 34; of accommodation: ibid., p. 47; Kerssenbroch, pp. 541, 557.

On the nature and extent of 'communism' at Münster: Ritschl.

Rothmann says Mine and Thine will disappear: Gresbeck, p. 31.

'all things were to be . . .': Cornelius (6) (OS), p. 373.

266 'Amongst us God . . .': Rothmann (2), pp. 70–71.

'The poorest amongst us . . .': quoted in Detmer (2), vol. II, p. 132.
'We in these parts . . .': Cornelius (2) (OS).

267 On the intensified repression of Anabaptism: Kerssenbroch, pp. 533-4, 566.
The unlearned will redeem the world: e.g. Rothmann (2), p. 14.
Books destroyed: Kerssenbroch, pp. 523, 564.
On the end of Matthys: ibid., pp. 568-70.

268 Bockelson gulled by the deserter: ibid., pp. 762 sq.
For Bockelson's declaration of faith: Cornelius (7) (OS), p. 402.
For the numbers of inhabitants and of able-bodied men: Gresbeck, p. 107.
These estimates are confirmed, more or less, by other sources.
For the appointment of the Elders: Kerssenbroch, p. 576.
The new legal code is given in full in Kerssenbroch, pp. 577 sq.
On the direction of labour: Blanke, p. 22; Detmer (2), vol. II, pp. 137-8.

269 For Knipperdollinck's appointment: Kerssenbroch, p. 573, 583.
For the regulations governing sexual relations: ibid., p. 580; and cf.
Cornelius (8) (OS), pp. 457 sq.
On Bockelson's arguments for polygamy: Gresbeck, p. 59; Kerssenbroch,
p. 619. It is however merely Kerssenbroch's bias that makes him say that
Rothmann and other preachers were as eager as Bockelson to introduce
polygamy. Dorp's *Historia* and various confessions of captured Ana-
baptists agree that Bockelson had much difficulty in persuading the
preachers.
On the revolt and the executions: Cornelius (6) (OS), pp. 372-3;
Kerssenbroch, pp. 621 sq.

270 On the institution of polygamy at Münster: Gresbeck, pp. 59, 79;
Kerssenbroch, pp. 625 sq. Cf. Detmer (2) (MW), vol. III.
On the defecting mercenaries: Kerssenbroch, p. 616, and Note 2 thereto;
and for examples of the leaflets: ibid., pp. 586-8, 613-16.

271 For particulars concerning the defence: Gresbeck, pp. 36-8, 51, 80-81;
Kerssenbroch, pp. 582 sq., 592, 594, 671-2.

The messianic reign of John of Leyden

271 The present account of Dusentschur's action is based on Kerssenbroch,
pp. 633 sq. Bockelson, in his two confessions of July 1535, and January
1536 (Cornelius (6) and (7) (OS)), denied that there was any secret
understanding between Dusentschur and himself. But he certainly began
to exercise his kingly prerogatives with complete self-confidence and great
ruthlessness.

272 Bockelson's speech is given in Kerssenbroch, pp. 336-8; and cf. Niesert
(1) (OS), p. 34.
On the re-naming of the streets: Gresbeck, pp. 154 sq.; Kerssenbroch,
p. 774.
On the naming of the children: Gresbeck, pp. 156-7.
For the inscriptions on the coins: Kerssenbroch, pp. 666-7.
For the emblem: ibid., p. 652.
On the organization of the court: Gresbeck, pp. 83 sq.; Kerssenbroch,
650 sq.

273 On Bockelson's ceremonial appearances: Fabricius, p. 99; Gresbeck,
pp. 90 sq.; Kerssenbroch, pp. 662 sq.
On the confiscation of 'surplus' clothing: Gresbeck, p. 96; Kerssenbroch, p. 638; Ramert (attrib.), p. 242.

On the mistrust between the 'king' and his subjects: Detmer's Note 3 to pp. 771–2 of Kerssenbroch.

For Bockelson's self-justification and promises: Gresbeck, p. 88.

274 Rothmann's pamphlets: Rothmann (2) and (3). For a full analysis of their argument: Stayer (2). It was in answer to the *Restitution* that Urbanus Rhegius produced his two refutations, the one a popular pamphlet in the vernacular, the other a learned treatise in Latin; see Rhegius (1) and (2). On the relation between Rothmann's 'restitutionism' and other sixteenth-century versions of the idea: Williams, pp. 375–8, and the works listed there.

'The glory of all the Saints . . .': Rothmann (3), p. 69.

On the Kingdom of the Saints see Rothmann (2), cap. i, xiii, xiv, and (3) *passim*; and cf. Niesert (2).

275 On the performance in the cathedral-square: Gresbeck, pp. 103 sq. *Newe zeitung, von den Widerteuffern zu Münster*, p. 257.

On the executions in Münster: Kerssenbroch, pp. 824–5; Niesert (4), p. 502.

276 On the sending out of the 'apostles': Gresbeck, pp. 111–12; Kerssenbroch, pp. 703 sq.; and on their fate: ibid., pp. 709 sq.

On the attempt to raise mercenaries: report in Löffler (OS), pp. 194–5. The attempt was denied by Bockelson in both his confessions.

Mass risings planned: cf. Cornelius (2) (OS).

For the rising in Groningen and its fate: reports from the Bishop of Münster to the Imperial Diet and of the Imperial Stadtholder to the Bishop, both in Keller, pp. 326 sq.

277 On other risings: Kerssenbroch, pp. 792 sq.

'To kill all monks and priests . . .': quoted in Ritschl, p. 60.

The plans betrayed: Kerssenbroch, p. 724.

On the attitude of Anabaptists in the Netherlands: Cornelius (2); Mellink (1) and (2).

The famine begins: Gresbeck, pp. 140, 174–5.

278 Food reserved for the court: Cornelius (4) (OS), p. 343; Gresbeck, p. 141; Kerssenbroch, p. 804; and cf. Detmer's Note 1 to p. 805.

The extremes of famine: Gresbeck, p. 189; Kerssenbroch, p. 798.

For Bockelson's prophecies: Cornelius (6) (OS), p. 373; Kerssenbroch, pp. 793, 803; report in Löffler, p. 195.

On the public amusements: Gresbeck, pp. 131 sq., 150 sq., 168.

On the fate of the emigrants: Cornelius (3) and (4) (both OS); Gresbeck, p. 189; Kerssenbroch, pp. 805 sq.

279 On the last stages of the terror: Cornelius (3) and (4) (both OS); Kerssenbroch, pp. 772 sq., 784, 820.

On the fall of Münster: Cornelius (5) (OS); Gresbeck, pp. 194–5, 200–201, 205 sq.; Kerssenbroch, pp. 833 sq.

280 On the execution of Bockelson: Corvinus (OS), p. C ii.

On Willemsen: Bouterwek, pp. 34–5.

Appendix

The Free Spirit in Cromwell's England: the Ranters and their literature

287 Brief accounts of the Ranters have been given by e.g. R. M. Jones (MW), pp. 467–81; and by C. E. Whiting, *Studies in English Puritanism from*

the Restoration to the Revolution, 1660–88, London, 1931, pp. 272–7. Bibliographical particulars of the seventeenth-century works mentioned below and in the Appendix itself will be found in e.g. D. Wing, *Short-title catalogue of books printed in England ... 1641–1700*, 3 vols., New York, 1945–51.

On Winstanley's millenarianism see e.g. W. Schenk, *The concern for social justice in the Puritan revolution*. London, 1948, pp. 96–111.

288 'it is no new work ...': John Taylor, *Ranters of both Sexes ... taken and imprisoned ...*, 1651, p. 4.

'high attainers': Richard Baxter, *Plain Scripture Proof of Infants Church Membership*, third edition, 1653, p. 148.

'high professors': George Fox, *Journal*, vol. I, London, 1902, p. 198.

Officers and soldiers whipped: *The Arraignment and Tryall with a Declaration of the Ranters*, 1650, p. 6.

289 Quakers were almost identified with Ranters not only by the bellicose Ephraim Pagitt (*Heresiography*, fifth edition, 1654, p. 143), but even by, for instance, the tolerant Baxter (*Reliquiae Baxterianae*, 1696, p. 77).

'When I came into the jail ...': Fox, *Journal*, vol. I, pp. 47–8.

'were very rude ...': ibid., vol. I, p. 199.

For the meeting at Reading: ibid., vol. I, p. 231.

For the Ranters at Charing Cross: ibid., vol. I, p. 212.

'ran quite out ...': ibid., vol. II, p. 7.

'if God had not raised up ...': ibid., vol. I, p. 95.

294 Parliament gives signs of concern in 1648: *Journals of the House of Lords*, vol. X, p. 240.

295 Parliament appoints a committee, 14th June, 1650: *Journals of the House of Commons*, vol. VI, p. 423.

The committee reports back, 21st June: ibid., p. 427.

The Bill debated: ibid., pp. 430, 437, 440, 443–4, 453–4.

The committee revived: ibid., p. 493.

303 The passages quoted from *The Light and Dark sides of God* are to be found at pp. 1–4, 6, 9–11, 14, 18, 33, 35, 36, 38–9, 46–7, 49–50, 53.

306 The passages quoted from *Heights and Depths* are to be found in the Preface and at pp. 2, 6, 9, 10, 17, 23–6, 28, 30, 52.

309 Clarkson's career is described by himself in *The Lost sheep found*; for the earlier part of it see also Thomas Edwards, *Gangraena*, 1646 (second edition, enlarged), pp. 104–5. In *The Routing of the Ranters*, 1650, p. 2, Clarkson is mentioned along with Coppe as being a 'chief Ringleader of this viperous generation'. For a modern account see the article by C. W. Sutton on Claxton or Clarkson in the *Dictionary of National Biography*.

'There was few of the clergy ...': *The Lost sheep found*, p. 23.

The committee reports on *A Single Eye*: *Journals of the House of Commons*, vol. VI, p. 427; is ordered to report in more detail: ibid., p. 444; makes its final report, with the result that Clarkson is sentenced: ibid., pp. 474–5.

The passages quoted from *The Lost sheep found* are at pp. 24–8.

For Clarkson's arrest and examination: ibid., pp. 29–31.

316 The account of Coppe's guilt-obsessed adolescence is taken from *Copp's Return to the wayes of Truth*, First Error. On Coppe's later career see Baxter, *Plain Scripture Proof*, pp. 147–8; Anthony à Wood, *Athenae Oxonienses*, second edition, vol. II, London, 1721, pp 500–502. For a modern account see the article by Alexander Gordon on Coppe in the *Dictionary of National Biography*.

God 'is in Heaven, Earth ...': *Copp's Return*, Fourth Error.

317 Coppe at Charing Cross: Fox, *Journal*, vol. I, p. 212.

For Coppe's swearing in church and tavern: *The Ranters Ranting*, 1650, pp. 5–6.

Parliament orders the *Rolls* to be seized: *Journals of the House of Commons*, vol. VI, p. 354.

On Coppe's behaviour during interrogation: *The Routing of the Ranters*, p. 2.

Bibliography

Abbreviations

Fuller descriptions of the works of reference and collections of sources listed below will be found in the body of the Bibliography.

ABAW	*Abhandlungen der königlich bayerischen Akademie der Wissenschaften (Historische Classe).* Munich
ADB	*Allgemeine Deutsche Biographie*
BHPF	*Bulletin de la société de l'histoire du protestantisme français.* Paris
CCF	*Corpus chronicorum Flandriae*
CDS	*Chroniken der deutschen Städte*
CEH	*Cambridge Economic History*
CMH	*Cambridge Medieval History*
ERE	*Encyclopaedia of Religion and Ethics*
FRA	*Fontes rerum Austriacarum*
FRG	*Fontes rerum Germanicarum*
GBM	*Geschichtsquellen des Bistums Münster*
MGHS	*Monumenta Germaniae Historica, Scriptores*
PG	*Patrologiae cursus completus, series Graeca*
PL	*Patrologiae cursus completus, series Latina*
RHC	*Recueil des Historiens des Croisades. (Historiens Occidentaux)*
RHF	*Recueil des Historiens des Gaules et de la France*
RPT	*Realencyclopädie für protestantische Theologie und Kirche*
RS	*Rolls Series*
SGUS	*Scriptores rerum Germanicarum in usum scholarum.* (See under *Monumenta Germaniae Historica* in Bibliography)
SPAW	*Sitzungsberichte der königlichen preussischen Akademie der Wissenschaften.* Berlin
ZKG	*Zeitschrift für Kirchengeschichte.* Gotha

1 Original Sources and Collections of Sources

ADSO OF MONTIER-EN-DER. *Epistola ad Gerbergam reginam de ortu et tempore Antichristi,* in Sackur, pp. 104–13 (also in PL, vol. CI).

AENEAS SILVIUS (Enea Silvio de' Piccolomini; Pope Pius II). *De ortu et historia Bohemorum,* in *Omnia opera,* Basle, 1551.

AIMO OF SAINT-PIERRE-SUR-DIVES. *Epistola ad fratres Totesberiae,* in PL, vol. CLXXXI, cols. 1707–8.

ALBERIC OF TROIS-FONTAINES. *Chronicon,* in RHF, vol. XVIII.

ALBERT OF AIX. *Liber Christianae expeditionis pro ereptione, emundatione et restitutione Sanctae Hierosolymitanae Ecclesiae,* in RHC, vol. IV.

ALBERT OF STADE. *Annales Stadenses,* in MGHS, vol. XVI.

ALBERTUS MAGNUS. *Compilatio de novo spiritu,* in Preger (1) (MW), vol. I, pp. 461–9. For emendations: Haupt (3).

Aliscans, ed. Wienbech et al., Halle, 1903.

ALVARUS OF CORDOVA. *Indicolus luminosus,* in PL, vol. CXXI.

AMBROSE, ST (1). *In Psalmum CXVIII expositio,* in PL, vol. XV.

AMBROSE, ST (2). *De officiis ministrorum,* in PL, vol. XVI.

'AMBROSIASTER'. *Commentaria in Epistolam ad Colossenses,* in PL, vol XVI.

ANDREW OF BÖHMISCHBROD (Andreas de Broda). *Tractatus de origine Hussitarum,* in Höfler, vol. VI of FRA, pp. 327–53.

ANDREW OF REGENSBURG (Andreas Ratisbonensis). *Chronicon,* in Eckhart, vol. I.

Annales Agrippenses, in MGHS, vol. XVI.

Annales Altahenses maiores, in MGHS, vol. XX.

Annales Austriacorum, continuations of, in MGHS, vol. IX:
    Continuatio Praedicatorum Vindobonensium
    Continuatio Claustroneoburgensis V
    Continuatio Florianensis

Annales Basileenses, in MGHS, vol. XVII.

Annales Blandinienses, in MGHS, vol. V.

Annales breves Solmenses, in FRG, vol. IV.

Annales Cameracenses, in MGHS, vol. XVI.

Annales capituli Cracoviensis, in MGHS, vol. XIX.

Annales Casineses, in MGHS, vol. XIX.

Annales Colbazenses, in MGHS, vol. XIX.

Annales Colmarienses maiores, in MGHS, vol. XVII.

Annales Frankofurtani, in FRG, vol. IV.

Annales Gandenses, in MGHS, vol. XVI.

Annales Herbipolenses, in MGHS, vol. XVI.

Annales Lubicenses, in MGHS, vol. XVI.

Annales Mellicenses, continuations of, in MGHS, vol. IX:
    Continuatio Mellicensis
    Continuatio Zwetlensis III
    Continuatio Sancrucensis II

Annales Monasterii de Burton, in RS 36 (*Annales Monastici*), vol. I, 1864.

Annales Monasterii de Oseneia, in RS 36 (*Annales Monastici*), vol. IV, 1869.

Annales Monasterii de Waverleia, in RS 36 (*Annales Monastici*), vol. II, 1865.

Annales Parchenses, in MGHS, vol. XVI.

Annales Rodenses, in MGHS, vol. XVI.

Annales S. Blasii Brunsvicenses, in MGHS, vol. XXIV.

Annales S. Jacobi Leodiensis minores, in MGHS, vol. XVI.

Annales S. Justinae Patavini, in MGHS, vol. XIX.

Annales Tielenses, in MGHS, vol. XXIV.

Annales Veterocellenses, in MGHS, vol. XVI.

ANNALISTA SAXO, in MGHS, vol. VI.

Anonimalle Chronicle, ed. Galbraith, Manchester, 1927.

Anonymi Gesta Francorum et aliorum Hierosolimitorum (ed. Bréhier as *Histoire anonyme de la première Croisade,* in: *Les classiques de l'histoire de France au Moyen Âge,* vol. IV), Paris, 1924.

ANONYMOUS OF MAINZ-DARMSTADT. *Memorial,* in Neubauer and Stern, vol. II.

Archiv český čili staré písemné památky české i moravské (The Bohemian archives, or old Bohemian and Moravian chronicles), ed. Palacký. 6 vols., Prague, 1840–72.

ARNOLD, Dominican. *De correctione Ecclesiae Epistola*, ed. Winkelmann, Berlin, 1865.

Articuli et errores Taboritarum, in *Archiv český* (OS), vol. III, pp. 218–25.

AUGUSTINE, ST. *De Civitate Dei contra paganos*, ed. Welldon. 2 vols., London, 1924.

BALDWIN OF AVESNES (attrib.). *Chronique attribuée à Baudoin d' Avesnes*, in RHF, vol. XXI.

BALDWIN OF NINOVE. Chronicon, in MGHS, vol. XXV.

BALUZE, E. (1). *Vitae paparum Avinoniensium*, ed. Mollat. 4 vols., Paris, 1914–27.

BALUZE, E. (2). *Miscellanea*. 4 vols., Paris, 1678–83.

BARACK, K. A. (ed.). Documents concerning Hans Böhm, 'the Drummer of Niklashausen'. See Barack (MW), pp. 50–108.
Document 3 (pp. 53–4) is *Handell Hannssen Behem zu Niclaeshussenn*.

BARONIUS, C. and RAYNALDUS, O. *Annales ecclesiastici una cum critica historico-chronologica*, Lucca, 1738–59.

Baruch-Apocalypse (= II Baruch or *The Syriac Apocalypse of Baruch*), ed. and trans. Charles, in Charles, vol. II.

BASZKO OF POZNAN. *Chronicon Poloniae*, in *Silesiacarum rerum scriptores*, vol. II, Breslau, 1730.

BAUDRI OF DOL. *Hierosolymitanae Historiae libri quatuor*, in PL, vol. CLXVI.

BEAUMANOIR, PHILIPPE DE RÉMI, Sire de. *Les Coutumes du Beauvoisis*, ed. Salmon, 2 vols., Paris, 1899.

BENEDICT OF MOUNT SORACTE. *Chronicon*, in PL, vol. CXXXIX.

BENEDICT, ST, OF NURSIA. *The Rule of Saint Benedict in Latin and English*, Ed. and trans. Abbot Justin McCann, London, 1952.

BENESSIUS KRABICE OF WEITMÜHL. *Chronicon*, in *Fontes rerum Bohemicarum*, vol. IV.

BENZO OF ALBA. *Ad Heinricum IV Imperatorem libri VII*, in MGHS, vol. XI.

BERNARD, ST. *Omnia opera*, ed. Picard, Paris, 1609. Includes, *inter alia:*
(1) *In Cantica Canticorum*, Sermo LXV, cols. 759–62.
(2) *Epistola ad Gaufridum Carnotensem episcopum*, col. 1441.
(3) *Epistola ad episcopum, clerum et populum Spirensem*, cols. 1637–9.
(4) *Epistola ad Henricum Moguntinum archiepiscopum*, cols. 1639–40.

BERNOLD OF CONSTANCE. *Chronicon*, in MGHS, vol. V.

BIRLINGER, A. (ed.). *Ein wunder nützes disputieren von einem ersamen bihter und siner bihtohter*, in *Alemannia*, vol. III, Bonn, 1875, pp. 15–45.

BOENDAELE, JAN (Jan de Klerk). *Brabantsche Yeesten*, ed. Willems, 3 vols., Brussels, 1839–69.

BOGAERT, HENDRIK vanden (Pomerius). *De origine monasterii Viridisvallis una cum vita B. Joann. Rusbrockii*, ed. de Smet, in *Analecta Bollandiana*, vol. IV, Paris and Brussels, 1885.

BRANDT, O. H. *Thomas Müntzer. Sein Leben und seine Schriften*. Jena, 1933. Includes, *inter alia* and in addition to Müntzer's pamphlets (for which see Müntzer), the following in modernized spelling:
(1) *Die Historie Thomä Müntzers*, pp. 38–50.
(2) Extract from Marcus Wagner's booklet on Storch, Erfurt, 1597, pp. 53–9.
(3) Müntzer's call to the people of Allstedt of April 1525, pp. 74–6.
(4) Müntzer's letter to the Count of Mansfeld of May 1525, pp. 77–8.
(5) Müntzer's confession, pp. 80–83.

BRANT, SEBASTIAN. *Das Narrenschiff*, ed. Zarncke, Leipzig, 1854.

Breve chronicon Flandriae, in CCF, vol. III.

BRUNO OF OLMÜTZ. *Relatio*, ed. Höfler, in ABAW, vol. IV, 1846, pp. 27 sq

BUCER, MARTIN. Letter to Margaret of Navarre, in Calvin, *Omnia opera*, vol. X b, col. 215.

CAESARIUS OF HEISTERBACH. *Dialogus miraculorum*, ed. Strange, vol. I, Cologne, 1851.

Calendar of the Close Rolls preserved in the Public Record Office. London, 1892 ff.

CALVIN, JEAN. *Omnia opera*, ed. Baum *et al.*, Brunswick, 1864–1900.

    (1) vol. I. *Institutio religionis Christianae*.

    (2) vol. VII. *Brieve Instruction pour armer tous bons fideles contre les erreurs de la secte des Anabaptistes*.

    (3) vol. XII. Letter to Margaret of Navarre, cols. 64–8.

    (4) vol. XXXV. *Contre la secte phantastique et furieuse des Libertins qui se nomment spirituelz*.

    (5) vol. XXXV. *Epistre contre un certain Cordelier suppost de la secte des Libertins*.

CAMENTZ, CASPAR. *Acta aliquot Francofurtana*, in FRG, vol. IV.

Chanson d'Antioche, ed. P. Paris, 2 vols., Paris, 1848.

Chanson de Roland, ed. Bédier, Paris, 1937.

CHAPTER OF UTRECHT. *Epistola ad Fridericum archiepiscopum Coloniensem de Tanchelmo seductore*, in Duplessis d'Argentré, vol. I, pp. 11–12.

CHARLES IV, Emperor (1). Decree appointing Kerlinger inquisitor, in Mosheim (2) (MW), pp. 343–62.

CHARLES IV, Emperor (2). Letter to Kerlinger, in Mosheim (2) (MW), pp. 368–75.

CHARLES, R. H. (ed.). *The Apocrypha and Pseudepigrapha of the OldTestament*, 2 vols., Oxford, 1913.

CHARLIER, GILLES (Aegidius Carlerus). *Liber de legationibus concilii Basiliensis pro reductione Bohemorum*, in *Monumenta Conciliorum generalium secul' XV. Scriptorum*, vol. I, Vienna, 1857.

Chronica de Mailros, ed. Stevenson (Bannatyne Club), Edinburgh, 1835.

Chronica minor auctore minorita Erphordiensi, in MGHS, vol. XXIV.

Chronica regia Coloniensis, in MGHS, vol. XVII.

Chronica regia Coloniensis, Continuatio II, in MGHS, vol. XXIV.

Chronica universalis Mettensis, in MGHS, vol. XXIV.

Chronicon Andrensis monasterii, in RHF, vol. XVIII.

Chronicon anonymi Laudunensis canonici, in RHF, vol. XVIII.

Chronicon Britannicum in collectione MS Ecclesiae Nannetensis, in RHF, vol. XII.

Chronicon comitum Flandrensium, in CCF, vol. I.

Chronicon Elwacense, in MGHS, vol. X.

Chronicon Normanniae, in RHF, vol. XXIII.

Chronicon rhythmicum Austriacarum, in MGHS, vol. XXV.

Chronicon Rotomagense, in RHF, vol. XXIII.

Chronicon S. Andreae Castri Camaracesii, in MGHS, vol. VII.

Chronicon S. Catharinae de Monte Rotomagi, in RHF, vol. XXIII.

Chronicon S. Laudi Rotomagensis, in RHF, vol. XXIII.

Chronicon S. Martini Turonensis, Continuatio, in MGHS, vol. XXVI.

Chronicon S. Medardi Suessionensis, in RHF, vol. XVIII.

Chronicon S. Petri vulgo Sampetrinum Erfurtense, in *Geschichtsquellen de Provinz Sachsen*, vol. I, Halle, 1870.

Chronicon Turonense, in RHF, vol. XVIII.

Chronicon universale anonymi Laudunensis, in MGHS, vol. XXVI.

Chroniken der deutschen Städte vom 14 bis ins 16 Jahrhundert, Leipzig, 1867–1917. (Pub. *Königlich bayerische Akademie der Wissenschaften*.)

Chronique anonyme des Rois de France, in RHF, vol. XXI.

Chroniques de Saint-Denis, in RHF, vol. XXI.

CLEMENT V, Pope (1). Bull *Ad nostrum* (*Constitutiones Clementis* ("Clementines"), lib. V, tit. III, cap. iii), in *Corpus juris canonici*, vol. II, cols. 1183–4.

CLEMENT V, Pope (2). Bull *De quibusdam* (*Constitutiones*, lib. III, tit. XI, cap. i), in *Corpus juris canonici*, vol. II, col. 1169.

CLEMENT VI, Pope. Bull against Flagellants, in Baronius and Raynaldus, vol. XXV, pp. 493 sq.

CLEMENT OF ALEXANDRIA. *Stromata*, in PG, vols. VIII, IX.

CLOSENER, FRITSCHE. *Strassburgische Chronik*, in CDS, vol. VIII.

COMMODIANUS (1). *Instructiones*, ed. Dombart, in *Corpus Scriptorum Ecclasiasticorum Latinorum*, vol. XV, Vienna, 1887.

COMMODIANUS (2). *Carmen apologeticum* (as for Commodianus (1)).

Concilium Lateranense IV, in Mansi, vol. XXII.

Conquête de Jerusalem, ed. Hippeau, Paris, 1868.

CONRAD OF MEGENBERG (Conradus de Monte Puellarum). *De erroribus Begehardorum et Beginarum* (fragment), in *Bibliotheca veterum patrum*, ed. Despont, vol. XXV, Lyons, 1677, p. 310.

CORNELIUS, C. A. (ed.). *Berichte der Augenzeugen über das münsterische Wiedertäuferreich*, in GBM, vol. II, Münster, 1852. Includes, *inter alia:*
 (1) Gresbeck (q.v.).
 (2) Erasmus Schetus, Letter to Erasmus of Rotterdam, p. 315.
 (3) Letter of Justinian of Holtzhausen of 21 May 1535, pp. 334–7.
 (4) Letter of Justinian of Holtzhausen of 29 May 1535, pp. 341–7.
 (5) Letter of Sigmund of Buineburg, pp. 367–9.
 (6) Confession of Jan Bockelson of July 1535, pp. 369–76.
 (7) Confession of Jan Bockelson of January 1536, pp. 398–402.
 (8) *Bekenntnis des Glaubens und Leben der Gemeinde Christi zu Münster*, pp. 445–64.

Corpus chronicorum Flandriae, ed. de Smet, 4 vols., Brussels, 1837–65.

Corpus juris canonici, ed. Friedberg, 2 vols., Leipzig, 1879, 1881.

CORVINUS, ANTON. *De miserabili Monasteriensium anabaptistarum obsidione ... epistola ad Spalatinum*, Wittenberg, 1536.

COSMAS OF PRAGUE. *Chronica Boemorum*, in MGHS, new series, vol. II.

CYPRIAN, ST. *Liber de opere et eleemosynis*, in PL, vol. IV.

DAMIAN, PETER (1). *Epistola ad Petrum Cerebrosum monachum*, in PL, vol. CXLIV.

DAMIAN, PETER (2). *Vita S. Romualdi*, in PL, vol. CXLIV.

Decretales Pseudo-Isidorianae, ed. Hinschius, Leipzig, 1858.

DENIFLE, H. S. and CHATELAIN, E. *Chartularium Universitatis Parisiensis*, vol. I, Paris, 1889.

Descripto qualiter Karolus Magnus clavum et coronam Domini a Constantinopoli Aquisgrani detulerit ..., in Rauschen (MW), pp. 103–25.

Detmar-Chronik, ed. Koppmann, in CDS, vol. XIX.

Deutsche Chroniken (Scriptores qui vernacula lingua usi sunt). (Part of *Monumenta Germaniae Historica*.)

Dialogue of Dives and Pauper, ed. Pynson, 1493.

DIODORUS SICULUS. *Bibliothecae Historicae libri qui supersunt*, 2 vols., Amsterdam, 1746.

DÖLLINGER, I von. *Beiträge zur Sektengeschichte*, vol. II, Munich, 1890.

DORP, HEINRICH. *Warhafftige Historia wie das Evangelium zu Münster angefangen, und darnach durch die Wiedertäufer verstört, wider auffgehört*, ed. Merschmann, Magdeburg, 1847.

DORSTEN, JOHANNES. *Quaestio de tertio statu*, in Kestenberg-Gladstein (MW), pp. 266–95.

DU FAYT, JEAN. *Contra Flagellatores*, in Fredericq (2) (MW).

DUPLESSIS D'ARGENTRÉ, C. de. *Collectio judiciorum de novis erroribus*, 3 vols., Paris, 1755.

ECKBERT OF SCHÖNAU. *Sermones contra Catharos*, in PL, vol. CXCV.

ECKHART, J. G. *Corpus historicum medii aevi*, 2 vols., Leipzig, 1723.

ÉGASSE DU BOULAY, C. *Historia universitatis Parisiensis*, 6 vols., Paris, 1665–73.

EKKEHARD OF AURA (1). *Hierosolymita*, ed. Hagenmeyer, Tübingen, 1877.

EKKEHARD OF AURA (2). *Chronicon universale*, in MGHS, vol. VI.

ELIEZER BAR NATHAN. *Relation*, in Neubauer and Stern, vol. II.

ELLENHARD OF STRASBOURG (1). *Bellum Waltherianum*, in MGHS, vol. XVII.

ELLENHARD OF STRASBOURG (2). *Chronicon*, in MGHS, vol. XVII.

ENNEN, L. and ECKERTZ, G. *Quellen zur Geschichte der Stadt der Köln*, 6 vols., Cologne, 1860–79

EPHRAIM BAR JACOB. *Relation*, in Neubauer and Stern, vol. II.

Erphurdianus Antiquitatum Variloquus, ed. Thiele (*Geschichtsquellen der Provinz Sachsen*, vol. XLII), Halle, 1906.

Errores bechardorum et begutarum, in Haupt (7) (MW), pp. 88–90.

Errores sectae hominum intelligentiae, in Baluze (2), vol. II, pp. 277–97.

ESPINAS, G. and PIRENNE, H. *Recueil de documents relatifs à l'histoire de l'industrie drapière en Flandre*, Part I, vol. III, Brussels, 1920.

EULOGIUS, Archbishop of Toledo. *Memorialis sanctorum*, in PL, vol. CXV.

Ezra-Apocalypse (= 4 Ezra or 2 Esdras), ed. and trans. Box in Charles, vol. II.

FABRICIUS, DIETRICH. Report on mission to Münster, in *Mitteilungen aus dem Germanischen Nationalmuseum*, vol. II, Nuremberg, 1885, pp. 99–102.

FAREL, GUILLAUME. *Le Glaive de la Parolle veritable*, Geneva, 1550.

Flores temporum, Imperatores, in MGHS, vol. XXIV.

Fontes rerum Austriacarum (Österreichische Geschichtsquellen), Section I. *Scriptores*, Vienna, 1849 ff.

Fontes rerum Bohemicarum, ed. Emler, Prague, 1873 ff.

Fontes rerum Germanicarum, ed. Boehmer, 4 vols., Stuttgart, 1843–68.

FÖRSTEMANN, C. E. (ed.). *Neues Urkundenbuch zur Geschichte der evangelischen Kirchenreformation*, Hamburg, 1842.

FRANCIS OF PRAGUE. *Secundus tractatus chronicae Pragensis*, in FRA, Section 1, vol. VIII.

FRANCK, SEBASTIAN. *Chronica, Zeÿtbüch und Geschÿchtbibel*, Strasbourg, 1531.

FREDERICHS J. (ed.). *Summa doctrinae quorundam hominum, qui nunc . . . Loistae . . . nunc Libertini . . . appellantur*, in Frederichs (1) (MW), pp. 1 sq.

FREDERICQ, P. *Corpus documentorum Inquisitionis haereticae pravitatis Neerlandicae*, 4 vols., Ghent, 1889–1900.

FRIES, LORENZ. *Historie der Bischöffen zu Wirtzburg*, in Ludewig, *Geschichtsschreiber von dem Bischoffthum Wirtzburg*, Frankfort, 1713.

FROISSART, JEAN. *Chroniques*, ed. Luce and Raynaud, 11 vols., Paris, 1869–99.

FULCHER OF CHARTRES. *Gesta Francorum Jerusalem expugnantium*, in RHC, vol. III.

GAGUIN, ROBERT. *Compendio de Francorum gestis*, Paris, 1500.

GARNIER OF ROCHEFORT (attrib.). *Contra Amaurianos*, ed. Baeumker, in *Beiträge zur Geschichte der Philosophie des Mittelalters*, vol. XXIV, Heft 5–6, Münster, 1926.

GERSON, JEAN CHARLIER de. *Opera omnia*, ed. Dupin, 3 vols., Antwerp, 1706. Includes, *inter alia:*

(1) vol. I.   *De examinatione doctrinarum.*
(2)   *De distinctione verarum visionum a falsis.*
(3)   *De libris caute legendis.*
(4) vol. II. *Epistola missa Magistro Vincento O.P. . . . contra se flagellantes.*
(5)   *Tractatus contra sectam Flagellantium.*
(6) vol. III. *Tractatus contra Romantium de Rosa.*
(7)   *Considerationes theologiae mysticae.*
(8)   *De mystica theologica speculativa.*
(9)   *Considérations sur Saint Joseph.*
(10)   *Sermo de Spiritu Sancto.*
(11)   *Sermo die festo S. Ludovici.*

Geschichtsquellen des Bisthums Münster, vols. II, V, VI, Münster, 1852, 1899, 1900.

Gesta abbatum Trudonensium, in MGHS, vol. X.

Gesta archiepiscoporum Magdeburgensium, Continuatio I, in MGHS, vol. XIV.

Gesta Baldevvini Treverensis archiepiscopi, in Baluze (2), vol. I.

Gesta Ludovici VIII, in RHF, vol. XVII.

Gesta Treverorum, Continuatio I, in MGHS, vol. VIII.

GILLES VAN DER HOYE. *Dicta in quodam sermone ad populum*, ed. Berlière, in 'Trois traités inédits sur les Flagellants', *Revue Bénédictine*, vol. XXV, Maredsous, 1908, pp. 334–57.

GIRALDUS CAMBRENSIS. *Liber de instructione principum*, in RS 21, 1891 (vol. VIII of *Opera*).

GLASSBERGER, NICOLAUS. *Chronica*, in *Analecta Franciscana*, vol. II, Quaracchi, 1887, pp. 423–6.

GOWER, JOHN. *Vox clamantis*, in Latin Works, ed. Macaulay, Oxford, 1902.

Grandes chroniques de France, ed. P. Paris, vols. V, VI, Paris 1836–8.

GRATIAN. *Decretum*, in PL, vol. CLXXXVII.

GREGORY, ST, OF TOURS. *Historia Francorum*, in MGHS *rerum Merovingicarum*, vol. I.

GREGORY XI, Pope (1). Letter to Kerlinger and others, in Baronius and Raynaldus, vol. XXVI, p. 228.

GREGORY XI, Pope (2). Letter to Emperor Charles IV, in Baronius and Raynaldus, vol. XXVI, pp. 240–41.

GRESBECK, H. *Summarische Ertzelungk und Bericht der Wiederdope und wat sich binnen der Stat Monster in Westphalen zugetragen im Iair MDXXXV*, in Cornelius, *Berichte*, pp. 3–214.

GROOT, GERHARD. *Gerardi Magni Epistolae XIV*, ed. R. Acquoy, Amstel, 1857.

GUI, BERNARD (1). *E Floribus Chronicorum*, in RHF, vol. XXI.

GUI, BERNARD (2). *Vita Clementis V*, in Baluze (1), vol. I.

GUI, BERNARD (3). *Vita Joannis XXII*, in Baluze (1), vol. I.

GUIBERT OF NOGENT (1). *Gesta Dei per Francos, sive Historia Hierosolymitana*, in RHC, vol. IV.

GUIBERT OF NOGENT (2). *De vita sua*, in RHF, vol. XII.

Haereses sectatorum Amalrici, in Denifle and Chatelain, pp. 71–2.

HARTMANN, CHRISTOPH. *Annales Heremi Deiparae Matris Monasterii in Helvetia*. Freiburg in Breisgau, 1612.

HARTZHEIM, J. and SCHANNAT, J. F. *Concilia Germaniae*, 11 vols., Cologne, 1759–90.

HENRY OF DIESSENHOFEN (Heinrich Truchsess). *Historia ecclesiastica* or *Chronicon*, in FRG, vol. IV.

HENRY OF HEIMBURG. *Annales*, in MGHS, vol. XVII.

HENRY OF HERFORD. *Liber de rebus memorabilioribus sive chronicon*, ed. Potthast, Göttingen, 1859.

HENRY OF VIRNENBURG. *Contra Beggardos et Beggardas*, in Fredericq (OS), vol. I, pp. 151 sq.

HERMANN OF ALTAHA. *Annales*, in MGHS, vol. XVII.

HILDEGARD, ST (1). *Scivias sive visionum ac revelationum libri tres*, in PL, vol. CXCVII.

HILDEGARD, ST (2). *Epistola ad praelatos Moguntinenses*, in PL, vol. CXCVII, cols. 218–43.

HIPPOLYTUS (attribution uncertain). *De consummatione mundi ac de Antichristo*, in PG, vol. X, cols. 904–52.

HÖFLER, C. A. C. von. *Geschichtsschreiber der husitischen Bewegung in Boehmen*, in FRA, Section 1, vols. II, VI, VII, Vienna, 1856–66.

HUGH OF REUTLINGEN (Spechtshart). *Weltchronik*, ed. Gillert, München, 1881.

IBN AL-QALĀNISĪ. *Continuation of the Chronicle of Damascus: The Damascus Chronicle of the Crusades*. Selected and trans. Gibb, London, 1932.

IBN VERGA, SOLOMON. *Shebet Yehuda*. German trans. Wiener, Hanover, 1856.

INNOCENT VI, Pope. Bull appointing inquisitors in France, in Baronius and Raynaldus, vol. XXV, p. 589.

Invectiva contra Hussitas, in Höfler, vol. II of FRA, pp. 621–32.

IRENAEUS, ST. *Adversus haereses*, in PG, vol. VII.

JEAN DE MEUN. *Le Roman de la Rose*, ed. Langlois, 5 vols. Paris, 1914–24.

JEAN DES PREIS DIT D'OUTREMEUSE. *Ly Myreur des Histors*, ed. Bormans, Brussels, 1887.

JEAN LE FÈVRE. *Les Lamentations de Matheolus*, ed. van Hamel, Paris, 1892.

JOBST OF EINSIEDELN. Report on the Wirsberg brothers, ed. Kürschner, in *Archiv für oesterreichische Geschichte*, vol. XXXIX, Part I, Vienna, 1868, pp. 280 sq.

JOHN, canon of St Victor. *Vita Joannis XXII*, in Baluze (1).

JOHN XXII, Pope. Letter to Seneschal of Beaucaire, in Baronius and Raynaldus, vol. XXIV, pp. 136–7.

JOHN OF COLUMNA. *E Mari Historiarum*, in RHF, vol. XXIII.

JOHN OF DÜRBHEIM (1). Pastoral letter, 1317, in Mosheim (2) (MW), pp. 255–61 (where attributed to John of Ochsenstein).

JOHN OF DÜRBHEIM (2). Letter to the Bishop of Worms, in Mosheim (2) (MW), pp. 267–9.

JOHN OF HAGEN (Joannes de Indagine). *De his, qui se vulnerunt...*, in Stumpf (MW), Document 6.

JOHN OF ROQUETAILLADE (Rupescissa). *Vade mecum in tribulatione*, in G. Orthuinus, *Fasciculum rerum expetendarum et fugiendarum*, ed. Edward Brown, vol. II, London, 1690, pp. 496–508.

JOHN OF TAYSTER. *Annales*, in MGHS, vol. XXVIII.

JOHN OF VIKTRING. *Liber certarum historiarum*, in SGUS, 1909–10, 2 vols.

JOHN OF YPRES. *Chronicon Sythiense S. Bertini*, in RHF, vol. XVIII.

JOHN OF WINTERTHUR. *Chronica*, in MGHS, new series, vol. III.

JOHN, Abbot of St Victor. Sermon, in Hauréau (MW), pp. 93–4, Note 1.

JOSEPH HA-COHEN. *Emek ha Bakha* (*The Valley of Tears*). German trans Wiener, Leipzig, 1858.

JOSEPHUS FLAVIUS. *The Jewish War*, trans. Whiston and Shilleto, 2 vols., London, 1890.

JUSTIN MARTYR. *Dialogus cum Tryphone Judaeo*, in PG, vol. VI.

Kalendarium Zwetlense, in MGHS, vol. IX

KAMNITZER, H. (ed.). *Dokumente des grossen deutschen Bauernkrieges*, in Meusel (MW), pp. 185–332.

KERVYN DE LETTENHOVE, C. B. (ed.). *Récits d'un bourgeois de Valenciennes* (1254–1366), Louvain, 1877.

KERSSENBROCH, HERMANN von. *Anabaptistici furoris Monasterium inclitam Westphaliae metropolim evertentis historica narratio*, ed. Detmer, in GBM, vols. V and VI.

Klingenberger Chronik, ed. Henne von Sargans, Gotha, 1861.

KNIGHTON, HENRY. Continuation of his *Chronicon*, in RS 92, 1895.

KÖRNER, HERMANN (Cornerus). *Chronica novella*, in Eckhart, vol. II.

KURFESS, A. (ed.). *Sibyllinische Weissagungen*, Munich, 1951.

LACOMBLET, T. J. *Urkundenbuch für die Geschichte des Niederrheins*, 4 vols., Düsseldorf, 1840–58.

LACTANTIUS FIRMIANUS (1). *Divinae Institutiones*, in PL, vol. VI.

LACTANTIUS FIRMIANUS (2). *Epitome Divinarum Instutionum ad Pentadium fratrem*, in PL, vol. VI.

LANGLAND, WILLIAM. *The Vision of William concerning Piers the Plowman*, ed. Skeat, 2 vols., Oxford, 1886.

LANGLOIS, C. V. (ed.). *Instrumenta facta super examinacione M. Porete*, in *Revue historique*, vol. LIV, Paris, 1894, pp. 296–7.

LAWRENCE OF BŘEZOVÁ (Vavřince z Březové). *De gestis et variis accidentibus regni Boemiae*, in Höfler, vol. II of FRA, pp. 321–534. (Also, with Czech as well as Latin text, in vol. V of *Fontes rerum Bohemicarum*.)

LAZIUS, WOLFGANG. *Fragmentum vaticinii cuiusdam . . . Methodii, episcopi Ecclesie Patarensis*, Vienna, 1547.

LEA, H. C. (ed.). Sentence on Margaret of Porette, in Lea (MW), Appendix, pp. 575–8.

LE BEL, JEAN. *Chronique*, ed. Viard and Deprez, 2 vols., Paris, 1904–5.

Litera de civitate Pragensi . . ., in Höfler, vol. VI of FRA, pp. 311–19.

LÖFFLER, K. *Die Wiedertäufer zu Münster 1534–5*, Jena, 1923. (Contains much of the material translated into modern German.)

LUCIAN OF SAMOSATA. *Saturnalian Letters*.

LUTHER, MARTIN, *Werke* (*Kritische Gesamtausgabe*), Weimar, 1883–1908.
  (1) vol. XV.   *Brief an die Fürsten zu Sachsen von dem aufrührischen Geist*, pp. 199 sq.
  (2) vol. XVIII. *Wider die mörderischen und räuberischen Rotten der Bauern*.
  (3)   *Sendschreiben an die Christen zu Antwerpen*, 1525, pp. 547 sq.

Magdeburger Schöppenchronik, in CDS, vol. VII.

Majestas Carolini, in *Archiv český*, vol. III, pp. 68–180.

MANSI, J. D. *Sacra conciliorum collectio*, Paris and Leipzig, 1902–13.

MARTÈNE, E. and DURAND, U. *Veterum Scriptorum at Monumentum amplissima collectio*, 9 vols., Paris, 1724–33.

MARTIN OF TROPPAU (Martinus Polonus). *Chronicon expeditissimum*, Antwerp, 1574.
  Continuations to Martin's *Chronicon pontificum et imperatorum*:
    Continuatio Anglica, in MGHS, vol. XXIV.
    Continuatio Brabantina, in MGHS, vol. XXIV.

MATILDA OF MAGDEBURG. *Das fliessende Licht der Gottheit*, ed. Morel Regensburg, 1869.

MATTHEW OF NEUENBURG. *Chronica*, in FRG, vol. IV.

MICHAEL DE LEONE. *Annotata historica*, in FRG, vol. I.

MONK OF WESTMINSTER. Continuation to Higden's *Polychronicon*, in RS 41, vol. IX, 1886.

Monumenta Boica. Munich, 1763 ff.

Monumenta Germaniae Historica, ed. Pertz, Mommsen *et al.*, Hanover and Berlin, 1826 ff.

   Scriptores, 1826 ff.

   Scriptores rerum Germanicarum in usum scholarum, 1839 ff.

   Scriptores rerum Germanicarum, new series, Berlin, 1922 ff.

MOUSKES, PHILIPPE (Mousket). *Chronique rimée*, ed. Reifenberg, vol. II, Brussels, 1838.

MUISIS, GILLES LI. *Chronica*, in CCF, vol. II.

MÜNTZER, THOMAS. *Schriften*, ed. Brandt (see also Brandt (OS)). Includes, *inter alia*, in modernized spelling:

   (1) *Von dem gedichteten Glauben . . .*

   (2) *Protestation oder Entbietung Thomas Müntzers . . .*

   (3) *Die Fürstenpredigt*

   (4) *Ausgedrückte Entblössung . . .*

   (5) *Hoch verursachte Schutzrede . . .*

MÜNTZER, THOMAS. *Thomas Müntzers politische Schriften*, ed. Hinrichs, Halle, 1950.

MÜNTZER, THOMAS. *Thomas Müntzers Briefwechsel*, ed. Böhmer and Kirn, Leipzig, 1931.

NAUCLERUS, JOANNES. *Chronica*, Cologne, 1544.

NEUBAUER, A. and STERN, M. (ed.). *Hebräische Berichte über die Judenverfolgungen während der Kreuzzüge*, in *Quellen zur Geschiche der Juden in Deutschland*, vol. II, Berlin, 1892. (Hebrew, with German translations.)

Newe zeitung, von den Widerteuffern zu Münster, in *Zeitschrift für vaterländische Geschichte und Altertumskunde*, vol. XXVII, Münster, 1867, pp. 255–66.

NIDER, JOHANN. *Formicarius*, Strasbourg, 1517.

NIESERT, J. *Münsterische Urkundensammlung*, vols, I, II, Koesfeld, 1826. Includes, *inter alia*:

   (1) vol. I.   Confession of Johannes Beckemann, pp. 33–7.

   (2)   Confession of Zillis Leitgen, pp. 136–49.

   (3)   Confession of Jacob of Osnabrück, pp. 154–66.

   (4) vol. II. *Newe zeittunge vonn Münster*, pp. 499–504.

Notae Colonienses, in MGHS, vol. XXIV.

OPEL, O. (ed.). 'Zur Geschichte des Bauernkrieges', in *Neue Mitteilungen aus dem Gebiete historisch-antiquarischer Forschungen*, vol. XII, Halle and Nordhausen, 1869. (Documents concerning Thomas Müntzer.)

OSWALD DER SCHREIBER (of Königsberg in Hungary), ed. Zarncke, in 'Der Priester Johannes', *Abhandlungen der sächsischen Gesellschaft der Wissenschaften, Philologisch-historische Klasse*, vol. VII, Leipzig, 1879.

OTTO OF FREISING. *Gesta Friderici I Imperatoris*, in SGUS, 1912, 3rd edn.

OTTOKAR. *Österreichische Reimchronik, 1250–1300*, in *Deutsche Chroniken*, vol. V.

OVID. *Metamorphoses.*

PAPIAS. *De expositione oraculorum dominicorum* (fragments), in PG, vol. V.

PARIS, MATTHEW. *Chronica majora*, in RS 57, 7 vols., 1872–83.

Patrologiae cursus completus. Series Latina, ed. J. P. Migne, Paris, 1844–55.

Patrologiae cursus completus. Series Graeco-Latina, ed. J. P. Migne, Paris, 1857–66.

PELAYO, ALVAREZ (Alvarus Pelagius). *De Planctu Ecclesiae*, 2 vols., Ulm, 1474.

PETER OF ZITTAU. *Die Königsaaler Geschichtsquellen (Chronica Aulae regiae libri tres)*, in FRA, vol. VIII.

PFEIFFER, F. (ed.). *Swester Katrei Meister Ekehartes Tohter von Strâzburc*, in *Deutsche Mystiker des vierzehnten Jahrhunderts*, vol. II, Leipzig, 1857, pp. 448–75.

POCQUE, ANTOINE. Mystical treatise, quoted in Calvin (4), cols. 225–42.

*PORETE, MARGUERITE. *Le Mirouer des simples ames anienties et qui seulement demourent en vouloir et desir d'amour*, ed. Guarnieri, in *Il Movimento del Libero Spirito*, Rome, 1965. (Replaces edition by Guarnieri, Rome, 1961.)

PREGER, W. (ed.) (1). *Compilatio de novo spiritu* (anonymous), in Preger (1) (MW), pp. 469–71.

PREGER, W. (ed.) (2). *Tractatus ... contra quosdam articulos erroneos*, in Preger (2) (MW), pp. 62–3.

PRIMAT, Monk of Saint-Denis. *Chronique de Primat*, translated from the (lost) Latin original by John of Vignay, in RHF, vol. XXIII.

Pseudo-Methodius, in Sackur, pp. 59–96.

PTOLOMY (Tholomeus) OF LUCCA. *Vita Clementis V*, in Baluze (1), vol. I.

PULKAVA OF RADENIN (Przibico). *Chronica Boemorum*, with Continuations, in G. Dobner, *Monumenta historica Boemiae*, vols. III, IV.

RADULPH GLABER. *Historiarum libri quinque*, in PL, vol. CXLII.

RAMERT, HERMANN (attrib.). *Die Ordnung der Wiedertäufer zu Münster, item was sich daselbst nebenzu verloffen hat*, in *Zeitschrift für vaterländische Geschichte und Altertumskunde*, vol. XVII, Münster, 1856, pp. 240–49.

RAYMOND OF AGUILERS. *Historia Francorum qui ceperunt Jerusalem*, in RHC, vol. III.

Recognitiones (S. Clementis Romani), in PG, vol. I.

Recueil des Historiens des Croisades, Historiens Occidentaux. Publ. *Académie des Inscriptions et Belles-Lettres*, 5 vols., Paris, 1844–95.

Recueil des Historiens des Gaules et de la France (Rerum Gallicarum et Francicarum scriptores), ed. Bouquet *et al.*, Paris, 1738–1876.

Reformation Kaiser Sigmunds, ed. Beer (*Beiheft zu den deutschen Reichtagsakten*), Stuttgart, 1933.

REGENBOGEN (attrib.). *Meistersingerlied*, in Schultheiss (MW), pp. 55–8.

REIFFERSCHEID, A. (ed.). *Neun Texte zur Geschichte der religiösen Aufklärung in Deutschland während des 14-ten und 15-ten Jahrhunderts*, Griefswald, 1905.

REINERUS. *Annales S. Jacobi Leodiensis*, in MGHS, vol. XVI.

Renart le Contrefait, ed. Raynaud and Lemaître, vol. II, Paris, 1914.

REUSS, F. A. 'Die Wallfahrt nach Niklashausen im Jahre 1476', in *Archiv des historischen Vereins von Unterfranken und Aschaffenburg*, vol. X, 3, Würzburg, 1858, pp. 300–18. (Collection of documents.)

RHEGIUS, URBANUS (1). *Widderlegung der münsterischen newen Valentinianer und Donatisten Bekentnus*, Wittenberg, 1535.

RHEGIUS, URBANUS (2). *De restitutione regni Israëlitici, contra omnes omnium seculorum Chiliastas: in primis tamen contra Miliarios Monasterienses*, Zell, 1536.

RICHARD OF POITIERS. *Chronicon*, in RHF, vol. XII.

RICHERUS. *Gesta Senoniensis Ecclesiae*, in MGHS, vol. XXV.

RIGORD. *Gesta Philippi Augusti*, in RHF, vol. XVII.

RITTER, G. (ed.). 'Zur Geschichte des häretischen Pantheismus in Deutschland im 15-ten Jahrhundert', in ZKG, vol. XLIII (1924), new series, vol. VI. Includes:

(1) *Articuli confessi per Johannem Lolhardum*, pp. 150 sq.

(2) *Articuli informatoris de heresi circa Egram anno 1467*, pp. 158–9.

ROBERT OF AUXERRE. *Chronologia*, in RHF, vol. XVIII.

ROBERT OF AVESBURY. *De gestis mirabilibus regis Edwardi tertii*, in RS 93, 1889.

Rolls Series (*Rerum Britannicarum medii aevi scriptores*). Published under direction of the Master of the Rolls, London, 1858 ff.

ROTHE, JOHANNES. *Thüringische Chronik*, ed. von Liliencron, vol. III of *Thüringische Geschichtsquellen*, Jena, 1854 ff.

ROTHMANN, BERNT (1). *Bekentnisse van beyden Sacramenten* (first printed in Münster, 1533), in H. Detmer and R. Krumbholtz (MW).

ROTHMANN, BERNT (2). *Eyne Restitution edder Eine wedderstellinge rechter unnde gesunder Christliker leer* ... (first printed in Münster, 1534), in *Neudrucke deutscher Literaturwerke*, nos. 77 and 78, Halle, 1888.

ROTHMANN, BERNT (3). *Eyn gantz troestlick bericht van der Wrake unde straffe des Babilonischen gruwels* ... (first printed in Münster, 1534), in K. W. Bouterwek (MW).

RUUSBROEC, JAN VAN. *Werken*, ed. Reypens and Schurmans, 4 vols., Mechelen and Amsterdam, 1932–4. Includes, *inter alia*, in order of composition:

(1) *Vanden Vier Becoringhen*, in vol. III.

(2) *Die Gheestelike Brulocht*, in vol. I.

(3) *Vanden VII Sloten*, in vol. III.

(4) *Een Spieghel der eewigher Salicheit*, in vol. III.

(5) *Dat Boecsken der Verclaringhe*, in vol. III.

(6) *Van den XII Beghinen*, in vol. IV.

RYMER, T. *Foedera et acta publica*, ed. A. Clarke *et al.*, vol. I, London, 1816.

Rýmovaná kronika česká (with *Di tutsch kronik von Behemlant*), in *Fontes rerum Bohemicarum*, vol. III, Prague, 1882.

SACKUR, E. *Sibyllinische Texte und Forschungen: Pseudomethodius, Adso und die tiburtinische Sibylle*, Halle, 1898.

SALIMBENE OF PARMA. *Cronica*, in MGHS, vol. XXXII.

SALOMO BAR SIMEON. *Relation*, in Neubauer and Stern, vol. II.

SCHEDEL, HARTMAN. *Liber cronicarum cum figuris et ymaginibus ab inicio mundi*, Nuremberg, 1493.

SCHMID, KONRAD (1). *Prophetica ... Schmid haeresi Flagellatorum infecti*, in Stumpf (MW), Document 2, pp. 16–24.

SCHMID, KONRAD (2). *Articuli ab ... flagellantium Praedicatore conscripti*, in Stumpf (MW), Document 3, pp. 24–6.

SCHMIDT, KARL. *Nicolaus von Basel*, Vienna, 1866. Includes:

(1) *Confession of Martin of Mainz*, pp. 66–9. (In Latin. For emendations see Haupt (4) (MW).)

(2) *Buch von den zwei Mannen*, pp. 205–77.

SCHNEIDER, FEDOR (ed). *Fünfundzwanzig lateinische weltliche Rhythmen aus der Frühzeit*, Rome, 1925.

SENECA. *Epistolae morales*.

SIEGFRIED OF BALNHUSIN (Grossballhausen in Saxony). *Historia universalis*, in MGHS, vol. XXV.

SIGEBERT OF GEMBLOUX. *Chronographia*, in MGHS, vol. VI. Continuations to Sigebert's chronicle:

Continuatio Gemblacensis, in MGHS, vol. VI.

Continuatio Praemonstratensis, in MGHS, vol. VI.

Auctarium Gemblacense, in RHF, vol. XIII (also in MGHS, vol. VI).

ROBERT OF TORIGNY (Robertus de Monte). *Chronica*, in MGHS, vol. VI.

SIMON OF TOURNAI. *Collectio de scandalis Ecclesiae*, ed. Stroick, in *Archivum Franciscanum Historicum*, vol. XXIV, Florence, 1931, pp. 33 sq.

Sollicitudo sacerdotum Thaboriensium, in Höfler, vol. VI of FRA (as Chapter 2 of Part I of the *Chronicon Taboritarum*.)

Staří letopisové čeští (Old Czech chronicles), *1378–1527*, ed. Palacký, Prague, 1829 (vol. III of *Scriptores rerum Bohemicarum*). (A more recent edition is now available, ed. F. Šimek and M. Kaňák, Prague, 1959.)

STEPHEN OF BOURBON. *Tractatus de diversis materiis predicabilibus*, ed. Lecoy de la Marche, in *Anecdotes historiques d'Étienne de Bourbon*, Paris, 1877.

STOLLE, KONRAD. *Thüringisch-erfurtische Chronik*, ed. Thiele (*Geschichtsquellen der Provinz Sachsen*, vol. XXXIX), Halle, 1900.

SUSO, HEINRICH. *Deutsche Schriften*, ed. Bihlmeyer, Stuttgart, 1907. Includes:
  (1) *Leben*.
  (2) *Das Büchlein der Wahrheit*.

Synod of Cologne, 1353, in Hartzheim and Schannat, vol. IV.

Synod of Cologne, 1357, in Hartzheim and Schannat, vol. IV.

Synod of Magdeburg, 1261, in Mansi, vol. XXIV.

Synod of Mainz, 1259, in Mansi, vol. XXIII.

Synod of Mainz, 1310, in Mansi, vol. XXV.

Synod of Paris, 1209, in Denifle and Chatelain, p. 70.

Synod of Rheims, 1157, in Mansi, vol. XXI.

Synod of Rome, in Tangl.

Synod of Trier, 1277, in Mansi, vol. XXIII.

Synod of Trier, 1310, in Mansi, vol. XXV.

Synod of Utrecht, 1357, in Fredericq (OS), vol. II, p. 142.

TANGL, M. *Die Briefe des heiligen Bonifatius und Lullus*, Berlin, 1916 (MGH *Epistolae Selectae*, vol. 1).

TAUBE OF SELBACH, HEINRICH. *Chronica*, in MGHS, new series, vol. I.

THOMAS OF CHANTIMPRÉ. *Bonum universale de apibus*, Douai, 1627.

THOMAS OF ECCLESTON. *Liber de adventu Minorum in Angliam*, in MGHS, vol. XXVIII.

Tiburtina, in Sackur, pp. 177–87.

TILEMANN ELHEN OF WOLFHAGEN. *Die Limburger Chronik*, in *Deutsche Chroniken*, vol. IV.

TOBLER, A. (ed.). *Li proverbe au Vilain*, Leipzig, 1895.

Tractatus contra errores (Picardorum), in Döllinger (OS), pp. 691–700. (Also in Höfler, vol. II of FRA, pp. 434–41.)

TRITHEMIUS, JOHANNES (1). *Annales Hirsaugienses*, St Gall, 1690.

TRITHEMIUS, JOHANNES (2). *De viris illustribus ordinis S. Benedicti*, Cologne, 1575.

TROGUS, POMPEIUS GNAEUS, in *Juniani Justini Epitoma Historiarum Philippicarum Pompei Trogi*.

TWINGER OF KÖNIGSHOFEN, JACOB. *Chronik*, in CDS, vols. VIII, IX.

ULANOWSKI, B. (ed.). *Examen testium super vita et moribus Beguinarum ... in Sweydnitz*, in *Scriptores Rerum Polonicarum*, vol. XIII, Cracow, 1889, pp. 233–55.

URBAN V, Pope (1). Bull appointing inquisitors in Germany, in Mosheim (2) (MW), pp. 336–7.

URBAN V, Pope (2). Bull against Beghards in France, in Mosheim (2) (MW), p. 412.

USQUE, SAMUEL. *Consolaçam ás Tribulaçoens de Israel*, ed. Mendes dos Remédios, in *Subsidios para o estudo da Historia da Litteratura Portuguesa*, Coimbra, 1906–7.

Visitationes Odonis Rigaudi archiepiscopi Rothomagensis, in RHF, vol. XXI.

Vita Henrici II archiepiscopi (Treverensis) altera, in MGHS, vol. XXIV.

Vita S. Norberti A, in MGHS, vol. XII.

Vita S. Norberti B, in *Acta Sanctorum Bollandiana, Junii I*, 6 June.

WADDING, L. *Annales Minorum*. 2nd edn., Rome, 1731–45.

WALSINGHAM, THOMAS. *Historia Anglicana*, RS 28, vol. II, 1869.

WASMOD, JOHANN, OF HOMBURG. *Contra hereticos Bekardos Lulhardos et swestriones*, in Haupt (3) (MW), pp. 567–76.

WATTENBACH, W. 'Uber die Sekte der Brüder vom freien Geiste', in SPAW, vol. XXIX (1887), pp. 517–44. Includes:
  (1) Confession of John of Brünn, pp. 529–37.
  (2) Confession of Johann Hartmann, pp. 538–43.
            (Both in Latin.)

WIDMAN, GEORG. *Chronika*, in *Württembergische Geschichtsquellen*, vol. VI, Stuttgart, 1904.

WILLIAM OF EGMONT. *Chronicon*, in Antonius Matthaeus, *Veteris Aevi Analecta*, vol. II, The Hague, 1723.

WILLIAM OF NANGIS (1). *Gesta Ludovici IX*, in RHF, vol. XX.

WILLIAM OF NANGIS (2). *Chronicon*, with *Continuationes I, II, III*, ed. Géraud, 2 vols., Paris, 1843.

WILLIAM OF NEWBURGH. *De rebus Anglicis*, in RHF, vol. XIII.

WILLIAM THE BRETON. *Gesta Philippi Augusti*, ed. Delaborde, in *Oeuvres de Rigord et de Guillaume le Breton*, vol. I, Paris, 1882.

WOLF, JOHANN. *Lectionum memorabilium et reconditarum centenarii XVI*, Lauingen, 1600.

WYCLIF, JOHN. *Tractatus de civili dominio. Liber primus*, ed. Poole, London, 1885.

WYKES, THOMAS. *Chronicon*, in RS 36 (*Annales Monastici*), vol. IV, 1869.

ZANTFLIET, CORNELIUS. *Chronicon*, in Martène and Durand, vol. V.

ZENO, ST, OF VERONA. *Tractatus* (or *Sermones*), in PL, vol. XI.

2 Modern Works

ADLER, GEORG. *Geschichte des Sozialismus und Kommunismus von Plato bis zur Gegenwart*, Part I, Leipzig, 1899.

AEGERTER, E. *Les hérésies du Moyen Âge*, Paris, 1939.

Allgemeine Deutsche Biographie, ed. von Liliencron and Wegele, Leipzig, 1875–1912.

ALLIER, R. 'Les frères du libre esprit', in T. Reinach *et al.*, *Religions et sociétés*, Paris, 1905, pp. 109–53.

ALPHANDÉRY, P. (1). *Les idées morales chez les hétérodoxes latins au début du XIIIe siècle*. (*Bibliothèque de l'École des Hautes Études, Sciences religieuses*, vol. XVI, fasc. 1), Paris, 1903.

ALPHANDÉRY, P. (2). 'De quelques faits de prophétisme dans les sectes latines antérieures au joachimisme', in *Revue de l'histoire des religions*, vol. LII, Paris, 1905, pp. 177–218.

ALPHANDÉRY, P. (3). 'Les croisades d'enfants', in *Revue de l'histoire des religions*, vol. LXIII, Paris, 1916. pp. 259–82.

ALPHANDÉRY, P. (4). *Notes sur le messianisme médiéval latin (XIe–XIIe siècles)* Paris, 1912.

ALPHANDÉRY, P. (5). 'Les foules religieuses', in *La Foule* (papers read to the *Centre international de synthèse*, 1932), Paris, 1934, pp. 53–76.

ALPHANDÉRY, P. and DUPRONT, A. *La Chrétienté et l'idée de Croisade*, 2 vols., Paris, 1954, 1959.

ALTMEYER, J. J. *Les précurseurs de la Réforme aux Pays-Bas*, Paris, 1886.

ALVERNY, M. T. d'. 'Un fragment du procès des Amauriciens', in *Archives d'histoire doctrinale et littéraire du Moyen Âge*, vol. XVIII, Paris, 1950–51, pp. 325–6.

ANDREAS, W. *Deutschland vor der Reformation*, Stuttgart and Berlin, 1934.

BACHMANN, R. *Niclas Storch*, Zwickau, 1880.

BAERWALD, R. *Die Schlacht bei Frankenhausen*, Mühlhausen in Thuringia, 1925.

BAETHGEN, F. *Der Engelpapst*, Leipzig, 1943.

BAHLMANN, P. *Die Wiedertäufer zu Münster. Eine bibliographische Zusammenstellung*, Münster, 1894.

BAINTON, R. H. *David Joris*, Leipzig, 1937.

BARACK, K. A. 'Hans Böhm und die Wallfahrt nach Niklashausen im Jahre 1476', in *Archiv des historischen Vereines von Unterfranken und Aschaffenburg*, vol. XIV, 3, Würzburg, 1858, pp. 1–108.

BARON, S. W. *A social and religious history of the Jews*, vol. II, New York, 1937.

BARTOŠ, F.-M. (1). 'Žižka a pikarti', in *Kalich*, vol. IX, fasc. 3–4, Prague, 1924, pp. 97–108.

BARTOŠ, F.-M. (2). 'Kněze Petra Kǎnyše vyznǎni víry a večeře Páně z r. 1421', in *Jihočeský sborník historický*, vol. I, Tabor, 1928, pp. 2–5.

BARTOŠ, F.-M. (3). 'Picards et "Pikarti"', in BHPF, vol. LXXX (1931), pp. 465–86; vol. LXXXI (1932), pp. 8–28.

BAX, E. B. *Rise and fall of the Anabaptists*, London, 1903.

BEAUSOBRE, I. de. 'Dissertation sur les Adamites de Bohème', in J. Lenfant, *Histoire de la guerre des Hussites*, vol. I, Amsterdam, 1731, pp. 304–49.

BEMMANN, R. *Thomas Müntzer, Mühlhausen in Thüringen und der Bauernkrieg*, Leipzig, 1920.

BENZ, E. *Ecclesia Spiritualis. Kirchenidee und Geschichtstheologie der franziskanischen Reformation*, Stuttgart, 1934. (2nd edn., 1964.)

BERGER, E. *Histoire de Blanche de Castille, reine de France*, Paris, 1895.

BERNHEIM, E. *Mittelalterliche Zeitanschauungen in ihrem Einflus auf Politik und Geschichtschreibung*, Tübingen, 1918.

BERNHEIMER, R. *Wild men in the Middle Ages*, Cambridge, Mass., 1952.

BETTS, R. R. 'Correnti religiose nazionali ed ereticali dalla fine del secolo XIV alla metà del XV', in *Storia del Medioevo* (MW), pp. 403–513. (In English.)

BEUZART, P. *Les hérésies pendant le Moyen Âge dans la région de Douai, d'Arras et au pays de l'Aller*, Le Puy, 1912.

BEZOLD, F. von (1). *Zur Geschichte des Hussitentums*, Munich, 1874.

BEZOLD, F. von (2). 'Die Lehre von der Volkssouveränität während des Mittelalters', 1876. Reprinted in *Aus Mittelalter und Renaissance*, Munich and Berlin, 1918, pp. 1–48.

BEZOLD, F. von (3). 'Die "armen Leute" und die deutsche Literatur des späteren Mittelalters', 1879. Reprinted in *Aus Mittelalter und Renaissance*, Munich and Berlin, 1918, pp. 49–81.

BEZOLD, F. von (4). 'Zur deutschen Kaisersage', in *Sitzungsberichte der königlich bayerischen Akademie der Wissenschaften. Philosophisch-philologische Klasse*, vol. XIV, Munich, 1884, pp. 560–606.

BEZOLD, F. von (5). *Geschichte der deutschen Reformation*, Berlin, 1890.

BIDEZ, J. *La Cité du Monde et la Cité du Soleil*, Paris, 1932.

BIGNAMI-ODIER, J. *Études sur Jean de Roquetaillade (Johannes de Rupescissa)*, Paris, 1952.

BLANKE, F. 'Das Reich der Wiedertäufer zu Münster 1534–1535', in *Archiv für Reformationsgeschichte*, vol. XXXVII, Berlin, 1940, pp. 13–37.

BLOCH, M. (1). *Les rois thaumaturges: Étude sur le caractère surnaturel attribué à la puissance royale particulièrement en France et en Angleterre*, Strasbourg, 1924.

BLOCH, M. (2). *Les caractères originaux de l'histoire rurale française*, Oslo, 1931.

BLOCH, M. (3). *La société féodale: la formation des liens de dépendance*, Paris, 1939.

*BLOOMFIELD, M. W. 'Joachim of Flora. A critical survey of his canon, teachings, sources, biography, and influence', in *Traditio*, vol. XIII, New York, 1957, pp. 249–311.

BLOOMFIELD, M. W. and REEVES, M. E. 'The penetration of Joachism into northern Europe', in *Speculum*, vol. XXIX, Cambridge, Mass., 1954, pp. 772–93.

BOAS, G. *Essays on Primitivism and related ideas in the Middle Ages*, Baltimore, 1948.

BOEHMER, H. (1). *Studien zu Thomas Müntzer*, Leipzig, 1922.

BOEHMER, H. (2). 'Thomas Müntzer und das jüngste Deutschland', in *Gesammelte Aufsätze*, Gotha, 1924.

BORST, A. *Die Katharer (Schriften der Monumenta Germaniae Historica*, vol. XII), Stuttgart, 1953.

BOSSERT, G. *et al. Württembergische Kirchengeschichte*, Calw and Stuttgart, 1893.

BOUSSET, W. (1). *The Antichrist legend, a chapter in Christian and Jewish folklore*, trans. Keane, London, 1896.

BOUSSET, W. (2). 'Beiträge zur Geschichte der Eschatologie', in ZKG, vol. XX (1900), pp. 103–31, 262–90.

BOUTERWEK, K. W. *Zur Literatur und Geschichte der Wiedertäufer, besonders in den Rheinlanden*, Bonn, 1864.

BRUNO DE JÉSUS-MARIE *et al.* 'La confession de Boullan', in *Satan (Études carmélitaines*, vol. VI), Paris, 1949.

BULARD, M. *Le scorpion, symbole du peuple juif dans l'art religieux des XIVe, XVe, XVIe siècles*, Paris, 1935.

BURDACH, K. *Vom Mittelalter zur Reformation*, Berlin, 1893–1937.
    (1) vol. II, part I: *Rienzo und die geistige Wandlung seiner Zeit.*
    (2) vol. III, part 2: *Der Dichter des Ackermann aus Böhmen und seine Zeit.*

BURDACH, K. (3). *Reformation, Renaissance, Humanismus*, Berlin, and Leipzig, 1926.

BURDACH, K. (4). *Der Longinus-Speer im eschatologischem Lichte*, in SPAW, vol. IX, 1920, pp. 294–321.

*BÜTTNER, Th. and WERNER, E. *Circumcellionen und Adamiten. Zwei Formen mittelalterlicher Häresie. (Forschungen zur mittelalterlichen Geschichte*, vol. II) Berlin, 1958, pp. 73–134.

CAHOUR, A. *Baudouin de Constantinople. Chronique de Belgique et de France*, Paris, 1850.

Cambridge Economic History of Europe, Cambridge, 1942–52.
  vol. I: Agrarian life of the Middle Ages, ed. J. H. Clapham and E. Power.
  vol. II: Trade and industry in the Middle Ages, ed. M. Postan and E. E.
  Rich.
Cambridge Medieval History, 8 vols., Cambridge, 1913–36.
CAPELLE, G. C. *Amaury de Bène, étude sur son panthéisme formel*, Paris, 1932.
CAREW HUNT, R. H. 'Thomas Müntzer', in *Church Quarterly Review*, London,
  vol. CXXVI (1938), pp. 213–44; vol. CXXVII (1939), pp. 227–67.
CARLYLE, R. W. and CARLYLE, A. J. *A history of medieval political theory in
  the West*, 6 vols., Edinburgh, 1903–36.
CARO, G. *Sozial- und Wirtschaftsgeschichte der Juden im Mittelalter und der
  Neuzeit*, 2 vols., Frankfort-on-Main, 1920–24.
CARUS-WILSON, E. 'The woollen industry', in CEH, vol. II, chap. 6,
  pp. 355–428.
CASE, S. J. *The millennial hope*, Chicago, 1918.
CHALANDON, F. *Histoire de la première Croisade*, Paris, 1925.
CHALUPNÝ, E. 'Adamité a Žižka', in *Jihočeský sborník historický*, vol. I,
  Tabor, 1928, pp. 51–2.
*COHN, N. *Warrant for Genocide. The Myth of the Jewish world-conspiracy
  and the Protocols of the Elders of Zion*, London and New York, 1967.
*COMBES, A. *Essai sur le critique de Ruysbroeck par Gerson*, 3 vols., Paris,
  1945–59.
CORNELIUS, C. A. (1). *Geschichte des Münsterischen Aufruhrs*, 2 vols.,
  Leipzig, 1855–60.
  vol. I: *Die Reformation*.
  vol. II: *Die Wiedertaufe*.
CORNELIUS, C. A. (2). *Die niederländischen Wiedertäufer während der
  Belagerung Münsters 1534 bis 1535*, Munich, 1869.
CORNELIUS, C. A. (3). 'Johann Bokelson', in ADB, vol. III, pp. 91–3.
CORNELIUS, C. A. (4). 'Bernt Knipperdollinck', in ADB, vol. XVI, pp.
  293–5.
CORNELIUS, C. A. (5). 'Jan Mathyszoon', in ADB, vol. XX, pp. 600–602.
COULTON, G. G. *The Black Death*, London, 1929.
CUMONT, F. 'La fin du monde selon les mages occidentaux', in *Revue de
  l'histoire des religions*, vol. CIII, Paris, 1931, pp. 29–96.
CURSCHMANN, H. H. W. F. *Hungersnöte im Mittelalter*, Leipzig, 1900.
DELACROIX, H. *Le mysticisme en Allemagne au 14e siècle*, Paris, 1900.
DEMPF, A. *Sacrum Imperium: Geschichts- und Staatsphilosophie des Mittel-
  alters und der politischen Renaissance*, Munich and Berlin, 1929.
*DE SMET, J.-M. 'De monnik Tanchelm en de Utrechtse Bisschopszetel in
  1112–1114', in *Scrinium Lovaniense, Mélanges historiques Etienne van
  Cauwenbergh*, Louvain, 1961, pp. 207–34.
DE STEFANO, A. *Riformatori ed eretici del medioevo*, Palermo, 1938.
DETMER, H. (1). *Hermann von Kerssenbrochs Leben und Schriften*, Münster,
  1900.
DETMER, H. (2). *Bilder aus den religiösen und sozialen Unruhen in Münster*,
  3 vols.,Münster, 1903–4.
  vol. I: Johann von Leiden.
  vol. II: Bernhard Rothmann.
  vol. III: Uber die Auffassung von der Ehe ... während der Täuferherr-
    schaft.
DETMER, H. and KRUMBHOLTZ, R. *Zwei Schriften des Münsterischen
  Wiedertäufers Bernhard Rothmann*. With historical introduction, Dortmund,
  1904.

DEVIC, C. and VAISSÈTE, J. J. *Histoire générale de la province de Languedoc*, ed. Molinier, vol. IX, Toulouse, 1885.

*DE VOOGT, P. *L'hérésie de Jean Hus* (*Bibliothèque de la Revue d'Histoire ecclésiastique*, fasc. 34), Louvain, 1960.

DICKENS, A. G. *Reformation and society in sixteenth-century Europe.* London, 1966.

Dictionnaire de Théologie Catholique, ed. Vacant and Mangenot, Paris, 1899–1950.

DOBROWSKÝ, J. 'Geschichte der Bömischen Pikarden und Adamiten', in *Abhandlungen der königlich böhmischen Gesellschaft der Wissenschaften*, vol. IV, Prague and Dresden, 1788, pp. 300–343.

*DOHNA, Graf LOTHAR zu,. *Reformatio Sigismundi. Beiträge zum Verständnis einer Reformschrift des fünfzehnten Jahrhunderts* (*Veröffentlichungen des Max-Planck-Instituts für Geschichte*, no. 4), Göttingen, 1960.

DÖLLINGER, I. von. 'Der Weissagungsglaube und das Prophetentum in der christlichen Zeit', in *Historisches Taschenbuch*, fifth series, vol. I, Leipzig, 1871, pp. 259–370.

DOREN, A. 'Wunschräume und Wunschzeiten', in *Vorträge der Bibliothek Warburg*, vol. IV, Leipzig, 1927, pp. 158–205.

DU CANGE, C. DU FRESNE. *Glossarium ad scriptores mediae et infimae Latinitatis*, ed. Henschel, Paris, 1840–50.

DUPRÉ THESEIDER, E. *Introduzione alle eresie medievali*, Bologna, 1953.

ELBOGEN, I. 'Zu den hebräischen Berichten über die Judenverfolgungen im Jahre 1096', in *Festschrift zum 70-ten Geburtstage Martin Philippsons*, Leipzig, 1917.

ELIADE, M. *The myth of the eternal return*, trans. Trask, London, 1955.

Encyclopedia of religion and ethics, ed. Hastings and Selbie, Edinburgh, 1908–26.

ERBKAM, H. W. *Geschichte der protestantischen Sekten im Zeitalter der Reformation*, Hamburg and Gotha, 1848.

*ERBSTÖSSER, M. and WERNER, E. *Ideologische Probleme des mittelalterlichen Plebejertums. Die freigeistige Häresie und ihre sozialen Wurzeln*, Berlin, 1960.

ERDMANN, C. (1). 'Endkaiserglaube und Kreuzzugsgedanke im 11-ten Jahrhundert', in ZKG, vol. LI (1932), pp. 384–414.

ERDMANN, C. (2). *Die Entstehung des Kreuzzugsgedankens*, Stuttgart, 1935.

ESSEN, L. van der. 'De ketterij van Tanchelm in de XIIde eeuw', in *Ons Geloof*, vol. II, Antwerp, 1912, pp. 354–61.

FLADE, P. 'Römische Inquisition in Mitteldeutschland', in *Beiträge zur sächsischen Kirchengeschichte*, vol. IX, Leipzig, 1894.

FOLZ, R. *Le souvenir et la légende de Charlemagne dans l'Empire germanique médiéval*, Paris, 1950.

FÖRSTEMANN, E. G. *Die christlichen Geisslergesellschaften*, Halle, 1828.

FRANZ, G. *Der deutsche Bauernkrieg*, Munich and Berlin, 1933.

FREDERICHS, J. (1). *De secte der Loïsten, of Antwerpsche Libertijnen* (1525–1545), Ghent and The Hague, 1891.

FREDERICHS, J. (2). 'Un luthérien français devenu libertin spirituel: Christophe Herault et les Loïstes d'Anvers (1490–1544)', in BHPF, vol. XLI (1892), pp. 250–69.

FREDERICQ, P. (1). *De secten der geeselars en der dansers in den Nederlanden tijdens de 14de eeuw*, Brussels, 1897.

FREDERICQ, P. (2). 'Deux sermons inédits de Jean du Fayt', in *Bulletin de l'Académie royale de Belgique Classe des Lettres*, vols. IX, X, Brussels, 1903, pp. 688–718.

GILSON, E. *La philosophie au Moyen Âge*, Paris, 1944.

GOTHEIN, E. *Politische und religiöse Volksbewegungen vor der Reformation*, Breslau, 1878.

GRAETZ, H. *Geschichte der Juden*, vols. VI, VII, Leipzig, 1873.

GRAUERT, H. von (1). 'Zur deutschen Kaisersage', in *Historisches Jahrbuch*, vol. XIII, Leipzig, 1892, pp. 100–143.

GRAUERT, H. von (2). 'Das Schulterkreuz der Helden mit besonderer Beziehung auf das Haus Wettin', in *Ehrengabe deutscher Wissenschaft (für Prinz Johann Georg)*, ed. Fessler, Freiburg in Breisgau, 1920, pp. 703–20.

GRAUS, F. *Chudina městská v době předhusitské*, Prague, 1949.

GROUSSET, R. *Histoire des croisades et du royaume franc de Jérusalem*, vol. I, Paris, 1934.

GRUNDMANN, H. (1). *Studien über Joachim von Fiore*, Leipzig and Berlin, 1927.

GRUNDMANN, H. (2). *Religiöse Bewegungen im Mittelalter*, Berlin, 1935.

GRUNDMANN, H. (3). *Neue Forschungen über Joachim von Fiore* (Münstersche Forschungen I), Marburg, 1950.

*GRUNDMANN, H. (4). *Neue Beiträge zur Geschichte der religiösen Bewegungen im Mittelalter*. (Supplement to new edition of *Religiöse Bewegungen im Mittelalter*, Hildesheim, 1961.)

*GRUNDMANN, H. (5). *Ketzergeschichte des Mittelalters*, Göttingen, 1963. (Reprinted from vol. II of *Die Kirche in ihrer Geschichte*, ed. K. D. Schmidt and E. Wolf.)

*GRUNDMANN, H. (6). *Bibliographie zur Ketzergeschichte des Mittelalters, 1900–1966*. (*Sussidi Eruditi* no. 20), Rome, 1967.

*GRUNDMANN, H. (7). 'Ketzerverhöre des Spätmittelalters als quellenkritisches Problem,' in *Deutsches Archiv für Erforschung des Mittelalters*, vol. XXI, Cologne and Graz, 1965, pp. 519–575.

GRY, L. *Le millénarisme dans ses origines et son développement*, Paris, 1904.

*GUARNIERI, R. (1). *Il movimento del Libero Spirito. Testi e documenti*, Rome, 1965.

*GUARNIERI, R. (2). 'Frères du libre esprit', in M. Viller *et al.*, *Dictionnaire de Spiritualité*, vol. V, Paris, 1966, cols. 1241–68.

HAAGEN, F. *Geschichte Aachens*, vol. I, Aachen, 1873.

HAGENMEYER, H. *Peter der Eremite*, Leipzig, 1879.

HAHN, C. U. *Geschichte der Ketzer im Mittelalter*, vols. II, III, Stuttgart, 1845.

HAMPE, K. 'Eine frühe Verknüpfung der Weissagung vom Endkaiser mit Friedrich II und Konrad IV' in *Sitzungsberichte der Heidelberger Akademie der Wissenschaften (Philosophisch-historische Klasse)*, Abhandlung VI, 1917.

HARTING, D. *De munstersche Furie*, Enkhuizen, 1850.

HAUCK, A. *Kirchengeschichte Deutschlands*, vol. V, Leipzig, 1911.

HAUPT, H. (1). *Die religiösen Sekten in Franken*, Würzburg, 1882.

HAUPT, H. (2). 'Ein Beghardenprozess in Eichstädt vom Jahre 1381', in ZKG, vol. V (1882), pp. 487–98.

HAUPT, H. (3). 'Beiträge zur Geschichte der Sekte vom freien Geiste und des Beghardentums', in ZKG, vol. VII (1885), pp. 503–76. (Includes emendations to Albertus Magnus, *Compilatio*, from another MS.)

HAUPT, H. (4). 'Zur Biographie des Nicolaus von Basel', in ZKG, vol. VII (1885), pp. 508–11. (Includes emendations to confession of Martin of Mainz.)

HAUPT, H. (5). 'Zur Geschichte der Geissler', in ZKG, vol. IX (1888), pp. 114–19. (Includes emendations to Sonderhausen articles from another MS.)

HAUPT, H. (6). 'Husitische Propaganda in Deutschland', in *Historisches Taschenbuch*, 6th series, vol. VII, Leipzig, 1888, pp. 235–304.

HAUPT, H. (7). 'Zwei Traktate gegen Beginen und Begharden', in ZKG, vol. XII (1891), pp. 85–90.

HAUPT, H. (8). *Ein oberrheinischer Revolutionär aus dem Zeitalter Kaiser Maximilians I.* (*Westdeutsche Zeitschrift für Geschichte und Kunst*, Ergänzungsheft VIII), Trier, 1893, pp. 77–228.

HAUPT, H. (9). 'Beginen und Begarden', in RPT, vol. II, pp. 516–26.

HAUPT, H. (10). 'Brüder des freien Geistes', in RPT, vol. II, pp. 467–72.

HAUPT, H. (11). 'Kirchliche Geisselung und Geisslerbruderschaften', in RPT, vol. VI, pp. 432–44.

HAUPT, H. (12). 'Konrad Schmid', in ADB, vol. XXXI, p. 683.

HAUPT, H. (13). 'Wirsberg: Janko (Johannes) und Livin (Levin) von W.', in ADB, vol. XLIII, pp. 518–20.

HAURÉAU, B. *Histoire de la philosophie scolastique*, Part II, vol. I, Paris, 1880.

HEATH, R. *Anabaptism from its rise at Zwickau to its fall in Münster*, London, 1895.

HECKER, J. F. C. *The epidemics of the Middle Ages*, trans. Babington, London, 1859.

HEER, F. *Aufgang Europas: eine Studie zu den Zusammenhängen zwischen politischer Religiosität, Frömmigkeitsstil und dem Werden Europas im 12-ten Jahrhundert*, Vienna and Zurich, 1949.

HEIDELBERGER, F. *Kreuzzugsversuche um die Wende des 13-ten Jahrhunderts*, Berlin and Leipzig, 1911.

HEISIG, K. 'Die Geschichtsmetaphysik des Rolandsliedes und ihre Vorgeschichte', in *Zeitschrift für romanische Philologie*, vol. LV, Halle, 1935, pp. 1–87.

HEYER, F. *Der Kirchenbegriff der Schwärmer* (*Schriften des Vereins für Reformationsgeschichte*, vol. LXVI), Leipzig, 1939.

HEYMANN, F. G. *John Žižka and the Hussite revolution*, Princeton, 1955.

*HILLERBRAND, H. J. *Bibliographie des Täufertums 1520–1630*. (*Quellen zur Geschichte der Täufer, vol. X*), Gütersloh, 1962.

HINRICHS, C. *Luther and Müntzer, ihre Auseinandersetzung über Obrigkeit und Widerstandsrecht*. Berlin, 1952

HOCHHUT, W. H. 'Landgraf Philipp und die Wiedertäufer', in *Zeitschrift für die historische Theologie*, vol. XXIX, Hamburg and Gotha, 1859.

HOENIGER, R. *Der schwarze Tod in Deutschland*, Berlin, 1882.

HOLINKA, R. 'Sektářství v Cechách před revolucí husitskou, Bratislava, 1929.

HOLL, K. 'Luther und die Schwärmer', in his *Gesammelte Aufsätze zur Kirchengeschichte*, vol. I, Tübingen, 1923.

HORSCH, J. 'The rise and fall of the Anabaptists of Münster', in *Mennonite Quarterly Review*, vol. X, Goshen, Indiana, 1935, pp. 92–103, 129–43.

HÜBNER, A. *Die deutschen Geisslerlieder*, Berlin and Leipzig, 1931.

HÜBSCHER, A. *Die grosse Weissagung. Texte, Geschichte und Deutung der Prophezeiungen von den biblischen Propheten bis auf unsere Zeit*, Munich, 1952.

HUGENHOLTZ, F. W. N. *Drie boerenopstanden uit de veertiende eeuw*, Haarlem, 1949.

HUNDESHAGEN, C. B. 'Der Communismus und die ascetische Socialreform im Laufe der christlichen Jahrhunderte', in *Theologische Studien und Kritiken*, vol. XVIII, Gotha, 1845, pp. 535–607, 821–72.

HYAMSON, A. M. 'Pseudo-messiahs', in ERE, vol. VIII, pp. 581–7.

Il Movimento dei disciplinati nel settimo centenario dal suo inizio (Perugia 1260). Deputazione di storia patria per l'Umbria. Appendici al Bolletino no. 9, Perugia, 1960.

JANSSEN, H. Q. 'Tanchelijn', in *Annales de l'Académie d'archéologie de Belgique*, vol. XXIII, Antwerp, 1867, pp. 374–450.

JOHNSON, A. R. *Sacral kingship in Ancient Israel*, Cardiff, 1955.

JONES, ERNEST. *On the nightmare. Part II: The connections between the nightmare and certain medieval superstitions*, London, 1931.

JONES, R. M. *Studies in mystical religion*, London, 1909.

JORDAN, R. *Zur Schlacht bei Frankenhausen* (*Zur Geschichte der Stadt Mühlhausen in Thüringen*, vol. IV), Mühlhausen in Thuringia, 1908.

OURDAIN, C. 'Mémoire sur les sources philosophiques des hérésies d'Amaury de Chartres et de David de Dinant', in *Mémoires de l'Académie des Inscriptions et Belles-Lettres*, vol. XXVI, Paris, 1870, pp. 467–98.

JUNDT, A. *Histoire du panthéisme populaire au Moyen Âge et au 16e siècle*, Paris, 1875.

JUSSERAND, J. J. *English wayfaring life in the Middle Ages*, trans. L. T. Smith, London, 1950 (first published 1889).

KAHN, SALOMON. 'Les juifs de Montpellier au Moyen Âge', in *Revue des études juives*, vol. XXII, Paris, 1891, pp. 264–79.

*KAMINSKY, H. (1). 'Hussite radicalism and the origins of Tabor 1415–1418', in *Medievalia et Humanistica*, vol. X, Boulder, Colorado, 1956, pp. 102–30.

*KAMINSKY, H. (2). 'Chiliasm and the Hussite Revolution', in *Church History*, vol. XXVI, New York, 1957, pp. 43–71.

*KAMINSKY, H. (3). 'The Free Spirit in the Hussite Revolution', in *Millennial Dreams in Action* (MW), pp. 166–86.

KAMPERS, F. (1). *Die deutsche Kaiseridee in Prophetie und Sage*, Munich, 1896.

KAMPERS, F. (1A). *Kaiserprophetien und Kaisersagen im Mittelalter*, Munich, 1895. (Same as Kampers (1) but with Appendices.)

KAMPERS, F. (2). *Vom Werdegang der abendländischen Kaisermystik*, Leipzig and Berlin, 1924.

KAUTSKY, K. *Communism in Central Europe in the time of the Reformation*, trans. Mulliken, London, 1897.

KAWERAU, P. *Melchior Hoffmann als religiöser Denker*, Haarlem, 1954.

KELLER, L. *Geschichte der Wiedertäufer und ihres Reiches zu Münster*, Münster, 1880.

KERVYN DE LETTENHOVE, C. B. (1). 'Bertrand de Rays', in *Biographie nationale de Belgique*, vol. I, pp. 338–42.

KERVYN DE LETTENHOVE, C. B. (2). *Histoire de Flandre*, 6 vols., Brussels, 1847–50.

KESTENBERG-GLADSTEIN, R. 'A fifteenth-century polemic against Joachism, and its background', in *Journal of the Warburg and Courtauld Institutes*, vol. XVIII, London, 1955, pp. 245–95.

KISCH, G. *The Jews in medieval Germany*, Cambridge, 1950.

*KLASSEN, P. J. *The economics of Anabaptism, 1525–1560* (*Studies in European History*, no. 3), The Hague, 1964.

KLAUSNER, J. *The messianic idea in Israel*, trans. Stinespring, London, 1956.

KLOSE, S. B. *Von Breslau. Dokumentirte Geschichte und Beschreibung*, vol. II, Breslau, 1781.

KNOX, R. A. *Enthusiasm, a chapter in the history of religion*, Oxford, 1950.

KÖHLER, W. 'Münster, Wiedertäufer', in RPT, vol. XIII, pp. 539–53.

*KONRAD, R. (1). *De ortu et tempore Antichristi. Antichristvorstellung und Geschichtsbild des Abtes Adso von Montier-en-Der.* (*Münchener Historische Studien, Abteilung Mittelalterliche Geschichte*, vol. I), Kallmütz b. Regensburg, 1964.

*KONRAD, R. (2). 'Das himmlische und das irdische Jerusalem im mittelalterlichen Denken. Mystische Vorstellung und geschichtliche Wirkung', in *Speculum historiale*, ed. C. Bauer, L. Boehm and M. Müller, Freiburg i. Br. and Munich, 1965, pp. 523–40.

KRACAUER, I. *Die politische Geschichte der Frankfurter Juden bis zum Jahre 1349*, Frankfort-on-Main, 1911.

KRAFT, H. 'Gab es einen Gnostiker Karpokrates?', in *Theologische Zeitschrift*, vol. VIII, Basle, 1952, pp. 434–43.

KRIEHN, G. 'Studies in the sources of the social revolt of 1381', in *American Historical Review*, vol. VII, New York, 1901–2, pp. 254–85, 458–84.

KROFTA, K. (1). 'Bohemia in the fourteenth century', in CMH, vol. VII, chap. 6, pp. 155–82.

KROFTA, K. (2). 'John Hus', in CMH, vol. VIII, chap. 2, pp. 45–64.

KROFTA, K. (3). 'Bohemia in the fifteenth century', in CMH, vol. VIII, chap. 3, pp. 65–115.

*KULCSÁR, Z. *Eretnekmozgalmak a XI–XIV. században*, Budapest, 1964. (An exhaustive bibliography of heretical movements from the eleventh to the fourteenth centuries.)

LANCHESTER, H. C. O. 'Sibylline Oracles', in ERE, vol. II, pp. 496–500.

LATOMUS, JOANNES. *Corsendonca*, Antwerp, 1644.

LEA, H. C. *A history of the Inquisition of the Middle Ages*, vol. II, London, 1888.

LECHNER, K. 'Die grosse Geisselfahrt des Jahres 1349', in *Historisches Jahrbuch*, vol. V, Munich, 1884, pp. 437–62.

*LECLERCQ, J., VANDENBROUCKE, P., and BOUYER, L. *La spiritualité du moyen âge* (vol. II of *Histoire de la spiritualité chrétienne*), Paris, 1959.

*LEFF, G. *Heresy in the Later Middle Ages. The relation of heterodoxy to dissent, c. 1250–c. 1450*, 2 vols., Manchester and New York, 1967.

LEFRANC, A. *Les idées religieuses de Marguérite de Navarre*, Paris, 1898.

LEMPP, E. 'Sekte von Hall', in RPT, vol. VII, pp. 363–5.

LEVASSEUR, E. *Histoire des classes ouvrières françaises et de l'industrie en France avant 1789*, vol. I, Paris, 1900.

LINDSAY, P. and GROVES, R. *The Peasants' Revolt of 1381*, London, 1950.

LOCHNER, G. W. C. *Geschichte der Reichsstadt Nürnberg zur Zeit Kaiser Karls IV*, Berlin, 1873.

LOEB, I. 'Josef Haccohen et les chroniqueurs juifs', in *Revue des études juives*, vol. XVI, Paris, 1888, pp. 28–56, 209–23.

LOHMANN, A. *Zur geistigen Entwicklung Thomas Müntzers*, Leipzig and Berlin, 1931.

LOVEJOY, A. O. 'The communism of St Ambrose', in his *Essays in the History of Ideas*, London, 1949.

LOVEJOY, A. O. and BOAS, G. *Primitivism and related ideas in Antiquity*, Baltimore, 1935.

LÖWITH, K. *Meaning in History: the theological implications of the Philosophy of History*, Cambridge, 1950.

LUCAS, H. S. 'The great European famine of 1315, 1316 and 1317', in *Speculum*, vol. V, Cambridge, Mass., 1930, pp. 343–77.

LÜTZOW, F. H. H. W. *The life and times of Master John Hus*, London, 1909.

MACCULLOCH, J. A. (1). 'Eschatology', in ERE, vol. V, pp. 373–91.

MACCULLOCH, J. A. (2). *Medieval faith and fable*, London, 1932.

MAČEK, J. (1). *Ktož jsú boží bojovníci (Who are God's warriors)*, Prague, 1951.

MAČEK, J. (2). *Husitské revoluční hnutí*, Prague, 1952.

*MAČEK, J. (3). *The Hussite Movement in Bohemia*, Prague, 1958; London and Prague, 1965 (trans. of Maček (2), by V. Fried and I. Milner).

MCDONNELL, E. W. *The Beguines and Beghards in medieval culture*, New Brunswick, 1954.

MELLINK, A. F. (1). *De Wederdopers in de Noordelijke Nederlanden (1531–1544)*, Groningen, 1953.

*MELLINK, A. F. (2). 'The mutal relations between the Münster Anabaptists and the Netherlands', in *Archiv für Reformationsgeschichte*, vol. I, Berlin, 1959, pp. 16–33.

**Mennonite Encyclopedia*. 4 vols., Scottdale, Pennsylvania, 1955–9.

MERX, O. *Thomas Münzer und Heinrich Pfeiffer, 1523–5. Ein Beitrag zur Geschichte des Bauernkrieges in Thüringen*, Göttingen, 1889.

MEUSEL, A. *Thomas Müntzer und seine Zeit*, Berlin, 1952.

MEYER, CHRISTIAN (1). 'Zur Geschichte der Wiedertäufer in Ober-schwaben', in *Zeitschrift des historischen Vereins für Schwaben und Neuburg*, vol. I, Augsburg, 1874, pp. 271 sq.

MEYER, CHRISTIAN (2). 'Der Widertäufer Nikolaus Storch und seine Anhänger in Hof', in ZKG, vol. XVI (1896), pp. 117–24.

MEYER, VICTOR. *Tile Kolup (der falsche Friedrich) und die Wiederkunft eines ächten Friedrich, Kaisers der Deutschen*, Wetzlar, 1868.

MIRET Y SANS, J. 'Le massacre des Juifs de Montclus en 1320', in *Revue des études juives*, vol. LIII, Paris, 1907, pp. 255–66.

MOHR, W. 'Tanchelm von Antwerpen. Eine nochmalige Überprüfung der Quellenlage', in *Annales Universitatis Saraviensis, Philosophie-Lettres*, vol. III, Saarbrucken, 1954, pp. 234–47.

*MOLNÁR, A. (1). 'Eschatologická naděje česke reformace' (The eschato-logical hope in the Czech Reformation), in Hromáda *et al.*, *Od reformace k zítřku* (From Reformation to Tomorrow), Prague, 1956, pp. 11–101.

*MOLNÁR, A. (2). 'Le mouvement préhussite et la fin du temps', in *Communio Viatorum*, vol. I, Prague, 1958, pp. 27–32.

MORGHEN, R. *Medioevo cristiano*, Bari, 1951.

MOSHEIM, J. L. von (1). *Institutiones historiae ecclesiasticae Novi Testamenti*, vol. I, Helmstadt, 1764.

MOSHEIM, J. L. von (2). *De Beghardis et Beguinabus commentarius*, Leipzig, 1790.

MÜLLER, EWALD. *Das Konzil von Vienne, 1311–12. Seine Quellen und seine Geschichte*, Münster, 1934.

MÜLLER, KARL (1). *Kirchengeschichte*, vol. I, Freiburg in Breisgau, 1892.

MÜLLER, KARL (2). 'Calvin und die "Libertiner"', in ZKG, vol. XL (1922), pp. 83–129.

MUNRO, D. C. 'The Children's Crusade', in *American Historical Review*, vol. XIX, London, 1914, pp. 516–24.

NABHOLZ, H. 'Medieval society in transition', in CEH, vol. I, chap. 8, pp. 493–562.

NATUSIUS, M. von. *Die christlich-socialen Ideen der Reformationszeit und ihre Herkunft*, Gütersloh, 1897.

*NEUMANN, E. G. *Rheinisches Beginen- und Begardenwesen. (Mainzer Abhand-lungen zur mittleren und neueren Geschichte*, vol. IV), Meisenheim am Glan, 1960.

NEWMAN, A. H. *A history of anti-pedobaptism*, Philadelphia, 1897.

NIESEL, W. 'Calvin und die Libertiner', in ZKG, vol. XLVIII (1929), pp. 58–74.

NIGG, W. (1). *Das ewige Reich*, Berlin and Munich, 1944.

NIGG, W. (2). *Das Buch der Ketzer*, Zurich, 1949.

NOHL, J. *The Black Death*, trans. Clarke, London, 1926.

OESTERLEY, W. O. E. and ROBINSON, T. H. *Hebrew religion, its origin and development*, London, 1949.

OLIGER, L. *De secta Spiritus Libertatis in Umbria saeculo XIV. Disquisitio et Documenta. (Storia e Letteratura, Raccolta di Studi e Testi*, vol. III), Rome, 1943.

OMAN, C. *The Great Revolt of 1381*, Oxford, 1906.

OWST, G. R. *Literature and pulpit in medieval England*, Cambridge, 1933.

PALACKÝ, F. *Geschichte von Boehmen*, vol. III, Prague, 1845.

PARKES, J. W. *The Jew in the medieval community*, London, 1938.

PAYNE, E. A. *The Anabaptists of the 16th century*, London, 1949.

PEARSON, K. 'The Kingdom of God', in *Modern Review*, vol. V, London, 1884, pp. 29–56, 259–83.

PETIT-DUTAILLIS, C. (1). 'Introduction historique' to A. Réville, *Le soulèvement des travailleurs en Angleterre en 1381* Paris, 1898.

PETIT-DUTAILLIS, C. (2). 'Causes and general characteristics of the rising of 1381', in *Studies and notes supplementary to Stubbs' Constitutional History*, vol. II, Manchester, 1914, pp. 252–304.

PEUCKERT, W. E. *Die grosse Wende. Das apokalyptische Saeculum und Luther*, Hamburg, 1948.

PFANNENSCHMID, H. 'Zur Geschichte der deutschen und niederländischen Geissler', in P. Runge, *Die Lieder und Melodien der Geissler des Jahres 1349*, Leipzig, 1900.

PHILIPPEN, L. J. M. 'De Heilige Norbertus en de strijd tegen het Tanchelmisme te Antwerpen', in *Bijdragen tot de Geschiedenis*, vol. XXV, Antwerp, 1934, pp. 251–88.

PIRENNE, H. (1). *Le soulèvement de la Flandre maritime de 1323–1328*, Brussels, 1900.

PIRENNE, H. (2). 'Tanchelm et le projet de démembrement du diocèse d'Utrecht vers 1100', in *Bulletin de l'Académie royale de Belgique, Classe des Lettres*, fifth series, vol. XIII, Brussels, 1927, pp. 112–19.

PIRENNE, H. (3). *A history of Europe from the Invasions to the sixteenth century*, trans. Miall, London, 1952.

PORGÈS, N. 'Les relations hébraïques des persécutions des Juifs pendant la première croisade', in *Revue des études juives*, Paris, vol. XXV (1892), pp. 181–201; vol. XXVI (1893), pp. 183–97.

POTTHAST, A. *Bibliotheca historica Medii Aevi*, 2 vols., Berlin, 1896.

POWER, E. 'The position of women', in *Legacy of the Middle Ages*, ed. Crump and Jacob, chap. VII, Oxford, 1926, pp. 401–34.

PRA, M. DAL. *Amalrico di Bena*, Milan, 1951.

PREGER, W. (1). *Geschichte der deutschen Mystik im Mittelalter*, vol. I, Leipzig, 1874.

PREGER, W. (2). *Beiträge zur Geschichte der religiösen Bewegung in den Niederlanden in der zweiten Hälfte des vierzehnten Jahrhunderts*, in ABAW, vol. XXI, Part 1, Munich, 1894.

PREUSS, H. *Die Vorstellungen vom Antichrist im späteren Mittelalter bei Luther und in der konfessionellen Polemik*, Leipzig, 1906.

RADCKE, F. *Die eschatologischen Anschauungen Bernhards von Clairvaux*, Langensalza, 1915.

RAUSCHEN, G. (ed.), *Die Legende Karls des Grossen im 11-ten und 12-ten Jahrhundert* Leipzig, 1890.

Realencyklopädie für protestantische Theologie und Kirche, 3rd edn, Leipzig, 1896–1913.

REEVES, M. E. (1). 'The *Liber Figurarum* of Joachim of Fiore', in *Medieval and Renaissance Studies*, vol. II, London, 1951, pp. 57–81.

*REEVES, M. E. (2). 'Joachimist influences on the idea of a Last World Emperor', in *Traditio*, vol. XVII, New York, 1961, pp. 323–70.

REMBERT, C. *Die Wiedertäufer im Herzogtum Jülich*, Berlin, 1899.

REUTER, H. *Geschichte der religiösen Aufklärung im Mittelalter*, vol. II, Berlin, 1877.

RÉVILLE, A. *Le soulèvement des travailleurs en Angleterre en 1381 (Mémoires et documents publiés par la Société de l'École des Chartes,* II), Paris, 1898.

RIGAUX, B. *L'Antéchrist et l'opposition au Royaume Messianique dans l'Ancien et le Nouveau Testament,* Gembloux and Paris, 1932.

RITSCHL, H. *Die Kommune der Wiedertäufer in Münster,* Bonn and Leipzig, 1923.

ROHR, J. 'Die Prophetie im letzten Jahrhundert vor der Reformation als Geschichtsquelle und Geschichtsfaktor', in *Historisches Jahrbuch,* vol. XIX, Munich, 1898, pp. 29–56, 423–66.

RÖHRICHT, R. (1). 'Die Pilgerfahrten nach dem Heiligen Lande vor den Kreuzzügen', in *Historisches Taschenbuch,* fifth series, vol. V, Leipzig, 1875, pp. 323–96.

RÖHRICHT, R. (2). 'Bibliographische Beiträge zur Geschichte der Geissler', in ZKG, vol. I (1877), pp. 313–21.

RÖHRICHT, R. (3). 'Die Pastorellen (1251)', in ZKG, vol. VI (1884), pp. 290–95.

RÖHRICHT, R. (4). *Geschichte des ersten Kreuzzuges,* Innsbruck, 1901.

ROSENKRANZ, A. 'Prophetische Kaisererwartungen im ausgehenden Mittelalter', in *Preussische Jahrbücher,* vol. CXIX, Berlin, 1905, pp. 508–24.

ROTH, C. 'The Jews in the Middle Ages', in CMH, vol. VII, chap. 22, pp. 632–63.

ROUSSET, P. (1). *Les origines et les caractères de la première Croisade,* Neuchâtel, 1945.

ROUSSET, P. (2). 'L'idée de croisade chez les chroniqueurs d'Occident', in *Storia del Medioevo* (MW), pp. 547–63.

RUNCIMAN, S. (1). *The Medieval Manichee,* Cambridge, 1947.

RUNCIMAN, S. (2). *A history of the crusades,* 3 vols., Cambridge, 1951–4.

*RUPP, E. G. 'Thomas Müntzer, Hans Huth and the Gospel of all creatures', in *Bulletin of the John Rylands Library,* vol. XLIII, Manchester, 1960–61, pp. 492–519.

*RUSSELL, J. B. (1). 'Saint Boniface and the Eccentrics', in *Church History,* vol. XXXIII, no. 3, Chicago, 1964, pp. 235–47.

*RUSSELL, J. B. (2). *Dissent and Reform in the Early Middle Ages,* Berkeley and Los Angeles, 1965.

RUSSO, F. *Bibliografia Giochimita (Biblioteca di Bibliografia Italiana,* vol. XXVIII), Florence, 1954.

SAULNIER, V. L. (ed.). Marguerite de Navarre: *Théâtre profane.* With commentary, Paris, 1946.

SCHAAB, A. *Diplomatische Geschichte der Juden zu Mainz,* Mainz, 1855.

SCHÄFFLER, A. 'Hans Böhm', in ADB, vol. III, pp. 62–4.

SCHIFF, O. (1). 'Thomas Münzer und die Bauernbewegung am Oberrhein', in *Historische Zeitschrift,* vol. CX, Munich, 1913, pp. 67–90.

SCHIFF, O. (2). 'Die Wirsberger. Ein Beitrag zur Geschichte der revolutionären Apokalyptik im 15-ten Jahrhundert', in *Historische Vierteljahrschrift,* vol. XXVI, Dresden, 1931, pp. 776–86.

SCHMIDT, KARL. *Histoire et doctrine de la secte des Cathares ou Albigeois,* 2 vols., Paris, 1848–9.

SCHREIBER, H. *Der Bundschuh zu Lehen im Breisgau,* Freiburg in Breisgau, 1824.

SCHUBERT, H. von. *Der Kommunismus der Wiedertäufer in Münster und seine Quellen,* Heidelberg, 1919.

SCHULTHEISS, F. G. *Die deutsche Volkssage vom Fortleben und der Wiederkehr Kaiser Friedrichs II,* Berlin, 1911.

*SEIBT, F. (1). 'Die Hussitenzeit als Kulturepoche' in *Historische Zeitschrift*, vol. CVC, Munich, 1962, pp. 21–61.

*SEIBT, F. (2). *Hussitica. Zur Struktur einer Revolution*, Cologne and Graz, 1965.

SETTON, K. M. and BALDWIN, M. W. (ed.). *A history of the crusades*, vol. I: *The first hundred years*, Philadelphia, 1955.

SIMON, O. *Überlieferung und Handschriftsverhältnis des Traktates 'Schwester Katrei'*, Halle, 1906.

SMIRIN, M. M. *Der Volksaufstand des Thomas Müntzer und der grosse Bauernkrieg*, Berlin, 1952. (Translated from the Russian.)

SMITHSON, R. J. *The Anabaptists*, London, 1935.

SÖDERBLOM, N. *La vie future d'après le mazdéisme: étude d'eschatologie comparée*, Paris, 1901.

SOMMARIVA, L. 'Studi recenti sulle eresie medievali (1939–52)', in *Revista storica italiana*, vol. LXIV, fasc. II, Naples, 1952, pp. 237–68.

SONNE, I. 'Nouvel examen des trois Relations hébraïques sur les persecutions de 1096', in *Revue des études juives*, vol. XCVI, Paris, 1933, pp. 113–56.

SPITZER, L. 'Turlupin', in *Modern Language Notes*, vol. LXI, Baltimore, 1946, pp. 104–8.

*STAYER, J. M. (1). 'Hans Hut's doctrine of the sword: an attempted solution', in *Mennonite Quarterly Review*, vol. XXXIX, Goshen, Indiana, 1965, pp. 181–91.

*STAYER, J. M. (2). 'The Münsterite rationalization of Bernhard Rothmann', in *Journal of the history of ideas*, vol. XVIII, Lancaster (Penn.) and New York, 1967, pp. 179–92.

STEEL, A. *Richard II*, Cambridge, 1941.

STEVENSON, W. B. 'The First Crusade', in CMH, vol. V, chap. 7, pp. 265–99.

Storia del Medioevo. Vol. III of the Proceedings of the Tenth International Congress of Historical Sciences, Florence, 1955.

STRAUCH, P. 'Nicolaus von Basel', in ADB, vol. XXIII, pp. 620–21.

STUMPF, A. *Historia Flagellantium, praecipue in Thuringia*. Written in 1780 but first appeared (ed. Erhard) in vol. II, *Neue Mitteilungen aus dem Gebiet historisch-antiquarischer Forschungen*, Halle and Nordhausen, 1836.

*STUPPERICH, R. *Das Münsterische Täufertum. Ergebnisse und Probleme der neueren Forschung*, Munster i. W., 1958.

*SUMBERG, L. A. M. 'The *Tafurs* and the First Crusade', in *Medieval Studies* (University of Toronto), vol. XXI, London, New York, 1959, pp. 224–46.

SVÁTEK, J. *Culturhistorische Bilder aus Böhmen*, Vienna, 1879.

SYBEL, H. von. *Geschichte des ersten Kreuzzuges* Leipzig, 1881.

TAMASSIA, N. *La famiglia italiana nei secoli XV e XVI*, Milan, Palermo, Naples, 1910.

TAUBES, J. *Abendländische Eschatologie*, Bern, 1947.

THALAMAS, A. *La société seigneuriale française, 1050–1270*, Paris, 1951.

THOMA, A. 'Der Pfeifer von Niklashausen', in *Preussische Jahrbücher*, vol. LX, Berlin, 1887, pp. 541–79.

TRACHTENBERG, J. *The Devil and the Jews. The medieval conception of the Jew and its relation to modern anti-semitism*, New Haven, Conn., 1944.

TREVELYAN, G. M. *England in the age of Wycliffe*, London, 1899.

TROELTSCH, E. *The social teaching of the Christian Churches*, trans. Wyon, 2 vols., 3rd edn., London, 1950.

TURBERVILLE, A. S. *Medieval heresy and the Inquisition*, London, 1920.

VERNET, F. 'Les frères du libre esprit', in *Dictionnaire de Théologie Catholique*, vol. VI, Paris, 1920, cols. 800–809.

VOEGELIN, E. *The new science of politics*, Chicago, 1952.

VOIGT, GEORG. 'Die deutsche Kaisersage', in *Historische Zeitschrift*, vol. XXVI, Munich, 1871, pp. 131–87.

VÖLTER, D. 'Die Secte von Schwabisch-Hall und der Ursprung der deutschen Kaisersage', in ZKG, vol. IV (1881), pp. 360–93.

VULLIAUD, P. *La fin du monde*, Paris, 1952.

WAAS, A. 'Die grosse Wendung im deutschen Bauernkrieg', in *Historische Zeitschrift*, Munich, 1938, vol. CLVIII, pp. 457–91; vol. CLIX, pp. 22–53.

WADSTEIN, E. *Die eschatologische Ideengruppe: Antichrist, Weltsabbat, Weltende und Weltgericht*, Leipzig, 1896.

WALTER, G. *Histoire du Communisme*, vol. I, *Les origines judaïques, chrétiennes, grecques, latines*, Paris, 1931.

WALTER, L.-G. *Contributions à l'étude de la formation de l'esprit révolutionnaire en Europe: Thomas Munzer et les luttes sociales à l'époque del a Réforme*, Paris, 1927.

WAPPLER, P. *Die Täuferbewegung in Thüringen von 1526-1584*, Jena, 1913.

WEBER, M. (1). *Gesammelte Aufsätze zur Religionssoziologie*, vols. I, II, Tübingen, 1920.

WEBER, M. (2). *Wirtschaft und Gesellschaft*, Tübingen, 1925.

WELLER, K. 'König Konrad IV und die Schwaben', in *Württembergische Vierteljahrshefte für Landesgeschichte*, new series, vol. V, Stuttgart, 1896, pp. 113–60.

*WERNER, E. (1). 'Popular ideologies in late medieval Europe: Taborite chiliasm and its antecedents', in *Comparative Studies in Society and History*, vol. II, The Hague, 1959–60, pp. 344–63.

*WERNER, E. (2). 'Messianische Bewegungen im Mittelalter', in *Zeitschrift für Geschichtswissenschaft*, vol. X, Berlin, 1962, pp. 371–96, 598–622.

*WERNER, E. and ERBSTÖSSER, M. 'Sozial-religiöse Bewegungen im Mittelalter', in *Wissenschaftliche Zeitschrift der Karl-Marx-Universität Leipzig, Gesellschafts- und Sprachwissenschaftliche Reihe*, no. 7, 1957–8, pp. 257–82.

WERUNSKY, E. *Geschichte Kaiser Karls IV und seiner Zeit*, Innsbruck, 1882.

WEYDEN, E. *Geschichte der Juden in Köln am Rhein*, Cologne, 1867.

WICKERSHEIMER, E. 'Les accusations d'empoisonnement portées pendant la première moitié du XIVe siècle contre les lépreux et les juifs', in *Bulletin du quatrième Congrès international d'histoire de la médicine*, Brussels, 1923 (published 1927).

WILKINSON, B. 'The Peasants' Revolt of 1381', in *Speculum*, vol. XV, Cambridge, Mass., 1940, pp. 12–35.

*WILLIAMS, G. H. *The Radical Reformation*, London, 1962.

WINKELMANN, E. 'Holzschuh', in ADB, vol. XV, pp. 792–3.

*WOLF, G. (ed.). *Stupor Mundi. Zur Geschichte Friedrichs II von Hohenstauffen*, Darmstadt, 1966.

WOLFF, T. *Die Bauernkreuzzüge des Jahres 1096*, Tübingen, 1891.

WORKMAN, H. B. *John Wiclif*, 2 vols., Oxford, 1926.

*ZIEGLER, P. *The Black Death*, London, 1969.

ZÖCKLER, O. *Kritische Geschichte der Askese*, Frankfort-on-Main and Erlangen, 1863.

*ZSCHÄBITZ, G. *Zur mitteldeutschen Wiedertäuferbewegung nach dem grossen Bauernkrieg*, Berlin, 1958.

3 General Works on Millenarian and Messianic Movements in the World

ANDERSSON, E. *Messianic popular movements in the Lower Congo*, Uppsala, 1958.

Archives de sociologie des religions, vol. IV (*Messianismes et millénarismes*) and vol. V (*Les messianismes dans le monde*), Paris, 1957–8.

BURRIDGE, K. O. L. *New Heaven, new earth: a study of millenarian activities*, Oxford, 1969.

*COHN, N. 'Reflexions sur le millénarisme', in *Archives de sociologie des religions*, vol. V, Paris, 1958, pp. 103–7.

COHN, N. 'Medieval Millenarism: its bearing on the comparative study of millenarian movements,' in *Millennial Dreams in Action*, pp. 31–43.

DESROCHE, H. 'Messianismus', in *Die Religion in Geschichte und Gegenwart*, vol. IV, Tübingen, 1960.

GUARIGLIA, G. *Prophetismus und Heilserwartungs-Bewegungen als völkerkundliches und religionsgeschichtliches Problem*. (*Wiener Beiträge zur Kulturgeschichte und Linguistik*, vol. XIII) Vienna, 1959.

HOBSBAWM, E. J. *Primitive Rebels*, Manchester, 1959.

LANTERNARI, V. *The religions of the oppressed. A study of modern messianic cults*, trans. Sergio, London, 1963.

Millennial Dreams in Action, ed. S. L. Thrupp (*Comparative Studies in Society and History, Supplement II*), The Hague, 1962.

MÜHLMANN, W. E. *Chiliasmus und Nativismus. Studien zur Psychologie, Soziologie und historischen Kasuistik der Umsturzbewegungen*, Berlin, 1961.

SUNDKLER, B. *Bantu Prophets in South Africa*, London, 1948.

WORSLEY, P. *The trumpet shall sound. A study of 'Cargo' Cults in Melanesia*, London, 1957.

Index

Acts of the Apostles, on community of goods, 194, 197, 200, 241, 259

Adam-cult, and the Free Spirit, 180–1, 210; amongst Adamites, 220; and Böhm, 233

Adamites, Bohemian, 219–21

'Adam-Moses', Adamite leader, 220–1

Adso, monk, on Antichrist, 78

Albertus Magnus, on the Free Spirit, 163

Aldebert, heresiarch, 42–4; claims sainthood, 43; his following, 42–3; condemned by synods, 43

Amaurians: leadership, 152–3; apostolate and doctrine, 154–6; female followers, 160

Amaury of Bène, philosopher, 153–4

Ambrose, St, on community of goods, 193, 200

'Ambrosiaster', on freedom and slavery, 192

Anabaptism, and Müntzer, 250–1, 284; general characteristics of, 253–4; millenarian and communistic, 254–5, 258–80. (See also Münster, revolutionary)

Antichrist, Biblical origins of the idea of, 33–4; medieval ideas of, 35; expectations of, in Middle Ages, 35–6, 85–6; during First Crusade, 75; amongst followers of Vincent Ferrer, 145; amongst Taborites, 205–6; amongst Anabaptists, 254, 261; prophecies concerning, in Lactantius, 28; in Commodianus, 28; in *Tiburtina*, 31; in *Pseudo-Methodius*, 32; in Adso, 78; by Benzo, 72; in Roquetaillade, 105; in Joachim of Fiore, 110; by Brother Arnold, 112; by Milič, 205–6; by Matthew of Janov, 205–6; by Storch, 236; dramas about, 79, 136; ministers of Antichrist: Moslems, 75; Jews, 78–9; 86; clergy, 80–1, 83–4, 112, 145, 223; the rich, 101, 215; Lutherans and Catholics, 253–4; Pope as, 80–1, 83–4, 112, 156, 211, 243; Frederick II as, 112–13, 114; and Satan, 34, 86; as a Jew, 78–9; Babylon the birthplace of, 74, 77, 215

Antiochus Epiphanes, persecutes Judaism, 21; in Book of Daniel, 33, 34

Apostolic life, as ideal, 38; its appeal, 37–9

Aquinas, St Thomas, on property, 100

Aristotle, banned at Paris, 153–4

Arnold, Brother, prophecy by, 112–13, 118, 130

Artisans, in local industry, 58; in export industry, 58–9. (See also Cloth-workers; Guilds; Poor, the revolutionary)

Augustine, St, discredits millenarianism, 29; on equality, 193

Aurelius, Bishop of Le Puy, 42

Avaritia, 101, 121, 122, 158, 203, 225, 227, 242

Babylon, as symbol of evil, in Sibylline prophecies, 74; in *Book of a Hundred Chapters*, 121; in Revelation, 215–16; in Rothmann's pamphlets, 274; associated with Church of Rome, 81, 274; with Holy Roman Empire, 111; with the

Müntzer—(contd.)
of, 240–1, 247–8; pamphlet against
the rich, 241–2; and against
Luther, 242–4; at Mühlhausen,
244–5; role of, in the Peasants'
War, 246–50; letter to followers at
Allstedt by, 247–8; capture and
execution of, 250; posthumous
fame of, 250–1; and flagellants,
147, 237. (See also Luther;
Storch)

Neo-Platonism, and the Free Spirit,
153, 154, 172, 179
Nicholas of Basle, adept of the Free
Spirit, 165–6, 181
Nietzsche, Friedrich, 148–9
Nimrod, as originator of private pro-
perty, 248, 258
Norbert, St, 40; opposes Tanchelm,
47; biography of, 49–50; volun-
tary poverty of, 100
Novus dux, in Joachite prophecy,
110, 112

Origen, discredits millenarianism, 29
Ovid, on Golden Age, 187
Owst, G. R., translation of Brom-
yard by, 201

Papias, 'Apostolic Father', mil-
lenarian prophecy by, 26–7
Paschal II, Pope, 47
Pastoureaux (see Crusade of the
Shepherds, in 1251, 1320)
Paul, St, on Antichrist, 33–4
Peasantry, social situation of, 54–6,
99; and English Peasants' Revolt,
198; and Taborites, 209, 218;
and Böhm, 231; in German Pea-
sants' War, 245, 249; little inclined
to millenarianism, 55, 126, 245
Peasants' Revolt, English, 198, 242,
245
Peasants' War, German, 245–6,
248–9, 254, 257
Pepin, Frankish king, 43–4
Persian religion, 19, 34
Peter the Hermit, 62, 67, 94, 129
Pfeiffer, Heinrich, revolutionary of
Mühlhausen, 244, 245, 247, 249,
250
Philip II (Augustus) of France, 90,
94, 156; as 'second Charlemagne',
94

Philip V of France, 102–3
Philip V of France, bans flagellants,
140
Philip, Landgrave of Hesse, 248–50
Philippa of Hainaut, Queen of England, 164
Pikarti: arrival of Picards in Bohemia, 211; radical Taborites,
219–20, 224, 260
Pirenne, Henri, 105
Plotinus, and the Free Spirit, 172–4
Poor, the revolutionary, social situation of, 58–60, 87–8; salvationist
tendencies amongst, 83; see themselves as Elect ('Saints'), 65, 85;
hostility of, towards Jews, 75,
78–9, 80; towards clergy, 80–1,
83–4; towards the rich, 98–101,
116–17; associated with First
Crusade, 62–9, 72–3; with Second
Crusade, 69–70, 73–4; with Fulk
of Neuilly, 89; with Pseudo-
Baldwin, 92–3; with Shepherds'
Crusade of 1251, 95; with
Caputiati, 100; with later popular
crusades and revolts, 101–5;
with Frederick II, 112–13;
with Pseudo-Frederick, 114–15;
with resurrected Frederick II,
116–17; with flagellants, 128, 130,
137–40, 144–7; with Pruystinck,
170; with English Peasants'
Revolt, 203–4; with Taborites,
208–9; with Böhm, 226, 228–9;
with Bundschuh, 234; with Müntzer, 237, 246–7; with Münster,
259, 266; role ascribed to, by
Roquetaillade, 105; by Brother
Arnold, 112; in Reformation of
Sigismund, 118–19; in Book of a
Hundred Chapters, 121; by Ball,
199; by Bromyard, 201–2; by
Böhm, 228; by Müntzer, 242,
244–5; by Rothmann, 266, 274;
by Bockelson, 273–4. (See also
Artisans; Cloth-workers; Peasantry)
Population, surplus, in Flanders,
57–60; in Bohemia, 208–9; other
references, 59, 63, 87–8, 107, 204,
237
Porete, Marguerite, adept of the
Free Spirit, 149, 163, 183–6. (See
also Mirouer des simples ames)

PHILOSOPHY

CONFUCIUS D. Howard Smith   75p
An introduction to the Way of Confucius – the system of belief
which was the inspiration behind one of the richest and noblest
civilisations the world has known.

MAGIC AND THE MILLENNIUM Bryan Wilson   £2.50
'Civilised' man's impact on the Third World has thrown up many
strange millenarian religions. This classic of the sociology and
anthropology of religion casts light on the very bases of man's
hopes and fears for the future and for redemption.

MARX'S GRUNDRISSE David McLellan   50p
A substantial set of extracts from the classic work in which Marx
develops an account of the process of alienation, analyses the nature
of work and develops a vision of the fully automated society in
which social wealth could be devoted to the all-round development
of the faculties of each individual. Edited by one of Britain's
leading Marxist scholars.

THE SOCIAL PHILOSOPHERS Robert Nisbet   £2.50
This provocative absorbing essay in social and intellectual history
shows that Western social philosophy has been preoccupied with
man's perennial quest for community: military, religious,
revolutionary, ecological and plural.

THE ROSICRUCIAN ENLIGHTENMENT
Frances A. Yates   £1.50
The Rosicrucians stood midway between the Dark Ages and the
scientific Renaissance: the Hermetic tradition of magic, alchemy
and the Kabbalah revealed.

RHYTHMS OF VISION Lawrence Blair   £1.95
A discussion of most of the current beliefs and theories relating to
modern mysticism, from the Great Pyramid to Kirlian photography.

CONSCIOUSNESS AND SOCIETY H. Stuart Hughes   75p
The re-orientation of European social thought from 1890 to 1930;
the ideas and works of Freud, Croce, Bergson, Jung, Sorel, Weber,
Durkheim, Proust, Mann, Gide, Hesse etc.

SOCIOLOGY

THE CHILDREN OF THE DREAM Bruno Bettelheim 75p
The dream is the kibbutz, one of the most enduring modern
attempts to create a Utopian human society. Bruno Bettelheim
examines the products of that dream and goes on to look at the
Western middle-class ideal of family.

CONSCIOUSNESS AND SOCIETY H. Stuart Hughes 75p
The re-orientation of European social thought from 1890 to 1930;
the ideas and works of Freud, Croce, Bergson, Jung, Sorel, Weber,
Durkheim, Proust, Mann, Gide, Hesse etc.

EDUCATION IN EVOLUTION John Hurt 60p
A classic of the history of education up to the Elementary
Education Act of 1870.

ETHNIC MINORITIES IN BRITAIN Ernest Krausz 50p
Dr. Krausz examines the root causes of the wide-spread prejudice
and outright hostility that have rapidly greeted the large-scale
immigration to Britain of Jews, Irish, Poles, Cypriots, and now
West Indians and Pakistanis.

THE FEMALE EUNUCH Germaine Greer 75p
The book that caused a revolution, the central focus of the
Women's Liberation movement.

FOLK DEVILS AND MORAL PANIC Stan Cohen 50p
Teddy Boys, Mods and Rockers, Hell's Angels, football
hooligans, Skinheads, student militants, drugtakers: these are the
folk devils of our time. A classic study of deviancy sociology.
Illustrated.

HOMO HIERARCHICUS Louis Dumont 90p
Ostensibly a study of the caste system in India, Louis Dumont
sheds new light on Western notions of equality and democracy: a
classic of Anthropology.

THE INTERNATIONAL URBAN CRISIS
Thomas L. Blair 60p
A lucid and disturbing analysis of the facts behind planning blight,
suburban sprawl, traffic congestion, and human alienation.

CRIME AND PERSONALITY   H. J. Eysenck £1.25
A revised edition of the controversial and classic study of race and intelligence.

LINGUISTICS AT LARGE   Noel Minnis 75p
Linguistics: a semantic jungle or a valuable key to the problems of sociology, anthropology, education, literary criticism, and psychology? Fourteen lectures presented to the ICA.

THE LORE AND LANGUAGE OF SCHOOLCHILDREN
Iona and Peter Opie £2.50
The classic study of the mysterious world and underworld of schoolchildren – the games, the chants, the rites and the rituals performed generation after generation by children all over Britain.

MAGIC AND THE MILLENNIUM   Bryan Wilson £2.50
'Civilised' man's impact on the Third World has thrown up many strange millenarian religions. This classic of the sociology and anthropology of religion casts light on the very bases of man's hopes and fears for the future and for redemption.

MYTHOLOGIES   Roland Barthes 50p
An entertaining and elating introduction to the science of semiology – the study of the signs and signals through which society expresses itself, from the leading intellectual star.

THE NEW TOWN STORY   Frank Schaffer 75p
A comprehensive review of the whole of Britain's post-war New Town movement from its early origins to likely developments in the year 2000 and beyond.

LITERATURE

THE COUNTRY AND THE CITY Raymond Williams £1.50
A study of responses in English literature and social thought to the
two kinds of human settlement: the 'country' and the 'city'.

THE ENGLISHMAN'S FLORA Geoffrey Grigson £1.95
A latterday herbal of the medicinal and culinary purposes of the
flowers and plants of the English countryside: magic, myth, lore
and truth. Illustrated.

THE ENGLISH NOVEL FROM DICKENS TO LAWRENCE
Raymond Williams 60p
A brilliant interpretation of a crucial period in the evaluation of the
novel. Raymond Williams vividly and compassionately portrays the
triumph of art in a time of crisis. 'A splendid corrective to the
wide-spread academic urge to separate literature from life.'
Angus Wilson.

THE RETURN OF THE VANISHING AMERICAN
Leslie A. Fiedler 50p
A classic definition of the myths which give a special character to
art and life in America: A stimulating venture in literary
anthropology.

THE STRANGER IN SHAKESPEARE Leslie A. Fiedler 90p
A completely radical analysis of Shakespeare's work which
illuminates the sub-surface psychological tensions.

THE WORLD AND THE BOOK Joseph Joapovici 75p
The author shows how the modern artist seeks to shake us out of
our habitual response to the world as a repository of meaning and
makes us see it for what it is: something irreducibly other,
incapable of being grasped by the imagination.

SHAKESPEARE THE MAN A. L. Rowse £1.25
The identity of the dark lady of the sonnets is revealed, and
Shakespeare is set in the context of his friends, patrons and
contemporaries – not merely of his plays.

A VIEW OF THE ENGLISH STAGE Kenneth Tynan £1.75
The very best of Kenneth Tynan's theatre criticism from 1948 to
1968. Waspish, funny, prophetic and outrageous.

TRAVEL

DAFFODIL AND GOLDEN EAGLE   Jonathan Yeatman   £1.00
In the best tradition of British devil-may-care eccentricity, the
authors decided to float across the Sahara in two hot-air balloons.
Illustrated in full colour.

THE FEARFUL VOID   Geoffrey Moorhouse   £1.25
There is a fearful void out there in the empty quarter of the
Sahara Desert, but more terrifying still is the void within our
minds – the fear of loneliness and failure. One man's search to
conquer his own self-distrust. Illustrated in full colour.

JOURNEY THROUGH BRITAIN   John Hillaby   75p
It was a magical idea to walk through the over-industrialised land
of Britain from Land's End to John O'Groats, avoiding all centres
of population. Britain's master walker made his reputation with this
book. Illustrated.

JOURNEY THROUGH EUROPE   John Hillaby   75p
John Hillaby gives a splendid potpourri of factual account, lively
anecdote, mythology and private comment in this account of his
walk from the Hook of Holland via the Alps to Nice. Illustrated.

JOURNEY TO THE JADE SEA   John Hillaby   75p
Tired of city-living and ashamed of his toleration of boredom,
John Hillaby made a three-month safari from the Northern Frontier
District of Kenya to the legendary Jade Sea. Illustrated.

ARCHAEOLOGY

BEFORE THE DELUGE   Herbert Wendt   90p
Palaeontology sets out to find the point in the past when life began
to exist on our planet, how it developed, and when man first
appeared. This is the story of how palaeontology developed as a
science and what it now tells us about the planet on which we live.
Illustrated.

THE BOG PEOPLE   P. V. Glob   75p
In a peat bog in Schleswig, Denmark, the body of a fourteen-year-
old girl was found. It was almost 2,000 years old and had been
perfectly preserved by the strange chemical properties of the peat.
An authoritative account of one of the most remarkable
archaeological finds ever. Illustrated.

THE CHANGING FACE OF BRITAIN   Edward Hyams   £1.50
Illustrated general study of how the geological structure of the land,
our climate, our social history and our industries have contributed
to the shape of our landscape.

THE DAWN OF EUROPEAN CIVILISATION
V. Gordon Childe   £1.00
The last edition of the classic archaeological work that continues to
dominate all explanations of the growth of European prehistory.
Illustrated.

INDUSTRIAL ARCHAEOLOGY   Arthur Raistrick   75p
The 'forgotten' aspect of archaeology; both an introduction and an
essential reference work from Britain's leading authority.
Illustrated.

MYSTERIOUS BRITAIN   Janet and Colin Bord   £1.50
All over the British countryside are totems and indications of lost
civilisations and knowledge, scattered in a rich profusion if only the
eye can see. This book looks into the past while suggesting some
startling research for the future. Illustrated.

THE PILTDOWN MEN   Ronald Millar   75p
The case study of the most notorious hoax in the history of
archaeology. Illustrated.

SCIENCE

ALBERT EINSTEIN Banesch Hoffman £1.00
Written with the co-operation of Einstein's personal secretary, this
is the most authoritative account of the 20th Century's greatest
scientist. Illustrated.

THE ALCHEMISTS F. Sherwood Taylor £1.25
Before it became regarded as a branch of the occult, alchemy was in
the forefront of the search for human knowledge and led to the
founding of modern chemistry. Illustrated.

DICTIONARY FOR DREAMERS Tom Chetwynd 60p
A comprehensive key to the baffling language of dream symbolism.
Over 500 archetypal symbols give essential clues to understanding
the ingeniously disguised, life-enriching, often urgent messages to
be found in dreams.

A DICTIONARY OF DRUGS
Richard Fisher and George A. Christie 95p
From everyday aspirin and vitamin, to the powerful agents
prescribed for heart disease and cancer, this is a reference guide to
the gamut of drugs in today's pharmaceutical armoury.

A DICTIONARY OF SYMPTOMS Dr. Joan Gomez £1.50
Although not a full alternative to medical opinion, this is a
thorough-going and authoritative guide to the interpretation of
symptoms of human disease.

DRUGS OF HALLUCINATION Sidney Cohen 60p
A lucid account of the discovery and first synthesis of LSD, its use
and dangers in experimental psychiatry, and self-induced
transcendental experiences.

EARTH'S VOYAGE THROUGH TIME David Dineley £1.75
A revolution has taken place in geology. The first readable account
of what we know of Earth's past, present and future life.
Illustrated.

THE END OF ATLANTIS J. V. Luce 95p
New light on an old legend. Archaeologists, volcanologists,
seismologists, show a double story – a gigantic myth and a gigantic
cataclysm. Illustrated.

POLITICS

AFRICA IN HISTORY Basil Davidson £1.50
A complete introduction to the history of the 'Dark Continent'.
Illustrated.

ANEURIN BEVAN VOLS 1 & 2 Michael Foot £2.50 each
The classic political biography of post-war politics.

CRIME AND PERSONALITY H. J. Eysenck £1.25
A revised edition of the controversial and classic study of race and
intelligence.

THE FEMALE EUNUCH Germaine Greer 75p
The book that caused a revolution, the central focus of the
Women's Liberation movement.

THE IMPERIAL ANIMAL Lionel Tiger and Robin Fox £1.00
The authors assert that humans are fundamentally undemocratic,
adulterous, acquisitive and status-seeking. A controversial
biogrammar of human behaviour by two brilliant anthropologists.

THE INTERNATIONAL URBAN CRISIS
Thomas L. Blair 60p
A lucid and disturbing analysis of the facts behind planning blight,
suburban sprawl, traffic congestion, and human alienation.

INTERVENTION AND REVOLUTION
Richard J. Barnet 75p
A biting critique of America's attempt at acting as world
policeman, guarding against the myth of the international conspiracy
of communism.

MARX'S GRUNDRISSE David McLellan 50p
A substantial set of extracts from the classic work in which Marx
develops an account of the process of alienation, analyses the nature
of work and develops a vision of the fully automated society in
which social wealth could be devoted to the all-round development
of the faculties of each individual. Edited by one of Britain's leading
Marxist scholars.

HISTORY

AFRICA IN HISTORY   Basil Davidson   £1.50
A complete introduction to the history of the 'Dark Continent'.
Illustrated.

THE ALCHEMISTS   F. Sherwood Taylor   £1.25
Before it became regarded as a branch of the occult, alchemy was in
the forefront of the search for human knowledge and led to the
founding of modern chemistry. Illustrated.

ANATOMY OF THE SS STATE
Helmut Krausnick and Martin Brozat   60p
The inside story of the concentration camps, 'probably the most
impressive work on the Nazi period ever to appear'. THE TIMES
EDUCATIONAL SUPPLEMENT.

ART AND THE INDUSTRIAL REVOLUTION
Francis D. Klingender   £1.50
One of the most original and arresting accounts of the impact of
the new industry and technology upon the landscape of England and
the English mind. 'There is no book like it.' *John Betjeman.*
Illustrated.

ASPECTS OF THE FRENCH REVOLUTION
Alfred Cobban   75p
The origins of the Revolution, the role of the Enlightenment, *The
Parlement*, the diamond necklace affair. 'A tremendous and enviable
achievement of scholarship.' *David Thomson.*

THE BORGIAS   Michael Mallett   90p
The rise and fall of one of the most notorious families in
European history: Legends of poisoning, incest, and political
contrivance. Illustrated.

CONSCIOUSNESS AND SOCIETY   H. Stuart Hughes   75p
The re-orientation of European social thought from 1890 to 1930;
the ideas of Freud, Croce, Bergson, Jung, Sorel, Weber, Durkheim,
Proust, Mann, Gide, Hesse etc.

HISTORY

EUROPE'S INNER DEMONS   Norman Cohn   £1.75
The history of the vilification of minority groups as scapegoats, by
the author of THE PURSUIT OF THE MILLENNIUM

SHAKESPEARE THE MAN   A. L. Rowse   £1.25
The identity of the dark lady of the sonnets is revealed, and
Shakespeare is set in the context of his friends, patrons and
contemporaries – not merely of his plays.

EVOLUTION OF THE HOUSE   Stephen Gardiner   £1.50
A history of dwelling places and domestic architecture from the
cave onwards. Fully illustrated.

MARX   David McLellan   £2.25
A major new biography by Britain's leading Marxist historian.
Marx is shown in his private and family life as well as in his
political contexts.

A HISTORY OF WESTERN MUSIC
Christopher Headington   £1.95
A fully illustrated account of the development of song, opera, of
various musical instruments, musicians and music itself.

THE FORMATION OF ENGLAND   H. P. R. Finberg   75p
Part of the new Paladin History of England series. This volume
deals with the reign of Victoria and the effects of the industrial
revolution, colonialism and incipient social change.

THE CRISIS OF IMPERIALISM   Richard Shannon   £1.25
England in the realm of Victoria. A time of development,
expansion, colonisation, enormous social upheavals and reform.

PEACE, PRINT AND PROTESTANTISM
C. S. L. Davies   £1.50
Third in the Paladin History of England series. C. S. L. Davies'
book deals with the period 1450–1558 encompassing the reign of
the Tudors and the breakaway from the Church of Rome.

THE EDWARDIANS   Paul Thompson   £1.95
A marvellous collage of interviews and reminiscences of living
Edwardians of all classes. This is social history at its best – a superb
analysis of a misinterpreted era.

THE PALADIN HISTORY OF ENGLAND
A new nine-volume history of England from pre-Roman to modern
times.

ARTS

MYTHOLOGIES   Roland Barthes   50p
An entertaining and elating introduction to the science of
semiology – the study of the signs and signals through which
society expresses itself, from the leading intellectual star.

THE SORROW AND THE PITY   Marcel Ophuls   £1.00
The chronicle of a French city under the German occupation,
the text and illustrations from the film.

THE VOICES OF SILENCE   Andre Malraux   £1.90
The ultimate exposition of all art from prehistory to modern
photography and cinema: The museum without walls.
600 illustrations.

FUNNY WAY TO BE A HERO   John Fisher   £1.50
An illustrated exploration of British comedians in the music hall
tradition, from Dan Leno, through Will Hay and Max Miller to
Morecambe and Wise.

THE LONG VIEW   Basil Wright   £2.95
A complete history of the international cinema by a man who has
been involved in film-making for 50 years. Comprehensive, massive,
informative and entertaining.

A SONG FOR EVERY SEASON   Bob Copper   £1.25
A year in the life of a Sussex farming family . . . their work, their
traditions and above all their music and their songs.